SHAWNEE HERITAGE I
Shawnee Genealogy and Family History

by Don Greene

Copyright: © 2008

Shawnee Heritage I
Shawnee Genealogy and Family History

Frontpiece (below) and other paintings by Hal Sherman. Used with permission.

Hal Sherman email:
hsherman@donet.com
Gallery
http://shawnee-bluejacket.com/Gallery.htm

The Death of Moluntha

Author's Foreword

Welcome to the research that represents in part the contributions I made to the Shawnee Traditions site. The following 2,000 plus names are of Shawnee and those with some degree of Shawnee blood that were born, lived or died in the turbulent 1700s. These Shawnee represent only a portion of an Encyclopedia of the Natives of the 1700s, east of the Mississippi that I originally envisaged. Currently I have nearly 20,000 entries from all the tribes, 4,000+ of them being partly or entirely Shawnee. Since research like this is always an ongoing project, I am sure that as I search the various historical documents and histories, many more will be discovered. Likewise, as new information becomes known some of these listings may be changed to some degree.

You will see that the individuals' names are listed in Shawnee, English, French and sometimes two or more of these. I have also listed the conflicts and raids in which they are known or were likely to have taken part and the treaties and councils in they were involved. Sadly, most of the women are known in history from being widows. I have tried especially hard to follow some of the better known families, like those of Cornstalk, Blue Jacket, Black Fish, Black Hoof, Tecumseh, and others, since they are of more interest to the public than the lesser known Shawnee. Whenever possible, I have shown the percentage of Shawnee blood by the use of a fraction, like ½ or ¼th, etc... I have used the term Metis to show that a person has some degree of white ancestry. Adopted whites are generally included only if they left Metis children or were notable in some other way.

Since the Shawnee listed here may be of interest to genealogists, historians and others, it has been my goal to gather as many names as possible in one place. While I originally intended to stop the listings at about 2,000, in the cases of important or more interesting families I have followed their lines further -- please forgive my enthusiasm. Most lived and were known as Shawnee, but many lived with and were considered to be members of other tribes or had the blood of other tribes or even whites running in their veins. These Shawnee, and the rest of the nearly 20,000 + listings for my proposed Encyclopedia, represent the last of the free Natives east of the Mississippi and their brave but futile struggle to stop the encroachment of the whites.

So please have a look. Maybe some questions will be answered; or some new questions will arise. Either way I hope the readers will enjoy the opportunity to see over 2,000+ of our pre-removal Shawnee and those with Shawnee bloodlines all collected in one place.

Contents

Author's Forward... 3
Introduction... 5
Section I   A: Adair to Aweekone..................................... 9
Section II   B: Baby to Black Wolf.................................... 14
Section III   B (cont): Blackburn to Buzzard........................... 33
Section IV   C: Caesar to Conawapa.................................... 51
Section V   C (cont): Conner to Cuts Corn............................ 70
Section VI   D: Dancing Deer to Dusquene.............................. 86
Section VII   E – F: Eats Buffalo to Fults............................. 95
Section VIII   G – H: Gauthier to Hurrican Tom.......................... 113
Section IX   I – K: Ice to Kyanthawtha................................ 135
Section X   L: Laathska to Lynch..................................... 149
Section XI   M: MacIntosh to Musquanako............................... 165
Section XII   N – O: Nahaasema to Oxonoxy.............................. 187
Section XIII   P: Paciter to Pyatt...................................... 202
Section XIV   Q – R: Quaghoquona to Runs With Ax....................... 215
Section XV   S: Sachachewa to Silversmith............................. 239
Section XVI   S (c ont.): Singing Crow to Sykes........................ 256
Section XVII   T: Tahchee to Two Clouds................................. 272
Section XVIII   U – W: Ugly Man to White Bark............................ 293
Section XIX   W (cont.) – Z: White Beaver to Young..................... 317

APPENDIX I:
Introduction to Shawnee Names *by Noel Schutz*............................ 337

APPENDIX II:
Guide to Pronoucing Shawnee Names *by Noel Schutz*.................... 350

ENDNOTES:
Analysis of Selected Shawnee Names *by Noel Schutz*....................... 352

Paintings by Hal Sherman

Frontpiece: Death of Moluntha.. 2
Otha-he-waugh-Pi-Qua ('Pekwa Man rising from the ashes')................ 8
Blue Jacket at Fort Miami..36
Portrait of Cornstalk... 74
Tecumseh meets General Brock... 277
Endpiece: Greeneville Treaty, 1795... 333

Introduction to the first edition

Oh my, what an optimistic little monkey I was in those days. As my research into the Shawnee has progressed, I have come to realize that this great tribe alone is enough work for a lifetime.

To begin with let me explain my use of the term *metis*. It is simply a French word (métis) used from the earliest days of European contact to indicate that a person has some degree of both white and native blood. It is short, easy to type repeatedly and expresses, in my use, that an individual has some white blood. So let's not get off on some "French-blood" kick.

The fractions I use indicate the amount of Shawnee blood a person has. I list the other tribes in their ancestry also, but do not always take the time to hash out all the degrees of such bloodlines. You can do that yourself if you care to. Many of these people lived as members of a tribe other than their own and some lived as whites. My desire is to reflect the amount of Shawnee blood they possess in an effort to show that they may have possibly held some cultural connection to the Shawnee in the years and generations that had passed until their time.

It has become clear over the years that in order to completely understand the important role of the Shawnee in American history and to fully appreciate their widespread influence on not only the other tribes but also the colonization of America, I must go back to the arrival of the Europeans on this continent. I am now in that the process of doing that and that the work continues almost daily.

The descendants of the Shawnee truly appear everywhere in the time frame covered here, from east of the Appalachians, to as far west as Missouri, Kansas and Oklahoma, from as far north as Pennsylvania and the Great Lakes to as far south as Alabama, Georgia, and even Florida. Some are intermarried with so many pioneer families as to almost disappear from sight. They mingle with and play roles in so many other tribes so as to almost fade into the woodwork.

With lots of perseverance and not just a little luck, I will continue to uncover the Shawnee that have for so many years been hidden in our midst.

I well know that many will be unhappy with my lack of footnotes and/or listed sources. My answer is simple — though apparently lazy. I just do not feel like spending nearly as much time listing sources and writing footnotes as I do compiling the entries. As the names have grown into the thousands it has become apparent that maintaining a running list of sources, with the required footnotes, would take up far too much of my limited and valuable time, not to mentin uping the printing costs beyond reason. So I have bypassed those steps in the interest of sanity. Take my work for what you will. If you feel the need for such things, then by all means do the research for your own benefit. These individuals are out there; it is not easy to locate them, but I encourage any of the completists among us Shawnee descendants to jump right in and dig for yourself, using my listings as your starting point. Then feel free to go to the Shawnee Traditions website and share your information on the Forum there.

Being free of academic restraints and, so far, rather oblivious to critics, I have been formulating some theories concerning our Shawnee. It appears to me like they are the remnants of a great, half a continent-spanning culture that flourished from the time of the Mississippian mound-builders through the Ft. Ancient times into the time of the European invasion. It is almost impossible to think otherwise when you consider that the Shawnee were found from the Susqehanna River and Delaware Bay to the Mississippi River and from the Great Lakes to the Gulf of Mexico by the earliest white invaders.

The sad lack of a credible recorded history of the Shawnee — which ideally would have been written at a time when such history would have been recalled clearly and more accurately and most properly done by actual Shawnee – has, of course, biased our knowledge of them.

Much of what we are told of the Shawnee, other than notes or remembrances by the whites, has been gleaned from the observations or recollections of other tribes that were once more or less subservient to the great Shawnee and, who through their compliance and co-operation with the invading whites, came to be better off in some ways than the noble Shawnee who opposed the whites vehemently.

As the old truism goes, "History belongs to the victors" and our Shawnee unfortunately were not the victors and so they didn't have the chance to write their own history. Instead, we have been fed a string of tales by other tribes, usually reflecting their own biases and playing on their roles as alleged friends of the whites. How sad for the descendants of such a proud and notable culture.

I truly hope that by following my listings the readers can begin to understand and appreciate the important roles played by the Shawnee in the history of this nation, not just as an anti-Europeans tribe, but as friends, traders, teachers, preachers, leaders of their communities, spouses and parents.

So many of our Shawnee ancestors simply faded into the pioneer communities, passing as some sort of immigrants from Europe, be it Irish, Scottish, Dutch, French, or just some strangers to an area that spoke English rather poorly, kept to themselves and tried their best to survive.

In the process, of course, they began the long history of denying they were Shawnee. After all, who would want to be aligned with such vigorous anti-whites as Cornstalk, Black Fish, or the dozens and hundreds of others, up through Blue Jacket and Tecumseh that were put in the position of having to kill the whites in trying to defend their homeland?

If our ancestors expected to either stay alive or at least to stay on the land where they lived, they had to simply not be Shawnee and so claimed different ancestry, rather claiming to be from another tribe that was better accepted by the whites from some nation other than England.

Of all the tribes, the Shawnee may have been the most welcoming and the most open to allowing others to intermingle with them by marriage or adoption. The long, well documented history of this is clear. From the earliest days of Spanish and French explorers right into the massive English invasion the Shawnee freely and openly accepted the white Europeans, as well as blacks both free and slave. The descendants of those adopted and intermarried Europeans and blacks simply became one and the same as the original Shawnee.

Regretably we are once again under attack as some spurious people are backtracking into history and claiming our Shawnee as members of an alleged Muslim pioneer culture or community based on some wildy speculative, erroneously interpreted, and at times totally imaginary information. Once again the lack of a factual, detailed Shawnee history has come back to haunt us by allowing these people to make their fantstically unsubstantiated claims.

If my humble efforts can in some way help clarify the history of the Shawnee by identifying who they were and where they were then all of the years involved will be rewarded.

So once again, welcome to my Great Work. Take it as you may, reject it if you must. Hopefully you will find something of some value to you.

Bear in mind that I grew up and have lived among people like myself, country born and raised, with Metis roots that go back for literally hundreds of years. Our way of life is so much like those of our forefathers that we take it for granted. We don't live in teepees or wigwams, we don't wear feathers much or speak in a stumbling, halting manner, but we do all seem to hold a love for the land and nature in our hearts and are most comfortable when allowed to spend our days in the quietness, solitude and beauty of a rural environment. Many of my friends and neighbors do seem to have anaffintiy for wearing turquoise, maybe as an outward expression of some soul felt yearning for an earlier time.

This Great Work of mine is a labor of love, for history, for America, for our noble Shawnee and for factual, honest reflection of all of those. I hope you enjoy reading it as much as I love creating it.

Sincerely,
Don Greene
6-15-2007

Pi-Qua
Otha-he-waugh-Pi-Qua 'Pekwa Man rising from the ashes'
The first Pekowi Man (Piqua) from Shawnee tradition

Section I
A - Adair to Aweekonee

A

1. **Abbott, James** - adopted-white born about 1725 IRE-died after 1774 - fur trader on the frontier, husband about 1765 OH of **Chalakatha Woman**/50, father of James Abbott Jr/66, Robert Abbott/68, Samuel Abbott/70, Elizabeth Abbott/72, Ruth Abbott/74-all 1/2 Chalakatha-Metis.

2. Adair, Walter Scott Black Wat - 1/8th Thawikila-**Cherokee**-Metis born 1783 GA-died 1835 OK - son of **Nancy Gahoga Lightfoot**/60 & **John Adair**/53, with U.S. Army-War 1812, Treaty 1817, 1819, husband 1804 of **Rachel Thompson**/86-1/4th Chalakatha-Metis, father of George Washington Adair/1804, Mary Adair/1805, John Thompson Adair/1806, Nancy Adair/1808, Sarah Thompson Adair/1810, Rachel Adair/1812-all 3/16th Chalakatha-Thawikila-Cherokee-Metis

3. Adair, Walter Scott Red Wat - 1/32nd Chalakatha-Thawikila-**Cherokee**Metis born about 1791-died 1851 - son of **Elizabeth Scott**/69 & **Edward Adair**/55-Cherokee Metis, 1st Master of the 2nd Masonic Lodge in OK, husband 1824 of **Nancy Harris** (McCoy)/1807-1/16th Chalakatha-Cherokee-Metis, children unknown

4. **Adkins, Charity Adkins** – 15/32nd Chalakatha-Mekoche-**Metis** born 1768 PA-died 1820 Cabell Co WV - daughter of **Mary Blue Sky Cornstalk**/50 & **Parker V. Adkins**/20-white (or Metis, granddaughter of **Cornstalk**10, wife 1788 of 1st cousin **Randolph Adkins**-white (or Metis) born 1742 VA-died 1818 Cabell Co. WV-(nephew of **Parker V. Adkins**/20-son of his brother **William Adkins**/21), mother of Parker Adkins/89, Randolph Sprang Adkins/90, Nancy Adkins/94, William Adkins/95, Jane Adkins/1804, Richard Adkins/1805, Rhoda Adkins/1810, Sylvester Adkins/1812, Price Adkins/1819 & John T. Adkins/1816-all 15/64th Chalakatha-Mekoche-Metis

5. Adkins, Littleberry – 15/32nd Chalakatha-Mekoche-**Metis** born 1767 Ft. Pitt area PA-died 1848 Mercer Co. WV - son of **Mary Blue Sky Cornstalk**/50 &

Parker V. Adkins/20-white (or Metis), grandson of **Cornstalk**/10, husband 1790 Franklin Co VA of 1st cousin **Nancy Adkins**/67-white (or Metis), father of Jesse Adkins/91, Isom Adkins/95, Hezekiah Adkins/1800, Littleberry Adkins Jr/1801, Christina Adkins/1805, Dicey Adkins/1806, Priscilla Adkins/1810 & Vicey Adkins/1811-all 15/64th Chalakatha-Mekoche-Metis

6. Adkins, White Wing Cornstalk aka **Nancy Adkins-Big Nancy** - granddaughter of **Cornstalk**/10, wife 1st 1784 VA of **Elijah Adkins**-white (or possible Metis) born 1764 VA-died after 1799 TN-son of **Parker V. Adkins**/20 & **Mary Polly Alexander**/20, mother of Lewis Adkins/84, Elijah Adkins Jr/86, Richard Adkins/88 & Nancy Adkins/90-all 15/64th Chalakatha-Mekoche-**Metis**, abandoned children 1790 when she left Elijah for **Tecumseh** (except Nancy/90)

7. Ailstock, Abraham aka Abraham Cornstalk – 7/16th ChalakathaMekoche-Black-**Metis** born about 1750 OH-died after 1790 VA - 4th son of **Julia**/20-adopted-Mulatto & **Cornstalk**/10, took surname when he returned to whites 1775, abandoned Chalakatha Wife & children 1775, husband 1st 1770 OH of **Chalakatha Woman**/55, 2nd 1779 VA of **Pekowi-Metis Woman**/60, 3rd 1784 of **Isabel Radcliff**/65-white, father **with Chalakatha** of 3 children/70-74, **with Pekowi-Metis** of Rebecca Ailstock/80 & Virginia Ailstock/82-both 15/32nd Chalakatha-Pekowi-Mekoche-Black-Metis, any children **with Radcliff** unknown

8. Ailstock, Absalom - 7/16th Chalakatha-Mekoche-Black-**Metis** born about 1748 OH-died after 1814 VA - 3rd son of **Julia**/20-adopted-Mulatto & **Cornstalk**/10, took surname when returned to whites 1775, abandoned Chalakatha Wife & children 1775, Augusta Co-VA Militia-**with U.S. Army**Revolution, husband 1st 1768 OH of **Chalakatha Woman**/53, 2nd 1782 VA of **Sally Going**/69-white (sister of Rebecca Going-wife of his brother Michael), father **with Chalakatha** of 4 children/68-74, **with Going** of Katy Ailstock/83, John Ailstock/84, Polly Ailstock/85, Lawrence Ailstock/86, Elizabeth Ailstock Ailstock/87, Andrew Ailstock/88, David Ailstock/90, James Ailstock/92, Absalom Ailstock Jr/93, William Ailstock/94 & Thomas Ailstock/98-all 7/32nd Chalakatha-Mekoche-Black-Metis

9. Ailstock, John - 7/32nd Chalakatha-Mekoche-**Black**-Metis born about 1784 VA-died after 1860 WV - 1st son of **Sally Going**/69-white & **Absalom Ailstock**/48, grandson of Julia/20-adopted-Mulatto & **Cornstalk**/10, living in Mason Co. WV by 1840, husband 1st about 1805 of **Polly Mekoche-BlackMetis**/80, 2nd about 1814 of **Arsella Mekoche-Black-Metis**/83, father **with Polly** of Mary Ailstock/1808, **with Arsella** of Rebecca Ailstock/1815, Mary Ailstock/1820, Susanna Ailstock/1825-all

10. Ailstock, Mary - 23/64th Chalakatha-Mekoche-**Black**-Metis born about 1820 VA-died after 1870 WV - daughter of **John Ailstock**/84 & **Arsella Mekoche-Black-Metis**/83, living with **John & Arsella** in Mason Co. WV by 1850, living 1870 with sister **Susanna-Susan Ailstock**/1825 & brother in law **John E. Cordell**/1812-white, mother by **Mr. Moss** of Harriet Jane Moss/1854

11. Ailstock, Michael aka Michael Cornstalk - 7/16th Chalakatha-MekocheBlack-**Metis** born about 1752 OH-died about 1791 VA - 5th son of **Julia**/20adopted-Mulatto & **Cornstalk**/10, took surname when returned to whites about 1775, abandoned Chalakatha Wife & children 1775, husband 1st 1772 of **Chalakatha Woman**/56, 2nd 1776 VA of **Rebecca Going**/60-white (sister of **Sally Going**-wife of his brother **Absalom Ailstock**), father with Chalakatha of 2 children/72-74, **with Going** of Mary Ailstock/76, Joseph Ailstock/77, Susanna Ailstock/78, Michael Ailstock Jr/79, Absalom Ailstock/80 & Elizabeth Ailstock/81-all 7/32nd Chalakatha-Mekoche-Black-Metis, grandfather of Rebecca Ailstock/85-1/8th Shawnee-Black-Scot Metis

12. Ailstock, Susanna aka Susan - 23/64th Chalakatha-Mekoche-Black-**Metis** born about 1825-died after 1870 - daughter of **Arsella Mekoche-Black-Metis**/83 & **John Ailstock**/84, living with parents in Mason Co. WV 1850, wife before 1870 of **John E. Cordell**/12-white

13. Akepee – Mekoche born about 1775 OH-died after 1817 - Fallen Timber/94, a warrior at Wapaghonettat 1817, Treaty 1817

14. Alawaymotakah – Mekoche born about 1770 OH-died after 1817 - raiding Ohio River valley 1788, Blue Jacket War/87-94, a warrior at Wapaghonettat 1817, Treaty 1817

15. Alder, Jonathan - adopted-white born 1773 MD-died 1849 OH - captured 1781 VA, translator, trader, adopted son of **Succopanus**/40-Seneca & **Winecho**/40-Kishpoko, Blue Jacket War/87-92, raiding KY with band 1787-92, raiding Ohio River valley 1788, Harmar/90, returned to whites about 1805, Capt. of Plain City OH Militia-War of 1812, husband 1st about 1795 of **Barshaw Turtle**/65, 2nd 1807 of **Mary Blont**/90-white, children unknown

16. Alibanan – Mekoche born about 1720 IL-died after 1757(OH?) - captured by French in IL & questioned 1747, French-Indian War/54-57, Braddock/55, raiding New-Shenandoah River valleys/55

17. All Bones aka All Bones White Owl-**All Bones Carpenter**-KalahuSawanugi-Shawano-Sawnook-Swanugi-Flying Squirrel - 7/16th

ChalakathaCherokee-Metis born 1720 Great Tellico TN-died after 1797 TN - son of **White Owl Carpenter**/1678 & **Nancy Rainmaker**/1683, could cipher, read & write English, Wolf Clan Cherokee, from the Lower Towns & Cheowee NC, advisor to his cousin **Oconastota Rainmaker**/02, raiding Ohio-New River valleys/58, husband 1735 Chota TN of (possible cousin) **Tame Deer Muskrat**/20Chalakatha-Pekowi, father of All Bones Carpenter (2)/50-23/32nd Chalakatha-Pekowi-Cherokee-Metis

18. Ant - Kishpoko born before 1790 OH-died after 1825 - Prophet's Town/1811, Brownstown/1812-Monguagon/1812-1st Amherstburg/1812Frenchtown/1813-Ft. Meigs/1813-2nd Amherstburg/1813 & Thames/1813 with **Tecumseh**, moved to CAN 1815, returned to OH 1825, moved to KS with **Prophet** & **Paukeesaa** 1826, wife & children unknown

19. Aqueloma – Thawikila born about 1670 GA-died after 1730 (PA?) - a Thawikila Chief in western PA/eastern OH before 1720

20. Aquashequa aka Aquesheka-Aquashequa Logan-Akwashekwa - 15/16th Mekoche-Kishpoko-Pekowi-Creek-Metis born about 1793 (OH?) -died after 1822 - son of **Capt. John Logan-Big Horn**/74 & **Blue Bird Mekoche**/75, a Mekoche warrior at Wapaghonettat 1817, Treaty 1817, brother of Red Leaf Logan/90, Cageshee Logan/95, half-brother of James Logan/1805, grandson of **Tecumapease Puckenshinwa**/58 & **Mink**/40

21. Ash, George - adopted-white born about 1765-died after 1801 – son of **John Ash**, adopted 1770 with brother **Abraham Ash**/51, adopted son of **Young Black Fish**, returned to whites 1795, Blue Jacket War/80-94, raiding Ohio River valley/88-92, associated with **Blue Jacket** & family, husband 1st about 1785 of **She Bear**/65-Chalakatha, 2nd about 1801 of **Hannah Combs**/80-adopted-white, father **with She Bear** of George Ash Jr/90-1/2 Chalakatha-Metis, children **with Combs** unknown

22. Asheseka - Chalakatha born about 1770 OH-died after 1817 – Blue Jacket War/88-94, a Chalakatha warrior from Wapaghonettat 1817, Treaty 1817

23. Ashkunigha – adopted-Delaware born about 1730 PA-died after 1782 - wife about 1745 (PA-OH) of **Pekowi Man**/25, widow 1774, children unknown

24. Assaragoa - Chalakatha born about 1710 PA-died after 1755 - raiding PA/40, French-Indian War/54, Council Logstown 1752, Braddock/55

25. Ationokonee aka Ateeonokonee – Chalakatha born about 1740 PA-died after 1786 – Cornstalk War/58-77, raiding Ohio-New River valleys/58, Pontiac War/62-66, Bushy Run/63, raiding Greenbrier-Jackson River valleys/63, raiding Ohio-Little Kanawha-Big Sandy-New River valleys/72, Point Pleasant/74-75-78, raiding OH-KY-VA/75-81, Blue Jacket War/77-86, Crawford/82, Treaty 1786

26. Atshena – Chalakatha born about 1770 OH-died after 1817 – Blue Jacket War/87-94, raiding Ohio River valley 1788, a warrior at Lewistown 1817, Treaty 1817

27. Attakullakulla aka **Attakullakulla Carpenter-Leaning Wood**[1]-Little Carpenter-Little Cornplanter-Ookunaka-Chugonanto Tom-Thomas Carpenter (6)-Chukenanta Warrior-Truconita-White Owl (2)-Attagulagula-Little Tom – 7/16th Chalakatha-**Cherokee**-Metis born 1706 Great Tellico TN-died 1777 Nachestown TN in battle – son of **Savannah Tom Carpenter (1)-Moytoy (3)**/1680 & **Nancy Rainmaker**/1683, stepson 1711 of his uncle **White Owl Carpenter**/1678, Wolf Clan Cherokee, delegation to ENG 1730, captive of **Ottawa or Chippewa** in north 1738-45, (wrongly called a Chippewa or Ottawa due to his 8 years of captivity in the north which some thought to be at least partially voluntary), raiding Ohio Valley/58, sent warriors to Point Pleasant/74, Treaty Sycamore Shoals 1775, a **Principal Chief of Cherokee 1763-1775**, husband 1st 1734 of his 2nd cousin/niece (daughter of his 1st cousin) **Ollie Nionee Oconastota**/20-1/2 Chalakatha-Thawikila-Creek-Cherokee, father **with Ollie Nionee before captivity** of Dragging Canoe/34, White Owl (3)/36 & Tahchee Carpenter/38-all 15/32nd Chalakatha-Thawikila-Creek-Cherokee-Metis, (possibly father of children/38-45 with a Chippewa (?) during his captivity in the north-see **Marie Lesperance**), father **with Ollie Nionee after captivity** of Shoe Boots/50, Ollie Mollie/54, Turtle At Home/58 & Wurtegua Carpenter/60-all 15/32nd Chalakatha-Thawikila-Creek-Cherokee-Metis, **(adopted father after captivity of** Badger Hop/39, Black Fox Hop/41, Little Owl Hop/43 & Sugi-Suki Hop/45all ½ Chalakatha-Thawikila-Creek-Cherokee-born during his captivity = **children of Young Hop**/15 & **Ollie Nionee**), also **adopted father** & **father in law** of **Alexander Cameron** aka **Scotchee**/30-white

28. Attakullakulla, Ollie Mollie aka Ollie Mollie Carpenter –15/32nd Chalakatha-Thawikila-Creek-**Cherokee**-Metis born 1748 Great Tellico TN-died after 1810 Cherokee Nation TN – daughter of **Attakullakulla Carpenter**/08 & **Ollie Nionee Oconastota**/20, Wolf Clan Cherokee, wife 1st 1769 Great Tellico TN of **Alexander Scotchee Cameron**/30-adopted-white (he dies 1781 GA), 2nd

1780 Great Tellico TN of **James Dougherty**/42-1/4th Chalakatha-PekowiCherokee-Metis (widowed 1791), 3rd 1795 Cherokee Nation TN of **Thomas Harrison**/36-white, mother **with Cameron** of Susanne Cameron/70, Archibald Cameron/72 & David Cameron/74-all 15/64th Chalakatha-Thawikila-CreekCherokee-Metis, **with Dougherty** of Annie Crying Bear (Dougherty)/80, James Dougherty Jr/82, Susan Dougherty/84, Elizabeth Dougherty/86, Elsie Dougherty/88, Rachel Dougherty/90, Mary Dougherty/92 (born after death of James)-all 23/64th Chalakatha-Thawikila-Creek-Cherokee-Metis, any children **with Harrison** unknown

29. Aupawimawat aka Opaweemawat – Pekowi born about 1760 OH-**killed** 1782 OH – Blue Jacket War/77-82, raiding KY-VA-OH/77-81, Point Pleasant/78, Boonesboro/78, killed at Crawford/82

30. Auseewantuwah aka Oseewantoowah – Pekowi born about 1785 OHdied after 1813 - Prophet's Town/1811, Brownstown/1812-Monguagon/1812-1st Amherstburg/1812-Frenchtown/1813-Ft. Meigs/1813-2nd Amherstburg/1813 & Thames/1813 **with Tecumseh**

31. **Autumn Leaf aka Pahkotasisqui**[2]-Pahkotaseeskwee – Pekowi born about 1760 OH-died after 1782 - wife 1774 OH of **Pekowi Man**/54, widow 1774

32. Awabaneshekaw – Mekoche born about 1775 OH-died after 1817 - Fallen Timber/94, a warrior at Wapakonetta 1817, Treaty 1817

33. **Aweekonee aka Oweekonnee**[3] - Mekoche born about 1750 OH-died after 1786 – Cornstalk War/68-77, raiding Ohio- Kanawha-Big Sandy-New River valleys/72, Point Pleasant/74-75-78, Blue Jacket War/77-86, Boonesboro/78, raiding KY-OH-VA/75-81, Crawford/82, Treaty 1786.

Section II B - Baby to Black Wolf

B

34. Baby, Jacques Duperon aka Jacques Duperon Baubee – adopted-French Canadian born 1733-died 1789 - French-Indian War/54-63, Braddock/55, Pontiac War/62-66, husband 1st (unmarried) 1749 of **Pekowi Woman**/35, 2nd (unmarried) 1755 of **Angelique Crevier**/39-1/2 Kishpoko-Metis, 3rd 1760 of **Suzanne Reaume**/40-1/2 Pekowi-Metis, 4th (unmarried) by 1773 of **Kishpoko**

Woman/59, had 11 legitimate children & 11 illegitimate children/50-89, father with **Pekowi** of Clear Water Baby/50-(wife of **Blue Jacket**), Ms. Baby/52-(wife of **Wabete Opessa**) & a child/54-all illegitimate 1/2 Kishpoko-Métis, **with Crevier** of Suzanne Baby/60-(wife of **William Caldwell**)-1/4th Kishpoko-Metis, **with Reaume** of James Baby/62, Suzanne Baby/66, Therese Baby/67, Francios Baby/68, Jean Baptiste Baby/70, Archangel Baby/74, Anthony Baby/75, Pierre Baby/76, Monica Baby/77, Daniel Baby/78 & Louis Baby/82-all 1/4th PekowiMetis, **with Kishpoko** of Mamate Baby/74- (wife of **Tecumseh**) -1/2 Kishpoko-
Metis (six other illegitimate Metis children)

35. **Bad Eagle** aka **Waughapelethee**[4] – Kishpoko born about 1735-died after 1775 – Cornstalk War/58-75, raiding Ohio-New River valleys/58, Pontiac War/62-66, Bushy Run/63, raiding Big Sandy-Little Kanawha-Ohio-New River valleys/72, Point Pleasant/74-75, raiding Ohio-New River valleys/75, husband 1755 OH of **Kishpoko Woman**/40, father of Young Eagle-Peekshinoah/55

36. Bad Hand – Chalakatha born about 1750 OH-died after 1781 - wife 1765 OH of **Chalakatha Man**/45, crippled in one hand, widow 1781, children unknown

37. Bad Snake aka **Matchemento**[5] - Mekoche born 1745 OH-died after 1788 – son of **Great Snake**/25 & **Mekoche Woman**/30, Cornstalk War/63-77, Pontiac War/63-66, Bushy Run/63, raiding New-Jackson-Greenbrier River valleys/63, raiding Ohio-Little Kanawha-Big Sandy-New River valleys/72, Point Pleasant/74-75-78, Blue Jacket War/77-88, Boonesboro/78, raiding KY-VA-OH/75-81, Crawford/82, raiding Ohio River valley/88, wife & children unknown

38. Badger (1) aka **Badger Hop**-Badger Attakullakulla-**Ookuhmuh (1)**Akumneh-Oguma – ½ Chalakatha-Thawikila-Creek-**Cherokee**- born 1738 Great
Tellico TN-died after 1804 Great Tellico TN – son of **Young Hop**/15 & **Ollie Nionee Oconastota**/20, adopted son 1746 of **Attakullakulla Carpenter**/06, from the Overhills, Wolf Clan & Red Paint Clan Cherokee, raiding NewShenandoah River valleys/55, raiding Ohio-New River valleys/58, Pontiac War/62-66, Point Pleasant/74, Cherokee War/75, Treaty Sycamore Shoals/75, Pigeon Co-Cherokee scouts-**with U.S. Army**-Revolution, diplomatic missions to Detroit & Canada/83-84, Council Eustinali 1788, Council Estinawa 1792, delegate to D.C./91, Treaty 1791, Treaty 1792, husband 1759 Great Tellico TN of **Nancy Great Eagle Carpenter**/45-7/32nd Chalakatha-Cherokee-Metis, father of Badger (3)-Young Ookuhmuh-Young Badger/60, Nancy Ookuhmuh/68, Jennie Ookuhmuh/70, Johnson Ookuhmuh/76, John Welch Ookuhmuh/82-all

23/64th Chalakatha-Thawikila-Creek-Cherokee-Metis

39.　Badger (2) – Kishpoko born about 1740 OH-**killed** before 1770 - husband about 1760 KY of **Wife of Badger (1)**/40-Cherokee, Cornstalk War/5863, raiding Ohio-New River valleys/58, Pontiac War/62-66, Bushy Run/63, raiding New-Jackson-Greenbrier River valleys/63, killed while raiding, husband of **Badger's Wife**/46-Cherokee, father of several 1/2 Kishpoko-Cherokee children- possibly named Badger

40.　Baker, Boling aka **Kikpelethee**[6] - adopted- ½ Shawano-Metis born about 1735 on New River NC-died about 1810 OH - son of **Andrew Baker** white & **Shawano Wife**, captured-adopted 1755 at Point Pleasant after deserting whites at Braddock/55, Cornstalk War/58-77, raiding Ohio-New River valleys/58, Pontiac War/62-66, Bushy Run/63, raiding New-Jackson-Greenbrier River valleys/63, raiding Big Sandy-Little Kanawha-Kanawha-New River valleys/72, Point Pleasant/74-75-78, Blue Jacket War/77-88, Boonesboro/78, raiding Ohio River valley/88, left children to be raised by Cornstalk family after death of Aracoma even though he remained among the tribe/clan, lived among Natives & mixed community in Lawrence Co. OH across the Ohio River from the mouth of the Big Sandy River/Huntington WV, visited Aracoma's grave annually until his death, son in law of **Cornstalk**/10, husband 1758 OH of **Aracoma Cornstalk**/42-15/16th Chalakatha-Mekoche-Metis, father of sons Running Deer (Baker)/64, Laughing Water (Baker)/66, Running Water (Baker)/72 & Blue Feather (Baker)/74 & daughters Snow Lily (Baker)/68 & Raindrop-Rain Falling (Baker)/70-all 23/32nd Chalakatha-Mekoche-Shawano-Metis, other children said to have died young

41.　Baker, Davy aka **Peektoo** - Mekoche born about 1770 OH-died after 1817 - raiding Ohio River valley/88-92, Blue Jacket War/87-94, scout-**with U.S. Army**-Prophet's Town/1811-War 1812-Thames/1813, a warrior at Wapaghonettat 1817, Treaty 1817, wife & children unknown

42.　Bald – Chalakatha born about 1790 OH-died after 1817 - Prophet's Town/1811, Brownstown/1812-Monguagon/1812-1st Amherstburg/1812Frenchtown/1813-Ft. Meigs/1813-2nd Amherstburg/1813 & Thames/1813 with
Tecumseh, a warrior at Lewistown 1817, Treaty 1817

43.　Baptikutee aka Bapticute – Mekoche born about 1780 OH-died after 1817 – **with U.S. Army**-Thames/1813, a warrior at Wapaghonettat 1817, Treaty 1817

44.　Baptiste – adopted-Seneca - born about 1780 OH-died after 1832 – **with**

U.S. Army-Thames/1813, Treaty 1832, moved to KS 1832, husband 1800 OH of **Mekoche Woman**/85, children unknown

45. Barbareau - 1/2 Thawikila-Spanish-**Metis** born about 1740 MO-IL?)died after 1778 – son of **Daughter of Thawikila Chief** & **Spanish Soldier**, raiding Ohio-New River valleys/58, Pontiac War/62-66, Bushy Run/63, raiding Greenbrier-Jackson River valleys/63, raiding Big Sandy-Little Kanawha-OhioNew River valleys/72, Point Pleasant/74, living in Apple Creek MO 1778

46. Barking Fox – Kishpoko born about 1750 OH-died after 1783 – Cornstalk War/68-74, raiding Little Kanawha-Big Sandy-Ohio-New River valleys/72, Point Pleasant/74-75-78, Blue Jacket War/77-82, raiding KY-OH-VA/77-81, Boonesboro/78, Blue Licks/82, Crawford/82

47. Barnes, April Tkikami Hop aka April Tkikami Turkey - wife 1718 of **Richard Barnes**-white born 1695 VA-died after 1750 Upper Hiwassee VA, mother of Mary Barnes/20 & Charity Barnes/26-both 1/2 Chalakatha-**Metis**

48. Barnes, Charity - 1/2 Chalakatha-**Metis** born 1726 Chota TN-died 1788 Cherokee Nation East - daughter of **April-Tkikami Hop**/1690-Chalakatha & **Richard Barnes**/1695-white, 2nd wife 1744 of **Edward Vann**/20-1/2 Cherokee-Metis, mother of Clement Vann/44, Thomas Vann/46, Avery Vann/48, Edith Vann/50, Susanna Vann/52-all 1/4th Chalakatha-**Cherokee-Metis**

49. Barnes, Mary - 1/2 Chalakatha-**Metis** born 1720 Chota TN-died 1744 Davidson Co. NC (TN) - daughter of **April-Tkikami Hop**/1690-Chalakatha & **Richard Barnes**/1695-white, wife 1738 of **Edward Vann**/20-1/2 CherokeeMetis, mother of Joseph Vann/38, Jennie Vann/40, James Vann/42 & Edward
Ned Vann/44-all 1/4th Chalakatha-**Cherokee-Metis**

50. Barshaw aka Barshaw Turtle - Chalakatha born about 1765 OH-died after 1830 - from the **Black Fish** band, sister of **Big Turtle**/50, wife 1st about 1780 OH of **Chalakatha Man**/60, widowed 1794, 2nd 1795 OH of **Jonathan Alder**/73-adopted white, 3rd of **Shawnee Man**/70, widow of 3rd husband in 1830, children unknown

51. Barton, Joab - adopted-white born about 1767 VA-died 1829 MO - adopted about 1775, moved to MO before 1799-when met there by Daniel Boone possibly with early Thawikila, son of **Joshua Barton**, brother of **Violet Barton**/75-(wife of **Alexander Brown Jr**/65), husband 1st about 1796 of **Eetahaha**/80-Thawikila, 2nd 1807 of **Anna Musick**/80 (possible Metis or adopted Shawnee), father **with Eetahaha** of Jane Jenny Barton/98 & Marcy

Barton/1800-both 1/2 Thawikila-**Metis**, **with Anna** of Susannah Barton/1808 & Abraham Barton/1810-both white

52. Bastard Son - 1/2 Kishpoko-Metis born about 1750-died after 1778 - son of **Kishpoko Woman** & **White Trader**, raiding Big Sandy-Little Kanawha-Ohio-New River valleys/72, Point Pleasant/74-75-78, raiding KY-OH-VA/77, known for his red hair & beard, husband 1770 OH of **Pekowi Woman**/55, children unknown

53. Battease – Chalakatha born about 1780-died after 1817 – **with U.S. Army**-Thames/1813, a warrior at Lewistown 1817, Treaty 1817

54. Bayles, Mary - adopted-white (or Metis?) born 1763-died 1822 WV – daughter of **Jesse Bayles**/36 & **Margaret Elizabeth Marie Moniaine**/35, adopted 1774-returned 1778 with 1/2 Kishpoko-Metis son, wife 1776 OH of **Peekishinoah-Young Eagle**/55, mother of Teliskwatawa Bayles-Son of Peekishinoah-Son of Young Eagle-Tecumseh Bayles/77-1/2 Kishpoko-Metis, wife 2nd 1782 WV of **Andrew Ice**-white born 1757 WV-died 1849 WV, (Andrew Ice returned Teliskwatawa/77 to the Shawnee 1795)

55. Bean, William aka Old Bean - adopted-1/2 Ottawa-**Metis** born about 1710-died after 1772 (TN?) - son of **Ottawa Woman** & **Trader Bean**-white, adopted by Shawnee by 1760, French-Indian War/54-63, Braddock/55, raiding New-Shenandoah River valleys/55, raiding Ohio-New River valleys/58, Pontiac War/62-66, Bushy Run/63, raiding New-Jackson-Greenbrier River valleys/63, living on the TN-NC border by 1769, called "one of the worst characters on the frontier", husband (at least 2nd?) before 1760 (OH-VA?) of **Chalakatha Woman**/45, 3rd by 1769(VA?) of **Lydia Russell**-white, father **with Chalakatha** of Peggy Bean/60, William Bean Jr/62, Robert Bean/64 & maybe John Bean/66all 1/2 Chalakatha-Ottawa-Metis, **with Russell** of Russell Bean/about 70 & maybe another John Bean/about 72

56. Bear Cub – Chalakatha born about 1745 OH-died after 1775 - Pontiac War/62-66, Bushy Run/63, raiding Little Kanawha-Big Sandy-Ohio-New River valleys/72, Point Pleasant/74-75

57. Bear Fat – adopted-Cherokee born about 1730 TN-died after 1756 - living in OH 1756, wife about 1745 TN of **Chalakatha Man**/25, children unknown

58. Beauchemie, Mackinaw aka Mackinac – adopted-1/2 Chippewa-**Metis** born about 1770-died 1848 - son of **Maune**/30-adopted-Chippewa & **Col. Beauchemie**-white, husband 1st about 1790 of **Mary Rogers**/74-daughter of Lewis Rogers, 2nd about 1795 MO of **Polly Rogers**/80-daughter of Henry Rogers, 3rd 1800 of **Elizabeth Rogers**/84-daughter of Lewis Rogers, 4th 1814 of her sister

Parlie Rogers/86-daughter of Lewis Rogers-all 1/2 ChalakathaMekoche-Pekowi-Metis, any children/90-95 **with Mary**/70, children/95-1800 **with Polly**/80 or children 1800-1814 **with Elizabeth**/80 unknown, father **with Parlie**/86 of Annie Beauchemie/1815, Alexander Beauchemie/1816, William Beauchemie/1817, Martha Beauchemie/1818, Louisa Beauchemie/1819, Julia Ann Beauchemie/1820 & John Beauchemie/1822-all 1/4th Chalakatha-Mekoche-Chippewa-Metis

59. Beaulieu, Catherine Montagnais aka Short Hair – Mekoche born about 1755-died after 1773 - wife 1768 of **Francois Beaulieu**/40-adopted French/Canadian, mother of Francois Beaulieu Jr/69, Chatte Beaulieu/70, Denoyan Beaulieu/72-all 1/2 Mekoche-Metis

60. Beaulieu, Denoyan - 1/2 Mekoche-Metis born about 1772-died after 1797 - son of **Francois Beaulieu**/40-adopted-Canadian & **Catherine Montagnais-Short Hair**/55, raiding Ohio River valley/88, Blue Jacket War/8894

61. Beaulieu, Francois - adopted-French/Canadian born about 1740 CANdied 1812 – Cornstalk War/62-77, Pontiac War/62-66, Bushy Run/63, raiding Ohio-Little Kanawha-Big Sandy-New River valleys/72, Point Pleasant/74, Boonesboro/78, Blue Licks/82, Crawford/82, raiding Ohio River valley/88, Blue Jacket War/77-94, husband 1768 of **Catherine Montagnais-Short Hair**/55, father of Francois Jr/69, Chatte/70, Denoyan/72-all ½ Mekoche-Metis

62. Beausoliel aka **Joseph Brosard** - adopted-1/2 Ottawa-**Metis** born about 1730-died after 1778 - son of **Joseph Brossard** aka **Beausoliel**/02-French/Canadian & **Ottawa Woman**, associated **with Gauthier family, Louis Herbert & LeMaigre**, French-Indian War/54-63, Cornstalk War/55-77, Braddock/55, raiding New-Shenandoah River valleys/55, raiding PA/55-56, raiding Ohio-New River valleys/58, Pontiac War/62-66, raiding GreenbrierJackson River valleys/63, Bushy Run/63, raiding Ohio-Little Kanwha-Big
Sandy-New River valleys/72, Point Pleasant/74, Boonesboro/78, husband about 1750 OH of **Chalakatha Woman**/35, father of several 1/2 Chalakatha-Ottawa-Metis children/50-78

63. **Beaver aka Amaghqua**[7] – Kishpoko born about 1740 OH-died after 1778 – Cornstalk War/58-77, raiding Ohio-New River valleys/58, Pontiac War/62-66, Bushy Run/63, raiding Greenbrier-Jackson River valleys/63, raiding Ohio-Big Sandy-Little Kanawha-New River valleys/72, Point Pleasant/74-75-78, raiding KY-OH-VA/77-78

64. Beaver Blanket – adopted-Delaware born about 1750-died after 1780 - wife 1765 OH of **Mekoche Man**, widow in 1780

65. Bell, David (1) - 1/2 Pekowi-**Metis** born about 1760 VA-died after 1800 (KY?) - son of **Thomas Bell**-white (that played fiddle at marriage of **Corn Blossom Doublehead** & **Big Jake Troxell**) & **Pekowi Woman**, husband 1777 VA of **Elizabeth Hughes**/62, father of James Bell/78, John Bell/82, Thomas Bell/87 & other children-all 5/8th Chalakatha-Pekowi-Metis

66. Benge, Robert aka **Chief Benge**-Bench – 21/64th Chalakatha-Pekowi**Cherokee**-Metis born 1761 Toqua TN-**killed** 1794 Stone Mountain VA - son of **Wurteh Watts**/44 & **John Trader Benge**/35-white, Red Paint Clan Cherokee, a Chickamauga, half-brother of **Chief John Jolly**/57, **Sequoyah**/58 & **Tahlonteeskee (2)**/60, known for his red hair, lived at Toquo village TN, Benge's Field AL & **with Shawnee in OH**, raiding/77 **with Cheeseekau**-brother of Tecumseh, Boonesboro/78, Blue Licks/82, raiding KY-OH-VA/77-81 **with Dragging Canoe**, Crawford/82, raiding Ohio valley-OH-WV-KY/82-90, raiding TN-KY-VA-OH/91-94, from the Overhills, killed in VA after KY raid/94, husband 1781 (TN?) of **Dorcas Lightfoot**/66-1/4th Thawikila-Cherokee-Metis, 2nd 1784 Running Water TN of **Kishpoko Woman**/69, 3rd 1786 Benge's Field GA of **Daughter of Black Fox**/62-1/4th Chalakatha-Thawikila-Creek-CherokeeMetis, father **with Lightfoot** of Edmund Benge-Edmund Duncan/82 & Houston Benge/84-9/32nd Chalakatha-Pekowi-Cherokee-Metis, **with Kishpoko** of Mary Polly (1)-Ooloosta Benge/85 & Robert Benge Jr/86-both 21/32nd ChalakathaKishpoko-Pekowi-Cherokee-Metis, **with Black Fox** of Richard Benge (2)/86, John Wagonmaster Benge/88, Mary Polly Benge (2)/90, Nancy Agnes Benge/92all 9/32nd Chalakatha-Pekowi-Thawikila-Creek-Cherokee-Metis

67. Berry – Chalakatha born about 1750 OH-died after 1778 – Cornstalk War/68-77, raiding Ohio-Little Kanawha-Big Sandy-New River valleys/72, Point Pleasant/74, raiding KY-VA-OH/77, Boonesboro/78

68. Berrystain – adopted-Cherokee born about 1730 TN-died after 1768 - wife 1745 TN of **Chalakatha Man**/25, widow in 1768

69. Berthiuame, Marie - 7/64th Chalakatha-Mekoche-Pekowi-Cherokee**Metis** born about 1795-died after 1816 - daughter of **Francois Bertiaume**/64white & **Daughter of Beauvais**/70, great-granddaughter of **Black Beard**/30, great-great-granddaughter of **Cornstalk**/10, 3rd wife 1810 of **Peter Lorimier**/48adopted-

Shawnee Heeritage

French/Canadian-Metis, wife 2nd 1813 of **John Logan (Rennicks) Jr**/99-3/4th Pekowi-Mekoche-Metis, mother **with Lorimier** of Manuel Lorimier/1808-3/64th Chalakatha-Mekoche-Pekowi-Cherokee-Metis, **with Rennicks-Logan** of Louisa Villars Logan/16-27/64th Chalakatha-Mekoche-Pekowi-Cherokee-Metis

70. Big Ash – adopted-Seneca born about 1770 OH-died after 1832 KS - raiding Ohio River valley/88-92, Blue Jacket War/88-94, scout-**with U.S. Army**Prophet's Town/1811-War 1812-Thames/1813, Treaty 1832, move to KS 1832, husband about 1790 OH of **Mekoche Woman**/75, father of several 1/2 Mekoche-
Seneca children/90-1815

71. Big Black (1) aka African-L'African-LeGross Noire-Big Black - adopted-Black born about 1700 Africa-died after 1755 (OH?) - runaway slaveadopted 1724 PA, over 6' tall & heavy built, raiding PA/40, French-Indian War/54, Braddock/55, associated with the Canadian Metis, husband 1725 PA of **Kishpoko Woman**/10, father of Infidel/25, Black Butcher/30, Red Beast/35-all 1/2 Kishpoko-Black

72. Big Black (2) aka Big Negro-LeGrand Negre - adopted-1/2 PottawameeBlack-Metis born about 1730-died after 1756 - son of **Mulatto**/1700-adopted Pottawamee & **Pottawamee Woman**/15, French-Indian War/54, Braddock/55, raiding New-Shenandoah River valleys/55, raiding PA/55-56, over 6' tall, husband about 1750 (IN?) of **Mekoche Woman**/35, father of three 1/2 Mekoche-
Pottawamee-Black-Metis children/50-55

73. Big Dog - adopted-Creek born about 1740 AL-died after 1778 - living **with Thawikila** in OH 1762, Pontiac War/62-66, Bushy Run/63, raiding Greenbrier-Jackson River valleys/63, raiding New-Ohio-Little Kanawha-Big Sandy River valleys/72, Point Pleasant/74, raiding KY-OH-VA/77, moved to MO with band about 1779, husband about 1760 (AL?) of **Thawikila Woman**/45, father of at least six 1/2 Thawikila-Creek children/60-78

74. Big Eyes - adopted-Delaware born about 1740 (PA?)-died after 1777 - Pontiac War/62-66, Bushy Run/63, raiding New-Jackson-Greenbrier River valleys/63, raiding New-Ohio-Big Sandy-Little Kanawha River valleys/72, Point Pleasant/74, raiding VA-OH-KY/75-77, husband about 1760 OH of **Pekowi Woman**/45, father of at least six 1/2 Pekowi-Delaware children/60-77

75. Big French aka Big Frenchman - adopted-1/2 Wyandot-Metis born about 1735 OH-died after 1780 - son of **Coureur deBois** & **Wyandot Woman**,

Cornstalk War/55-77, French-Indian War/54-63, Braddock/55, raiding NewShenandoah River valleys/55, raiding PA/55-56, raiding Ohio-New River valleys/58, Pontiac War/62-66, Bushy Run/63, raiding New-Greenbrier-Jackson River valleys/63, raiding Little Kanawha-Big Sandy-New River valleys/72, Point Pleasant/74-78, Blue Jacket War/77-89, raiding KY-VA-OH/77-80, husband about 1755 OH of **Chalakatha Woman**/40, father of nearly a dozen 1/2 Chalakatha-Wyandot Metis children/55-80

76.   Big Halfbreed – ½ Chalakatha-**Cherokee** born 1750 TN-died after 1789 – son of **Chalakatha Woman**/30 & **Cherokee Man**/25, husband 1st 1771 TN of **Hannah Qualiluka Guulisi Critterden**/56-1/4th Chalakatha-Pekowi-Cherokee-Metis, divorced Hannah 1789 when she became a Christian, husband 2nd 1790 TN of **Unknown Woman**, father **with Critterden** of Daughter/72, Daughter/74, Lydia Halfbreed/76, Pigeon Halfbreed/78, Susannah Halfbreed/80, Jennie Halfbreed/82, Elizabeth Halfbreed/84, Chinosa Halfbreed/86 & Jesse Halfbreed/88-all 3/8th Chalakatha-Cherokee-Metis, children **with Unknown Woman** unknown

77.   Big Head aka David Bighead - adopted-white born about 1740-died after 1777 - adopted by 1750-returned to whites-returned to tribe 1765, Cornstalk War/58-77, raiding Ohio-New River valleys/58, Pontiac War/62-66, Bushy Run/63, raiding New-Jackson-Greenbrier River valleys/63, raiding Ohio-Big Sandy-Little Kanawha-New River valleys/72, Point Pleasant/74, raiding KY-OHVA/75-77, husband about 1765 OH of **Chalakatha Woman**/50, father of several
1/2 Chalakatha-Metis children/65-74

78.   Big Hole – Mekoche born about 1730 PA-**killed** 1764 - French-Indian War/54-63, Braddock/55, Cornstalk War/55-64, raiding New-Shenandoah River valleys/55, raiding PA/55-56, raiding Ohio-New River valleys/58, Pontiac War/62-64, Bushy Run/63, raiding New-Jackson-Greenbrier River valleys/63, killed/64 by some Kickapoo, husband of **Mekoche Woman**/35, father of Big Hole's Son/50

79.   Big Hole's Son – Mekoche born about 1750 OH-died after 1777 - son of **Big Hole**/30 & **Mekoche Woman**/35, Cornstalk War/68-77, raiding Ohio-Little Kanawha-Big Sandy-New River valleys/72, Point Pleasant/74, raiding VA-OH-KY/75-77

80.   **Big Hominy aka Great Huminy-Big Hanoana-MisemeathaquathaMissemediqueety**[8] – Pekowi born about 1690-died about 1758 OH in epidemic - raiding PA/40, a **Pekowi Chief** in PA by 1740, moved to

Ohio valley 1744, in OH 1748 with **Peter Chartier**, Council Shawnee Town 1750, Logstown 1752

81. Big Horns aka **Capt. Logan**-Capt. John Logan-High Horn-Spencialawbe-**Spemica Lawba**[9] - born 1774 OH-died of wounds 1812 OH - 7/8th Mekoche-Kishpoko-Pekowi-Creek-Metis - son of **Tecumapease Puckenshinwa**/58 & **Mink Mekoche**/40, a Mekoche warrior, captured at Moluntha's village 1786, raised & given white name by **Col. Benjamin Logan**white, translator, scout-**with U.S. Army**-Prophet's Town/1811 & War 1812, killed in battle with **Winnemak**-Pottawamee & British supporters, 1st cousin of
Tecumseh/68, **Big Capt. Johnny**/65, **Bright Horn**/70, **Otter**/70, husband 1st 1789 OH of **Blue Bird**/75-Mekoche, 2nd 1804 OH of **Spamaghlebee**/90Mekoche, father **with Blue Bird** of Red Leaf/90, Cagashee/96, Aqueshka/95 & **with Spamaghlebee** of James Logan/1805-all 15/16th Mekoche-Kishpoko-
Pekowi-Creek-Metis

82. Big Jim aka **Bedeedee** – Chalakatha born about 1750 OH-died shortly after 1832 KS - raiding New-Ohio-Little Kanawha-Big Sandy River valleys/72, Point Pleasant/74-75-78, Blue Jacket War/77-94, raiding OH-VA-KY/75-81, Boonesboro/78, Blue Licks/82, Crawford/82, raiding Ohio River valley/88-92, scout-**with U.S. Army**-War 1812, captured at Ft. Meigs/1813 & released by **Tecumseh**, Treaty 1831, move to KS 1832

83. Big Knife aka **Chupehekaw** – Mekoche born about 1750 OH-died after 1832 KS - Cornstalk War/68-77, raiding Ohio-Big Sandy-Kanawha-New River valleys/72, Point Pleasant/74-75-78, Boonesboro/78, raiding KY-OH-VA/75-81, Blue Jacket War/77-94, Blue Licks/82, Crawford/82, raiding Ohio River valley/88-92, a elder from Wapakonetta 1817, Treaty 1831, move to KS 1832, husband about 1770 of **Mekoche Woman**/55, father of Sam Big Knife/75, George Big Knife/80, Tom Big Knife/88, John Big Knife/90, Fanny Knife/95, Younger Son/1800 & Youngest Son/1805

84. Big Little aka **Petitegros** - 1/2 Mekoche-Metis born about 1730 IN-died after 1770 - daughter of **Mekoche Woman** & **Coureur deBois**, wife about 1745 IN of **Mekoche Man**/25, widow 1763, mother of eight 3/4th Mekoche-Metis children/45-63-names unknown

85. Big Man aka Thawquotsaway-**Thawkwotsaway** – Kishpoko born about 1770 OH-died after 1832 - over 6'6" tall & big built, raiding Ohio River valley/88-92, Blue Jacket War/88-94, Prophet's Town/1811-

Brownstown/1812Monguagon/1812-1st Amherstburg/1812-Frenchtown/1813-Ft. Meigs/1813-2nd Amherstburg/1813 & Thames/1813 **with Tecumseh**, Treaty 1831, husband 1790 OH of **Chalakatha Woman**/75, children unknown

86. Big Moccasin - adopted-Ottawa born about 1745-died after 1778 - Cornstalk War/62-77, Pontiac War/62-66, Bushy Run/63, raiding NewGreenbrier-Jackson River valleys/63, raiding New-Ohio-Little Kanawha-Big Sandy River valleys/72, Point Pleasant/74-75-78, raiding VA-KY-OH/75-78, husband about 1765 OH of **Kishpoko Woman**/50, father of five 1/2 Kishpoko-Ottawa children/65-78

87. Big Nicholas aka Big Nickels – Chalakatha born about 1735 PA-died after 1778 OH – Cornstalk War/55-77, French-Indian War/54-63, Braddock/55, raiding New-Shenandoah River valleys/55, raiding PA/55-56, raiding Ohio-New River valleys/58, Pontiac War/62-66, Bushy Run/63, raiding New-Ohio-Little Kanawha-Big Sandy River valleys/72, Point Pleasant/74-75, Boonesboro/78 (**not Big Nicholas-Big Nigger-**the Delaware-Black)

88. Big Owl – Chalakatha born about 1750-died about 1783 – Cornstalk War/68-77, raiding Ohio-New-Big Sandy-Little Kanawha River valleys/72, Point Pleasant/74-75-78, Blue Jacket War/77-82, raiding KY-OH-VA/75-81, Crawford/82

89. **Big Rabbit aka Sepettekenathe**[10] – Thawikila born about 1740-died after 1777 – Cornstalk War/58-77, raiding Ohio-New River valleys/58, Pontiac War/62-66, Bushy Run/63, raiding New-Jackson-Greenbrier River valleys/63, raiding Ohio-Little Kanawha-New-Big Sandy River valleys/72, Point Pleasant/74-75, raiding OH-VA-KY/75-77, not in group that moved to AL 1774, (**not Blue Jacket**)

90. Big Rock - adopted-Cherokee born about 1750 TN-died after 1782 (OH?) – Cornstalk War/70-77, raiding Big Sandy-Little Kanawha-New River valleys/72, Point Pleasant/74, raiding KY-VA-OH/77-81, Blue Jacket War/7782, Boonesboro/78, Crawford/82, husband about 1770 KY of **Kishpoko Woman**/55, father of five 1/2 Kishpoko-Cherokee children/70-82

91. **Big Snake aka Shemepoo-Shemenetu-Shemenetoo**[11]-Schmentu - Mekoche born about 1720 PA-died about 1810 OH - brother of **Helizikinopo**/15, **Green Snake**/17 & **Great Snake**/25, raiding PA/40, Cornstalk War/55-77, French-Indian War/54-63, Braddock/55, raiding New-Shenandoah River valleys/55, raiding Ohio-New River valleys/58, Pontiac War/62-66, Bushy Run/63, raiding New-Jackson-Greenbrier River valleys/63, raiding Ohio-NewLittle Kanawha-Big Sandy River valleys/72, Point Pleasant/74-78, Blue

Jacket War/77-81, raiding KY-VA-OH/77-81, Crawford/82, signed Complaint to U.S.
1809 with sister **Helizikinopo**/15, son **Capt. Snake**/60, **Black Hoof**/30, **Wahappi**-Delaware & **Beaver**-Delaware, brother in law of **Cornstalk**/10, husband about 1740 of **Mekoche Woman**/25, father of Major Snake/40, Young Snake/45, John Snake/50, Thomas Snake/55, Capt. Snake/60

92. Big Snake (2) aka **Capt. Snake**-Shemepoo-Shemenetoo[8]-Shemenetu-Schemutu - Mekoche born about 1760 OH-died 1838 KS - son of **Big Snake (1)**/20 & **Mekoche Woman**/25, raiding KY-VA-OH/77-81, Point Pleasant/78, Crawford/82, raiding Ohio River valley/88-92, Blue Jacket War/78-94, signed Complaint to U.S. 1809 with father **Big Snake**/20, aunt **Helizikinopo Cornstalk**/15, **Black Hoof**/30, **Wahappi**-Delaware & **Beaver**-Delaware, a **Mekoche Chief** at Wapakonetta 1817, Treaty 1815, 1817, 1818, nephew of **Cornstalk**/10, moved to KS 1826 with **Prophet & Paukeesaa**, husband 1780 OH of **Kishpoko Woman**/65, children unknown

93. Big Sturgeon – Chalakatha born about 1740-died after 1782 OH – Cornstalk War/58-77, raiding Ohio-New River valleys/58, Pontiac War/62-66, Bushy Run/63, raiding New-Greenbrier-Jackson River valleys/63, raiding NewOhio-Little Kanawha-Big Sandy River valleys/72, Point Pleasant/74-78, raiding
KY-OH-VA/75-81, Blue Jacket War/77-82, Crawford/82

94. Big Swamp – Kishpoko born about 1750 OH-died after 1795 OH - Cornstalk War/68-77, raiding New-Ohio-Big Sandy-Little Kanawha River valleys/72, Point Pleasant/74-78, Blue Jacket War/77-92, Boonesboro/78, raiding KY-VA-OH/77-81, Blue Licks/82, Crawford/82, raiding Ohio River valley/88-92

95. Big Tooth – Kishpoko born about 1740 OH-died after 1780 – Cornstalk War/58-77, raiding Ohio-New River valleys/58, Pontiac War/62-66, Bushy Run/63, raiding New-Greenbrier-Jackson River valleys/63, raiding Ohio-Little Kanawha-Big Sandy-New River valleys/72, Point Pleasant/74-78, raiding KY-VA-OH/77-80

96. Big Tree (2) aka **Young Big Tree** – Thawikila born about 1760 OH-died after 1843 KS - son of **Big Tree (1)**/20, Point Pleasant/78, Blue Jacket War/7791, raiding KY-VA-OH/77-81, Crawford/82, raiding Ohio River valley/88, Harmar/90, St. Clair/91, scout-**with U.S. Army**-Fallen Timbers/94-War of 1812, living in Apple Creek MO 1815, moved to KS by 1832

97. **Big Turtle aka Shekaghkela**[12] – Chalakatha born about 1750 OH-died after 1817 - from the **Black Fish** band, brother of **Barshaw Turtle**/65, Cornstalk War/68-77, raiding Little Kanawha-Big Sandy-Kanawha River valleys/72, Point

Pleasant/74-75-78, raiding KY-OH-VA/75-81, Blue Jacket War/77-94, Boonesboro/78, Blue Licks/82, Crawford/82, raiding Ohio River valley/88-92, a **Chalakatha Chief** in OH by 1787, wounded at Ft. Recovery/94, Treaty 1817, husband 1770 OH of **Chalakatha Woman**/55, children unknown (**not Daniel Boone**)

98. Big Wife - adopted-Cherokee born about 1760 TN/NC-died after 1798 MO - wife about 1775 KY of **Kishpoko Man**/55, mother of nine or ten 1/2 Kishpoko-Cherokee children/75-95, widow 1798

99. Big Yankee Jim - adopted-Seneca born about 1780 OH-died after 1832 KS - scout-**with U.S. Army**-Prophet's Town/1811 & War 1812-Thames/1813, moved to KS 1832, husband about 1800 OH of **Chalakatha Woman**/85, father of several 1/2 Chalakatha-Seneca children/1800-20

100. Bigby, Mary Hicks - Wolf Clan Cherokee, wife 1st (of 3) 1775 of **Samuel Bigby**-white born 1750-died after 1778, mother of Susan Bigby/76 & James Bigby/78-both 1/16th Chalakatha-Thawikila-Cherokee-Creek Metis

101. Bilyeu, Mariya Pekowi aka Margaritia Pekowi - wife about 1728 of **Peter Bilyeu (1)**-white born 1700-died after 1750, mother of Hendrick Bilyeu (1)/29, Peter Bilyeu (2)/31, Euryda Bilyeu/33, Abraham Bilyeu/36, Mareytje Bilyeu/38, Stintye Bilyeu/40, John Bilyeu (1)/43, Aeltje Bilyeu/48 & Jonathan Bilyeu/50-all 1/2 Pekowi-Metis

102. Bird, Margaret - adopted white born about 1722-died 1765 - adopted 1757-returned 1765, died shortly return, wife 2nd 1757 OH of **Chalakatha Man**/17, mother **with Chalakatha** of Molly Bird/58, John Bird/60 & Nalupa Bird/62-all 1/2 Chalakatha-Metis

103. Biting Bug - Kishpoko born about 1770 OH-died after 1794 - raiding Ohio River valley/88-92, Blue Jacket War/88-94

104. **Black Bear aka Mugwa**[13] – Chalakatha born about 1750 OH-**murdered** 1774 WV - raiding Ohio-New-Little Kanawha-Big Sandy River valleys/72, murdered by Greathouse gang

105. Black Beaver – Mekoche born about 1750-died after 1778 – Cornstalk War/68-77, raiding Little Kanawha-Big Sandy-Ohio-New River valleys/72, Point Pleasant/74-75-78, raiding KY-OH-VA/75-78

106. Black Bobb aka **Wawahchepaehai**-John Bobb- Chalakatha born about 1775 OH-died 1864 - moved to MO about 1795, a **Chalakatha Chief** in MO, moved to OK/AR 1826 to avoid arrival of Ohio Shawnee, leader of Black Bobb's

Shawnee Heeritage

Band, husband 1st 1795 of **Thawikila Woman**/80, 2nd about 1816 of **Mathanahse-Martha Scarlett**/1800-Thawikila, children **with Thawikila** unknown, father **with Scarlett** of Julia Bobb/1827

107. **Black Body aka Cottawahcothi-Black Body**[14] LaForce - 3/4th Chalakatha-Mekoche-Black-Metis born about 1788 OH-died 1846 KS - son of **Mekoche Man**/63 & **Rachel LaForce-Apple-laPomme**/68, moved to KS 1832, Joseph Parks Co-**with U.S. Army**-Seminole War/1837, husband 1st by 1808 OH of **Chalakatha Woman**/90, 2nd by 1822 OH of **Mekoche Woman**/1807, children 1808-22 **with Chalakatha** unknown, father **with Mekoche** of Elizabeth Black Body/1822, other children likely

108. Black Buffalo - adopted-Miami born about 1740 OH-died after 1775 – Cornstalk War/58-75, raiding Ohio-New River valleys/58, Pontiac War/62-66, Bushy Run/63, raiding New-Jackson-Greenbrier River valleys/63, raiding OhioLittle Kanawha-Big Sandy-New River valleys/72, Point Pleasant/74-75, husband about 1760 OH of **Pekowi Woman**/45, father of about eight 1/2 Pekowi-Miami children/60-75

109. Black Bull - adopted-Cherokee born about 1730 TN-died after 1777 – Cornstalk War/55-77, French-Indian War/54-63, Braddock/55, raiding NewShenandoah River valleys/55, raiding PA/55-56, raiding Ohio-New River valleys/58, Pontiac War/62-66, Bushy Run/63, raiding New-Jackson-Greenbrier River valleys/63, raiding New-Ohio-Big Sandy-Little Kanawha River valleys/72, Point Pleasant/74, raiding KY-OH-VA/77, husband about 1750 TN of **Chalakatha Woman**/35, father of several 1/2 Chalakatha-Cherokee children/5077

110. Black Butcher - 1/2 Kishpoko-Black born 1730 (PA?)-died after 1765 - son of **African**/1700-adopted-black & **Kishpoko Woman**/10, Cornstalk War/5565, French-Indian War/54-63, Braddock/55, raiding New-Shenandoah River valleys/55, raiding PA/55-56, raiding Ohio-New River valleys/58, Pontiac War/60-65, Bushy Run/63, raiding New-Jackson-Greenbrier River valleys/63, a dark skinned, unattractive man, an especially viscous warrior, husband 1750 OH of **Kishpoko Woman**/35, father of several 3/4th Kishpoko-Black children/50-65

111. **Black Cat (1) aka Piktwaposetha-Pekatwaposetha**[15] – Chalakatha born about 1745 OH-died after 1790 – Cornstalk War/63-75, Pontiac War/63-66, Bushy Run/63, raiding New-Jackson-Greenbrier River valleys/63, raiding Ohio-Little Kanawha-Big Sandy-New River valleys/72, Point Pleasant/74-75, Blue Jacket War/77-90, husband about 1765 OH of **Chalakatha Woman**/49, father of Black Cat (2)/90

112. Blacked Eyes – Kishpoko born about 1755 OH-died after 1775 - Point

Pleasant/74-75, raiding in Ohio-New River valley/75

113. Black Face aka Black Face Caesar - 1/2 Thawikila-Black born 1740 OHdied after 1778 - son of **Caesar (2)-Black Caesar**/10 & **Thawikila Woman**/25, brother of **Yellow Legs**/45 & **Young Caesar**/50, raiding Ohio-New River valleys/58, Pontiac War/62-66, Bushy Run/63, raiding New-Jackson-Greenbrier River valleys/63, raiding New-Ohio-Little Kanawha-Big Sandy River valleys/72,
Point Pleasant/74, raiding VA-OH-KY/77, moved to MO 1778, husband about 1760 OH of **Thawikila Woman**/45, father of about eight 3/4th Thawikila-Black children/61-78

114. Black Feather aka **Peckandoughalisid**-Pekandohaleesee – Thawikila(adopted **Delaware then Wea**) born about 1750 OH-died after 1835 KS – Cornstalk War/68-77, **Chief of Wea village** 1778 when he **surrendered to George Rogers Clark**, Council Detroit 6-1778, allied with **Black Hoof**/30, **refused Tecumseh**, John Logan's scouts-**with U.S. Army**-War 1812, **a sub-chief of Hog Creek** 1835 under **John Perry**/75 & **William Perry**/70, associated with **Joshua Renicks**/46 & with mixed-tribe Mingoes, husband 1st about 1770 OH of **Delaware Woman**/55, 2nd by 1777 IN of **Wea Woman**/62, father **with Delaware** of several 1/2 Thawikila-Delaware children/70-76, **with Wea** of several 1/2 Thawikila-Wea children/77-1805

115. **Black Fish** aka **Chiungulla**- Paheataheaseka-**Makadaywahmayquah**[16] – Chalakatha-Mekoche born about 1725 PA-**killed** 1779 KY - son of **Chalakatha Chief**/05 & **Mother of Black Fish**/10-Mekoche, raised Chalakatha by father's family after father's death 1739, Cornstalk War/55-77, French-Indian War/54-63, Braddock/55, raiding New-Shenandoah River valleys/55, raiding Ohio-New River valleys/58, Pontiac War/62-66, Bushy Run/63, raiding Greenbrier-Jackson River valleys/63, Grand Council 1763, raiding Ohio-Big Sandy-Little Kanawha-New River valleys/72, Point Pleasant/74, **succeeded Cornstalk as Head Chief of Chalakatha & All Shawnee** in 1777, led 300+ warriors at Point Pleasant/78 **with Half King**-Wyandot, Boonesboro/78, **killed** in KY raid/79, step-half-brother (through marriage of his Mother/10 to Pride Opessa/10 who was also married to Rising Sun/15) of **Blue Jacket**/35, was referred to as the **uncle of Tecumseh**/68), husband 1745 OH of **Watmeme Opessa**/30-Pekowi, father **with Watmeme** of Chinwa/46, Black Fish (2)-Young Black Fish (1)/48, Pimegeezhigoqua/52, Black Fish (3)-Young Black Fish (2)/54, Parlie/56, Lamateshe/58 & Cheletha/60-all Chalakatha-Mekoche-Pekowi, adopted father 1778 & father in law of **Capt. Joseph Duquesne**/50-adopted-1/2 Pekowi-Wyandot-Metis, **Lewis Rogers**/50-white & **Henry Rogers**/55-white, adopted father of **William Jackson-Fish**/70-white & **Stephen Ruddle-Big**

Fish/68-white

116. Black Fish, Chelatha – Chalakatha-Mekoche born about 1760 OH-died after 1790 - daughter of **Black Fish**/25 & **Watmeme**/30, called a relative of **Tecumseh**, wife about 1775 OH of **Henry Rogers**/55-adopted white, mother of Polly Rogers/80 & William Rogers/85-both 1/2 Chalakatha-Mekoche-Metis

117. Black Fish, Chinwa – Chalakatha-Mekoche-Pekowi born about 1746 OH-**killed** 1774 Pt. Plsnt. WV - son of **Black Fish**/25 & **Watmeme Opessa**/30, Cornstalk War/63-74, Pontiac War/63-64, Bushy Run/63, raiding GreenbrierJackson-New River valleys/63, raiding Ohio-Little Kanawha-Big Sandy-New
River valleys/72, Point Pleasant/74, killed in battle at Point Pleasant/74, called a relative of **Tecumseh**, husband about 1765 OH of **Chalakatha Woman**/50, father of several children/65-74-(likely surnamed Blackfish)

118. Blackfish, Lemateshe aka **Lematashe**[17]-Launatashe-Auqualanaux – Chalakatha-Mekoche born about 1758 OH-died after 1800 - daughter of **Black Fish**/25 & **Watmeme Opessa**/30, called a relative of **Tecumseh**, wife 1st about 1778 OH of **Capt. Joseph Dusquene**/55-1/2 Pekowi-Wyandot-Metis, 2nd about 1784 OH of his half-brother **Anthony Shane**/63-1/4th Kishpoko-CreekWyandot-Metis, mother with **Dusquene** of David Deshane/80-1/2 Chalakatha-Mekoche-Pekowi-Wyandot-Metis, **with Shane** of David Dushane/85 & John Shane/90, Charles Chesne/95 & 2 daughters/96-1800-5/8th Chalakatha-Kishpoko-Mekoche-Pekowi-Creek-Wyandot-Metis

119. Black Fish, Parlie – Chalakatha-Mekoche-Pekowi born about 1756 OHdied after 1799 (MO?) - daughter of **Black Fish**/25 & **Watmeme**/30, called a relative of **Tecumseh**, wife about 1771 OH of **Lewis Rogers**/50-adopted white, mother of Nancy Rogers/72, Martha Rogers/74, James Rogers/78, Polly Rogers /82, Lewis Rogers/86-all 1/2 Chalakatha-Mekoche-Pekowi-Metis

120. Black Fish, Pimegeezhigoqua – Chalakatha-Mekoche-Pekowi born about 1752 OH-died after 1826 - daughter of **Black Fish**/25 & **Watmeme**/30, Shawnee name unknown, went by Chippewa name after marriage to Dusquene, called a relative of **Tecumseh**, wife 1779 OH of **Capt. Joseph Dusquene**/56-1/2 PekowiWyandot-Metis, mother of Joseph Dusquene Jr/80, Jean Baptiste Dusquene/85,
Isabella Dusquene/90 & Susanne Dusquene/95-all 1/2 Chalakatha-Mekoche-Pekowi-Wyandot-Metis

121. Blackfish, Watmeme Opessa – wife 1745 OH of **Black Fish**/25, mother of Chinwa/46, Black Fish (2)/48, Pimegeezhigoqua/52, Black Fish (3)/54,

Parlie/56, Lamatashe/58 & Cheletha/60-all Chalakatha-Mekoche-Pekowi, adopted mother & mother in law of **Capt. Joseph Dusquene**/55, **Lewis Rogers**/50 & **Henry Rogers**/55, adopted mother of **William Jackson Fish**/70 & **Stephen Ruddle**/68, moved to MO with adopted son Stephen Ruddle 1779, Ruddle returned to whites upon her death/97

122. Black Fish, Young (1) aka **Black Fish (2)** – Chalakatha-MekochePekowi born about 1748 OH-died after 1794 - son of **Black Fish**/25 & **Watmeme Opessa**/30, Cornstalk War/66-77, raiding Ohio-Little Kanawha-NewBig Sandy River valleys/72, Point Pleasant/74-75-78, Blue Jacket War/77-94, Boonesboro/78, Blue Licks/82, raiding KY-OH-VA/77-81, Crawford/82, raiding Ohio River valley/88, called a relative of **Tecumseh**, husband 1770 OH of **Chalakatha Woman**/55, father of Eli Black Fish/90-Chalakatha-MekochePekowi, adopted father of **George Ash**/65-adopted white

123. Black Fish, Young (2) aka **Black Fish (3)** – Chalakatha-Mekoche-Pekowi born about 1754 OH-**killed** 1788 KY - son of **Black Fish**/25 & **Watmeme Opessa**/30, Cornstalk War /72-77, raiding Ohio-Little Kanawha-Big Sandy-New River valleys/72, Point Pleasant/74-78, raiding Ohio-New River valleys/75, Blue Jacket War/77-88, Boonesboro/78, raiding KY-VA-OH/77-81, Blue Licks/82, Crawford/82, killed/88 in KY raid, with group that captured **John Taylor**/81-white, called a relative of **Tecumseh**, husband about 1774 OH of **Chalakatha Woman**/59, father of Young Black Fish (3)/80 & Joseph Black Fish/85-both Chalakatha-Mekoche-Pekowi

124. Black Fish, Young (3) – Chalakatha-Mekoche-Pekowi born about 1780 OH-died after 1837 KS - son of **Young Black Fish (2)**/54 & **Chalakatha Woman**/65, moved to MO about 1800, moved to KS before 1832, Capt. John Brown Co-**with U.S. Army**-Creek War/1813 & Joseph Parks Co-**with U.S. Army**-Seminole War/1837, husband about 1800 MO of **Chalakatha Woman**/85, father of Colatha Black Fish/1809

125. Black Foot - Kishpoko born about 1750 OH-died after 1794 – Cornstalk War/68-77, raiding New River valley/72, Point Pleasant/74-78, Blue Jacket War/77-94, Boonesboro/78, Blue Licks/82, raiding Ohio River valley/88-92

126. Black Fox aka **Black Fox Hop**-Black Fox Attakullakulla- Inali-Fox**Capt. Fox**-Black Fox Attakullakulla – ½ Chalakatha-Thawikila-Creek-**Cherokee** born 1740 Great Tellico TN-died 1811 KY – son of **Young Hop**/15 & **Ollie Nionee Oconastota**/20, adopted son 1746 of **Attakullakulla Carpenter**/06, Wolf Clan Cherokee, Cornstalk War/58-74, raiding Ohio-New River valleys/58, Pontiac War/62-66, Point Pleasant/74, Cherokee War/75, Pigeon Co-Cherokee

scouts-**with U.S. Army**-Revolution, assistant **Chickamauga Chief** under **Dragging Canoe** 1788-90, delegate to D.C./91, Treaty 1791, 1805, 1806, 1807, **Principal Chief** 1802-06 upon death of **Little Turkey-Standing Turkey (2)**/15, sided with **Double Head**/40 1806-10-deposed 1806(officially by 1810)succeeded 1806 by **Path Killer**, reinstated 1810-11, husband 1759 Great Tellico TN of **Grand Priber**/37-7/32nd Chalakatha-Cherokee-Metis, father of Young Black Fox /60, Daughter/62, Mary Ann Black Fox-Mary Ann Fox/64-all 1/4th Chalakatha-Thawikila-Creek-Cherokee-Metis

127. Black Hatchet - Kishpoko born about 1755 OH-died after 1781 - Point Pleasant/74-75, Blue Jacket War/77-81, Boonesboro/78, raiding on Ohio River/75-81

128. Black Heart - adopted-Cherokee born about 1740 TN-died after 1788 – Cornstalk War/58-77, raiding Ohio-New River valleys/58, Pontiac War/62-66, Bushy Run/63, raiding New-Ohio-Big Sandy-Little Kanawha River valleys/72, Point Pleasant/74-75-78, Blue Jacket War/77-88, Boonesboro/78, Blue Licks/82, Crawford/82, raiding Ohio River valley/88, husband about 1760 KY of **Chalakatha Woman**/45, father of about ten 1/2 Chalakatha-Cherokee children/60-88

129. **Black Hoof aka Catahekassa**[18] - Thawikila born 1730 (FL-AL?)-died 1831 OH - with Thawikila in SC-AL-FL with Creeks 1740, Cornstalk War/5577, French-Indian War/54-63, Braddock/55, raiding New-Shenandoah River valleys/55, raiding PA/55-56, raiding Ohio-New River valleys/58, Pontiac War/62-66, Bushy Run/63, raiding New-Jackson-Greenbrier River valleys/63, a **Thawikila Chief** in OH 1764, raiding Ohio-Little Kanawha-New-Big SandyNew River valleys/72, Point Pleasant/74, went south to Creeks with Thawikila late in 1774-returned about 1777, Blue Jacket War /77-94, Boonesboro/78, stayed in OH when most of Thawikila moved to MO starting in 1779, **succeeded Black Fish as Head Chief of All Shawnee** 1779-(when **leadership splits between Black Hoof**-Head Chief of the Thawikila faction & **Moluntha**-Head Chief of the Chalakatha & Mekoche faction), Blue Licks/82, raiding Ohio River valley/88-89, Treaty Greenville 1795-never opposed the whites again, Delegation to Congress 1779, 1802, Grand Council 1763, 1782, 1791, 1805, 1815, signed Complaint to U.S. 1809 with **Helizikinopo Cornstalk**/15, her brother **Big Snake**/20, **Capt. Snake**/60-all Mekoche, **Wahappi**-Delaware & **Beaver**Delaware, **refused Tecumseh**, succeeded 1831 as Chief by **John Perry**, brother of **Wife of Moluntha**/15, **Black Stump**/20, **Kikusgowlawa**/22, **Weasau**/24,
Capt. Johnny-Kekewepelethee/26, **Yellow Hawk**/28, **Kishkalwa-Tiger Tail**/35, husband 1st 1750 OH of **Thawikila Woman**/35, 2nd about 1790 OH of

Rabbit (2) -Nenexsa/70-Mekoche, father **with Thawikila** of Quasakee/60, Daughter/61, Falling Tree-Peaitchtha/63, Young Black Hoof/e70, Little Fox/80all Thawikila, **with Rabbit** of Thomas Blackhoof/90, Mary Blackhoof/1810, Eli Blackhoof/1820-Thawikila-Mekoche, many other children by both wives very likely

130. Black Hoof, **Falling Tree** aka Peaitchtha- Pht-**Peethatha**[19] – Thawikila born about 1764 OH-died 1832 OH - son of **Black Hoof**/30 & **Thawikila Woman**/35, moved south to AL Creeks 1774 with family, returned to OH 1777, Blue Jacket War /82-94, Blue Licks/82, Crawford/82, raiding Ohio River valley/88, never opposed whites after 1795, a **Thawikila Head Chief** at Hog Creek 1817, Treaty 1817, 1831.

131. Black Hoof, Little Fox aka Naecimo - Thawikila born about 1780 OHdied after 1835 KS - youngest son of **Black Hoof**/30 & **Thawikila Woman**/35, a Thawikila warrior at Hog Creek 1817, Treaty 1831, moved to KS 1832, **a subchief** in KS 1835 under **John Perry**/75 & **William Perry**/70, wife & children unknown

132. Black Hoof, Quasakee - Thawikila born about 1760 OH-died 1853 KS - oldest son of **Black Hoof**/30 & **Thawikila Woman**/35, moved to AL Creeks 1774 with family, returned to OH 1777, Blue Jacket War /78-94, raiding KYVA-OH/78-81, Boonesboro/78, Blue Licks/82, Crawford/82, raiding Ohio River valley/88-92, never opposed whites after 1795, delegate to D.C. 1802 with **Wayweleapee**/60, **John Perry**/75, **Spy Buck**/70, **Joseph Parks**/90 & **Francois Duchoquet**/66, an elder at Wapaghonettat 1817, Treaty 1817, moved to KS 1832 after death of father, husband 1780 OH of **Rabbit (1)-Nenuxse**/64, father of Thomas Blackhoof (1) -Quasakee (2)/85

133. Black Hoof, **Rabbit (1) aka Nenuxse-Nenookse**[20] – Mekoche, granddaughter of **Big Snake**/20, wife 1780 OH of **Quasakee Black Hoof**/60, mother of Thomas Blackhoof (1) –Young Quasakee/85

134. Black Hoof, **Rabbit (2) aka Nenexsa-Neneksa**[21] – Mekoche, 2nd wife about 1790 OH of **Black Hoof**/30, moved to KS 1832 after death of Black Hoof/30 with extended family, mother of Thomas Blackhoof (2)/90, Mary Blackhoof /1810, Eli Blackhoof/20 & others-all Thawikila-Mekoche

135. Black Hoof, Young - Thawikila born about 1770 OH-died after 1854 KS - son of **Black Hoof**/30 & **Thawikila Woman**/35, moved south to AL Creeks 1774 with family, returned to OH 1777, Blue Jacket War /88-94, raiding Ohio River valley/88-92, never opposed Americans after Fallen Timber/94, a Thawikila warrior 1817, moved to KS before 1832, Treaty 1854, wife & children unknown

136. Black Log in Water - Chalakatha born about 1740 PA-died after 1774 – Cornstalk War/58-74, raiding Ohio-New River valleys/58, Pontiac War/62-66, Bushy Run/63, raiding New-Jackson-Greenbrier River valleys/63, raiding NewOhio-Little Kanawha-Big Sandy River valleys/72, Point Pleasant/74

137. **Black Loon aka Cawtawawwawqua-Kahtahwawwahkwah**[22] – adopted-Mohawk born about 1762 (OH-died after 1794 - son of **Coohcoochee**/45-adopted-Mohawk & **Cokundiawtah**/40-adopted-Mohawk, joined Shawnee 1769 OH with mother, father, brothers **White Loon**/70 & **Wapunno**/65 & sister **Sotonegoo**/60, adopted brother 1792-93 (6 months) of **Oliver Spencer**-white, raiding KY-VA-OH/81, Blue Jacket War/80-94, Blue Licks/82, Crawford/82, raiding Ohio River valley/88-92, husband about 1780 of **Kishpoko Woman**/65, father of several 1/2 Kishpoko-Mohawk children/80-94

138. Black Oak aka Black Wood-Black Tree - Chalakatha born about 1725 PA-died after 1808 OH – brother of **Tall Oak**/20, half-brother of **Moose-Big Deer**/30, uncle of **Little Oak**/40 & **Leaning Oak**/45, relative/same clan as **Cornstalk**/10, Cornstalk War/55-77, French-Indian War/54-63, Braddock/55, raiding New-Shenandoah River valleys/55, raiding PA/55-56, raiding Ohio-New River valleys/58, Pontiac War/62-66, Bushy Run/63, raiding New-JacksonGreenbrier River valleys/63, a **Chalakatha Chief** by 1763, raiding Big SandyLittle Kanawha-Ohio-New River valleys/72, Point Pleasant/74-78, Blue Jacket War/77-94, Boonesboro/78, Blue Licks/82, Crawford/82, raiding Ohio River valley/88-92, Council 1808 with **Capt. Johnny** & **Buffalo**, wife & children unknown

139. Black Pigeon - adopted-Cayuga born about 1740-died after 1780 - Cornstalk War/58-77, raiding Ohio-New River valleys/58, Pontiac War/54-63, Bushy Run/63, raiding New-Greenbrier-Jackson River valleys/63, raiding Ohio-Big Sandy-Little Kanawha-New River valleys/72, Point Pleasant/74-75-78, Blue Jacket War/77-80, raiding KY-VA-OH/77-80, husband about 1760 OH of **Chalakatha Woman**/45, father of several 1/2 Chalakatha-Cayuga children/60-80

140. Black Skin aka LePeau Noire-Black Skin French - 3/4th ChalakathaBlack-Metis born 1741 Running Water TN-died after 1790 (WI?) - son of **Chalakatha Woman**/17 & **Capt. French**/12, came north with raiders & never returned to the south, Cornstalk War/58-77, raiding Ohio-New River valleys/58, Pontiac War/62-66, Bushy Run/63, raiding New-Jackson-Greenbrier River valleys/63, raiding Ohio-New-Little Kanawha-Big Sandy River valleys/72, Point Pleasant/74-75-78, Blue Jacket War/77-90, raiding KY-VA-OH/77-81, Boonesboro/78, Crawford/82, raiding Ohio River valley/88-90, Harmar/90, moved north-west 1790, husband about 1760 OH of **Kishpoko Woman**/45, father of several 7/8th Chalakatha-Kishpoko-Black-Metis children/60-90

141. **Black Snake aka Shemeneto**[23]- Kishpoko born about 1735 OH-died after 1818 – Cornstalk War/55-77, French-Indian War/54-63, a **Kishpoko War Chief** in 1755, Braddock/55, raiding New-Shenandoah River valleys/55, raiding Ohio-New River valleys/58, a general War Chief in 1760, Pontiac War/62-66, Bushy Run/63, raiding New-Jackson-Greenbrier River valleys/63, raiding NewOhio-Big Sandy-Little Kanawha River valleys/72, Point Pleasant/74-75-78, **succeeded Puckenshinwa as Head Chief of Kishpoko** 1774, Blue Jacket War/77-85, a **Civil Chief** in **Black Hoof** faction 1779, Crawford/82, stepped down as Chief 1785, succeeded by **Blue Jacket** (Kishpoko-Pekowi) as War Chief & **Yellow Hawk** (Thawikila) as Civil Chief in **Black Hoof** faction, Grand Council Sept. 1762, 1782, Treaty Camp Charlotte 1774, Greenville 1795, 1814, 1815, 1818, married a couple of times, father **with Later Kishpoko Wife** of Black Snake (2)-Young Black Snake/95

142. Black Stump aka **Ciuxa**-Keyooksa – Thawikila born about 1720 AL died after 1787 MO - raiding PA/40, Cornstalk War/55-74, French-Indian War/54-63, Braddock/55, raiding New-Shenandoah River valleys/55, raiding PA/55-56, raiding Ohio-New River valley/58, Pontiac War/62-66, Bushy Run/63, raiding New-Jackson-Greenbrier River valleys/63, raiding Ohio-Little KanwhaBig Sandy-New River valleys/72, Point Pleasant/74, Grand Council June 1762, a **Thawikila Chief** before 1762, Treaty Camp Charlotte 1774, move south to AL
Creeks late 1774-returned to OH 1777-moved to MO 1779 with (likely relatives) **Red Eagle** & **Red Snake**, brothers **Kikusgowlawa**, **Yellow Hawk** & 400 families, brother of **Wife of Moluntha**/15, **Kikusgowlawa**/22, **Weasau**/24, **Capt. Johnny**/26, **Yellow Hawk**/28, **Black Hoof**/30 & **Kishkalwa-Tiger Tail**/35, wife & children unknown

143. Black Thing aka Something Black - adopted-Cherokee (maybe Cherokee-Black?) born about 1750 TN-died after 1795 (OH?) - Cornstalk War/70-77, raiding Ohio-Little Kanawha-Big Sandy-New River valleys/72, Point Pleasant/74-75-78, Boonesboro/78, Blue Jacket War/77-94, raiding KY-VAOH/77-81, Crawford/82, raiding Ohio River valley/88-92, husband about 1770
(TN-KY?) of **Chalakatha Woman**/55, father of several 1/2 Chalakatha-Cherokee children/70-95

144. Black Turtle – Pekowi born about 1750 OH-died after 1795 – Cornstalk War/68-77, raiding Little Kanawha-Big Sandy-Kanawha-New River valleys/72, Point Pleasant/74-75-78, Blue Jacket War/77-94, Crawford/82, raiding Ohio River valley/88-92, Fallen Timber/94

145. Black Warrior - adopted-Cherokee (possibly adopted-Creek or CreekCherokee) born about 1740 (AL-TN?)-died after 1784 (OH?) – Cornstalk War/60-77, raiding Ohio-New River valleys/58, Pontiac War/62-66, Bushy Run/63, raiding Greenbrier-Jackson River valleys/63, raiding Ohio-New-Little Kanawha-Big Sandy River valleys/72, Point Pleasant/74-75-78, Blue Jacket War/77-84, Boonesboro/78, raiding KY-VA-OH/77-81, Crawford/82, husband about 1760 (AL-OH?) of **Chalakatha Woman**/45, father of several 1/2 Chalakatha-Cherokee children/60-84

146. Black Wasp – Kishpoko born about 1755-died after 1795 – Cornstalk War/72-77, raiding Ohio-Little Kanawha-Big Sandy-New River valleys/72, Point Pleasant/74-75-78, Blue Jacket War/77-94, raiding KY-VA-OH 1777-81, Blue Licks/82, raiding Ohio River valley/88-92

147. Black Willows - adopted-Cherokee born about 1760 TN-died after 1795 (OH?) – wife about 1775 TN of **Kishpoko Man**, mother of about seven 1/2 Kishpoko-Cherokee children/75-90, widow 1790

148. Black Wolf (1) aka **Peshkatewah Petwekwa** – Pekowi born about 1720 PA-**killed** 1786 OH - raiding PA/40, Cornstalk War/55-77, a **Pekowi Chief** in PA by 1750, French-Indian War/54-63, Braddock/55, raiding New-Shenandoah River valleys/55, raiding Ohio-New River valleys/58, moved to OH by 1760, Pontiac War/62-66, Bushy Run/63, raiding New-Jackson-Greenbrier River valleys/63, raiding Ohio-Little Kanawha-Big Sandy-New River valleys/72, Point Pleasant/74-78, Blue Jacket War/77-86, killed when kicked by a horse, wife & children unknown

149. Black Wolf, Soldier (1) aka **Maunahpeykaw**-Black Wolf's Son – 15/32nd Chalakatha-Mekoche-Pekowi-**Pottawatamee**-Metis born 1770 OH-died after 1832 KS - son of **Black Wolf Cornstalk (1)**/40 & **Pottawatamee Woman**/54, grandson of **Cornstalk**/10, raiding Ohio River valley/88-92, Blue Jacket War/88-94, scout-**with U.S.** Army-War 1812-Thames/1813-(against his sons), captured at Ft. Meigs/1813 & released by **Tecumseh**, Treaty 1832, moved to KS 1832, husband 1789 (IN-OH?) of **Pottawatamee Woman**/74, father of Soldier Black Wolf (2)/90-15/64th Chalakatha-Mekoche-Pekowi-PottawatameeMetis

Section III

B -Blackburn to Buzzard

B (Continued)

150. Blackburn, Mary Vann - 1st (known) wife about 1808 of **Lewis Blackburn**/78-1/4th Chalakatha-Cherokee-Metis, mother of Richard Blackburn/1808, Elizabeth Blackburn/1813, Frances H. Blackburn/1816, Louisa Jane Blackburn/1817 & Mary Ann Blackburn/1818-all 7/16th Chalakatha-Pekowi-Cherokee-Metis

151. Blanchard, Jean Jacques - adopted-French-(later adopted-Wyandot) born about 1720 FRA-died 1802 - French-Indian War/54-63, Braddock/55, living **with Shawnee** in OH by 1760, living **with Wyandot** in OH by 1780, Pontiac War/62-66, Bushy Run/63, raiding New-Jackson-Greenbrier River valleys/63, Point Pleasant/74, husband 1st before 1750 CAN of **French/Canadian Woman**, 2nd before 1760 (OH?) of **Native Woman** (likely Shawnee), 3rd before 1780 OH of **Mekoche Woman**/60, 4th after 1780 OH of **Wyandot Woman**, children **with French/Canadian** & **Native Wife**/50-80 likely surname Blanchard unknown, father **with Mekoche**/60 of Francis Blanchard/80-1/2 Mekoche-Metis-(Wyandot)

152. **Blanket Man aka Aquewelene**[24] – Pekowi born about 1730 PA-died after 1777 – Cornstalk War/55-77, French-Indian War/54-63, Braddock/55, raiding New-Shenandoah River valleys/55, raiding PA/55-56, raiding Ohio-New River valleys/58, Pontiac War/62-66, Bushy Run/63, raiding New-JacksonGreenbrier River valleys/63, raiding Ohio-Little Kanawha-New-Big Sandy River valleys/72, Point Pleasant/74-75, raiding KY-VA-OH/77

153. Blevins, Lucretia - Cherokee-Metis born 1800 VA-died after 1833 AR - daughter of **Jonathan Blevins**/79-Cherokee-Metis & **Charlotte Muse**/80-white, 2nd wife 1814 of **James Cooper**/96, mother of Julia Cooper/1822, Martha G. Cooper/1826, Edith Cooper/1833 & other children/1814-32-all 1/32nd Chalakatha-Thawikila-Creek-Cherokee-Metis

154. Blevins, Mahala Jane - Cherokee-Metis born 1801 VA-died after 1870 AL - daughter of **Jonathan Blevins**/79-Cherokee-Metis & **Charlotte Muse**/80white, wife 1823 of **Isaac Cooper**/1804, mother of Sarah Cooper/1818, William Cooper/1820, James Cooper/1822, Jackson Cooper/1825, Susan Elizabeth Cooper/1826, John Cooper/1828, Harmon Cooper/1830, Mary Polly Cooper/1831, Gaines Cooper/1833, Jemima H. Cooper/1839 & Nancy Frances Cooper/1842-all 1/32nd Chalakatha-Thawikila-Creek-Cherokee-Metis

155. Blind Chief - 3/4th Pekowi-Metis born about 1710 PA-died of smallpox

1759 OH - son of **Pekowi Chief** & **1/2 Pekowi-Metis Woman**, French-Indian War/54-59, Braddock/55, raiding Ohio-New River valleys/58, **a Pekowi Chief in OH** by 1759, blinded in one eye during battle with whites, husband about 1730 PA of **Pekowi Woman**/15, father of several 7/8th Pekowi-Metis children/30-59 names unknown

156. Blondeau - 1/2 Pekowi-**Metis** born about 1710 (IN?)-died after 1755 - son of **Pekowi Woman** & **Coureur deBois**-(name possibly assumed after the more famous **Maurice Blondeau**), raiding PA/40, French-Indian War/54, Braddock/55, raiding New-Shenandoah River valleys/55, husband about 1730 (IN-OH?) of **Pekowi Woman**/15, father of several 3/4th Pekowi-Metis children/30-55

157. Blondeau, Maurice - adopted-Chippewa-**Metis** born about 1735-died after 1790 - French-Indian War/54-63, Braddock/55, raiding New-Shenandoah River valleys/55, raiding PA/55-56, raiding Ohio-New River valleys/58, Pontiac War/62-66, Bushy Run/63, raiding New-Jackson-Greenbrier River valleys/63, raiding Ohio-Little Kanawha-Big Sandy-New River valleys/72, Point Pleasant/74, Boonesboro/78, associated **with Capt. Joseph Dusquene** & **Antoine Francois Maisonville**, brother of **Joseph Blondeau**/40, brother in law of **Gabriel Cotte**/40-adopted-French/Canadian & **William Joseph LeMothe**/301/2 Shawnee-Metis, Blondeau, Cotte & LeMothe married Shawnee sisters, husband of **Shawnee Sister (2)**/42-Kishpoko, father of several 1/2 Kishpoko-
Chippewa-Metis children/60-80

158. Blondine - 1/2 Mekoche-**Metis** born about 1750 (IN)-died after 1782 - son of **Mekoche Woman** & **French/Canadian Man**, Cornstalk War/68-77, raiding Ohio-Little Kanawha-Big Sandy-New River valleys/72, Point Pleasant/74, Boonesboro/78, raiding OH-KY-VA/75-81, Blue Jacket War/77-82, Crawford/82, husband about 1770 OH of **Mekoche Woman**/55, father of several 3/4th Mekoche-Metis children/70-82

159. **Bloody Fellow aka Nenetooyah-Ninatoogah**[25]-Nanetooquah-Nonetooquh-Nontuaka-Nittooktees-Northward-Looks Northward-**Iskagua-Clear Sky**-Ikegwa-Great Day - Kishpoko born 1740 Running Water TN-died 1794 Tsisdunagi Village NC - Cornstalk War/58-74, raiding Ohio-New River valleys/58, Pontiac War/62-66, Bushy Run/63, raiding New-Jackson-Greenbrier River valleys/63, raiding New-Ohio-Big Sandy-Little Kanawha River valleys/72, Point Pleasant/74, Cherokee War/75, Treaty Sycamore Shoals 1775, raiding KYOH-VA/77, Boonesboro/78, allied **1st with Dragging Canoe** & **Chickamauga, then with Americans**, delegate to Philadelphia-met **George**

Washington 1791, Council Coyatee 1792, Council Hanging Maw Town- survived attack by **John Beard's** renegade militia 1793, Council Tellico 1794, a Commissioner during Line Survey 1797, from Running Water (Shawnee) village, Treaty 1791, 1792, 1794, husband 1st 1758 Running Water TN of **Kishpoko Woman**/45, 2nd 1760 Great Tellico TN of **Wurteh Watts**/44-21/32nd Chalakatha-Pekowi-Cherokee-Metis, father **with Kishpoko** of Bloody Fellow (2)-Young Bloody Fellow/58Kishpoko, **with Wurteh Watts** of Tahlonteeskee/60-53/64th Kishpoko-Chalakatha-Pekowi-Cherokee-Metis

160. Bloody Vulture aka **Pisquisholees**-Peeskweeholeez – Kishpoko born about 1765 OH-died after 1794 – Blue Jacket War/82-94, Crawford/82, raiding Ohio River valley/88-92

161. Blue aka Blue Color-**Blue Man** – Kishpoko born about 1780 OH-died after 1817 - raiding OH-KY-VA/99-10, Prophet's Town/1811, Brownstown/1812-Monguagon/1812-1st Amherstburg/1812-Frenchtown/1813-Ft. Meigs/1813-2nd Amherstburg/1813 & Thames/1813 **with Tecumseh**, a warrior at Lewistown 1817, Treaty 1817, husband about 1800 OH of **Chalakatha Woman**/85

162. **Blue Bird aka Piskipahcah Ouiskelotha**[26]-Peeskeepahkah Weeskeelohtha – Mekoche born about 1775 OH-died after 1830 - captured by whites at **Col. Benjamin Logan**'s attack on **Moluntha**'s village 1786, stayed with whites until marriage/89, 1st wife about 1789 OH of **Capt. John Logan Big Horn**/74-7/8th Mekoche-Kishpoko-Pekowi-Creek-Metis, a widow at Wapaghonettat 1817, mother of Red Leaf/90, Aqueeshka/95, Cagashee Logan/96-all 15/16th Mekoche-Kishpoko-Pekowi-Creek-Metis

163. Blue Corn aka **Wapanoosa** - adopted-Miami born about 1750 OH-died after 1789 - wife about 1765 OH of **Mekoche Man**/50, mother of several 1/2 Mekoche-Miami children/65-82, widowed at Crawford/82

164. Blue Crane – Chalakatha born about 1740 PA-died after 1774 – Cornstalk War/58-74, raiding Ohio-New River valleys/58, Pontiac War/62-66, Bushy Run/63, raiding New-Jackson-Greenbrier River valleys/63, raiding Ohio-Little Kanawha-Big Sandy-New River valleys/72, Point Pleasant/74

165. Blue Feather (1) – Mekoche born 1745-**killed** 1778 Point Pleasant WV – nephew of **Helizikinopo Mekoche**-wife of **Cornstalk**, Cornstalk War/62-74, Pontiac War/62-66, Bushy Run/63, raiding New-Jackson-Greenbrier River valleys/63, raiding Little Kanawha-Big Sandy-Ohio-New River valleys/72, Point

Pleasant/74-75, raiding KY-VA-OH/77, killed Point Pleasant/78, wife & children unknown

166. Blue Fish – Pekowi born about 1760 OH-died after 1778 - raiding KYVA-OH/77, Point Pleasant/78, Boonesboro/78

167. Blue Fog – Pekowi born about 1730 (AL?)-died after 1775 – Cornstalk War/55-75, French-Indian War/54-63, Braddock/55, raiding New-Shenandoah River valleys/55, raiding PA/55-56, raiding Ohio-New River valleys/58, Pontiac War/62-66, Bushy Run/63, raiding New-Jackson-Greenbrier River valleys/63, raiding Ohio-Little Kanawha-Big Sandy-New River valleys/72, Point Pleasant/74-75, raiding Ohio-New River valleys/75

168. Blue Hawk – Kishpoko born about 1755 OH-died after 1777 - Point Pleasant/74-75, raiding KY-VA-OH/75-77

169. Blue Hen on Nest - adopted-Delaware born about 1730 OH-died after 1780 - wife about 1745 OH of **Chalakatha Man**/25, mother of several 1/2 Chalakatha-Delaware children/45-70, widow 1780

170. Blue Heron - adopted-Kickapoo born about 1750 (IN?)-died after 1777 - wife about 1765 of **Kishpoko Man**/45, mother of several 1/2 Kishpoko-Kickapoo children/65-76, widow 1777

171. Blue Jacket [27] aka **Weyapiersenwha**[28], **Wehyehpiherhsehnwah Whirlpool-(Sepettekenathe**[29]**-Big Rabbit-in youth)** – Pekowi-Kishpoko born 1735 PA-died 1809 OH - son of **Pride Opessa**/10-Pekowi & **Rising Sun**/15-Kishpoko, trading with Ohio Fur Co. in PA by early 1750's with brothers **Lawagqua**/33 & **Wabete-Elk**/37, Pekowi by birth but reverted to Kishpoko family with his mother upon death of Pride, Cornstalk War/55-77, French-Indian War/54-63, Braddock/55, raiding New-Shenandoah River valleys/55, raiding PA/55-56, raiding Ohio-New River valleys/58, Pontiac War/62-66, Bushy Run/63, raiding New-Jackson-Greenbrier River valleys/63, raiding Little Kanawha-Big Sandy-Ohio-New River valleys/72, Point Pleasant/74-75, led **Blue Jacket War**/77-94 = allied **with British-**Revolution/76-83, Vincennes/78, Point Pleasant/78, Boonesboro/78, Martin & Ruddle Stations KY/80, Lochery/81, Blue Licks/82, Crawford/82, Ft. Finney/86, raiding KY-TN/86, raiding Ohio River valley/88-92, Harmer/90, Dunlap Station/91, St. Clair/91, Ft. Recovery/94, defeated by Anthony Wayne & American Army at Fallen Timbers 1794, established Blue Jacket Town on Deer Creek of Sciota River OH by 1773, Treaty Camp Charlotte 1774, Council Ft. Pitt 1775 **with Cornstalk**/10, **Silverheels**/30, **Nimwha**/26 & **Wryneck**/25, Treaty Ft. Pitt 1776, Council Miami Jan. 1786, attended Treaty Ft. Finney 1786, a **Pekowi Chief** in OH by 1772, **succeeded Black Snake as War Chief** 1785-stepped down 1794, **succeeded Moluntha as Head of Chalakatha-Mekoche led faction** 1786, **succeeded Little Turtle** Miami **1794 as leader of United Tribes with Turkey Foot (1)**/50-adopted Ottawa, Treaty Greenville 1795, never opposed whites after 1795, Grand Council 1782, 1791, Sept. 1792, 1805, Treaty 1805, **refused Tecumseh** in early ventures but was supportive later, brother of Lawagqua/33, Wabete-Elk/37 & Sally/39-all Kishpoko-Pekowi, half-brother-(by 2nd marriage of Rising Sun to Kishpoko Man) of **No Worries-Marie Louise Sanschagrin**/54-(2nd wife of **Col. Matthew Elliott**) & **Yellow Britches-Edna Rising Sun**/56-(2nd wife of **Col. Alexander McKee**)-both Kishpoko, half-brother -(by 3rd marriage of Rising Sun/15 to Mohawk) of **Sarah Rising Sun**/59-1/2 Kishpoko-Mohawk-wife of **Brother of Mink**=mother of **Bright Horn** aka **Sarah Caldwell**-wife of **William Caldwell**=mother of **Billy Caldwell** aka wife of **James Colwell** aka wife of **William Vance**, half-brother (by marriage of Pride/10 to the Mother of Black Fish/10) of **Red Pole**/40-Pekowi-Mekoche, step-half-brother (by marriage 1739 of Pride Opessa/10 to Mother of Black Fish/10) of **Black Fish**/25, 1st cousin of **Watmeme Opessa**/30 & **Metheotashe Opessa**/40-(fathers were brothers), double-uncle of **Tecumseh**/68 (as 1st cousin of **Metheotashe** & brother-in-law of **Puckenshinwa**), husband 1st 1755 of **Older Sister of Puckenshinwa**/39-1/2 Kishpoko-Creek-Metis, 2nd 1762 OH of **Margaret Moore**/46-adopted-white, 3rd

1765 OH of **Clear Water Baby**/50-1/2 Pekowi-Metis, father **with Sister of Puckenshinwa** of Young Blue Jacket/56, Spybeech/58, Wayweleapee/60 & George Blue Jacket (1)/62-all 3/4th Pekowi-Kishpoko-Creek-Metis, **with Moore** of Joseph Moore-Blue Jacket/63 & Nancy Moore-Stewert/65-both 1/2 PekowiKishpoko-Metis, **with Clear Water** of James Blue Jacket/66, Son/70, Marie
Louise Blue Jacket/74, Sally Blue Jacket/76, Nancy Blue Jacket/78, George Blue Jacket/80-all 3/4th Pekowi-Kishpoko-Metis

172. Blue Jacket, Clear Water Baby - 3rd wife 1765 OH of **Blue Jacket**/35, moved to KS with family 1832, mother of James Blue Jacket/66, Son/70, Marie Louise Blue Jacket/74, Sally Blue Jacket/76, Nancy Blue Jacket/78 & George Blue Jacket/80-all 3/4th Pekowi-Kishpoko-Metis

173. Blue Jacket, Eliza aka Chowapea (Sarcoxie) – Pekowi born 1818 OHdied after 1857 KS – 2nd wife by 1837 KS of **Henry Blue Jacket**/99, moved to KS 1832, mother **with Henry** of Stephen/1838, Thomas Bluejacket/1841, Sarah E. Bluejacket/1844, Silas Armstrong Bluejacket/1848, Isaac Bluejacket/1852, Emma Bluejacket/1854, Joseph Bluejacket/1856-all 15/16th Pekowi-Kishpoko-Wyandot-Metis

174. Blue Jacket, George (1) aka Son of Blue Jacket- 3/4th Pekowi-KishpokoCreek Metis born 1762 OH-**killed** 1813 Kingston CAN – 4th son of **Blue
Jacket**/35 & **Older Sister of Puckenshinwa**/39, Blue Jacket War/80-94, raiding Ohio valley/88-92, **with British Army**-War 1812, killed at Kingston CAN 1813, 2nd cousin of **Tecumseh**, disowned by the sons of Clear Water Baby after the death of Blue Jacket for some reason, husband 1st about 1782 OH of **Catherine Hon**/68-adopted white, 2nd 1795 OH of **Kishpoko Woman**/80, father **with Hon** of about five 3/8th Pekowi-Kishpoko-Creek-Metis children/82-94 names unknown, **with Kishpoko** of about eight children/96-1812 (all may have been called Blue Jacket's)

175. Blue Jacket, George (2) - 3/4th Pekowi-Kishpoko-Metis born 1780 Mad
River OH-died 1829 Piqua OH – younger son of **Blue Jacket**/35 & **Clear Water Baby**/50, Blue Jacket War/86-94, translator-**with British Army**-War of 1812Thames/1813 with 2nd cousin **Tecumseh**, husband about 1798 OH of **Kishpoko
Woman**/84, father of Henry Bluejacket/99, George Bluejacket Jr- Nawahtahtha /1802, Betsy Bluejacket/1806, Kate Bluejacket/1810, John Bluejacket/1814, Charles Bluejacket/1816-all 7/8th Kishpoko-Pekowi-Metis, other children likely

176.   Blue Jacket, George Jr aka Nawahtahtha[30] - 7/8th Kishpoko-PekowiMetis born 1802 Piqua OH-died 1867 Johnson Co KS – 2nd son of **George Blue Jacket (2)**/80 & **Kishpoko Woman**/84, grandson of **Blue Jacket**/35, moved to
KS 1832, Treaty 1854, husband by 1837 (KS?) of **Mary Blackhoof**/1810-Thawikila-Mekoche, father of William George Bluejacket/1838, Charles Bluejacket/1846, Mary Bluejacket/1849, James Bluejacket/1851-all 15/16th Kishpoko-Pekowi-Thawikila-Mekoche-Metis

177.   Blue Jacket, Henry - 7/8th Kishpoko-Pekowi-Metis born 1799 Huron
River MI-died 1855 Johnson Co KS – oldest son of **George Blue Jacket (2)**/80 & **Kishpoko Woman**/84, grandson of Blue Jacket/35, **with British Army**-War 1812, Brownstown/1812-Monguagon/1812-1st Amherstburg/1812-Frenchtown/1813-Ft. Meigs/1813-2nd Amherstburg/1813 & Thames/1813 with 3rd cousin/uncle **Tecumseh**, moved to KS 1832, husband 1st about 1820 OH of **Kishpoko Woman**/1805, 2nd by 1837 Johnson Co KS of **Eliza Chowapea**/1818-Pekowi, children/1820-38 **with Kishpoko** unknown, father **with Eliza** of Stephen Bluejacket/1838, Thomas Bluejacket/1841, Sarah E. Bluejacket/1844, Silas Armstrong Bluejacket/1848, Isaac Bluejacket/1852, Emma Bluejacket/1854, Joseph Bluejacket/1856-all 15/16th Pekowi-KishpokoWyandot-Metis, adopted father of Eliza's son **George Sarcoxie**/1836-1/2 Pekowi-Metis

178. Blue Jacket, James aka Thucusca-**Teaskoota**- Teawascoota - 3/4th Pekowi-Kishpoko-Metis born 1766 Scioto River OH-died about 1845 KS – older son of **Blue Jacket**/35 & **Clear Water Baby**/50, Blue Jacket War/83-94, raiding Ohio River valley/88-92, Prophet's town/1811, Brownstown/1812-Monguagon/1812-1st Amherstburg/1812-Frenchtown/1813-Ft. Meigs/1813-2nd Amherstburg/1813 & Thames/1813 with 2nd cousin **Tecumseh**, Treaty 1814, 1817, moved to KS with Wyandot 1842, husband 1784 of **Wyandot Woman**/70, father of James Patexie Bluejacket/85 & Charles Bluejacket (1)/90-3/8th Pekowi-Kishpoko-Wyandot-Metis

179. Blue Jacket, James Jr aka Patexie - 3/8th Pekowi-Kishpoko-WyandotMetis born 1785 Maumee Rapids OH-died 1848 KS – older son of **James
Teaskoota Blue Jacket**/65 & **Wyandot Woman**/70, grandson of **Blue Jacket**/35, Brownstown/1812-Monguagon/12-1st Amherstburg/12Frenchtown/13-Ft. Meigs/13-2nd Amherstburg/13 & Thames/13

with 3rd cousin/uncle **Tecumseh**, moved to KS 1832, husband about 1805 of **Pekowi Woman**/90, 2nd 1834 KS of **Mathahpease**/90-1/2 Pekowi-Wyandot, father **with Pekowi** of David Blue Jacket/1805-11/16th Pekowi-Kishpoko-Metis, **with Mathahpease** of Mary Wahpanasee Bluejacket/1835, Stephen Bluejacket/1840 & Rebecca Bluejacket/1848-all 7/16th Pekowi-Kishpoko-Wyandot-Metis

180. Blue Jacket, Jim aka Little Blue Jacket - 3/8th Pekowi-Kishpoko-CreekMetis born about 1790 OH-**killed** 1812 - son of **Young Blue Jacket**/56 & **Maria Knodler Hon**/50-adopted white, Prophet's Town/1811, with 3rd cousin/uncle **Tecumseh**, killed by **Beaver**-Delaware while attempting to assassinate **William Henry Harrison**, any wife & children unknown

181. Blue Jacket, Joseph Moore - 1/2 Pekowi-Kishpoko-Metis born 1763 Scioto River OH-died before 1817 likely OH - son of **Blue Jacket**/35 & **Margaret Moore**/46-adopted white, raised by Blue Jacket after Margaret returned to the whites, Blue Jacket War/80-94, Prophet's town/1811, Brownstown/1812-Monguagon/1812-1st Amherstburg/1812-Frenchtown/1813-Ft. Meigs/1813-2nd Amherstburg/1813 & Thames/1813 with 2nd cousin **Tecumseh**, husband about 1783 OH of **Pekowi Woman**/66, no known descendants

182. Blue Jacket, Margaret Moore - adopted-white, 2nd wife 1762 OH of **Blue Jacket**/35, returned to whites 1765 under treaty with Bouquet while pregnant with Nancy, returned to OH about 1804 with Nancy & son in law James Stewert, lived in Lewistown OH village, mother of Joseph Moore Blue Jacket/63 & (after return to whites) Nancy Blue Jacket Moore (Stewert)/65-both 1/2 Pekowi-Kishpoko-Metis

183. Blue Jacket, Maria Louise aka Mary Blue Jacket - 3/4th PekowiKishpoko-Metis born 1774 OH-died 1806 Detroit MI – oldest daughter of **Blue Jacket**/35 & **Clear Water Baby**/50, 2nd cousin of **Tecumseh**, wife 1790/church marriage 1801 Detroit MI of **Jacques-Coco Lassalle**/67-Metis, mother of Marie Antoinette Lassalle/91, Jacques Lassalle Jr/1801, Susannah Lassalle/1804, Julia Lassalle/1806-all 3/8th Pekowi-Kishpoko-Metis

184. Blue Jacket, Mary Black Hoof - wife by 1837 of **George Blue Jacket Jr**/1802, moved to KS 1832, mother of William George Bluejacket/1838, Charles Bluejacket/1846, Mary Bluejacket/1849, James Bluejacket/1851-all 15/16th Pekowi-Kishpoko-Thawikila-Metis

185. **Blue Jacket, Mathahpease**[31] - ½ Pekowi-**Wyandot** born 1800 OH-died

1855 KS – daughter of **Pekowi Woman** & **Wyandot Man**, wife 1834 KS of **James Patexie Blue Jacket**/85, had moved to KS 1832, former wife of **Rev. Lewis McNiff**-white, mother **with McNiff** of Emily McNiff-Blue JacketWyandot-Metis, mother **with James-Patexie** of Mary Wahpanasee/1835, Stephen/1840 & Rebecca Blue Jacket/1848-3/16th Pekowi-Kishpoko-WyandotMetis

    186.   Blue Jacket, Nancy Moore - 1/2 Pekowi-Kishpoko-**Metis** born 1765
Hampshire Co WV-died 1840 Logan Co OH - daughter of **Blue Jacket**/35 & **Margaret Moore**/46-adopted white, sister of Joseph/62, born after Margaret returned to the whites, moved to OH about 1804, living at Lewistown OH 1817, 2nd cousin of **Tecumseh**, wife about 1785 WV of **James Stewert**/65-white, mother of Elizabeth Stewert/86, Henry Stewert/88, Margaret Stewert/90, John Stewert/92 & Sarah Ann Stewert/94-all 1/4th Pekowi-Kishpoko-Metis

    187.   Blue Jacket, Nancy **Wanasee** - 3/4th Pekowi-Kishpoko-Metis born 1778 OH-died 1876 Wyandotte Co KS – 3rd daughter of **Blue Jacket**/35 & **Clear
Water Baby**/50, 2nd cousin of **Tecumseh**, moved to KS 1832, never married

    188.   Blue Jacket, Older Sister of Puckenshinwa aka Kishpoko Wife, 1st wife
1755 OH of **Blue Jacket**/35, left Blue Jacket when he married **Margaret Moore**-white in 1762, mother of Young Blue Jacket/56, Spybeech/58, Wayweleapee/60, George Blue Jacket (1)/62-all 3/4th Pekowi-Kishpoko-CreekMetis

    189.   Blue Jacket, Sally - 3/4th Pekowi-Kishpoko-Metis born 1778 OH-died after 1823 MI – 2nd daughter of **Blue Jacket**/35 & **Clear Water Baby**/50, wife 1st 1794 of **William Short**/74-white, abandoned by Short when he returned to
ENG, 2nd 1799 **Charles Wilson**/82-5/32nd Chalakatha-Kishpoko-Thawikila-Black-Creek-Cherokee-Metis, left Wilson when she joined followers of Tecumseh to go to CAN 1815, mother **with Short** of Thomas Short/95-3/8th Pekowi-Kishpoko-Metis & **with Wilson** of Thomas Wilson (3)/1800-29/64th Chalakatha-Kishpoko-Thawikila-Black-Creek-Cherokee-Metis

    190.   Blue Jacket, Spy Beech - 3/4th Pekowi-Kishpoko-Creek-Metis born 1758 OH-died after 1817 (KS?) – 2nd son of **Blue Jacket**/35 & **Older Sister of**

Shawnee Heeritage

Puckenshinwa/39, Blue Jacket War/77-94, raiding KY-VA-OH/77-81, Point Pleasant/78, Boonesboro/78, Blue Licks/82, Crawford/82, raiding Ohio River valley/88-92, delegate to D.C. 1802 with **Wayweleapee/60, John Perry/75, Spy Buck/70, Joseph Parks/90 & Francois Duchoquet**/66, Prophet's Town/1811, Brownstown/1812-Monguagon/1812-1st Amherstburg/1812-Frenchtown/1813-Ft. Meigs/1813-2nd Amherstburg/1813 & Thames/1813 with 2nd cousin **Tecumseh**, disowned after the death of Blue Jacket by the sons of Clear Water Baby for some reason, an elder at Wapaghonettat 1817, husband 1778 OH of **Chalakatha Woman**/63, children unknown

191.   Blue Jacket, Wayweleapee aka Waywalapee-Waywalaapee-Wayweleapee- Clearwater - 3/4th Pekowi-Kishpoko-Creek-Metis born 1760 OHdied 1843 KS – 3rd son of **Blue Jacket**/35 & **Older Sister of Puckenshinwa**/39, Blue Jacket War/77-94, raiding KY-VA-OH/77-81, Point Pleasant/78, Crawford/82, raiding Ohio River valley/88-92, 2nd cousin of **Tecumseh**, scout**with U.S. Army**-War 1812, delegate to D.C. 1802 with **John Perry**/75,
Quaskee Black Hoof/60, **Spy Buck**/70, **Joseph Parks**/90 & **Francois Duchoquet**/66, 3rd **chief 1833** under **John Perry**/75, an Elder at Wapaghonettat 1817, Treaty 1817, moved to KS 1832, disowned by the sons of Clear Water Baby after Blue Jacket's death for some reason, husband 1780 OH of **Mekoche Woman**/65, children unknown

192.   Blue Jacket, Young aka Blue Jacket (2) -Son of Blue Jacket - 3/4th
Pekowi-Kishpoko-Creek-Metis born 1756 OH-**killed** 1792 OH – oldest son of **Blue Jacket**/35 & **Older Sister of Puckenshinwa**/39, Cornstalk War/74-77, Point Pleasant/74-75-78, Blue Jacket War/77-92, Boonesboro/78, Crawford/82, raiding Ohio River valley/88-92, Harmar/90, St. Clair/91, killed in raid, not acknowledged by the sons of Clear Water Baby for some reason, **2nd cousin of Tecumseh**, husband 1st about 1776 of **Pekowi Woman**/60, 2nd 1780 of **Maria Knodler Hon**/50-adopted-white, children **with Pekowi**/76-92 names unknown likely (may have been called Blue Jackets), father **with Hon** of Jim Blue Jacket/90-3/8th Pekowi-Kishpoko-Creek-Metis, other children/80-92 **with Hon** names unknown likely (may have been called Blue Jackets)

193.   Blue Pocket aka **Marmaduke Swearingen**-Duke Swearingen-White Snake-Blue Jacket - adopted-white born 1763 MD-died about 1824 (OH?) - brother of "Indian" **Van Swearingen**-white, adopted about 1775-never fully returned, Blue Jacket War/77-94, Blue Licks/82, raiding KY-OH-VA/75-81,
Crawford/82, raiding Ohio River valley/88-92, raiding KY-OH-VA/95-1810,

Prophet's Town/1811, Brownstown/1812-Monguagon/1812-1st Amherstburg/1812-Frenchtown/1813-Ft. Meigs/1813-2nd Amherstburg/1813 & Thames/1813 **with Tecumseh**, husband 1783 OH of (Blue Jacket's niece) **Swan-Wapehti Opessa**/68-3/4th Pekowi-Metis, children unknown

194. Blue Pocket, Swan Opessa aka Wapehti-Daughter of Elk-Swan Swearingen – niece of **Blue Jacket**/35-daughter of his brother **Wabete-Elk Opessa**/37, wife about 1783 OH of **Blue Pocket-Marmaduke Swearingen**/63adopted white, children unknown

195. Blue Turtle (1) - adopted-Kickapoo born about 1730 IN-died after 1774
(AL?) – moved to AL with Chalakatha band by 1755, returned to OH 1758, Cornstalk War/58-74, French-Indian War/58-63, raiding Ohio-New River valleys/58, Pontiac War/62-66, Bushy Run/63, raiding New-Jackson-Greenbrier River valleys/63, raiding Ohio-Little Kanawha-Big Sandy-New River valleys/72, Point Pleasant/74, moved to AL with band 1774, husband about 1750 OH of **Chalakatha Woman**/35, father of Young Blue Turtle/55 & several other children/50-75-all ½ Chalakatha-Kickapoo

196. Blue, Charity Marshall aka **Talithcuny** - wife by 1774 of **Barnabas Blue**-white born about 1757-died 1827 OH (possibly Barnabas Bilyeu?), mother of Fredrick Blue/74, Martha Patsy Blue/75, Uriah Blue/82, Solomon Blue/84,
Barnabas Blue Jr/87, Mary Blue/90, Esther Hetty Blue/92-all 1/4th ChalakathaMetis

197. Bonah – Chalakatha born about 1750 OH-died after 1778 - a Chalakatha warrior, Cornstalk War/68-77, raiding Little Kanawha-Big Sandy-Ohio-New River valleys/72, Point Pleasant/74-75-78, **captured Simon Kenton**, raiding
Ohio-New River valleys/75-78

198. Bone Digger – Mekoche born about 1740 OH-died after 1782 – Cornstalk War/58-77, raiding Ohio-New River valleys/58, Pontiac War/62-66, Bushy Run/63, raiding New-Jackson-Greenbrier River valleys/63, raiding Ohio-Little Kanawha-Big Sandy-New River valleys/72, Point Pleasant/74-75-78, Blue Jacket War/77-82, raiding KY-VA-OH/77-81, Boonesboro/78, Crawford/82

199. Bone Splitter - adopted-Cherokee born about 1750 TN-died after 1778 (OH?) – Cornstalk War/70-77, raiding Ohio-Little Kanawha-Big Sandy-New River valleys/72, Point Pleasant/74, raiding KY-OH-VA/75-77, Boonesboro/78, husband about 1770 TN of **Kishpoko Woman**/55, father of six 1/2 Kishpoko-

Cherokee children/70-82

200.   Bone, John - Mekoche-(adopted **Seneca**) - born about 1780-died after
1832 KS - scout-**with U.S. Army**-Prophet's Town/1811-War 1812-Thames/1813, Treaty 1832, move to KS 1832, husband about 1800 OH of **Seneca Woman**/85, father of ten 1/2 Mekoche-Seneca children/1800-30-(likely surname Bone)

201.   **Boney Legs aka Hokantitakarchi**[32] - Pekowi born about 1745 PA-died after 1779 - wife about 1760 OH of **Pekowi Man**/40, widow 1779

202.   Bonhomme, Andre - adopted-Ottawa-**Metis** born about 1725-died after
1766 - son of **Ottawa Woman** & **French/Canadian**, French-Indian War/54-63, Braddock/55, raiding Ohio-New River valleys/58, Pontiac War/62-66, Bushy Run/63, husband about 1750 (IN?) of **Mekoche Woman**/35, father of seven 1/2 Mekoche-Ottawa Metis children/50-66

203. Bonnisui - 1/2 Kishpoko-Ottawa born about 1775 OH-died after 1815 - son of **Kishpoko Man** & **Ottawa Woman**, brother in law of **Billy Dragoo**/75adopted white, Fallen Timber/94, visited white Dragoo family 1804 with Billy
Dragoo, brother of Billy's wife, husband about 1794 OH of **Kishpoko Woman**/79, children unknown

204. Boots aka Little Boots-Little White Boots – Thawikila born about 1750 OH-died after 1775 - wife about 1765 OH of **Thawikila Man**/45, widow in 1775

205. Bores In aka Kakinathucca (2) -**Borer**-Kekanathuko-Young Kakinathucca – Thawikila born about 1760 OH-died after 1802 - son of **Kakinathucca**/40 & **Metsigemewa**/45, Blue Jacket War/77-94, Point Pleasant/78, raiding KY-VA-OH/77-81, Blue Licks/82, Crawford/82, raiding Ohio River valley/88-92, Council 1797 **with Capt. Johnny, Black Beard, Buffalo & Capt. Mayne**-ENG, brother of **Altowesa**/70, adopted brother of **Boosisi**/60-adopted-Black & **Thomas Ridout**/70-adopted white

206. Bouganville, Charlotte Pemanich - 1/2 Mekoche-Metis born about 1758died 1808 - daughter of **Pemanich Pemenpiah**/35-Mekoche & **Louis Antoine Bouganville**/30-white-(adopted-Iroquois), wife 1st 1773 of **Mekoche Man**/53, widowed by 1778, 2nd 1783 of **Peter Lorimier**/48 aka Louis Lorimier-adoptedMetis, children/73-78 **with Mekoche** unknown, adopted mother 1778 of **Joseph
Jackson**/65-white, mother **with Lorimier** of Louis Lorimier Jr/84, Maria Louise Lorimier/86, Augusta Bouganville Lorimier/90, Agatha Lorimier/91, Verneuil

Raphael Lorimier/94, Victor Lorimier/96, Lisette Lorimier/1800-all 1/4th Mekoche-Metis

207. Bowl, Chief aka **Chief John Bowles (1)**-Bold Hunter-ToowayellahDuwali-John Watts (4) – 11/16th Chalakatha-Pekowi-Metis - born 1756 Settico TN-**killed** in battle 1839 TX - son of **Ghigoneli Bowles**/23 & **John Watts Sr**/04, took white name of his grandfather **John Bowles (1)**/1700-Scot upon his murder in 1769, as a 13 year old Bowl hunted down the murders & killed them, Blue Holly Cherokee-Red Paint Clan (by marriage?), great-nephew of Old Hop,
Treaty 1791, 1805, 1836, **Chief** 1786 of **Little Hiwassee Town** NC & **Chief** 1790 of **Running Water TN**, a Chickamaugua, moved to mouth of St. Francis River AR-(LA Territory) 1795-joined Shawnee-Cherokee already there, **Chief of St. Francis AR village before 1800**, settlement destroyed by 1811 earthquakemoved to between Arkansas & White Rivers-continued as **Head Chief of AR Cherokee** 1800-1813, Capt. John MacIntosh Co-**with U.S. Army**-Creek War/1813, moved to TX when he was excluded from Treaty 1819, **Head Chief TX Cherokee** 1827-39, founding member of Tahlequah OK Masonic Lodge, **killed 1839 in battle with Mexicans in TX**, most of family/band moved back to OK/1839, husband 1st 1776 Little Hiawassee TN of **Red Paint Woman**/60Cherokee, 2nd 1783 Running Water TN of **Ooloosta Tahchee**/60-15/64th
Chalakatha-Thawikila-Creek-Cherokee-Metis, 3rd 1794 Running Water TN of **Jennie Due**/64-19/64th Chalakatha-Cherokee¯Metis, 4th 1804 St. Francis AR of **Otiyu Vann**/86-5/8th Chalakatha-Pekowi-Black-Cherokee-Metis, children/76-83 **with Red Paint Woman** unknown, father **with Tahchee** of Lightning Bug Bowles/84, Tunooneski Bowles/86, Standing Man Bowles/88, Quatini Bowles/90 & Tsagina Bowles/92-all 29/64th Chalakatha-Pekowi-Thawikila-Creek-Cherokee-Metis, **with Due** of John Bowles Jr-Little Bowl/96, French Bowles/97, Nellie Bowles/98, Standing Bowels/99 & James Bowles/1800-all 3/8th Chalakatha-Pekowi-Cherokee-Metis, **with Vann** of Samuel Bowles/1805, Rebecca Bowles/1806, Standing In The Middle Bowles/1808, Nancy Bowles/1810, Catherine Bowles/1812 & Eliza Bowles/1813-all 21/32nd Chalakatha-Pekowi-Black-Cherokee-Metis

208. Bowman, Billy aka Two Goose-Neshwaueshwa[33] - ½ Mekoche-Metis born about 1757-died after 1777 - son of **Christian Bowman**/36-adopted-white & **Mekoche Woman**/40, half-brother of John Bowman/51-white, wife & children unknown

209. Brand aka Branded - adopted-Cherokee born about 1755 KY-died after 1778 (OH?) – branded while held captive by whites, Point

Pleasant/75-78, raiding KY-OH-VA/75-78, Boonesboro/78, lived **with OH-KY Shawnee**, husband about 1775 OH of **Kishpoko Woman**/60, father of some 1/2 Kishpoko-
Cherokee children/75-78

210.   Brant, Powlus - 1/4th Chalakatha-**Mohawk**-Metis - born about 1778 OHdied after 1832 KS - only son of **Joseph Brant**/42-Mohawk & **Christine Croghan**/58, lived with Ohio Shawnee-Seneca, Treaty 1832, move to KS 1832, husband about 1798 of **1/2 Chalakatha-Seneca Woman**/82, father of Susan
Brant/1800-3/8th Chalakatha-Seneca-Mohawk-Metis

211.   Brashears, Hannah Owens - wife 1783/church marriage 1802 of **Thomas
Brashears**-white born about 1752-died after 1804, mother of Sarah Brashears/83, Nancy Brashears/85, Elizabeth Brashears/90, William Brashears/97, Judith Susan Brashears/1802, George W. Brashears/1803, Owen Brashears/1804-all 5/16th Pekowi-Seneca-Metis

212.   Brave Boy – Kishpoko born about 1770 OH-died after 1794 - raiding
Ohio River valley/88-92, Blue Jacket War/88-94

213.   Breaks Bones - 1/2 Kishpoko-Cherokee-(adopted **Wyandot**) - born about
1750 Running Water TN-died after 1790 (OH?) – son of **Kishpoko Man** & **Cherokee Woman**, a big, burley man, noted for his strength & roughness, raiding Ohio-Little Kanawha-Big Sandy-New River valleys/72, Point Pleasant/74-78, raiding KY-OH-VA/75-81, Blue Jacket War/77-90, Boonesboro/78, Crawford/82, raiding Ohio River valley/88-90, Harmar/90, later lived with Wyandots, husband about 1770 OH of **Kishpoko Woman**/55, later of **Wyandot Woman**, father of several children/70-90

214. Breaks Bow – Thawikila born about 1735-died after 1779 - a Thawikila warrior, Cornstalk War/55-74, French-Indian War/54-63, Braddock/55, raiding New-Shenandoah River valleys/55, raiding PA/55-56, raiding Ohio-New River valleys/58, Pontiac War/62-66, Bushy Run/63, raiding New-Jackson-Greenbrier River valleys/63, raiding Ohio-New-Little Kanawha-Big Sandy River valleys/72, Point Pleasant/74, moved south to AL Creeks 1750-returned 1755-moved again 1774-returned to OH 1778-moved to MO 1779, husband about 1755 of **Creek Woman**/40, father of several 1/2 Thawikila-Creek children/55-79

215. Brewer, Susannah Fields (Walker) - Blind Savannah Clan **Cherokee**, wife 1797 of **George Brewer**-white born 1765-died after 1807, mother of Thomas Brewer/99, John Brewer/1801, Aky Brewer/1803 & Sarah Brewer/1805all 1/4th Chalakatha-Pekowi-Metis

216. **Bright Horn** aka Thothweillew-**Waskweela-Wathethewela**[34] - 3/4th Mekoche-Kishpoko-Mohawk born 1772 OH-died 1826 OH - son of **Sarah Rising Sun**/59 & **Brother of Mink**/50-Mekoche, grandson of **Rising Sun**/15 (mother of Blue Jacket/35), half-nephew of **Blue Jacket**/35, raiding Ohio River valley/88-92, Blue Jacket War/90-94, scout-**with U.S. Army-**War of 1812Thames/1813, a warrior at Wapaghonettat 1817, Treaty 1817, 1831, abandoned by Sarah & raised by family members, cousin of **Big Capt. Johnny**/65, **Tecumseh**/68, **Big Horn-Capt. John Logan**/74, **Otter**/70, husband 1787 of
Mekoche Woman/73, father of John Bright Horn/88-7/8th Mekoche-Kishpoko-Mohawk

217. Brock, Aaron aka **Red Bird** Carpenter (1) -Red Bird Great Eagle-Taleonteeskee-Cusawah-Tuchuwor-Tsisquaya-Totsuwha-Dotsuwa-TochuwarQuagi – 7/32nd Chalakatha-**Cherokee**-Metis born 1727 Great Tellico TN**murdered** 1796 Clay Co. KY - son of **Great Eagle Carpenter**/02 & **Wurteh Tawsee Fox**/05, Red Paint Clan Cherokee, **Chief of Taluegue**-Red Bird village, could speak, read & write English & cipher white style, Pontiac War/62-66, allied **with Cornstalk**/62-77, Point Pleasant/74, Cherokee War/75, Blue Licks/78, a Chickamauga, Pigeon Co-Cherokee scouts-**with U.S. Army**Revolution after 1778, took white-Christian name for marriage from about 1749after 1764, returned to Native name after death 1764 of Susanna Caroline Priber, moved to Barrens TN 1778, moved back to KY 1789, **murdered by whites** with friend Crippled Will-Cherokee, husband 1748 Great Tellico TN of his half-niece
Susanna Caroline Priber/30-7/32nd Chalakatha-Cherokee-Metis, father of Red Bird (2)-Aaron Brock Jr-Little Red Bird/48, Mahala Susannah/50, Jesse/52, George/54, Reuben/56, John/58, Mary Polly/60, James/62 & Amon Brock/64-all 7/32nd Chalakatha-Cherokee-Metis

218. Brock, James (1) aka Thunderstorm-Unalasgiunula – 7/32nd ChalakathaCherokee-**Metis** born 1759 Taluegue KY-died 1831 Cumberland Co KY - son of **Aaron Brock (1)-Red Bird Carpenter**/31 & **Susanna Caroline Priber**/36, **raised by John McLemore (3)**/1740- 1/8th Chalakatha-Cherokee-Metis (nephew of Charles McLemore/09) after the death 1764 of his mother, Cherokee scout & 10th NC Regiment-**with U.S. Army**-Revolution with brothers **Jesse Brock** &

John Brock & **John Euskulacau McLemore**/60, husband 1st 1780 NC/VA of **Matilda Crane**/56-white, 2nd 1788 TN of her sister **Mildred Crane**/58-white, father **with Matilda** of Elizabeth Brock (1)/82, Ann Brock/84, Joel Brock/86, **with Mildred** of George Ambrose Brock/89, Mary Polly Brock (3)/91, Allen Brock/94, Malinda Brock/96, Matilda Brock/1800-all 7/64th Chalakatha-Cherokee-Metis

219. Broken Knife – Chalakatha born about 1745 OH-died after 1782 - from **Okowellos-Cornstalk** band, Cornstalk War/62-77, Pontiac War/62-66, Bushy Run/63, raiding New-Jackson-Greenbrier River valleys/63, raiding Ohio-Little Kanawha-Big Sandy-New River valleys/72, Point Pleasant/74-75-78, Blue Jacket War/77-82, raiding KY-VA-OH/75-81, Crawford/82

220. Broken Path aka Follows Broken Path - 1/2 Thawikila-Creek born about 1755 AL-died after 1792 – son of **Thawikila Woman** & **Creek Man**, from Souvanogee (Shawnee) village AL, raiding KY-VA-OH **with Shawnee** & Cherokee/75-90, Blue Jacket War/77-91, Harmar/90 & St. Clair/91, may have returned to the South about 1792, husband about 1775 AL of **Creek-Black Woman**/60-(a McQueen?), father of several 1/4th Thawikila-Creek-Black children/75-92

221. Broken Stick - Chalakatha born about 1770 (OH-KY?)-**killed** 1810 Yahoo Falls KY - raiding Ohio River valley/88-92, Blue Jacket War/87-94, living **with Shawnee-Cherokee** in KY 1792-1810, associated with **Big Jake Troxell**, husband about 1790 KY of **Cherokee Woman**/75, father of several 1/2 Chalakatha-Cherokee children/90-1810 (that may have died at Yahoo Falls)

222. Broom, Little - Cherokee born about 1775-died after 1816 - son of **Tauchee Dutch Broom (2)**/27 aka Chief Broom (2) & **Ajosta Cherokee**/30, Wolf Clan Cherokee, grandson of Nancy Rainmaker (Carpenter White Owl)/1683 & Tauchee Dutch Broom (1)/1680, nephew of Kaiyateehee Broom/29 & Nancy Broom (1)/31-Cherokee, family had long association with the Shawnee, husband about 1816 of **Jennie Brown**/80-1/4th Chalakatha-Cherokee-Metis, children unknown

223. Brown Bird – Kishpoko born about 1780 OH-died after 1814 - wife about 1795 of **Kishpoko Man**/75, widowed at Thames/1813

224. Brown, Charlotte (1) - 1/4th Pekowi-Metis-(**Wyandot**) born about 1782 OH-died after 1855 KS - daughter of **Adam Brown**/47-adopted-white-(Wyandot) & **Daughter of Samuel Sanders**/62-1/2 Pekowi-Metis, wife 1st 1799 of **Thomas McKee**/70-1/2 Kishpoko-Metis, 2nd after 1800 of **Isaac Williams**/65Wyandot, moved to KS about 1843, mother **with McKee** of Thomas

McKee/1800-3/8th Kishpoko-Pekowi-Metis, mother **with Williams** of some 1/8th Pekowi-Wyandot-Metis children

225. Brown, Daughter of Samuel Sanders - wife 1775 OH of **Adam Brown**/47-white-(adopted-Wyandot), mother of Mary Brown/75, Joseph Brown/78, Theresa Brown/79, Samuel Brown/80, Charlotte Brown/81, John D. Brown/83, James Brown/84, Daughter/85, Adam Brown Jr/86, Matthew Brown/87, Daughter/88 & Julia Ann Brown/90-all 1/4th Pekowi-Metis-(Wyandot)

226. Brown, John (1) aka **Drowning Bear (1)**-YanungunskiYahnugungyahski-Yanaguska-Yonuguyasgi- Junalusky-Tsunulahunski-Gulkalaski-Tried But Failed (1) – adopted-white born 1700 (IRE?)-died after 1755 – husband 1st 1723 Chota TN of **Nionee Beamer**/04-1/2 Chalakatha-Metis (daughter of **Quatsis Hop & John Beamer**), 2nd 1738 Running Water TN of her half-sister **Quatsis Fox**/08-1/2 Chalakatha-Cherokee (daughter of **Quatsis Hop & Smallpox Conjurer-Tsula Fox**), father **with Nionee** of John Drowning Bear Brown (2)/24 & Samuel Brown/26-both 1/4th Chalakatha-Metis, **with Quatsis** of Alexander Brown/45, Mary Brown/47, Robert Brown/49 & John Drowning Bear Brown (3)-Junaluska (1)/51-all 1/4th Chalakatha-Cherokee-Metis

227. Brown, John (2) aka **Drowning Bear (2)**-YanungunskiYahnugungyahski-Yanaguska-Yonuguyasgi- Junalusky- TsunulahunskiGulkalaski-Tried But Failed (2) – 1/4th Chalakatha-Metis born 1724 Chota TNdied 1818 - son of **John Drowning Bear Brown (1)**/1700-white & **Nionee Beamer**/04, husband 1st 1744 of **Cherokee Woman**/30, 2nd 1752 of **Quatsis Oconastota**/36-1/2 Chalakatha-Cherokee (i.e. son in law of Oconastota), children/44-51 **with Cherokee** unknown, father **with Oconastota** of John Drowning Bear Brown (4)/53, Jennie Brown/55 & Patsy Brown/60-all 3/8th Chalakatha-Cherokee-Metis

228. Brown, John (3) aka Drowning Bear (3)-**Junaluska (1)**-**Yonaguska**Yanungunski-Yahnugungyahski-Yanaguska-Yonuguyasgi-Junalusky-Tsunulahunski-Gulkalaski-Tried But Failed – 1/4th Chalakatha-**Cherokee**-Metis born 1751 Running Water TN-died 1839 AR - son of **John Drowning Bear Brown (1)**/1700-white & **Quatsis Fox**/08, grandson of **Quatsis Hop**/1684 & **Tsula Fox-Smallpox Conjurer**/1670, refused Tecumseh, with U.S. **Army**Creek War/1813, saved **Andrew Jackson** at Horseshoe Bend/1814, **Head Chief NC Cherokee** 1832-39-(succeeded Big Bear aka Yanegwa), **Head Chief AR**

Cherokee Spring 1839, husband 1st 1770 TN of **Gowhistiski**/55-Cherokee, 2nd 1783 of **Lucy Benge**/68-21/64th Chalakatha-Pekowi-Cherokee--Metis, 3rd about 1794 **Lizzie Timberlake**/80-5/16th Kishpoko-Chalakatha-Thawikila-Pekowi-Creek-Cherokee-Metis, father **with Gowhistiski** of Witch Drowning BearKahtolstah/70 & Junaluska Drowning Bear (2)-Tsunuluhsgi/75-both 1/8th Chalakatha-Cherokee-Metis, **with Benge** of Junaluska Drowning Bear (3)/84 & daughter Katolista Drowning Bear/85-both 9/32nd Chalakatha-Pekowi-CherokeeMetis, **with Timberlake** of Big Witch Drowning Bear/95, Sarah Drowning Bear/96, Jennie Drowning Bear/98, Highanee Drowning Bear/1800-all 9/32nd Chalakatha-Kishpoko-Thawikila-Pekowi-Creek-Cherokee-Metis

229. Brown, John (4) aka Drowning Bear (4)-**Capt. John Brown** - 3/8th Chalakatha-**Cherokee**-Metis born 1753 Chota TN-died after 1817 Creek Path AL – son of **John Drowning Bear Brown (2)**/24 & **Quatsis Oconastota**/36, a trader with the Cherokee & Chickasaw, Capt-**with U.S. Army**-Creek War/1813, husband 1st 1773 TN of **Cherokee Woman**/58, 2nd 1797 of **Sarah Cherokee**/70, children/73-97 **with Cherokee** unknown, father **with Sarah** of David Brown/983/16th Chalakatha-Cherokee-Metis

230. Brown, Robert - 1/4th Chalakatha-**Cherokee**-Metis born 1749 Running Water TN-died 1835 Trail of Tears - son of **John Drowning Bear Brown (1)**/1700-white & **Quatsis Fox**/08, Colonel-**with U.S. Army**-Creek War/1813, Treaty 1806, 1817, 1819, husband 1st about 1770 of **Cherokee Woman**/55, 2nd 1786 of **Sarah Gosaduisga Hicks**/58-1/8th Chalakatha-Thawikila-CreekCherokee-Metis, father **with Cherokee** of Nancy Brown/78, Judge James Brown/79, Jennie Brown/80, Capt. John Brown/82, Isabella Brown (1)/84-all 1/8th Chalakatha-Cherokee-Metis, **with Hicks** of Charley Gosuisga Brown/90, Susan Brown/92, Mary Brown/94, Isabella Brown (2)/96, Isaac Brown/98 & Charlotte Brown/1800-all 3/16th Chalakatha-Thawikila-Creek-Cherokee-Metis

231. Brown, Theresa - 1/4th Pekowi-Metis-(**Wyandot**) born about 1779 (OH?)-died after 1820 - daughter of **Adam Brown**/47-adopted-white-(Wyandot) & **Daughter of Samuel Sanders**/62, wife 1st 1795 of **Andrew Clark**/60adopted-white-(Shawnee-Wyandot), 2nd 1800 of **Joseph Williams**/75-adopted-Mulatto-(Wyandot), mother **with Clark** of Alexander Clark/96, Thomas Clark/98 & George P. Clark/1800-all 1/8th Shawnee-Metis-Wyandot, children/1800-1820 **with Williams** unknown

232. Buffalo aka **Moothooshwah**[35]-Capt. Buffalo – Chalakatha born about 1750 OH-died after 1815 - raiding Ohio-New-Little Kanawha-Big Sandy River

valleys/72, Point Pleasant/74-75-78, raiding KY-OH-VA/75-81, Blue Jacket War/77-94, Crawford/82, raiding Ohio River valley/88-92, Council 1797 **with Capt. Johnny, Black Beard, Borer** & Capt. Mayne-ENG, Council 1808 **with Capt. Johnny** & **Black Oak**, living **with Munsee**-(mixed Shawnee-Delaware) on the Thames 1815, husband 1770 OH of **Delaware Woman**/55, children unknown

233. Buffalo Girl - adopted-Delaware born about 1740 PA-died after 1778 - wife about 1755 OH of **Chalakatha Man**/35, mother of several 1/2 Chalakatha-Delaware children/55-74, widow 1774

234. Buffalo Hump - adopted-Cherokee born about 1760 TN-died after 1795 (OH?) – Blue Jacket War/80-94, raiding KY-VA-OH/77-81, Point Pleasant/78, Crawford/82, raiding Ohio River valley/88-92, husband about 1780 KY of **Kishpoko Woman**/65, father of several 1/2 Kishpoko-Cherokee children/80-95

235. Buffalo's Daughter aka Wife of Red Giant – Chalakatha born about 1750 in Great Lakes area-died after 1788 – parents unknown, wife 1766 (OH-IN-MI?) of **Red Giant**/50, about 6' tall & heavy, widow 1788 OH, mother of Long Stepper/67, Big Corn/69, River Willow/71 & Little Giant/73-all over 6'6" tall

236. Buffington, Ezekial (1) - adopted-Scot born about 1740 SCO-died after 1813 - brother of **Joshua Buffington**/45-adopted white, raiding with Shawnee 1788, lived on edge of white & Native cultures, husband by 1777 Tomatley TN of **Mary Emory**/46, 2nd 1813 of her niece **Mary Due**/72, father **with Emory** of Ellis Buffington/78, Jennie Buffington/80, Elizabeth Buffington/82, Thomas Buffington/84, Susannah Buffington/86, Annie Buffington/88 & Mary Buffington/90-all 3/64th Chalakatha-Cherokee-Metis, children **with Due** unknown

237. **Bukangolas**[36] aka Bukangolas Hokolesqua-Bukangolas OkowellosBukangolas-Bukanghelas-**Breaks to Pieces**-Buckongahlas-Beloved Leader-He Who Fulfills – 3/8th Chalakatha-**Delaware**-Metis born 1720 PA-died 1804 OH - son of **Okowellos Hokolesqua**/1674 & **Delaware Wife**/1695, went to AL with father 1725, returned to PA by 1731, in OH before 1758, raiding PA/40, Cornstalk War /55-77, French-Indian War/54-63, Braddock/55, raiding NewShenandoah River valleys/55, raiding PA/55-56, raiding Ohio-New River valleys/58, Grand Council Sept. 1762, Pontiac War/62-66, Bushy Run/63, raiding New-Jackson-Greenbrier River valleys/63, Council 1763, a **Major Delaware Chief** by mid-1760's, raiding Ohio-New-Big Sandy-Little Kanawha River valleys/72, an **emissary to the Delaware for Cornstalk** 1774, scarred on left cheek-left ear cut off in battle by sword blow before 1778, Point Pleasant/74-78, Blue Jacket War /77-94, Council Detroit Nov. 1781, Grand Council 1782, Treaty 1785, Council Miami Jan. 1786 & Aug. 1786, Grand Council 1792, Treaty

Greenville 1795, Council Swan Creek OH 1795 with Capt. Johnny, Black Beard & George Ironside, Treaty 1803 & 1804, **refused Tecumseh** in early ventures, husband 1740 PA of **Delaware Woman**/25, father of many 3/16th Chalakatha-Delaware-Metis children/40-70

238. Bull Head aka Capt. Bullhead – adopted-Delaware - born about 1770 OH-died after 1843 KS - raiding Ohio River valley/88, Blue Jacket War/88-94, scout-**with U.S. Army**-War 1812--Thames/1813, Treaty 1832, move to KS 1832, husband about 1790 OH of **Mekoche Woman**/75, father of several 1/2 Mekoche-Delaware children/90-1815

239. Burnt Hands – Pekowi born about 1755 OH-died after 1780 - wife about 1770 OH of **Pekowi Man**/50, widow 1780

240. **Bushy Head** (1) aka Bushyhead Hop-**Chiesatebe**[37]-Bushyhead RavenBushyhead Moytoy-Bushyhead Greenwood – Chalakatha-Pekowi born 1718 Nickajack TN-died 1760 Nickajack TN - son of **Ahneewakee Muskrat**/04 & **Raven Hop**/1680, adopted son of **John Cheesquatalone Greenwood**/03, Blind Savannah Clan Cherokee, could cipher, read & write English, 2nd husband 1743 Great Tellico TN of **Nancy Greenwood**/20, father of Posetha-Posie Greenwood/49-31/32nd Chalakatha-Pekowi-Kishpoko-Black-Metis

241. Bushy Head (2) aka Bushyhead Carpenter-**Chicsatihi**-Bushy Head White Owl-Chicsatere-Chiksatere-Chiksateehee – 7/16th Chalakatha-**Cherokee**-Metis born 1724 Great Tellico TN-died shortly after 1814 OK - son of **White Owl Carpenter**/1678 & **Nancy Rainmaker**/1683, Wolf Clan Cherokee, could cipher, read & write English, husband 1st (her 2nd of 4) 1746 Great Tellico TN of **Nancy Augustus Hop**/26-Chalakatha-Pekowi, 2nd 1755 of **Unknown Woman**, father **with Nancy** of Bushyhead Carpenter (2)/50-7/32nd Chalakatha-Pekowi-Cherokee-Metis, other children unknown

242. Bushy Head (3) aka Bushyhead Stuart-**Oonodutu** -Donodutu - 3/64th Chalakatha-**Cherokee**-Metis born 1760 Great Tellico TN-died after 1835 OK - son of **Susannah Emory (1)**/44 & **Col. John Stuart**/30-white, Long Hair Clan Cherokee, **with U.S. Army**-Creek War/1813, husband 1st 1780 TN of **Cherokee Woman**/65, 2nd 1803 of **Nancy Gourd Foreman**/86-19/64th Chalakatha-Pekowi-Cherokee-Metis, children/80-1802 **with Cherokee** unknown, father **with Foreman** of Jesse Bushyhead/1804, Isaac Bushyhead/1808, George Bushyhead/1810, Nancy Otahki Bushyhead/1811, Charles Bird Bushyead/1814, Jacob Bushyhead/1816, Susan C. Bushyhead/1818-all 11/64th Chalakatha-Pekowi-Cherokee-Metis

243. Butcher – Kishpoko born 1740 OH-died after 1782 OH – Cornstalk War/58-77, raiding Ohio-New River valleys/58, Pontiac War/62-66, Bushy Run/63, raiding New-Jackson-Greenbrier River valleys/63, raiding Ohio-NewLittle Kanawha-Big Sandy River valleys/72, raiding Ohio River valley/81 **with**
Chief Logan, Point Pleasant/74-75-78, Blue Jacket War/77-82, Boonesboro/78, Blue Licks/82, raiding KY-OH-VA/75-81, Crawford/82

244. Butler, Capt. aka **Tamenatha**[38] - 7/16th Chalakatha-Mekoche-Metis born about 1763 OH-died about 1834 KS - son of **Nonhelema Hokolesqua**/18 & & **Richard Butler**/42-white-(adopted-Seneca), a Chalakatha warrior, raiding KY-VA-OH/81, nephew of **Cornstalk**/10, grandson of **Okowellos**/1680, Blue Licks/82, Crawford/82, raiding Ohio River valley/88-92, Blue Jacket War/82-94, **refused Tecumseh**, scout-**with U.S. Army**-Prophet's Town/1811-War 1812Thames/1813, Treaty 1814, 1815, moved to KS about 1832, half-brother of Nonhelema's Elder Daughter/45, Younger Daughter/50, Chieska/55, Youngest Daughter/57 & Capt. Johnny/59, wife & children unknown

245. Butler, Fanny – 3/16th Chalakatha-Creek-Metis born about 1755-died after 1781 - daughter of **Elizabeth Hokolesqua**/26 & **John Butler (1)Sugantah-Lodging Pole**/30-white-(adopted-Seneca), adopted daughter of her aunt **Nonhelema**/18, listed as prostitute 1781, niece of **Cornstalk**/10, granddaughter of **Okowellos**/1680, any husband & children unknown

246. Butler, Polly – 3/16th Chalakatha-Creek-Metis born about 1765 OH-died about 1854 KS - daughter of **Catherine Hokolesqua**/28 & **William Butler (1)**/44-white-(adopted-Seneca), known for her blue eyes & attractiveness, halfniece of **Cornstalk**/10, granddaughter of **Okowellos Hokolesqua**/1674, accused 1805 with Daughter/83 of being witches by followers of the Prophet, saved by a
Quaker Missionary, wife 1st 1779 OH of 1st cousin (son of mother's sister) **Chieska Moluntha**/55-15/16th Chalakatha-Mekoche-Metis, 2nd 1782 OH of **Joshua Logan Renicks**/46-adopted-white, mother **with Chieska** of Spy Buck Moluntha/80-9/16th Chalakatha-Mekoche-Creek-Metis, **with Joshua** of Daughter of Renicks/83-3/32nd Chalakatha-Creek-Metis

247. Butler, Tommy – 3/16th Chalakatha-Creek-Metis born 1760 OH-died 1833 KS - son of **Elizabeth Hokolesqua**/26 & **John Butler-Lodging Pole**/30white-(adopted-Seneca), nephew of **Cornstalk**/10, raiding KY-VA-OH/77-81,
Crawford/82, raiding Ohio River valley/88-92, Blue Jacket War/77-94, moved to KS 1832, wife & children unknown

248. Buzzard aka **Wewasee** – Chalakatha born about 1745 OH-died after 1775 – Cornstalk War/65-75, raiding Ohio-Little Kanawha-Big Sandy-New River valleys/72, raiding Ohio River valley/74 **with Chief Logan**, Point Pleasant/74, raiding Ohio-New River valleys/75

Section IV
Caesar to Conawapa (C)

C

249. Caesar (2) aka **Black Caesar**-Old Caesar-Caesar - adopted-Black born about 1710-died after 1778 - escaped slave, (**no connection to Caesar (1)Thomas Greenwood**/1680), adopted by the Thawikila by 1739, blacksmith for the tribe, Cornstalk War/55-74, French-Indian War/54-63, Braddock/55, raiding New & Shenandoah River valleys/55, raiding PA/55-56, raiding Ohio River valley/58, Pontiac War/62-66, Bushy Run/63, raiding New-Greenbrier-Jackson River valleys/63, refused to return to whites 1765, raiding Ohio-Little Kanawha-
Big Sandy-New River valleys/72, Point Pleasant/74, refused to return to whites 1775, Council Ft. Pitt-George Morgan 1776 **with Cornstalk, Nimwha, Ellinipsico, Capt. Johnny, Blue Jacket & Cawechile**, moved to MO 1778, husband by 1740 of **Thawikila Woman**/25, father of Black Face/40, Yellow Legs/45 & Young Caesar -Caesar (4)/50-all 1/2 Thawikila-Black

250. Caesar (3) – adopted-Black born about 1740 VA-died after 1812 MO - **escaped slave**-adopted 1774 (OH?),(**no connection to Caesar (1)-Thomas Greenwood**/1680 or to **Caesar (2)-Black Caesar**/10), Blue Jacket War/77-94, Point Pleasant/75-78, Boonesboro/78, Blue Licks/82, Crawford/82, raiding Ohio River valley/88-92, moved to MO 1812, husband 1774 OH of **Sally Kishpoko**/60, father of Caesar (6)/75, Sally's White Son/80, Sally's Black Son/85 & others/76-1805-all 1/4th Kishpoko-Black-Metis

251. Caesar (4) aka **Young Caesar**-John Caesar-**Juan Bautista Caesar** - 1/2 Thawikila-Black born 1750-died after 1795, son of **Caesar (2)-Black Caesar**/10adopted Black & **Thawikila Woman**/25, brother of **Black Face**/40 & **Yellow Legs**/45, Cornstalk War/68-77, raiding Ohio-Little Kanawha-Big Sandy-New
River valleys/72, Point Pleasant/74-75-78, raiding Ohio-New River valleys/75, Blue Jacket War/77-94, raiding KY-OH-VA/77-81, Crawford/82, raiding Ohio

River valley/88-92, moved to Spanish MO 1795, husband 1770 of **Thawikila Woman**/55, father of Caesar (5)/70, James Caesar/72, Nancy Caesar/74 & Lucy Caesar/76 & other 3/4th Thawikila-Black children/71-95

252. Cagashee aka Cagashee Logan - 15/16th Mekoche-Kishpoko-PekowiCreek-Metis born about 1795 OH-died after 1822 - daughter of **Capt. John Logan-Big Horn**/74 & **Blue Bird**/75, a Mekoche, sister of Red Leaf/90 & Aqueshkaa/93, half-sister of James Logan/1805, granddaughter of Tecumapease/58 & Mink/40, living at Wapaghonettat 1817, husband & children unknown

253. Calawesa – Mekoche born about 1770 OH-died after 1817 - raiding Ohio River valley/88-92, Blue Jacket War/78-94, a warrior at Wapaghonettat 1817, Treaty 1817

254. Caldwell, Billy aka Sauganash-Speaks English – 1/4th KishpokoMohawk-Metis-(adopted **Chippewa**) born 1777 OH-died 1841 IA - son of **Sarah Rising Sun**/59 & **William Caldwell (1)**/50-white, grandson of **Rising Sun**/15Kishpoko & **Mohawk Man**/10, abandoned 1779 by mother, educated at Jesuit monastery/84-92, half-nephew of Blue Jacket/35, **with Tecumseh & British Army**-War of 1812, secretary for cousin **Tecumseh**, Brownstown/1812Monguagon/1812-1st Amherstburg/1812-Frenchtown/1813-Ft. Meigs/1813-2nd Amherstburg/1813 **with Tecumseh**, sent on errand by Tecumseh before Thames/1813, Treaty Greenville 1795, 1829, 1832, 1833, husband 1st 1796 OH of his niece **LaNannette Tecumapease** aka **Maryanne-Nanette**/80 (niece of Tecumseh), 2nd 1803 of **Daughter of Robert Forsythe**/80-Chippewa-Metis, 3rd 1805 of **French Woman**/80-Chippewa-Metis, father of Alexander Caldwell, Elizabeth Caldwell & 6 more children

255. Caldwell, LaNannette Tecumapease aka Maryanne-Nanette - daughter of **Stands Firm**/60-adopted Chippewa & **Tecumapease**/58, granddaughter of **Metheotashe**/40 & **Puckinshinwa**/35 & granddaughter of **White SturgeonNamegousee**/30-Chippewa, niece of **Tecumseh**/68 (brother of her mother) & niece of **Mad Sturgeon**/65-Chippewa (brother of her father),1st wife about 1796 of her uncle (cousin of her mother) **Billy Caldwell**/77, any children uncertain

256. Caldwell, Thomas - 1/8th Kishpoko-**Metis** born about 1788 Sandwich CAN-died after 1838 - son of **Suzanne Baby**/60 & **William Caldwell**/50-white, scout-**with British /Army**-War of 1812, husband 1817

Sandwich CAN of his half-niece **Marie Antoinette Lassalle**/91, father of John Caldwell/1818, Charles Caldwell/1819, Mary Adeline Caldwell/1820, Francis Xavier Caldwell/1823,
William Charles Caldwell/1826, Anthony Edward Caldwell/1827, Joseph Hubert Caldwell/1830, Teresa Caroline Caldwell/1832, Susanne Emily Caldwell/1838all 1/4th Kishpoko-Pekowi-Metis

257.   Callahan, Mahala Susannah Brock - wife 1767 VA of **Edward Ned
Callahan** white born 1745 VA-died after 1800 KY, mother of John William Callahan/68, Jenny Jane Callahan/70, Zilphia Callahan/76, Charlotte Callahan/79, Elizabeth Callahan/83, Isaac Callahan/84-all 7/64th Chalakatha-Cherokee-Metis

258.   Calloway, Micagah aka Cager – adopted-white born about 1750-died after 1830 IN - adopted about 1760-returned to whites 1765-adopted 2nd time 1778-returned to whites about 1790, raiding Ohio River valley/81 **with Joseph Brant** & **George Girty**, scout- **with U.S. Army** -Fallen Timber/94, husband about 1775 (OH-KY?) of **Mekoche Woman**/60, father of 2 sons & 5 daughters/1775-1820-all ½ Mekoche-Metis

259.   Calossetee – Chalakatha born about 1770-died after 1817 - raiding Ohio
River valley/88-92, Blue Jacket War/87-94, a warrior at Lewistown 1817, Treaty 1817

260.   Cameron, Alexander aka Scotchee – adopted-white born 1730 SCO-died
1781 GA - 1st husband 1769 Great Tellico TN of **Ollie Mollie Attakullakulla Carpenter**/54, **adopted brother of Dragging Canoe**/34 (brother of Ollie Mollie), British Agent to Cherokee, raised Tory band among the Chickamauga during Revolution, father **with Ollie Mollie**/54 of Susanne Cameron/70, Archibald Cameron/72 & David Cameron/74-all 15/64th Chalakatha-Thawikila-Creek-Cherokee-Metis

261. Campbell, Elizabeth Watts – Red Paint Clan **Cherokee**, wife 1779 (AL?) of **William R. Campbell**

262. Sr.-white born 1755-died after 1824, mother of William R. Campbell Jr/80, Lucy Campbell/82, child/84, Elizabeth Campbell/86, Diana Campbell/88all 21/64th Chalakatha-Pekowi-Cherokee-Metis

263. Canacke – Thawikila born about 1770 OH-died after 1817 - raiding Ohio River valley/88-92, Blue Jacket War/88-94, a warrior from Hog Creek 1817, Treaty 1817

264. Canaqua aka Kanakwa – Mekoche born about 1775-died after 1817 - Fallen Timber/94, a warrior from Wapakoneta 1817, Treaty 1817

265. Candy, Samuel (2) aka Sam Candy Jr - 3/64th Chalakatha-CherokeeMetis born 1768 Chota TN-died 1837 TN - son of **Catherine Kingfisher**/52 & **Samuel Candy (1)**/44-white, Wolf Clan Cherokee, husband about 1790 of **Elizabeth West**/74-1/2 Chalakatha-Metis, father of Thomas Tsatagadihi Candy/92, Ollie Candy/93, Nancy Candy/96, George W. Candy/99, Samuel Candy (3)/1800, John Walker Candy/1803 & Peggy Candy/1808-all 17/64th Chalakatha-Cherokee-Metis

266. Caneshomo – Mekoche born about 1770 OH-died after 1817 - raiding Ohio River/88-92, Blue Jacket War/88-94, a warrior at Wapakoneta 1817, Treaty 1817

267. Canowun aka Canown – Mekoche born about 1780 OH-died after 1817 - a warrior at Wapakoneta 1817, Treaty 1817

268. Capain – Chalakatha born about 1770 OH-died after 1817 – Blue Jacket War/88-94, a warrior from Lewistown 1817, Treaty 1817

269. Capea – Mekoche born about 1775 OH-died after 1817 – Fallen Timer/94, a warrior at Wapakoneta 1817, Treaty 1817

270. Capeah – Mekoche born about 1775 OH-died after 1817 - Fallen Timber/94, a warrior at Wapakoneta 1817, Treaty 1817

271. Capeea – Mekoche born about 1755 OH-died after 1817 – Blue Jacket War/77-94, an Elder at Wapakoneta 1817, Treaty 1817

272. Capt. America aka American Chief – Mekoche born about 1760 OH-died after 1815 - scout-**with U.S. Army**-Revolution-War of 1812, living in MO 1815

273. Capt. Bill – Mekoche born about 1790 OH-**killed** 1838 OH - scout-**with U.S. Army**-War of 1812, **murdered Peter Cornstalk Sr.**/55 with Doc Bill/95 & Sam Loon/1800-both Shawnee, **killed by Peter Cornstalk Jr.**/85 in revenge

274. Capt. Billy – Chalakatha born about 1750 OH-died after 1817 - Point Pleasant/74-75-78, raiding Ohio-New River valleys/75, raiding KY-OH-VA/7781, Crawford/82, raiding Ohio River valley/88-92, Blue Jacket War/77-94, scout**with U.S. Army**-War 1812, Treaty 1817

275. Capt. Johnny (1) aka **Kekewepelethee**[39]-Kekewapiletee-Kakawipilathee**Tame Hawk**-Aholdkawah-Scares Up Game – Thawikila born about 1726 ALdied shortly after 1810 likely MO – moved from AL to OH 1755, Cornstalk

War/55-77, French-Indian War/55-63, raiding New-Shenandoah River valleys/55, Braddock/55, raiding New-Shenandoah River valleys/55, raiding PA/55-56, raiding Ohio-New River valleys/58, Pontiac War/62-66, Bushy Run/63, raiding New-Jackson-Greenbrier River valleys/63, a **Thawikila Chief** by 1766, raiding Ohio-Little Kanawha-Big Sandy-New River valleys/72, Point Pleasant/74, moved south with Thawikila band/74-returned to OH/79, Blue Jacket War/77-94, Crawford/82, Council 1785 Wapakonetta with **Alexander McKee**, **Matthew Elliott** & **James Sherlock**, Council Miami Jan. 1786, Treaty Ft. Finney 1786, became a **Principal Chief of Moluntha** faction 1786 upon death of Moluntha (**Blue Jacket** was leader of the other faction), Grand Council Nov. 1792, moved to MO after 1792 & leadership split again, Council Swan Creek OH with **Black Beard**, **Bukangolas** & **George Ironside**, Council with **Black Beard**, **Borer**, **Buffalo** & Capt. Mayne-ENG, Council 1808 with **Black Oak** & **Buffalo**, Council Brownstown 1810, brother of **Wife of Moluntha**/15, **Black Stump**/20, **Kikusgowlawa**/22, **Weasau**/24, **Yellow Hawk**/28, **Black Hoof**/30 & **Kishkalwa-Tiger Tail**/35, husband 1st about 1745 AL of **Thawikila Woman**/30, 2nd 1755 OH of **Adopted White Woman**/25, children/45-50 **with Thawikila** unknown, children/55-75 **with Adopted White** unknown

276. Capt. Johnny (2) aka **Johnny Tanacharisson-Straight Arm** Welepachon-Heylepacheion-Assilcius-Isreal- 1/2 Pekowi-**Seneca** born about 1722 PA-died after 1764 (OH?) - son of **Tanacharisson**/1700-Seneca & **Pekowi Woman**/05, scout-**with Colonial Army**-French-Indian War/54-63-Braddock/55, Treaty 1764, husband 1755 PA of **Seneca Woman**/30, children unknown

277. Capt. Johnny (3) aka Capt. Johnny Moluntha- Big Capt. Johnny-Capt. John-**Big John** – 15/16th Chalakatha-Mekoche-Metis born 1759 OH-died after 1815 OH - son of **Nonhelema Hokolesqua**/18 & **Moluntha**/10, grandson of **Okowellos**/1680, nephew of **Cornstalk**/10, a Chalakatha warrior, attended Council 1785 with **Alexander McKee** & **Matthew Elliott**, Blue Jacket War/7794, scout-Capt. John Logan Co-**with U.S. Army**-War of 1812, **killed Winnemak**-Pottawamee, nearly 7' tall, cousin of **Capt. John Logan-Big Horn**/74, **Otter**/70 & **Bright Horn**/70, half-brother of **Nonhelema's Elder Daughter**/45, **Younger Daughter**/50 & **Capt. Butler**/60, brother of **Chieska**/55 & **Nonhelema's Youngest Daughter**/57, husband about 1785 OH of **Rachel Kizer**/61-1/2 Chalakatha-Metis, father of two known 23/32nd Chalakatha-Mekoche-Metis children/86-90

278. Capt. Reed aka Red Man-Wawathethaka-Pathekoussia-WeeasesakaWacasesaka-Wathawakshua – Mekoche born about 1750 OH-died after 1825 - raiding Ohio-Little Kanawha-Big Sandy-New River valleys/72, Point

Pleasant/74-75-78, raiding KY-OH-VA/77-81, Crawford/82, raiding Ohio River valley/88-92, Blue Jacket War/77-94, listed as a leader in 1799, scout-**with U.S. Army**-War 1812, Treaty Greenville 1795, 1815, 1817, 1825, a **Mekoche Chief at Wapakoneta** 1817, husband 1st about 1770 of **Chalakatha-Cherokee Woman**/55, 2nd about 1797 OH of **Rachel McKee**/82-1/4th Kishpoko-BlackMetis, 3rd 1799 OH of **Mekoche Woman**/80, children/70-96 **with ChalakathaCherokee** unknown, father **with McKee** of Susannah Melinda Reed/98-3/4th Mekoche-Kishpoko-Black-Metis, **with Mekoche**/80 of Nancy Reed/1820

279. Capt. Will (1) aka **William Webber** (3) -Red-haired Will - ½ Chalakatha-Kishpoko-Metis born 1740 Chota TN-died after 1796 TN - son of **Lucy Ward (2)**/25 & **William Webber (2)**/12, adopted son 1751 of his aunt **Catherine Webber**/10 & **May Apple**/1690-Kishpoko upon death of his parents, called a half-brother of **Ostenaco Oconastota**/19, from Nequassee & Running Water TN, raiding New-Ohio-Little Kanawha-Big Sandy River valleys/72, Point Pleasant/74, raiding KY-OH-VA/77, Treaty 1785, Council with Blount 1792, moved west 1796, husband about 1760 (TN?) of **Sarah Bird Clan**/45-Cherokee, father of William Webber (4)/62, other children/63-71, Susan Webber/72, Robert Webber/74, Archibald Webber/76, David Webber/78, Elizabeth-Betsy Webber/80-all 1/4th Chalakatha-Kishpoko-Cherokee-Metis

280. Capt. Will (2) aka **William Emory Jr** - 7/64th Chalakatha-**Cherokee**Metis born 1744 Great Tellico TN-**murdered** 1788 Great Tellico TN - son of **Mary Grant**/26 & **William Emory**/20-white, tall, muscular, fair skinned, red hair, spoke-read-wrote English fluently, lived with & raided with the Shawnee, living in **Black Fish** (Chalakatha) village OH by 1772, Cornstalk War/72-77, raiding Ohio-Little Kanawha-Big Sandy-New River valleys/72, raiding Ohio River valley/74 **with Chief Logan**, Point Pleasant/74, raiding Ohio-New River valleys/75, raiding KY-OH-VA/77-78, with group that captured **Daniel Boone** 1778, murdered with **Old Abram** & **Old Tassel** , Long Hair Clan Cherokee, known husband 1764 Running Water TN of **Chalakatha Woman**/50, 1770 OH of **Adopted Mulatto Woman**/55, 1778 Great Tellico TN of **Deer Clan Woman**/60-Cherokee, several reported children **with Chalakatha** & **with Adopted Mulatto** unknown, father **with Deer Clan Woman** of Thomas-Long Tom Emory/79-3/64th Chalakatha-Cherokee-Metis

281. Capt. Will (3) - Chalakatha-**Cherokee**-Metis born about 1750 TN-**killed** about 1778 PA – parents unknown but known to be Chalaaktha-Cherokee-Metis, raiding Ohio-Little Kanawha-Big Sandy-New River valleys/72, raiding Ohio River valley **with Chief Logan**/74, Point Pleasant/74, raiding Ohio-New River valleys/75-78, Boonesboro/78, killed while raiding in PA/78, namesake of Will's

Knob PA, husband about 1770 KY of **Kishpoko Woman**/55, children unknown

282. Capt. Wolf - Mekoche-(adopted-**Delaware**-Mingo) - born 1755 OH-died after 1829 - Point Pleasant/74-75-78, raiding Ohio-New River valleys/75, raiding KY-VA-OH/77-81, Boonesboro/78, Blue Licks/82, Crawford/82, raiding Ohio River valley/88-92, Blue Jacket War/77-94, scout-**with U.S. Army-**War of 1812-Thames/1813, lived in Mingo village OH, husband about 1775 OH of **Delaware Woman**/60, father of several 1/2 Mekoche-Delaware children/75-1800

283. Captain (1) - born about 1725 PA-died about 1782 - raiding PA/40, French/Indian War/54-63, Braddock/55, raiding New-Shenandoah River valleys/55, raiding PA/55-56, raiding Ohio-New River valleys/58, Pontiac War/62-66, Bushy Run/63, raiding New-Greenbrier-Jackson River valleys/63, raiding Ohio-Little Kanawha-Big Sandy-New River valleys/72, Point Pleasant/74, raiding KY-VA-OH/77-81, Crawford/82, husband 1745 of **Captain's Wife**/30, children unknown

284. Captain (2) aka **Little Captain (1)**-Little Captain Powder Horn– 3/4th Thawikila-Metis born about 1770 OH-died after 1848 KS – son of **Powder Horn (1)**/40 & **Thawikila Woman**/45, moved to MO before 1800, a **minor chief** in MO, associated with **James Rogers (1)**/78-1/2 Chalakatha-Mekoche-PekowiMetis & **Jimmy Rogers (1)**/70-adopted white, Blue Jacket War/87-94, Fallen Timber/94, scout-**with U.S. Army-**War 1812-Thames/13, Treaty 1817, 1819, moved to KS 1832, husband 1st about 1790 of **Mekoche Woman**/75, 2nd 1848 of

Phoebe Perry/1828-1/2 Mekoche-Metis, father **with Mekoche** of Little Captain (2)/1809, Martha Captain/1814 & other children/90-1820-all 7/8th Mekoche-Thawikila-Metis

285. Capuchin - 1/2 Kishpoko-**Metis** born about 1740-died after 1777 - son of **Kishpoko Woman**/25 & **French/Canadian Soldier**/15 (associated with **Jean Baptiste Campeau**/11), Cornstalk War/62-77, Pontiac War/62-66, Bushy Run/63, raiding New-Jackson-Greenbrier River valleys/63, stirring trouble in OH 1767, raiding Ohio-New River valleys/72, Point Pleasant/74-75, brother in law of **Antoine Campeau**/39-1/2 Ottawa-Metis (married sister of Wife of Campeau/46), husband 1760 of **Kishpoko Woman**/44, father of several 3/4th Kishpoko-Metis children/60-77

286. Carpenter, Thomas Pashmere aka Thomas Carpenter (1)-**Corn Planter (1)** – adopted-white born 1607 Plymouth ENG-died 1675 Running Water TN – husband 1630 Shawnee village VA of **Pride Chalakatha**/1615, taught children to read, speak & cipher in English, father of Thomas-Trader Tom Carpenter (1)Moytoy (1)/35 & Pashmere Carpenter (1)/1637-both ½ Chalakatha-Metis

287. Carpenter, Trader Tom (1) aka Thomas Carpenter (2)-**Moytoy (1)-Corn Planter (2)**– ½ Chalakatha-Metis born 1635 VA-died 1693 Great Tellico TN – son of **Pride Chalakatha**/1615 & **Thomas Pashmere Carpenter-Corn Planter (1)**/1607-white, could cipher, read & write English, husband by 1658 Shawnee village VA of **Locha Chalakatha**/1640, father of Thomas-Trader Tom Carpenter (2)-Corn Planter (3)-Moytoy (2)/1660-3/4th Chalakatha-Metis

288. Carpenter, Trader Tom (2) aka Thomas Carpenter (3)-**Moytoy (2)-Corn Planter (3)-Wrosetasatow**– 3/4th Chalakatha Metis born 1660 Running Water TN-died 1734 ENG – son of **Trader Tom Carpenter (1)-Moytoy (1)-Corn Planter (2)**/1635 & **Locha Chalakatha**/1640, could cipher, read & write English, husband 1678 Running Water TN of **Nancy Chalakatha**/1664-(an aunt of **Old Hop** & his siblings), father of sons White Owl Carpenter-White Owl Raven-Moytoy (4)/1678, Thomas Carpenter (3)-Savannah Tom (1)-Corn Planter (4)-Moytoy (3)/1680 & daughter Pashmere Carpenter (2)/1681-all 7/8th Chalakatha-Metis & adopted father 1694 of daughters **Quatsis Hop**/1682, **Swan-Wapiti Hop**/1686, **April-Tkikami Hop**/1690-all Chalakatha & adopted father 1694 of sons **Raven (of Hiwassee) Hop**/1680, **Standing Turkey-Old Hop**/1688-both Chalakatha & adopted father 1698 of son **Oshasqua-MuskratMoytoy (5)**/1686- (likely a cousin of the Hop family, either the son of their father's sister or their mother's brother)

289. Cassik aka Kaseeka – Chalakatha born about 1770 OH-died after 1817 - raiding Ohio River valley/88-92, Blue Jacket War/88-94, a warrior from Lewistown 1817, Treaty 1817

290. Castle, Jacob (1) aka **White Tassel**-Hunter-**Taumee Elene-Corn Man**[40] – white born 1717 Lancaster Co PA-died 1789 Holston River VA – associated 1749 in VA **with John Downing, John Foreman, Charles Sinclair/St. Clair & John Vance**-all whites with Native/Shawnee wives), moved 1738 to Orange Co VA, purchased a Negro Wench 1740 from estate of **Jacob Stover, with U.S. Army**-Revolution-King's Mountain/80, husband 1st 1736 Lancaster Co PA of **Sowege-Gliding Swan-Mary Elizabeth**/22-Pekowi, 2nd 1759 Russell Co VA of **Wapehti-Swan**/44-Kishpoko, 3rd 1772 Russell Co VA of **Waupahathee**/56-½ Kishpoko-Cherokee, 4th 1787 Russell Co VA of ½ **Chalakatha-KishpokoCherokee Woman**/71, possibly some other Native or Metis wives yet unknownwith unknown children, father **with Sowege** of Valentine Castle/36-PA, Mary-Cawakawachi Castle/38-PA, Rachel Castle/40-VA, Elijah Castle/42, Catherine Castle/44, Benjamin Castle/46, Jacob Castle Jr/48, Littleton Castle/52, Joseph Castle/55 & others-all ½ Pekowi-Metis, **with Wapehti-Swan** of Bazel Castle/60,

Mary Castle/62, Henry Castle/64, John Castle/66 & Rachel Castle/68-all ½ Kishpoko-Metis, **with Waupahathee** of Abraham Castle/73, Joseph Castle/75, George Castle/77 & other children/74-87-all 1/4th Kishpoko-Cherokee-Metis, **with Chalakatha-Kishpoko-Cherokee** of David Castle/88-1/4th ChalakathaKishpoko-Cherokee-Metis, three other wives possible, children unknown

    291.   Castle, Jacob (2) aka **Jacob Castle Jr** – ½ Pekowi-**Metis** born 1748 Augusta Co VA-died about 1804 Russell Co VA – son of **Sowege-Gliding Swan**/22-Pekowi & **Jacob-White Tassel Castle**/17-white, husband 1769 PA of **Mary Shane**/54-1/2 Pekowi-Wyandot-Metis, father of Margaret Castle/70, Joseph Jacob Castle/75, Zedekiah Castle/80, Benjamin Castle/85, Zachariah Castle/87, Lydia Castle/89, John Joshua Castle/91, Elijah Castle/93, James Castle/95, William Castle/97, Mary Polly Castle/99, Inman Castle/1801 & others-all ½ Pekowi-Wyandot-Metis

    292.   Castle, Mary (1) aka **Cawakawachi** – ½ Pekowi-Metis born 1738 Lancaster Co PA-died after 1765 – daughter of **Sowege-Gliding Swan**/22 & **Jacob White Tassel Castle**/17-white, forced to return to whites-returned to Shawnee 1765, wife 1755 PA of **Pekowi Man**/35, mother of several 3/4th Pekowi-Metis children/55-65 names unknown

    293.   Catateehee, Nancy Ookummuh - wife 1785 Great Tellico TN of **Catateehee Cherokee**-born 1765-died after 1816, mother of Rebecca Naka Catateehee/93, Grasshopper-Wahchucha Catateehee/94, Young Catateehee/98, Celey Catateehee/1803, Jennie Catateehee /1804, Lucy Catateehee /1806, Ulayoha Catateehee/1808-all 11/64th Chalakatha-Thawikila-Creek-**Cherokee**-Metis - see **Nancy Ookuhmuh**/68

    294.   Cat Face – Chalakatha born about 1730 PA-died after 1764 - wife 1745 PA of **Chalakatha Man**/25, widow 1764

    295.   Catesikan aka Kateseekan - Chalakatha born about 1710-died after 1751 – living in PA 1725, raiding PA/40, living with Creeks in AL 1751

    296.   Catfish (1) aka **Tangookqua** – Chalakatha born about 1710 PA-died after 1759 OH - raiding PA/40, French-Indian War/54-63, Braddock/55, raiding Shenandoah-New River valleys/55, raiding PA/55-56, raiding Ohio-New River valleys/58, Council Philadelphia Dec. 1759, husband 1730 PA of **Chalakatha Woman**/15, father of Young Catfish/50 & other children

297. Catfish, Young – Chalakatha born about 1750 OH-died after 1778 – son of **Catfish-Tangookqua**/10 & **Chalakatha Woman**/15, Cornstalk War/68-77, raiding Little Kanawha-Big Sandy-Kanawha-New River valleys/72, Point Pleasant/74-75-78, raiding Ohio-New River valleys/75, raiding KY-VA-OH/7778

298. Catondemoilly - Pekowi born about 1730 PA-died after 1766 - FrenchIndian War/54-63, Braddock/55, raiding Shenandoah-New River valleys/55, raiding PA/55-56, raiding Ohio-New River valleys/58, Pontiac War/62-66,
Bushy Run/63, raiding New-Jackson-Greenbrier River valleys/63

299. Cat's Eye - Kishpoko born about 1760 OH-died after 1794 - Point Pleasant/78, raiding KY-OH-VA/77-81, Crawford/82, raiding Ohio River valley/88-92, Blue Jacket War/77-94

300. Cawaweskula aka Cawaweskucka-Kawaweskula-Kawawskuka – Mekoche born about 1770 OH-died after 1817 - raiding Ohio River valley/88-92, Blue Jacket War/88-94, a warrior at Wapakoneta 1817, Treaty 1817

301. Chakata – Mekoche born about 1770 OH-died after 1817 – Blue Jacket War/88-94, a warrior at Wapakoneta 1817, Treaty 1817

302. Chalakatha, Katie – Chalakatha born 1684 Nickajack TN-died 1738 Great Tellico TN - wife 1698 Nickajack TN of **Thomas Greenwood (2)-Caesar-Skiagunsta**/1680-7/8th Chalakatha-Kishpoko-Metis, mother of Thomas (3)Sutichettchee Greenwood/1698, John (2)-Cheesquatalone Greenwood/1700, daughters Quatsis Atawaya Greenwood/12, Nancy Greenwood/23 & Ankee Greenwood/29-all 15/16th Chalakatha-Kishpoko-Metis

303. Chalakatha, Locha – Chalakatha born 1640 Shawnee Nation-southwest VA-died 1692 Great Tellico TN – wife by 1658 Shawnee Nation-western VA of **Trader Tom Carpenter (1)-Moytoy I**/1635, mother of Trader Tom Carpenter (2)-Moytoy (2)/1660-3/4th Chalakatha-Metis

304. Chalakatha, Mikona – Chalakatha born 1644 Shawnee Nation-southwest VA-died 1695 Running Water TN, wife 1659 Shawnee Nation-southwestern VA of **Thomas Greenwood (1)-Skootekitehi (1)**/1641-1/2 Chalakatha-Metis, mother of Joseph (1)-Gorhaleke-Winter Fever Greenwood/1660, RichardGohoma Greenwood/1662, Martin-Owasta Greenwood/1664, David-Calunna-Raven Greenwood/1666, Killer-Nellawgitchi Greenwood/1668 & Hawk-Sinnawa-Tlanuwa Greenwood/1670-all 3/4th Chalakatha-Metis

305. Chalakatha, Nancy – born 1664 Running Water TN-died 1732 ENG - wife 1678 Running Water TN of **Trader Tom Carpenter (2)-Moytoy**

II/1660³/4ᵗʰ Chalakatha-Metis, mother of White Owl Carpenter-Raven-Moytoy IV/1678, Savannah Tom Carpenter(1)-Moytoy III/1680 & daughter Pashmere Carpenter (2)/1681-all 7/8ᵗʰ Chalakatha-Metis & adopted daughters Quatsis (Elder Sister Hop)/1684, Wapiti-Swan (Middle sister Hop)/1686 & April-Tkikami (Younger Sister Hop)/1691-all Chalakatha & adopted sons Oshasqua-Muskrat-Moytoy V/1686-Pekowi & Standing Turkey-Old Hop/1690-Chalakatha

306. Chalakatha, **Nepikeweewa**[41] – Chalakatha born 1625 Shawnee Nation southwestern VA-died 1680 Running Water TN - sister of **Pride Chalakatha**/1615, wife 1640 Shawnee Nation-southwestern VA of **John Greenwood (1)-Spemcia Elene-Big Man**/1619-adopted white, mother of Thomas Greenwood (1)-Skootekitehi/1641-1/2 Chalakatha-Metis

307. Chalakatha, Pride – Chalakatha born 1615 Shawnee Nation-southwestern VA-died 1679 Running Water TN – sister of **Nepikeweewa Chalakatha**/1625, wife 1630 Shawnee Nation-southwestern VA of **Thomas Pashmere Carpenter/Corn Planter (1)**-white born 1607 Plymouth ENG-died 1675 Running Water TN, mother of son Trader Tom Carpenter (1)-Moytoy I/1635 & daughter Pashmere Carpenter (1)/1637-both ½ Chalakatha-Metis

308. Chalakatha, Sedano – Chalakatha born about 1715 Rockingham Co VA died after 1774 – wife about 1735 southwest VA of **Matthew Fulk**/15-white, mother of Adam Fulk/36, David Fulk/38 & John Fulk/40-all ½ Chalakatha-Metis

309. Chalequa aka Chalekwa – Mekoche born about 1775 OH-died after 1817 - Fallen Timber/94, a warrior at Wapakoneta 1817, Treaty 1817

310. **Change of Feathers** aka **Penegashegan**[42] – Chalakatha born about 1715 PA-died 1805 OH - raiding PA/40, French-Indian War/54-63, Braddock/55, raiding Shenandoah-New River valleys/55, raiding PA/55-56, raiding Ohio-New River valleys/58, Pontiac War/62-66, Bushy Run/63, raiding New-Jackson Greenbrier River valleys/63, a **Chalakatha prophet** in his older years & forerunner of **Lalawethika-Tenskawatawa-Shawnee Prophet**/74

311. Chartier, Anna - 3/4ᵗʰ **Pekowi**-Metis born about 1730 PA-died after 1779 (PA?) - daughter of **Peter Chartier**/1690 & **Snow White Opessa**/1695, wife about 1750 PA of **David Troxell**/30-white, mother of child/52, Solomon Troxell/54, George Troxell/56, **Jacob-Big Jake Troxell**/58, John Troxell/60, Fredrick Troxell/62, twins Mary & Elizabeth Troxell/64, **Peter Jacob-Little Jake Troxell**/66, Abraham Troxell/68, David Troxell Jr/70 & Catherine Troxell/72-all 3/8ᵗʰ Pekowi-Metis

312. Chartier, Francois - 3/4th **Pekowi**-Metis born about 1712 PA-died after 1740 - son of **Peter Chartier**/1690 & **Snow White Opessa**/1695-Pekowi, husband about 1734 of **Younger Daughter of Poxinosa**/20-Pekowi, father of Nancy Chartier aka Nadachine/35-7/8th Pekowi-Metis

313. Chartier, Martin - adopted-French born 1655 FRA-died 1718 PA - arrived in America 1667 with **father Rene Chartier, brother Pierre Chartier & a sister** (possibly Rene-Jeanne Chartier), deserted in OH while on expedition to Illinois territory with LaSalle, in IL 1683-88, a fur-trader on Cumberland River TN 1689, in east TN-NC 1690, in PA 1700, husband 1687 IL of **Sewatha Straight-tail** aka Seaworth/1660, father of Mary Chartier/1688, Peter Chartier/90, Jacquette Chartier/1692 & likely other unrecorded children-all 1/2 Pekowi-Metis

314. Chartier, Mary aka Maria - 1/2 Pekowi-**Metis** born about 1688 (INTN?)-**killed** 1732 PA - daughter of **Martin Chartier**/1655-adopted-French & **Sewatha Straight-tail**/1660, **sister of Peter Chartier**/1690, **killed in Native attack with 7 of 12 children**, wife by 1705 PA of **Jean DeBert** aka John Burtwhite/1685, mother of Charles Christopher Dibert/20 & eleven other 1/4th Pekowi-Metis children (4 that survived Native attack-5 total)

315. Chartier, Mary aka Mary Chartteyr - 7/8th Pekowi-**Metis** born about 1770-died after 1790 - daughter of **Pale Stalker-Rene Chartier**/25 & **Pekowi Woman**/30, 1st wife about 1790 of **Francois Monjennier**/70-French-Canadian-Metis, children unknown

316. Chartier, Nancy aka Nadachine - 7/8th Pekowi-**Metis** born about 1735 PA-died about 1787 NC - daughter of **Francois Chartier**/12 & **Younger Daughter of Poxinosa**/20-Pekowi, wife about 1750 of **John Three Rivers Yaunts**/18-1/4th Pekowi-Delaware-Metis, mother of John Yaunts Jr/51-9/16th Pekowi-Delaware-Metis

317. Chartier, Pale Stalker aka Rene Chartier-Pale Croucher-Son of Peter Chartier - 3/4th **Pekowi**-Metis born about 1725 PA-died after 1775 (OH?) - son of **Peter Chartier**/1690 & **Snow White Opessa**/1695-Pekowi, a Pekowi warrior, French-Indian War/54-63, Braddock/55, raiding New-Shenandoah River valleys/55, raiding PA/55-56, raiding Ohio-New River valleys/58, Pontiac War/62-66, Bushy Run/63, raiding New-Jackson-Greenbrier River valleys/63, raiding Ohio-Little Kanawha-Big Sandy-New River valleys/72, Point Pleasant/74-75, husband about 1745 of **Pekowi Woman**/30, father of Elizabeth Chartier./60, Mary Chartier/70 & other unrecorded 7/8th Pekowi-Metis children/46-74

318. Chartier, Peter aka Wokonuckshenoah-Wacanackshina[43]-Shirtier-SartierSartee-Cortee-Chertier, Shirtee-Sirier - 1/2 **Pekowi**-Metis born about 1690 TNdied shortly after 1759 PA/OH - son of **Martin Chartier**/1655-adopted-French
& **Sewatha Straight-tail**/1660, French-Indian War/54-59, a **Pekowi Chief in PA** 1737, signed **Petition to PA 1738** with **Pride Opessa**/10, **Tecomteh Opessa**/1700 & **George Miranda**/1700, with band in IL & Detroit 1748-when French doubted his control over the band, in AL with band 1751 to 1755, in PA with band 1759, died either just before the band moved to OH or just after, husband about 1710 PA of **Snow White Opessa**/1695-Pekowi, father of Francois Chartier/12, Pale Stalker-Rene Chartier/25, Anna Chartier/30 & other children-all 3/4th Pekowi-Metis

319. Chartier, Sewatha Straight-tail aka Seaworth – a Pekowi, wife 1686 IL of **Martin Chartier**/1655-adopted French, mother of Mary Chartier/1688, Peter Chartier/1690, Jacquette Chartier/1692 & others-all 1/2 Pekowi-Metis.

320. Chatown – Kishpoko born about 1790-died after 1817 – Prophet's Town/1811, Brownstown/1812-Monguagon/1812-1st Amherstburg/1812Frenchtown/1813-Ft. Meigs/1813-2nd Amherstburg/1813 & Thames/1813 **with Tecumseh**, Treaty 1817, moved west 1825 with **Prophet** & **Paukeesa**, wife & children unknown

321. Chavinon aka Shawenese-Chaveenon - Kishpoko-(adopted **Ottawa**) born about 1730 OH-died after 1797 - French-Indian War/54-63, Braddock/55, Cornstalk War/55-77, raiding New-Shenandoah River valleys/55, raiding PA/5556, raiding Ohio-New River valleys/58, Pontiac War/62-66, Bushy Run/63, raiding New-Jackson-Greenbrier River valleys/63, Point Pleasant/74, raiding Ohio-New River valleys/75, raiding KY-VA-OH/77-81, Crawford/82, Council Detroit Sept. 1761, May 1763, Niagara July 1764, Detroit June 1778, husband about 1750 (IN-MI?) of **Ottawa Woman**/35, father of several 1/2 Kishpoko-
Ottawa children/50-80

322. Chawquawee aka Chawkwee-Chawkwawee – Kishpoko born about 1780 OH-died after 1831 - Prophet's Town/1811, Brownstown/1812-Monguagon/1812-1st Amherstburg/1812-Frenchtown/1813-Ft. Meigs/1813-2nd Amherstburg/1813 & Thames/1813 **with Tecumseh**, moved to CAN 1815returned 1825, Treaty 1831, husband about 1800 OH of **Chalakatha Woman**/84

323. Cheeseekau[44] aka Chiksika-Cheeseequa-Sting-Snakebite-Passquannakeek, Passquankake[45]-Gunshot-Shawnee Warrior (1)-Cheeseekau

Puckenshinwa - 3/4th Kishpoko-Pekowi-Creek-Metis born about 1756 AL-**killed 1792 TN** - oldest son of **Puckenshinwa**/35 & **Metheotashe Opessa**/40, a **Kishpoko War Chief**, Point Pleasant/74-75-78, Blue Jacket War/77-92, raiding KY-VA-OH/77-81 **with Dragging Canoe**/34 & **Chief Bob Benge**/62, Boonesboro/78, Blue Licks/82, Crawford/82, Council Miami Jan. 1786, raiding Ohio River valley/88, Harmar/90, St. Clair/91, led Shawnee contingent & was **killed at Buchanan Station** 1792, living in Running Water (Shawnee) village 1789-92 with brother **Tecumseh**, a Chickamauga, husband 1st about 1776 OH of **Kishpoko Woman**/60, 2nd about 1780 of **Daughter of Dragging Canoe**/563/16th Shawnee-Creek-Cherokee-Metis, father **with Kishpoko** of Tecumqualuska aka Graybeard (Cheeseekau)/77 & Great Shawnee Warrior (2)/80-both 7/8th Kishpoko-Pekowi-Creek-Metis & other child or two, father **with Daughter of Dragging Canoe** of Teciekeapease-Teseekeapease-Genevieve Marie (Cheeseekau)/90 & another child/92-both 31/64th Kishpoko-Pekowi-Chalakatha-Thawikila-Creek-Cherokee-Metis, other children likely

324. Chekposa – Kishpoko born about 1780 OH-died after 1817 - raiding OHKY-VA-TN/99-1810, Prophet's Town/1811-Brownstown/1812-Monguagon/1812-1st Amherstburg/1812-Frenchtown/1813-Ft. Meigs/1813-2nd Amherstburg/1813 & Thames/1813 **with Tecumseh**, Treaty 1817, a warrior at Wapaghonettat 1817, husband about 1800 OH of **Mekoche Woman**/85

325. Cherokee - 1/2 Kishpoko-Cherokee born about 1750 KY-died after 1788 OH – son of **Kishpoko Man** & **Cherokee Woman**, Cornstalk War/68-77, raiding Ohio-New River valleys/72, Point Pleasant/74-75-78, Blue Jacket War/77-88, Boonesboro/78, raiding KY-VA-OH/75-81, Crawford/82, raiding Ohio River valley/88, husband about 1770 KY of **Kishpoko Woman**/55, father of several 3/4th Kishpoko-Cherokee children/70-88

326. Chesne, Isadore aka Shetoon-Hayanemadae - 1/2 Wyandot-**Metis**(adopted-Chippewa) - born about 1735-died 1828 - son of **Catherine Sauvage**/1695-Wyandot & **Charles Chesne (1)**/1690-French/Canadian(adopted-Chippewa), some action in Cornstalk War/55-77, French-Indian War/54-63, Braddock/55, Pontiac War/62-66, Point Pleasant/74, Boonesboro/78, Crawford/82, some role in Blue Jacket War/77-94, Council Detroit 6-1778, 41781, 12-1781, 2-1782, 5-1782, 4-1783, 5-1790, Sandusky 10-1791, 9-1783, **met with Tecumseh** 6-1812 near Ft. Wayne, **Head Wyandot Chief of CAN**, succeeded by Solomon Warrow as Wyandot chief, brother of **Antoine Chesne**/30 & **Elleopelle-Mini Chesne**/25, husband 1st about 1754 OH of **Younger Daughter of Loyparkoweh Opessa**/38-Pekowi, 2nd by 1759 OH of **Older Sister of Puckenshinwa**/39-1/2 Kishpoko-Creek-Metis-(same clan as Tecumseh), 3rd 1774 of **Therese Becquet**/40-Ottawa-Metis, father **with Opessa**

of **Capt. Joseph Dusquene**/55-1/2 Pekowi-Wyandot-Metis, **with Puckenshinwa** of Anthony Shane/63 & Joseph Shane/65-both 1/2 Kishpoko-Wyandot-Metis & **with Becquet** of **Mary Josette Chesne**/75-Ottawa-Wyandot-Metis

327. Chestnut aka **Tillehaweh** – adopted-Cherokee born about 1750 TN-died after 1813 - from Hiwassee, Cornstalk War/72-77, raiding Ohio-New-Little Kanawha-Big Sandy River valleys/72, Point Pleasant/74, Cherokee War/75, Treaty Sycamore Shoals 1775, raiding KY-OH-VA/77-81, Booneboro/78, Crawford/82, raiding Ohio River valley/88-92, Blue Jacket War/77-94, Capt. John Speers Co-**with U.S. Army**-Creek War/1813, husband about 1770 KY of **Kishpoko Woman**/55, father of several 1/2 Kishpoko-Cherokee children/70-1800

328. Chieska aka Chieska Moluntha- **Capt. Chieska**-Young King-Young Moluntha-**Capt. Tom**-Capt. Tommy-Cheachisika-Jakeshaw-Chakalakek-Cheacksca-Chiachisika-Capt. Shigsta – 15/16th Mekoche-Chalakatha-Metis born 1755 OH-died of cholera 1833 - son of **Moluntha**/10-Mekoche & **Nonhelema Hokolesqua**/18, a Mekoche, over 6' tall, Blue Jacket War/77-94, raiding KYVA-OH/77-81, Point Pleasant/78, Crawford/82, raiding Ohio River valley/88-92, scout-Capt. John Logan Co-Anthony Shane Co-William Wells Co-**with U.S. Army**-War of 1812, a **Chalakatha Chief** at Wapaghonettat 1817, Treaty 1804, 1817, 1818, 1831, husband 1st 1779 OH of 1st cousin (daughter of mother's sister) **Polly Butler**/65-3/16th Chalakatha-Creek-Metis, 2nd 1780 OH of **Chalakatha Woman**/65, father **with Polly** of Spy Buck Moluntha/80-9/16th Mekoche-Chalakatha-Creek-Metis, children **with Chalakatha**/65 unknown

329. Chikatakyen aka Cheekatakien - Kishpoko-(adopted-Chippewa) born about 1750 IN-died after 1795 – Cornstalk War/72-77, raiding Ohio-New-Little Kanawha-Big Sandy River valleys/72, raiding Ohio River valley/74 **with Chief Logan**, Point Pleasant/74-75-78, Blue Jacket War/77-94, raiding KY-VAOH/77-81, Crawford/82, raiding Ohio River valley/88-92, husband about 1770 (MI?) of **Chippewa Woman**/55, father of several 1/2 Kishpoko-Chippewa children/70-95

330. Chikatommo aka Cheekatommo – ½ Chalakatha-Creek born about 1725 AL-died after 1790 OH – son of **Creek Man** & **Chalakatha Woman**, Cornstalk War/55-77, French-Indian War/54-63, Braddock/55, raiding New-Shenandoah River valleys/55, raiding PA/55-56, raiding Ohio-New River valleys/58, Pontiac War/62-66, Bushy Run/63, raiding New-Greenbrier-Jackson River valleys/63, raiding Ohio-Little Kanawha-Big Sandy-New River valleys/72, Point Pleasant/74-75-78, Blue Jacket War/77-90, raiding KY-OH-VA/77-81, Crawford/82, raiding Ohio River valley/88-90, Harmar/90, possibly returned to the south, husband about 1745 of **Chalakatha Woman**/30, children unknown

331. **Child in Blanket aka Aquewa Apetotha**[46] – Mekoche born 1757 OH**murdered** 1774 - murdered by Greathouse party

332. Chilosee aka Cheelosee – Mekoche born about 1770-died after 1817 – Blue Jacket War/88-94, a warrior at Wapakoneta 1817, Treaty 1817

333. Chisholm, Ignatius - 1/8th Chalakatha-Cherokee-**Metis** born about 1777died 1817 - son of **Patsy Brown**/60 & **John D. Chisholm**/40-white, husband 1st 1798 of **Daughter of Corn Tassel Carpenter**/80-7/32nd Chalakatha-CherokeeMetis, 2nd 1811 of **Martha Rogers**/83-9/64th Chalakatha-Cherokee-Metis, father **with Carpenter** of Jesse/1800, John/1806 & William Chisholm/1808-all 11/64th
Chalakatha-Cherokee Metis, **with Rogers** of Martha/1812, Nelson/1813 & George Chisholm/1814-all 1/8th Chalakatha-Cherokee-Metis

334. Chisholm, Jesse – 11/64th Chalakatha-Cherokee-**Metis** born 1800-died 1868 - son of **Daughter of Old Corn Tassel Carpenter**/80 & **Ignatius Chisholm**/77, husband 1st 1818 of **Chalakatha Woman**/1802, 2nd 1825 of **Eliza Edwards**/1805-5/64th Chalakatha-Kishpoko-Thawikila-Black-Creek-Cherokee-Metis, 3rd 1828 of **Sari Sakkahkee McQueen**/1810-1/4th Thawikila-CreekBlack-Metis, any children/1818-25 **with Chalakatha** unknown, father **with Edwards** of William Edwards Chisholm/1827-1/8th Chalakatha-KishpokoThawikila-Black-Creek-Cherokee-Metis, **with McQueen** of Jennie Chisholm
/1830, Joseph Chisholm /1831, George Chisholm /1833 & Shawnee Bob Chisholm/1835-all 13/64th Chalakatha-Thawikila-Creek-Black-Cherokee-Metis

335. Chisholm, John D. – white born 1740 SCO-died 1818 Hot Springs AR - Council Coyatee 1792, husband 1st about 1771 of **Chalakatha Woman**/55, 2nd 1776 of **Patsy Brown**/60-1/4th Chalakatha-Cherokee-Metis, 3rd 1778 of **Betsy Sims**/65-white, 4th 1792 of **Martha Holmes**/50-1/4th Chalakatha-Metis, father **with Chalakatha** of George/72 & James Chisholm/74-both 1/2 ChalakathaMetis, **with Brown** of Ignatius Chisholm/77-1/8th Chalakatha-Cherokee-Metis, **with Sims** of John Chisholm Jr/79, Elizabeth Chisholm/80, Deborah Chisholm/82 & Elijah Chisholm/84-all white, **with Holmes** of Thomas Chisholm/93, James Chisholm/94, Joseph Chisholm/95, Dennis Chisholm/96 & Isaac Chisholm/97-all 1/8th Chalakatha-Metis

336. Chissekaw aka Cheeseekaw – Kishpoko born about 1780 OH-died after 1831 KS - raiding OH-KY-VA/99-1810, Prophet's Town/1811, Brownstown/1812-Monguagon/1812-1st Amherstburg/1812-Frenchtown/1813-Ft. Meigs/1813-2nd Amherstburg/1813 & Thames/1813 **with Tecumseh**, Treaty

1831

337.	Chiuxa aka Cheeooksa – Chalakatha born about 1740-died after 1812 - a
Chalakatha village Chief, succeeded **Panther-Meshepesha** 1791, Cornstalk War/55-77, raiding Ohio-New River valleys/58, Pontiac War/62-66, Bushy Run/63, raiding New-Greenbrier-Jackson River valleys/63, raiding Ohio-NewLittle Kanawha-Big Sandy River valleys/72, Point Pleasant/74-75-78, raiding
Ohio-New River valleys/75, Blue Jacket War/77-94, Boonesboro/78, Blue Licks/82, Crawford/82, raiding Ohio River valley/88-92, Treaty Greenville 1795, living near Simon Kenton in **Logan Co OH** 1812

338.	Choate, Younger Daughter of Samuel Sanders – wife 1779 (VA?) of
Moses Choate-white born 1750 Halifax Co VA-died 1810 MS, mother of Silas Choate/80, Edward Choate /82, Sanders Choate /84 & James Choate/88-all 1/4th Pekowi-Metis

339.	Cholutha – Chalakatha born about 1750 OH-**murdered** 1781 OH - raiding Ohio-New River valleys/72, Point Pleasant/74-75-78, Boonesboro/78, raiding KY-OH-VA/77-81, murdered 1781 by **Martin Wetzel**, husband 1770 OH of **Chalakatha Woman**/55, children unknown

340.	Chouteau, Cyprian – Osage-**Metis** born 1804 (MO?)-died 1879 St. Louis
MO – son of **Jean Pierre Chouteau**/58 & **Osage Woman**, husband (possibly) 1st 1830 MO of **Miss Rogers**/1815, (at least) 2nd 1852 MO of **Nancy Natawakomse Francis**/1825, father **with Rogers** of Benjamin C. Chouteau/1835 & Miss Chouteau/1837-both 5/16th Chalakatha-Thawikila-Mekoche-PekowiOsage-Metis, **with Francis** of Fredrick Louis Chouteau/1853-(husband of Adele
Cornatzer), Mary Frances Chouteau/1855-(wife of Carl Guinnott Jr), Francis Edmund Chouteau/1859-(husband of Clarice Irene Billinglsey)-all 11/64th Chalakatha-Mekoche-Wyandot-Osage-Metis

341.	Chouteau, Frederick - white born 1809-died 1891 - son of **Jean Pierre**
Chouteau/58-white & **Brigitte Saucier**/78-white, husband 1st 1827 of **Elizabeth Tooley**/1810-3/4th Chalakatha-Metis, 2nd 1832 of **Nancy Renicks Logan**/1810-3/4th Pekowi-Metis, 3rd 1845 of **Matilda White**/1828-1/4th Mekoche-SenecaMetis, 4th 1855 of **Elizabeth Carpenter**/1835-1/4th Chalakatha-Metis, 5th 1861 of

Elizabeth Ware/1841-white, father **with Tooley** of William Meyers Chouteau/1828, Benjamin Chouteau/1829 & Franklin Chouteau/1830-all 3/8th Chalakatha-Metis, **with Logan** of William Chouteau/1833, Benjamin Chouteau/1835, Amanda Chouteau/1837 & Francis Xavier Chouteau/1839-all 3/8th Pekowi-Metis, **with White** of Fredrick Chouteau Jr/1845, Peter Chouteau/1846, Loho Chouteau/1848, Charles Pierre Chouteau/1849, Emily Chouteau/1850 & Julia Chouteau/1851-all 1/8th Mekoche-Seneca-Metis, **with Carpenter** of Alexander J. Chouteau/1855 & Peter Chouteau/59-both 1/8th Chalakatha-Metis, **with Ware** of Minnie Chouteau/1861 & Fredrick Walker Chouteau/63-both white

342. Chuluxca aka Choolookska - Chalakatha born about 1745 OH-died after 1785 – Cornstalk War/63-77, raiding New-Greenbrier-Jackson River valleys/63, raiding Ohio-Big Sandy-Little Kanawha-New-River valleys/72, Point Pleasant/74-75-78, raiding Ohio-New River valleys/75, Blue Jacket War/77-82, raiding OH-KY-VA/77-81, Boonesboro/78, Blue Licks/82, Crawford/82

343. Civil Man aka **Auonasechla**-Haoonaseechla – Mekoche born about 1750 OH-died after 1817 - Cornstalk War/68-77, raiding Ohio-New-Little Kanawha-Big Sandy River valleys/72, Point Pleasant/74-75-78, Blue Jacket War/77-94, raiding KY-OH-VA/77-81, Crawford/82, raiding Ohio River valley/88-92, Treaty 1805, husband 1770 of **Mekoche Woman**/55, father of Civil Man's Son/80 & other children/70-95

344. Civil Man's Son – Mekoche born about 1780-**killed** 1813 Thames CAN – son of **Civil Man-Auonasechla**/50 & **Mekoche Woman**/55, raiding KY-OH-VA/99-1810, Prophet's Town/1811, Brownstown/1812-Monguagon/1812-1st Amherstburg/1812-Frenchtown/1813-Ft. Meigs/1813 & 2nd Amherstburg/1813, killed at Thames/1813 **with Tecumseh**, wife & children unknown

345. Clark, Andrew (1) – adopted-white-(**Wyandot**) - born before 1760**killed** 1813 Thames - adopted before 1765-returned to whites-returned to tribe 1765, Blue Jacket War/78-94, raiding Ohio River valley/88-92, Prophet's Town/1811, Brownstown/1812-Monguagon/1812-1st Amherstburg/1812Frenchtown/1813-Ft. Meigs/1813-2nd Amherstburg/1813, killed at Thames/1813 **with Tecumseh**, husband 1st 1780 of **Kishpoko Woman**/65, 2nd 1795 OH of **Theresa Brown**/80-1/4th Pekowi-Metis-(Wyandot), children/80-95 **with Kishpoko** unknown, father **with Brown** of Alexander McKee Clark/96, Thomas Clark/98, George P. Clark/1800-all 1/8th Pekowi-Metis-(Wyandot)

346. Clay, Henry Nolesimo aka Nolesimo Wolf-Henry Clay Wolf – 31/32nd Chalakatha-Mekoche-Pekowi-Metis born before 1781 OH-died 1846 KS - son of

John Wolf Cornstalk/50 & **Chalakatha Woman**/55, grandson of **Cornstalk**/10, Treaty 1831, moved to KS 1832, **sub-chief** 1835 KS under **John Perry**/75 & **William Perry**/70, husband 1st about 1801 OH of **Chalakatha Woman**/85, 2nd 1820 OH of **Daughter of Jeremiah McClene**/80-white, 3rd 1833 KS of **Ottawa Woman**/1815, children/1801-20 **with Chalakatha** unknown, father **with McLene** of William Clay/1822, Susan Clay/1832 & 2 sons/1823-31 all 31/64th Chalakatha-Mekoche-Pekowi-Metis, **with Ottawa** of Henry Clay Jr/1833-31/64th Chalakatha-Mekoche-Pekowi-Ottawa-Metis

347. Clears Field – adopted-Delaware born about 1720 PA-died after 1763 - wife about 1735 PA of **Chalakatha Man**/15, widow 1763, mother of several 1/2 Chalakatha-Delaware children/35-63

348. Clock, Hale – ½ Chalakatha-Mekoche-Metis born about 1780-died after 1817 – son of **Chalakatha-Mekoche Woman** & **White Man**, raiding KY-OH-VA/99-1810, Prophet's Town/1811, Brownstown/1812-Monguagon/1812-1st Amherstburg/1812-Frenchtown/1813-Ft. Meigs/1813-2nd Amherstburg/1813 & Thames/1813 **with Tecumseh**, a warrior at Lewistown 1817, Treaty 1817, husband 1800 OH of **Chalakatha Woman**/85, children unknown

349. Club Foot aka Reel Foot – Chalakatha born about 1730 PA-**killed** 1790 OH – named for deformed foot, Cornstalk War/55-77, French-Indian War/54-63, Braddock/55, raiding New-Shenandoah River valleys/55, raiding PA/55-56, raiding Ohio-New River valleys/58, a **Chalakatha Chief** 1763, Pontiac War/6266, Bushy Run/63, raiding New-Greenbrier-Jackson River valleys/63, raiding Ohio-New-Little Kanawha-Big Sandy River valleys/72, Point Pleasant/74-75-78, raiding Ohio-New River valleys/75, Blue Jacket War/77-90, raiding OH-KYVA/77-81, Crawford/82, raiding Ohio River valley/88, **killed at Harmar**/90, relative/same clan as **Cornstalk** & **Tall Oak**, wife & children unknown

350. Cohun, Nancy Rogers - wife by 1810 MO of **John Cohun**-Delaware born about 1770 OH-died after 1830 KS, mother of George Cohun/1825-1/4th Chalakatha-Mekoche-Pekowi-Delaware-Metis- see **Nancy Rogers**/72

351. Cokundiawthah aka Kokoondeeawtha - adopted-Mohawk born about 1740-**killed** 1790 – Cornstalk War/57-77, French-Indian War/57-63, raiding Ohio-New River valleys/58, Pontiac War/62-66, Bushy Run/63, raiding NewJackson-Greenbrier River valleys/63, **joined Ohio Shawnee 1769**, raiding Ohio-

Little Kanawha-Big Sandy-New River valleys/72, Ohio River valley/74 **with Chief Logan**, Point Pleasant/74-75-78, Blue Jacket War/77-90, raiding OhioNew River valleys/75, raiding KY-VA-OH/77-81, Crawford/82, raiding Ohio river valley/88-99, **killed 1790 at Harmar**, husband of **Cookoochee**/45-adoptedMohawk, father of Sotonegoo (Girty Ironside Peters)/60, Black Loon/62, White Loon/64 & Wapunno/66-all adopted-Mohawk, grandfather of Simon Girty JrKedzawsaw-Simon Peters/76 & Quasay Girty/78-both adopted-1/2 MohawkMetis

352. Colbert, Ishtonnarhay Doublehead – wife 1788 TN of **William Chooshemataha Colbert**/60-1/2 Chickasaw-Metis, sister of **Corn Blossom**/65wife of **Jacob Troxell**, sister of **Tuskiahooto**/59 & **Seeleechie Doublehead**/62, half-sister of **Nancy Doublehead**-all wives of **George Colbert**, mother of Tooklaishtubbee Colbert/89, Ballarchubbee Colbert/90, Meharchubbee Colbert/91, Nossaecachubbee Colbert/92, Immarhollchetubbee Colbert/93, Logan Colbert/94, Shemarhoyeacher Colbert/95, Wilekee Colbert/96, Schimmarhoye Colbert/97, Onnarhotetay Colbert/98, Apalartubbee Colbert/99, Nacknitubbee Colbert/1800-all 7/64th Chalakatha-Cherokee-**Chickasaw**-Metis

353. Colbert, Nancy Doublehead – 3rd wife 1807 Colbert Co AL of **George Tootemastubbee Colbert**/64, half-sister of **Tuskiahooto & Seleechie**, mother of Susan-Sukey Colbert (2)/1810-5/64th Chalakatha-Pekowi-Cherokee-**Chickasaw**Metis

354. Colbert, Seleechie Doublehead aka Shelaecher Doublehead - 2nd wife 1794 Colbert Co AL (church married 1807) of **George Tootemastubbee Colbert**/64-1/2 Chickasaw-Metis, sister of **Corn Blossom (Troxell)**/65, **Ishtonnarhay**/66-(wife of **William Colbert**) ,**Tuskiahooto**/59-1st wife of George Colbert & half-sister of **Nancy Doublehead**-3rd wife of George Colbert, mother of John Colbert/95, Jane Colbert/96, Samuel Pitman Colbert/97, Susan Colbert/99 & Levica-Visa Colbert/1800-all 7/64th Chalakatha-Cherokee**Chickasaw**-Metis

355. Colbert, Tuskiahooto Doublehead aka Sukey - 1st wife 1785 AL of **George Tootemastubbee Colbert**/64-1/2 Chickasaw-Metis, sister of **Corn Blossom (Troxell)**/65 & 2nd wife **Seleechie**/63-2nd wife of George & **Ishtonnarhay**/66-(wife of William Colbert) & half-sister of **Nancy Doublehead**/91-3rd wife of George, mother of George Colbert Jr/85-7/64th

Chalakatha-Cherokee-Chickasaw-Metis

356.	Cold Water (1) aka **Wepenipe**[47] – Chalakatha born about 1715 PA-died after 1774 OH - raiding PA/40, Cornstalk War/55-77, French-Indian War/54-63, Braddock/55, raiding New River valley/55, raiding PA/55-56, raiding Ohio-New
River valleys/58, Pontiac War/62-66, Bushy Run/63, raiding New-GreenbrierJackson River valleys/63, raiding Ohio-New-Little Kanawha-Big Sandy River valleys/72, Point Pleasant/74, brother in law of **Cornstalk**/10, husband about 1735 PA of **Cawechile Hokolesqua**/18-7/8th Chalakatha-Mekoche-Metis, father of Young Cold Water/40, Lacumtequa Cold Water/44 & other children/42-62-all 15/16th Chalakatha-Mekoche-Metis

357.	Cold Water (2) aka **Young Cold Water-Young Wepenipe** – 15/16th
Chalakatha-Mekoche-Metis born 1740 OH-died after 1778 – son of **Cold Water-Wepenipe**/15 & **Cawechile Hokolesqua**/18, Cornstalk War/58-74, Point Pleasant/74-75-78, husband of **Chalakatha Woman**/45, father of Cold Water (3)/60 & John Cold Water/70-both 31/32nd Chalakatha-Mekoche-Metis

358.	Cold Water (3) – 31/32nd Chalakatha-Mekoche-Metis born 1760 OHdied after 1832 KS - son of **Young Cold Water**/40 & **Chalakatha Woman**/45, a Chalakatha warrior, Blue Jacket War/78-94, Crawford/82, raiding Ohio River valley/83-89, Capt. Shoe Boots Co-**with U.S. Army**-Creek War/1813, Treaty
1831, great-nephew of **Cornstalk**/10, moved to KS about 1832, husband about 1780 OH of **Mekoche Woman**/64

359. Cold Water, Cawechile Hokolesqua aka Younger Daughter of Okowellos-Sister of Cornstalk-Wife of Cold Water - sister of **Cornstalk**/10, wife 1735 PA of **Cold Water (1)-Wepenipe**/15, mother of Young Cold Water/40, Lacumtequa/44 & other children/42-62-all 15/16th Chalakatha-Mekoche-Metis

360.	Cold Water, Lacumtequa – 15/16th Chalakatha-Mekoche-Metis born about 1744 OH-died after 1786 – daughter of **Cold Water-Wepenipe**/15 &
Cawachile Hokolesqua/18 – wife about 1760 OH of **Moluntha**/10, living in Moluntha village OH 1786, children unknown

361.	Coldiron, John - 1/2 Chalakatha-Metis born 1790 Rowan Co NC-1844 Harlan Co KY - son of **Chalakatha Woman** & **Mr. Coldiron** aka **Cold Iron**/40adopted-white, husband 1812 KY of **Sarah Brock**/94, father of William

Shawnee Heritage

Coldiron/1812, Mary Polly Coldiron/1817, Elizabeth Coldiron/1821 & Jesse Brock Coldiron/1828-all 19/64th Chalakatha-Cherokee-Metis

362.   Colesetos aka Koleseetos – Chalakatha born about 1790 OH-died after 1826 KS - Prophet's Town/1811, Brownstown/1812-Monguagon/1812-1st Amherstburg/1812-Frenchtown/1813-Ft. Meigs/1813-2nd Amherstburg/1813 & Thames/1813 **with Tecumseh**, a warrior from Lewistown 1817, Treaty 1817, moved to KS 1826 **with Prophet** & **Paukeesaa**, husband 1810 OH of **Kishpoko Woman**/95, children unknown

363.   Collins, Jane (1) - 1/2 Pekowi-**Metis** born 1768 WV-died after 1800 (WV?) - daughter of **Tecumoplas Margaret Opessa**/42-Pekowi-(daughter of Sister of Metheotashe/27) & **Rupert Collins**/40-white, 2nd cousin/niece of **Tecumseh**, wife by 1790 (WV-OH?) of **Lewis Full**/70-white, mother of Joseph Full/91, Absalom Full/95, Andrew Full/99, Amelia Full/1803, Reuben Full/1806 & 5 more children-all 1/4th Pekowi-Metis-(all 3rd cousins of **Tecumseh**)

364.   Colored Skirt – adopted-Mohawk-Metis born about 1765-died after 1785 - daughter of **Mohawk Woman** & **Scot**-Canadian Man, wife about 1780 OH of **Kishpoko Man**/60, adopted by marriage, widow 1785, mother of 1 son & 1 daughter/80-85-both 1/2 Kishpoko-Mohawk-Metis

365.   Colosetee aka Kolosetee - Mekoche-(adopted-**Seneca**) - born about 1780 OH-died after 1832 – scout-**with U.S. Army**-War 1812-Thames/1813, Treaty 1832, move to KS 1832, husband 1800 OH of **Seneca Woman**/85, father of several 1/2 Mekoche-Seneca children/1800-30

366.   Comforter – Mekoche born about 1740 OH-died after 1770 - wife about 1755 OH of **Mekoche Man**/35, widow 1770, mother of several children/55-70

367. Conawapa aka Konawapa - adopted-Cree born about 1740 CAN-died after 1774 (OH?) – Cornstalk War/60-74, Pontiac War/62-66, Bushy Run/63, raiding New-Jackson-Greenbrier River valleys/63, raiding Ohio-Little KanawhaBig Sandy-New River valleys/72, Point Pleasant/74, moved south-east before 1760-living **with Shawnee** in OH 1774, likely moved back to north-west about 1774, husband about 1760 OH of **Chalakatha Woman**/45, father of several 1/2 Chalakatha-Cree children/60-74

Section V

Conner to Cuts Corn

C (*continued*)

368. Conner, James – white-Shawnee born 1771 OH-died after 1795 - son of **Richard Conner**/18-white & **Margaret Boyer**/52-adopted-white, husband about 1790 OH of **Pekowi Woman**/75, children unknown

369. Conner, Margaret Boyer - wife 1769 OH of **Richard Conner**-white born about 1718 MD-died 1808 MI, mother of James Conner/71-(married a Pekowi), John Conner/73-(married a Delaware), William Conner/75-(married a Delaware), Henry Conner/77, daughter/79, Thomas Conner/81 & Susannah Conner/83-all white Shawnee or white Delaware

370. Conogonoee aka Conogoniony - 1/2 Chalakatha-Metis born about 1745 OH-died after 1778 - son of **Adopted White Woman** & **Chalakatha Man**, returned to whites-returned to tribe 1765, Cornstalk War/62-77, Pontiac War/62-66, Bushy Run/63, raiding New-Greenbrier-Jackson River valleys/63, raiding Ohio-New-Little Kanawha-Big Sandy River valleys/72, Point Pleasant/74, raiding KY-VA-OH/75-78, husband about 1765 OH of **Chalakatha Woman**/50, father of several children/65-78-all 3/4th Chalakatha-Metis

371. Conrad, Gunrod aka Untoolah-Butler-Dihyundula-Untoola-Ahyundula - 1/4th Chalakatha-Thawikila-Creek-**Cherokee**-Metis born 1746 Chota TN**murdered** before 1817 - son of **Jennie Oconastota**/24 & **Johann Conrad**/20white, Wolf Clan Cherokee, Point Pleasant/74, Cherokee War/75, raiding KYVA-OH/77-81, Crawford/82, raiding Ohio River valley/88-92, Blue Jacket War/77-94, Treaty 1785, husband 1770 of **Ollie-Arle Bird Clan**/55-Cherokee, father of Rattling Gourd Conrad/72, Young Wolf-Kanaugh Conrad/74, HairDegoska Conrad/76, Terrapin Head Conrad/78 & Quatie Conrad/80-all 1/8th Chalakatha-Thawikila-Creek-Cherokee-Metis

372. Conrad, Nancy aka Nayehi - 1/4th Chalakatha-Thawikila-Creek**Cherokee**-Metis born 1743 Chota TN-died 1797 GA - daughter of **Jennie Oconastota**/24 & **Johann Conrad**/20-white, granddaughter of Oconastota/02, Wolf Clan Cherokee, wife 1759 of **Nathan Hicks**/35-white, mother of Sarah Gosaduisga Hicks/58, Elizabeth Hicks (1)/59, Mary Hicks /60, Chief Charles Hicks /62, Nathan Hicks Jr/64, Elizabeth Hicks (2)/68 & Chief William Abraham Hicks/69-all 1/8th Chalakatha-Thawikila-Creek-Cherokee-Metis

373. Consontha – Chalakatha born about 1710 PA-died about 1758 Oh in epidemic - raiding PA/40, Council Ft. Pitt Nov. 1753, Braddock/55, raiding

NewShenandoah River valleys/55, raiding PA/55-56, raiding Ohio-New River valleys/58

374. Constant Sorrow – Kishpoko born about 1750 OH-died after 1794 - wife of **3 Kishpoko Men**, widow 1774, 1782, 1794, mother by all 3 husbands of several children/64-92

375. Coody, Edith Vann - wife 1765 Davidson Co NC (TN) of **Arthur Archibald Coody**/40-white born 1740-died 1782, mother of Joseph Coody (1)/66, Arthur Archer Coody/68, Lewis Coody/70, James Coody/72, Edward Ned Coody/74, Zephaniah Coody/76, Elizabeth Coody/78, Rachel Coody/79, Charity Coody /80 & Joseph Coody (2)/82-all 1/8th Chalakatha-Cherokee-Metis

376. Coody, Joseph (1) - 1/8th Chalakatha-Cherokee-**Metis** born 1766 Davidson Co NC (TN)-died after 1800 - son of **Edith Vann**/50 & **Arthur Archibald Coody**/40-adopted-white, husband 1782 Great Tellico TN of **Elizabeth Tassel (2)**/60-7/64th Chalakatha-Cherokee-Metis, father of Sarah Coody/83, Elizabeth Coody /86, Nancy Coody/90-all 7/64th Chalakatha-Cherokee-Metis

377. Coody, Joseph (2) - 1/8th Chalakatha-Cherokee-**Metis** born 1782 VA (?)died after 1814 - son of **Edith Vann**/50 & **Arthur Archibald Coody**/40adopted-white, husband 1805 of **Jennie Ross**/87-1/8th Chalakatha-CherokeeMetis, father of Letitia Coody/1806, Elizabeth Coody/1814-both 1/8th Chalakatha-Cherokee-Metis

378. Coody, Sarah – 7/64th Chalakatha-Cherokee-**Metis** born 1783 Great Tellico TN-died after 1860 OK - daughter of **Elizabeth Tassel (2)**/60 & **Joseph Coody (1)**/66, 3rd wife 1802 TN of **Capt. George Fields**/70-3/64th ChalakathaCherokee-Metis, mother of Dempsey Fields/1806, Richard George Fields/1808,
Nancy Fields/1810, Rider Fields/1812, Ruth Fields/1815, Martha Fields/1818 & John Fields/1824-all 5/64th Chalakatha-Cherokee-Metis

379. Coohunt – Chalakatha born about 1770 OH-died after 1817 - raiding Ohio River valley/88-92, Blue Jacket War/88-94, raiding OH-KY-VA/95-1810, Prophet's Town/1811, Brownstown/1812-Monguagon/1812-1st Amherstburg/1812-Frenchtown/1813-Ft. Meigs/1813-2nd Amherstburg/1813 & Thames/1813 **with Tecumseh**, a warrior at Lewistown 1817, Treaty 1817

380. Coon, John aka **Coonaha** - adopted-white-(later **Wyandot**) born about 1740-died after 1812 - adopted before 1755-never fully returned to whites, Cornstalk War/60-77, Pontiac War/62-66, Bushy Run/63, raiding NewJacksonGreenbrier River valleys/63, raiding Little Kanawha-Big Sandy-Ohio-

New River valleys/72, Point Pleasant/74-75-78, raiding Ohio-New River valleys/75, Blue Jacket War/77-94, raiding KY-VA-OH/77-81, Crawford/82, raiding Ohio River valley/88-92, living in Logan Co OH near Simon Kenton 1812, husband 1st 1760 OH of **Mekoche Woman**/45, 2nd about 1785 OH **Wyandot Woman**/65, father **with Mekoche** of Abraham Coon/65, John Isatouque Coon/72 & Lewis Coon/75-all 1/2 Mekoche-Metis, **with Wyandot** of Aaron Coon/86, Robert Coon/90 & John Coon Jr (1)/95-all 1/2 Wyandot-Metis

381. Cooper, Daughter of Young Black Fox - wife 1795 of **Isaac Cooper**white born about 1775-died after 1840 TN, mother of James Cooper/95, Mary Polly Cooper/97, Isaac Cooper Jr/1800, Sarah Cooper/1801, Nancy Cooper/1803, William Cooper/1807 & Harmon Cooper/1811-all 1/16th Chalakatha-Thawikila-Creek-Cherokee-Metis

382. Copper, Jean - 1/2 Pekowi-Metis born about 1730 PA-died after 1794 - son of **Pekowi Woman** & **French Trader**, French-Indian War/54-63, Cornstalk War/55-74, Braddock/55, raiding New-Shenandoah River valleys/55, raiding Ohio-New River valleys/58, Pontiac War/62-66, Bushy Run/63, raiding New-Jackson-Greenbrier River valleys/63, messenger/translator-**with U.S. Army**Revolution, husband about 1750 PA of **1/2 Pekowi-Delaware Woman**/35, father of several 1/2 Pekowi-Delaware-Metis children/50-80

383. Cordery, Susannah Sonicooie aka Sonigui - Blind Savannah Clan Cherokee, wife 2nd 1782 GA (legally in 1785) of **Thomas Cordery**-white born about 1763-died 1840, mother of Sarah Sonicooie/82, Lucy Elizabeth Sonicooie/84, Nancy Ann Cordery/86, Charlotte Cordery/90, David Cordery/92, Hetty Cordery/94, Early Cordery/97 & Susan Cordery/98-all 1/8th Chalakatha-Thawikila-Creek-Cherokee-Metis

384. Corn Cob – Chalakatha born about 1720 PA-died after 1768 OH – from the **Hokolesqua-Okowellos-Corn Stalk** band, raiding PA/40, Cornstalk War/5568, French-Indian War/54-63, Braddock/55, raiding New-Shenandoah River valleys/55, raiding PA/55-56, Pontiac War/62-66, Bushy Run/63, raiding NewGreenbrier-Jackson River valleys/63, a **Chalakatha Chief** in OH by 1755, traveled with **Rene-Pale Stalker Chartier** to Detroit 1768, husband 1st about 1740 PA of **Chalakatha Woman**/25, 2nd 1763 of **Adopted-White Woman**/50, father **with Chalakatha** of several children/40-64, **with White Woman** of three known 1/2 Chalakatha-Metis children/64-68

Corn Island aka Corn on Island – adopted-Cayuga born about 1740 (OH?)-died after 1794 – Cornstalk War/60-77, raiding Ohio-New River valleys/58, Pontiac

War/62-66, Bushy Run/63, raiding New-Greenbrier-Jackson River valleys/63, raiding Ohio-New-Little Kanawha-Big Sandy River valleys/72, Point Pleasant/74, Boonesboro/78, raiding KY-VA-OH 1777-81, Crawford/82, raiding Ohio River valley/88-92, Blue Jacket War/77-94, husband 1760 OH of **Mekoche Woman**/46, father of several 1/2 Mekoche-Cayuga children/60-85

Corn Stalk aka Corn Stalk Hokolesqua[48]-Corn Stalk Okowellos-Stalk of Corn-Stalk of Plant-Hokolesqua (3)-Hokoleshka (3)-Okowellos (2)-Akulusska-Wneypuechsika[49]-Waynaypooechseeka-Stout Man-Keightughqua[50]-SimaquanSeemakwan – 7/8th Chalakatha-Mekoche-Metis born 1710 PA-**murdered** 1777

Point Pleasant WV - son of **Okowellos Hokolesqua**/1674 & **Katee Mekoche**/1680, went to AL with father by 1725, in PA by 1730-(married 1st 1730 PA), in TN by 1734-(married 2nd in Running Water TN 1734), a **Chalakatha Chief** in PA by 1740, raiding PA/40, (married 3rd in PA 1741), in OH about 1745, a **major Chalakatha chief** in OH by 1749, Council Ft. Pitt Nov. 1753, read, wrote, spoke & ciphered in English, Cornstalk War/55-77, French-Indian War /54-63, in AL 1754-55, returned to OH in 1755, lead Shawnee in Braddock/55, **led raiding** of New-Shenandoah River valleys & PA/55-56, negotiated Treaty 1757 at mouth of Big Sandy River with **Thomas Lewis** & **William Preston**, in AL for a while 1757-58-(mentioned as **a Chief of the Shawnee among the Creeks**), returned to OH in 1758, **led raiding** of Ohio-New River valleys/58, associated with **John Swift, Dragging Canoe, Double Head, Red Bird, John Watts & Nathaniel Gist** in silver-mines-counterfeiting 1755-69 furnishing silver to Shawnee & confederacy, **Head Chief of Chalakatha & All Shawnee** 1755-77, **Head Chief of 20 tribe Northern Confederacy** 1760-74, Council Ft. Pitt June 1762, **Head Shawnee Chief** in Pontiac War/62-66, **led Shawnee** at Bushy Run/63, **led raiding** of New-Greenbrier-Jackson River valleys/63, Council with **Col. Bouquet** Oct. 1764, hostage of Col. Bouquet winter 1764-65 with brothers **Wakeeampea**/04, **Ewikunwee**/08, **Naythakeina**/15 & **Red Hawk**/22, negotiated Treaty Spring 1765 with Col. Bouquet, last home at Cornstalk's village on Sippio Creek of Scioto River OH from early 1770's, **sent raiders** to Ohio-Little Kanawha-Big Sandy-KanawhaNew River valleys/72, traveled & sent emissaries 1774 to Shawnee in **VA-NC-SC-AL-TN-KY-MO-IL-IN-OH-PA-MD-NY** enlisting support for upcoming Battle of Point Pleasant/74, sought support/74 of **nephew Dragging Canoe**, **Head Chief of Northern Confederacy** at Point Pleasant/74, negotiated Treaty

Camp Charlotte 1774 with **Lord Dunmore**, Council Ft. Pitt 1775 with **Nimwha, Silver Heels, Wryneck & Blue Jacket**, Council Ft. Pitt-George Morgan 1776 with **Nimwha, Ellinipsico, sister Cawechile, Capt. Johnny, Blue Jacket & Black Caesar**, Council 1776 with **White Eyes-Delaware, John Montour-Seneca-Metis, Wyandot Half-King & William Wilson**, Council Ft. Pitt 1777, **murdered** by whites at Ft. Randolph-Point Pleasant/77 with brother **Red Hawk**, son **Ellinipsico** & son in law/adopted son **Petella**, husband 1st 1730 PA of **Helizikinopo Snake**/15Mekoche, 2nd 1734 Running Water TN of **Ounaconoa Muskrat**/16-Chalakatha-Pekowi, 3rd 1741 PA of **Julia Mulatto**/20-adopted-Mulatto, (at least) 4th 1763 OH of

Catherine Vanderpoole See/25-adopted-white, (other wives/30-77 possible), father **with Helizikinopo** of Walker-Pomeatha/30, Wolf/32, Catherine (Petella)/34, Chenusaw/36, Newa/38, Greenbrier (Kennison)/40, Aracoma (Baker)/42, Elizabeth (Swift-Petella)/44,Young Cornstalk/46, Ellinipsico/48, Mary-Blue Sky (Adkins)/50, Esther (Soward)/51, Oceana/52-all 15/16th Chalakatha-Mekoche-Metis, **with Ounaconoa** of Black Beard/36, Black Wolf/40, John Wolf (Cornstalk)/50, Peter Cornstalk/55 & Susannah Cornstalk/57-all 15/16th Chalakatha-Mekoche-Pekowi-Metis, **with Julia** of Sun Fish/42, Elijah Cornstalk/44, Abraham Cornstalk "Ailstock"/48, Absalom Cornstalk "Ailstock"/50 & Michael Cornstalk "Ailstock"/52-all 7/16th Chalakatha-Mekoche-Black-Scot-Metis, **with Catherine** of Mary (Cornstalk) See/64-7/16th Chalakatha-Mekoche-Metis, **adopted father** about 1740 PA **of Petella**/30-white, 1763 OH **of Elizabeth See**/54 & **John See**/59-white, (unknown children with all wives likely & a Creek Wife about 1755 also likely).

385.   Cornstalk (2) aka Nenpemeshequa-Neenpeemeesheekwa-Wneypuechsika-Wynaypooeechseeka-Stout Man – see **Young Cornstalk**/46-15/16th Chalakatha-Mekoche-Metis

386.   Cornstalk, Aracoma aka Corn Flower-Aracoma Hokolesqua-Aracoma
Baker – 15/16th Chalakatha-Mekoche-Metis born 1742 OH-**killed** in battle 1780 **Logan Co. WV** - 2nd daughter of **Cornstalk**/10 & **Helizikinopo**/15, established village near Logan WV 1760 with family & clan at current site of **Logan WV**, a **Chalakatha village Head Woman** before 1780, about 6' tall, killed in battle defending the village, wife 1758 OH of **Boling Baker** aka **Kikpelethee**/30adopted-white (or NC Metis), mother of son Running Deer (Baker_/64, son Laughing Water (Baker)/66, daughter Snow Lily (Baker)/68, daughter Raindrop
(Baker)/70, son Running Water (Baker)/72 & son Blue Feather (baker)/74-all 15/32nd Chalakatha-Mekoche-Metis-Metis, 4 other children that may have died of disease

387.   Cornstalk, Black Beard (1) aka Wesekahnee-WeeseekahneeWissekapoway-Weeseekapoway-Black Beard Hokolesqua-**Black Beard (1)** - 15/16th Chalakatha-Mekoche-Pekowi-Metis born 1730 PA/AL-died after 1808 MO - oldest son of **Cornstalk**/10 & **Ounaconoa Muskrat**/16, about 6' tall & burly, known for rare black beard like brother Black Wolf/40, read, wrote, spoke & ciphered in English, Cornstalk War/55-77, French-Indian War/54-63, Braddock/55, raiding New-Shenandoah River valleys/55, raiding PA/55-56, raiding Ohio-New River valleys/58, Pontiac War/62-66, Bushy Run/63, raiding New-Greenbrier-Jackson River valleys/63, a **Chalakatha Chief** in OH by 1768, Council March 1768, raiding Little Kanawha-Big Sandy-Ohio-New River valleys/72, **an emissary for Cornstalk** 1774, Point Pleasant/74-75, raiding OhioNew River valleys/75, Blue Jacket War/77-94, raiding KY-VA-OH/77-81, Point
Pleasant/78, Booneboro/78, **2nd Chalakatha Chief** to **Black Hoof** 1779, Crawford/82, raiding Ohio River valley/88-92, Treaty Greenville 1795, Council Swan Creek OH 1795 with **Capt. Johnny, Bukangolas & George Ironside**, moved to MO 1796, Council 1797 with **Capt. Johnny, Borer, Buffalo & Capt. Mayne**-ENG, visited relatives among the Cherokee in south 1808, husband 1755 Running Water TN of **Katee Killaqua**/37-7/32nd Chalakatha-Cherokee-Metis, father of Daughter of Black Beard/55, Young Black Beard Cornstalk/60 & other children/55-77 names unknown-all 15/32nd Chalakatha-Mekoche-Pekowi-Cherokee-Metis

388.	Cornstalk, Black Wolf (1) aka Benewiska-Beeneeweeska-**Black Wolf (2)** - 15/16th Chalakatha-Mekoche-Pekowi-Metis born 1740 OH-died 1830 OH - 2nd son of **Cornstalk**/10 & **Ounaconoa Muskrat**/16, read, wrote, spoke & ciphered in English, Cornstalk War/58-77, raiding Ohio-New River valleys/58, Pontiac War/62-66, Bushy Run/63, raiding New-Greenbrier-Jackson River valleys/63, a **Chalakatha Chief** in OH by 1763, Grand Council 1763, Council Logstown 1765, Council Stanwix Oct. 1768, raiding Ohio-Little Kanawha-Big Sandy-New River valleys/72, **an emissary for Cornstalk** 1774, Point Pleasant/74-75, Blue Jacket War/77-94, raiding KY-OH-VA/77-81, Point Pleasant/78, Crawford/82, raiding Ohio River valley/88-92, a **Chalakatha Chief** at Wapakoneta 1817, Treaty 1814, 1815, 1817, 1818, about 6' tall & burly, known for rare black beard like brother Black Beard/30, husband 1st 1758 Running Water TN of **Nikkee Killaqua**/38-7/32nd Chalakatha-Cherokee-Metis, 2nd 1769 OH of **Pottawamee Woman**/54, (possibly father of a child 1787 with **Jenny Sellards Wiley**/60-adopted white), 3rd 1800 OH of **Miss Fish** aka Daughter of William Jackson-Fish/81-adopted-white, other wives possible, father **with Killaqua** of Black Wolf (2)/60 & other children/61-85-all 15/32nd Chalakatha-Mekoche-Pekowi-Cherokee-Metis, name & gender of child **with Wiley** unknown but born after Jenny's return to the whites, **with Pottawamee** of Soldier Black Wolf/70, Young Black Wolf/86 & other children/71-1800-all 15/32nd Chalakatha-Mekoche-Pekowi-Pottawamee-Metis, children **with Miss Fish** unknown

389.	Cornstalk, Catherine Vanderpool (Sharpe See) - adopted 1763 OHreturned to whites 1765, wife 3rd (of 4) 1763 OH of **Cornstalk**/10, mother before captivity **with Fredrick See** of Margaret Peggy See/44 (wife of Walker Cornstalk), Lois Sarah See/46 (wife of Newa Cornstalk), Mary Catherine See/48 (wife of Ellinipsico Cornstalk), Elizabeth See/54 (wife of Young Cornstalk) & John See/58-all adopted-whites, mother **with Cornstalk** of Mary (Cornstalk) See/64-1/2 7/16th Chalakatha-Mekoche-Metis

390.	Cornstalk, Chenusaw – 15/16th Chalakatha-Mekoche-Metis born 1736 PA-died after 1778 likely OH - 3rd son of **Cornstalk**/10 & **Helizikinopo**/15, a Chalakatha warrior, spoke some English (taught by stepmother & white captors), Cornstalk War/55-77, French-Indian War/54-63, Braddock/55, raiding NewShenandoah River valleys/55, raiding PA/55-56, raiding Ohio-New River valleys/58, Pontiac War/62-66, Bushy Run/63, raiding New-Jackson-Greenbrier River valleys/63, raiding Little Kanawha-Big Sandy-Ohio-New River valleys/72, **an emissary for Cornstalk** 1774, Point Pleasant/74-75-78, **hostage of**

Virginians 1775-76, husband 1756 OH of **Chalakatha Woman**/40, children unknown

391. Cornstalk, Elijah – 7/16th Chalakatha-Mekoche-Black-Metis born 1744 OH-**killed** 1760 OH - 2nd son of **Cornstalk**/10 & **Julia Mulatto**/20-adoptedMulatto, a **Chalakatha warrior**, over 6' tall, **shot by whites** near Marietta OH while with his uncle **Silverheels**/24, died unmarried

392. Cornstalk, Elizabeth – 15/16th Chalakatha-Mekoche-Metis born 1744 OH-died after 1777 likely OH - 5th daughter of **Cornstalk**/10 & **Helizikinopo**/15, over 6' tall, a **Christian Chalakatha**, may have served as a translator-messenger for the whites, wife 1st 1760 OH of **John Swift**-white, 2nd by 1770 OH of **Petella Cornstalk**/30-adopted white, mother **with Swift** of four 15/32nd Chalakatha-Mekoche-Metis children/60-62-64-66 names unknown but surname may have been Cornstalk, children/70-77 **with Petella** unknown, often confused in white histories with her sisters or aunts

393. Cornstalk, Elizabeth See - adopted 1763 OH-returned to whites 1775 - adopted daughter of **Cornstalk**/10, adopted 1763 with mother Catherine Vanderpoole Sharpe See/20, sisters Margaret Peggy See/44, Lois Sarah See/46, Mary Catherine See/48 & brother John/56, wife 1768 OH of **Young Cornstalk**/44, mother **with Young Cornstalk** of White Wing/70 & Cornstalk (3)/72-both 15/32nd Chalakatha-Mekoche-Metis

394. Cornstalk, **Ellinipsico aka Helinipsiko-Heleeneepseeko**[51]-Native Warrior – 15/16th Chalakatha-Mekoche-Metis born 1748 OH-**murdered** 1777 Point Pleasant WV - youngest son of **Cornstalk**/10 & **Helizikinopo**/15, over 6' tall, spoke some English (taught by stepmother & white wife, Cornstalk War/6577, Pontiac War/65-66, raiding Ohio-New-Little Kanawha-Big Sandy River valleys/72, **an emissary for Cornstalk** 1774, Point Pleasant/74-75, a **Chalakatha Chief** in OH 1777, **murdered by whites** at Point Pleasant WV/Ft. Randolph 1777 with father **Cornstalk**/10, brother in law/adopted brother **Petella** & uncle **Red Hawk**/22, husband 1st 1763 OH of **Mary Catherine See**/49adopted white, 2nd 1765 OH of **Chalakatha Woman**/50, 3rd 1772 OH of **Adopted White Woman**/55, father with **Mary Catherine** of Margaret Peggy See (2)/64-15/32nd Chalakatha-Mekoche-Metis, children/65-77 **with Chalakatha**/50 & children/72-77 **with White Woman**/55 unknown

395. Cornstalk, Esther – 15/16th Chalakatha-Mekoche-Metis born 1751 OHdied before 1836 PA - 6th daughter of **Cornstalk**/10 & **Helizikinopo**/15, about 6' tall & attractive, a **Christian Chalakatha**, Shawnee name unknown, may have served as a translator-messenger for the whites, wife 1768 OH/PA of **Thomas Sowards**/46-white, mother of Griffin Sowards/73, Thomas Sowards

Jr/75, Robert Sowards/80, Esther Sowards/81, Jacob Sowards/83, John B. Sowards/84, twins Rosannah & Diannah Sowards/86, Rebecca Sowards/90, George Sowards/92-all 15/32nd Chalakatha-Mekoche-Metis, often confused in white history with her sisters & aunts

396. Cornstalk, Greenbrier – 15/16th Chalakatha-Mekoche-Metis born 1740 PA-died after 1777 (OH?) - 3rd daughter of **Cornstalk**/10 & **Helizikinopo**/15, a **Christian Chalakatha**, about 6' tall & attractive, likely a translator-messenger for the whites, associated in later years with (white) McComas family-maybe in laws through marriage of a daughter?, wife by 1757 WV of **Reuben Kennison**white/37, widow 1776, children/57-76 (likely surname Kennison including a Reuben Jr & a young Greenbrier) unknown, often confused in white history with her sisters & aunts

397. Cornstalk, Helizikinopo Snake - Mekoche born 1715 PA-died shortly after 1809 OH - **sister of Big Snake**/20, 1st wife 1729 PA of **Cornstalk**/10, signed Complaint to U.S. 1809 with brother **Big Snake**/20, nephew **Young Snake**/60, **Black Hoof**/30, **Wahappi**-Delaware & **Beaver**-Delaware, mother of **daughters** Catherine/34, Greenbrier/40, Aracoma/42, Elizabeth/44, Mary-Blue Sky/50, Esther/51 & Oceana/52 & of **sons** Walker-Pomeatha/30, Wolf-Cutenwha/32, Chenusaw/36, Newa/38, Young Cornstalk/46, Ellinipsico/48, other unknown children/30-60 (probably daughters) possible, **adopted mother** 1740 PA of Petella/30-white, 1763 OH of John See/59 & Elizabeth See/54-white, 1778 OH of Martin Wetzel/62-white

398. Cornstalk, John (1) aka **Lawathtucheh**-Lawathtoochee-**John Wolf** – 15/16th Chalakatha-Mekoche-Pekowi-Metis born 1750 OH-died 1834 OH - 3rd son of **Cornstalk**/10 & **Ounaconoa Muskrat**/16, spoke, read & ciphered in English, Cornstalk War/68-77, raiding Little Kanawha-Big Sandy-Kanawha-New River valleys/72, **an emissary for Cornstalk** 1774, Point Pleasant/74-78, Blue Jacket War/77-94, raiding KY-VA-OH/77-81, Crawford/82, a **Chalakatha Chief** in OH by 1787, raiding Ohio River valley/88-92, Treaty 1817, husband 1780 of **Chalakatha Woman**/65, father of daughter-Black Poddee Wolf/75, sons Peter Temestehee Wolf/70, Henry Nolesimo Clay/80, John Wolf Cornstalk (2)/92 & Peter Cornstalk (3)/94-all 31/32nd Chalakatha-Mekoche-Pekowi-Metis

399. Cornstalk, Julia Mulatto aka Black Wife of Cornstalk - adopted-Mulatto born about 1720-died after 1775 OH – father may have been from Scotland & mother a Black slave woman, about 6' tall & said to be very pretty, capturedadopted 1740 PA by **Chief Intu** (some connection to Cornstalk family?), wife 1741 PA of **Cornstalk**/10, stayed with tribe in OH 1775 when 3 younger sons returned to whites, mother of Sun Fish Cornstalk/42, Elijah Cornstalk/44,

Shawnee Heritage

Absalom Cornstalk "Ailstock"/48, Abraham Cornstalk "Ailstock"/50 & Michael Cornstalk "Ailstock"/52-all 7/16th Chalakatha-Mekoche-Black-Metis, other unknown children/41-65 (probably daughters) likely

400. Cornstalk, Mary (1) aka **Blue Sky** - 15/16th Chalakatha-Mekoche-Metis born 1750 OH-died 1775 Ft. Pitt area PA/OH/WV - 4th daughter of **Cornstalk**/10 & **Helizikinopo**/15, about 6' tall & attractive, a **Christian Chalakatha**, wife 1766 of **Parker V. Adkins**/20-white (or Shawano-Metis), met while Adkins was in the Military in PA-abandoned by Adkins when he returned east, Adkins returned for children after her death, mother **with Adkins** of Littleberry Adkins/67 & Charity Adkins/68-both 15/32nd Chalakatha-Mekoche-Metis, often confused in white history with her sisters & aunts

401. Cornstalk, Newa – 15/16th Chalakatha-Mekoche-Metis born 1738 PAdied after 1778 (OH?) - 4th son of **Cornstalk**/10 & **Helizikinopo**/15, a **Chalakatha warrior**, spoke some English (taught by stepmother & white captors), Cornstalk War/58-76, raiding Ohio-New River valleys/58, Pontiac War/62-66, Bushy Run/63, raiding New-Greenbrier-Jackson River valleys/63, raiding Ohio-Little Kanawha-Big Sandy-New River valleys/72, **an emissary for Cornstalk** 1774, Point Pleasant/74-78, **hostage of Virginians** 1775-76, husband 1st 1757 OH of **Chalakatha Woman**/42, 2nd 1763 OH of **Lois Sarah See**/46adopted-white, children/57-87 **with Chalakatha** unknown, father **with See** of Son of Newa/64-15/32nd Chalakatha-Mekoche-Metis (Son stayed with Newa when mother returned to whites 1765)

402. Cornstalk, Oceana aka Ceanna-Cianna-Zeanna – 15/16th ChalakathaMekoche-Metis born 1752 OH-died 1770 WV - youngest daughter of **Cornstalk**/10 & **Helizikinopo**/15, about 6' tall & said to be very pretty, died after falling from a cliff on her way to visit her sister **Aracoma**/42, namesake of Oceana WV, died single

403. Cornstalk, Ounaconoa Muskrat aka Ounaconoa Moytoy-Cherokee Wife of Cornstalk - wife 1734 Chota TN of **Cornstalk**/10, mother of Black Beard Cornstalk/35, Black Wolf Cornstalk/40, John Wolf Cornstalk (1)/50, Peter Cornstalk (1)/55 & Susannah Cornstalk/57-all 15/16th Chalakatha-MekochePekowi-Metis, likely other unknown children/36-60 (probably daughters)

404. Cornstalk, Peter (1) aka Comes Flying-Peytehthator-**Pehathawtaw** – 15/16th Chalakatha-Mekoche-Pekowi-Metis born 1755 AL/OH-**murdered** 1832 OH - youngest son of **Cornstalk**/10 & **Ounaconoa Muskrat**/16, about 6'6" tall, raiding Ohio-New-Little Kanawha-Big Sandy River valleys/72, **an emissary for Cornstalk** 1774, Point Pleasant/74-78, Blue Jacket War/77-94, raiding KY-

VAOH/77-81, Crawford/82, raiding Ohio River valley/88-92, a **Chalakatha Elder** at Wapaghonettat 1817, Treaty 1817, 1831, **murdered** by Doc Bill/95, Capt. Bill/90 & Sam Loon/1800-all Shawnee or Shawnee-Metis, husband 1st 1775 OH of **Chalakatha Woman**/60, 2nd by 1784 OH of **Mary Frances Avery**/65-white, children/75-83 **with Chalakatha**/60 unknown, father **with Avery** of Peter Cornstalk (2)/85 & Mary Cornstalk/96 & other children/87-1805-all 15/32nd Chalakatha-Mekoche-Pekowi-Metis

405. Cornstalk, Peter (2) aka **Wyamwiman**-Wiamweemaw-Peter Cornstalk Jr – 15/32nd Chalakatha-Mekoche-Pekowi-Metis born 1785 OH-**murdered** 1841 KS - son of **Peter Cornstalk (1)**/55 & **Mary Frances Avery**/65-white, Treaty 1825, about 6'6" tall, moved to KS by 1832, returned from MO/KS to OH 1832 & killed Capt. Bill/95 & Sam Loon/1800 in revenge for murdering his father but spared Doc Bill/90, a **Chalakatha Chief** in OH by 1815, moved to MO about 1815 but living with Miami in 1825 (IN?), **murdered** by Peter A. Tyler- former friend of the family, husband by 1805 OH of **Chalakatha Woman**/90, father of Peter Cornstalk (4)/1805, Daughter/1810, John B. Cornstalk/1820 & other children/1805-20-all 47/64th Chalakatha-Mekoche-Pekowi-Metis

406. Cornstalk, Sun Fish aka Ionoca-Hionoca Cornstalk – 7/16th ChalakathaMekoche-Black-Metis born 1742 PA-**killed** 1774 Point Pleasant WV - oldest son of **Cornstalk**/10 & **Julia Mulatto**/20-adopted-Mulatto, a **Chalakatha warrior**, Cornstalk War/58-74, raiding Ohio-New River valleys/58, Pontiac War/62-66,
Bushy Run/63, raiding New-Jackson-Greenbrier River valleys/63, raiding OhioNew-Big Sandy-Little Kanawha River valleys/72, **an emissary to the Delaware for Cornstalk** 1774, husband 1760 OH of **Delaware Woman**/45, father of six or seven 7/32nd Chalakatha-Mekoche-Delaware-Black-Metis children/60-74

407. Cornstalk, **Walker aka Pomeatha-Passes By**[52]-Pomeseh – 15/16th Chalakatha-Mekoche-Metis born 1730 PA-died before 1825 OH – oldest son of **Cornstalk**/10 & **Helizikinopo**/15, over 6' tall, Cornstalk War/55-77, FrenchIndian War/54-63, Braddock/55, raiding New-Shenandoah River valleys/55, raiding PA/55-56, raiding Ohio-New River valleys/58, Pontiac War/62-66, Bushy Run/63, raiding New-Greenbrier-Jackson River valleys/63, raiding OhioNew-Big Sandy-Little Kanawha River valleys/72, a **Chalakatha Chief** in OH before 1774, **an emissary for Cornstalk** 1774, Point Pleasant/74-78, **captive of Virginians 1775-76**, Blue Jacket War/77-94, raiding KY-WV-OH/77-81,

Crawford/82, raiding Ohio valley/88-92, an **Elder Chalakatha Chief** at Wapakoneta 1817, Treaty 1814, 1817, 1818, husband 1st 1751 Great Tellico TN to **Oousta White Owl Carpenter**/22-7/16th Chalakatha-Cherokee-Metis, 2nd 1755 OH of **Chalakatha Woman**/40, 3rd 1763 OH of **Margaret Peggy See**/44adopted-white, father **with Carpenter** of John Walker/52-11/16th ChalakathaMekoche-Cherokee-Metis, father **with Chalakatha** of Capt. Walker/60 & others/55-85-all 31/32nd Chalakatha-Mekoche-Metis, father **with Margaret**
Peggy See (1) of Son of Walker/64-15/32nd Chalakatha-Mekoche-Metis

408. Cornstalk, White Wing aka Nancy Adkins-**Big Nancy** – 15/32nd Chalakatha-Mekoche-Metis born 1770 OH-died before 1825 CAN - daughter of **Young Cornstalk**/44 & **Elizabeth See**/54-adopted white, about 6' tall, a Chalakatha, an occasional translator for Tecumseh, moved to CAN 1815 with Tecumseh followers and died before they returned in 1825, wife 1st 1784 Montgomery Co VA(=southern WV) of **Elijah Adkins**/64-white, 2nd 1793 OH of **Tecumseh**/68-3/4th Kishpoko-Pekowi-Creek-Metis, abandoned Adkins & sons 1790 to become involved with Tecumseh, left daughter Nancy/90 with Cornstalk family when she married Tecumseh, mother **with Adkins** of Lewis Adkins/84, Elijah Adkins Jr/86, Richard Adkins/88 & Nancy Adkins aka Little Nancy/90-all 15/64th Chalakatha-Mekoche-Metis, **with Tecumseh** of Paukeesaa Tecumseh/94, Adjala Tecumseh/96 & Serena Tecumseh/98-all 39/64th Chalakatha-Mekoche-Kishpoko-Pekowi-Creek-Metis

409. Cornstalk, Wolf aka **Cutenwha**-Kootenwha – 15/16th ChalakathaMekoche-Metis born 1732 PA-died after 1817 (likely OH) - 2nd son of
Cornstalk/10 & **Helizikinopo**/15, Cornstalk War/55-77, French-Indian War/5463, Braddock/55, raiding New-Shenandoah River valleys/55, raiding PA/55-56, raiding Ohio-New River valleys/58, Pontiac War/62-66, Bushy Run/63, raiding New-Jackson-Greenbrier River valleys/63, a **Chalakatha Chief** in OH by 1770, raiding Ohio-Little Kanawha-Big Sandy-New River valleys/72, **an emissary for Cornstalk** 1774, Point Pleasant/74-78, captive of whites 1775-76, Blue Jacket
War/77-88, raiding KY-VA-OH/77-81, Crawford/82, raiding Ohio River valley 1788, husband 1750 OH of **Chalakatha Woman**/35, children unknown

410. Cornstalk, Young aka Cornstalk (2)-Stout Man-Nenpemeshequa-Neenpeemeesheekwa-Wneypuechsika-Wynaypooeechseeka-Winaypooeachseeka – 15/16th Chalakatha-Mekoche-Metis born 1746 OH-died 1833 KS - 5th son of **Cornstalk**/10 & **Helizikinopo Mekoche**/15, about 6'6" tall & big built,

Cornstalk War/55-77, French-Indian War/54-63, Braddock/55, raiding NewShenandoah River valleys/55, raiding PA/55, raiding Ohio-New River valleys/58, Pontiac War/62-66, Bushy Run/63, raiding New-Greenbrier-Jackson River valleys/63, raiding Ohio-Big Sandy-Little Kanawha-New River valleys/72, **an emissary for Cornstalk** 1774, a **Chalakatha Chief** in OH 1774, Point Pleasant/74-78, Blue Jacket War/77-94, raiding KY-VA-OH/77-81, Crawford/82, raiding Ohio River valley/88-92, Treaty 1814, 1817, an elder/warrior at Wapakoneta 1817, moved to KS about 1828 **with William Perry**/70, **4th Chief in KS** 1833 under **John Perry**/75, husband 1st 1766 OH of **Chalakatha Woman**/50, 2nd 1769 OH of **Elizabeth See**/54-adopted-white, no record of children/66-95 **with Chalakatha**, father **with Elizabeth See** of White Wing Cornstalk/70 & Son of Young Cornstalk/72-both 15/32nd Chalakatha-MekocheMetis

411. Corn Tassel (1) aka Corn Tassel Carpenter (1)-**Old Corn Tassel**-Old Tassel-Utsidsata-Koateehee-First To Kill-**Onitositah**-Thistle Head-George Tassel – 7/16th Chalakatha-**Cherokee**-Metis born 1708 Great Tellico TN**murdered** 1788 Chuhowa TN - son of **Savannah Tom Carpenter (1)-Moytoy (3)**/1680 & **Nancy Rainmaker**/1683, **stepson of his uncle White Owl Raven**/1678, Wolf Clan Cherokee, **associated with** Cornstalk, John Watts Sr, John Swift, Samuel Blackburn, Dragging Canoe, Doublehead & Nathaniel Gist, French-Indian War/54-63, Pontiac War/62-66, Point Pleasant/74, Cherokee War/75, Treaty Sycamore Shoals 1775, Treaty Long Island 1777, Treaty 1785, from Chota, a **Principal Chief under Old Hop**-Standing Turkey 1751-61, a **Principal Chief & counselor under Oconastota** 1761-83 & also the **leading counselor under Kitegista** 1783-88, visited Philadelphia 1787-met Benjamin Franklin, **murdered by whites** while under a flag of truce with 2nd wife Kaiyatahee (Hanging) Maw/40, sons Double Tassel/40, Young Tassel/45 & one other relative, husband 1st 1730 of **Tsigilili (Hanging) Maw**/15-Cherokee, 2nd by 1779 of **Kaiyatahee (Hanging) Maw**/40-Cherokee (both sisters of Hanging Maw), father **with Tsigilili** of Double Tassel-Corn Tassel (3)/40, Young TasselCorn Tassel (4)/45 & Susannah Corn Tassel/49 & **with Kaiyatahee** of Daughter of Corn Tassel/80-all 7/32nd Chalakatha-Cherokee-Metis

412. Corn Tassel (2) aka Corn Tassel Carpenter (2) -**Rayetaeh**-Corn Tassel Great Eagle – 7/32nd Chalakatha-**Cherokee**-Metis - born 1730 Great Tellico TNdied 1783 Great Tellico TN - son of **Great Eagle Carpenter**/02 & **Wurteh Tawsee Fox**/04, **namesake of his uncle Old Corn Tassel Onitositah Carpenter (1)**/10-(brother of his father), raiding New-Ohio River valleys/58,

Pontiac War/62-66, raiding New-Jackson-Greenbrier River valleys/63, Point Pleasant/74, Cherokee War/75, Pigeon Co-Cherokee scouts-Revolution **with U.S. Army**, Red Paint Clan Cherokee, husband 1750 Great Tellico TN of **Tali Cherokee**/35, father of Elizabeth Tassel Carpenter (2)/60, Corn Tassel Carpenter (5)/65 & other children/50-80-all 7/64th Chalakatha-Cherokee-Metis

413.   Corn Tassel (3) aka **Double Tassel** Carpenter-Corn Tassel Carpenter (3)
– 7/32nd Chalakatha-**Cherokee**-Metis - born 1740 Great Tellico TN-**murdered** 1788 Chuhowa TN - son of **Corn Tassel Carpenter (1)**/09 & **Tsigilili (Hanging) Maw**/15, Bird Clan Cherokee, Pontiac War/62-66, raiding NewJackson-Greenbrier River valleys/63, Point Pleasant/74, Cherokee War/75, raiding KY-VA-OH/77-81, Crawford/82, **murdered by whites** with his father, step-mother, brother & one other relative while under a flag of truce, husband 1760 Great Tellico TN of a **Cherokee Woman**/45, children unknown

414. Corn Tassel (4) aka Young Corn Tassel Carpenter-Corn Tassel Carpenter (4)–**Young Tassel**-Corn Tassel Jr-**Kunokeski** – 7/32nd Chalakatha-**Cherokee**Metis - born 1745 Great Tellico TN-**murdered** 1788 Chuhowa TN - son of **Corn Tassel Carpenter (1)**/09 & **Tsigilili (Hanging) Maw**/15, Bird Clan Cherokee, raiding New-Ohio River valleys/58, Pontiac War/62-66, raiding New-JacksonGreenbrier River valleys/63, Point Pleasant/74, Cherokee War/75, raiding KYVA-OH/77-81, Crawford/82, **murdered by whites** with his father, step-mother, brother & one other relative under a flag of truce, husband 1765 Great Tellico
TN of a **Cherokee Woman**/50, children unknown

415. Corn Tassel (5) aka Corn Tassel Carpenter (5) -**Corn Tassel Great Eagle (2)**-Young Rayetaeh – 7/64th Chalakatha-**Cherokee**-Metis - born 1765 Great Tellico TN-**died by hanging** 1830 - son of **Corn Tassel Rayetaeh Carpenter**/30 & **Tali Cherokee**/35, Little Turtle War/90-94, raiding TN-KYVA-OH/90-1810, associated **with White Path** (Benge) **Rebellion**, **hung by whites** 1830, husband 1785 Great Tellico TN of **Unknown Woman,** children unknown

416. Cotte, Gabriel - adopted-French-Canadian born about 1740 CAN-died after 1780 – Cornstalk War/58-77, raiding Ohio-New River valleys/58, Pontiac War/62-66, Bushy Run/63, raiding New-Jackson-Greenbrier River valleys/63, raiding Ohio-Little Kanawha-Big Sandy-New River valleys/72, Point Pleasant/74, Boonesboro/78, associated **with Antoine Francois Maisonville**/50, brother in law of **Maurice Blondeau**/35 & **William Joseph LeMothe**/30, all 3 married Shawnee sisters, husband about 1760 (OH?) of **Kishpoko Sister**/44, father of several 1/2 Kishpoko-Metis children/60-80 surname Cotte

Shawnee Heeritage

417. Cougar, Catherine - adopted-white born 1732 NJ-died 1801 OH – captured-adopted by 1744 PA, early white woman in OH 1744, wife 1746 OH of **Cougar**/25-Chalakatha, widow in 1800, mother of several 1/2 Chalakatha-Metis children/47-77 names unknown

418. Coyle, Margaret - 1/2 Pekowi-Metis born about 1740 PA-died about 1780 - daughter of **Judith Stoneking**/25 & **Thomas Coyle**/20-adopted-white, wife about 1760 of **Gardner Red Wolf Green**/40-1/2 Chalakatha-Cherokee, mother of Benjamin Franklin Green/61, William Green/65, Paul Green/72 & John Green/75-all ½ Chalakatha-Pekowi-Cherokee-Metis

419. Crawfish – Pekowi born about 1730 PA-died after 1772 – Cornstalk War/55-72, French-Indian War/54-63, Braddock/55, raiding New-Shenandoah River valleys/55, raiding PA/55-56, raiding Ohio-New River valleys/58, Pontiac War 62-66, Bushy Run/63, raiding New-Greenbrier-Jackson River valleys/63, raiding Ohio-New-Little Kanawha-Big Sandy River valleys/72

420. Critterden, Hannah Qualiluka Guulisi - 1/4th Chalakatha-Pekowi**Cherokee**-Metis born 1756 Nickajack TN-died after 1838 OK - daughter of **Jennie Dougherty**/40 & **Critter Den**/35-Cherokee, Blind Savannah Clan Cherokee, wife 1st 1771 (TN?) of **Big Halfbreed**/50-1/2 Chalakatha-Cherokee, divorced 1789 by Big Halfbreed when she became a Christian, 2nd 1789 of **Jack Fields (1)**/60-1/2 Chalakatha-Pekowi-Metis, mother **with Halfbreed** of Daughter/72, Daughter/74, Lydia Halfbreed/76, Pigeon Halfbreed/78, Susannah Halfbreed/80, Jennie Halfbreed/82, Elizabeth Halfbreed/84, Chinosa Halfbreed/86 & Jesse Halfbreed/88-all 3/8th Chalakatha-Cherokee-Metis, **with Fields** of Neki Fields/90-3/8th Chalakatha-Pekowi-Cherokee-Metis

421. Croghan, Catherine aka **Adonwentishon** - 1/2 Chalakatha-Metis born about 1759 OH-died 1837 - daughter of **Chalakatha Woman**/40 & **George Croghan**/25-adopted-Irish, 4th wife 1782 of **Chief Joseph Brant**/42-Mohawk, (sister of 3rd wife Christine Croghan/58), mother **with Brant** of Joseph Brant Jr/83, Jacob Brant/86, Mary Brant/87, Catherine Brant/91, John Anthony Brant/94 & Elizabeth Brant/96-all 1/4th Chalakatha-**Mohawk**-Metis

422. Croghan, Christine aka **Ohtowakheson** - 1/2 Chalakatha-Metis born about 1758 OH-died about 1779 - daughter of **Chalakatha Woman**/40 & **George Croghan**/25-adopted-Irish, 3rd wife about 1772 of **Chief Joseph Brant**/42-Mohawk, (sister of 4th wife Catherine Croghan/59), mother **with Brant** of Powlus Brant/80-1/4th Chalakatha-**Mohawk**-Metis

423. Crooked Eyes – Mekoche born about 1730 OH-died after 1760 - wife about 1745 OH of **Shawnee Man**/25, widow 1760

424. Crooked Legs - adopted-white born about 1750-died after 1777 - adopted about 1755-returned to whites-returned to tribe 1765, Cornstalk War/68-77, raiding Little Kanawha-Big Sandy-Ohio-New River valleys/72, Point Pleasant/74-75, raiding Ohio-New River valleys/75, raiding KY-VA-OH/77, husband 1770 OH of **Thawikila Woman**/55, father of several 1/2 Thawikila-Metis children/70-77

425. Crooked Stick – Chalakatha born about 1790 OH-died after 1817 - Prophet's Town/1811, Brownstown/1812-Monguagon/1812-1st Amherstburg/1812-Frenchtown/1813-Ft. Meigs/1813-2nd Amherstburg/1813 & Thames/1813 **with Tecumseh**, a warrior at Lewistown 1817, Treaty 1817

426. Cross Crow – Kishpoko born about 1770 OH-died after 1805 - wife about 1785 OH of **Kishpoko Man**/65, widow 1805

427. Cross Face – Pekowi born about 1730 (MD?)-died after 1785 - wife about 1750 OH of **Pekowi Man**/30, widow 1785

428. Crow – Chalakatha born about 1755 OH-died after 1817 – Cornstalk War/72-77, raiding Ohio-Little Kanawha-Big Sandy-New River valleys/72, Point Pleasant/74- 75-78, Blue Jacket War/77-94, raiding KY-VA-OH/77-81, Boonesboro/78, Crawford/82, raiding Ohio River valley/88-92, Fallen timber/94, a warrior at Lewistown 1817, Treaty 1817

429. Crutchfield, Edmund Rock - 1/8th Chalakatha-Cherokee-**Metis** born 1786 Running Water TN-died 1826 (GA?) - son of **Susanna Vann**/52 & **John Crutchfield**/50-white, grandson of **Edward Vann**/20 & **Charity Barnes**/26, husband 1st 1804 of **Ticanahila Tiger**/84-Cherokee-(sister of **Tarcheechee Tiger**-Cherokee), 2nd 1806 of **Nancy Love**/86-white, 3rd 1819 of **Miss Murray**/1800-white, children unknown

430. Crutchfield, Joseph - 1/8th Chalakatha-Cherokee-**Metis** born 1788 Running Water TN-died 1855 TX - son of **Susanna Vann**/52 & **John Crutchfield**/50-white, husband 1st 1809 of **Margaret Peggy Scott**/80, 2nd 1822 of **Chinosa Halfbreed**/92-1/8th Chalakatha-Pekowi-Cherokee-Metis, no children of record **with Scott** but **step-father** to David Vann/99, Judge John Vann/1801, Lucy Ayouku Vann/1803, Little John Vann/1805, Elizabeth Vann/1807 & James Vann/1809-all children of **Margaret Peggy Scott**/80 & **Chief James Vann**/66, father **with Chinosa** of John Crutchfield/1822, Richard McLeod Crutchfield/1826, Susan Crutchfield/1828 & Dixon Crutchfield/1830-all 1/8th Chalakatha-Pekowi-Cherokee-Metis

431. Crutchfield, Rachel - 1/8th Chalakatha-Cherokee-**Metis** born 1784 Running Water TN-died after 1810 - daughter of **Susanna Vann**/52 & **John Crutchfield**/50-white, wife 1800 of **John Tyner**/70-1/2 Chalakatha-Metis, mother of Jackson Tyner/1824, Andrew Tyner/1830 & others-all 5/16th Chalakatha-Cherokee-Metis

432. Cunningham, Joseph aka **Injun Joe** - adopted-white born about 1770died after 1796 - adopted with brother William/73 1779 OH-returned to whites 1795, raiding Ohio River valley/88-92, Blue Jacket War/88-94, husband about 1790 of **Chalakatha Woman**/75, father of a couple of 1/2 Chalakatha-Metis children/90-95, abandoned Shawnee Wife & Metis children when he returned to whites 1795

433. Cunningham, William aka **Bloody Bill** - adopted-white born about 1773died after 1818 - adopted with brother Joseph/70 1779 OH-returned to whites 1795, raiding Ohio River valley/88-92, Blue Jacket War/90-94, scout-Capt.
William Caldwell Sr. & sons-**with British Army-**War of 1812, about 1818 killed **John Caldwell**/98 (son of William Caldwell Sr-white & Suzanne Baby), a man of huge size, tall & heavy, husband about 1793 of **Chalakatha Woman**/79, father of a couple of 1/2 Chalakatha-Metis children/93-95, abandoned Shawnee Wife & Metis children when he returned to whites 1795

434. Cussabool aka General Cussabool – Mekoche born about 1770 OH-died after 1817 - raiding Ohio River valley/88-92, Blue Jacket War/88-94, scout-**with U.S. Army-**War 1812-Thames/1813, a warrior at Lewistown 1817, Treaty 1817

435. Cut Finger - ½ Mekoche-**Seneca** born about 1795 OH-died after 1832 KS - son of **Cut Finger's Mother**/80-Mekoche & **Seneca Man**/75, moved to KS 1832, wife & children unknown

436. Cut Finger's Mother - Mekoche-(adopted-**Seneca**) born about 1780 OHdied after 1832 KS - Treaty 1832, move to KS 1832, wife 1794 of **Seneca Man**/75, widow 1832, mother of Cut Finger/95-1/2 Mekoche-Seneca

437. Cutoff Ear - Kishpoko-(adopted-**Cayuga**) born about 1750 OH-died after 1794 – Cornstalk War/68-77, raiding Little Kanawha-Big Sandy-Ohio-New River valleys/72, raiding Ohio River valley/74 **with Chief Logan**, Point Pleasant/74-75-78, raiding KY-OH-VA/75-81, Blue Jacket War/77-94, Crawford/82, raiding Ohio River valley/88-92, ear cut off in battle about 1772, husband 1770 of **Cayuga Woman**/55, father of several 1/2 Kishpoko-Cayuga children/70-94

438. Cuts Corn aka Cutting Corn - adopted-Cayuga born about 1720 (PA?)died after 1753 - wife about 1735 (PA-OH?) of **Pekowi Man**/15, widow 1753, mother of several 1/2 Pekowi-Cayuga children/35-52

Section VI
Dancing Deer to Dusquene (D)

D

439. Dancing Deer – adopted-Creek born about 1720 AL-died after 1761 - wife about 1735 AL of **Thawikila Man**/15, widow 1761, mother of several 1/2 Thawikila-Creek children/35-61

440. Daugherty, James (1) aka **James Dougherty (2)-James Dougherty Jr (1)** - 1/8th Chalakatha-Pekowi-**Cherokee**-Metis born about 1760 NC-died 1830 AL - son of **James Dougherty (1)**/42 & **Cherokee Woman**/45, husband 1783 of **Mary Jane Stafford**/65-white, father of Sarah Daugherty/84, James Daugherty (2)/86, Hugh Daugherty/88, Noble Daugherty/90, Charles Daugherty/92, Virginia Janet Daugherty/95, Margaret Daugherty/1800, Eudocia Daugherty/1806, John Daugherty/1808-all 1/16th Chalakatha-Pekowi-CherokeeMetis

441. Dauphin - 1/2 Kishpoko-Chippewa-**Metis** born about 1740-died after 1775 - son of **Kishpoko Woman & 1/2 Chippewa-French/Canadian-Metis**, Cornstalk War/58-74, raiding Ohio-New River valleys/58, Pontiac War/62-66, Bushy Run/63, raiding New-Greenbrier-Jackson River valleys/63, raiding OhioBig Sandy-Little Kanawha-New River valleys/72, raiding Ohio River valley/74 **with Chief Logan**, Point Pleasant/74, husband about 1760 OH of **Kishpoko Woman**/45, moved to north-west (MI-WI?) 1775, father of several 3/4th Kishpoko-Chippewa-Metis children/60-75

442. Davis, James **Coonwasaliskee** – Kishpoko-(adopted **Cherokee**) born about 1750 (VA?)-died after 1805 - Treaty 1805, husband (1st or 2nd?) 1777 of **Cherokee Woman**/60, father of Thomas Davis/78, Easter Davis/80, Susanna Davis/82, Daniel Abraham Davis/85, Frances Davis/90, Fannie Davis/95, John Porum Davis/1800 & Mary Davis/1803-all 1/2 Kishpoko-Cherokee

443. Dead Tree aka **Mishawaka** – Kishpoko born about 1790 OH-died after 1834 - daughter of **Elk Heart**/70, wife about 1810 OH of **Kishpoko Man**/90, widow in 1834 (possibly from War of 1812?)

444. Deaf Jim – Mekoche born before 1790 OH-died after 1820 KS - scout **with U.S. Army-**War 1812-Thames/1813, moved to KS after 1820

445. Debolt, George (1) aka Dibert-Debert-Deburt - 5/8th Pekowi-**Metis** born 1745 Bedford Co PA-died after 1790 - son of **Charles Christopher Dibert** aka Debolt/18 & **Eve Elizabeth (Ney)** /22-Pekowi, grandson of **Mary Chartier**/1687-1/2 Pekowi-Metis, husband 1765 of **Ann Long**/50-white, father of Noah Debolt/66, Jacob Debolt/68, Jeremiah Debolt/70, George Debolt (3)/72, Elizabeth Debolt/74, Charity Debolt/76, Priscilla Debolt/78, Rhoda Debolt/80, Harriet Debolt/82, Mary Debolt/84, Catherine Debolt/86, Martha Debolt/88 & Sarah Debolt/90-all 5/16th Pekowi-Metis

446. Deer aka **Pisakethe**[53] – Thawikila born about 1745OH-died after 1774 (AL?) – from the **Black Hoof** band, Cornstalk War/62-74, Pontiac War/62-66,
Bushy Run/63, raiding New-Jackson-Greenbrier River valleys/63, raiding Ohio-New-Big Sandy-Little Kanawha River valleys/72, Point Pleasant/74, moved to AL with Creeks 1774

447. Dequindre, Antoine – adopted-Ottawa-Metis born about 1743-died 1784
– Cornstalk War/62-77, Pontiac War/62-66, Bushy Run/63, raiding Ohio-Little Kanawha-Big Sandy-New River valleys/72, Point Pleasant/74, Blue Jacket War/77-80, Boonesboro/78, raiding OH-KY-VA/77-80, husband by 1779 (OH?) of **Kishpoko Woman**/65, father of Angelique Dequindre/80-1/2 Kishpoko-Ottawa-Metis

448. Deuquot – Kishpoko born about 1770 OH-died about 1821 CAN - raiding Ohio River valley/88-92, Blue Jacket War/87-94, raiding OH-KYVA/95-1810, Prophet's Town/1811, Brownstown/1812-Monguagon/1812-1st Amherstburg/1812-Frenchtown/1813-Ft. Meigs/1813-2nd Amherstburg/1813 & Thames/1813 **with Tecumseh**, moved to CAN 1815, likely died in CAN about 1821, wife & children unknown

449. Dibert, Charles Christopher aka Deburt-Debert-Debolt - 1/4th Pekowi**Metis** born 1718 PA-**killed** 1757 Bedford Co PA in Native attack - son of **Mary Chartier**/1687-1/2 Pekowi-Metis & **John Deburt**/1685-white, grandson of **Martin Chartier**/1655-adopted-French, nephew of **Peter Chartier**/1690-1/2 Pekowi-French-Metis, husband 1737 Bedford Co PA of **Eve Elizabeth (Ney?)** /22-Pekowi, father of Michael Dibert/39, Adam Dibert/41, Margaret Dibert/43, George Debolt (1)/45, John Dibert/46, Charles Christopher Dibert Jr/47, Sophia Dibert/48, Fredrick Dibert/50 & Mary Debolt/51- all 5/8th Pekowi-Metis

450. Dickerson, Ben aka Capt. Dickerson-Shawnee Ben - adopted-white born about 1730 (PA?)-**killed** about 1785 OH - trading in OH by 1756, associated with **Blue Jacket, Blue Shadow & Succopanus family**, French-Indian War/5463, Braddock/55, raiding New-Shenandoah River valleys/55, raiding PA/55-56, Pontiac War/62-66, Bushy Run/63, raiding New-Greenbrier-Jackson River valleys/63, raiding Ohio-Little Kanawha-New-Big Sandy River valleys/72, Point Pleasant/74-75-78, Boonesboro/78, Council with Bouquet-Ft. Pitt 1765, living at Great Island 1768, killed by John Hardin expedition-head cut off, husband 1st by 1756 OH of **Kishpoko Woman**/40, 2nd by 1783 OH of **Hannah Succopanus**/70-1/2 Kishpoko-Seneca, children/57-83 **with Kishpoko** unknown, father **with Succopanus** of Hannah Dickerson aka Hannah Succopanus (2)/84-1/4th Kishpoko-Seneca-Metis

451. Digging Dog – Kishpoko born about 1770 OH-died before 1825 CAN - raiding Ohio River valley/88-92, Blue Jacket War/88-94, raiding KY-VAOH/95-1810, Prophet's Town/1811, Brownstown/1812-Monguagon/1812-1st Amherstburg/1812-Frenchtown/1813-Ft. Meigs/1813-2nd Amherstburg/1813 & Thames/1813 **with Tecumseh**, moved to CAN 1815

452. Disponet, Joseph – white born 1743 Fredrick Co VA-died 1797 Rockingham Co VA – husband 1st 1763 western VA of **Chalakatha Woman**/48, 2nd 1791 of **Margaret Rust**/45, father **with Chalakatha** of Jacob Disponet/64, John Disponet/66, Elizabeth Disponet/68, Adam Disponet/70, Margaret Disponet/72, Barbara Disponet/74, Mary Magdalene Disponet/82 & others-all ½ Chalakatha-Metis

453. Doc Bill – Chalakatha born about 1795 OH-died after 1838 KS - **murdered Peter Cornstalk**/55 with **Capt. Bill**/90 & **Sam Loon**/1800-both Mekoche, only 1 of the 3 that was not killed by **Peter Cornstalk Jr**/85 in revenge, some clan connection to the Cornstalk family, moved to KS

454. Doe Skin – adopted-Cayuga born about 1760 OH-died after 1790 - wife about 1775 OH of **Pekowi Man**, widow 1790, mother of several 1/2 Pekowi-Cayuga children/75-90

455. Dog in House – adopted-Miami born about 1750 OH-died after 1780 - wife 1770 OH of **Mekoche Man**/50, widow in 1778, mother of three 1/2 Mekoche-Miami children/70-78

456. Dog Rib – adopted-Chippewa born about 1755 (MI?)-died after 1780 - raiding Little Kanawha-Big Sandy-Kanawha River valleys/72, raiding Ohio River valley/74 **with Chief Logan**, Point Pleasant/74-78, raiding KY-OHVA/77-80, husband about 1775 OH of **Kishpoko Woman**/60, father of two 1/2 Kishpoko-Chippewa children/75-78

457. Double Ax - Kishpoko-(adopted-**Cherokee**) born about 1745 OH-died after 1777 – Cornstalk War/62-77, Pontiac War/62-66, Bushy Run/63, raiding New-Greenbrier-Jackson River valleys/63, raiding Big Sandy-New-Ohio-Little Kanawha River valleys/72, Point Pleasant/74, raiding KY-OH-VA/77, husband about 1765 east KY of **Cherokee Woman**/50, father of several 1/2 Kishpoko-Cherokee children/65-77

458. Double Head aka Doublehead Carpenter-Taltsuska-TultsuskaChuquilatague-Two Heads-Autowee-Kill Baby-Ahtowhee-Walking ManDhuqualutauge-Dsugweladegi-Taliwuaskaskule – 7/32nd Chalakatha-**Cherokee**Metis born about 1740 Great Tellico TN-**murdered** 1807 Hiawassee Ferry TN - son of **Great Eagle Carpenter**/02 & **Wurteh Tawsee Fox-(Smallpox Conjurer)**/05-Cherokee, Red Paint Clan Cherokee, **associated with Dragging Canoe** & **Cornstalk in John Swift silverming**/60-69, Point Pleasant/74, raiding KY-VA-OH/77-81, Crawford/82, Ish Station-Cavett Station 1793, Blue Jacket War/77-94, **a Chickamauga** with Dragging Canoe, from the Overhills, Center Star & Muscle Shoals AL, delegate to D.C./91, Treaty Sycamore Shoals 1775, 1791, 1792, 1794, 1805, 1806, Council Hanging Maw Town-survived attack by John Beard's renegade militia 1792, Conference at Henry's Station 1793, 3rd Treaty of Tellico 1806 with brother Red Bird/31, **murdered 1807** by **John Ridge** & nephews **Alexander Jeremiah Sanders** & **James Sanders** allegedly for signing 3rd Treaty of Tellico 1806 giving away Cherokee land, husband 1st 1757 of half-1st cousin **Great Priber**/39-1/2 Chalakatha-Cherokee-Metis, 2nd 1787 of 3rd cousin/niece **Nancy Drumgoole**/67 aka Nannie the Pain-7/64th Chalakatha-Pekowi-Cherokee-Metis, 3rd 1795 of 5th cousin/niece **Margaret Peggy Scott**/80-1/8th Chalakatha-Thawikila-Creek-Cherokee-Metis, 4th 1797 of 4th cousin/niece **Kateeyah Wilson (2)**/80-5/32nd Chalakatha-Thawikila-Kishpoko-Black-Creek-Cherokee-Metis, 5th 1800 of 5th cousin/niece **Sarah Scott**/86-1/8th Chalakatha-Thawikila-Creek-Cherokee-Metis (sister of Margaret Peggy/83), 6th 1805 GA of **Jennie Foster**/79-1/8th Shawnee-Cherokee-Metis, father **with Priber** of Corn Blossom/58, Tuskiahoote/59, Soney/60, Tuckahoe/61, Seeleechie/63, Nigodigeyu/64, Gulustiyu/66, Ishtonnarhay/68, Tahlejewsco Doublehead/70 & a Daughter/72-all 15/64th Chalakatha-Cherokee-Metis, **with Drumgoole** of Bird aka Bird Tail/90 & Nancy Doublehead/92-both 5/32nd Chalakatha-Pekowi-Cherokee-Metis, **with Margaret Peggy Scott** of Two Heads Doublehead/96 & Double Head (2)/97-both 9/64th Chalakatha-Thawikila-Creek-Cherokee-Metis, **with Wilson** of Tassel/97, Alcy/98, Susannah/99 & Peggy Doublehead/1800-all 3/16th Chalakatha-Thawikila-Kishpoko-Black-

Creek-Cherokee-Metis, **with Sarah Scott** of William Doublehead/1800 & Double Head (3)/1801-both 9/64th Chalakatha-Thawikila-Creek-Cherokee-Metis, **with Foster** of Tom Doublehead/1806-11/64th Chalakatha-Cherokee-Metis

459. Dougherty, James (1) - 1/4th Chalakatha-Pekowi-**Cherokee**-Metis born 1742 Nickajack TN-died 1791 Charleston SC - son of **Ahneewakee Muskrat**/04 & **Cornelius Dougherty**/1700, Blind Savannah Clan Cherokee, husband 1st 1759 Nickajack TN of **Cherokee Woman**/44, 2nd 1780 Great Tellico TN of 2nd cousin **Ollie Mollie Carpenter**/54-15/32nd Chalakatha-Thawikila-Creek-CherokeeMetis, father **with Cherokee** of James (2)/60 & several other Dougherty children/62-80- all 1/8th Chalakatha-Pekowi-Cherokee-Metis, **with Carpenter** of Annie Crying Bear/80, James Dougherty (3)/82, Susan Dougherty/84, Elizabeth Dougherty/86, Elsie Dougherty/88, Rachel Dougherty/90, Mary Dougherty/92all 23/64th Chalakatha-Pekowi-Thawikila-Creek-Cherokee-Metis

460. Dougherty, John (1) aka **Long John** - ½ Chalakatha-Pekowi-**Cherokee**Metis born 1744 Nickajack TN-died after 1805 - son of **Ahneewakee Muskrat**/04 & **Cornelius Dougherty**/1700, Blind Savannah Clan Cherokee, Treaty 1805, husband 1st 1764 Nickajack TN of **Cherokee Woman**/50, 2nd 1775 Chota TN of half-niece (daughter of half-sister) **Nellie Parris**/60-31/64th Chalakatha-Pekowi-Kishpoko-Black-Metis, children/65-82 **with Cherokee** unknown, father **with Parris** of Catherine Dougherty/84, John Oogama Dougherty/86, Leaf Oogahloguh Dougherty/88 & children/76-83-all 31/64th Chalakatha-Pekowi-Kishpoko-Black-Cherokee-Metis

461. Dougherty, John (2) aka **Long John** - 1/2 Mekoche-**Seneca** born about 1780-died after 1832 - son of **Louis Dougherty**/60-Seneca & **Mekoche Woman**/65, scout-**with U.S. Army**-War 1812, Treaty 1832, move to KS 1832, wife & children unknown

462. Dougherty, Louis aka Lewis Dougherty – adopted-Seneca born about 1760-died after 1832 - scout-**with U.S. Army**-Revolution, Treaty 1832, move to KS 1832, husband 1st 1779 OH of **Mekoche Woman**/65, 2nd 1810 of **Pekowi Woman**/90, father **with Mekoche** of John-Long John Dougherty/80, Joseph Dougherty/85, Jake Dougherty/90 & Nancy Dougherty/95-all ½ MekocheSeneca, **with Pekowi** of Julia Ann Dougherty/1815-1/2 Pekowi-Seneca

463. Downing, Cash - 5/16th Kishpoko-Pekowi-Creek-Cherokee-**Metis** born about 1812-died after 1836 - son of **Moses Downing**/88 & **Lydia**

Tecumseh/90, grandson of **Tecumseh**/68 & **Dark Star -Tahneh-Naomi**/75- Chickamauga, husband about 1830 of **Elizabeth Gooden**/1810-white, children unknown

464.   Downing, Celia (2) - 5/16th Kishpoko-Pekowi-Creek-Cherokee-**Metis** born about 1814-died about 1858 - daughter of **Lydia Tecumseh**/90 & **Moses Downing**/88, granddaughter of **Tecumseh**/68 & **Tahneh-Naomi-Dark Star**/75- Chickamauga, 2nd wife about 1835 of **William Proctor**/1806-white, mother of Adam Proctor/1836, Archibald Proctor/1839, Rachel Proctor/1842 & Nancy Proctor/1844-all 5/32nd Kishpoko-Pekowi-Creek-Cherokee-Metis (all greatgrandchildren of **Tecumseh**/68)

465.   Downing, Dicey aka Disi - 5/16th Kishpoko-Pekowi-Creek-Cherokee**Metis** born about 1808-died after 1844 - daughter of **Lydia Tecumseh**/90 & **Moses Downing**/88, granddaughter of **Tecumseh**/68 & **Tahneh-Naomi-Dark Star**/75-Chickamauga, 1st wife 1824 of **William Proctor**/1806-white, mother of Sarah Proctor/1824, Johnson Proctor/1828, Ezekial Proctor/1831, Elizabeth Proctor/1834-all 5/32nd Kishpoko-Pekowi-Creek-Cherokee-Metis (all greatgrandchildren of **Tecumseh**/68)

466.   Downing, John (1) aka **John Jr** - 1/2 Kishpoko-Metis born about 1742 VA-died after 1812 - son of **Hanna Falling Leaf**/20-Kishpoko & **Major John Downing**/10-white, Wolf Clan Cherokee, husband 1st about 1762 VA-TN of **Chalakatha Woman**/46, 2nd 1772 of **Jennie Cherokee**/56, children/62-72 **with Chalakatha** unknown, father **with Jennie** of John Downing/72, Samuel Downing/80, Catherine Downing/82, Sarah Downing/84, William Downing/86 & Moses Downing /88-all 1/4th Kishpoko-Cherokee-Metis

467.   Dragging Canoe aka Dragging Canoe Carpenter-Tsiyigunsini-Drags Canoe-Dragon-Dragging Canoe Attakullakulla-Chuconsene-CheucunseeKunnesee – 15/32nd Chalakatha-Thawikila-Creek-**Cherokee**-Metis – born 1734
Great Tellico TN-**died from wounds** 1792 Running Water TN – oldest son of **Attakullakulla Carpenter**/08 & **Ollie Nionee Oconastota**/20, Wolf Clan Cherokee, over 6' tall, broad-shouldered, muscular & pox-marked, raiding Ohio-New River valleys/58, Pontiac War/62-66, raiding New-Jackson-Greenbrier River valleys/63, associated with **Cornstalk**/10 & **Doublehead**/35 **in John Swift silverming**/60-69, raiding Ohio-Little Kanawha-Big Sandy-New River

Shawnee Heritage

valleys/72, Point Pleasant/74, raiding Ohio-New River valleys/75, attended but didn't sign Treaty Sycamore Shoals 1775, started Cherokee War/75 **with Abraham-Ooskiah**/21-Cherokee-Metis (half-brother of Hanging Maw), raiding VA-KY-OH-TN/77-92 **with Cheeseekau** /56 & **Chief Bob Benge**/62, adopted brother of **Alexander Cameron** aka **Scotchee**/30-white (husband of his sister Ollie Mollie Carpenter/54), Crawford/82, Harmar/90, St. Clair/91, died from wounds received at Buchanan Station/92, from the Overhills & Running Water (Shawnee) village TN, headman from Great Island TN, **Principal Chief of the Chickamauga 1775-92**, succeeded as Chickamauga Chief by **John Watts Jr**/48 & **Little Turkey Hop**/15, protested Treaty Sycamore Shoals/75, husband 1749 TN of **Leaf Cherokee**/35, father **with Leaf** of Sarah Naky/50, Young Dragging Canoe-Dragging Canoe (2)/52, Little Owl Dragging Canoe/54, Daughter-Wife of Cheeseekau/56 & other children/57-80-all 15/64th Chalakatha-Thawikila-Creek-Cherokee-Metis

468. Dragging Canoe, Little Owl aka Little Owl Canoe – 15/64th ChalakathaThawikila-**Creek**-Cherokee-Metis born 1750 Great Tellico TN-**killed** Buchanan
Station TN 1792 - son of **Dragging Canoe**/34 & **Leaf Cherokee**/35, Point Pleasant/74, Cherokee War/75, a Chickamauga warrior, raiding KY-OH-VATN/77-92, scout-**with British Army**-Revolution, called **Chief of a Creek village**, husband 1774 of **Creek Woman**/60, father of several children/74-92-all 7/64th Chalakatha-Thawikila-Creek-Cherokee-Metis

469. Dragging Canoe, Sarah aka Naky Canoe – 15/64th ChalakathaThawikila-Creek-**Cherokee**-Metis born 1754 Great Tellico TN-died after 1775 Running Water TN - daughter of **Dragging Canoe**/34 & **Leaf Cherokee**/35, wife 1764 of **Alexander Brown**/45-1/4th Chalakatha-Cherokee-Metis, mother of Alexander Brown Jr -Sawny/65-15/64th Chalakatha-Thawikila-Creek-CherokeeMetis

470. Dragging Canoe, Young aka Dragging Canoe (2)-Young Canoe – 15/64th Chalakatha-Thawikila-**Creek**-Cherokee-Metis born 1752 Great Tellico TN-died after 1814 (TN?) – son of **Dragging Canoe**/34 & **Leaf Cherokee**/35, from Lookout Mountain, a Chickamauga warrior, Point Pleasant/74, Cherokee War/75, raiding VA-OH-KY-TN/77-92 **with father, Cheeseekau**/56 & **Chief Bob Benge**/62, scout-Revolution **with British Army**, Capt. James Foster Co-**with U.S. Army**-Creek War/1813, husband 1st 1769 Running Water TN of **SajimaSagee**/55-Cherokee, 2nd 1808 of **Nancy Hughes**/74-3/4th Chalakatha-PekowiMetis, 3rd **of Jennie Pinson**, father **with Sajima** of Dragging Canoe (3)/70, Daughter/72 & other children/72-90-all 7/64th Chalakatha-Thawikila-Creek-
Cherokee Metis, children **with Hughes** & **with Pinson** unknown

471. Dragoo, Billy - adopted-white-(**Ottawa**) born 1775-died 1856 - adopted by Shawnee 1783 OH-married into Ottawa 1793-returned with sons to visit white family 1804-returned to whites with sons 1806 when wife died, Fallen Timber/94, had nose & ears pierced, lived in Ottawa village, husband 1st about 1793 of **Bonnisui's Sister**-1/2 Kishpoko-Ottawa, 2nd 1815 of **Rebecca Metheny**white, father **with Bonnisui's Sister** of John Dragoo/94, Elder Daughter/96, Younger Daughter/98, Isaac Dragoo/1802-all 1/4th Kishpoko-Ottawa-Metis,
(daughters stayed with tribe 1806, Isaac returned to tribe 1817, John died of TB 1823)

472. Dreaded Warrior – Kishpoko born about 1735 Running Water TN-died after 1777 (NC?) – pro-French faction in French-Indian War/54-63, Braddock/55, Cornstalk War/55-77, raiding New-Shenandoah River valleys/55, raiding Ohio-New River valleys/58, Pontiac War/62-66, Bushy Run/63, raiding New-Greenbrier-Jackson River valleys/63, raiding Ohio-Big Sandy-Little Kanawha-New River valleys/72, Point Pleasant/74, a **Chickamauga**, raiding KY-VA-OH/77 **with Dragging Canoe, Cheeseekau & Chief Bob Benge**, an especially vicious warrior, from the Middle Towns, a Principle Man of Jore (NC?), husband about 1755 TN of **Cherokee Woman**/39, children unknown

473. Drouillard, George aka Pierre George Drouillard - 1/2 Chalakatha-Metis born 1773 MI-**killed** 1810 MN - son of **Asoundechris**/53-Chalakatha & **Pierre Drouillard**/50-adopted-white, translator with Lewis & Clark/04, well educated(could read & write French, English & speak several Indian languages), **killed by**
Blackfeet Indians, nephew of **Peter Lorimier**/48-adopted-Metis & **Straight Ahead**/52, no known wives or children

474. Drouillard, Inioipiaichika aka Eeneoepeaechika-Niece of Lorimier - 1/2 Chalakatha-Metis born about 1775-died after 1805 - daughter of **Asoundachris**/53 & **Pierre Drouillard**/50-adopted-white, living in Apple Creek MO 1805, niece of **Straight Ahead**/50 & **Peter Lorimier**/48-adopted-Metis, husband & children unknown

475. Drowning Bear, Junaluska (2) aka Tsunuluhusgi - 1/8th Chalakatha**Cherokee**-Metis born about 1775 NC-died 1858 TN - son of **John Drowning Bear Brown (3)-Junaluska (1)**/51 & **Gowhistiski**/55-Cherokee, **with U.S.**
Army-Creek War/13-Horseshoe Bend/14, husband 1st 1795 of **Wallee**/80Cherokee, 2nd about 1840 of **Nisuh-Nicie Tsigia**/1820-Cherokee, father **with**

Wallee of Katakiska Drowning Bear/95, Witch Drowning Bear (2)/96, Junaluska Drowning Bear (4)/97 & other children/99-1840, **with Nicie** of Jimmy Drowning Bear/1846, Nalih Drowning Bear/1847, Sicqueyu Drowning Bear/1849-all 1/16th Chalakatha-Cherokee-Metis

476. Drowning Bear, Junaluska (3) – 9/32nd Chalakatha-Pekowi-**Cherokee**Metis born about 1784-died after 1831 - son of **Junaluska (1)-John Drowning Bear Brown (3)**/51 & **Lucy Benge**/68, **with U.S. Army**-Creek War/1813, husband 1st about 1804 of **Cherokee Woman**/85, 2nd 1822 of **Sokinney Cherokee**/1802, children/1804-22 **with Cherokee** unknown, father **with Sokinney** of Chulaoheh/1823, Young Bird/1825, Jennie Yonegooska/1829 & John Pendergrass/1831-all 9/64th Chalakatha-Pekowi-Cherokee-Metis

477. Drowns Turkey – adopted-Cayuga born about 1740 OH-died after 1782 - raiding Ohio-New River valleys/58, Pontiac War/62-66, Bushy Run/63, raiding New-Greenbrier-Jackson River valleys/63, raiding Ohio-Big Sandy-Little Kanawha-New River valleys/72, raiding Ohio River valley/74 **with Chief Logan**, Point Pleasant/74-78, Blue Licks/82, husband about 1760 OH of **Mekoche Woman**/44, children unknown

478. Drumgoole, Alexander (2) – 7/32nd Chalakatha-Cherokee-**Metis** born 1736 Great Tellico TN-died 1824 Great Tellico TN – son of **Oousta Carpenter**/22-7/16th Chalakatha-Cherokee-Metis & **Alexander Drumgoole (1)**/10-white, husband 1st 1755 Running Water TN of **Margaret Elizabeth French**/40-3/4th Chalakatha-Black-Metis, 2nd 1757 Great Tellico TN of **Nancy Augustus Hop-Moytoy**/24-Chalakatha-Pekowi, 3rd 1764 Great Tellico TN of **Nancy Foreman**/45-7/32nd Chalakatha-Cherokee-Metis, 4th 1762 Crowtown NC **Nionee Bird Clan**/47, 5th 1792 Davidson Co NC (TN) to **Lucy Parker**/?, 6th 1795 Sullivan Co TN of **Isabella Elliott (Shelby)**/70-1/2 Kishpoko-Metis, 7th 1809 TN of **Ann Baltzell**/90-1/4th Thawikila-Creek-Metis, children/55-59 **with French** of James Drumgoole/56-27/64th Chalakatha-Black-Cherokee-Metis, father **with Hop-Moytoy** of Chenelernkee Drumgoole/58-19/32nd ChalakathaPekowi-Cherokee-Metis, **with Foreman** of Nancy Drumgoole (1)/64-7/32nd Chalakatha-Cherokee-Metis, **with Nionee** of Alexander Drumgoole(3)-Wihu/62, Ruth Drumgoole (1)/64 & Nancy Drumgoole (2)/67-all 7/64th ChalakathaPekowi-Cherokee-Metis, children/92-95 **with Parker** unknown, **with Elliott**/70 of John Drumgoole/96 & Sarah Drumgoole/98-both 19/64th Chalakatha-Kishpoko-Cherokee-Metis, children **with Baltzell** unknown

479. Duchouquet, Francois aka **Sowahquothe** - 1/4th Kishpoko-Chippewa**Metis** born about 1766 Kaskaskia IN-died 1836 – son of **Francois Lafleur Duchoquet**/1700 & **Therese Celeste Louise Barrios**/37-Chippewa-Metis, adopted son of **Blue Jacket**/35, Crawford/82, raiding Ohio River valley/88-92, Blue Jacket War/82-94, **delegate to D.C. 1802** with Wayweleapee/60, John Perry/75, Quasakee Black Hoof/60, Spy Buck/70 & Joseph Parks/90, translator**with U.S. Army-**War of 1812, Treaty 1808, 1815, 1818, 1828, husband 1786
OH of **Kishpoko Woman**/70, father of Francois Duchouquet (2)/88-5/8th Kishpoko-Chippewa-Metis

480. Due, Robert aka Chief Jolly-Jaulee aka Dew's Son-Robert Dews - 1/2 Chalakatha-Metis born about 1737 (TN?)-died after 1777 - son of **Trader Jaulee**/10-French & **Dew**/20-Chalakatha, husband 1st 1757 Great Tellico TN of **Wurteh Watts**/44-21.32nd Chalakatha-Pekowi-Cherokee-Metis, 2nd 1760 (TN?) of **Susanna Catherine Red Horse**/42-Cherokee, 3rd 1763 Great Tellico TN of **Elizabeth Emory**/48-7/64th Chalakatha-Cherokee-Metis, 4th about 1773 of **Cherokee Woman**/55, 5th about 1778 of **Cherokee Woman**/60 & 6th (their 2nd marriage) 1785 Running Water TN of **Elizabeth Emory**/48-7/64th ChalakathaCherokee-Metis, father **with Wurteh** of Chief John Jolly/58-37/64th ChalakathaPekowi-Cherokee-Metis, with **Red Horse** of Tobacco Will/61-1/4th ChalakathaCherokee-Metis, **with Emory** (1st marriage) of Jennie Due/64 & Mary Due/70both 19/64th Chalakatha-Cherokee-Metis, no record of 1/4th ChalakathaCherokee-Metis children/73-85 with **Cherokee Women**, father with **Emory** (2nd marriage) of Betsy Houston (Due)/86 & Jennie Houston (Due)/88-both 19/64th
Chalakatha-Cherokee-Metis

481. Dushane, David aka David Shane-David Dusquene-David Duchene – 5/8th Chalakatha-Kishpoko-Mekoche-Creek-Wyandot-Metis born about 1785died after 1854 - son of **Anthony Shane**/63 & **Lamateshe Blackfish**/58, scoutAnthony Shane Co-**with U.S. Army-**War 1812, Treaty 1854, brother of John
Shane/90, Charles Chesne/95 & 2 Daughters of Lematashe Shane, half-brother of David Deshane/80, grandson of **Black Fish**/25 & grandson of **Isadore Chesne**/35-1/2 Wyandot-Metis, wife & children unknown

482. Dusquene, Capt. Joseph aka Joseph Chesne-Capt. Dusquene-Joseph Duchene-Mushkedewin-Prairie Man – adopted-1/2 Pekowi-Wyandot-Metis-(adopted Chippewa) born about 1756 OH-died after 1835 - son of **Isadore Chesne**/35 & **Younger Daughter of Loyparkoweh Opessa**/38, raiding Ohio

River valley/74 **with Chief Logan**, Point Pleasant/74, raiding OH-KY-VA/7581, Blue Jacket War/77-94, Boonesboro/78, raiding Ohio River valley/81 **with Joseph Brant**, Crawford/82, raiding Ohio River valley/88-92, employed in fur trade 1795-1827, became U.S. citizen 1818, half-brother of Anthony Shane/60 & Joseph Shane/65, half-brother of Mary Josette Chesne/75-Wyandot-OttawaMetis, adopted son 1778 & (double) son in law 1779-80 of **Black Fish**/25, husband 1st 1779 OH of **Lamateshe Blackfish**/58, 2nd 1780 OH of her sister **Pimegeezhigoqua Blackfish**/52-both Chalakatha-Mekoche-Pekowi, father **with Lamateshe** of David Deshane/80 & **with Pimegeezhigoqua** of Joseph Dusquene Jr/81, Jean Baptiste Dusquene/85, Isabella Dusquene/90 & Susanne Dusquene/95-all 1/2 Chalakatha-Mekoche-Pekowi-Wyandot-Metis

483. Dusquene, David aka **David Deshane**-David Shane-David Duchene – 1/2 Chalakatha-Mekoche-Pekowi-Wyandot-Metis born about 1780-died after 1854 - son of **Lamateshe Blackfish**/58 & **Capt. Joseph Dusquene**/55, raiding OH-KY-VA/99-1810, Prophet's Town/1811, Brownstown/1812-Monguagon/1812-1st Amherstburg/1812-Frenchtown/1813-Ft. Meigs/1813-2nd Amherstburg/1813 & Thames/1813 with uncle/3rd cousin **Tecumseh**, Treaty 1854, stepson of (his uncle) **Anthony Shane**/63, half-brother of David Dushane/85, John Shane/90, Charles Chesne/90 & 2 Daughters of Anthony Shane, husband about 1800 of **Chippewa Woman**/85, children unknown

Section VII
Eats Buffalo to Full (E – F)

E

484. Eats Buffalo – adopted-Cherokee born about 1730 TN-died after 1774 – Cornstalk War/55-74, French-Indian War/54-63, Braddock/55, raiding NewShenandoah River valleys/55, raiding PA/55-56, raiding Ohio-New River valleys/58, Pontiac War/62-66, Bushy Run/63, raiding New-Greenbrier-Jackson River valleys/63, raiding Ohio-Big Sandy-Little Kanawha-New River valleys/72, Point Pleasant/74, lived with KY-OH Shawnee, husband 1750 TN of **Chalakatha Woman**/35, father of several 1/2 Chalakatha-Cherokee children/5074

485. Egotakumshequa – Mekoche born about 1770 OH-died after 1817 – Blue Jacket War/88-94, a warrior at Wapakoneta 1817, Treaty 1817

486. Eight Minks – Thawikila born about 1760 OH-died after 1795 - wife 1775 OH of **Thawikila Man**/56, widow in 1795

487. Eitinipsiko aka Heeteeneepseeko – Chalakatha born about 1720 PA-died about 1758 OH in epidemic - French-Indian War/54-63, Braddock/55, raiding New-Shenandoah River valleys/55, raiding PA/55-56

488. Ekouachika aka Hekooachika – Pekowi born about 1790 OH-died after 1815 - Prophet's Town/1811, **left Tecumseh & Prophet** after Prophet's Town, living in Apple Creek MO 1815

489. **Elk aka Wabete**[54] (1) – Mekoche born about 1715 OH-**killed** 1786 OH - brother of **Moluntha**/10, raiding PA/40, Cornstalk War/55-74, French-Indian War/54-63, Braddock/55, raiding New-Shenandoah River valleys/55, raiding PA/55-56, raiding Ohio-New River valleys/58, Pontiac War/62-66, Bushy Run/63, raiding New-Greenbrier-Jackson River valleys/63, raiding Ohio-NewLittle Kanawha-Big Sandy River valleys/72, Point Pleasant/74-78, **killed in Col. Benjamin Logan's attack on Moluntha's village**, husband 1735 OH of **Mekoche Woman**/20, father of Little Elk/40

490. Elk Heart – Kishpoko born about 1770 OH-died about 1834 KS - raiding Ohio River valley/88-92, Blue Jacket War/88-94, raiding OH-KY-VA/95-1810, Prophet's Town/1811, Brownstown/1812-Monguagon/1812-1st Amherstburg/1812-Frenchtown/1813-Ft. Meigs/1813-2nd Amherstburg/1813 & Thames/1813 **with Tecumseh**, moved to CAN 1815-returned to OH 1825-moved to KS 1826 **with Prophet & Paukeesaa**, husband 1790 OH of **Kishpoko Woman**/75 by 1790, father of Dead Tree/90

491. Elk in Water aka **Tekuntequa**-Tecuntequah-Tekuntekwa - Kishpoko born about 1770 OH-died after 1818 – a Kishpoko warrior, raiding Ohio River valley/88-92, Blue Jacket War/88-94, raiding OH-KY-VA/95-1810, Prophet's Town/1811, Brownstown/1812-Monguagon/1812-1st Amherstburg/1812Frenchtown/1813-Ft. Meigs/1813-2nd Amherstburg/1813 & Thames/1813 **with Tecumseh**, Treaty 1818, relative/same clan as **Tecumseh**, wife & children unknown

492. Elliott, Alexander McKee - 1/2 Kishpoko-Metis born about 1780-died after 1815 - son of **Col. Matthew Elliott**/30-adopted-Irish & **Mary Louise Sanschagrin-No Worries Rising Sun**/49, raiding OH-KY-VA/99-1810, **with British Army**-War of 1812, wife & children unknown

493. Elliott, Capt. Matthew aka Matthew Jr-Capt. Elliott - 1/2 Kishpoko-Metis born 1772 OH-**killed** 1812 - son of **Marie Louise Sanschagrin-No Worries Rising Sun**/49 & **Col. Matthew Elliott Sr**/30-adopted-Irish, Capt-**with British Army**-War 1812, killed with **Winnemak II-Pottawamee** by **Capt. John Logan**-Big Horn/74, **Big Capt. Johnny**/65 & **Bright Horn**/70, husband 1792 OH of **Kishpoko Woman**/75, father of John Elliott (2)/95 & other children/90-1812 likely surname Elliott-all 3/4th Kishpoko-Metis

494. Elliott, Col. Matthew aka Col. Elliot - adopted-Irish born 1730 IRE-died 1814 CAN - came to America 1761, trader-agent, Pontiac War/62-66 **with Colonial Army**, moved to OH about 1766, in Chillicothe village during Point Pleasant/74, **with Natives** Boonesboro/78-off & on raiding KY-OH/77-81Crawford/82-Blue Jacket War/77-94, **with British Army**-Revolution, Council Coshocton 1776, Council with British 1779 with **Col. Alexander McKee**/25, **William Caldwell**/50, **Simon Girty**/41, **George Girty**/46, **James Girty**/43, **Simon Surphet**-cousin of McKee, **Wryneck**/25, **Savenooka Raven**/20, **Weed**/50-Iroquois & **River Bottom**/50-Seneca-Mingo, Grand Council 1791, Lt. Colonel **with British Army**-War of 1812, husband 1st 1763 PA of **Pekowi Woman**/46, 2nd 1769 PA of **Marie Louise Sanschagrin-No Worries Rising Sun**/49-Kishpoko, father **with Pekowi** of James Elliott/64, Daniel Elliott/66, John Elliott/68-all ½ Pekowi-Metis, **with Sanschagrin** of Isabella Elliott/70, Capt. Matthew Jr/72, William/75 & Alexander Elliott/80-all 1/2 Kishpoko-Metis

495. Elliott, Daniel - 1/2 Pekowi-Metis born about 1766 PA/OH-**killed** 1793 OH-KY - son of **Col. Matthew Elliott**/30-adopted-Irish & **Pekowi Woman**/46, trading in OH 1785, raiding Ohio River valley/88-92, Blue Jacket War/86-93, killed in raid/93, husband about 1785 OH of **Kejiah LaForce**/60-adoptedMulatto, father of four 1/4th Pekowi-Black-Metis children/86-92 likely surname Elliott

496. Elliott, Isabella - 1/2 Kishpoko-Metis born 1770 OH-died 1822 TN - daughter of **Col. Matthew Elliott**/30 & **Mary Louise Sanschagrin-No Worries Rising Sun**/49, sent south with Kishpoko or Irish relatives to escape the OH violence, wife 1st 1787 Sullivan Co TN of **Evan Shelby Jr**/19-Welsh, 2nd (his 3rd of 3) 1795 Sullivan Co TN of **Alexander Drumgoole (2)**/36-7/32nd ChalakathaCherokee-Metis, mother **with Shelby** of James Shelby/88, Letitia Shelby/90 &
Eleanor Shelby/92-all 1/4th Kishpoko-Metis, **with Drumgoole** of John Drumgoole/96 & Sarah Drumgoole/98-both 19/64th Chalakatha-Kishpoko-Cherokee-Metis

497. Elliott, James (1) aka Capt. James - 1/2 Pekowi-Metis born about 1764

PA-died before 1815 - son of **Col. Matthew Elliott**/30-adopted-Irish & **Pekowi Woman**/46, raiding OH-KY-VA/81, Crawford/82, raiding OH-KY-VA/88-92, Blue Jacket War/82-94, scout-William Wells Co-**with U.S. Army**-War of 1812, husband 1785 OH of **Kishpoko Woman**/70, father of several 3/4th Kishpoko-Pekowi-Metis children/85-1812 likely surname Elliott

498. Elliott, Joseph aka **Joseph LaForce** – adopted-Mulatto born 1758-died after 1829 - son of **Betty LaForce**/34-adopted-Mulatto & **White Man** (likely Rene LaForce), former LaForce slave, taken 1780-Martin's Station, given to Matthew Elliott Sr/30-adopted-white, freed before 1795 & stayed with tribe, took surname Elliott & moved south, living **with Cherokee** by 1806, husband about 1797 of **Martha Winford**/80-Cherokee-Metis, father of Mahala Elliott/98, Elizabeth Elliott/1800, James Elliott/1801, Josiah Elliott/1803, John Jack Elliott/1807, George Elliott/1811, David Elliott/1814, Mary Elliott/1816, Caroline Elliott/1829-all Black-Cherokee-Metis

499. Elvira – ½ Chalakatha-Cherokee born about 1770 (VA?)-died after 1800 Monroe Co. WV – daughter of **Chalakatha Man** & **Cherokee Woman**, living in Monroe Co. WV before 1800, sister of **Popsikona**, wife by 1800 of a **Free Black Man**, children unknown

500. Emory, Elizabeth – 7/64th Chalakatha-**Cherokee**-Metis born 1748 Great Tellico TN-died after 1790 on Hiwassee River TN - daughter of **Mary Grant**/26 & **William Emory**/20-white, Long Hair Clan Cherokee, wife 1st 1762 Tomatly TN of **Tahlonteeskee (1)**/42-7/32nd Chalakatha-Cherokee-Metis, 2nd 1763 Great Tellico TN of **Robert Due-Chief Jaulee-Jolly**/40-1/2 Chalakatha-Metis, 3rd by 1773 (TN?) of **John Headman Rogers**/40-white, 4th 1782 Great Tellico TN of **Unknown Man** –(possibly a **Houston**), 5th (2nd time) 1785 Running Water TN of **Robert Due**/40-1/2 Chalakatha-Metis, mother **with Tahlonteeskee (1)** of Tahlonteeskee (3) -Aaron Price/63-5/32nd Chalakatha-Cherokee-Metis, **with Due** of Jennie Due/64 & Mary Due/72-both 19/64th Chalakatha-Cherokee-Metis, **with Rogers** of Charles Rogers/74, Aky Ulusquatogu Rogers/76, John Hellfire Rogers/78, Nancy Rogers/80 & James Rogers/82-all 3/64th ChalakathaCherokee-Metis, children/83-85 **with Unknown Man** unknown –(but may have been Betsy & Jennie), **with Due** (2nd marriage) of Betsy Houston (Due)/86 & Jennie Houston (Due)/88-both 19/64th Chalakatha-Cherokee-Metis

501. Emory, Elizabeth – 35/64th Chalakatha-**Cherokee**-Metis born 1765 Running Water TN-died after 1818 AR – daughter of **Capt. Will Emory**/44 & **Chalakatha Woman**/50, 2nd wife 1782 Great Tellico TN of **Chief John Jolly**/58, mother of William Jolly/83 & John Jolly Jr/85-both ½ Chalakatha-Pekowi-Cherokee-Metis

502. Emory, Mary – 7/64th Chalakatha-**Cherokee**-Metis born 1746 Tomatly TN-died after 1800 (TN?) - daughter of **Mary Grant**/26 & **William Emory**/20white, Long Hair Clan Cherokee, wife 1st 1764 Tomatly TN of **Joseph Martin**/40-1/4th Pekowi-Metis, 2nd 1765 Tomatly TN of **Richard Fawling**/40adopted white, 3rd 1777 Tomatly TN of **Ezekial Buffington**/40-adopted Scot, mother **with Martin** of Samuel Martin/65-11/64th Chalakatha-Pekowi-CherokeeMetis, **with Fawling** of William Fawling/66, Ailsey Fawling/68, John Fawling/70 & Edmund Fawling/72-all 3/64th Chalakatha-Cherokee-Metis, **with Buffington** of Ellis Buffington/78, Jennie Buffington/80, Elizabeth Buffington/82, Thomas Buffington/84, Susannah Buffington/86, Annie Buffington/88 & Mary Buffington/90-all 3/64th Chalakatha-Cherokee-Metis

503. Emory, Susannah (1) – 7/64th Chalakatha-**Cherokee**-Metis born 1744 Tomatly TN-died after 1826 – daughter of **Susannah Catherine Grant**/28 & **John Robert Emory**/25-white, wife 1758 Great Tellico TN of **Col. John Stuart**-white born 1730 SCO-died 1779 FL, mother of Bushyhead Oonodutu Stuart/60 & Susan Wurteh Stuart/62-both 3/64th Chalakatha-Cherokee-Metis

504. Emory, Susannah (2) – 7/64th Chalakatha-**Cherokee**-Metis born 1750 Tomatly TN-died 1796 Tugaloo GA - daughter of **Mary Grant**/26 & **William Emory**/20-white, Long Hair Clan Cherokee, wife 1st 1764 Tomatly TN of **Richard "Texas Dick" Fields**/30-white, left Fields after he married her sister Nancy, 2nd by 1780 Great Tellico TN of **Col. John Martin**/52-1/4th PekowiMetis, mother **with Fields** of John Fields (1)/65, Chief Richard Fields/67, Jack Fields (2)/69, Capt. George Fields/71, Turtle Fields/73-all 3/64th Chalakatha-Cherokee Metis, **with Martin** of Judge John Calvin Martin/81, Nancy Martin/84 & Rachel Martin/88-all 9/64th Chalakatha-Pekowi-Cherokee-Metis

505. Emory, Susannah Catherine Grant – wife 1743 Great Tellico TN of **John Robert Emory**-white born 1725 ENG-died 1790 Charleston SC, mother of Susannah Emory (1)/44-7/64th Chalakatha-Cherokee-Metis

506. Enata aka Henata – Chalakatha born about 1775 OH-died after 1817 - Fallen Timber/94, a warrior at Lewistown 1817, Treaty 1817

507. Epaumee – Thawikila born about 1770 OH-died after 1817 – Blue Jacket War/88-94, a warrior from Hog Creek 1817, Treaty 1817

508. Epinoosa aka Epeenoosa-Hepeenoosa – Chalakatha born about 1750 OH-died after 1774 - raiding Little Kanawha-Big Sandy-Ohio-New River valleys/72, **fired 1st shot of Point Pleasant/74**, wife & children unknown

509. Ermatinger, Catherine McKee – 2nd wife 1803 Ontario CAN of **George**

Ermatinger-white born 1774 Ontario CAN-died 1841 CAN, mother of Jemima Ermatinger/1805, Thomas McKee Ermatinger/1806 & James Rough Ermatinger/1808-all 3/16th Kishpoko-**Chippewa**-Metis

510. Essquaseeto aka Heskwaseeto – Chalakatha born about 1775-died after 1817 – Fallen Timber/94, a warrior from Lewistown 1817, Treaty 1817

511. Ethanakeeptha – Pekowi born about 1730 PA-died after 1766 – Cornstalk War/55-66, French-Indian War/54-63, Braddock/55, raiding NewShenandoah River valleys/55, raiding PA/55-56, raiding Ohio-New River valleys/58, Pontiac War/62-66, Bushy Run/63, raiding New-Greenbrier-Jackson River valleys/63

512. Ethowakosee – Mekoche born about 1770 OH-died after 1817 – Blue Jacket War/88-94, Fallen Timber/94, a warrior at Wapakoneta 1817, Treaty 1817

513. Ewing, Black aka Ewing Slave - adopted-Mulatto born about 1745-died after 1782 – said to be son of **James Ewing** & **Black Woman**, adopted 1763 with owner's son/half-brother **John Ewing**/47, never returned to whites, Cornstalk War/66-77, raiding Ohio-Little Kanawha-Big Sandy-New River valleys/72, Point Pleasant/74-75-78, raiding Ohio-New River valleys/75, Blue Jacket War/77-82, raiding KY-VA-OH/77-81, Crawford/82, husband 1765 OH of **Chalakatha Woman**/52, father of several 1/2 Chalakatha-Black-Metis children/67-82

514. Ewing, John aka **Petabob**-Injun John - adopted-white born about 1747 Orange Co. VA-died 1824 **Gallia Co. OH** - son of sea captain **James Ewing**, adopted 1763 **with Slave** (half-brother) **Ewing**/45, returned to whites 1766 at Ft. Pitt, adopted brother of **White Otter**/40, adopted mother **White Otter's Mother** died of smallpox 1765, returned to Greenbrier Co. WV 1767, traveled back & forth to Indian country/67-74, living in Gallia Co. OH with Ann & children 1801, husband 1774 Gallia Co OH of **Ann Smith**/59-1/2 Chalakatha-Metis, father of William Ewing/75, Susanna Ewing/76, Andrew Ewing/77, John Smith Ewing/78, Elizabeth Ewing/79, Nancy Ann Ewing/80, Jeanette Ewing/81, Sarah Ewing/82, Lydia Ewing/83 & Samuel Ewing/84-all 1/4th Chalakatha-Metis

515. Eyengeking – Chalakatha born about 1740 PA-died after 1772 - Cornstalk War/58-72, raiding Ohio-New River valleys/58, Pontiac War/62-66, Bushy Run/63, raiding New-Greenbrier-Jackson River valleys/63, raiding Little Kanawha-Big Sandy-Ohio-New River valleys/72

F

516. Falling Leaf, Hanna aka **Hanna Fawling** - Kishpoko born about 1720 VA-died after 1746 – adopted-Wolf Clan Cherokee, wife by 1740 VA of **Major John Downing**/10-white, mother of George Downing/40, John DowningJr/42, William Downing/44 & Nancy Fawling Downing/46-all 1/2 Kishpoko-Metis

517. Falling Star – Chalakatha born about 1780 OH-died after 1817 - raiding OH-KY-VA-TN/95-1810, Prophet's Town/1811, Brownstown/1812-Monguagon/1812-1st Amherstburg/1812-Frenchtown/1813-Ft. Meigs/1813-2nd Amherstburg/1813 & Thames/1813 **with Tecumseh**, a warrior at Lewistown 1817, Treaty 1817

518. Father's Ax - Chalakatha born about 1735 PA-died after 1767 - FrenchIndian War/54-63, Braddock/55, raiding New-Shenandoah River valleys/55, raiding PA/55-56, raiding Ohio-New River valleys/58, Pontiac War/62-66, Bushy Run/63, raiding New-Greenbrier-Jackson River valleys/63, wife & children unknown

519. Fawling, John – 3/64th Chalakatha-Cherokee-**Metis** born 1770 Tomatley TN-**killed** 1807 - son of **Mary Emory**/46 & **Richard "Rim" Fawling**/40-white, killed in duel with his brother-in-law **Chief James Vann**/66, Long Hair Clan Cherokee, husband 1st 1799 of **Annie Rogers**/85-9/64th Chalakatha-CherokeeMetis, 2nd 1802 of **Katie Killachulla**/86-Cherokee, 3rd 1804 of **Nancy Vann**/743/8th Chalakatha-Pekowi-Cherokee-Metis-(sister of Chief James Vann/66), any children/99-1802 **with Rogers** unknown, father **with Killachulla** of John Fawling Jr/1803 & Mary Fawling/1804-both 1/64th Chalakatha-Cherokee-Metis, **with Vann** of Ruth Fawling/1805-13/64th Chalakatha-Pekowi-Cherokee-Metis

520. Featherstone, John – Chalakatha born about 1770 OH-died after 1830 - raiding Ohio River valley/88-92, Blue Jacket War/88-94, scout-**with U.S. Army**War 1812-Thames/1813, son in law of **Silverheels-Halowas Hokolesqua**/30, husband 1790 OH of **Sarah Silverheels**/75, children unknown

521. Featherstone, Sarah Silverheels - daughter of **Silverheels-Halowas**/30, granddaughter of **Okowellos**/1680, niece of **Cornstalk**/10, wife 1790 OH of **John Featherstone**/70, children unknown

522. Ferre, Jean aka John Iron-Iron John – adopted-1/2 Chippewa-Metis born about 1720 (MI?)-died after 1755 - son of **Chippewa Woman** & **Coureur deBois**, raiding PA/40, French-Indian War/54-55, Braddock/55, raiding NewShenandoah River valleys/55, husband 1740 PA of **Chalakatha Woman**/25, children unknown

523. Fields, Chief Richard aka Richard Jr-Kula-Gas – 3/64th Chalakatha**Cherokee**-Metis born 1767 TN-**executed** 1827 Nacogdoches TX - son of
Richard "Texas Dick" Fields/30-white & **Susannah Emory**/50, Long Hair Clan Cherokee, Capt.-Creek War/13 **with U.S. Army**, moved to TX 1819-**Head Chief TX Cherokee 1819-27, executed 1827 by Mexicans by order of Chief Bowl-John Bowles**, husband 1st about 1789 of **Elizabeth Hicks (1)**/66-1/8th Chalakatha-Thawikila-Creek-Cherokee-Metis, 2nd 1793 of his 1st cousin **Jennie Buffington**/80-3/64th Chalakatha-Cherokee-Metis, 3rd 1799 of **Nancy Brown**/78-1/8th Chalakatha-Cherokee-Metis, 4th by 1814 of **Frances Grapp**/90-Cherokee-Metis, father **with Hicks** of George Fields/90, Elizabeth Fields/91, John Fields (2)/92-all 5/64th Chalakatha-Thawikila-Creek-Cherokee-Metis, **with Buffington** of Nancy Fields/93 & Moses Fields/95-both 3/64th Chalakatha-Cherokee-Metis, **with Brown** of Lucy Brown Fields/1800, Susan Fields/1802, Ezekial Fields/1804, James Fields/1805, Dempsey Fields/1806, Henry Fields/1808, Delilah Fields/1810, Isabel-Ibba Fields/1812-all 5/64th Chalakatha-Cherokee-Metis, any children/1814-27 **with Grapp** unknown

524. Fighting Fish – Kishpoko born about 1730 AL-died after 1775 – Cornstalk War/55-74, French-Indian War/54-63, Braddock/55, raiding NewShenandoah River valleys/55, raiding PA/55-56, raiding Ohio-New River valleys/58, Pontiac War/62-66, raiding New-Greenbrier-Jackson River valleys/63, raiding Ohio-Little Kanawha-Big Sandy-New River valleys/72, crippled by wound Point Pleasant/74

525. Fire Heart (1) aka **Skootekitehi** (1)^{55}-**Thomas Greenwood**-PapapanaweLightning Fire – ½ Chalakatha-Metis born 1641 Shawnee Nation-western VAdied 1704 Running Water TN – son of **John Spemcia Elene-Big Man Greenwood**/1619-adopted white & **Nepikeweewa Chalakatha**/1625, husband
1659 of **Mikona Chalakatha**/1644, father of Joseph Gorhaleke-Winter Fever Greenwood/1660, Richard-Gohoma Greenwood/1662, Martin-Owasta Greenwood/1664, David-Calunna-Raven Greenwood/1666, Killer-Nellawgitchi Greenwood/1668 & Hawk-Sinnawa-Tlanuwa Greenwood/1670-all 3/4th Chalakatha-Metis

526. Fire Heart (2) aka Skootekitehi (2)-Skootekitehi Hop-Young Skootekitehi – 31/32nd Chalakatha-Kishpoko-Metis born 1752 Chota TN-**killed 1782 OH** – son of **Savanooka Hop (1)**/20 & **Cheekee Greenwood**/28, raiding Ohio-Little Kanawha-Big Sandy-New River valleys/72, Point Pleasant/74-75-78, raiding KY-OH-VA/77-81, Boonesboro/78, killed in Ohio valley 1782 by

Martin Wetzel, wife & children unknown

527. Fish aka **William Jackson**-Capt. Fish - adopted-white born about 1760died 1833 - adopted son before 1778 OH of **Black Fish**/25, raiding Ohio River valley/88, Blue Jacket War/78-94, living in MO before 1828, succeeded adopted brother **Lewis Rogers**/50 **as Chief of Band**, husband 1st about 1780 OH of **Elizabeth Bishop**/65-adopted-white, 2nd about 1789 OH of **Chalakatha Woman**/74, 3rd 1797 OH of **Martha Rogers**/82-1/2 Chalakatha-MekochePekowi-Metis (granddaughter of his adopted father Black Fish), father **with Bishop** of Daughter of Fish/81, Joseph Jackson/83, William Jackson Jr/85-all white-Shawnee, **with Chalakatha** of Arch Fish/90, Isaac Fish/92, Andrew Fish/94, Jesse Fish/96, Betsy Jane Fish/98-all 1/2 Chalakatha-Metis, **with Rogers** of Elizabeth Nakease Fish/98, William Jackson Jr/1800, Miss Fish/1802, Pascal Fish/1804, John Ficklin Fish/1806 & Charles Salahnewe Fish/1808-all 1/4th Chalakatha-Mekoche-Pekowi-Metis

528. Fish, Nathaniel - 7/64th Chalakatha-Pekowi-Kishpoko-Black-CherokeeMetis born about 1799 NC-died 1895 - son of **Zachariah Fish**/64 & **Elizabeth Ahtewattah** /74, husband 1st 1820 of **Mary Ann Francis Spicer**/1801, 2nd (simultaneously) 1825 of her sister **Elizabeth Walah Spicer**/1804, father **with Mary** of Levi Fish/1821, Crawford Fish/1823, Hannah Fish/1825, Sarah Ann Fish/1828, Mary Jane Fish/1831, Amanda Fish/1842, Eliza Jane Fish/1844, Kalitsa Fish/1847, Tsiguwi Fish/1849 & Nancy Fish/1851, **with Elizabeth** of Araminta Fish/1835-all 11/64th Chalakahta-Kishpoko-Mekoche-Pekowi-Black-Creek-Seneca-Cherokee-Metis

529. Fish, Paschal aka **Pascal Fish**-Paschal Jackson - 1/4th Chalakatha-Mekoche-Pekowi-Metis born 1804 OH-died 1893 KS - son of **William Jackson Fish**/60-adopted-white & **Martha Rogers**/82, Treaty 1854, **Principal Chief of Fish-Rogers band** 1860 with William Rogers/85, husband 1st 1824 OH of **Julia Parks**/1806-1/4th Thawikila-Metis, 2nd 1830 OH of **Jane Hohthawakawe**/1815Thawikila, 3rd 1842 KS of **Hester Jane Armstrong**/1800-Wyandot-Metis, 4th
1847 KS of **Mary Ann McClure (Steele)**-5/64th Chalakatha-Thawikila-PekowiCreek-Cherokee-Metis, 5th after 1852 of **Martha Captain**/1814-7/8th MekocheThawikila-Metis, father **with Parks** of Locust Paschal Fish/1825-1/4th Chalakatha-Mekoche-Pekowi-Thawikila-Metis, **with Hohthawakawe** of Obediah Fish/1842-5/8th Chalakatha-Thawikila-Mekoche-Pekowi-Metis, **with Zane** of Eudora Fish/1845-1/8th Chalakatha-Mekoche-Pekowi-Wyandot-Metis, **with McClure-Steele** of Leander Fish-Leading Turtle/1848-5/32nd

ChalakathaMekoche-Thawikila-Pekowi-Creek-Cherokee-Metis, **with Captain** of Mary T.
Fish/1854-9/16th Chalakatha-Mekoche-Pekowi-Metis

530. Fish, Zachariah aka **Oochaatahwah**-Fish – 15/64th Chalakatha-PekowiKishpoko-Black-**Cherokee**-Metis born 1762 Chota TN-died after 1839 (OKAR?) - son of **John Sour Mush Greenwood**/28 & **Long Hair Woman**/32, Capt. Shoe Boots Co-**with U.S. Army**-Creek War/1813, lived **with Wyandot** after moving west, husband 1st 1782 Chota TN of **Cherokee Woman**/67, 2nd 1798 NC of **Elizabeth Ahtewattah**/74-Cherokee, children/82-98 **with Cherokee** unknown, father **with Ahtewattah** of John Fish/98, Nathaniel Fish/99 & Simon Fish/1800-all 7/64th Chalakatha-Pekowi-Kishpoko-Black-Cherokee-Metis

531. Five Killer aka Shayaqustuego-**Francis Ward**-Raven of Chota-Kollanah – adopted-white born 1712 ENG-died 1755 Nachestown TN in battle – son of **Edmund Ward**/1680-white & **Mrs. Ward**/1685-white, brother of **James Ward (1)/1700, Lucy Ward (1)/14** & **Bryant Ward**/10, emigrated 1732 to VA with father James & brother Bryant, delegation to ENG later, killed in same battle as his son in law **Kingfisher**, husband 1735 Chota TN of **Tame Doe Carpenter**/167/16th Chalakatha-Cherokee-Metis, father of Long Fellow Ward-Fivekiller/36,
Nancy Wild Rose Ward-Fivekiller/38 & Little Fellow Ward-Fivekiller/40-all 7/32nd Chalakatha-Cherokee-Metis

532. Five Killer, Nancy aka Nancy Ward (1)-Nanyehi-Tsistungishe-Wild Rose-Beloved War Woman – 7/32nd Chalakatha-**Cherokee**-Metis born about 1738 Chota TN-died 1824 TN – daughter of **Tame Doe Carpenter**/16 & **Francis-Five Killer Ward**/12, Wolf Clan Cherokee, a female village leader in later years, War Woman, from the Overhills, Chota & Woman-killer Ford, led Women's War Council after 1755, Treaty Sycamore Shoals 1775, **betrayed the Chickamauga at least in 1772 & 1776**, niece of **Great Eagle**/05, **Elizabeth Tassel**/06, **Attakullakulla**/08 & **Old Corn Tassel**/10, raised by her uncle **Oconastota**/02 & his 3rd wife **Lucy Ward**/20-adopted-white, wife 1st 1751 Chota TN of **Tsula Kingfisher**/25-Cherokee, 2nd 1756 of her uncle **Bryant Ward**/10-white, mother **with Kingfisher** of Catherine Kingfisher/52 & Fivekiller-Little Fellow Kingfisher/55-both 7/64th Chalakatha-Cherokee-Metis, **with Ward** of Elizabeth Ward (1)/57-7/64th Chalakatha-Cherokee-Metis

533. Fisher, Billy aka **Shawnee Billy** - ½ Chalakatha-Metis born 1786-died after 1817 – son of **Fredrick Fisher**/40-adopted-white & **Chalakatha Woman**/65, scout-**with U.S. Army**-War of 1812, a warrior from Lewistown

1817, Treaty 1817, husband about 1806 of **Chalakatha Woman**/90, children unknown

534. Flat Head - 1/2 Kishpoko-Kickapoo-Metis born about 1750 (IL?)-died after 1780 - son of **Kickapoo-Metis** & **Kishpoko Woman**, Cornstalk War/68-77, raiding Ohio-Little Kanawha-Big Sandy-New River valleys/72, Point Pleasant/74-75, raiding KY-OH-VA/77-80, Boonesboro/78, husband 1770 OH of **Kishpoko Woman**/55, children unknown

535. Flat Nose - adopted-white born about 1750-died after 1778 - adopted about 1755 (likely in VA raids)-returned to whites-returned to tribe 1765, Cornstalk War/68-77, raiding Ohio-Little Kanawha-Big Sandy-New River valleys/72, Point Pleasant/74-75-78, raiding KY-VA-OH/77, Boonesboro/78, husband about 1770 OH of **Chalakatha Woman**/55, father of several 1/2 Chalakatha-Metis children/70-78

536. Flea (1) aka **LePuce** – Thawikila born about 1750 OH-died after 1815 (MO?) – a Thawikila warrior, Cornstalk War/68-77, raiding Ohio River valley/72, Point Pleasant/74-75-78, moved to MO about 1779, living in Apple Creek MO 1815

537. **Flea (2) aka Pepiqua**[56] – Thawikila born about 1760 OH-died after 1820 (IN?) – Point Pleasant/78, moved to MO 1779, a well thought of **minor Chief**, advised by **Big Ears-LeGrand Orielles**/60

538. **Flying Cloud aka Payakootha aka Paytakootha**[57] –Thawikila born about 1735-died after 1779 MO – Cornstalk War/55-77, French-Indian War/5463, Braddock/55, raiding New-Shenandoah River valleys/55, raiding PA/55-56, raiding Ohio-New River valleys/58, Pontiac War/62-66, Bushy Run/63, raiding New-Greenbrier-Jackson River valleys/63, raiding Ohio-Big Sandy-Little Kanawha-New River valleys/72, Point Pleasant/74-78, moved to AL 1774-back to OH 1778-to MO 1779, husband 1755 OH of **Thawikila Woman**/40, father of
Young Payakootha-Flying Cloud (2)/60

539. Flying Cloud (2) aka **Payakootha (2)-Young Payakootha** – Thawikila born 1768 OH-died 1838 Montgomery Co IN – son of **Flying Cloud (1)Payakootha**/35 & **Thawikila Woman**/40, living in Apple Creek MO 1810, husband 1788 OH of **Little Vine**/73-Thawikila, father of daughter Ulethi Kisathwa/1810

540. Flying Crane – Kishpoko born about 1780 OH-died after 1815 - raiding KY-OH-VA/99-1810, Prophet's Town/1811, Brownstown/1812-Monguagon/1812-1st Amherstburg/1812-Frenchtown/1813-Ft. Meigs/1813-2nd

Amherstburg/1813 & Thames/1813 **with Tecumseh**, may not have moved to CAN with band 1815, wife & children unknown

541. Flying Fox – Mekoche born about 1740 OH-died after 1778 - wife 1755 OH of **Mekoche Man**/35, widow by 1778

542. Flying Goose – Thawikila born about 1770 OH-died after 1795 - wife 1785 OH of **Thawikila Man**/65, widowed at Fallen Timber/94

543. Flying Squirrel (3) aka **Sawanugi**-Shawnano-Sawnook-Shawnee-All Bones White Owl (3)-All Bones Carpenter (3) – 23/64th Chalakatha-PekowiCherokee-Metis born 1770 Chota TN-**killed** 1814 AL at Horseshoe Bend - son of **All Bones Carpenter (2)-Flying Squirrel (2)**/50 & **Cherokee Woman**/55, with U.S. Army/Creek War/1813-killed at Horseshoe Bend/1814, husband 1st 1790 Chota TN of **Cherokee Woman**/75, 2nd 1810 of **Sarah Drowning Bear**/969/32nd Chalakatha-Kishpoko-Thawikila-Pekowi-Creek-Cherokee-Metis, children/90-1810 **with Cherokee** unknown, father **with Drowning Bear** of Flying Squirrel (4)-Callehigh/1814-5/16th Chalakatha-Pekowi-Kishpoko-Thawikila-Creek-Cherokee-Metis

544. Flying Squirrel (4) aka **Calleehigh** – 5/16th Chalakatha-PekowiKishpoko-Thawikila-Creek-**Cherokee**-Metis born 1810-died 1875 NC - son of **All Bones (3)-Flying Squirrel (3)**/70 & **Sarah Drowning Bear**/96, **Head Chief NC Cherokee** 1868-75-(before they became Eastern Cherokee), wife & children unknown

545. Flying Swan – Kishpoko born about 1780 OH-died after 1815 CAN - wife about 1795 OH of **Kishpoko Man**/75, widowed at Thames/1813, moved to CAN with followers of Tecumseh bout 1815, apparently died in CAN

546. Flying Turkey aka **Pemethata-Turkey Flying By**[58] – Chalakatha born about 1770 OH-died after 1814 – Blue Jacket War/88-94, raiding OH-KYVA/95-1810, Prophet's Town/1811, Brownstown/1812-Monguagon/1812-1st Amherstburg/1812-Frenchtown/1813-Ft. Meigs/1813-2nd Amherstburg/1813 & Thames/1813 **with Tecumseh**, Treaty 1814

547. Folsom, Susan Dougherty (Downing) - wife 2nd about 1810 of **Edmund Folsom** Cherokee-Creek-Choctaw-Metis-born about 1780-died after 1810-(son of **Edmund Folsom**-Creek-Choctaw-Metis & **Cherokee Woman**), mother of Ruth Folsom/1810-9/64th Chalakatha-Kishpoko-Thawikila-Pekowi-Creek-Cherokee-Choctaw-Metis

548. Fool Actor – adopted-Cherokee born about 1740 TN-died after 1794 – Cornstalk War/58-77, raiding Ohio-New River valleys/58, Pontiac War/62-66, Bushy Run/63, raiding New-Greenbrier-Jackson River valleys/63, raiding OhioBig Sandy-Little Kanawha-New River valleys/72, Point Pleasant/74, Blue Jacket War/77-94, raiding KY-VA-OH/77-81, Boonesboro/78, Crawford/82, raiding Ohio River valley/88-92, lived **with Shawnee in OH-KY**, husband about 1765 TN of **Chalakatha Woman**/50, father of several ½ Chalakatha-Cherokee children/65-94

549. Foreman, John Anthony (1) - white born 1720 Ontario CAN-died 1784 Lower Towns TN - husband 1st (of 4) 1737 Great Tellico TN of **Oousta (White Owl) Carpenter**/23-7/16th Chalakatha-Cherokee-Metis, 2nd 1743 Great Tellico TN of **Nancy Augustus Hop-Moytoy**/26-Chalakatha-Pekowi, father **with Oousta** of Thomas Foreman/37 & Nancy Foreman/39-both 7/32nd Chalakatha-Cherokee-Metis, **with Nancy Augustus** of John Anthony Foreman (2)/44 & Mary Foreman/46-both ½ Chalakatha-Pekowi-Metis

550. Foreman, John Anthony (2) – ½ Chalakatha-Pekowi-Metis born 1744 Great Tellico TN-died 1817 McMinn Co. TN - son of **Nancy Augustus Hop-Moytoy**/26 & **John Anthony Foreman (1)**/20-white, Blind Savannah Clan Cherokee, lived in Ooyougilogi village GA, husband 1st 1764 Great Tellico TN of **Unknown Woman**/50-Cherokee 2nd 1775 Great Tellico TN of his half-sister (daughter of his mother) **Chenelernkee Drumgoole**/58-19/32nd ChalakathaPekowi-Cherokee-Metis, 3rd 1779 Great Tellico TN of **Susie Teetarskeeskee-Rattling Gourd**/60-Red Paint Clan Cherokee, 4th 1781 Great Tellico TN of (half-sister of Chernelernkee & daughter of his sister) **Nancy Drumgoole (1)**/64-7/32nd Chalakatha-Cherokee-Metis, 5th 1784 Great Tellico TN of (half-sister of Chernelernkee & Nancy) **Ruth Drumgoole (1)**/69-7/64th Chalakatha-Pekowi-Cherokee-Metis, 6th 1799 Great Tellico TN of (the niece of Susie) **Elizabeth Watie Gurdaygle**/72-Red Paint Clan Cherokee, father of unknown children/6475, father **with Chenelernkee** of John Anthony Foreman (3)/78-35/64th Chalakatha-Pekowi-Cherokee-Metis, **with Susie** of John Anthony Foreman (4)/80, Thomas Foreman/82, Catherine Foreman/85, Sarah Foreman/87 & Richard Bark Foreman/89-all 1/4th Chalakatha-Pekowi-Cherokee-Metis, no known children **with Nancy**/64, **with Ruth** of Nancy Gourd Foreman/85-19/64th Chalakatha-Pekowi-Cherokee-Metis, **with Elizabeth** of Archibald Foreman/1800, Elsie Foreman/1804, Stephen Foreman/1807, Edward Foreman/1809, Mary Foreman/1812 & Alexander Drumgoole Foreman/1816-all

1/4th Chalakatha-Pekowi-Cherokee-Metis

551. Foreman, John Anthony (3) – 35/64th Chalakatha-Pekowi-**Cherokee**Metis born 1778 Great Tellico TN-died 1807 - son of **John Anthony Foreman (2)**/44 & **Chenelernkee Drumgoole**/58, Red Paint Clan Cherokee, husband 1st by 1800 of his half-1st cousin (granddaughter of Nancy Augustus Hop) **Nancy Drumgoole (3)**/85-7/64th Chalakatha-Pekowi-Cherokee-Metis, 2nd 1806 of **Jennie Foster**/79-1/8th Thawikila-Cherokee-Metis, 3rd by 1807 of his half-1st cousin (sister of Nancy/85) **Nanquese-Ruth (2) Drumgoole**/90-7/64th Chalakatha-Pekowi-Cherokee-Metis, father **with Nancy** of Richard Foreman/1800, John Jack-John Anthony (4) Foreman/1802, Elizabeth Foreman/1804 & James Foreman/1806-all 21/64th Chalakatha-Pekowi-Cherokee-Metis-(double-great-grandchildren of Nancy Augustus Hop/26), **with Foster** of Elizabeth Foster Foreman/1807-21/64th Chalakatha-Pekowi-Thawikila-Cherokee-Metis, **with Nanquese-Ruth** of Johnson Foreman/1808-21/64th Chalakatha-Pekowi-Cherokee Metis-(double-great-grandson of Nancy Augustus Hop/26)

552. Foreman, Richard – 21/64th Chalakatha-Pekowi-**Cherokee**-Metis born about 1800-died 1862 AR - son of **John Anthony Foreman (3)**/80 & **Nancy Drumgoole (2)**/85, a Chickamaugua, husband 1st 1820 of **Dorcas Bell Rattling Gourd**/1801-1/16th Chalakatha-Thawikila-Creek-Cherokee-Metis, 2nd 1846 of her sister **Sarah Gotane Rattling Gourd**/1811-1/16th Chalakatha-ThawikilaCreek-Cherokee-Metis, father **with Dorcas** of Anthony Foreman/1825, Lucinda
Foreman/1826, John Foreman/1827, Lewis Foreman/1828, Amos Foreman/1830, William Henderson Foreman/1832, Thomas Foreman/1834, Ruth Foreman/1836, Edward Foreman/1838, George Foreman/1840 & Emily Foreman/1842-all 29/64th Chalakatha-Pekowi-Thawikila-Creek-Cherokee-Metis, any children **with Sarah** unknown

553. Forest Man aka Forester-Man of the Forest-L'Homme de Foret - 1/2 Kishpoko-Chippewa-Metis born about 1720 (IN?)-died after 1763 - son of **Kishpoko Man** & **Chippewa-Metis Woman**, raiding PA/40, French/Indian War/54-63, Braddock/55, raiding New-Shenandoah River valleys/55, raiding PA/55-56, raiding Ohio-New River valleys/58, Pontiac War62-63, moved to north-west about 1763, husband about 1740 IN of **Mekoche Woman**/25, father of several 3/4th Mekoche-Kishpoko-Chippewa-Metis children/40-63-(possibly named Forest or Forester)

554. Foster, James Jr- 1/8th Thawikila-Cherokee-**Metis** born about 1778-died 1843 - son of **Nancy Gahoga Lightfoot**/60 & **James Foster**/50-white, Deer Clan Cherokee, Capt. of Foster Co-**with U.S. Army**-Creek War/13--Horseshoe Bend/14, Treaty 1829, husband 1st 1799 of **Katie Killachulla**/86-Cherokee, 2nd

1800 of **Lydia Halfbreed**/76, 3rd 1810 of **Betsy Spaniard**/85-Spanish-CreekMetis, father **with Killachulla** of Tiana Foster/1800-1/16th Thawikila-Cherokee-
Metis, **with Halfbreed** of John Tyler Foster/1801, Wat Foster/1803 & Tom Foster/1804-all 1/4th Chalakatha-Thawikila-Pekowi-Cherokee-Metis, **with Spaniard** of Hannah Foster/1811-1/16th Thawikila-Creek-Spanish-CherokeeMetis

555. Foster, Jennie aka Jennie Lightfoot-Jennie Gahoga-Jennie Doublehead - 1/8th Thawikila-**Cherokee**-Metis born 1779 TN-died 1812 TN - daughter of **Nancy Gahoga Lightfoot**/60 & **James Foster**/50-white, Deer Clan Cherokee, wife 1st by 1793 of **John Clement Vann(1)**/71, 2nd 1797 of his half-1st cousin(father's were half-brothers) **Chief James Vann**/66, 3rd 1805 GA of **Doublehead Carpenter**/40, 4th 1806 of **John Anthony Foreman (3)**/80, mother **with John Clement** of John Clement Vann (2)/93-1/4th Chalakatha-Thawikila-Pekowi-Cherokee-Metis, **with Chief James** of Sarah Vann/97-1/4th Chalakatha-Thawikila-Pekowi-Cherokee-Metis, **with Doublehead** of Tom Doublehead/1805-11/64th Chalakatha-Cherokee-Metis, **with Foreman** of Elizabeth Foster Foreman/1807-21/64th Chalakatha-Pekowi-Thawikila-CherokeeMetis

556. Foster, Nancy Gahoga Lightfoot – Deer Clan Cherokee, wife 1st about 1777 of **James Foster**/50-white-born about 1750-died after 1782), Deer Clan Cherokee, mother of James Foster Jr/78, Jennie Foster/79 & John Foster/80-all 1/8th Thawikila-Cherokee-Metis

557. Four Arms – Kishpoko born about 1740 OH-died after 1777 - raiding Ohio-New River valleys/58, Pontiac War/62-66, Bushy Run/63, raiding NewGreenbrier-Jackson River valleys/63, raiding Ohio-Big Sandy-Little Kanawha-
New River valleys/72, Point Pleasant/74, raiding KY-VA-OH/77

558. **Four Fingers aka Niewekilechi**[59]-Neeooekeelechee – Pekowi born about 1750 PA-**killed** 1781 – lost one finger in battle, Cornstalk War/68-77, raiding Ohio-New river valleys/72, Point Pleasant/74-75-78, raiding KY-VA-OH/77-81, killed by **Martin Wetzel** 1781

559. **Fox aka Wahkoceethee**[60] - born about 1740 Mekoche -died after 1778 – Cornstalk War/58-77, raiding Ohio-New River valleys/58, Pontiac War/62-66, Bushy Run/63, raiding New-Jackson-Greenbrier River valleys/63, raiding Ohio-

Big Sandy-Little Kanawha-New River valleys/72, Point Pleasant/74, raiding KYVA-OH/77, Boonesboro/78, husband 1760 OH of **Mekoche Woman**/45, father of Young Fox/60

560. Fox, Young aka Young Wahkoceethee - born about 1760 OH-died after 1778 - son of **Fox-Wahkoceethee**/40 & **Mekoche Woman**/45, raiding KY-VA-OH/77, Point Pleasant/78, Booneboro/78

561. Fox Tail – Thawikila born about 1740 (OH?)-died after 1780 - wife 1756 OH of **Thawikila Man**/36, widow in 1780

562. Fox, Quatsis aka Quatsis Smallpox Conjurer-**Daughter of Quatsis Hop**Niece of Standing Turkey - 1/2 Chalakatha-**Cherokee** born 1708 Settico TNdied after 1760 - daughter of **Quatsis Hop**/1682-Chalakatha & **Tsula FoxSmallpox Conjurer**/1670-Cherokee, wife 1st 1724 Settico TN of **John Watts Sr**/04-7/8th Chalakatha-Pekowi-Metis (left 1735 Watts when he married Unknown White Woman), 2nd (his 2nd of 3) 1735 Chota TN of 1st cousin **Oconastota Rainmaker**/02-1/2 Chalakatha-Cherokee (left Oconastota 1738 when he married Lucy Ward (1)/14-white) 3rd 1738 Running Water TN of **John Drowning Bear Brown (1)**/1700-white, mother **with Watts** of Terrapin Watts/26, Bark Watts/28 & others/29-34, **with Oconastota** of Quatsis Oconastota/36- ½ Chalakatha-Cherokee, **with Brown** of Alexander Brown/45, Mary Brown/47, Robert Brown/49 & John Drowning Bear Brown (3)-Junaluska (1)/51-all 1/4th Chalakatha-Cherokee-Metis

563. Fox, Wurteh Tawsee aka Wurteh Tawsee Smallpox Conjurer-Wurteh Tawsee Conjurer-Daughter of Quatsey - Cherokee born 1705 Tellico Plains TNdied 1764 Great Tellico TN - daughter of **Smallpox Conjurer**/1680 & **Quatsey (2)-Susan Rainmaker**/1682-both Cherokee, Wolf Clan through Quatsey-Red
Paint Clan Cherokee through Smallpox Conjurer (?), wife 1726 Tellico Plains TN of her 1st cousin (son of Quatsey's sister Nancy) **Great Eagle Carpenter**/02-7/16th Chalakatha-Cherokee-Metis, mother of Red Bird-(Aaron Brock) Carpenter/27, Corn Tassel Carpenter/30, Standing Turkey Carpenter/38, Double Head Carpenter/40, Pumpkin Boy Carpenter/41 & Nancy Great Eagle Carpenter/45, Older Daughter/49-(wife of Cabin Smith) & Younger Daughter/52-(wife of Leech Cherokee)-all 7/32nd Chalakatha-Cherokee-Metis, other children possible

564. Fox-Taylor, Jennie Oconastota - wife 3rd 1753 of **Charles Fox-Taylor (1)**-white born 1720 ENG-died 1773 West Indies, mother of Charles Fox-Taylor (2)/54 & Thomas Fox-Taylor (1)/60-both 1/4th Chalakatha-Thawikila-Creek-

Cherokee-Metis

565. Frame, Bill - adopted-white born about 1760 PA-**killed** 1791 KY - adopted before 1770, Blue Jacket War/77-91, raiding KY-OH-VA/77-81, Point Pleasant/78, Boonesboro/78, Blue Licks/82, Crawford/82, raiding Ohio River valley/88-91, Harmar/90, **killed in KY raid**/91, husband about 1780 OH of **Chalakatha Woman**/65, ½ Chalakatha-Metis children/80-91 unknown

566. Francis, David aka **Mumagechee** – 7/16th Chalakatha-Mekoche-Metis(adopted-**Creek**) born 1740 PA/OH-died after 1805 AL - son of **Older Daughter of Okowellos**/12 & **Mr. Francis**/1700-white British Officer, nephew of **Cornstalk**/10, adopted son of **Red Shoes (1)**/20-Creek-Metis & **Creek Woman**/25 (some connection of **Okowellos** & **Red Shoes** families **through Okowellos' Creek wife**?), Treaty 1790, 1805, uncle (by marriage) of **Tecumseh**/68, husband 1759 of **Younger Sister of Puckenshinwa**/44, father with **Younger Sister of Puckenshinwa** of John Francis/60, Josiah Francis/65, Joseph Francis/70, Susan Francis/75-all 15/32nd Chalakatha-Mekoche-Kishpoko-Creek-Metis

567. Francis, John (1) – 7/16th Chalakatha-Mekoche-Metis born 1745 PA/OHdied after 1785 - son of **Older Daughter of Okowellos**/12-7/8th ChalakathaMekoche-Metis & **Mr. Francis**/1700-white British Officer, nephew of **Cornstalk**/10, husband 1765 of half-niece (granddaughter of half-brother) **Daughter of Silver Heels (2)-Aroas**/50-31/32nd Chalakatha-Mekoche-Metisadopted-Seneca, father of John Francis (3)/80-45/64th Chalakatha-Mekoche-Metis-adopted-Seneca

568. Francis, John (2) – 15/32nd Chalakatha-Mekoche-Kishpoko-**Creek**-Metis born 1760 AL-died after 1790 - son of **David Francis**/40 & **Younger Sister of Puckenshinwa**/44, delegate to D.C. 1790, Treaty 1790, brother of Josiah Francis/65 & Joseph Francis/70, great-nephew of **Cornstalk**/10, 1st cousin of **Tecumseh** (by mother) & 2nd cousin of **Osceola** (by mother's half-sister), wife & children unknown

569. Francis, John (3) aka **Tapatacatha** – 45/64th Chalakatha-MekocheMetis-(adopted **Seneca**) born 1780 OH-died 1848 KS - son of **John Francis (1)**/45 & **Daughter of Silverheels (2)-Aroas**/50, with U.S. Army-War 1812Thames/1813, **last traditional Chief of Shawnee**, double-great-grandson of **Okowellos**/1680, great-nephew of **Cornstalk**/10, 1st cousin of **Josiah Francis** (by his uncle David) & cousin of **Tecumseh** (by his uncle David's brother in law

Puckenshimwa), husband about 1800 of **Wyandot Woman**/82, father of Mary Ann Francis/1801, Nancy Francis/1825 & others-all 11/32nd Chalakatha-Mekoche-Wyandot-Metis

570. Francis, Joseph – 15/32nd Chalakatha-Mekoche-Kishpoko-**Creek**-Metis born 1770 AL-**killed** 1813 AL - son of **David Mumagechee Francis**/40 & **Younger Sister of Puckenshinwa**/44, Creek Prophet with brother Josiah, greatnephew of **Cornstalk**/10, 1st cousin of **Tecumseh**/68 & 2nd cousin of **Osceola**/1802 (by mother's half-sister), a Red Stick, **with Natives**-Creek War/13, killed in attack on Ft. Sinquefield, wife & children unknown

571. Francis, Josiah aka **Hillis Hadja** – 15/32nd Chalakatha-MekocheKishpoko-**Creek**-Metis born 1765 AL-**hung** 1818 - son of **Younger Sister of Puckenshinwa**/45 & **David Mumagechee Francis**/40, Creek Prophet with brother Joseph Francis/70, a Red Stick, **with Natives**-Creek War/1813-Burnt Corn-Ft. Mims, visit ENG 1816, brother in law of **Sam Moniac**/78-Creek-Black Metis, 1st cousin of **Tecumseh**/68-(by mother's brother) & 2nd cousin/uncle of **Osceola**/02-(by mother's half-niece), great-nephew of **Cornstalk**/10-(by father), **hung by whites 1818**, husband 1799 of **Hannah Moniac**/80-Creek-Black-Metis, father of Millie Francis/1800 & Earle Francis-Jim Earley/1816-both 15/64th
Chalakatha-Mekoche-Kishpoko-Creek-Metis

572. Fredrick, Thomas aka **Keesawsoso** - adopted-white born about 1745 PAdied 1808 OH - adopted about 1750-returned to whites about 1765, translator, trader, husband about 1765 of **Margaret A. Tibbon**/40-white (possibly a former adopted-Shawnee), children unknown

573. French, Capt. aka Cappee French-Cappee Hop-Nephew of Old Hopadopted son of Old Hop – 1/2 Chalakatha-Black-Metis born 1712 Chota TN-died after 1775 Tomatley NC – son of **Ghigoneli Hop**/1694 & **French-Canadian Mulatto**/1690-(or possible Meluneon?), brother of **John French**/10, half-brother of **Ninihica Mayapple**/21 & **Laskigitchi Mayapple**/23-both Chalakatha-
Kishpoko, adopted son 1720 of uncle **Old Hop**/1688-Chalakatha & **Sugi Rainmaker**/1690-Cherokee, **allied with Savannah Tom Carpenter (2)**/1698, **John Lantaniak**/20, brother **John French**/10, **Rainmaker (3)**/06, **Muskrat (2)**/18 & **Robert-Thigh-Cauquillehaneh McLemore**/31 in pro-French faction during French-Indian War/54-63, Cornstalk War/55-75, could cipher, read & write English & French, Pontiac War/62-66, Point Pleasant/74, delegation to English **with Attakullakulla**, Treaty Sycamore Shoals 1775, from Chota TN & Tomatley NC, mistakenly identified as a slave by British of the time, husband 1st

1732 Running Water TN of **Chalakatha Woman**/17, 2nd 1759 Chota TN of **Cherokee Woman**/44, father **with Chalakatha** of Choosahete French/37, Margaret Elizabeth French/39-(wife 1755 of **Alexander Drumgoole (2)**/36), Black Skin French/41, Catherine French/48-(wife 1765 of **John Cherokee Vann**/44), Daughter/55-(wife 1770 of **Capt. Will Emory**/44)-all 3/4th Chalakatha-Black-Metis, children **with Cherokee** unknown

574. French, Catherine aka Catherine Hop-Catherine Metis – 3/4th Chalakatha-Black-Metis born 1748 Running Water TN-died 1785 Running Water TN – daughter of **Capt. French**/12 & **Chalakatha Woman**/17, 2nd wife 1765 Running Water TN of **John Cherokee Vann**/44-1/2 Chalakatha-Pekowi-Cherokee-Metis, mother of John Oowayne Vann/66, Rebecca Vann/74, Otiyu Vann/76, Lucinda Vann/80 & other children/67-84-all 5/8th Chalakatha-Pekowi-Black-Cherokee-Metis

575. French, John aka Jean French-French John Hop-Nephew of Old Hopadopted son of Old Hop – 1/2 Chalakatha-Black-Metis born 1710 Chota TN-died after 1775 - son of **Ghigoneli Hop**/1694 & **French-Canadian Mulatto**/1690-(or
a Melungeon?), adopted son 1720 of uncle **Old Hop**/1690, allied with **Savannah Tom Carpenter (2)**/1698, brother **Cappee Hop**/12, **John Lantaniak**/20, **Rainmaker (3)**/06, **Muskrat (2)**/18 & **Robert-ThighCauquillehanah-McLemore**/31 in pro-French faction during French-Indian War/54-63, from the Overhills, could cipher, read & write English & French, chief French agent at Ft. Toulouse AL & Chota TN, Cornstalk War/55-74,
Pontiac War/62-66, Point Pleasant/74, Cherokee War/75, half-brother of Ninihica Mayapple/23 & Laskigitchi Mayapple/25, mistakenly identified as a slave by British of the time, husband 1st 1730 Running Water TN of **Chalakatha Woman**/15, 2nd 1759 Chota TN of **Cherokee Woman**/44, children unknown

576. French Girl-**LaFranchise** - 1/2 Mekoche-Metis born about 1735 IL-died after 1760 - daughter of **Mekoche Woman** & **Coureur deBois**-Canadian, wife 1750 IL of **Mekoche Man**/30, mother of Totasquithetha-French Girl/55-3/4th
Mekoche-Metis

577. French Girl aka **Totasquithetha** - 3/4th Mekoche-Metis born about 1755
(IL?)-died after 1780 - daughter of **Mekoche Man**/30 & **LaFranchise**/35-1/2 Mekoche-Metis, wife 1765 (OH?) of **Kishpoko Man**/45, widowed 1774 (likely at Point Pleasant/74), children unknown

578.	French Man – ½ Chalakatha-Metis born about 1770 OH-died after 1817 – son of **Chalakatha Woman & Canadian Man**, raiding Ohio River valley/88-92, Blue Jacket War/88-94, Brownstown/1812-Monguagon/1812-1st Amherstburg/1812-Frenchtown/1813-Ft. Meigs/1813-2nd Amherstburg/1813 & Thames/1813 **with Tecumseh**, a warrior at Lewistown 1817, Treaty 1817, husband about 1790 of **Chalakatha Woman**/74

579.	Frog Hunter – Chalakatha born about 1750 OH-died after 1782 - Cornstalk War/68-77, raiding Ohio-New River valleys/72, Point Pleasant/74-7578, Blue Jacket War/77-82, raiding KY-VA-OH/77-81, Boonesboro/78, Blue Licks/82, Crawford/82

580.	Frozen aka **Sokutchmah**-Sokootchmah – Chalakatha born about 1770 OH-died after 1814 - raiding Ohio River valley/88-92, Blue Jacket War/88-94, raiding OH-KY-VA/95-1810, Prophet's Town/1811, Brownstown/1812Monguagon/1812-1st Amherstburg/1812-Frenchtown/1813-Ft. Meigs/1813-2nd
Amherstburg/1813 & Thames/1813 **with Tecumseh**, Treaty 1814

581.	Fry, Jim aka **Wakoskaka Tecumseh** - 13/16th Kishpoko-Pekowi-CreekMetis born about 1818-died 1865 - son of **Naythahwaynah Tecumseh**/90 & **Socomse**/95-Kishpoko, grandson of **Tecumseh & Mamate Baby**, husband 1st about 1835 KS of **Pahkepease**/1815-Kishpoko, 2nd about 1851 KS of **Chaneyqua**/1820-Pekowi, father **with Pahkepease** of Sam Fry/1836, Jim Fry Jr/37-both 29/32nd Kishpoko-Pekowi-Creek-Metis, **with Chaneyqua** of Joe Longhorn/52-29/32nd Pekowi-Kishpoko-Creek-Metis

582.	Fulk, Adam (1) – ½ Chalakatha-Metis born about 1736 Rockingham Co VA-**killed** 1774 Point Pleasant WV – son of **Sedano Chalakatha**/15 & **Matthew Fulk**/13-adopted white, husband by 1760 Russell Co VA of **Chalakatha Woman**/40, father of sons John **Fults**/61 & Obediah **Fults**/67 & daughters/63-65-69-71-73-all 3/4th Chalakatha-Metis

583.	Fulk, John (1) aka Old John – ½ Chalakatha-**Metis** born about 1740 Rockingham Co VA-died 1820 VA – son of **Sedano Chalakatha**/15 & **Matthew Fulk**/13-adopted-white, stayed in VA when father Matthew & brother Adam went to Battle of Point Pleasant/74, husband 1st 1760 Rockingham Co VA of **Catherine Castle**/44-1/2 Pekowi-Metis, 2nd by 1774 Rockingham Co VA of **Eve Beeler**/49-white, children/60-74 **with Castle** of Jacob Castle Fulk/73 & others/60-73-all ½ Chalakatha-Pekowi-Metis, father **with Beeler** of Adam Fulk/75, John H. Fulk/80, Catherine Fulk/84, George Fulk/85, twins Eva & Christian Fulk/86, Charles Fulk/90, Daniel Fulk/92, Elizabeth Fulk/94 & David

Fulk /96-all 1/4th Chalakatha-Metis

584. Fulk, Senado Chalakatha – wife 1735 VA of **Matthew Fulk**-white born about 1713 Europe-**killed** 1774 Point Pleasant WV, mother of Adam Fulk/36, David Fulk/38 & John Fulk/40-all ½ Chalkatha-Metis

585. Full, Absalom - 1/4th Pekowi-**Metis** born 1795 WV-died after 1840 WV - son of **Jane Collins**/68 & **Lewis Full**/65-white, grandson of Tecumoplas Margaret Opessa/42, nephew/3rd cousin of **Tecumseh**, living in **Mason Co. WV** before 1840, husband 1st by 1815 of **Iowa Lyons**/95-1/2 Delaware-Black-Metis, 2nd by 1820 of **Mahala Shepherd**/99-9/32nd Thawikila-Chalakatha-Creek-Cherokee-Metis (sister of Mary-wife of his brother Joseph), children unknown

586. Full, Amelia – 1/4th Pekowi-**Metis** born 1803 WV-died 1876 WV – daughter of **Jane Collins**/68 & **Lewis Full**/65, wife 1823 WV of **Samuel Shepperd**/1803-white, mother of Nancy Shepperd/1824, Jonathan Shepperd/1826, Martha Shepperd/1829, Clarissa Shepperd/1831, Rebecca Shepperd/1832, Lewis Shepperd/1837, Margaret Shepperd/1839 & Addison Hite Shepperd/1843-all 1/8th Pekowi-Metis

587. Full, Andrew - 1/4th Pekowi-**Metis** born 1799 WV-died 1867 WV - son of **Jane Collins**/68 & **Lewis Full**/65-white, grandson of Tecumoplas Margaret Opessa/42, nephew/3rd cousin of **Tecumseh**, living in **Mason Co. WV** before 1840, husband about 1820 of **Emma Jane Hartley**/1800-white, children unknown

588. Full, Jane Collins - daughter of **Tecumoplas** aka Margaret Opessa/42Pekowi & **Rupert Collins**-white, 2nd cousin/niece of **Tecumseh**, wife by 1790
WV of **Lewis Full**-white-born about 1765-died after 1803 WV, mother of Joseph Full/91, Absalom Full/95, Andrew Full/99, Amelia Full/1803, Reuben Full/1806 & 5 other children-all 1/4th Pekowi-Metis

589. Full, Joseph - 1/4th Pekowi-**Metis** born 1791 WV-died 1885 WV - son of **Jane Collins**/68 & **Lewis Full**/65-white, grandson of **Tecumpolas-Margaret Opessa**/42, 3rd cousin/nephew of **Tecumseh**, living in **Mason Co. WV** by 1840, husband about 1812 WV of **Mary Shepherd**/97-9/32nd Thawikila-ChalakathaCreek-Cherokee-Metis (sister of Mahala-wife of his brother Absalom Full), children unknown

590. Full, Reuben – 1/4th Pekowi-**Metis** born 1806 WV-died 1866 Wirt Co WV – son of **Jane Collins**/68 & **Lewis Full**/65, husband of **Unknown Woman**, father of Lewis Full/1848 & 10 other children-all 1/8th Pekowi-Metis

591. Fults, Obediah – 3/4th Chalakatha-**Metis** born 1767 Russell Co VA-died 1845 Carter Co KY – son of **Adam Fulk**/38 & **Chalakatha Woman**/40, husband 1787 Bedford Co VA of **Martha Blankenship**/75 (Metis?), father of Priscilla Fultz/88, John Fultz/90, Joseph Fultz/94, Hezekiah Fultz/96, Arthur Fultz/98, Martha Fultz/1800, Ralph Fults/1802, Robert Fultz/1805, Elizabeth Fultz/1811 & Wesley Fults/1815-all 3/8th Chalakatha-Metis

Section VIII
Gauthier to Hurrican Tom (G – H)

G

592. Gauthier, Charles - 1/2 Thawikila-**Metis** born about 1730-died after 1779 - son of **Louis Gauthier**/1700-adopted white & **Charlotte-Red Skies**/10, Cornstalk War/55-77, French-Indian War/54-63, Braddock/55, raiding NewShenandoah River valleys/55, raiding PA/55-56, raiding Ohio-New River valleys/58, Pontiac War/62-66, Bushy Run/63, raiding New-Greenbrier-Jackson River valleys/63, raiding Ohio-Big Sandy-Little Kanawha-New River valleys/72, Point Pleasant/74, raiding KY-VA-OH/77, moved to MO about 1779, husband by 1754 OH of **Thawikila Woman**/35, father of Charles Gauthier Jr/55-3/4th Thawikila-Metis

593. Gauthier, Charles Jr - 3/4th Thawikila-Metis born about 1755 (OH?)-died after 1788 - son of **Charles Gauthier**/30 & **Thawikila Woman**/35, raiding KYOH-VA/77-81, Point Pleasant/78, Boonesboro/78, moved to MO about 1779, husband about 1775 of **Madeline Paschel**/60-white

594. Gauthier, Charlotte Red Skies – Thawikila born about 1710-died after 1750 - wife by 1729 of **Louis Gauthier**/1700-adopted French/Canadian, mother of Charles/30, Jean/35, Joseph/40-all 1/2 Thawikila-Metis - see **Red Skies aka Charlotte**/10

595. Gauthier, Jean - 1/2 Thawikila-Metis born about 1735-died after 1765 - son of **Louis Gauthier**/1700-adopted white & **Charlotte-Red Skies**/10, FrenchIndian War/54-63, Braddock/55, raiding New-Shenandoah River valleys/55, wife
& children unknown

596. Gauthier, Joseph - 1/2 Thawikila-Metis born about 1750-died after 1779

- son of **Louis Gauthier**/1700-adopted white & **Charlotte-Red Skies**/10, Cornstalk War/68-77, raiding Ohio-Big Sandy-Little Kanawha-New River valleys/72, Point Pleasant/74, raiding KY-VA-OH/77-79, Boonesboro/78, moved to MO about 1779, husband about 1770 OH of **Therese Misk**/55-white

597. Geant, Jean aka **Big John**-Giant John-John the Giant - 3/4th ChalakathaPekowi-**Metis** born about 1730 (OH?)-died after 1755 - son of **Chalakatha Woman**/10 & **Coureur deBois**/1700-1/2 Pekowi-Metis, nearly 7' tall, FrenchIndian War/54-63, Braddock/55, raiding New-Shenandoah River valleys/55, may have moved north-west after 1755, husband by 1748 OH of **Chalakatha Woman**/32, children unknown

598. General Wayne aka Wayne – Mekoche born about 1780 OH-died after 1820 - scout-**with U.S. Army-**War 1812-Thames/1813, a warrior at Wapakoneta 1817, Treaty 1817

599. Gentry, Aky Rogers (Hicks) – 2nd wife (her 2nd of 3) about 1813 of **David Gentry**-white-born about 1780-died after 1820, mother **with Gentry** & 3rd husband **Daniel Vickery** of 2 daughters & 2 sons 1813-22

600. Gentry, Mary Due – 1st wife 1808 of **David Gentry**-white-born about 1780-died after 1820, mother of Elizabeth Gentry/1808, Isabel Gentry/1810 & Patience Gentry/1812-all 9/64th Chalakatha-Cherokee-Metis

601. Gentry, Tiana Rogers – 3rd wife 1817 of **David Gentry**-white-born about 1780-died after 1820, children unknown

602. George aka **Tegosbea** – Mekoche born about 1780-died after 1817 - scout-**with U.S. Army-**War 1812-Thames/13, a warrior at Wapakoneta 1817, Treaty 1817 (not the same as Shawnee George/70)

603. George, Shawnee – Chalakatha born about 1770-died after 1817 – Blue Jacket War/88-94, scout-**with U.S. Army-**War 1812, a warrior from Lewistown 1817, Treaty 1817 **(not the same as George-Tegosbea/80)**

604. Ghost Face – adopted-white born about 1725-died after 1766 - adopted about 1740 (possibly in PA raids)-stayed with tribe 1765, wife 1740 (PA-OH?) of **Chalakatha Man**, mother of several 1/2 Chalakatha-Metis children/40-66, widow/66 during Pontiac War

605. Gibson, John (1) aka Horsehead – adopted-white- (Kishpoko-Seneca) born 1740 PA-died 1822 - adopted 1763-returned to whites 1764, son of **George**

Gibson/04 & **Elizabeth de Vinez**, adopted son of **Widow Shawnee**, translator/scout/spy-**with U.S. Army**-Revolution, trader, Indian Agent, Gen. of PA Militia, delegate to PA Constitutional Convention, Commander Ft. Pitt/8181, Acting Governor of Indiana Territory/1800-13, namesake of Gibson Co. IN, Allegheny Co. PA Judge, husband 1st by 1770 OH of **Kooney Shikellimus**/50-Seneca-(sister of Chief Logan), 2nd 1775 PA of **Mary Brent**/60-1/2 PekowiMetis, 3rd about 1780 PA of **Ann Mingo**/65-Kishpoko, father **with Shikellimus** of Ann Grayson Gibson/73 & Joseph Gibson/74-1/2 Seneca-Metis, **with Brent** of John Gibson (2)/76, James Gibson/78 & Hugh Gibson/80-all 1/4th PekowiMetis, **with Ann** of Thomas Gibson/80, Mary Gibson/82, Eleazer Gibson/84,
Esther Gibson/86 & Elsie Gibson/88-1/2 Kishpoko-Metis

606. Girty, Betsy – Kishpoko born about 1748 OH-died before 1804 - wife before 1770 of **James Girty**/43-adopted-white, mother of James Girty Jr/70, Nancy Ann Girty/72 & Mary Girty/75-all 1/2 Kishpoko-Metis

607. Girty, George (1) - white-(adopted-**Delaware**) born about 1746 PA-died 1796 OH - son of **Simon Girty Sr & Mary Eckerlin (Newton Turner)**, captured-adopted by Delaware 1756 with mother Mary/20, brothers Simon/41 & James Girty/43 & half-brother John Turner/54, Lt.-**in Continental Army**deserted when his brothers joined the Natives, Blue Jacket War/78-94, Point Pleasant/78, Boonesboro/78, raiding Ohio River valley/81 **with Joseph Brant** & his brother **James Girty**, Blue Licks/82, Crawford/82, Council with British 1779 with **Alexander McKee**/25, **William Caldwell**/50, **Matthew Elliott**/30, **Simon Surphet**-cousin of McKee, brothers **Simon**/41 & **James**/43, **Wryneck**/25Pekowi, **Savenooka Raven Hop**/20, **Weed**/50-Iroquois & **River Bottom**/50Seneca, Grand Council 1782, 1791, associated often with Shawnee, husband 1st
1769 of **Delaware Woman**/54, 2nd 1779 of **Pekowi Woman**/63, father **with Delaware** of George Girty Jr (1)/70-1/2 Delaware-Metis, **with Pekowi** of George Girty Jr (2)/80, Isaac Girty/85, Jack Panther Girty/90 & likely other children-all 1/2 Pekowi-Metis

608. Girty, James (1) - adopted-white born 1743 PA-died 1817 CAN - son of **Simon Girty Sr & Mary Eckerlin (Newton Turner)**/20, captured-adopted by Shawnee 1756 (with mother Mary/20, brothers Simon/41 & George/46 & halfbrother John Turner Jr/54)-never fully returned, Cornstalk War/63-77, raiding Ohio-Big Sandy-Little Kanawha-New River valleys/72, Point Pleasant/78, Blue Jacket War/77-94, raiding KY-VA-OH/77-81, Boonesboro/78, Blue Licks/82, Crawford/82, Council Coshocton 1776, Council with British 1779 with **Alexander McKee**/25, **William Caldwell**/50, **Matthew Elliott**/30, **Simon**

Surphlet-cousin of McKee, his brothers **Simon**/41 & **George**/46, **Wryneck**/25Pekowi, **Savenooka Raven Hop**/20, **Weed**/50-Iroquois & **River Bottom**/50Seneca, Grand Council 1782, 1791, raiding KY-OH-VA/81 **with Joseph Brant**
& brother **George Girty**, raiding Ohio River valley/88, trading post in OH 178394, move to CAN 1794, half-brother of **Michael Girty**/57-1/2 Kishpoko-Metis, husband by 1770 of **Betsy Kishpoko**/48, father of James Girty Jr/71, Nancy Ann Girty/72, Mary Girty/75-all 1/2 Kishpoko-Metis

609. Girty, Michael - 1/2 Kishpoko-Metis born 1757 OH-**killed** 1836 IL - son of **Mary Eckerlin Newton Girty Turner**/20-adopted white & **Kishpoko Man**/35, **stayed with father** when mother Mary/20 returned to whites, halfbrother of Simon/41, James/43, George Girty/46 & John Turner Jr/54, (later known & referred to as a son of Simon Girty but age of Simon (16) & of Simon's mother Mary (37) suggests he was actually a half-brother), Blue Jacket War/7794, Point Pleasant/78, raiding KY-OH-VA/77-81, Boonesboro/78, Crawford/82, raiding Ohio River valley/88-92, raiding OH-KY-VA/95-1810, Prophet's Town/1811, Brownstown/1812, Monguagon/1812, 1st Amherstburg/1812,
Frenchtown/1813, Ft. Meigs/1813, 2nd Amherstburg/1813 & Thames/1813 **with Tecumseh**, translator-Council June 1827, Black Hawk War/1832 **with Black Hawk**, in IL about 1821, found dead in the woods 1836-likely murdered by young white rogues, husband 1777 OH of **Kishpoko Woman**/60, father of James Girty (3)/78, Isaac Girty/79, John Girty/80 & other children/82-1800 (likely surname Girty)-all 3/4th Kishpoko-Metis

610. Girty, Simon aka **Katepakomen** -]'' vc[hite-(adopted-**Seneca**) born 1741 PA-died 1818 CAN - son of **Mary Eckerlin (Newton Turner)**/20 & **Simon Girty Sr**/1700, brother of James/43 & George Girty/46, half-brother of John Turner Jr/54 & Michael Girty/57, captured, then adopted by Seneca 1756, **with Colonial forces-**Pontiac War/62-66 & Point Pleasant/74, Blue Jacket War/77-94, raiding Ohio River valley/77-81, Boonesboro/78, Blue Licks/82, Crawford/82, raiding Ohio River valley/88-92, Grand Council 1763, 1782, 1791, Council Logstown 1765, Ft. Pitt 1774, 1776, Coshocton 1776, Council with British 1779 with **Alexander McKee**/25, **William Caldwell**/50, **Matthew Elliott**/30, **Simon Surphet**-cousin of McKee, brothers **George Girty**/46 & **James Girty**/43, **Wryneck**/25-Pekowi, **Savenooka Raven Hop**/20, **Weed**/50Iroquois & **River Bottom**/50-Seneca, long associated **with the Shawnee**, spoke
11 different languages & dialects, husband 1st (known) 1775 (OH?) of **Sotonegoo**/60-adopted-Mohawk, 2nd 1784 of **Catherine Mallot**/64-adoptedwhite-Shawnee, father **with Sotontgoo** of Simon Girty Jr-Simonee-

KedzawsawSimon Peters/76 & Quasay Girty/78-both adopted-1/2 Mohawk-Metis, **with**
Catherine of Nancy Ann Girty/86, Thomas Girty/88, Sarah Girty/91 & Prideaux Girty/97-all white

611.   Girty, Simon Jr aka Kedzawsaw-Simonee-**Simon Peters** - 1/2 adoptedMohawk-Metis born about 1776 OH-died after 1830 IN - son of **Simon Girty**/41-adopted-white-Seneca & **Sotonegoo**/60-adopted-Mohawk, grandson of **Coohcoochee** & **Cokundiawthah**, nephew of **Wapunnoo, White Loon** & **Black Loon**-all adopted Mohawk, stepson of **Isaac Peters**/60-adopted-Delaware, husband 1802 of **Angelique Dequindre**/80-1/2 Kishpoko-Ottawa-Metis

612.   Gist, Christopher aka Christopher Guess-Guest – adopted-white born 1705 Baltimore Co MD-died 1759 VA of smallpox - son of **Richard Gist** & **Zipporah Murray**-both white, scout, messenger, surveyor, expedition to OH 1751-52 with son Nathaniel for George Washington, **with Colonial Army** French-Indian War/54-59, Braddock/55, Council Logstown 1752, husband 1st 1728 PA of **White Rose**/14-Pekowi, 2nd 1731 Baltimore co MD of **Sarah Howard**/16-white, father **with Rose** of Richard Gist/29, Nathaniel Gist/30-1/2 Pekowi-Metis, **with Howard** of Violetta Gist/31, Nancy Anne Gist/33, Thomas Gist/35-all white, apparently returned to **White Rose** again in 1739 (MD?), father **with Rose** of Christopher Gist Jr/40, Jacob Gist/42, Samuel Gist/44, Elizabeth Gist/46, Polly Gist/48-all ½ Pekowi-Metis grandfather of **Sequoyah-George Gist**/58

613. Gist, Nathaniel aka Nathaniel Guess-Guest - 1/2 Pekowi-**Metis** 1730 MD-died 1810 Clark Co KY - son of **Christopher Gist**/05-white & **White Rose**/10-Pekowi, on OH expedition with his father 1751-52, **with Colonial Army**-Braddock/55, living with Overhill Cherokee/56-61-returned to whites/61, trading partner with **Richard Parris**-white in Cherokee country after 1763, Capt.-**with British Army**- associated with **Alexander Cameron** & **John Stuart** from before 1776 then switched to supporting the Americans, Col.-**with U.S. Army** 1777 on, 1777 took **Amoyah Pigeon Hop (3)**/57 & 16 others (i.e. Pigeon Co-Cherokee scouts) to be scouts for **George Washington with U.S. Army**, husband 1st 11758 TN-NC of **Wurteh Watts**/44-21/32nd Chalakatha-PekowiCherokee-Metis, 2nd 1783 Buckingham Co VA of **Judith Cary Bell**, father **with Wurteh of** George Gist-Sequoyah/58-37/64th Chalakatha-Pekowi-Cherokee-
Metis, **with Bell** of Sarah Howard Gist/83, Henry Cary Gist/86, Judith Bell Gist/88, Thomas Nathaniel Gist/90, Anna Maria Gist/91, Davidella C. Gist/93, Elizabeth Violet Gist/95, Maria Cecil Gist/97-all white

614. Goes Bare – Kishpoko born about 1750 OH-died after 1796 - wife about 1765 of **Kishpoko Man**/45, widow in 1796

615. Goes Quietly – Chalakatha born about 1770 OH-died after 1794 - raiding Ohio River valley 1788-92, Blue Jacket War/88-94

616. Goes to Front – Kishpoko born about 1760 OH-died after 1795 - Blue Jacket War/78-94, raiding KY-OH-VA/77-81, Boonesboro/78, raiding Ohio River valley/81 **with Joseph Brant** & **James Girty**, Crawford/82, raiding Ohio River valley/88-92

617. Golden – Chalakatha born 1730 PA-died after 1775 OH – Cornstalk War/55-75, French-Indian War/54-63, Braddock/55, raiding New-Shenandoah River valleys/55, raiding Ohio-New River valleys/58, Pontiac War/62-66, Bushy Run/63, raiding New-Greenbrier-Jackson River valleys/63, raiding Ohio-Little Kanawha-Big Sandy-New River valleys/72, Point Pleasant/74-75

618. Gosselin, Margaret – Shawnee born about 1750 OH-died 1808 - wife by 1770 (OH?) of **Michael Gosselin**-white, children unknown

619. Grant, Elizabeth Tassel aka **Elizabeth Euguinoote Carpenter** - Wolf Clan Cherokee, wife 1726 Great Tellico TN of **Ludovic Grant**-white-born 1698 SCO-died 1757 Charleston SC, mother of Mary Grant/26 & Susannah Catherine Grant/28-both 7/32nd Chalakatha-Cherokee-Metis

620. Gray Bird Sitting – Pekowi born about 1745 PA-died after 1774 - wife about 1760 OH of **Pekowi Man**/40, widowed at Point Pleasant/74

621. Gray Fox – Chalakatha born about 1761 OH-**murdered** 1791 OH - son of **Panther-Meshepeshe**/40 & **Chalakatha Woman**/45, a Chalakatha warrior, Blue Jacket War/78-91, Point Pleasant/78, Boonesboro/78, raiding KY-VAOH/77-81, Blue Licks/82, raiding Ohio River valley/88-90, Harmar/90, **murdered by whites** with father

622. Gray Hawk – Kishpoko born about 1760-died after 1795 – Blue Jacket War/77-94, raiding KY-VA-OH/77-81, Crawford/82, raiding Ohio River valley/88-92

623. Gray Pigeon – Chalakatha born about 1750 OH-died after 1774 - wife 1765 OH of **Chalakatha Man**/45, widowed at Point Pleasant/74

624. Gray, John – adopted-white born about 1720-died after 1770 – captured/adopted as a child, husband 1st by 1759 PA of **Pekowi Woman**/40, 2nd by 1769 PA of **Delaware Woman**/50, father **with Pekowi** of Sam Gray/60-1/2 Pekowi-Metis & **with Delaware** John Gray Jr/70-1/2 **Delaware**-Metis

625. Great Eagle aka **Great Eagle Carpenter**-Gray Eagle-WillenawahWoolenawah-Tifftoy of Tenase-Tiftoa-Woolochuoah – 7/16th **ChalakathaCherokee**-Metis born 1702 Great Tellico TN-died 1777 Great Tellico TN - son of **Savannah Tom Carpenter (1)-Moytoy (3)**/1680 & **Nancy Rainmaker**/1683, adopted son of uncle **White Owl Carpenter-Moytoy (4)** upon death of his father 1710, from the Overhills, Tenase & Great Tellico, delegation to ENG 1730, Wolf Clan Cherokee through mother-Blind Savannah Clan through father, FrenchIndian War/54-63, Braddock/55, Pontiac War/62-66, Point Pleasant/74, Cherokee War/75, protested but signed Treaty Sycamore Shoals 1775, adopted father of his half-sister **Oousta White Owl Carpenter**/23, husband 1726 Tellico Plains TN of his 1st cousin (daughter of mother's sister Quatsey) **Wurteh Tawsee Fox**/04Cherokee, father of Red Bird Carpenter-(Aaron Brock)/27, Corn Tassel Carpenter/30, Standing Turkey Carpenter/38, Double Head Carpenter/40, Pumpkin Boy Carpenter/41, Nancy Great Eagle Carpenter/45, Older Daughter/49-(wife of Cabin Smith) & Younger Daughter/52-(wife of Leech/25)all 7/32nd Chalakatha-Cherokee-Metis

626. Great Mountain - adopted-Cherokee born about 1740 Running Water TN-died after 1780 (OH?) - raiding Ohio-New River valleys/58, Pontiac War/62-66, raiding New-Greenbrier-Jackson River valleys/63, raiding Ohio-Little Kanawha-Big Sandy-New River valleys/72, Point Pleasant/74, raiding KY-VAOH/77-80, over 6' 6" tall & big, husband 1760 Running Water TN of **Kishpoko Woman**/45, children unknown

627. Great Shawnee Warrior aka Great Shawnee Warrior Cheeseekau-Great Shawnee Warrior (2) – 7/8th Kishpoko-Pekowi-Creek-Metis born 1780 OH**killed** 1810 Yahoo Falls KY - son of **Cheeseekau Puckenshinwa-Great Shawnee Warrior (1)**/56 & **Kishpoko Wife**/60, raiding KY-VA-TN/97-1810, **killed Yahoo Falls**/1810, nephew of **Tecumseh**/68, husband 1798 of **Cherokee Woman**/82, father of Tommy Bright Star/98-7/16th Kishpoko-Pekowi-Creek-Cherokee-Metis

628. Great Snake – Mekoche born about 1725 PA-died after 1795 OH – brother of **Helizikinopo**/15, **Green Snake**/17 & **Big Snake**/20, Cornstalk War/55-77, French-Indian War/54-63, Braddock/55, raiding New-Shenandoah River valleys/55, raiding Ohio-New River valleys/58, Pontiac War/62-66, Bushy Run/63, raiding New-Greenbrier-Jackson River valleys/63, raiding Ohio-Big

Sandy-Little Kanawha-New River valleys/72, Point Pleasant/74-75-78, Boonesboro/78, raiding KY-VA-OH/77-81, husband 1745 OH of **Mekoche Woman**/30, father of Bad Snake-Matchemento/45

629. Green, Gardner aka Red Wolf-Gigageiwaya – ½ Chalakatha-**Cherokee** born about 1740 TN-died 1835 GA – son of **Chalakatha Man** & **Cherokee Woman**, from the Overhills, a Chickamauga **with Dragging Canoe**, husband 1st by 1760 VA of **Margaret Coyle**/40-1/2 Pekowi-Metis, 2nd by 1780 TN of **Rachel Toalson**/60-1/2 Kishpoko-Metis, father **with Coyle of** Benjamin Franklin-Otter Gown Green/61, William Green/65, Paul Green/72 & John Green/75-all ½ Chalakatha-Pekowi-Cherokee-Metis, **with Toalson of** Letha Green/80, Mossie Green/82, Dicey Ann Green/87, Isaac Green/94, William Alonzo Green/95-all ½ Chalakatha-Kishpoko-Cherokee-Metis, other children by both wives likely

630. Green, Thomas – adopted-white born about 1720-died 1783 OH - adopted before 1740-never fully returned to whites, husband about 1755 VA of **Chalakatha Woman**/40, father of Mary Margaret Green/56 & John Green/60 both 1/2 Chalakatha-Metis

631. Greenham, Nicholas aka **Skipagetha** - adopted-white born about 1790 died after 1830 – **with U.S. Army-**War 1812-Thames/13, husband of **Mekoche Woman**/95, children unknown

632. Greenwood, John aka Cheesquatalone-Yellow Bird-CheeskioweeCuareto-Kealharfteke-First Yellow Bird – 15/16th Chalakatha-Kishpoko-BlackMetis born 1703 Nickajack TN-**murdered** 1760 Ft. Prince George/Keowee TN – son of **Thomas Caesar-Skiagunsta Greenwoood**/1680-7/8th ChalakathaKishpoko-Black-Metis & **Katie Chalakatha**/1684, a **Headman from the Lower Towns** & Estatoe, **murdered with David Swallow Tail Greenwood/18, Joseph Two Tails Greenwood/20** & **Robert Two Killer Greenwood/22** by whites while held captive, husband 1729 Chota TN of **Ahneewakee MuskratMoytoy**/04-Chalakatha-Pekowi, father of John Sour Mush Greenwood/30, Skienah Greenwood/32, Preachy Greenwood/34, Skiarow Greenwood/36, Cheekee Greenwood (2)/37, Ground Squirrel-Skiuka Greenwood/38-all 31/32nd Chalakatha-Pekowi-Black-Metis, **adopted father** of Bushyhead Hop-Moytoy/18, Savenooka Hop-Moytoy/20, Goohsohly Hop-Moytoy/22, Elizabeth HopMoytoy/24, Nancy Augustus Hop-Moytoy/26, Muskrat (3)-Moytoy (7)/28 & Amoyah Pigeon (3)/36-all children of Raven Hop-Moytoy)

633. Greenwood, John aka Sinnawa-Hawkhead-Chuchia-Johnny Sinawaska – 3/8th Chalakatha-**Cherokee**-Metis born 1695 Running Water TN-died after 1753 Tuskasegee AL – son of **Hawk Sinnawa Greenwood**/1670 & **Cherokee Woman**/1675, a **Headman from Tuskasegee**, wife & children unknown

634. Greenwood, John aka **Sour Mush-Ookoseta-Ogosata** – 31/32nd Chalakatha-Pekowi-Kishpoko-Black-Metis born 1730 Chota TN-died 1820 OK – son of **John Cheesquatalone Greenwood**/03 & **Ahneewakee Muskrat-Moytoy**/04, **pro-French** faction in French-Indian War/54-63, Pontiac War/62-66, Point Pleasant/74, raiding KY-VA-OH/77-81, Treaty 1785, 1804, 1805, 1806, 1816, 1817, Blind Savannah Clan Cherokee, husband 1748 Chota TN of **Long Hair Woman**/32-Cherokee, father of Bear Meat- Yonaheheweeah Greenwood/56, Tree Greenwood/58, Charley-Tsali Greenwood/60 & Zachariah Fish Greenwood/64-all 15/64th Chalakatha-Pekowi-Kishpoko-Black-CherokeeMetis

635. Greenwood, John aka Spemcia Elene-Big Man[61] – adopted-white born 1619 ENG-died1689 Nickajack TN - about 7' tall, immigrated to VA 1635, associated with **Thomas Pashmere Carpenter**/1607-adopted white, moved quickly into the mountains, husband 1640 Shawnee Nation-western VA of **Nepikeweewa Chalakatha**/1625, father of Thomas (1)-Skootekitehi Greenwood/1641-1/2 Chalakatha-Metis

636. Greenwood, Thomas Caesar aka **Capt. Caesar-Skiagunsta**-Three Nosed Warrior-Triple-nose Warrior-Old Caesar-Blind Warrior-**Breed Slave-catcher**Old Warrior – 7/8th Chalakatha-Kishpoko-Black-Metis born 1680 Nickajack TNdied 1775 Great Tellico TN – son of **Joseph Gorhaleke Greenwood**/1660-3/4th Chalakatha-Metis & **Quaghcunnega**/1662- ½ **Kishpoko-Black**, advisor to **Old Hop**/1688-Chalakatha & **Young Rainmaker**/1680-Cherokee, a **Headman of Chatuga** in Great Tellico faction, delegate to ENG 1730, **pro-British** faction**with George Washington** & **Colonial Army** in French-Indian War/54-63, from the Overhills & Chatuga TN, on Council 1741 of **Bad Water Muskrat-Moytoy (6)**/22, Treaty Sycamore Shoals 1775, husband 1700 Nickajack TN of **Katie Chalakatha**/1684, father of Thomas Sutichettchee Greenwood/01, John Cheesquatalone-Yellow Bird Greenwood/03, daughters Quatsis Atawaya Greenwood/12, Nancy Greenwood/20 & Ankee Greenwood/29-all 15/16th Chalakatha-Kishpoko-Black-Metis

637. Greenwood, Thomas Sutichettchee – 15/16th Chalakatha-KishpokoBlack-Metis born 1701 Nickajack TN-**killed** in battle 1760 TN – son of **Thomas**

Caesar Greenwood/1680-7/8th Chalakatha-Kishpoko-Black-Metis & **Katie Chalakatha**/1684, delegate to ENG 1730, husband 1718 Nickajack TN of **Wakuta Okowellos**/04-7/8th Chalakatha-Metis, father of David (2)-Swallow-tail Greenwood/18, Joseph (3)-Tallichama Greenwood/20, Robert-Tallitaha Greenwood/22, daughters Puki-Pequea Greenwood/24 & Cheekee Greenwood/28-all 29/32nd Chalakatha-Kishpoko-Black-Metis

638. Grenadier Squaw - see **Wife of Mr. Francis & Old Belt**/12, **Nonhelema Hokolesqua**/18, **Elizabeth Hokolesqua**/26 & **Catherine-Kitty Hokolesqua**/28sisters of **Cornstalk**/10

639. Grignon, Jean Baptiste (1) - 1/2 Chalakatha-Chippewa-Metis born about 1743-died after 1770 - son of **Pierre Grignon (1)**/10 & **Mary Ann Sauvagesse**/20, husband 1763 of **Marie Renee Moreau**/48-Chippewa-Metis, children unknown

640. Grignon, Jean Baptiste (2) - 1/4th Chalakatha-Chippewa-Ottawa-Metis born about 1785-died after 1832 - son of **Pierre Grignon (2)**/40 & **Louise Domitilde Langlade**/45-Ottawa-Metis, husband 1st about 1800 of **Quipiwa Chippewa**/85, 2nd about 1810 of **Noquas Chippewa**/90, 3rd about 1830 of **Cattish Maccabee**/1810-Pottawamee, children unknown

641. Grignon, Marie Olive - 1/2 Chalakatha-Chippewa-Metis born about 1754-died after 1775 - daughter of **Pierre Grignon (1)**/10 & **Mary Anne Sauvagesse**/20, husband & children unknown

642. Grignon, Mary Anne Sauvagesse- wife by 1740 of **Pierre Grignon (1)**/10-Chippewa-Metis, mother of Pierre Grignon (2)/40, Jean Baptiste Grignon (1)/43, Germaine Grignon/50, Mary Olive Grignon/54 & Louis Grignon/58-all 1/2 Chalakatha-Chippewa-Metis

643. Grignon, Pierre (2) aka **Pierre Grignon Jr** - 1/2 Chalakatha-ChippewaMetis born about 1740-died after 1795 - son of **Pierre Grignon (1)**/10 & **Mary Anne Sauvagesse**/20, Cornstalk War/58-77, Pontiac War/62-66, Bushy Run/63, Point Pleasant/74, Blue Jacket War/77-94, raiding KY-OH-VA/77-81, Crawford/82, husband 1st (known) about 1769 of **Marie Eechauwaukak**/55-Winnebego-Metis, 2nd about 1782 of **Charlotte Ambrosia**/65-PottawameeMetis, 3rd about 1784 of **Louise Domitilde Langlade**/45-Ottawa-Metis, 4th by 1789 of **Mary Menomonee**/70, father **with Eechauwaukak** of Perrish Grignon/70, Pierre Antoine-Fanfan Grignon/75, Charles Antoine Grignon/77 & Augustin Grignon/79-all 1/4th Chalakatha -Chippewa-Winnebago-Metis, **with**

Charlotte Ambrosia of Louis Grignon/83-1/4th Chalakatha - ChippewaPottawamee-Metis, **with Langlade** of Jean Baptiste Grignon/85 & Paul Grignon/89-both 1/4th Chalakatha -Chippewa-Ottawa-Metis, **with Mary** of Domitilde Grignon/90, Amable Grignon/95 & Charlotte Ambrosia Grignon/1800-all 1/4th Chalakatha-Chippewa-Menomonee-Metis

644. Guerineau, Susanne Cameron - wife 1790 of **Dr. Guerineau**-white born about 1760-died after 1802, mother of Sarah Amelia Guerineau /1802 & other children-all 7/64th Chalakatha-Thawikila-Creek-Cherokee-Metis

645. Gunter, Catherine Rising Fawn - Red Paint Clan **Cherokee**, wife 1795 TN of **John Gunter (2)**-Welsh born 1760 WAL-died 1835 AL, mother of Samuel Gunter/96, Aky Gunter/98, Martha Jane Gunter/1800, Edward Gunter/1803, Elizabeth Hunt Gunter/1804, John Gunter (3)/1806, Catherine Gunter/1810-all 21/64th Chalakatha-Pekowi-Cherokee-Metis

H

646. Half Day – adopted-Chippewa born about 1750 (MI?)-died after 1781 – Cornstalk War/68-77, raiding Ohio-Little Kanawha-Big Sandy-New River valleys/72, Point Pleasant/74-75-78, Blue Jacket War/77-81, raiding KY-VAOH/77-81, Boonesboro/78, husband about 1770 IN of **Mekoche Woman**/55, father of several 1/2 Mekoche-Chippewa children/70-81

647. Half Moon (1) – Chalakatha born about 1725 PA-died after 1765 OH - son of **Big Moon**/1700, raiding PA/40, Cornstalk War/55-65, French/Indian War/54-63, Braddock/55, raiding New-Shenandoah River valleys/55, raiding PA/55-56, Pontiac War/62-65, Bushy Run/63, raiding New-Jackson-Greenbrier River valleys/63

648. Half Moon (2) – Kishpoko born about 1740-**killed** 1782 OH - Cornstalk War/58-77, raiding Ohio-New River valleys/58, Pontiac War/62-66, Bushy Run/63, raiding New-Greenbrier-Jackson River valleys/63, raiding Ohio-Big Sandy-Little Kanawha-New River valleys/72, Point Pleasant/74-75-78, Blue Jacket War/77-82, raiding KY-VA-OH/77-81, killed at Crawford/82 (**not son of Half Moon/25**)

649. Halfbreed, Hannah Critterden aka Qualiluka Guulisi – Blind Savannah Clan **Cherokee**, wife 1774 of **Big Halfbreed**/50, divorced by Big Halfbreed when she was Christianized, mother with Halfbreed of Daughter/74, Lydia Halfbreed/76, Pigeon Halfbreed/78, Susannah Halfbreed/80, Jennie Halfbreed/82, Elizabeth Halfbreed/84, Chinosa Halfbreed/86, Jesse Halfbreed/88-all 3/8th Chalakatha-Pekowi-Cherokee-Metis

650. Halfbreed, Lydia aka Qualayuga-Chiuka-Zaeucka-Toocayeeha - 3/8th Chalakatha-Pekowi-**Cherokee**-Metis born about 1776-died 1849 - daughter of **Big Halfbreed**/50 & **Hannah Critterden**/56, Blind Savannah Clan Cherokee, wife 1st 1790 of **Leonard D. Shaw**/66-white, 2nd 1791 of **Chief William Abraham Hicks**/69-1/8th Chalakatha-Thawikila-Creek-Cherokee-Metis, 3rd 1793 of **Daniel McCoy**/70-white, 4th 1794 **James Chisholm**/74-1/2 Chalakatha-Metis, 5th 1800 of **James Foster Jr**/78-1/8th Thawikila-Cherokee-Metis, 6th 1821 of (brother of James/74) **George Chisholm**/72-1/2 Chalakatha-Metis, no children/90-91 of record **with Shaw**, mother **with Hicks** of George Augustus Hicks-Young Wolf-Woyehneeta/92-1/4th Chalakatha-Thawikila-Pekowi-CreekCherokee-Metis, **with McCoy** of Catherine Maria McCoy/93-3/16th ChalakathaPekowi-Cherokee-Metis, children/94-1800 **with James Chisholm** unknown, **with Foster** of John Tyler Foster/1801, Wat Foster/1803 & Tom Foster/1804-all 1/4th Chalakatha-Thawikila-Pekowi-Cherokee-Metis, **with George Chisholm** of
Nelson Chisholm/1822, Lydia Chisholm/24 & Polly Naomi Chisholm/26-all 7/16th Chalakatha-Pekowi-Cherokee-Metis

651. Hanging Maw aka **Skolakutta**-Hanging Man-Uskwaliguta-His Stomach Hangs Down - Cherokee born 1710-died 1794 – a brother or half-brother of **Abram-Oskuah-Ooskiah**/15, French-Indian War/54-63 **with George Washington & Colonial Army**, sent warriors to Point Pleasant/74, Cherokee War/75, Treaty Sycamore Shoals 1775, a seceding headman 1777, **Principle Chief of Cherokee** 1780-92, delegate to D.C. 1791, Treaty 1785, 1791, 1792, from the Overhills, Council Hanging Maw Town-wounded in attack by John Beard's renegade militia 1793, husband 1st 1730 of **Cherokee Woman**/15, 2nd 1749 of **Betsy Carpenter**/14-7/16th Chalakatha-Cherokee-Metis, father **with Cherokee** of Daughter/78-Cherokee, **with Carpenter** of Willico Maw/50, Thomas Maw/55, Nancy Oousta Hanging Maw/60-all 7/32nd Chalakatha-Cherokee-Metis

652. Hard Fish – Pekowi-(adopted-**Cayuga**) born about 1740 OH-died after 1778 (OH?) – Cornstalk War/58-77, raiding Ohio-New River valleys/58, Pontiac War/62-66, Bushy Run/63, raiding New-Jackson-Greenbrier River valleys/63, raiding Ohio-Big Sandy-Little Kanawha-New River valleys/72, raiding Ohio River Valley/74 **with Chief Logan**, Point Pleasant/74, Boonesboro, husband 1760 OH of **Cayuga Woman**/45

653. Hard Head aka **LeTete Dure** – Kishpoko-(adopted-**Ottawa**) born about 1720 (IN?)-died after 1759 – adopted-Ottawa 1740, raiding PA/40, FrenchIndian War/54-63, Braddock/55, raiding New-Shenandoah River valleys/55, raiding PA/55-56, raiding Ohio-New River valleys/58, husband 1740 (MI?) of

Ottawa Woman/25

654. **Hard Hickory** - Kishpoko born about 1745 OH-died after 1774 – Cornstalk War/62-74, Pontiac War/62-66, raiding New-Greenbrier-Jackson River valleys/63, raiding Ohio-Little Kanawha-Big Sandy-New River valleys/72, Point Pleasant/74, husband about 1765 (TN?) of **Cherokee Woman**/50, father of several 1/2 Kishpoko-Cherokee children/65-74

655. **Hard Man aka Kishanositee**[62]-Guschanatsi-Gieschantsi-BittamaughTrapped Raccoon - 1/2 Pekowi-Metis born about 1730 PA-died after 1779 (OH?) - son of **Pheasant(1)-Kakawatchekee (1)** /1680 & **Adopted White Woman**/10, Cornstalk War/55-77, French-Indian War/54-63, Braddock/55, raiding NewShenandoah River valleys/55, raiding PA/55-56, raiding Ohio River valley/58, Pontiac War/62-66, Bushy Run/63, raiding New-Greenbrier-Jackson River valleys/63, raiding Ohio-New-Big Sandy-Little Kanawha River valleys/72, Point Pleasant/74, a **Pekowi Chief** by 1764, Council with Bouquet 1764, living on Deer Creek of Sciota River OH 1773, removed as war chief 1774, a **Pekowi sachem** 1776, Treaty Ft. Pitt 1776, moved to MO about 1779, 1st cousin (through father) of **Young Pheasant-Kakawatchekee (2)**/30, **Pucksinekau**/35 & **Hard Striker**/40, husband 1755 OH of **Adopted White Woman**/35, father of several 1/4th Pekowi-Metis children/55-85 (children or grandchildren took the surname Hardman then some to Herdman)

656. **Hard Rain aka Hard Falling Rain** – Kishpoko (adopted-**Cherokee**) born about 1740 (KY?)-died after 1782 (OH?) – Cornstalk War/58-77, raiding OhioNew River valleys/58, Pontiac War/62-66, Bushy Run/63, raiding New-JacksonGreenbrier River valleys/63, raiding Ohio-New-Big Sandy-Little Kanawha River valleys/72, Point Pleasant/74, raiding KY-VA-OH/77 **with Bob Benge** & **Cheeseekau**, Boonesboro/78, raiding KY-VA-OH/81 **with Joseph Brant** & **James Girty**, Crawford/82, husband about 1760 (TN/KY?)of **Cherokee Woman**/45

657. **Hard Shell aka LeCoquille** - 1/2 Pekowi-**Miami**-Metis born about 1730died after 1780 - son of **Miami-Metis Man** & **Pekowi Woman**, Cornstalk War/55-77, French-Indian War/54-63, Braddock/55, raiding New River valley/55, raiding PA/55-56, raiding Ohio-New River valley/58, Pontiac War/62-66, Bushy Run/63, raiding New-Jackson-Greenbrier River valleys/63, raiding Ohio-Little Kanawha-Big Sandy-New River valleys/72, Point Pleasant/74, raiding KY-VA-OH/77-80, husband about 1750 OH of **Pekowi Woman**/35, father of several 3/4th Pekowi-Miami-Metis children/50-80.

658. **Hard Striker**[63] aka **Nephew of Pheasant**-Nephew of Kakawatchee-2nd Husband of Metheotashe-**Step-father of Tecumseh** – Pekowi born 1740 PA**killed** 1775 OH - son of **Sister of Kakawatchekee** aka Pheasant/1695-Pekowi & **Pekowi Man**, Cornstalk War/55-75, raiding Ohio-New River valleys/58, Pontiac War/62-66, Bushy Run/63, raiding New-Greenbrier-Jackson River valleys/63, raiding Ohio-New-Big Sandy-Little Kanawha River valleys/72, Point Pleasant/74, brother of **Young Pheasant**-Kakawatchekee(2)/30, **Pucksinekau**/35
& Sister/38, nephew of **Pheasant**-Kakawatchekee (1)/1680, 1st cousin of **Hard Man**/30, **killed by whites** while hunting, husband 1st 1760 OH of **Pekowi Woman**/45, 2nd 1775 OH of **Metheotashe Opessa**-(widow of Puckenshinwa)/40, children/60-75 **with Pekowi** unknown, **step-father of Tecumseh** & younger siblings for a short while, no child with Metheotashe known.

659. Harlan, Catherine Kingfisher (Candy Walker) – Wolf Clan **Cherokee**, wife 3rd 1773 Chota TN of **Ellis Harlan**-white born 1731 PA-died 1815 TN-son of **Hannah Osborne**/07 & **Ezekial Harlan Jr**/07, mother **with Harlan** of Nancy Harlan/74, George Harlan/76, Ezekial Harlan/78, Susanne Harlan/80, Ruth Harlan/82, Sarah Harlan/84, William Harlan/86, Ellis Harlan (2)/88, John T. Harlan/90, Elizabeth Harlan/92-all 3/64th Chalakatha-Cherokee-Metis

660. Harnage, Elizabeth Metis – ½ Chalakatha-Metis born by 1755-died after 1780 - daughter of **Chalakatha Woman** & **White Man**, wife by 1770 of **Mr. Harnage**-white, mother of Jacob Harnage/70 & Ambrose Harnage/80-both 1/4th Chalakatha-Metis

661. Harris, Lucy Fields- Long Hair Clan Cherokee, wife 1799 of **Capt. James Harris**-white born 1760 GA-died after 1803, mother of Nancy/1800 & Rachel Harris/1803-both 1/64th Chalakatha-**Cherokee**-Metis

662. Harris, Rebecca Sowards – (granddaughter of **Cornstalk**/10), wife 1805 of **Garrett Harris**-white born about 1790-died after 1810, mother of Garrett Harris Jr/1806, Lucinda Harris/1809-both 15/64th Chalakatha-Mekoche-Metis

663. **Hawk aka Hawkawepilathy-Hokawepeelathee**[64] – Thawikila born about 1730-died after 1786 – Cornstalk War/55-77, raiding Ohio-New River valleys/58, Pontiac War/62-66, Bushy Run/63, raiding New-Jackson-Greenbrier River valleys/63, raiding Ohio-New-Little Kanawha-Big Sandy River valleys/72, Point Pleasant/74-75-78, Blue Jacket War/77-86, raiding KY-VA-OH/77-81, Boonesboro/78, remained in OH with **Black Hoof** band in 1779 when most Thawikila moved to MO, Blue Licks/82, Crawford/82, Council Miami Jan. 1786, Treaty 1786, husband of **Thawikila Woman**/35, father of Young Hawk/52

664. Healeo - Thawikila born about 1750 OH-died after 1810 – a Thawikila warrior, raiding Cornstalk War/58-74, Ohio-Little Kanawha-Big Sandy-New River valleys/72, Point Pleasant/74, moved to AL 1774-returned to OH 1778, Blue Jacket War/78-94, raiding OH-KY-VA-PA/78-81, Crawford/82, raiding Ohio River valley/83-89, Fallen Timber/94, living in Apple Creek MO 1810

665. **Heap aka Akopee**[65]-Hapokee – Mekoche born about 1780 OH-died after 1817 - a warrior at Wapakoneta 1817, Treaty 1817

666. Heartless aka **Sansceour** – adopted-**Ottawa**-Metis born about 1720-died after 1766 – son of **Ottawa Woman** & **Coureur deBois**-Canadian, raiding PA/40, Cornstalk War/55-66, French-Indian War/54-63, Braddock/55, raiding New-Shenandoah River valleys/55, raiding PA/55-56, aiding Ohio-New River valleys/58, Pontiac War/62-66, Bushy Run/63, raiding New-Greenbrier-Jackson River valleys/63, husband about 1740 OH of **Chalakatha Woman**/25, children unknown

667. elton, Ruth - white born about 1784 VA-died after 1810 - sister of **Shadrack Helton**/85 & **Robert Helton**/94, 3rd wife about 1810 of **Judge John Calvin Martin**/81-11/64th Chalakatha-Pekowi-Cherokee-Metis, mother of Amelia Martin/1812-5/64th Chalakatha-Pekowi-Cherokee Metis

668. Henry, John – white-Shawnee born 1780 OH-died after 1833 KS - son of **Miss Collins**/50-adopted-white & **Moses Henry**/40-adopted white, moved to KS 1832, husband 1800 OH of **Chalakatha Woman**/85, father of Son of John Henry/1805, Mary Henry/1816 & several other 1/2 Chalakatha-Metis children/1800-30

669. Herbert, Louis - 1/2 Mekoche-Metis born about 1750 IN-died after 1777 – son of **Jean Herbert**/15-adopted-French/Canadian & **Mekoche Woman**/30, Cornstalk War/58-77, raiding Ohio-Little Kanawha-Big Sandy-New valleys/72, Point Pleasant/74, raiding KY-VA-OH/77, moved north-west after 1777, husband about 1770 OH of **Mekoche Woman**/55, children unknown

670. Hercules - 1/2 Kishpoko-Black born before 1780-died after 1820 - son of **Kishpoko Woman** & **Black French/Canadian**, Prophet's Town/1811, Brownstown/1812-Monguagon/12-1st Amherstburg/1812-Frenchtown/1813-Ft. Meigs/1813-2nd Amherstburg/1813 & Thames/1813 **with Tecumseh**, 2nd husband about 1805 of **Margaret Pelegia Campbell**/90-Sioux-Ottawa-Metis, children unknown

671.	Hicks, Charles Renatus - 1/8th Chalakatha-Thawikila-Creek-CherokeeMetis born about 1762 GA-died 1827 GA - son of **Nancy Conrad**/40 & **Nathan Hicks**/35-white, Wolf Clan Cherokee, delegate to D.C. 1819, Treaty 1819, Assistant Principal Chief **under Path Killer** 1817-27, **Principal Chief** of Cherokee 1827-short while between death of Path Killer & his own, husband 1st 1781 of **Wolf Clan Cherokee Woman**/67, 2nd 1793 of **Nancy Broom (2)-Anna Felicitas**/70-Wolf Clan Cherokee, father **with Cherokee** of John HIcks/82 & Nathan Wolf Hicks/94-both 1/16th Chalakatha-Thawikila-Creek-Cherokee-Metis, **with Broom** of Elsie Hicks/94, Charles Renatus Hicks Jr/95, Elijah Hicks/96, Elizabeth Hicks/97, Sarah Elizabeth Hicks/98, Jesse Hicks/99 & Leonard Looney Hicks/1800-all 1/16th Chalakatha-Thawikila-Creek-Cherokee-Metis

672.	Hisoskok – Chalakatha born about 1780 OH-died after 1817 - raiding OH-KY-VA/99-1810, Prophet's Town/1811, Brownstown/1812-Monguagon/1812-1st Amherstburg/1812-Frenchtown/1813-Ft. Meigs/1813-2nd Amherstburg/1813 & Thames/1813 **with Tecumseh**, a warrior from Lewistown 1817, Treaty 1817

673.	Hog Head – Chalakatha born about 1730 PA-died after 1774 – Cornstalk War/55-74, French-Indian War/54-63, Braddock/55, raiding New-Shenandoah River valleys/55, raiding Ohio-New River valleys/58, Pontiac War/62-66, Bushy Run/63, raiding New-Greenbrier-Jackson River valleys/63, raiding Ohio-Big Sandy-Little Kanawha-New River valleys/72, Point Pleasant/74, husband by 1755 OH of **Wind From Water**/40, children unknown

674.	Hokolesqua (1) – Chalakatha (or maybe ½ Chalakatha-Powhatan) born 1630 southwest VA-died 1696 west PA – son of **Chalakatha Man** & **Chalakatha Woman** (or possibly **Nikkiti Powhatan**), some connection/relation with **Straight Tail**-Pekowi, **Nepikeweewa Chalakatha**/1625-wife of John (Spemcia Helene-Big Man) Greenwood, **Pride Chalakatha**/1615-wife of Thomas Pashmere Carpenter, **Locha Chalakatha**/1640-wife of Trader Tom Carpenter & **Mikona Chalakatha**/1644-wife of Tom (Skootekitehi) Greenwood, **Pheasant**-Pekowi & **parents of Standing Turkey-Old Hop** family-Chalakatha, husband 1662 Running Water TN **of Pashmere Carpenter (1)**/1637-1/2 Chalakatha-Metis, father of Okowellos Hokolesqua/1674-3/4th Chalakatha-Metis

675.	Hokolesqua, Catherine (1) aka Kitty-Catherine Kitty OkowellosCatherine Kitty Cornstalk (1)-Sister of Cornstalk-Grenadier Squaw – 3/8th Chalakatha-Creek-Metis born 1728 Shawnee village AL-died after 1797 likely OH - daughter of **Okowellos Hokolesqua**/1674 & **Creek Wife**/09, a Christian

Chalakatha, about 6' tall & attractive, often a translator/messenger for the whites, wife 1st 1745 OH of **Wrynek-Aquilsa Shawnee**/25-Pekowi, 2nd (liaison) 1764 of **William Butler**/44-adopted white Seneca, children/45-65 **with Wrynek-Aquilsa** unknown, mother **with Butler** of Polly Butler/65-3/16th Chalakatha-Creek-Metis, often confused in white histories with her sisters & nieces

676. Hokolesqua, Cawechile[66] aka Younger Daughter of-Wife of Cold Water – 7/8th Chalakatha-Mekoche-Metis born 1716 PA-died after 1807 OH - daughter of **Okowellos Hokolesqua**/1674 & **Katee Mekoche**/1680, a Chalakatha, in later years the **Chief of the women's council**, speaker for the women & children, about 6' tall, Council Ft. Pitt 1776 with **Cornstalk, Nimwha, Ellinipsico, Blue Jacket, Capt. Johnny & Caesar** with George Morgan, Council Ft. Finney 1786 with **Moluntha, Capt. Johnny, Red Pole, Black Snake, Nianimissico (?), Wapachcawela (?), Nihipeewa & Nihinessiko**, , wife about 1735 of **Cold Water**/15-Shawnee, mother of Young Cold Water/40-15/16th Chalakatha-Mekoche-Metis & several other children

677. Hokolesqua, Counasona[67] aka Counasona Okowellos-Counasona BeltKoonasona – 15/16th Chalakatha-Mekoche-Metis born 1735 PA-died after 1778 likely OH - son of **Older Daughter of Okowellos**/12 & **Shawnee Man**/10, brother of **Silver Heels (2)-Aroas**/30, adopted son (after 1745) of **Old Belt**/1700Seneca, Mohawk by marriage, scout-spy **with Colonial Forces**-French-Indian War/54-63-Braddock/55-Pontiac War/62-66-Dunmore War/74-Point Pleasant/74, Council Detroit 1778, nephew of **Cornstalk**/10, husband about 1755 of **Mohawk Woman**/40, children unknown

678. Hokolesqua, Elizabeth aka Elizabeth Okowellos-Sister of CornstalkGrenadier Squaw - 3/8th Chalakatha-Creek-Metis born 1726 Shawnee village AL-died after 1817 OH- daughter of **Okowellos Hokolesqua**/1674 & **Creek Woman**/09, in PA by 1730 with father, appears to have not returned to AL 175558, a Christian Chalakatha, about 6' tall & attractive, often a translator/messenger for the whites, wife 1st about 1744 of **Chalakatha Man**/24, 2nd about 1754 of **Capt. John Butler**-Lodging Pole/30-adopted-white-Seneca, likely (or returned to 1st) 3rd 1760 of **Mekoche Man**/20, children/44-54 & 60/71 **with Shawnee husbands** unknown, mother **with John Butler** of Fanny Butler/55 & Tommy Butler/60-both 3/16th Chalakatha-Creek-Metis, often confused in white histories with her sisters & nieces

679. Hokolesqua, Ewikunwee aka Hewikunwee-Ewikunwee Okowellos – 3/8th Chalakatha-Delaware-Metis born 1716 PA-died after 1765 - son of

Okowellos/1674 & **Delaware Wife**/1695, **Cornstalk War** /55-65, French-Indian War/54-63, Braddock/55, raiding New-Shenandoah River valleys/55, a **Chief of the Shawnee among the Delaware** by 1755, raiding PA/55-56, raiding OhioNew River valleys/58, Pontiac War/62-65, Bushy Run/63, raiding New-JacksonGreenbrier River valleys/63, **hostage of Col. Bouquet** winter of 1764-65 with
Wakeeampea, **Cornstalk**, Naythakeina & **Red Hawk**, husband about 1736 of a **Delaware Woman**/19, children unknown

680. Hokolesqua, Katee Mekoche aka Katee Mekoche Okowellos - born 1680 PA-died 1725 OH – aunt of Moluntha/10-sister of Father of Moluntha, wife 1695 PA of **Okowellos Hokolesqua**/1674-3/4th Chalakatha-Metis, mother of daughters/96-02, daughter Wakuta/04-wife of Thomas Greenwood, child/06, child/08, son **Cornstalk**/10, daughter/12-wife of Mr. Francis & Old Belt, son Keeweeton/14, daughter Cawechile/16-wife of Cold Water, daughter **Nonhelema**/18, son Nimwha/20, son **Red Hawk**/22 & son **Silverheels**/24-all 7/8th Chalakatha-Mekoche-Metis

681. Hokolesqua, Keeweeton aka Keeweeton Okowellos-KeewetonKeywayton-Quiouiton-Quiwetahn-Keywetahn-Kiwitahn-Brother of Cornstalk –
7/8th Chalakatha-Mekoche-Metis born 1714 PA-died about 1804 OH - son of **Okowellos Hokolesqua**/1674 & **Katee Mekoche**/1680, moved to AL with father 1725-returned to PA by 1730-may have returned to AL for a short while in 1755, over 6' tall, raiding PA/40, **Cornstalk War** /55-77, French-Indian War/54-63, Braddock/55, raiding New-Shenandoah River valleys/55, raiding PA/55-56, raiding Ohio-New River valleys/58, a **Chalakatha Chief** in OH by 1763, Pontiac War/62-66, Bushy Run/63, raiding New-Greenbrier-Jackson River valleys/63, raiding Ohio-Little Kanawha-Big Sandy-New River valleys/72, **an emissary to the Shawnee for Cornstalk** 1774, Point Pleasant/74-78, raiding KY-OH-VA/7780, husband 1734 PA of **Chalakatha Woman**/18, children unknown

682. Hokolesqua, Naythakeina aka Neightthakeina-Naythakeina Okowellos – 3/8th Chalakatha-Delaware-Metis born 1718 PA-died after 1765 - son of **Okowellos Hokolesqua**/1674 & **Delaware Wife**/1695, raiding PA/40, a **Chief of the Shawnee among the Delaware** 1745, **Cornstalk War** /55-65, French/Indian War/54-63, Braddock/55, raiding New-Shenandoah River valleys/55, raiding PA/55-56, raiding Ohio-New River valleys/58, Pontiac War/62-64, Bushy Run/63, raiding Greenbrier-Jackson-New River valleys/63, **hostage of Bouquet 1765 with** Wakeeampea, **Cornstalk**, Ewikunwee & **Red Hawk**, husband 1738 of **Delaware Woman**/22, children unknown

683. Hokolesqua, Older Daughter of Okowellos aka Wife of Mr. Francis-Wife of Old Belt – 7/8th Chalakatha-Metis born 1712 PA-died after 1745 likely OH - daughter of **Okowellos**/1674 & **Katee Mekoche**/1680, wife 1st 1730 of **Shawnee Man**/10, 2nd 1739 of **Mr. Francis**-white/1700-British Officer, 3rd after 1745 of **Old Belt**/1700-Seneca, mother **with Shawnee** of Aroas-Silverheels (2)/32 & Counasona/35-both 15/16th Chalakatha-Mekoche-Metis-(later adopted Seneca), **with Francis** of David Francis/40 & John Francis (1)/45-both 7/16th Chalakatha-Mekoche-Metis, no known children **with Belt**

684. Hokolesqua, Silverheels (2) aka **Aroas (1)**-Haroas-Silverheels Okowellos (2) – 15/16th Chalakatha-Mekoche-Metis-adopted Seneca born 1732 OH/PA-**killed** 1770 IN/IL - son of **Daughter of Okowellos**/12 & **Shawnee Man**/10, **adopted son after 1745 of Old Belt**/1700-Seneca, brother of Counasona/35, grandson of Okowellos/1674, scout-spy **for whites**-French-Indian War/54-63-Ft. Necessity/54-Braddock/55--Pontiac War/62-66, translator-guide for George Morgan-white after Pontiac War, **killed about 1770 below Louisville KY**, husband 1752 OH of **Shawnee Woman**/35, father of Daughter/52, Aroas (2)-Silverheels Hokolesqua(3)/60-both 31/32nd Chalakatha-Mekoche-Metisadopted Seneca

685. Hokolesqua, Silverheels (3) aka **Aroas (2)** - 31/32nd ChalakathaMekoche-Metis born 1760 OH-died after 1825 - **son of Aroas-Silverheels (2)**/32 & **Shawnee Woman**/35, adopted Seneca, great-grandson of Okowellos/1674, translator-guide for George Morgan-white after death of his father, scout-spy **with whites**-Blue Jacket War/80-94-Crawford/82, Treaty 1809, husband 1780 IN of **Miami Woman**/65, children unknown

686. Hokolesqua, Wakeeampea aka Wakeeampea Okowellos – 3/8th Chalakatha-Delaware-Metis born 1714 PA-died after 1765 likely OH - son of **Okowellos Hokolesqua**/1674 & **Delaware Wife**/1695, raiding PA/40, **Cornstalk War** /55-65, French-Indian War/54-63, Braddock/55, raiding NewShenandoah River valleys/55, raiding PA/55-56, raiding Ohio-New River valleys/58, Pontiac War/62-65, Bushy Run/63, raiding New-Jackson-Greenbrier River valleys/63, a **Delaware Chief** by 1750, **hostage of Bouquet** 1765 with **Cornstalk**, Ewikunwee, Naythakeina & **Red Hawk**, husband by 1734 of **Delaware Woman**/19, children unknown

687. Hokolesqua, Wakuta – 7/8th Chalakatha-Mekoche-Metis born 1704 Running Water TN-died 1758 Running Water TN – daughter of **Okowellos**/1674 & **Katee Mekoche**/1680, wife 1718 Nickajack TN of **Thomas Sutichettchee Greenwood**/1698-15/16th Chalakatha-Kishpoko-Black-Metis, mother of sons David (2)-Swallow-tail Greenwood/18, Joseph (3)-Tallichama Greenwood/20,

Robert-Tallitaha Greenwood/22 & daughters Puki-Pequea Greenwood/24 & Cheekee Greenwood/28-all 29/32nd Chalakatha-Kishpoko-Mekoche-Black-Metis

688. Hole in Day aka **Thobequebah**-Eclipse – adopted-Chippewa born about 1750-died about 1817 – Cornstalk War/70-77, raiding Little Kanawha-Big Sandy-Ohio-New River valleys/72, Point Pleasant/74-78, raiding Oh-KY-VA/7781, Crawford/82, raiding Ohio River valley/88-92, Blue Jacket War/77-94, son in law of Broken Tooth/50-Chippewa, husband 1st 1770 IN of **Kishpoko Woman**/55, 2nd 1790 of **Daughter of Broken Tooth**/75-Chippewa, children unknown

689. Hollis, Job – adopted-white born about 1745-died after 1789 – adopted before 1755, raiding Ohio-Little Kanawha-Big Sandy-New River valleys/72, Point Pleasant/74, raiding Ohio-New River valleys/75-81, Crawford/82, brother of **John Hollis**/40, husband 1765 OH of **Pekowi Woman**/50, children unknown

690. Hollis, John – adopted-white born about 1740-**killed** 1778 – adopted before 1755, raiding Ohio-Little Kanawha-Big Sandy-New River valleys/72, Point Pleasant/74, raiding Ohio-New River valleys/75-78, killed in raid/78, brother of **Job Hollis**/45, husband about 1760 OH of **Pekowi Woman**/44, children unknown

691. Hooded Eyes aka **LeChapheron**-Hooded Man - 1/2 Kishpoko-**Metis** born about 1740 PA-died after 1794 - son of **Kishpoko Woman** & **Coureur deBois**, Cornstalk War/58-77, raiding Ohio-New River valleys/58, Pontiac War/58-63, Bushy Run/63, raiding New-Jackson-Greenbrier River valleys/63, raiding Ohio-Little Kanawha-Big Sandy-New River valleys/72, Point Pleasant/74, Blue Jacket War/77-94, Boonesboro/78, raiding KY-VA-OH/77-81, Crawford/82, husband about 1760 OH of **Kishpoko Woman**/45, children unknown

692. Hop, Old aka Kanagatoga-**Standing Turkey (1)** -Uka-Fire KingKanetekoka-Conarcorturer-Connecorte - Chalakatha born 1688 Chota TN (some records indicate Upper Hiwassee VA-where older siblings were born or further north-Ohio valley or further west in TN)-died 1761 Chota TN – parents unknown but died in 1694 VA, adopted son 1694 of **Trader Tom Carpenter (2)**-**Moytoy (2)**/1660 & **Nancy Chalakatha**/1664, Nancy/1664 referred to as an aunt of the Hop family i.e. a sibling of one of their parents, brother of **Raven Hop**/1680, **Quatsis Hop**/1682, **Elder Sister Hop**/1684, **Swan-Wapehti Hop**/1686, **AprilTkikami Hop**/1690, **Oolootah-Ulutse Hop**/1692 & **Ghigoneli Hop**/1694, could cipher, read & write English, Wolf Clan Cherokee, removed British appointed (Carpenter-Moytoy or Rainmaker?) leaders & united 4 (of 7) Cherokee

clans at Chota 1751, leader of pro- French faction in French-Indian War/54-61, sent warriors to Braddock/55, **Principal Chief 1751-61**, passed actual power/authority to his nephews **Kitegista Rainmaker**/10 & **Oconastota Rainmaker**/02 upon his death in 1761 even though his son **Little TurkeyStanding Turkey (2)**/09 succeeded him as titular Chief, husband by 1708 of **Sugi Rainmaker**/1690, known father of sons Little Turkey/09, Young Hop/15 & daughter Grasshopper Hop/25-all 1/2 Chalakatha-Cherokee, adopted father 1723 of nephews **John French**/10 & **Capt.-Cappee French**/12-both 1/2 Chalakatha-Black-French/Canadian-Metis-(nephews through his sister Ghigoneli/1694)

693. Hop, April **Tkikami** aka Middle Sister of Old Hop-Middle Sister of Standing Turkey-Wife of Richard Barnes - Chalakatha born 1690 Chota TN-died 1744 Upper Hiwassee TN – sister of **Old Hop-Standing Turkey (1)**/1688Chalakatha, adopted daughter 1694 of **Trader Tom Carpenter (2)-Moytoy (2)**/1660 & **Nancy Chalakatha**/1664, could cipher, read & write English, wife 1st 1705 Chota TN of **Unknown Man**, 2nd 1718 Chota TN of **Richard Barnes**/1695-white, children/05-17 **with Unknown Man** unknown, mother **with Barnes** of Mary Barnes/20 & Charity Barnes/26-both 1/2 Chalakatha-Metis

694. Hop, Elder Sister of Old aka Elder Sister of Standing Turkey-Wife of **Young Rainmaker**-Anigatagewi Woman-Wild Potato Woman-wife of **Smallpox Conjurer**-wife of Tsula Fox-Blind Savannah Woman - Chalakatha born 1684 Upper Hiwassee VA-died after 1741 TN - adopted daughter 1694 of **Rainmaker (1)**/1640-Cherokee, Blind Savannah Clan Cherokee, wife 1st 1700 of **Young Rainmaker**/1685-Cherokee, 2nd 1741 of **Tsula Fox-Smallpox Conjurer**/1670-Cherokee, mother **with Rainmaker** of son Oconastota Rainmaker/02, child/04, son Cloggoittah Rainmaker/06, daughter Ooloosta Rainmaker/08, sons Kitegista Rainmaker/10, Tathtowe Rainmaker/12, Wallenaeoa-Gray Eagle Rainmaker/14, Oukahoukah Rainmaker/16, Kallannah Rainmaker/18-all 1/2 Chalakatha-Cherokee, children **with Smallpox Conjurer** unlikely due to her age

695. Hop, Ghigoneli aka Younger Sister of Old - Chalakatha born 1694 Chota TN-died 1724 Chota TN – sister of **Old Hop-Standing Turkey (1)**/1688, adopted daughter 1694 of **Rainmaker (1)**/1640-Cherokee, Blue Holly Clan Cherokee by marriage (?), could cipher, read & write English, wife 1st 1707 of **Blue Holly Cherokee**/1685-(also husband of her sister **Oolootha**/92), 2nd by 1710 of **French-Canadian Mulatto**/1690-(or a Melungeon?), 3rd 1720 of **May Apple**/1690-Kishpoko, any children/07-10 **with Cherokee** unknown, mother **with Mulatto** of John French (French John)/10 & Capt. French (Cappee)/12-both

1/2 Chalakatha-Black-Metis, **with May Apple** of Ninihica Mayapple/21 & Laskigitchi Mayapple/23-both Chalakatha-Kishpoko

696.   Hop, Grasshopper aka Grasshopper Standing Turkey-Granny Hopper - 1/2 Chalakatha-**Cherokee** born 1725 Chota TN-died 1785 Chota TN - daughter of **Old Hop**/1688-Chalakatha & **Sugi Rainmaker**/1690-Cherokee, could cipher, read & write English, Wolf Clan Cherokee, wife 1st 1740 Chota TN of **Unknown Man**/20, 2nd 1752 Chota TN of **William David McDaniel**/20-SCO, children/4051 **with Unknown Man** unknown, mother **with McDaniel** of Catherine McDaniel/53, Alexander McDaniel /54, Lewis McDaniel /56, John McDaniel /58, Mary McDaniel /62, Nancy McDaniel /64, Elizabeth McDaniel /65, Susannah McDaniel /66, Rachel McDaniel /67, William McDaniel Jr/68-all 1/4th Chalakatha-Cherokee-Metis

697.   Hop, Little Turkey (1) aka Standing Turkey (2)-**Kanagatoga**-Standing Turkey Hop (2)-Kanitta-Gundigaduhnyi - 1/2 Chalakatha-**Cherokee** born 1709 Chota TN-died 1804 OH - son of **Standing Turkey (1)-Old Hop**/1688-Chalakatha & **Sugi Rainmaker**/1690-Cherokee, Wolf Clan Cherokee, succeeded father as **Principal Chief 1761** but actual authority-power was held by his cousins **Oconastota Rainmaker**/02 & **Kitegista Rainmaker**/10, Pontiac War/62-66, sent warriors to Point Pleasant/74, sent warriors raiding KY-VAOH/75-81, lost power among Cherokee about 1775, sent warriors raiding Ohio River valley/88-92, a **Chickamauga Principal Chief** 1792-1801, Treaty 1798, **living with Shawnee in TN** 1764-92, moved to northern KY with Chalakatha Wife about 1792 finally settling in OH about 1801, husband 1st about 1729 Chota TN of **Cherokee Woman**/15, 2nd 1760 of **Chalakatha Woman**/40, father **with Cherokee** of Little Turkey Hop (2) –Standing Turkey (4)/60-1/4th ChalakathaCherokee & several other children/36-60, **with Chalakatha** of Auquotaque Hop- Standing Turkey-Little Turkey/62-3/4th Chalakatha-Cherokee

698. Hop, Oolootah aka Oolootah Standing Turkey-Ulutse-Oolootsee-Wife of John Bowles – Chalakatha born 1692 Chota TN-died after 1756 TN - sister of **Old Hop**/1688, adopted daughter 1694 of **Rainmaker (1)**/1640 & **Quatsey (1)**/1650-both Cherokee, Blue Holly Clan Cherokee, lived with sister **Quatsis Hop-Beamer** from 1699-1705, wife 1st 1705 Chota TN of **Blue Holly Cherokee**/85-(also husband of her sister **Ghigoneli**/94), 2nd by 1722 Settico TN of **John Bowles**/1688-Scot, children/06-21 **with Cherokee** unknown, mother **with Bowles** of Ghigoneli Bowles/23-1/2 Chalakatha-Metis

699. Hop, Quatsis aka Quatsis Standing Turkey-Quatsis Aniwadi – Chalakatha born 1682 Great Tellico TN-died 1758 Tellico Plains TN – adopted daughter 1694 of **Trader Tom Carpenter (2)-Moytoy (2)**/1660-3/4th Chalakatha-Metis & **Nancy Chalakatha**/1664, sister of **Old Hop**/1688, could cipher, read & write English, niece of **Nancy Chalakatha**/1664-(wife of **Trader Tom Carpenter (2)-Moytoy (2)**/1660, aunt of **Savanooka**/20 & **Goohsohly**/22(sons of niece **Ahneewakee Muskrat-Moytoy**/04-Chalakatha-Pekowi & brother **Raven Hop**/1683), Red Paint Clan Cherokee, took in sister **Oolootah** from 16991710, wife 1st 1697 Great Tellico TN of **John Beamer**/1676-ENG, 2nd 1705 Settico TN of **Tsula Fox-Smallpox Conjurer**/1670-Cherokee (husband 1741 of her sister **Elder Sister of Old Hop**), 3rd 1709 Chota TN of **William Webber**/1680-ENG, mother **with Beamer** of Ooloosta Beamer/1698, John Beamer (2)/1700, Peggy Beamer/02 & Nionee Beamer/04, **with Fox-Conjurer** of Rising Fawn (1)-Rising Fawn Fox/06 & Quatsis Fox-Daughter of Quatsis/08both 1/2 Chalakatha-Cherokee, **with Webber** of Catherine Webber/10 & William Webber (2)/12-both ½ Chalakatha-Metis

700. Hop, Raven aka **Raven Moytoy**-Raven of Hiwassee-Collanah-CoraniCorane – Chalakatha born 1680 Upper Hiwassee VA-died 1756 Chewohe TN – adopted son 1694 of **Trader Tom Carpenter (2)-Moytoy (2)**/1660 & **Nancy Chalakatha**/1664, brother of Old Hop-Standing Turkey/1688 & siblings, could cipher, read & write English, Treaty 1684 with SC, delegation to ENG 1730, husband 1st 1700 Upper Hiwassee TN of adopted sister **Pashmere Carpenter (2)**/1681-7/8th Chalakatha-Metis, 2nd 1718 of **Ahneewakee Muskrat**/04, father **with Pashmere** of Amoyah Pigeon Hop (1)/15-15/16th Chalakatha-Metis, **with Ahneewakee** of Bushyhead Chiesatebe Hop-Moytoy/18, Savanooka Hop-Moytoy/20, Goohsohly Hop-Moytoy/22, Elizabeth-Raven's Sister HopMoytoy/24, Nancy Augustus Hop-Moytoy/26 & Amahetai Hop-Muskrat (3)-Moytoy (7)/28-all Chalakatha-Pekowi

701. Hop, **Swan aka Wapethi**[68] – Chalakatha born 1686 Upper Hiwassee TN-died 1754 Chota TN – sister of **Old Hop-Standing Turkey**/1688, adopted daughter 1694 of **Trader Tom Carpenter (2)-Moytoy (2)**/1660 & **Nancy Chalakatha**/1664, could cipher, read & write English, wife 1703 Running Water TN of her adopted brother (possible cousin/son of father's sister of mother's brother) **Oshasqua-Muskrat (1)**/1686-Pekowi, mother of daughters Ahneewakee Muskrat/04, Ounacona Muskrat/16, Tame Deer Muskrat/20 & son Bad Water Muskrat-Moytoy (6)/22-all ½ Chalakatha-Pekowi, adopted mother of **John Watts**/04-7/8th Chalakatha-Pekowi-Metis-(possible nephew/relative)

702. Hop, Young aka Young Hopper-Oukahulah - 1/2 Chalakatha-**Cherokee** born about 1715 Chota TN-died 1764 Chota TN - son of **Old Hop**/1688Chalakatha & **Sugi Rainmaker**/1690-Cherokee, Wolf Clan Cherokee, could cipher, read & write English, pro-French faction in French-Indian War, husband 1st 1738 Chota TN of **Ollie Nionee Oconastota** (apparent widow of Attakullakulla)/20-1/2 Chalakatha-Thawikila-Creek-Cherokee, 2nd 1745 Running Water TN of **Chalakatha Woman**/30, father **with Oconastota** of Badger/38, Black Fox/40, Little Owl/42 & Sugi-Suki Hop/44-all ½ Chalakatha-Thawikila-Creek-Cherokee & **all adopted 1746 by Attakullakulla**, children/45-64 **with Chalakatha** unknown

703. Horse Jockey – Mekoche born about 1765 OH-died after 1794 - Crawford/82, raiding Ohio River valley/88-92, Blue Jacket War/82-94

704. Howard, Elizabeth Brock - sister of **Mary Polly Brock**/97 & **Moses Brock**/99, wife 1833 of **Larkin Howard** born 1803 TN-died 1852 KY, mother of Mary Howard/1833, John J. Howard/1835, Matilda Howard/1837, Elizabeth Howard/1839, Larkin Howard Jr/1841, Comfort Howard/1843, Jane M. Howard/1845, Hester Howard/1847, Green A. Howard/1849 & America Howard/1852-all 3/64th Chalakatha-Cherokee-Metis

705. Howard, Margaret Reaume - wife about 1765 of **Joseph Howard**-white born about 1740-died about 1816, children unknown

706. Howard, Rebecca Osborne - wife before 1805 of **Andrew Howard**white born about 1780-died 1834-(son of **Samuel Howard**/62 & **Chloe Langley Osborne**/65), children unknown

707. Hughes, Sarah (1) – ½ Chalakatha-Pekowi-Metis born 1743 Nickajack TN-died after 1798 Cherokee Nation - daughter of **Elizabeth Hop-Raven's Sister**/24 & **Bernard Hughes (1)**/1719-white, Blind Savannah Clan Cherokee, niece of Chief **Sour Mush-Ookoseta-John Greenwood**/28 (half-brother of her mother), wife 1st by 1770 Nickajack TN of **Otter Lifter**/40-Cherokee, 2nd 1775 of **Col. Thomas Waters**/38-white, mother **with Otter Lifter** of Michael Otter Lifter-Michael Waters/72-1/4th Chalakatha-Pekowi-Cherokee-Metis, **with Waters** of Sally Waters/75 & George Morgan Waters/77-both 1/4th Chalakatha-Pekowi-Metis

708. Hughes, Sarah Godagewi aka Sarah Hughes (2)-Sally Hughes - 3/4th Chalakatha-Kishpoko-Pekowi-Metis born 1778 GA-died after 1838 (OK?) - daughter of **James Hughes (1)**/39 & **Elder Kishpoko Sister**/45, Blind Savannah Clan Cherokee, wife 1st 1794 of **Alexander Garvin** aka **Alexander Feather**/70Cherokee, 2nd 1797 of **Avery Vann (2)**/68-1/8th Chalakatha-Cherokee-Metis, 3rd

1800 of 1st cousin **George Hughes**/76, 4th 1808 of **James Critterden**/66-1/4th Kishpoko-Cherokee Metis, mother **with Garvin-Feather** of Betsy Feather/95, Jennie Feather/96, Polly Feather/97, Oogatutlih Feather/98-all 3/8th Chalakatha-Kishpoko-Pekowi-Cherokee-Metis, **with Vann** of James Clausee Vann/99 & Elizabeth Vann/1800-both 7/16th Chalakatha-Kishpoko-Pekowi-Cherokee-Metis, **with Hughes** of George Hughes Jr/1802 & Mary Hughes/04-both 3/4th Chalakatha-Kishpoko-Pekowi-Metis, **with Critterden** of Charles Critterden/1808, Richard Critterden/1810, Elizabeth Critterden/1812, Jack E. Critterden/1814, Peggy Critterden/1816 & Aelie Critterden/1818-all ½ Chalakatha-Kishpoko-Pekowi-Cherokee-Metis

709. Hurricane Tom – adopted-Delaware born about 1720 PA-died after 1756 - raiding PA/40, French-Indian War/54-63, Braddock/55, raiding NewShenandoah River valleys/55, husband 1740 PA of **Chalakatha Woman**/25, children unknown

Section IX
Ice to Kyanthawtha (I - K)

I

710. Ice, Mary (1) aka Red-haired Woman-**Red Hair**- adopted-white born 1737 WV-died shortly after 1825 OH - daughter of **Fredrick Ice**/1680 & **Mary Galloway**/1700-both white, adopted about 1740-returned to visit white family once in 1825, known for her long red hair, wife 1752 of **Pucksinekau**/35, mother of Young Pucksinekau/53, Red Hair/55 & other 1/2 Kishpoko-Pekowi-Metis children

711. Ice, William Galloway aka Indian Billy - adopted-white (**Mohawk**Kishpoko) born 1730 WV-died 1826 WV - son of **Fredrick Ice**/1680 & **Mary Galloway**/1700, adopted by Mohawk about 1740-returned to whites 1765, married into Kishpoko that lived with Mohawk, returned to whites with 1st wife Catherine & 6 children 1765, either Catherine died & Billy sent children back to the tribe or Catherine took them & left by 1766, husband 1st 1750 OH of

Catherine Pheasant/38-Kishpoko-Pekowi, 2nd 1766 WV of **Margaret Higginbotham**/46-white, 3rd 1802 of **Mary Higginbotham** (Scott McMullen)/48-(sister of Margaret/46), 4th 1804 WV of **Elizabeth Shreve**/78, father **with Pheasant** of Christian Ice/52, Elizabeth Ice/54, Eve Ice/56, John Ice/58, Lewis Ice/60 & Thomas Ice/62-all 1/2 Kishpoko-Pekowi-Metis, **with Margaret** of George Ice/66, Susannah Ice/68, Margaret Ice/70, Eve Ice/72, Mary Ice/74, John Ice/76, Thomas Ice/78, Abraham Ice/81, William Ice Jr/85, Sarah Ice/86 & Isaac Ice/90-white, children **with Mary** of Hayden Arden Bayles Ice/1803 & Margaret Ice/1804, **with Elizabeth** of James Shreve Ice/1805, Fredrick Ice/1806, Benjamin Ice/1807, Sally Ice/1808-all white

712. Infidel aka **L'Infidele**- Infidel African - 1/2 Kishpoko-Black born 1725 PA-died after 1763 (OH?) - son of **African**/1700-adopted-Black & **Kishpoko Woman**/10, Cornstalk War/55-63, French-Indian War/54-63, Braddock/55, raiding New-Shenandoah River valleys/55, raiding PA/55-56, raiding Ohio-New River valleys/58, raiding New-Jackson-Greenbrier River valleys/63, an especially violent warrior, associated with the Canadian Metis, husband 1745 OH of **Kishpoko Woman**/30, father of several 3/4th Kishpoko-Black children/45-63

713. Ireland, Catherine aka Big Kate-Irish Kate - 3/4th Chalakatha-MekocheMetis born about 1755 (KY-OH?)-died after 1790 (OH?) - daughter of **James Ireland**/30 & **Chalakatha Woman**/35 , known for her red hair, freckles, height of about 6' & attractiveness, wife about 1775 OH of **Chalakatha Man**/55, widow in 1790, mother of five or six 7/8th Chalakatha-Irish-Metis children/75-90

714. Ireland, James aka Irish-Irishman-L'Iriandais - 1/2 Mekoche-Metis born about 1730 (KY-OH?)-died after 1781 - son of **Irish-Canadian Trader** & **Mekoche Woman**, raiding Ohio-New River valleys/58, associated with **John Monday**/25-adopted French-Canadian & **Joshua McClintock**/30-adopted-white in **John Swift** silver-mines 1760-69 furnishing silver to **Cornstalk**/10, Cornstalk War/55-77, raiding Ohio-Little Kanawha-Big Sandy-New River valleys/72, Point Pleasant/74, raiding Ohio-New River valleys/75, Blue Jacket War/77-81, raiding KY-OH-VA/77-81, noted for his red hair & freckles, husband about 1750 OHKY of **Chalakatha Woman**/35, father of Catherine-Big Kate/55, Shamrock/60 & other 3/4th Chalakatha-Mekoche-Metis children, some with surname Ireland

715. Ireland, Shamrock - 3/4th Chalakatha-Mekoche-Irish-Metis born about 1760-died after 1794 - daughter of **James Ireland**/30-1/2 Mekoche-Irish-Metis & **Chalakatha Woman**/35, wife by 1775 of **Mekoche Man**/55, children unknown

716. Ironside, Alexander - 3/8th Kishpoko-Pekowi-Creek-Metis born about 1793-died after 1813 - son of **George Ironside**/60-adopted-Irish &

IsabellaVocemassussia Puckenshinwa/70 (sister of Tecumseh), **with British Army**War 1812-Thames/1813 **with uncle Tecumseh**, wife & children unknown

717.   Ironside, Annie – (Kishpoko?) born 1810-died 1902 - wife by 1830 of **George Ironside Jr**/1806, children unknown

718.   Ironside, George - adopted-Irish born about 1760 IRE-died 1830 - trading post 1789-94, Council Swan Creek OH 1795 with **Capt. Johnny, Black Beard & Bukangolas**, Indian Agent 1795-1830, **with British Army**-War of 1812, husband 1st about 1785 of **Sotonegoo Girty**/60-adopted Mohawk, 2nd 1792 (church wedding 1810) of **Vocemassussia-Isabella Puckenshinwa**/70-3/4th Kishpoko-Pekowi-Creek-Metis, any children/85-91 **with Sotonegoo** unknown, father **with Vocemassussia** of Alexander Ironside/93, George Ironside Jr/1806, 2 sons & 2 daughters/92-1815 all 3/8th Kishpoko-Pekowi-Creek-Metis.

719.   Ironside, George Jr - 3/8th Kishpoko-Pekowi-Creek-Metis born 1806died 1863 - son of **George Ironside**/60-adopted white & **Isabella-Vocemassussia**/70, Indian Agent after his father 1830-45, nephew of **Tecumseh**, husband by 1830 of **Annie (Kishpoko)**/1810

720.   Itahaha aka Hitahaha-Eetahaha – Thawikila born about 1780-died about 1807 - 1st wife about 1796 of **Joab Barton**/67-adopted white, mother of Jenny Jane Barton/98 & Marcy Barton/1800-both 1/2 Thawikila-Metis.

721. Itawachkomequa aka Hitawachomequa-Heewachkomeekwa – Pekowi born about 1720 PA-died about 1758 OH in epidemic - raiding PA/40, interrogated in South Carolina 53, 53, French-Indian War/54-58, Braddock/55, raiding New-Shenandoah River valleys/55, raiding PA/55-56, raiding Ohio-New River valleys/58

722. Ithathekaka aka Hitathekaka-Heethathekaka - Thawikila born about 1750-died after 1810 – Cornstalk War/68-74, raiding Ohio-Little Kanawha-Big Sandy-New River valleys/72, Point Pleasant/74, moved to AL 1774-returned to OH 1779, Blue Jacket War/79-94, Crawford/82, moved to Apple Creek MO about 1795

723. Itching Bug – Mekoche born about 1765 OH-died after 1795 - wife about 1780 of **Mekoche Man**/60, widow in 1795

J

724. Jackson, Joseph (1) – adopted-white born 1765 VA-died after 1844 KY - captured 1778-returned to whites 1799, Blue Jacket War/82-94, adopted 1778 by **Charlotte Pemenpiah Bourganville** (later **Lorimier**)/58, husband about 1785 OH of **Mekoche Woman**/70, father of several 1/2 Mekoche-Metis children/8599

725. Jackson, Joseph (2) aka Joseph Fish – white-Shawnee born about 1783 OH-died after 1812 - son of **William Jackson-Fish**/60-adopted white & **Elizabeth Bishop**/65-adopted white, brother of Miss Fish aka Daughter of Fish/81, moved to MO about 1800 **with Jimmy Rogers**/70-adopted white & **Charles Philips**/60-1/2 Pekowi-Metis, wife & children unknown

726. Jacquis aka Jakwee – Chalakatha born about 1790 OH-died after 1817 - Prophet's Town/1811, Brownstown/1812-Monguagon/1812-1st Amherstburg/1812-Frenchtown/1813-Ft. Meigs/1813-2nd Amherstburg/1813 & Thames/1813 **with Tecumseh**, a warrior from Lewistown 1817, Treaty 1817

727. Jaunisse, Genevieve aka Jaundiced Girl-Yellow-faced Girl - 1/2 PekowiBlack-Metis born about 1750-died after 1768 - daughter of **Canadian Mulatto & Pekowi Woman**, wife about 1765 of **Claude Reaume**/44-1/4th Pekowi-Metis, mother of Jean Baptiste Reaume/66, Agathe Reaume/67 & Charlotte Reaume/68all 3/8th Pekowi-Black-Metis

728. Jautard - 3/4th Chalakatha-Metis born about 1730-died after 1774 - son of **Chalakatha Man & 1/2 Chalakatha-Metis Woman**, Cornstalk War/55-74, French-Indian War/54-63, Braddock/55, raiding Ohio-New River valley/58, Pontiac War/62-66, Bushy Run/63, raiding New-Greenbrier River valley/63, raiding Ohio-Big Sandy-Little Kanawha-New River valleys/72, Point Pleasant/74, husband 1750 (OH?) of **Chalakatha Woman**/35, children unknown

729. Jeskakake – Pekowi born about 1710 PA-died after 1755 - raiding PA/40, French-Indian War/54, Braddock/55, raiding New-Shenandoah River valleys/55

730. Jim Jack – Mekoche born about 1775 OH-died after 1825 – Fallen Timber/94 **with Shawnee**, scout-**with U.S. Army**-War of 1812-Thames/1813

731. Joe, Shawnee – Chalakatha born about 1765 OH-died after 1832 KS – Blue Jacket War/83-94, raiding Ohio River valley/88-92, scout-**with U.S. Army**War 1812-Thames/13, a warrior from Lewistown 1817, Treaty 1817, moved to KS 1832

732.   John, King aka John King (1) - Mekoche born about 1750 PA-died after 1832 KS - Point Pleasant/74-78, raiding Ohio River valley/77-81, Crawford/82, **a minor Mekoche peace Chief** 1787, moved to MO 1787-moved to KS 1832, husband of **Mekoche Woman**, father of King John (2)-John King (2)/84

733.	John, Shawnee (1) – Chalakatha born about 1730 PA-**killed** 1766 (OH?)
– Cornstalk War/55-66, French-Indian War/54-63, Braddock/55, raiding New-Shenandoah River valleys/55, raiding Ohio-New River valleys/58, Pontiac War/62-66, Bushy Run/63, raiding New-Greenbrier-Jackson River valleys/63, **killed by the Kickapoo**, husband 1750 OH of **Mekoche Woman**/35, father of Shawnee John (2)/50-Chalakatha-Mekoche

734.	John, Shawnee (2) – Chalakatha-Mekoche born about 1750 OH-died after 1815 (MO?) - son of **Shawnee John (1)**/30 & **Mekoche Woman**/35, Cornstalk War/68-77, raiding Ohio-Little Kanawha-Big Sandy-New River valleys/72, Point Pleasant/74-75-78, moved to MO 1779, living in Apple Creek 1815, husband 1770 OH of **Thawikila Woman**/54, father of Shawnee John (3)/75-Chalakatha-Thawikila-Mekoche

735.	John, Shawnee (3) – Chalakatha-Mekoche-Thawikila born about 1775 OH-died after 1817 (KS?) – son of **Shawnee John (2)**/50 & **Thawikila Woman**/54, moved to MO 1779, Fallen Timber/94, moved back to OH before 1812, scout-**with U.S. Army**/War 1812

736.	Johnson, John aka **Apetathe** – white-Shawnee born about 1780-died after 1830 - son of **Mary Catherine See**/49-adopted white & **James Johnson**/45-white, husband about 1800 of **Chalakatha Woman**/85, children unknown

737.	Jolly, Chief John aka Kalanna-Akuludegee-Ooleteka-AnuludegiEulatakee-Throws Away The Drum-John Due-John Jaulee – 37/64th Chalakatha-Pekowi-**Cherokee**-Metis born 1758 Great Tellico TN-died 1838 AR - son of **Robert Due**-Chief Jolly/37 & **Wurteh Watts**/44, Long Hair Clan Cherokee (but should have been Red Paint through his mother?), moved to AR about 1810, succeeded half-brother **Tahlonteeskee (1)**/42 as **Head Chief of AR Cherokee** 1819-38, half-brother through **Wurteh** of **Sequoyah**/59, **Tahlonteeskee (2)**/60, **Robert-Chief Bench Benge**/61, **Richard Benge**/62, **Catherine Benge**/63, **Martin-Utana-Tail Benge**/64, **Tashliske Benge**/66 & **Lucy Benge**/68, halfbrother through Due of **Tobacco Will**/61, **Jennie Due**/64, **Mary Due**/70, **Betsy (Due) Houston**/86 & **Jennie (Due) Houston**/88, Treaty 1805, 1806, 1817, move to AR 1818, husband 1st 1779 TN of **Sarah Chickamauga**/62-1/2 ShawneeCherokee, 2nd 1782 Great Tellico TN of **Elizabeth Emory**/65-35/64th Chalakatha-Cherokee-Metis, father **with Sarah** of Girt Jolly/80, Rachel Jolly/82, Price Jolly/84, Elizabeth Jolly/86, Sarah Jolly (2)/88 & Golista Jolly/90-all 17/32nd Chalakatha-Pekowi-Cherokee Metis, **with Emory** of William Jolly/83 & John Jolly Jr/85-both ½ Chalakatha-Pekowi-Cherokee Metis, adopted father of **Sam Houston**/93-white-(some connection of Sam Houston/93 to Betsy/86 &

Jennie Due-Houston/88?)

738. Jolly, John Jr – ½ Chalakatha-Pekowi-**Cherokee**-Metis born 1785 Great Tellico TN-**killed** 1814 AL - son of **Elizabeth Emory**/65 & **Chief John Jolly**/58, Capt. John McLemore Co-**with U.S. Army**-Creek War/1813, killed at Horseshoe Bend/1814, wife & children unknown

739. Jolly, William – ½ **Chalakatha**-Pekowi-Cherokee-Metis born 1783 Great Tellico TN-died after 1810 (OH?) - son of **Elizabeth Emory**/65 & **Chief John Jolly**/85, brother of John Jolly Jr/85, moved north about 1803 to live **with Ohio Shawnee**, husband 1803 OH of **Chalakatha Woman**/85, children unknown

740. Joseph, Shawnee aka **Shawnee Joe** - Chalakatha born about 1770 OHdied after 1817 - raiding Ohio River valley/88-92, Blue Jacket War/88-94, scout**with U.S. Army**-War 1812-Thames/1813, a warrior at Lewistown 1817, Treaty 1817

741. Josey - 1/2 Mekoche-Metis born about 1780 OH-died after 1817 - son of **Mekoche Man** & **Adopted White Woman, with U.S. Army**-Thames/1813, Treaty 1817 **(not Joseph Parks)**

742. Journeycake, Charles Neshapanacumin – 1/8th Thawikila-**Delaware**Metis born 1811 OH-died 1894 Nowata Co OK – son of **Sally Williams**/92 & **Solomon Journeycake**/70, husband by 1832 of **Kate Blue Jacket**/1812, children unknown

743. Jumping Cat – adopted-Seneca born about 1740 (PA?)-died after 1780 - wife 1755 OH of **Chalakatha Man**/34, widow in 1780, children unknown

744. Justice, Ned – ½ Kishpoko-**Cherokee** born 1790 KY-died after 1851 – son of **Dick Justice-Uwenahi-Oowenahee-Tsusti-Just Man-Wealthy Man**-**Buffalo Horns**/55-Cherokee & **Kishpoko Woman** (his 2nd or 3rd of 3), husband 1810 of **Rachel Dougherty**/90, father of Uyawana-Ooyawana Justice/1815, Ned Justice Jr/1817, Utalana-Ootalana Justice/1819, Desogasgi-Tesoogerskee Justice/1821, Gunutagi-Kuntakee Justice/1823, Catherine Justice/1825, Going Back Justice/1827, Tseyanata-Cheyarnertah Justice/1829, John Justice/1831 & Skali Justice/1833-all 27/64th Chalakatha-Thawikila-Pekowi-Creek-CherokeeMetis

K

745. Kachschwuchdaniontee – Chalakatha born about 1720 PA-died about

1758 OH in epidemic - raiding PA/40, Braddock/55, raiding New-Shenandoah River valleys/55, raiding PA/55-56, raiding Ohio-New River valleys/58

746. Kaghsigwarante aka Kaghseegwarantee – Mekoche born about 1750 OH-died after 1785 – Cornstalk War/68-77, Point Pleasant/74, Blue Jacket War/77-82, raiding KY-VA-OH/77-81, Point Pleasant/78, Boonesboro/78, Blue Licks/82, Crawford/82

747. Kakawatchekee aka **Pheasant** (1)-Kawcowatchety-KawawachekeeCawcawatchety-Cockawatchy-Cochawitchakee – Pekowi born about 1680 INdied about 1752 OH – living in PA-MD by 1700, succeeded **Straight TailMeaurroway** as **Head Pekowi Chief** in PA-MD 1700-52, moved from PA to
OH 1744, succeeded as **Head Pekowi Chief** in PA by relative **Poxinosa**/1680 1744, succeeded as **Head Pekowi Chief** in OH by **Opessa**/1680 1752, husband 1st 1700 PA of **PekowiWoman**/85, 2nd before 1730 PA of **Adopted White Woman**/10 aka **Mother of Hard Man**, children/1700-30 **with Pekowi** unknown, father **with White Woman** of Hard Man/30 & other 1/2 Pekowi-Metis children

748. Kakinathucca (1) aka Kakeenathooka- Kekinathuka – Thawikila born about 1740 OH-died 1806 OH – Cornstalk War/58-77, French-Indian War/58-63, raiding Ohio-New River valleys/58, Pontiac War/62-66, Bushy Run/63, raiding New-Jackson-Greenbrier River valleys/63, raiding Ohio-Little Kanawha-Big Sandy-New River valleys/72, Point Pleasant/74, raiding Ohio-New River valleys/75, Blue Jacket War/77-94, raiding KY-VA-OH/77-81, raiding Ohio River valley/88, Treaty Greenville 1795, husband 1760 OH of **Metsigemewa**/45Thawikila, father of Bores In-Kekanathuko-Kakinathucca (2)/60 & Altowesa/70, adopted father of **Boosini**/60-Black & 1788 of **Thomas Ridout**/70-white

749. Kalkoo – Mekoche born about 1780 OH-died after 1817 - a warrior from Wapaghonettat 1817, Treaty 1817

750. Kalositah aka Kaloseetah – Kishpoko born about 1800 OH-died after 1838 - well known, successful & renowned professional wrestler in OH, over 6' tall & over 200 lb., possibly husband of a **Wyandot Woman**, children unknown

751. Kannawhaee aka Kannawhaee-Kanawhae - adopted-Cherokee born about 1750 TN-died after 1779 (OH?) – Cornstalk War/68-77, raiding Ohio-Big Sandy-Little Kanawha-New River valleys/72, Point Pleasant/74-75-78, raiding KY-VA-OH/77, Boonesboro/78, husband 1770 KY of **Chalakatha Woman**/55, children unknown

752. Kashtesh – Mekoche born about 1730 OH-died after 1766 - FrenchIndian War/54-63, Braddock/55, raiding New-Shenandoah River valleys/55, raiding Ohio-New River valleys/58, Pontiac War/62-66, Bushy Run/63, raiding New-Greenbrier-Jackson River valleys/63

753. Kaskee - 1/2 Kishpoko-Metis born about 1740 (IN?)-died after 1774 - son of **French-Canadian Man** & **Kishpoko Woman**, Cornstalk War/58-74, raiding Ohio-New River valleys/58, Pontiac War/62-66, Bushy Run/63, raiding New-Greenbrier-Jackson River valleys/63, raiding Ohio-New-Little KanawhaBig Sandy River valleys/72, Point Pleasant/74, living in OH **with Shawnee** 1765, husband 1760 (OH?) of **Kishpoko Woman**/45

754. Katewikacha aka Kateweekacha – Chalakatha born about 1790 OH-died after 1815 - Prophet's Town/1811, **left Tecumseh & Prophet** 1811, living in Apple Creek 1815

755. Kayoughshoutong – Chalakatha born about 1730 PA-died after 1766 - French-Indian War/54-63, Braddock/55, raiding New-Shenandoah River valleys/55, raiding PA/55-56, raiding Ohio-New River valleys/58, Pontiac War/62-66, Bushy Run/63, raiding New-Greenbrier-Jackson River valleys/63

756. Kaysewaesekah – Mekoche born about 1760 OH-died after 1795 – Blue Jacket War/77-94, raiding KY-VA-OH/77-81, Boonesboro/78, Blue Licks/82, raiding Ohio River valley/88-92, Treaty Greenville 1795

757. Keenateta – adopted-Delaware born about 1740 OH-died after 1784 – Cornstalk War/58-77, raiding Ohio-New River valleys/58, Pontiac War/62-66, Bushy Run/63, raiding New-Greenbrier-Jackson River valleys/63, raiding Ohio-New-Big Sandy-Little Kanawha River valleys/72, Point Pleasant/74-78, Blue Jacket War/77-84, Crawford/82, husband about 1760 OH of **Mekoche Woman**/45, father of several 1/2 Mekoche-Delaware children/60-84

758. Keeshequeatama aka Keeshekweeatama – Chalakatha born about 1720 PA-died about 1758 OH in epidemic - raiding PA/40, French-Indian War/54, Braddock/55, raiding New-Shenandoah River valleys/55, raiding PA/55-56, raiding Ohio-New River valleys/58

759. Keeweton aka Keeweton Hokolesqua-Keywayton-Quiouiton-QuiwetahnKeewetahn-Kwiwitahn - 7/8th Chalakatha-Mekoche-Metis born 1714 PA-died about 1804 OH - son of **Okowellos Hokolesqua**/1674 & **Katee Mekoche**/1680, moved to AL with father 1725, returned to PA by 1730, may have returned to AL for a short while in 1755, over 6' tall, raiding PA/40, Cornstalk War /55-77, French-Indian War/54-63, Braddock/55, raiding New-Shenandoah River valleys/55, raiding PA/55-56, raiding Ohio-New River

valleys/58, a **Chalakatha Chief** in OH by 1763, Pontiac War/62-66, Bushy Run/63, raiding NewGreenbrier-Jackson River valleys/63, raiding Ohio-Little Kanawha-Big SandyNew River valleys/72, **an emissary to the Shawnee for Cornstalk** 1774, Point
Pleasant/74-78, raiding KY-OH-VA/77-80, husband 1734 PA of **Chalakatha Woman**/18, children unknown

760. Keissinantchsa aka Keyeeseeantksa – Chalakatha born about 1720 PAdied after 1778 - raiding PA/40, Cornstalk War/55-77, French-Indian War/54-63, Braddock/55, raiding New-Shenandoah River valleys/55, raiding PA/55-56, raiding Ohio-New River valleys/58, Pontiac War/62-66, Bushy Run/63, raiding New-Greenbrier-Jackson River valleys/63, raiding Ohio-Big Sandy-Little Kanawha-New River valleys/72, Point Pleasant/74-78

761. Kekentha aka Kekenseh – Mekoche born about 1775 OH-died after 1817 - Fallen Timber/94, a warrior at Wapaghonettat 1817, Treaty 1817

762. Kempeno (1) aka Joseph Sovereigns-**Kemepeno**[69] Shawno-Joseph Sufferin-Joseph Severins - adopted-white born about 1750-**killed** 1789 - son of **Gower Sovereigns**/30-white, adopted about 1755-returned to whites 1765, lived mostly as a Native for remainder of life, messenger-translator for whites, brother of **John Sovereigns**/52, **Hannah Soverigns**/54 & 1 other child, scout **with George Rogers Clark** OH campaign 1782 with brother John, Council 1786, **murdered by whites**/89, husband about 1770 OH of ½ **Mekoche-Black Metis Woman**/54-(daughter of **Mekoche husband of Gower Sovereigns** & **Adopted Mulatto Woman**, i.e. his step-sister), father of Young Kemepeno/75 & several other children/70-89-all 1/4th Mekoche-Black-Metis

763. Kemepeno, Young aka Kemepeno Shawno-Joseph Sufferin – 1/4th Mekoche-Black-Metis born about 1775 OH-died after 1813 – son of **Joseph Sovereigns**/50-adopted-white & ½ **Mekoche-Black-Metis Woman**/54, mistakenly called a former slave due to color, translator, Fallen Timber/94, scoutwith U.S. Army-Thames/1813, husband 1795 OH of **Mekoche Woman**/79, children unknown

764. Kenzie, John aka **Shawneewakee**-Silversmith - adopted-white Shawnee(later **Delaware, Seneca** & **Pottawamee**) born 1763 QUE-died 1828 IL - translator, Indian Sub-agent, silversmith, trader, Treaty 1815, 1818, husband 1st 1790 of **Margaret Peggy Koothumpum** (McKenzie)/68-adopted white daughter of Delaware chief **Koothumpum**/10, 2nd 1798 of **Eleanor Little Cornplanter** (McKillop)/70-adopted white daughter of Seneca Chief **Corn Planter**-widow of David McKillop, father **with Margaret** of William Kenzie/89, Elizabeth Kenzie/92 & James Kenzie/93-all white (Shawnee-Pottawamee-Delaware)

765. Ketakatawish aka Ketakataweesh – Mekoche born about 1750 OH-died after 1774 – Cornstalk War/68-74, raiding Little Kanawha-Big Sandy-Kanawha-Ohio-New River valleys/72, Point Pleasant/74

766. Ketakatwitchie aka Ketakaweetchee – Chalakatha born about 1720 PAdied after 1774 - raiding PA/40, Cornstalk War/55-74, French/Indian War/54-63, Braddock/55, raiding New-Shenandoah River valleys/55, raiding PA/55-56, raiding Ohio-New River valleys/58, Pontiac War/62-66, Bushy Run/63, raiding New-Jackson-Greenbrier River valleys/63, raiding Ohio-Little Kanawha-Big Sandy-New River valleys/72, Point Pleasant/74, husband 1740 (PA?) of **French/Canadian Woman**/24, father of Jean Ketakawitchie/40-1/2 ChalakathaMetis

767. Ketakatwitchie, Jean - 1/2 Chalakatha-Metis born about 1740 (PA?)-died after 1765 - son of **French/Canadian Woman**/24 & **Ketakatwitchie**/20, raiding Ohio-New River valleys/58, Pontiac War/62-66, Bushy Run/63, raiding New-Greenbrier-Jackson River valleys/63, returned by force to whites-returned to tribe & wife 1765, husband 1760 OH of **Chalakatha Woman**/45, children unknown

768. Ketaksosa – Chalakatha born about 1775 OH-died after 1817 - Fallen Timber/94, a warrior from Hog Creek 1817, Treaty 1817

769. Kethekomree – Mekoche born about 1730 OH-died after 1760 - FrenchIndian War/54-63, Braddock/55, raiding New-Shenandoah River valleys/55,
Ohio-New River valleys/58, Council Ft. Pitt Aug. 1760

770. Ketoawsa aka Ketoawga – Thawikila born about 1760 OH-died after 1817 – Blue Jacket War/77-94, raiding KY-OH-VA/77-81, Boonesboro/78, Blue Licks/82, Crawford/82, raiding Ohio River valley/88-92, a warrior from Hog Creek 1817

771. Ketukepe aka Ketuchepa-Ketuckepe – Thawikila born about 1770 OHdied after 1817 - Fallen Timber/94, a warrior from Hog Creek 1817, Treaty 1817

772. Kewaytaka aka Kooaytaka-Cuaytaka – Chalakatha born about 1775 OHdied after 1817 - Fallen Timber/94, a warrior at Wapaghonettat 1817, Treaty 1817

773. Kewepea aka Cuapea-Kooapeea – Mekoche born about 1795 OH-died after 1832 KS – Joseph Parks Co-**with U.S. Army**-Seminole War/1832, husband 1820 OH of **Mekoche Woman**/1800, father of James Kewepea/1820, 2 other sons & one daughter

774. Keys, Elizabeth Riley - wife 1810 Roane Co TN of **Isaac Keys**-white born about 1794 VA-died 1863 OK, mother of Nancy Keys/1811, Judge Riley Keys/1813, Leroy Keys/1814, Letitia Keys/1815, Lydia Keys/1824, George W. Keys/1826, Thomas J. Keys/1828, Sarah Keys/1830, Samuel Houston Keys/1832, Electa Bosworth Keys/1834, Martha Jane Keys/1835, Isaac Wm. Keys/1836, Richard Riley Keys/1837, Rachel Keys/1838, Susan Keys/1840 & Elizabeth Keys/1842-all 3/64th Chalakatha-**Cherokee**-Metis

775. Keys, Mary Polly Riley - wife 1808 (TN?) of **Samuel Keys**-white born 1787 TN-died 1855 AL, mother of Katherine Anariah Keys/1809, Richard Keys/1814, Evaline Keys/1816, Samuel Riley Keys/1819, James Madison Keys/1822, Mary Keys/1828 & Eleanor Keys/1830-all 3/64th Chalakatha-**Cherokee**-Metis

776. Kiahquah aka Keeahkwah – Kishpoko born about 1770 OH-died after 1832 KS – Blue Jacket War/88-94, raiding Ohio River valley/88-92, raiding OHKY-VA/95-1810, Prophet's Town/1811, Brownstown/1812-Monguagon/1812-1st Amherstburg/1812-Frenchtown/1813-Ft. Meigs/1813-2nd Amherstburg/1813 & Thames/1813 **with Tecumseh**, move to CAN 1815, move back to OH 1826, Treaty 1832, moved to KS 1832, husband about 1790 OH of **Mekoche Woman**/74

777. Kicking Bird – Mekoche born about 1760 OH-died after 1792 - wife 1775 OH of **Mekoche Man**/55, widow in 1792

778. Kicking Doe – Chalakatha born about 1740 PA-died after 1774 - wife about 1755 OH of **Chalakatha Man**/35, widow in 1774

779. Kicking Elk aka **Musheemwa** – Chalakatha born about 1750 OH-died after 1795 – Cornstalk War/68-77, raiding Ohio-Little Kanawha-Big Sandy-New River valleys/72, Point Pleasant/74-78, Blue Jacket War/77-94, raiding KY-OH-VA/77-81, Crawford/82, raiding Ohio River valley/88-92

780. Kikusgowlawa aka Keekusgowlawa – Thawikila born 1722 AL-died after 1779 (MO?) - move to OH from AL/55, Cornstalk War/55-74, FrenchIndian War/55-63, Braddock/55, raiding New-Shenandoah River valleys/55, Ohio-New River valleys/58, Pontiac War/62-66, Bushy Run/63, raiding NewJackson-Greenbrier River valleys/63, raiding Ohio-Big Sandy-Little Kanawha River valleys/72, Point Pleasant/74, a **Thawikila Chief** in OH before 1763, move to AL/74-back to OH/78- on to MO/79 with **Black Stump, Yellow Hawk, Red Eagle, Red Snake** & 400 families, brother of **Wife of Moluntha**/15, **Black**

Stump/20, **Weasau**/24, **Capt. Johnny**/26, **Yellow Hawk**/28, **Black Hoof**/30 & **Kishkalwa-Tiger Tail**/35, wife & children unknown

781. Killaneca aka Killancea Carpenter-Killancea White Owl (1)-Buck (1)Killileenah-Killankea-Raven of Chota – 7/16th Chalakatha-**Cherokee**-Metis born
1712 Great Tellico TN-died after 1770 Chota TN - son of **White Owl Carpenter**/1678 & **Nancy Rainmaker**/1683, adopted son of **Young Rainmaker**/1685-Cherokee & **Elder Sister of Old Hop**/1685-Chalakatha, could cipher, read & write English, Wolf Clan Cherokee, from the Overhills & Tuskasegee, pro-English faction in French-Indian War/54-63, released from Ft. Prince George 1760 by British at request of **Attakullakulla**, husband of **Bird Clan Woman**/19, father of Killancea Carpenter (2)/40-7/32nd Chalakatha-Cherokee-Metis

782. Killaque aka Killaqua Carpenter-Killaqua White Owl – 7/16th Chalakatha-**Cherokee**-Metis born 1714 Great Tellico TN-died 1758 in battle with the Creeks - son of **White Owl Carpenter**/1678 & **Nancy Rainmaker**/1683, adopted son of **Elder Sister of Old Hop**/1685-Chalakatha & **Young Rainmaker**/1685-Cherokee, could cipher, read & write English, Wolf Clan Cherokee, from the Overhills & Tuskasegee, pro-English faction in FrenchIndian War/54-63, husband 1731 Great Tellico TN of **Nionee (Hanging) Maw**/15-Cherokee, father of Katee Killaqua/37, Nikkee Killaqua/39 & Spring Frog (Killaqua) Carpenter/54-all 7/32nd Chalakatha-Cherokee-Metis

783. Killaqua, Katee aka Katee Carpenter – 7/32nd Chalakatha-**Cherokee**-Metis born 1737 Great Tellico TN-died 1806 Shawnee Village OH – daughter of **Killancea Carpenter (1)** /14 & **Nionee Hanging Maw**/15, wife 1755 Running Water TN of **Black Beard Cornstalk**/35, mother of Daughter of Black Beard/55, Young Black Beard Cornstalk/60 & other children/55-77 names unknown-all 15/32nd Chalakatha-Mekoche-Pekowi-Cherokee-Metis

784. Killaqua, Nikkee aka Nikkee Carpenter – 7/32nd Chalakatha-**Cherokee**Metis born 1738 Great Tellico TN-died 1809 Shawnee Village OH – daughter of
Killaqua Carpenter (1) /14 & **Nionee Hanging Maw**/15, 1st wife 1758 Running Water TN of **Black Wolf Cornstalk**/40, mother of Young Black Wolf Cornstalk/60 & other children/61-85-all 15/32nd Chalakatha-Mekoche-Pekowi-Cherokee-Metis

785. Kincaid, Alley – adopted-white born 1746-died after 1765 - adopted 1755-returned to whites-returned to tribe 1765, wife 1760 OH of **Mekoche**

Man/40, mother of three 1/2 Mekoche-Metis children/61-64 (surname possibly Kincaid?)

786. King, John (2) – Mekoche born about 1784 PA-died 1864 WV - son of **John King (1)-King John**/50-Mekoche & **Mekoche Woman**/55, a Christian Shawnee, husband 1804 PA of **Christina Yeager**/85-3/4th Delaware-Metis, stayed in PA when father left for MO, living in **Mason Co. WV** about 1824, father of William Richard King/1805, Peter King/1807, John King Jr/1809, George King/1811, James King/1812, Elizabeth King/1813, Hugh King/1816, Levi King/1817, Jacob King/1818, Alexander King/1820, Mary King/1822, Francis King/1823, Delila King/1824, Christina King/1826, Sarah Martha King/1828, Catherine King/1831-all 1/2 Mekoche-Delaware-Metis

787. King, Mary (1) - ½ Thawikila-**Chickasaw** born about 1746 (AL?)-died 1836 SC - daughter of **Squirrel King**/10-Chickasaw & **Thawikila Woman**/10 - wife 1762 SC of **Edward Ned Vann (2)**/44, mother of Edward Ned Vann (3)/63, Margaret Vann/66, William Vann/70, Edith B. Vann/74, Vashti Vann/76 & Mason Vann/77-all 3/8th Chalakatha-Thawikila-**Cherokee**-Chickasaw-Metis

788. Kishkalawa (1) aka **Keeshkalawa**[70] - Chalakatha born about 1710 PAdied 1760OH - raiding PA/40, French-Indian War/54-60, Braddock/55, raiding New-Shenandoah River valleys/55, raiding PA/55-56, raiding Ohio-New River valleys/58

789. Kishkalawa (2) aka Young Kishkalawa – Chalakatha born about 1780 OH-died after 1825 KS - son of **Son of Kishkalwa**, scout-**with U.S. Army-**War 1812-Thames/1813, Treaty 1825, grandson of **Kishkalawa (1)**/10, moved to KS after 1825

790. Kishkalwa (1) aka **Tiger Tail**-Keeshkalwa – Thawikila born about 1735 OH-died before 1832 MO – Cornstalk War/55-74, Braddock/55, raiding NewShenandoah River valleys/55, raiding PA/55-56, raiding Ohio-New River valleys/58, Pontiac War/62-66, Bushy Run/63, raiding New-Greenbrier-Jackson River valleys/63, raiding Ohio-Big Sandy-Little Kanawha-New River valleys/72, Point Pleasant/74, a **Thawikila Chief** before 1770, moved to AL with Creeks/74 after Point Pleasant/74-returned to OH/79-moved to MO about 1790, took no part in Blue Jacket War or War 1812, Delegation to D.C. 1825, succeeded by **Jim Squire-Paylawestha** as **major chief in MO**, youngest brother of **Wife of Moluntha**/15, **Black Stump**/20, **Kikusglowlawa**/22, **Weasaau**/24, **Capt. Johnny**/26, **Yellow Hawk**/28 & **Black Hoof**/30, husband 1st by 1755 OH of **Thawikila Woman**/40, 2nd about 1773 OH of **Gray Eyes**/50-adopted white, father **with Thawikila** of Young-Kishkalwa/60, Pamaloois/70 & other

children/55-73, father **with Gray Eyes** of daughter Tohsi/74, son Seleetha/75 & 7 other sons-all 1/2 Thawikila-Metis

791.   Kishkalwa, **Gray Eyes** aka Wepayqueleequa-Weepaykweleekwa[71] - adopted-white born about 1750-died after 1825 - adopted about 1765-never returned to whites, 2nd wife about 1773 OH of **Kishkalwa**/35, moved with family to AL 1774-returned to OH 1779-moved to MO 1790, mother of daughter
Tohsi/74, son Seleetha/75 & 7 other sons-all 1/2 Thawikila-Metis

792.   Kishkalwa, Pamaloois – Thawikila born about 1770 OH-died after 1815
- daughter of **Kishkalwa (1)**/35 & **Thawikila Woman**/40, moved to MO about 1790, living in Apple Creek MO 1815, wife about 1785 OH of **Thawikila Man**/65

793. Kishkalwa, Seleetha - 1/2 Thawikila-Metis born about 1795 MO-died after 1825 - son of **Kishkalwa (1)**/35 & **Gray Eyes**/50-adopted white, brother of sister Toshi & 7 brothers, husband about 1815 of **Thawikila Woman**/1800

794. Kishkalwa, Tohshi - 1/2 Thawikila-Metis born about 1796 MO-died after 1825 - daughter of **Kishkalwa (1)**/35 & Gray Eyes/50-adopted white, a Thawikila, sister of Seleetha & 7 other brothers, wife about 1810 of **Thawikila Man**/90

795. Kishkalwa, Young aka **Young Tiger Tail** – Thawikila born about 1760 OH-died about 1838 KS - son of **Kishkalwa (1)**/35 & **Thawikila Woman**/40, a Thawikila warrior, moved to Creeks in AL with family/74-returned to OH/79moved to MO/90, took no part in Blue Jacket War or War of 1812, living at
Apple Creek MO 1815, move to KS about 1832

796. Kisinoutha aka Keeseenootha – Chalakatha born about 1730 PA-died after 1765 – Cornstalk War/55-65, French-Indian War/54-63, Braddock/55, raiding New-Shenandoah River valleys/55, raiding PA/55-56, raiding Ohio-New River valleys/58, Pontiac War/62-65, Bushy Run/63, raiding New-Greenbrier-Jackson River valleys/63, Council Logstown 1765

797. Kiskomonnetta aka Keeskomonetta – Pekowi born about 1680 IN-died after 1737 – in PA by 1700, living on the Allegheny River 1737

798. Kiskoquallah aka Keekokwallah – Pekowi born about 1690 TN-died after 1743 - raiding PA/40, a **Pekowi Chief** in PA before 1743

799. Kismichepilla aka Keesmeechepeella – Chalakatha born about 1710 PAdied after 1751 (AL?) - raiding PA/40, living with Creeks 1751

800. Kitegista aka Kitegista Rainmaker-Kittegunsta-**Skalilosken**-ShallelockePrince of Chota-Speaker-Nephew of Old Hop - 1/2 Chalakatha-**Cherokee** born 1710 Chota TN-**killed** 1792 Buchanan Station TN - son of **Elder Sister of Old Hop**/1684-Chalakatha & **Young Rainmaker**/1680-Cherokee, (mistakenly rumored to be son of his aunt Quatsey Rainmaker (2)/1682-Cherokee & John
Beamer/1676-white =1/2 Cherokee-Metis but is referred to as a **nephew of Old Hop**), from the Overhills-Middle towns & Chota, Blind Savannah Clan Cherokee, delegation to ENG 1730, shared power/authority with his brother **Oconastota** after death of **Old Hop** in 1761, Council with **Attakullakulla** & British, delegation to Philadelphia 1791, Council Coyatee 1792, a Chickamauga, killed at Buchanan Station 1792 with sons Young Kitegista/37 & Kiachatalee/35, husband 1st 1728 Chota TN of **Betty Turnbridge**/10-white, 2nd 1735 Chota TN of **Cherokee Woman**/20, father with **Turnbridge** of Kiachatalee KitegistaRainmaker/35-1/4th Chalakatha-Cherokee-Metis, **with Cherokee** of Johnny (of
Tenase) Kitegista-Rainmaker/36, Kitegista Rainmaker (2)/37, Betty Kitegista-Rainmaker/38-all 1/4th Chalakatha-Cherokee

801. Kizer, Charity (1) aka Charity Kaiser-Keezer - 1/2 Chalakatha-Metis born about 1785 OH-died after 1808 - daughter of **Polly Kizer**/42-adopted white & **Tom Lewis**/60, sister of **Little Lewis**/80, half-sister of **Rachel Kizer**/61 & **Mary Kizer**/75, wife 1808 of **Uriah Blue**/82-1/4th Chalakatha-Metis, children unknown

802. Kizer, Charity (2) - 3/4th Chalakatha-Metis born about 1805 OH-died after 1825 - daughter of **Ben Kizer**/82 & **Chalakatha Woman**/87, wife 1825 of **John McCullough**-white/1800, children unknown

803. Kizer, Mary aka Mary Kaiser-Keezer - 1/2 Chalakatha-Metis born about 1775 OH-died after 1800 - daughter of **Polly Kizer**/42-adopted-white & **Chalakatha Man**/35, sister of **Rachel Kizer**/61, half-sister of **Little Lewis**/80 & **Charity Kizer**/85, living in **Mason Co WV** by 1800, wife before 1800 of **Patrick Board**/50-white

804. Kizer, Polly aka Polly Kaiser-Keezer-Pollykizer - adopted-white born about 1742 NJ-died after 1817 OH - adopted about 1755-returned to whitesreturned to tribe 1765, a woman at Lewistown 1817, Treaty 1817, living in home of John & Mary Lewis 1817, wife 1st about 1755 of **Chalakatha Man**/35 (likely an uncle of **Tom & John Lewis**), 2nd about 1779 of **Tom Lewis**/60-Chalakatha, mother **with Chalakatha** of Rachel Kizer/61 & Mary Kizer/75,

other children likely-all 1/2 Chalakatha-Metis, **with Lewis** of Little Lewis/80, Ben Kizer/82 &
Charity Kizer/85-all 1/2 Chalakatha-Metis

805. Kizer, Rachel - 1/2 Chalakatha-Metis born about 1761 OH-died after 1800 - daughter of **Polly Kizer**/42-adopted white & **Chalakatha Man**/35 (likely an uncle of Tom & John Lewis), sister of **Mary Kizer**/75, half-sister of **Little Lewis**/80 & **Charity Kizer**/85, returned to whites-returned to tribe with Polly 1765, wife about 1785 of **Capt. Johnny Moluntha**/65-15/16th ChalakathaMekoche-Metis, mother of two known 23/32nd Chalakatha-Mekoche-Metis children/86-90

806. Kline, Suzette Lafrance - 1/2 Mekoche-Metis born about 1766 (IN-IL?)died after 1781 - daughter of **Mekoche Woman** & **Mr. Lafrance**-French/Canadian, wife 1781 of **Michael Kline**/60-white, children unknown

807. Knanakhih aka Kananakhee – Kishpoko born about 1760 OH-died after 1817 – Blue Jacket War/87-94, raiding KY-OH-VA/77-81, Crawford/82, raiding Ohio River valley/88-92, Fallen Timber/94

808. Knox's Son, Peter - 1/2 Mekoche-**Seneca**-Metis born about 1790-died after 1832 - son of **Mekoche Woman** & **Peter Knox**-1/2 Seneca-Metis, **with U.S. Army**-War 1812-Thames/1813, Treaty 1832, moved to KS 1832

809. Koghkela – Kishpoko born about 1790 OH-died after 1817 - Prophet's Town/1811, Brownstown/1812-Monguagon/1812-1st Amherstburg/1812Frenchtown/1813-Ft. Meigs/1813-2nd Amherstburg/1813 & Thames/1813 **with**
Tecumseh, Treaty 1817

810. Kulaquati aka Koolakwatee – Mekoche born about 1740 OH-died about 1802 OH – Cornstalk War/58-77, raiding Ohio-New River valleys/58, Pontiac War/62-66, Bushy Run/63, raiding New-Greenbrier-Jackson River valleys/63, raiding Ohio-Big Sandy-Little Kanawha-New River valleys/72, Point Pleasant/74-78, Blue Jacket War/77-82, raiding OH-KY-VA/77-81, Crawford/82, medicine man, allied with **Prophet & Tecumseh**, had **Beaver** & others killed

811. **Kumshaka**^{72} aka Kumshaka Puckenshinwa-Kunshauskau-**Cat Flying In Air** - 3/4th Kishpoko-Pekowi-Creek-Metis born 1770 OH-died before 1824 CAN - 5th son of **Puckenshinwa**/35 & **Metheotashe Opessa**/40, a Kishpoko warrior, raiding Ohio River valley/88-92, Blue Jacket War/87-94, raiding OH-KY-VATN/95-10, Prophet's Town/1811, Brownstown/1812-Monguagon/1812-1st Amherstburg/1812-Frenchtown/1813-Ft. Meigs/1813-2nd Amherstburg/1813 & Thames/1813 **with Tecumseh**, moved to CAN 1815, died before band returned

to OH 1825, husband about 1790 OH of **Kishpoko Woman**/74, children unknown

812. **Kwatooka aka Quatucka-He's Afraid-He Who Is Afraid**[73] – Chalakatha-Mekoche born about 1727 PA-died about 1758 OH in epidemic OH – son of **Father of Black Fish**/05 & **Mother of Black Fish**/10, brother of **Black Fish**/25 & Nakanapaseka/29, raiding PA/55, raiding New-Shenandoah valleys/55, Braddock/55, raiding PA/55-56, raiding Ohio-New River valleys/58, wife & children unknown

813. Kyanthawtah – Kishpoko born about 1790 OH-died 1850 KS - Prophet's Town/1811, Brownstown/1812, Monguagon/1812, 1st Amherstburg/1812, Frenchtown/1813, Ft. Meigs/1813, 2nd Amherstburg/1813 & Thames/1813 **with Tecumseh**, 1st husband (likely at least his 2nd) about 1835 KS of **Pasequahmease Tecumseh**/1822, son in law of **Naythahwaynah**, grandson in law of **Tecumseh**, children unknown

Section X
Laathska to Lowery (L)

L

814. Laathska aka Lahathska - Pekowi born about 1790 OH-died after 1817 - Prophet's Town/1811, Brownstown/1812-Monguagon/1812-1st Amherstburg/1812-Frenchtown/1813-Ft. Meigs/1813-2nd Amherstburg/1813 & Thames/1813 **with Tecumseh**, Treaty 1817.

815. LaForce, Ambrosia - 3/4th Chalakatha-Kishpoko-Black-Metis born about 1790-died after 1815 - daughter of **Grace LaForce** aka **Lavielle-Queen**/67 & **Kishpoko Man**/60, living in Apple Creek MO 1815, wife about 1805 (OH-MO?) of **Chalakatha Man**/85, mother of several 7/8th Chalakatha-Kishpoko-Black-Metis children/1805-15, names unknown

816. LaForce, Candis aka **Candis McKee** - 1/2 Chalakatha-Black-Metis born 1765-died after 1794 - daughter of **Hannah LaForce**/48 & **Chalakatha Man**, former LaForce slave, captured 1780 at Martin's Station KY, given to **Col. Alexander McKee**-adopted-white, never returned, slave-wife 1781 OH of **Col. Alexander McKee**/25-adopted white, mother of Rachel McKee/82-1/4th Chalakatha-Black-Metis

817. LaForce, Cottawahcothi aka Black Body⁷⁴ LaForce-**Black Body** - 3/4ᵗʰ Chalakatha-Mekoche-Black-Metis born about 1788 OH-died 1846 KS - son of **Mekoche Man**/63 & **Rachel LaForce-Apple-laPomme**/68, moved to KS 1832, Joseph Parks Co-**with U.S. Army**-Seminole War/1837, husband 1ˢᵗ by 1808 OH of **Chalakatha Woman**/90, 2ⁿᵈ by 1822 OH of **Mekoche Woman**/1807, children 1808-22 **with Chalakatha** unknown, father **with Mekoche** of Elizabeth Black Body/1822, other children likely

818. LaForce, **Flat Belly** aka LaPlatventra - 3/4ᵗʰ Chalakatha-Mekoche-BlackMetis born 1784-died after 1815 - daughter of **Rachel LaForce** aka **AppleLaPomme**/68 & **Mekoche Man**/63, living in Apple Creek MO 1815, wife about
1800 of **Mekoche Man**/80, mother of several 7/8ᵗʰ Mekoche-Chalakatha-BlackMetis children/1800-15, names unknown

819. LaForce, Grace aka **Lavielle-Queen** - 1/2 Chalakatha-Black-Metis born 1767-died after 1815 (MO?) - daughter of **Hannah LaForce**/48 & **Chalakatha Man**, former LaForce slave, taken 1780-Martin's Station, never returned, living in Apple Creek MO 1815, wife 1780 of **Kishpoko Man**/60, mother of Ambrosia LaForce/90 & several other 3/4ᵗʰ Chalakatha-Kishpoko-Black Metis children/80-1812, names unknown

820. LaForce, Hannah aka Hannah Fisher - adopted-Mulatto born about 1748died after 1780 - daughter of **Betty LaForce**/34 & **White Man** (likely Rene LaForce), former LaForce slave, captured 1780-Martin's Station, given to **Fredrick Fisher**-adopted white, freed by Fisher & never returned, wife 1ˢᵗ 1764 (PA-OH-WV?) of **Chalakatha Man**, 2ⁿᵈ 1780 of **Fredrick Fisher**/40-adoptedwhite, mother **with Chalakatha** of Candis LaForce/65, Job LaForce/66, Rachel
LaForce/67, Patrick LaForce/68, Grace LaForce/69-all 1/2 Chalakatha-Black-Metis, any children **with Fisher** unknown

821. LaForce, James aka **James Force** - adopted-Mulatto born 1752-died after 1824 - son of **Betty LaForce**/34 & **White Man** (likely Rene LaForce), former LaForce slave, captured 1780-Martin's Station, given to **Philip LeDuc**/40-white-(adopted-Chippewa), freed by LeDuc by 1800, husband 1805 (OH?) of **Mary Williams**/90-1/2 Wyandot-Metis, father of Sarah Force/1824 & other children/1805-30-all 1/4ᵗʰ Wyandot-Black-Metis

822. LaForce, Kijah aka Keggy-Kejiah-Kijah Elliott - adopted-Mulatto born about 1760-died after 1794 - daughter of **Betty LaForce**/34-adopted-Mulatto & **White Man** (likely Rene LaForce), former LaForce slave, taken 1780-Martin's Station, given to **Col. Matthew Elliott**/30-adopted-white, never returned, wife

about 1785 OH of Col. Elliott's son **Daniel Elliott**/67-1/2 Pekowi-Metis, widow 1794, mother of about four 1/4th Pekowi-Black-Metis children/85-94 named Elliott

823. LaForce, Rachel aka **Apple-Lapomme** - 1/2 Chalakatha-Black-Metis born 1768-died after 1815 (MO?) - daughter of **Hannah LaForce**/48 & **Chalakatha Man**, former LaForce slave, taken 1780-Martin's Station, stayed with tribe 1795, living in Apple Creek MO 1815, wife 1783 OH of **Mekoche Man**/63, mother of Flat Belly-Laplatventra/84, Black Body-Cottawahcothi/88 & several other 3/4th Chalakatha-Mekoche-Black-Metis children/84-1813

824. Lail, George (1) - adopted-white born 1773 N.C.-died 1853 MO - captured 1780 at Ruddle's Station KY-taken to MO-returned to whites 1795, son of **Margaret**/36 & **George Lail**/30-both white, nephew of **Henry Lail**/55, MO Mounted Militia-**with U.S. Army**-War of 1812, husband 1st about 1791 MO of **Kishpoko Woman**/75, 2nd about 1797 MO of **Louisa Wolf**/80-adopted white, father **with Kishpoko** of a George Lail Jr/92 & Margaret Lail/94-both 1/2 Kishpoko-Metis, children **with Wolf** unknown

825. Lail, Henry - adopted-white born about 1753-died 1830 AR - captured 1780 at Ruddle's Station KY-stayed with tribe, uncle of **George Lail**/71, husband about 1780 OH of **Kishpoko Woman**/65, father of Maria Lail/81, Elizabeth Lail/83, George Lail (2)/84, John Lail/86 & 3 more daughters/87-1800-all 1/2 Kishpoko-Metis

826. Lakose – Thawikila born about 1770 OH-died after 1817 – Blue Jacket War/87-94, a warrior at Hog Creek 1817, Treaty 1817

827. Lalahowcheka – Chalakatha born about 1770 OH-died after 1832 KS - raiding Ohio River valley/88-92, Blue Jacket War/87-94, raiding OH-KYVA/95-1810, Prophet's Town/1811, Brownstown/1812-Monguagon/1812-1st Amherstburg/1812-Frenchtown/1813-Ft. Meigs/1813-2nd Amherstburg/1813 & Thames/1813 **with Tecumseh**, moved to CAN 1815, moved back to OH about 1825, Treaty 1832, moved to KS 1832

828. Lame Buffalo – Chalakatha born about 1740 PA-died after 1786 – slightly crippled in one leg from wound in battle, Cornstalk War/58-77, raiding New-Ohio River valleys/58, Pontiac War/62-66, Bushy Run/63, raiding NewGreenbrier-Jackson River valleys/63, raiding Ohio-Big Sandy-Little KanawhaNew River valleys/72, Point Pleasant/74-78, Blue Jacket War/77-86, raiding KY-
VA-OH/77-81, Boonesboro/78, Crawford/82

829. Lame Doctor - adopted-Seneca born about 1780 OH-died after 1832 KS

- scout-**with U.S. Army**-War 1812-Thames/1813, Treaty 1832, move to KS 1832, husband by 1800 OH of **Mekoche Woman**/85

830. Lame Wife – Mekoche born about 1740 OH-died after 1775 (OH?) - limped from wound received from whites, wife 1755 OH of **Mekoche Man**/35, widow 1775

831. Lamkesheka – Mekoche born about 1785 OH-died after 1817 - a warrior from Wapaghonettat 1817, Treaty 1817

832. Lamotothe aka Lamatothe-Lamotoshe-Lamotoseh - Mekoche born about 1775 OH-died after 1832 KS – Fallen Timber/94, raiding OH-KY-VA/95-1810, Prophet's Town/1811, Brownstown/1812-Monguagon/1812-1st Amherstburg/1812-Frenchtown/1813-Ft. Meigs/1813-2nd Amherstburg/1813 & Thames/1813 **with Tecumseh**, a warrior from Wapaghonettat 1817, Treaty 1817, move to KS 1832

833. Lanawytuka – Chalakatha born about 1790 OH-died after 1817 - Prophet's Town/1811, Brownstown/1812-Monguagon/1812-1st Amherstburg/1812-Frenchtown/1813-Ft. Meigs/1813-2nd Amherstburg/1813 & Thames/1813 **with Tecumseh**, Treaty 1817

834. Langley, Uckteeyah aka Wakteeyah - **Creek**-Metis born about 1790-died about 1816 – likely daughter of **Noah Langley**-white & **Annie Self**-Creek-Metis, sister of **Wokteeyah Langley**/85-(3rd wife of **Sequoyah**), 1st wife 1815 (TNAR?) of **Teesey Gist**/88, mother of George Gist (3)/1815, Richard Gist (3)/1816, Joseph Gist (1)/1817, Wahlenetah Gist/1818, Wahlaloo Gist/1819, Lydia Gist/1820, Crawfish Gist/1821, Chuwanoskee Gist/1822 & Nancy Gist/23-all 13/64th Chalakatha-Pekowi-Creek-Cherokee-Metis

835. Langley, Wokteeyah aka Utiyuwokteeyah Langley Sequoyah - **Creek**Metis born about 1785-died after 1804 – likely daughter of **Noah Langley**-white & **Annie Self**-Creek-Metis, 3rd wife about 1798 of **Sequoyah-George Gist**/59, sister of **Uckteeyah Langley**/90-(1st wife of step-son **Teesey Gist**/88), mother of daughters Oolootsa Gist (2)/99 & Gooneki Gist (2)/1800-both 9/32nd Chalakatha-
Pekowi-Creek-Cherokee-Metis

836. Laskigitchi aka Laskigitchi Mayapple -Laskigitchi Hop-Nephew (4) of Standing Turkey-Old Hop – Chalakatha-Kishpoko born 1723 Settico TN-**killed** 1776 Ft. Pitt PA - son of **May Apple**/1690-Kishpoko & **Ghigoneli Hop**/1694-Chalakatha, from Settico, raiding New-Ohio valleys/58, Pontiac War/62-66,

Bushy Run/63, raiding New-Jackson-Greenbrier valleys/63, raiding New-Little Kanawha-Ohio-Big Sandy valleys/72, Point Pleasant/74, Cherokee War/75, **killed by Americans** while held captive, half-brother of **John French**/10 & **Cappee French**/12, husband 1743 Running Water TN of **Blind Savannah Woman**/30, children/44-76 unknown

837. LaPorte, Isabella Dusquene aka Isabella LaPrairie-Isabella Muskkodence – wife 1st by 1805 of **Joseph LaPorte**-white born about 1780 CAN-died after 1805, mother of Joseph LaPorte Jr/1805-1/4th Chalakatha-Mekoche-Pekowi-Wyandot-Metis

838. Lassalle, Jacques – 1/8th Pekowi-**Metis** born about 1767-died 1815 St. Antoine MI - son of **Jacques Lassale**/35 & **Therese Berthelet dit Savoyard**, Blue Jacket War/90-94, translator, Treaty Greenville 1795, son in law of **Blue Jacket**/35, husband 1790 OH (church marriage 1801 Detroit MI) of **Marie Louise Blue Jacket**/74, father of Marie Antoinette Lassalle/91, Jacques Lassalle Jr/1802, Susannah Lassalle/1804, Julia Lassalle/1806-3/8th Pekowi-KishpokoMetis

839. Lassalle, Marie Antoinette aka Maryanne-Nanette - 3/8th PekowiKishpoko-Metis born 1791 MI-died 1881 - daughter of **Marie Louise Blue Jacket**/74 & **Jacques Lassalle**/67, granddaughter of **Blue Jacket**/35, wife 1817 Sandwich CAN of her half-uncle **Thomas Caldwell**/88-1/8th Kishpoko-Metis, mother of John Caldwell/1818, Charles Caldwell/1819, Mary Adeline Caldwell/1820, Francis Xavier Caldwell/1823, William Charles Caldwell/1826, Anthony Edward Caldwell/1827, Joseph Hubert Caldwell/1830, Teresa Caroline Caldwell/1832, Susanne Emily Caldwell/1838-all 1/4th Kishpoko-Pekowi-Metis `

840. Lathawanomo – Mekoche born about 1780 OH-died after 1817 - a warrior from Wapaghonettat 1817, Treaty 1817

841. Lawaghanicke aka Lawaghaneeka - Chalakatha born about 1720 PA-died after 1751 - raiding PA/40, among Creek in AL 1751

842. Lawagqua aka Lawagqua Opessa-Lawoughqua-Lawagkwa-**Elder Brother of Blue Jacket** – Pekowi-Kishpoko born 1733 PA-died after 1774 – trading with Ohio Fur Co. in PA **with Blue Jacket** & **Wabete** by early 1750's, Cornstalk War/55-74, French-Indian War/54-63, Braddock/55, raiding New-Shenandoah River valleys/55, raiding Ohio-New River valley/58, Pontiac War/62-65, Bushy Run/63, raiding New-Greenbrier-Jackson River valleys/63, Council Logstown PA 1765, a **Pekowi Chief** in OH 1760's-70's, returned

captives to Ft. Pitt 1765, raiding Ohio-Little Kanawha-Big Sandy-New River valleys/72, Point Pleasant/74, wife & children unknown

843. Lawetcheto – Thawikila born about 1770 OH-died after 1817 - raiding Ohio River valley/88-92, Blue Jacket War/88-94, from Hog Creek 1817

844. Lawisimo aka Lawaeeseemo – Chalakatha born about 1730 PA-died after 1765 – Cornstalk War/55-65, French-Indian War/54-63, Braddock/55, raiding New-Shenandoah River valleys/55, raiding PA/55-56, raiding Ohio-New River valleys/58, Pontiac War/62-65, Bushy Run/63, raiding New-GreenbrierJackson River valleys/63, Council Logstown 1765

845. Lawitchetee aka Laweetchetee – Thawikila born about 1780 OH-died after 1817 - from Hog Creek 1817, Treaty 1817

846. Leaning Oak aka Leaning Wood-Leaning Tree – Chalakatha born about 1745-killed 1784 KY - son of **Tall Oak**/20, Cornstalk War/63-77, Pontiac War/63-66, raiding New-Greenbrier-Jackson River valleys/63, raiding Ohio-Big Sandy-Little Kanawha-New River valleys/72, Point Pleasant/74-75-78, Blue Jacket War/77-84, raiding KY-VA-OH/77-81, Boonesboro/78, Blue Licks/82, Crawford/82, a Chalakatha warrior, living in KY 1784 **with Shawnee-Cherokee**, brother of **Little Oak**/40, nephew of **Black Oak**/25 & **Moose**/30

847. LeBeace - 1/2 Chalakatha-**Ottawa**-Metis born about 1740-died after 1774 - son of **Ottawa-French/Canadian-Metis** & **Chalakatha Woman**, Cornstalk War/58-74, raiding Ohio-New River valleys/58, Pontiac War/62-66, Bushy Run/63, raiding Ohio-Little Kanawha-Big Sandy-New River valleys/72, Point Pleasant/74, husband about 1760 OH of **Chalakatha Woman**/45

848. LeChapaw - 1/2 Kishpoko-Mekoche-**Miami**-Metis born about 1750 (IN?)-died after 1778 - son of **1/2 Kishpoko-French/Canadian Metis** & **1/2 Mekoche-Miami Woman**, Cornstalk War/58-74, raiding Little Kanawha-Big Sandy-Ohio-New River valleys/72, Point Pleasant/74-78, raiding KY-VA-OH/77, husband by 1770 OH of **Kishpoko Woman**/54, children unknown

849. LeDagneau, Jean Baptiste - 1/2 Chalakatha-Metis born about 1730-died after 1768 - son of **Mr. Dagneau**-French/Canadian & **Chalakatha Woman**, Cornstalk War/55-68, French-Indian War/54-63, Braddock/55, raiding New-Shenandoah River valleys/55, raiding Ohio-New River valleys/58, Pontiac War/62-66, Bushy Run/63, raiding New-Greenbrier-Jackson River valleys/63, apparently moved north-west after Pontiac War

850. Leeso – Thawikila born about 1770 OH-died after 1817 - raiding Ohio River valley/88-92, Blue Jacket War/88-94, a warrior from Hog Creek 1817, Treaty 1817

851. LeFevre - 1/2 Mekoche-Metis born about 1740 IL-died after 1777 - son of **Coureur deBois** & **Mekoche Woman**, Cornstalk War/58-77, raiding OhioNew River valleys/58, Pontiac War/62-66, Bushy Run/63, raiding NewGreenbrier-Jackson River valleys/63, raiding Ohio-Little Kanawha-Big SandyNew River valleys/72, Point Pleasant/74, raiding KY-OH-VA/75-77, husband about 1760 (IN?) of **Mekoche Woman**/44

852. Lekuseh – Chalakatha born about 1775 OH-died after 1817 CAN - raiding OH-KY-VA/95-1810, Prophet's Town/1811, Brownstown/1812Monguagon/1812-1st Amherstburg/1812-Frenchtown/1813-Ft. Meigs/1813-2nd Amherstburg/1813 & Thames/1813 **with Tecumseh**, move to CAN 1815

853. LeMonier - 1/2 Kishpoko-**Chippewa**-Metis born about 1715 (OH?)-died about 1758 in epidemic - son of **Chippewa-French/Canadian-Metis** & **Kishpoko Woman**, raiding PA/40, French-Indian War/54-55, Braddock/55, raiding New-Shenandoah River valleys/55, raiding PA/55-56, raiding Ohio-New River valleys/58

854. LeMothe, William Joseph (1) - 1/2 Pekowi-Metis born about 1730-died 1799 - son of **Jean Baptiste LeMothe**/1680-white & **Pekowi Woman**, Cornstalk War/55-77, French-Indian War/54-63, Braddock/55, raiding New-Shenandoah River valleys/55, raiding PA/55-56, raiding Ohio-New River valleys/58, Pontiac War/62-66, Bushy Run/63, raiding New-Greenbrier-Jackson River valleys/63, raiding Ohio-Big Sandy-Little Kanawha-New River valleys/72, Point Pleasant/74, traveling 1776 in OH **with Antoine Maisonville**/50, Blue Jacket War/77-94, raiding KY-VA-OH/77-81, Boonesboro/78, Crawford/82, raiding Ohio River valley/88-92, half-brother of **Chopin LeMothe**/30-white, brother in law of **Maurice Blondeau**/35-Chippewa-Metis & **Gabriel Cotte**/40French/Canadian, all 3 married Shawnee sisters, husband about 1760 of **Kishpoko Sister** (1)/40

855. LeMothe, William Joseph (2) - 1/2 Mekoche-Metis born about 1760-died after 1788 - son of **Chopin LeMothe**/30-white & **Mekoche Woman**/45, Blue Jacket War/78-88, Boonesboro/78, raiding OH-KY-VA/77-81, Crawford, raiding Ohio River valley/88, nephew of **William Joseph LeMothe (1)**/30, husband 1780 of **Mekoche Woman**/64

856. Leonard, Katrina - adopted white born about 1762-died after 1786 - adopted 1780-returned to whites 1786, wife 1st 1779 of **Michael Leonard**-white born 1760-killed 1780, 2nd 1780 OH of **Mekoche Man**, mother **with Mekoche** of Michael Leonard Jr/81 & 2 other children/82-86-all 1/2 Mekoche-Metis

857. Lesheshe – Mekoche born about 1790 OH-died after 1817 - a warrior from Wapaghonettat 1817, Treaty 1817

858. Lesperance, Marie – Chippewa-**Metis** (or 7/32nd Chalakatha-CherokeeChippewa-Metis) born about 1770-died after 1795 – daughter of **Chippewa Woman** & **Mr. Lesperance**-Metis (or possibly the daughter of **Daughter of Attakullakulla** & **Mr. Lesperance** = granddaughter of Attakullakulla), wife about 1794 of **David Cameron**/74-15/64th Chalakatha-Thawikila-Creek-Cherokee-Metis

859. LeTart, James aka James LeTort - adopted-French born about 1700 France-died after 1765 WV - French-Indian War/54-63, Braddock/55-with Natives, Council Logstown 1765, 1st trader west of Allegheny mountains 1730, trading post at Big Bend of Ohio River in **Mason Co. WV** 1740, husband 1734 PA of **Pekowi Woman**/20, father of James LeTart Jr/35-1/2 Pekowi-Metis

860. LeTart, James Jr aka Cahiktodo-Kahiktodo - 1/2 Pekowi-Metis born about 1735 PA-died after 1775 – son of **James LeTart**/1700-French & **Pekowi Woman**/20, Cornstalk War/55-74, French-Indian War/54-63, Braddock/55, raiding PA/55-56, raiding Ohio-New River valleys/58, Pontiac War/62-66, Bushy Run/63, Point Pleasant/74, trading post & **Pekowi/Delaware Village Chief** in Big Bend of **Mason County WV** 1765, moved to OH before 1772, husband 1755 OH of **Letart's Wife**/40-Delaware

861. Letho aka Lethew – Chalakatha born about 1770 OH-died after 1835 KS – Blue Jacket War/88-94, raiding Ohio River valley/88-92, Prophet's Town/1811, Brownstown/1812-Monguagon/1812-1st Amherstburg/1812-Frenchtown/1813-Ft. Meigs/1813-2nd Amherstburg/1813 & Thames/1813 **with Tecumseh**, a warrior at Hog Creek village 1817, Treaty 1831, a **sub-chief** 1835 under **John Perry**/75 & **William Perry**/70

862. LeTulipe, Louis - 1/2 Mekoche-Metis born about 1730 (OH-IN?)-died after 1755 - son of **French/Canadian Man** & **Mekoche Woman**, French-Indian War/54, Braddock/55, raiding New-Shenandoah River valleys/55, husband 1750 of **Mekoche Woman**/34

863. Lewis, George – Chalakatha born about 1770 OH-died after 1815 - a warrior in Lewistown (OH) 1795, , brother of **Tom Lewis**/60 & **John Lewis**/65, Harmar/90 & St. Clair/91 with Shawnee, Piomingo's Chickasaw scouts-**with U.S. Army**-Fallen Timber/94, Prophet's Town/1811 with Prophet, **left Tecumseh** with brothers after Prophet's Town, scout-**with U.S. Army**-War 1812, living in Apple Creek 1815, husband about 1790 OH of **Madeline Shawnee**/75

864.   Lewis, John aka Capt. Lewis-Col. Lewis-**Quatawepay**-KaitwawypieLittle White Man – Chalakatha born about 1765 OH-died 1826 MO - raiding OH-VA-KY/81, Blue Licks/82, Crawford/82, raiding Ohio River valley/88-92, Harmar/90, St. Clair/91-all **with Shawnee**, with Piomingo's Chickasaw scouts**with U.S. Army**-Fallen Timber/94, **Chalakatha Chief** in Lewistown OH 1795, **traveled with Tecumseh** 1795-1808, **left Tecumseh** after Prophet's Town/1811, Capt.of scouts-**with U.S. Army**-War 1812-Thames/1813, Treaty 1808, 1814, 1815, 1817, 1825, brother of **Tom Lewis**/60 & **George Lewis**/70, husband about 1785 of **Mary Succopanus**/67-1/2 Kishpoko-Seneca, no children

865.   Lewis, Tom – Chalakatha born about 1760 OH-died after 1813 - a warrior in Lewistown OH 1795, brother of **John Lewis**/65 & **George Lewis**/70, raiding OH-VA-KY 1781-92, Harmar/90, St. Clair/91-all **with Shawnee**, with Piomingo's Chickasaw scouts-**with U.S. Army**-Fallen Timber/94, with Prophet at Prophet's Town/1811, **left Tecumseh** after Prophet's Town, scout-**with U.S. Army**-War 1812-Thames/1813, husband 1st 1779 OH of **Polly Kizer**/42-adopted white, 2nd 1786 OH of **Chalakatha Woman**/70, father **with Polly** of Little Lewis/80 & Charity Kizer/85-both 1/2 Chalakatha-Metis

866.   Liberty – Pekowi born about 1745 PA-died after 1786 – Cornstalk War/62-75, Pontiac War/62-66, Bushy Run/63, raiding New-Greenbrier-Jackson River valleys/63, raiding Ohio-Little Kanawha-Big Sandy-New River valleys/72, Point Pleasant/74, messenger/scout-**with U.S. Army**-Revolution

867.   Lightfoot, Wife of Capt. John - 1/2 Thawikila-**Cherokee** born about 1740-died after 1770 - daughter of **Thawikila Woman** & **Deer Clan Man**, Deer Clan Cherokee, wife about 1760 of **Capt. John Lightfoot**/30-white born about 1730-died after 1770, mother of Nancy Lightfoot/60, Dorcas Lightfoot/66, George Lightfoot/70-all 1/4th Thawikila-Cherokee-Metis

868.   Linn, Sarah aka Sarah Ruddle - 1/2 Chalakatha-Metis born 1781-died 1839 - daughter of **Chalakatha Man** & **Theodosia Linn**/60-adopted white, adopted daughter of **George Ruddle**/57-white, returned to whites 1795 with Theodosia/60, wife 1st 1797 of **Nicholas Anger**/77-white, 2nd 1812 of **Mr. Simmons**/80-white

869.   Little Black Cat aka Little Black Woman - 1/2 Chalakatha-Black-Metis born 1750 PA-died after 1771OH - daughter of **Chalakatha Woman**/35

Shawnee Heritage

& **Black Horse**/30-adopted-Mulatto, niece of **Julia**/20-wife of **Cornstalk**/10, known to be quite attractive & small, wife 1st 1765 OH of **Chalakatha Man**/45, widow 1771, wife 2nd 1772 OH of **Mr. Rose**-likely a Jewish trader, mother **with Chalakatha** of 2 or 3 children-all 3/4th Chalakatha-Black-Metis, children **with Rose** of Edward Rose/80-1/4th Chalakatha-Black-Metis

870. Little Bouquet - 1/2 Mekoche-Metis born about 1750 (IN?)-died after 1782 - daughter of **Mekoche Woman** & **French/Canadian Man**, wife 1765 of **Kishpoko Man**/40, widow 1782

871. Little Eagle aka **Kiskipelia** – adopted-Delaware born about 1720-**killed 1758 OH** - raiding PA/40, French-Indian War/54-58, Braddock/55, raiding NewShenandoah River valleys/55, raiding PA/55-56, raiding Ohio-New River valleys/58, **killed by John Gibson**-adopted white, husband 1740 PA of **Pekowi Woman**/25, children unknown

872. Little Eel in Hand - 1/2 Thawikila-Creek-Metis born about 1751 AL-died after 1775 OH - daughter of **Creek-Metis Woman**/35 & **Thawikila Man**/30, wife 1765 OH of **Thawikila Man**/45, widow living in OH 1775, children unknown

873. Little Fox aka **Oreroimo** – Chalakatha born about 1790 OH-died after 1832 KS - Prophet's Town/1811, Brownstown/1812-Monguagon/1812-1st Amherstburg/1812-Frenchtown/1812-Ft. Meigs/1813-2nd Amherstburg/1813 & Thames/1813 **with Tecumseh**, moved to CAN 1815, moved back to OH about 1825, moved to KS 1832

874. Little Lewis aka **Quashacough-Deshau** - 1/2 Chalakatha-Metis born about 1780 OH-died after 1832 KS - son of **Tom Lewis**/60 & **Polly Kizer**/42adopted white, a Chalakatha warrior, raiding OH-KY-VA-TN/99-1810, Prophet's Town/1811, Brownstown/1812-Monguagon/1812-1st Amherstburg/1812Frenchtown/1813-Ft. Meigs/1813-2nd Amherstburg/1813 & Thames/1813 **with Tecumseh**, moved to CAN 1815, returned to OH 1825, Treaty 1831, 1832, moved to KS 1832

875. Little Melon Vine – adopted-Seneca born about 1760 OH-died after 1790 - wife 1775 OH of **Mekoche Man**/55, widow 1790, children unknown

876. **Little Moon aka Tebethtakishthok**[75] – Thawikila born about 1750 OHdied after 1779 - wife 1765 OH of **Thawikila Man**/45, widow in 1778, moved to MO 1779

877. Little Mountain – Chalakatha born about 1745 OH-died after 1775 – short, heavy woman, wife 1760 OH of **Chalakatha Man**/40, widow in 1775, children unknown

878. Little Oak aka Little Wood-Little Tree – Chalakatha born about 1740 PA-died after 1795 - son of **Tall Oak**/20, a Chalakatha warrior, Cornstalk War/58-77, raiding Ohio-New River valley/58, Pontiac War/62-66, Bushy Run/63, raiding New-Jackson-Greenbrier River valleys/63, raiding Ohio-Little Kanawha-Big Sandy-New River valleys/72, Point Pleasant/74-78, Blue Jacket War/77-94, Boonesboro/78, raiding KY-OH-VA/77-81, Crawford/82, raiding Ohio River valley/88-92, relative/same clan as **Cornstalk**, nephew of **Black Oak**/25 & **Moose**/30, brother of **Leaning Oak**/45, wife & children unknown

879. Little Owl (1) aka Little Owl Hop-**Ookoosdi**-Little Owl Attakullakulla**Nahoolah**-White Mankiller-Unegadihi-Unakata-Ishettechi-Unakateehee – ½ Chalakatha-Thawikila-Creek-**Cherokee** born 1742 Great Tellico TN-**killed** 1792 Buchanan Station TN – son of **Young Hop**/15 & **Ollie Nionee Oconastota**/20, adopted son 1746 of **Attakullakulla Carpenter**/06, from the Overhills, Wolf Clan Cherokee, Cornstalk War/62-74, Pontiac War/62-66, Bushy Run/63, raiding New-Jackson-Greenbrier River valleys/63, raiding Ohio-Big Sandy-Little Kanawha-New River valleys/72, Point Pleasant/74, Boonesboro/78, a **seceding Headman** 1777, a **Chickamauga Chief**, raiding KY-OH-VA/77-81, Dragging Canoe's **emissary to the British** in Detroit & CAN, raiding Ohio River valley/88, husband 1762 Great Tellico TN of **Bird Clan Shawnee Woman**/47, children/62-92 unknown

880. Little Owl (2) aka Little Owl Dragging CanoeLittle Owl Canoe – 15/64th Chalakatha-Thawikila-Creek-**Cherokee**-Metis born 1750 Great Tellico TN**killed** Buchanan Station TN 1792 - son of **Dragging Canoe**/34 & **Leaf Cherokee**/35, Point Pleasant/74, Cherokee War/75, a Chickamauga warrior, raiding KY-OH-VA-TN/77-92, scout-**with British Army**-Revolution, called **Chief of a Creek village**, husband 1774 TN of **Creek Woman**/60, father of several children/74-92-all 7/64th Chalakatha-Thawikila-Creek-Cherokee-Metis

881. Little Rum Cup – adopted-1/2 **Seneca**-Metis born about 1760 PA-died after 1810 - daughter of **Rum Cup**/45-Seneca & **White Man**, wife 1st about 1775 OH of **White Man**, 2nd 1780 OH of **Mekoche Man**/60, mother **with White Man** of a couple of 1/4th Seneca-Metis children/75-80, **with Mekoche** of several 1/2 Mekoche-Seneca-Metis children/80-1800

882. Little Salt Bride – adopted-Chickamauga-Cherokee born about 1760 TNdied after 1794 - wife 1775 KY of **Kishpoko Man**/55, widow 1794, children unknown

883. Little Skirt – Mekoche born about 1790-died after 1815 – called very attractive, living in Apple Creek MO 1815, wife about 1805 MO of **Mekoche Man**/85, mother of 4 daughters & 1 son/1805-15

884. Little Snake aka Young Snake (1) – Mekoche born about 1745 OH-died after 1782 - son of **Big Snake (1)**/20 & **Mekoche Woman**/25, a Mekoche warrior, Cornstalk War/62-77, Pontiac War/62-66, raiding Ohio-Kanawha-Big Sandy-Little Kanawha-New River valleys/72, Point Pleasant/74-75-78, raiding KY-VA-OH/77-81, Blue Jacket War/77-82, Boonesboro/78, Blue Licks/82, Crawford/82, nephew of **Helizikinopo Cornstalk**/15, wife & children unknown

885. Little Spirit – Chalakatha born about 1750 OH-died after 1775 - wife 1765 OH of **Chalakatha Man**/45, widow in 1775

886. **Little Sun aka Kisathoitakishok**[76] – Thawikila born about 1760 OHdied after 1785 - wife 1775 (AL?) of **Thawikila Man**/55, widow in 1785

887. Little Vincennes – ½ Kishpoko-Metis born about 1770 OH-died after 1815 – son of **Kishpoko Woman** & **French-Canadian Man,** Blue Jacket War/87-94, raiding OH-KY-VA/95-1810, Prophet's Town/1811, **left Prophet** & **Tecumseh** after Prophet's Town, living in Apple Creek MO 1815

888. Little Voice – Chalakatha born about 1755 OH-died after 1782 - wife 1770 OH of **Chalakatha Man**/50, widow in 1782

889. Locket – Chalakatha born about 1750 OH-died after 1775 - wife 1765 OH of **Chalakatha Man**/45, widow in 1775

890. Logan, Chief aka John Logan-Talgayeeta-Branching Oak -Seneca born 1725 PA-**murdered** 1786 OH - son of **Skikellimus**/1700-Seneca, brother of **James Tahgahjute Logan**/30 & **Kooney Skikellimus-Logan**/50-both Seneca, raiding Ohio River valley/74, Point Pleasant/74, Grand Councils 6-1762 & 1782, refused to attend Treaty Camp Charlotte/75, husband 1st 1745 (PA?) of **Chalakatha Woman**/30, 2nd 1775 OH of **Sarah Brent**/58-1/2 Chalakatha-Metis, father **with Chalakatha** of Chief Logan Jr aka John Logan Jr/45-1/2 ChalakathaSeneca & other children/46-74 named Logan, **with Brent** of several 1/4th
Chalakatha-Seneca-Metis children/75-86 named Logan

891. Logan, Chief Jr aka John Logan Jr - 1/2 Chalakatha-Seneca born about 1745-**murdered** 1774 - son of **Chief Logan**/25-Seneca & **Chalakatha**

Woman/30, **murdered** 1774 with uncle James/30, aunt Kooney/50 & wifeYounger Daughter of Nonhelma/48 by Greathouse group, husband about 1768 of
Younger Daughter of Nonhelema/48, children/68-74 unknown

892. Logan, Chotschawanne - adopted-white born about 1725 (PA?)-died after 1786 OH - adopted before 1740 (PA?)-never returned to whites, Cornstalk War/55-77, French-Indian War/54-63, Braddock/55, raiding New-Shenandoah River valleys/55, raiding Ohio-New River valleys/58, Pontiac War/62-66, Bushy Run/63, raiding New-Greenbrier-Jackson River valleys/63, raiding Little Kanawha-Big Sandy-Ohio-New River valleys/72, Point Pleasant/74-78, Blue Jacket War/77-81, raiding KY-VA-OH/77-81, husband 1st 1760 OH of **Elder Daughter of Nonhelema**/44, 2nd about 1780 OH of **Delaware Woman**/60 (possibly a Shawnee among the Delaware), father **with Elder Daughter of Nonhelema** of several 15/32nd Chalakatha-Mekoche-Metis children/60-79, **with Delaware** of several ½ Delaware-Metis children/80-86+ all with possible surname Logan, adopted father 1783 of **Billy Dragoo**-white

893. Logan, James (3) - 15/16th Mekoche-Kishpoko-Pekowi-Creek-Metis born about 1805 OH-died after 1825 - son of **Capt. John Logan-Big Horn**/74 & **Spamaghlebee**/90, a Mekoche warrior, grandson of **Tecumapease**/58 & **Mink**/40, living at Wapaghonettat 1817

894. Logan, Nancy aka Nancy Renicks – 3/4th Pekowi-Metis born about 1810 OH-died about 1842 - daughter of **James Logan Renicks** aka James Logan/74 & **Pekowi Woman**/80, wife 1851 MO of **Fredrick Chouteau**/1809-white, mother of William Chouteau/1833, Benjamin Chouteau/1835, Amanda Chouteau/1837 & Francis Xavier Chouteau/1839-all 3/8th Pekowi-Metis

895. Loho – ½ Chalakatha-Cherokee born about 1748 TN-died after 1774 – son of **Marhalonak**/10-Cherokee & **Chalakatha Woman**/15, scout with father Marhalonak/10 & brothers Tok/42, Sak/44 & Sark/46 **with Andrew Lewis** & whites-Pontiac War/62-66, Bushy Run/63 & Point Pleasant/74, husband about 1768 VA of **Chalakatha Woman**/52, children unknown

896. Long Canoe – adopted-Seneca born about 1750 OH-died after 1775 - raiding Ohio-Big Sandy-Little Kanawha-New River valleys/72, raiding Ohio River valley/74 **with Chief Logan**, Point Pleasant/74-75, husband 1770 OH of **Chalakatha Woman**/55, children unknown

897. Long Fellow (1) aka Long Fellow Fivekiller (1)-Long Fellow WardTuskegatahu-Tuskegetchee-Tuckogee-Dasigidihi-Tuskogeekiller -7/32nd Chalakatha-**Cherokee**-Metis born 1736 Chota TN-died 1826 Cherokee Nation -

son of **Tame Doe Carpenter**/16 & **Francis-Five Killer-Ward**/12, Wolf Clan Cherokee, Cornstalk War/58-74, raiding New-Ohio valleys/58, Pontiac War/62-66, Bushy Run/63, raiding New-Jackson-Greenbrier River valleys/63, raiding New-Ohio-Little Kanawha-Big Sandy River valleys/72, Point Pleasant/74, Cherokee War/75, a seceding Chickamaugua headman 1777, Treaty Sycamore Shoals 1775, 1785, 1798, 1805, 1817, from the Valley Towns-Chota-ChistatoaOcoee, husband 1756 Chota TN of **Blind Savannah Woman**/40, father of Long Fellow Ward (2)-Young Long Fellow Fivekiller/65 & Robin Long Fellow/70both 23/64th Chalakatha-Cherokee-Metis

898. Long Fish – Pekowi born about 1760 OH-died after 1794 – Blue Jacket War/77-94, raiding KY-VA-OH/77-81, Boonesboro/78, Point Pleasant/78, raiding KY-OH-VA/77-81, Crawford/82, raiding Ohio River valley/88-92

899. Long Hair aka Gitlugunahita – adopted-Cherokee born about 1740 TNdied after 1795 - Point Pleasant/74-78, Blue Jacket War/77-94, raiding KY-VAOH/77-81, Boonesboro/78, Blue Licks/82, Crawford/82, raiding Ohio River valley/88-92, Fallen Timber/94, living with his band **with Shawnee in OH** 177495, husband 1st 1760 TN of **Cherokee Woman**/45, 2nd 1774 OH of **Kishpoko Woman**/60, children unknown

900. Long Leg Woman – Chalakatha born about 1740 (PA?)-died after 1780 - over 6' tall, wife about 1755 OH of **Chalakatha Chief**/20, widow in 1780

901. Long Log aka Long Log in Water – Chalakatha born about 1740 PA-died after 1778 – Cornstalk War/58-77, raiding Ohio-New River valleys/58, Pontiac War/62-66, Bushy Run/63, raiding New-Greenbrier-Jackson River valleys/63, raiding Ohio-Big Sandy-Little Kanawha-New River valleys/72, Point Pleasant/74, raiding OH-KY-VA/77, Boonesboro/78

902. Long Shanks aka **Waytheah** – Mekoche born about 1745 OH-died after 1795 – Cornstalk War/62-77, Pontiac War/62-66, Bushy Run/63, raiding NewJackson-Greenbrier River valleys/63, raiding Ohio-Little Kanawha-Big SandyNew River valleys/72, Point Pleasant/74-78, Blue Jacket War/77-94, raiding KYVA-OH/77-81, Boonesboro/78, Blue Licks/82, Crawford/82, raiding Ohio River valley/88-92, Treaty Greenville 1795

903. Long Tail aka **Chakalawa**[77] - Chaklaway-Chakalowah-Tail's End – Chalakatha born about 1770 OH-died after 1854 KS - raiding Ohio River valley/88-92, Blue Jacket War/88-94, a **Chalakatha Chief** at Wapaghonettat before 1817, Treaty 1817, 1818, 1854, moved to KS before 1832

904. Long Tailed Cat - 1/2 Kishpoko-Metis born about 1740 OH-died after 1782 - son of **White Trader** & **Kishpoko Woman,** Cornstalk War/58-77, raiding Ohio-New River valleys/58, Pontiac War/62-66, Bushy Run/63, raiding New-Greenbrier-Jackson River valleys/63, raiding Little Kanawha-Big SandyOhio-New River valleys/72, Point Pleasant/74-78, Blue Jacket War/77-82, raiding KY-VA-OH/77-81, Crawford/82, husband 1760 OH of **KishpokoWoman**/45, children unknown

905. Long Wolf – Chalakatha born about 1745 OH-died after 1778 – Cornstalk War/62-77, Pontiac War/62-66, Bushy Run/63, raiding NewGreenbrier-Jackson River valleys/63, raiding Ohio-New River valleys/72, Point Pleasant/74, raiding KY-VA-OH/77, Boonesboro/78

906. Long Woman - 1/2 Chalakatha-Metis born about 1730 (KY?)-died after 1764 - daughter of **Chalakatha Woman** & **French/Canadian Man**, about 6' tall, wife about 1755 OH of **Chalakatha Man**/22, widow in 1764

907. Loon aka **Magawa** - Mekoche born about 1745 OH-died after 1775 – Cornstalk War/62-75, Pontiac War/62-66, Bushy Run/63, raiding NewGreenbrier-Jackson River valleys/63, raiding Ohio-Little Kanawha-Big SandyNew River valleys/72, Point Pleasant/74-75, husband 1765 OH of **Mekoche Woman**/50, father of Young Loon/66-Mekoche

908. Loon, Sam – Mekoche born about 1790 OH-**killed** 1838 – son of **Young Loon**/66 & **Mekoche Woman**/70, scout-**with U.S. Army**-War 1812, murdered **Peter Cornstalk (1)**/55 with **Doc Bill**/95 & **Capt. Bill**/90, killed in revenge by **Peter Cornstalk Jr**/85

909. Loon, Young – Mekoche born 1766 OH-died after 1800 – son of **LoonMagawa**/45 & **Mekoche Woman**/50, Blue Jacket War/84-94, husband 1786 OH of **Mekoche Woman**/70, father of Sam Loon/90-Mekoche

910. Looney, John aka **Chief John Looney** – 1/8th Chalakatha-Thawikila-Creek-**Cherokee**-Metis born 1776 Great Tellico TN-died 1846 D.C. - son of **Daughter of Black Fox**/62 & **Joseph Looney**/52, Capt. John MacIntosh Co**with U.S. Army**-Creek War/1813, **Head Chief AR Cherokee** 1838 & 1839 (2 separate terms), husband 1st about 1795 of **Susan Cherokee**/80, 2nd about 1819 of **Elizabeth Webber**/80-1/4th Chalakatha-Cherokee-Metis, father **with Cherokee** of Eleanor Looney/1816 & Rachel Looney/1818-both 1/16th Chalakatha-Thawikila-Creek-Cherokee-Metis, **with Webber** of Eliza Abigail Looney/1824 & Nancy Looney/1828-both 3/16th Chalakatha-Thawikila-Creek-Cherokee-Metis

911. Lorimier, Charlotte Pemanich Bouganville – 2nd wife 1783 OH of **Peter Lorimier**/48-adopted-French-Canadian-Metis, mother **with Lorimier** of Louis Lorimier Jr/84, Maria Louisa Lorimier/86, Augustus Bouganville Lorimier/90, Agatha Lorimier/91, Verneuil Raphael Lorimier/94, Victor Lorimier/98, Lisette Lorimier/1800-all 1/4th Mekoche-Metis

912. Lorimier, Peter Louis aka Peter Loramie-Louis Lorimer-Pierre Louis de Lorimier-Louis de Lorimier-Don Lorimier - adopted-French-Canadian-Metis born about 1748-died 1812 MO - son of **Claude Nicholas Guillaume de Lorimier**/05-white & **Marie Louise Pailleur**/15-Metis, trading post in OH 1769-93, **with Black Fish** group that captured **Daniel Boone** 1778, move to MO 1793 after trading post was destroyed by U.S. troops, **Spanish Governor of MO Territory** 1793-1803, **U.S. Indian Agent** 1806-12, spoke 22 Native languages, namesake of Loramie Creek & Ft. Loramie in OH, brother in law of **Pierre Drouillard**/50, uncle of **George Drouillard**/73, husband 1st about 1769 OH of **Straight Ahead**/52-Chalakatha, 2nd 1783 OH of **Charlotte Pemanich Bouganville**/58-1/2 Mekoche-Metis, 3rd 1810 MO of **Maria Berthiaume**/85-7/64th Chalakatha-Mekoche-Pekowi-Cherokee-Metis, father **with Straight Ahead** of Peter Lorimier Jr/70, Elder Daughter/73, Middle Daughter/76, Younger Daughter/78, Guillaume-William Lorimier/81-all 1/2 Chalakatha-Metis, **with Charlotte** of Louis Lorimier Jr/84, Maria Louise Lorimier/86, Augustus Bouganville Lorimier/90, Agatha Lorimier/91, Verneuil Raphael Lorimier/92, Victor Lorimier/98, Lisette Lorimier/1800-all 1/4th Mekoche-Metis, **with Marie** of Manuel Lorimier/98-3/64th Chalakatha-Mekoche-Pekowi-Cherokee-Metis

913. Lorimier, Louis Jr - 1/4th Mekoche-Metis born about 1784 OH-died 1831 MO - son of **Peter Lorimier**/48-adopted Metis & **Charlotte Pemanich Bouganville**/58, Spanish Militia-Stoddard Co. MO, graduated from West Point, commissioned in 2nd U.S. Inf., **2nd in Command** of Ft. Osage, with **Lisa's Expedition to WY** 1811, husband 1816 of **Margaret Penny**/1800-white, father of Marsalette Lorimier/1818, Victor Steinbeck Lorimie/1820, Louisa D. Lorimier/1822, Louis Lorimier III/1824, Mary Lorimier/1826, Louis Charles Lorimier/1828, Archibald Lorimier/1829, Clement W. Lorimier/1831, Odele Lorimier/1832-all 1/8th Mekoche-Metis

914. Lorimier, Maria Berthiaume - 3rd wife 1810 MO of **Peter Lorimier**/48adopted-Metis, mother of Manuel Lorimier/1808-3/64th Chalakatha-Mekoche-Pekowi-Cherokee-Metis

915. Lorimier, Peter Jr aka Pierre Louis Lorimier II-Louis Lorimer II - 1/2

Chalakatha-Metis born about 1770 OH-died 1806 - son of **Straight Ahead**/52Chalakatha & **Peter Lorimier**/48-adopted Metis, raiding Ohio River valley/8892, Blue Jacket War/88-94, husband about 1790 OH of **Chalakatha Woman**/75, children/90-1806 unknown

916. Lorimier, Straight Ahead – Chalakatha, sister of **Asoundachris**/53-wife of **Pierre Drouillard**/50, aunt of **George Drouillard**/73, 1st wife 1768 OH of **Peter Lorimier**/48-adopted Metis, mother of Peter Lorimier Jr/70, Elder Daughter/73, Middle Daughter/76, Younger Daughter/78, Guillaume-William Lorimier/81-all 1/2 Chalakatha-Metis

917. Lowe, Cynthia Rogers - wife about 1838 of **John Lowe**-white born about 1810-died after 1850, mother of Julia Lowe/1846, John Lowe/1848, Sarah Alice Lowe/1850-all 5/32nd Chalakatha-Pekowi-Thawikila-Creek-**Cherokee**Metis

918. Lowe, Jenny Jane Barton - wife 1814 of **Charles Lowe**-white born about 1790-died after 1846, mother of Joab Lowe/1816, Malinda Lowe/1817, Nancy Lowe/1819, Jane Lowe/1820, Lucinda Lowe/1825, Isaac Lowe/1828, David Lowe/1832, Abraham Lowe/1834, Susannah Lowe/1836 & Elizabeth Ann Lowe/1838-all 1/4th Thawikila-Metis

919. Lowery, Major George Jr aka George Lowery (2)-Rising FawnAginagili-**Rising Man**-Agili-Ahgeehlim – 11/32nd Chalakatha-Pekowi-**Metis** born 1768 AL-died 1852 OK - son of **Nancy Watts**/48 & **George Lowery (1)**/40-white, Blue Holly Clan Cherokee, nephew & stepson of **Ghigoneli Watts** (Rising Fawn)/50, cousin of **Sequoyah**/59, delegate to **George Washington** on behalf of the Chickamauga 1791, 1st Cherokee National Convention 1814, Cherokee Constitutional Convention 1827 & 1839, Major-**with U.S. Army**Creek War/1813-Horseshoe Bend/1814, Treaty 1816, 1817, 1819, from Tuskegee & Will's Town, **assistant Principal Chief** 1828-1843-1847, moved to AR 1839, husband 1st 1791 of **Lucy Benge**/66-21/64th Chalakatha-Pekowi-Cherokee-Metis, 2nd 1796 of **Elizabeth Shorey**/62-Cherokee-Metis, 3rd about 1814 of **Cherokee Woman**/80, 4th about 1820 of **Annie Fields**/92-1/64th Chalakatha-Cherokee-Metis, father **with Benge** of James Lowery/91, Susan Lowery/93, George Lowery (3)/99, Lydia Lowery/1803, Rachel Lowery/1805, John Lowery/1808, Anderson Pierce Lowery/1811-all 21/64th Chalakatha-Pekowi-Cherokee-Metis, **with Shorey** of Peggy Lowery/96, Archibald Lowery (1)/97, Washington Lowery (1)/98, Charles Lowery (1)/1801-all 11/64th Chalakatha-Pekowi-Cherokee-Metis, **with Cherokee** of John Lowery (3)/1814, Anderson Lowery/1816, Archibald Lowery (2)/1818-all 11/64th Chalakatha-Pekowi-Cherokee-Metis, **with Fields** of Washington Lowery (2)/1820, Charles Lowery (2)/1825-both 11/64th Chalakatha-Pekowi-Cherokee-Metis

920. Lowery, Major John aka John (1) – 11/32nd Chalakatha-Pekowi-**Metis** born 1768 Nickajack TN-died 1817 TN - son of **Nancy Watts**/48 & **George Lowery (1)**/40-white, Blue Holly Clan Cherokee, Major-**with U.S. Army**-Creek War/1813-Horseshoe Bend/1814, Treaty 1806, 1816, husband 1st 1790 of **Ganelugi Run After McLemore**/75-15/64th Chalakatha-Kishpoko-BlackChippewa-Cherokee-Metis, 2nd 1794 of **Elizabeth Shorey**/62-Cherokee-Metis, father **with McLemore** of John Lowery (2)/90, Jennie Lowery/95 & Eliza Lowery/1800-all 9/32nd Chalakatha-Pekowi-Kishpoko-Black-ChippewaCherokee-Metis, **with Shorey** of Elizabeth Lowery/95-all 11/64th Chalakatha-Pekowi-Cherokee Metis

921. Lowery, Sarah – 11/32nd Chalakatha-Pekowi-Metis born 1774 TN-died after 1816 - daughter of **Nancy Watts**/48 & **George Lowery Sr**/40-white, Blue Holly Clan **Cherokee**, wife 1st 1789 of **Cherokee Man**/70, 2nd 1790 of **Bald Ridge**/50-Cherokee, 3rd 1798 of **Stayd Rope**/70-Cherokee, 4th 1799 of **Rattling Gourd Conrad**/72-1/8th Chalakatha-Thawikila-Creek-Cherokee-Metis, 5th by 1808 of **William R. Campbell Jr**/80-7/64th Chalakatha-Pekowi-Cherokee-Metis, 6th about 1816 of **Jack Tesquatanosti Cersingle**/75-Cherokee-Metis, mother **with Cherokee**/70 of Switzler Lowery/90, **with Bald Ridge**/50 of Bluefoot Baldridge/91, George Baldridge/92, Garnae Baldridge/93, Alsey Baldridge/94, Oolusta Baldridge/95, Garstochumlartoh Baldridge/96, William Baldridge/97 & Jennie Jane Baldridge/98, **with Rope**/70 of Tsagina Rope/99, **with Conrad** of Nona Lowery (Conrad)/1800 & Elizabeth Gourd (Conrad)/1801-all 15/64th Chalakatha-Pekowi-Thawikila-Creek-Cherokee-Metis, **with Campbell** of George William Campbell/1810 & Rope Campbell/1814-both 21/64th Chalakatha-Pekowi-Cherokee-Metis, children **with Cersingle** unknown

922. Lynch, Nancy Martin - wife about 1797 of **Jeter Lynch**-Irish born about 1756-died 1816, mother of Thomas Lynch/98, Martha Lynch/1801, Sally Lynch/1802, Berilla Lynch/1804, Joseph Martin Lynch/1806, Mary Lynch/1808, Sabra Lynch/1810, Rachel Lynch/1812 & Maria Lynch/1813-all 5/64th Chalakatha-Pekowi-Cherokee-Metis

Section XI
MacIntosh to Musquanako (M)

M

923.   MacIntosh, John Gotaquasgi – ½ **Chickasaw**-Metis born about 1770died after 1819 - son of **William MacIntosh Sr**/45-white & **Chickasaw Woman**/55, half-brother of **Hoagy MacIntosh**/72 & **William MacIntosh Jr**/75both Creek-Metis, Capt-**with U.S. Army**-Creek War/13, Treaty 1819, **associated with Shawnee**-among-the Creeks-Cherokee-Chickasaw, husband 1789 of **Jennie Walker**/71, father of John MacIntosh Jr/90, Nellie MacIntosh/92 & Maria MacIntosh/95-all 3/16th Chalakatha-Mekoche-Cherokee-Chickasaw-Metis

924.   MacIntosh, William H. Jr. aka White Warrior-White Eagle-Tustunnugee Huthee - 1/2 **Creek**-Metis born about 1775 SCO-**murdered** 1825 AL - son of **William H. MacIntosh**/45-white & **Creek Woman**/60, half-brother of **Hoagy MacIntosh**/72-Creek-Metis & of **John Gotaquasgi MacIntosh**/70-1/2 Chickasaw Metis, grew up with & **associated with Shawnee**-among-the-Creeks, **Head Chief** 1800 of the Coweta Creeks, Treaty 1805, 1814, 1818, 1821, 1824, **refused Tecumseh, murdered** 1825 with **Tommy Tustunnuggee**/75-Creek for signing Treaty that forced the Creeks to move west, husband 1st 1794 of **Eliza Grierson**/80-Creek-Metis, 2nd 1799 of **Susannah Rowe**/70-25/64th Chalakatha-Pekowi-Thawikila-Creek-Cherokee-Metis, 3rd 1809 of **Peggy Graves**/95-Cherokee-Metis, father **with Grierson** of Chilly MacIntosh/96, Delilah MacIntosh/97 & George MacIntosh/98-all Creek-Metis, **with Rowe** of Croesy MacIntosh/1800, Jane MacIntosh/1802 & Catherine MacIntosh/1804-all 3/16th Chalakatha-Pekowi-Thawikila-Cherokee-Creek-Metis, **with Graves** of Sarah MacIntosh/1809, Daniel Newton MacIntosh/1822-both Creek-Cherokee-Metis

925. Mad Porcupine – Kishpoko born about 1730 OH-died after 1774 – Cornstalk War/55-74, French-Indian War/54-63, Braddock/55, raiding New-Shenandoah River valleys/55, raiding Ohio-New River valleys/58, Pontiac War/62-66, Bushy Run/63, raiding New-Greenbrier-Jackson River valleys/63, raiding Ohio-Big Sandy-Little Kanawha-New River valleys/72, Point Pleasant/74

926. Mad Sturgeon - Chippewa born about 1765-died after 1813 - son of **White Sturgeon**/30-Chippewa, brother of **Stands Firm**/55 & **Yellow Cloud**/60both adopted-Chippewa, Blue Jacket War/82-94, Crawford/82, raiding Ohio River valley/83-89, raiding OH-KY-VA/95-1810, Prophet's Town/1811-Brownstown/1812-Monguagon/1812-1st Amherstburg/1812-Frenchtown/1813-Ft. Meigs/1813-2nd Amherstburg/1813-Thames/1813 **with son in law Tecumseh**, husband 1785 of **Chippewa Woman**/70, father of Winnipegoosqua Sturgeon/90(last wife of **Tecumseh**) & others

927. Maddox, Wife of Christopher – Kishpoko born about 1760 KY-died after 1800 **Mason Co. WV** - wife about 1775 KY of **Christopher Maddox**/55-Welsh, came from KY to Mason Co. WV 1788 with husband Christopher & **Daniel Boone**, mother of Son of Christopher/75, Tobias Maddox/91 & other 1/2 Kishpoko-Welsh-Metis children

928. Magalakutway aka Magalakootway – Pekowi born about 1730 PA-died after 1762 - French-Indian War/54-62, Braddock/55, raiding New-Shenandoah River valleys/55, raiding PA/55-56, raiding Ohio-New River valleys/58, Council Ft. Pitt 1762 & Lancaster Aug. 1762

929. Magotha – Mekoche born about 1775 OH-died after 1817 - no part in Fallen Timber/94 or War 1812, a warrior from Wapaghonettat 1817, Treaty 1817

930. Maisonville, Antoine Francois aka Antoine Francois Maisonville Rivard dit Loranger-Laculotte - adopted-1/2 Miami-French-Canadian-Metis born about 1750-died after 1819 - son of **Alexander Maisonville**/30 & **Miami Woman**/35, traveling in OH 1776 with **William Joseph LeMothe**/30, **Maurice Blondeau**/35 & **Gabriel Cotte**/40, **with British Army** 1778, Capt. of Ottawa & Miami Co. 1779, captured & scalped by **George Rogers Clark** forces 1779 with **Jean Baptiste Sanscriante**/30, living in Apple Creek MO by 1782, brother in law of **Tecumseh** & **Cheeseekau**, husband 1782 of **Menewalaukoose**/65-3/4th Kishpoko-Pekowi-Creek-Metis, father of Francois Maisonville/91-3/8th Kishpoko-Pekowi-Creek-French-Canadian Metis

931. Maisonville, Francois aka Francois Maisonville Rivard dit LorangerLacullotte - 3/8th Kishpoko-Pekowi-Creek-Metis born about 1791-died about
1756 - from Apple Creek MO, son of **Menewaulakoose**/65 & **Antoine Francois Maisonville**/50-adopted French-Canadian Metis, nephew of **Tecumseh**/68, nephew & son in law of **Cheeseekau**/56, husband 1808 MO of 1st cousin **Genevieve Marie-Teciekeapease Cheeseekau**/91-31/64th Kishpoko-PekowiChalakatha-Thawikila-Creek-Cherokee-Metis, father of Francois Maisonville Jr/1811, Modest Maisonville/1819 & Angelica Maisonville/1826 & 9 other children/1808-25-all 5/16th Kishpoko-Pekowi-Chalakatha-Thawikila-Creek-
Cherokee-Metis

932. Makes Peace – Pekowi born about 1720 PA-died after 1765 - raiding PA/40, Cornstalk War/55-65, French-Indian War/54-63, Braddock/55, raiding New-Shenandoah River valleys/55, raiding PA/55-56, raiding Ohio-New River valleys/58, Pontiac War/62-66, Bushy Run/63, raiding New-Greenbrier-Jackson River valleys/63

933. Makottaweloma – Chalakatha born about 1710 PA-died about 1758 OH in epidemic - raiding PA/40, Council Ft. Pitt Nov. 1753, Braddock/55, raiding New-Shenandoah River valleys/55, raiding PA/55-56, raiding Ohio-New River valleys/58

934. Mallot, Catherine - adopted-white born about 1754-died about 1840 CAN - daughter of **Peter & Sarah Mallot**, captured-adopted 1778 on Ohio River, living by 1784 with **Simon Girty**/41-adopted Seneca, then married 1791, mother of Nancy Ann Girty/86, Thomas Girty/88, Sarah Girty/91 & Prideaux Girty/97-all white

935. Mamate aka **Mamate Baby**-Mamate Baubee - 1/2 Kishpoko-Metis born 1774-died 1790 - daughter of **Kishpoko Woman**/59 & **Jacques Duperon Baby**/33, one of 11 illegitimate children of Baby & Native women, 2nd wife 1789 OH of **Tecumseh**/68, died shortly after birth of son, mother of Naythahwaynah-Panther Seizing Prey-Young Tecumseh/90-5/8th Kishpoko-Pekowi-Creek-Metis

936. Mamrehigh – Chalakatha born about 1730 PA-died after 1765 – Cornstalk War/55-65, French-Indian War/54-63, Braddock/55, raiding NewShenandoah River valleys/55, raiding PA/55-56, raiding Ohio-New River valleys/58, Pontiac War/62-66, Bushy Run/63, raiding New-Greenbrier-Jackson River valleys/63, Council Logstown 1765

937. Maney, Keziah Vann - wife about 1781 TN of **Martin Maney**-Irish born about 1748 IRE-died 1830 NC, mother of Nancy Maney/83, John J. Maney/85, William Maney/87, James Maney/90-all 7/32nd Chalakatha-Pekowi-Shawano-**Cherokee**-Metis

938. Manwealte – Chalakatha born about 1770 OH-died after 1817 - raiding Ohio River valley/88-92, Blue Jacket War/88-94, raiding OH-KY-VA/95-1810, Prophet's Town/1811, Brownstown/1812-Monguagon/1812-1st Amherstburg/1812-Frenchtown/1813-Ft. Meigs/1813-2nd Amherstburg/1813 & Thames/1813 **with Tecumseh**, a warrior at Lewistown 1817, Treaty 1817

939. Many Hands – Mekoche born about 1740 OH-died after 1767 - wife about 1755 OH of **Mekoche Man**/35, widow in 1767

940. Many Marks - adopted-Cherokee born about 1750 TN-died after 1795 OH - marked by smallpox scars, wife 1765 KY of **Chalakatha Man**/45, widow in 1795

941. Many Teeth – Thawikila born about 1750 (OH?)-died after 1782 - wife about 1765 OH of **Thawikila Man**/45, widow in 1782

942. Marhalonak - adopted-Cherokee born about 1710-died after 1755 - scout **for Andrew Lewis** & whites-French-Indian War/54-63 & Braddock/55, scout

with Andrew Lewis & Colonial forces-Pontiac War/62-66 & Bushy Run/63 & Point Pleasant/74 with sons **Tok**/42, **Sak**/44, **Sark**/46, **Loho**/48, husband 1730 TN of **Chalakatha Woman**/15, father of Tok/42, Sak/44, Sark/46 & Loho/48-all ½ Chalakatha-Cherokee

943. Marsh Bird – Mekoche born about 1760 OH-died after 1790 - wife about 1775 OH of **Mekoche Man**/55, widowed at Harmar/90

944. Marshall, Charity aka **Talithcuny** - 1/2 Chalakatha-Metis born about 1754 OH-died after 1792 - daughter of **Chalakatha Woman** & **Trader Marshall**-white, wife by 1774 of **Barnabas Blue**/57-white, mother of Fredrick Blue/74, Martha Patsy Blue/75, Uriah Blue/82, Solomon Blue/84, Barnabas Blue Jr/87, Mary Blue/90, Esther Hetty Blue/92-all 1/4th Chalakatha-Metis

945. Martin, John (2) - 5/16th Pekowi-Chalakatha-**Cherokee**-Metis born about 1776 TN-died after 1840 - son of **Elizabeth Ward**/57 & **Joseph L. Martin**/40, Quartermaster-**with U.S. Army**-Creek War/1813-wounded at Horseshoe Bend/1814, Treaty 1819, Wolf Clan Cherokee, husband 1st about 1800 of **Cherokee Woman**/80, 2nd about 1820 of **Eliza Vann**/1806, children unknown

946. Martin, Judge John Calvin – 11/64th Chalakatha-Pekowi-**Cherokee**Metis born 1781 GA-died 1840 OK - son of **Susannah Emory**/50 & **Col. John Martin**/52, Long Hair Clan Cherokee, Treaty 1819, delegate Cherokee Constitutional Convention 1827, **1**[st] **Treasurer** & **1**[st] **Chief Justice** of Cherokee Nation, husband 1st 1803 of **Eleanor McDaniel**/88-23/64th ChalakathaKishpoko-Black-Cherokee-Metis, 2nd 1808 of her sister **Lucy McDaniel**/9023/64th Chalakatha-Kishpoko-Black--Cherokee-Metis, 3rd about 1810 of **Ruth Helton**/84-white, father **with Eleanor** of Annie Martin/1804, Gabriel Martin/1806, Brice Martin/1808, Susannah Martin/1810, Martha Patsy Hammock Martin/1812, Richard Fields Martin/1814, Joseph Lynch Martin/1816 & Ellen D. Martin/1818, **with Lucy** of Charlotte Martin/1812, Jennie Martin/1816, Eliza Martin/1818, John Martin/1819, Nancy Martin/1820, Rachel Martin/1822, Cicero Martin/1823 & Pauline Martin/1824-all 17/64th Chalakatha-Pekowi-KishpokoBlack-Cherokee Metis, **with Helton** of Amelia Martin aka Amelia Matoy/1812-
5/64th Chalakatha-Pekowi-Cherokee-Metis

947. Martin, Nancy (1) - 5/16th Pekowi-Chalakatha-**Cherokee**-Metis born about 1778 TN-died 1837 - daughter of **Elizabeth Ward**/57 & **Joseph L. Martin**/40, Wolf Clan Cherokee, wife about 1800 of **Michael Hilderbrand**/81white, mother of Elizabeth Hilderbrand/1801, John Hilderbrand/1803, Jane Hilderbrand/1806, Margaret Peggy Hilderbrand/1811,

Delilah Nali Hilderbrand/1813, Elizabeth Katherine Hilderbrand/1815, Stephen P.
Hilderbrand/1816, Rachel Hilderbrand/1818, Nancy Hilderbrand/1820, Joseph Martin Hilderbrand/1822, Brice Hilderbrand/1824, Mary Polly Hilderbrand/1826-all 5/32nd Pekowi-Chalakatha-Cherokee-Metis

948. Martin, Samuel - 5/16th Pekowi-Chalakatha-**Cherokee**-Metis born 1765 Tomatley TN-died after 1835 OK - son of **Mary Emory**/46 & **Joseph L. Martin**/40, Long Hair Clan Cherokee, husband 1st about 1785 of **Cherokee Woman**/70, 2nd about 1808 of **Catherine Hilderbrand**/90-white, 3rd about 1820 of **Charlotte Wickett**/70-15/64th Chalakatha-Kishpoko-Black-Cherokee-Metis, father **with Cherokee** of Mary Ann Martin/1804 & George Martin/1806-both 5/32nd Pekowi-Chalakatha-Cherokee-Metis, **with Hilderbrand** of Joseph Brice Martin/1808, Lucinda Martin/1810, William A. Martin/1812, Elizabeth Martin/1814, John Martin/1816, Martha Martin/1818, James Martin/1820, Susan Martin/1821, Brice Martin/1822 & Ellen Martin/1823-all 5/64th Chalakatha-Pekowi-Cherokee Metis, **with Wickett** of Nellie Martin/1820-17/64th Chalakatha-Kishpoko-Pekowi-Black-Cherokee-Metis

949. Masikee aka Maseekee – Chalakatha born about 1710 PA-died after 1751 - raiding PA/40, living with Creeks in AL 1751, husband 1750 AL of **Creek Woman**/34

950. Maskenogi – adopted-Pottawamee born about 1740-died after 1774 - raiding Ohio-New River valleys/58, Pontiac War/62-66, Bushy Run/63, raiding New-Jackson-Greenbrier River valleys/63, raiding Ohio-Little Kanawha-Big Sandy-New River valleys/72, Point Pleasant/74, husband about 1760 (OH-IN?) of **Kishpoko Woman**/46

951. Mauler aka Mauls Him – Kishpoko born about 1740 OH-died after 1778 – Cornstalk War/58-77, raiding Ohio-New River valleys/58, Pontiac War/62-66, Bushy Run/63, raiding New-Greenbrier-Jackson River valleys/63, raiding Ohio-Little Kanawha-Big Sandy-New River valleys/72, Point Pleasant/74-78, raiding KY-VA-OH/77, Boonesboro/78

952. Maw, Betsy White Owl Carpenter – 2nd wife 1749 of **Hanging Maw**/10Cherokee, Wolf Clan Cherokee, mother of Willico Maw/50, Thomas Jacob
Maw/55 & Nancy Maw/60-all 7/32nd Chalakatha-**Cherokee**-Metis

953. Maw, Nancy aka Oousat Maw-Nancy Oousta Hanging Maw-Daughter of Hanging Maw - 7/32nd Chalakatha-**Cherokee**-Metis born 1760 Great Tellico TNdied after 1790 (TN?) – daughter of **Betsy White Owl Carpenter**/14 &

Hanging Maw/10-Cherokee, Wolf Clan Cherokee, 2nd wife 1779 Great Tellico TN of 1st cousin **John Watts Jr**/48-21/64th Chalakatha-Pekowi-Cherokee-Metis, mother **with Watts** of Thomas Watts/80, Two Wood Watts/82, Peach Eater Watts/84, Elizabeth Watts/86-all 7/16th Chalakatha-Pekowi-Cherokee-Metis

954. Maw, Willico (1) – 7/32nd Chalakatha-**Cherokee**-Metis born 1750 Great Tellico TN-died after 1826 OK – son of **Betsy White Owl Carpenter**/16 & **Hanging Maw**/10-Cherokee, Wolf Clan Cherokee, Pigeon Co-Cherokee scouts**with U.S. Army**-Revolution, husband 1st 1770 Great Tellico TN of **Ooloocha Cherokee**/55, 2nd 1800 Great Tellico TN of **Eliza Quedi-Quatie**/80-Cherokee, father **with Ooloocha** of Susie Maw/95 & Nellie Maw/97 & other younger children/70-94, **with Eliza** of Ruth Maw/1820, Nancy Maw/1821, Polly Maw/1822, Nettie Maw/1824 & Willico Maw Jr/1826 & other younger children/1801-19-all 7/64th Chalakatha-Cherokee-Metis

955. Mawentacheka –Mekoche born about 1780 OH-died after 1817 – no known part in War 1812, a warrior at Wapaghonettat 1817, Treaty 1817

956. Mawethaque – Mekoche born about 1775 OH-died after 1817 – Fallen Timber/94, no part in War 1812, a warrior at Wapaghonettat 1817, Treaty 1817

957. May Apple – Kishpoko born 1690 Running Water TN-died 1762 Keowee TN – husband 1st (known) 1720 Running Water of **Ghigoneli Hop**/1694, 2nd 1725 Running Water TN of **Catherine Webber**/08-1/2 Chalakatha-Metis, father **with Hop** of Ninihica Mayapple/21 & Laskigitchi Mayapple/23-both ½ Chalakatha-Kishpoko, no known children **with Webber** but adopted father 1751 of her nephew **Capt. Will-William Webber (3)**/40-1/2 Chalakatha-Kishpoko-Metis

958. Maywathekeha – Kishpoko born about 1780 OH-died after 1825 KS - raiding OH-KY-VA/99-1810, Prophet's Town/1811, Brownstown/1812Monguagon/1812-1st Amherstburg/1812-Frenchtown/1813-Ft. Meigs/1813-2nd Amherstburg/1813 & Thames/1813 **with Tecumseh**, move to CAN 1815, moved back to OH about 1825, Treaty 1825

959. McBragg, Antoinia – Pekowi-(adopted-Delaware) born about 1730 PAdied after 1751 - wife before 1751 (PA?) of **James McBragg**-white, children unknown

960. McClelland, Robert - adopted white born about 1771-died 1815 MO - adopted 1783, returned to whites 1792, with William Wells scouts-**with U.S. Army**-Fallen Timber/94, moved to MO before 1815, husband 1792 of **Nancy Pryor**/76-1/2 Chalakatha-Metis, father of James McClelland/93, Robert McClelland Jr/95, John McClelland/97 & others-all 1/4th Chalakatha-Metis

961. McClure, Susanna Dougherty - wife 1822 of **William McClure**-white born 1800 SC-died 1834, mother of James M. McClure/1823, John A. McClure/1825, Frances Eleanor McClure/1827 & Mary Ann McClure/1829-all 5/64th Chalakatha-Thawikila-Pekowi-Creek-Cherokee-Metis

962. McCoy, Alexander - 1/64th Chalakatha-**Cherokee**-Metis born about 1796-died before 1851 - son of **Lucy Fields**/79 & **Daniel McCoy**/70-white, Secretary of Cherokee Constitutional Convention 1827, Long Hair Clan Cherokee, husband 1st 1815 of **Nona Lowery**/1800-15/64th Chalakatha-PekowiThawikila-Creek-Cherokee-Metis, 2nd 1817 of **Sarah Elizabeth Hicks**/98-1/16th Chalakatha-Thawikila-Cherokee-Metis, 3rd 1820 of **Aky Gunter**/98-3/16th Shawnee-Cherokee-Metis, father **with Lowery** of John Lowery McCoy/18161/8th Chalakatha-Pekowi-Thawikila-Creek-Cherokee-Metis, **with Hicks** of Mary Ann McCoy/1829 & Araminta McCoy/1831 & earlier children/1817-28-all 1/32nd Chalakatha-Thawikila-Creek-Cherokee-Metis, **with Aky** of Lucy McCoy/1820-11/64th Chalakatha-Pekowi-Cherokee-Metis

963. McCoy, Catherine Maria - 3/16th Chalakatha-Pekowi-**Cherokee**-Metis born about 1793 GA-died 1839 - daughter of **Lydia Halfbreed**/76 & **Daniel McCoy**/70-white, Blind Savannah Clan Cherokee, wife 1st about 1807 of **Andrew Miller**/80-white, 2nd about 1819 of **Thomas Gann**/85-white, 3rd about 1830 of **Mr. Ferguson**/90-white, 4th about 1837 (his 2nd) of **Thomas Fields** (2)/99-1/64th Chalakatha-Cherokee Metis, mother **with Miller** of Elizabeth Queti Miller/1809-3/32nd Chalakatha-Pekowi-Cherokee Metis, children **with Gann, Ferguson & Fields** unknown

964. McDaniel, Alexander - 1/4th Chalakatha-**Cherokee**-Metis born 1754 Chota TN-died 1834 (Trail?) - son of **Grasshopper Hop**/25 & **William David McDaniel**/26-white, Wolf Clan Cherokee, husband 1st 1774 Chota TN of **Unknown Native Woman**/60, 2nd 1786 Chota TN of **Catherine Wilson**/70-31/64th Chalakatha-Kishpoko-Black-Metis, 3rd 1787 Chota TN of her sister **Mary Wilson**/72-31/64th Chalakatha-Kishpoko-Black-Metis, children/74-86 **with Unknown Native** unknown, father **with Catherine** of James McDaniel/90, Catherine-Katy McDaniel/96, Mary McDaniel/98 & John B. McDaniel/1800, **with Mary** of Lucy McDaniel/88, Eleanor-Nell McDaniel/90, Moses McDaniel/92 & Susan-Sukey-Sugi McDaniel/1813-all 23/64th Chalakatha-Kishpoko-Black-Cherokee-Metis

965. McDaniel, Grasshopper aka Granny Grasshopper-Grasshopper Hop - Wolf Clan **Cherokee**, wife 2nd 1752 Chota TN of **William David**

McDaniel white born 1720 SCO-died after 1787 (Wm. McDaniel bought 140 acres in Ashe
Co. NC in 1787), mother of Catherine McDaniel/53, Alexander McDaniel/54, Lewis McDaniel/56, John McDaniel/58, Mary McDaniel/62, Nancy McDaniel/64, Elizabeth McDaniel/65, Susannah McDaniel/66, Rachel McDaniel/67, William David Jr/68-all 1/4th Chalakatha-Cherokee-Metis

966. McDaniel, Jim – Mekoche-(adopted-**Seneca**) born about 1770 OH-died after 1832 – Blue Jacket War/87-94, **with U.S. Army**-War 1812-Thames/1813, Treaty 1832, move to KS 1832, husband about 1790 OH of **Seneca Woman**/75

967. McDonald, James aka James McDonnell - 3/4th Chalakatha-Metis born about 1765-died after 1832 - son of **John McDonald**/35 & **Chalakatha Woman**/40, Blue Jacket War/82-94, **with U.S. Army**-War 1812-Thames/1813, Treaty 1815, 1831, moved to KS 1832, wife & children unknown

968. McDonald, John Titasgisgi - 1/2 Chalakatha-Metis born 1735 PA-died 1824 - son of **William McDonald**/10-adopted white & **Chalakatha Woman**/14, **with British Army**-Revolution, British Agent-trader among Chickamauga, from Lookout Mountain, husband 1st 1755 of **Chalakatha Woman**/40, 2nd 1769 **Annie Shorey**/45-Cherokee-Metis, father **with Chalakatha** of James McDonald/65-3/4th Chalakatha-Metis, **with Shorey** of Mary McDonald/70, Mollie McDonald/72, Charles McDonald/74 & George McDonald/76-all 1/4th Chalakatha-Cherokee-Metis

969. McDonald, Joseph - 1/2 Chalakatha-Metis-(adopted **Delaware & Chippewa**) born about 1737 PA-died after 1795 - son of **William McDonald**/10-adopted white & **Chalakatha Woman**/14, Cornstalk War/58-77, raiding Ohio-New River valleys/58, Pontiac War/62-66, Bushy Run/63, raiding New-Jackson-Greenbrier River valleys/63, raiding Ohio-Little Kanawha-Big Sandy-New River valleys/72, Point Pleasant/74, raiding Ohio-New River valleys/75-81, Blue Jacket War/77-94, Crawford/82, raiding Ohio River valley/88-92, husband about 1st about 1759 OH of **Chalakatha Woman**/40, 2nd before 1770 OH of **Delaware Woman**/50, 3rd before 1780 (OH?) of **Chippewa Woman**/60, father **with Chalakatha** of William McDonald (2)/60-3/4th Chalakatha-Metis, **with Delaware** of Delaware Son of Joseph McDonald/70 1/4th Chalakatha-Delaware-Metis, **with Chippewa** of Chippewa Son of Joseph McDonald/80-1/4th Chalakatha-Chippewa-Metis

970. McDonald, William (1) – adopted-white born about 1710 SCO-died after 1750 – adopted before 1735 PA, husband 1735 PA of **Chalakatha Woman**/14, father of John McDonald/35 & Joseph McDonald/37-both 1/2 Chalakatha-Metis

971.   McDonald, William (2) - 3/4th Chalakatha-Metis born about 1760-**killed** 1813 Thames - son of **Joseph McDonald**/37 & **Chalakatha Woman**/40, raiding OH-KY-VA/77-81, Point Pleasant/78, Crawford/82, raiding Ohio-New River valleys/88-92, Little Turtle War/90-94, raiding OH-KY-VA/95-1810, Prophet's Town/1811, Brownstown/1812-Monguagon/1812-1st Amherstburg/1812Frenchtown/1813-Ft. Meigs/1813-2nd Amherstburg/13, **killed at Thames/1813 with Tecumseh**, husband about 1777 OH of **Kishpoko Woman**/60 (same family as Tecumseh), children unknown

972. McDougall, George Jr aka **Squekawpowee**-Skoapowa - adopted white born about 1766-died about 1854 KS - son of **Francoise Navarre**/35 & **George McDougall**/30-white, **with U.S. Army**-War 1812-Thames/1813, a warrior at Wapaghonettat 1817, Treaty 1817, 1831, 1854, moved to KS 1832, husband 1st about 1786 OH of **Mekoche Woman**/70, 2nd about 1821 OH of **Polly Stewitaniba Adams**/1807-Chalakatha, children unknown

973. McKee, Alexander aka White Elk-**Wapimescheu**-Wapeemeshoo-**Col. Alexander McKee** - adopted-Irish born 1725 IRE-died 1799 Ontario CAN - son of **Thomas McKee**/1695 & **Elizabeth Gordon**/1700-both Irish, grandson of **Alexander McKee**/1665 & **Catherine**/1670-both Irish, nephew of **Patrick McKee**/1690 & two other uncles, brother of **Thomas-Pelewiechen McKee**/20adopted-white-Delaware, half-brother of **Alexander McKee**/33, **Nancy McKee**/40, **Hugh McKee**/42, **John McKee**/54 & James McKee/55-all 1/2
Pekowi-Metis, moved to Lancaster Co PA before 1735 with grandfather **Alexander McKee**/1665, father **Thomas McKee**/1695, uncle **Patrick McKee**/1690, 2 other uncles & brother **Thomas Pelewiechen McKee**/20, trader, agent, translator, replaced **George Croghan** as Deputy Indian Agent 1772, Grand Council 1763, 1782, 1791, Grand Council Coshocton 1776, Council Ft. Pitt 1777, Council Detroit 1778, Council with British 1779 with **Wryneck**/25Pekowi, **William Caldwell**/50, **Matthew Elliott**/30, **Simon**/41, **George**/46 &
James Girty/43, cousin **Simon Surphet**, **Savenooka Hop**/20, **Weed**/50-Iroquois & **River Bottom**/50-Seneca, Capt.-**with Colonial Army**-French-Indian War/54-63, Colonel-**with British Army**-Revolution, Col. Bird's expedition 1780 (Ruddle's, Martin's stations, Council Detroit 1781, raiding Ohio valley **with Joseph Brant** 1781, Council Zanesville 1782, moved to Ontario CAN 1796 when British surrender Detroit, husband 1st 1745 PA of **Shawnee Woman** (not identified yet), 2nd 1769 PA of **Yellow Britches-Edna Rising Sun**/55-Kishpoko, owner/husband 1780 OH of **Candis LaForce**/65-1/2 Chalakatha-Black-Metis,

children/45-68 **with Shawnee** unknown, father **with Yellow Britches** of Thomas McKee/70, Elizabeth McKee/72, Alexander McKee/75, Catherine McKee/80 & at least 2 other 1/2 Kishpoko-Metis children by 1780, **with Candis** of Rachel McKee/82-1/4th Chalakatha-Black-Metis

 974. McKee, Alexander - 1/2 Pekowi-Metis born about 1738 PA-died 1799 - son of **Thomas McKee**/1695 & **Margaret Tecumsapah Opessa**/25, brother of **Nancy McKee**/40, **Hugh McKee**/42, **Catherine McKee**/44, **Thomas McKee**/50, **John McKee**/54 & **James McKee**/55, half-brother of **ThomasPelewiechen McKee**/20-adopted-Delaware & **Col. Alexander-Wapimescheu McKee**/25-adopted-Shawnee, wife & children unknown

 975. McKee, Alexander - 1/2 Pekowi-Metis born about 1740 PA-died after 1760 - son of **Patrick McKee**/1690-Irish & **Mary Brown**/20-Pekowi, grandson of Alexander McKee/1665 & Catherine, husband about 1760 of **Pekowi Woman**/45, father of Catherine McKee/60-3/4th Pekowi-Irish-Metis

 976. McKee, Catherine - 1/2 Kishpoko-Metis born 1780 OH-died after 1850 - daughter of **Col. Alexander McKee**/25-adopted Irish & **Yellow Britches-Edna Rising Sun**/55, namesake of great-grandmother Catherine-wife of Alexander/1665, wife 1818 OH (a possible earlier marriage indicated by age but not found yet) of **Thomas George Waters (2)**/98-white, mother of Alexander Joseph Waters/1820, twins James & John Waters/1822 & Thomas George Waters (3)/1825-all 1/4th Kishpoko-Metis

 977. McKee, Catherine Quoqua aka Katie-Tomame - Wyandot born 1805 OH-died 1876 KS - daughter of **Chief Quoqua**-Wyandot, wife 1st before 1838 of **Thomas McKee**/1800-3/8th Kishpoko-Metis, (wife 2nd about 1845 of **James Clark**-Wyandot-Metis), mother of Mary McKee/38-3/16th Kishpoko-WyandotMetis

 978. McKee, Charlotte Brown - wife 1799 of **Alexander McKee**/75-1/2 Kishpoko-Metis, mother of

 979. Thomas McKee/1800-3/8th Kishpoko-Pekowi-Metis-(Wyandot)

 980. McKee, Mary aka Tarema-Carrying a Lake - 3/16th Kishpoko-Wyandot-

Metis born 1838-died 1922 - daughter of **Thomas McKee**/1800-3/8th KishpokoMetis & **Catherine Quoqua**/1805-Wyandot, moved to KS about 1843, husband
& children unknown

  981. McKee, Rachel - 1/4th Chalakatha-Black-Metis born 1782 CAN- died
1864 OH - daughter of **Col. Alexander McKee**/25-adopted-Irish & **Candis LaForce**/65-1/2 Chalakatha-Black-Metis, wife 1st about 1797 OH of **Capt. Reed**/50-Mekoche, 2nd about 1804 OH of **Rev. Francis Reno**/80-Mulatto, mother **with Reed** of Susannah Melinda Reed/98-3/4th Chalakatha-MekocheBlack-Metis, **with Reno** of daughters Phyllis Reno/1805, Rhoda Reno/1817,
Lelia Reno/1819, Rosanna Reno/1820 & Anna Reno/1824, sons Robert Reno/1810, Joseph Reno/1812, Francis Reno Jr/1815, Edwin Reno/1818, Abram Reno/1821, Lewis Reno/1822 & William Francis Reno/1823-all 1/8th Chalakatha-Black-Metis

  982. McKee, Tecumsapah Margaret Opessa - wife 1737 PA of **Thomas
McKee**/1695-adopted-Irish, mother of Alexander McKee/38, Nancy McKee/40, Hugh McKee/42, Catherine McKee/44, child/46, child/48, Thomas McKee/50, child/52, John McKee/54, James McKee/55-all 1/2 Pekowi-Metis, step-mother of **Thomas-Pelewiechen McKee**/20-adopted-Delaware & **Col. Alexander-Wapimescheu-White Elk McKee**/25-adopted-Shawnee

  983. McKee, Therese Askin - wife 1790 of **Thomas McKee**/70-1/2 Kishpoko-Metis, mother of Catherine McKee/91 & Alexander McKee/92-3/8th Kishpoko-Chippewa-Metis

  984. McKee, Thomas aka **Wahbemeshawa**-Capt. Thomas - 1/2 KishpokoMetis born 1770 OH-**killed** 1814 - son of **Col. Alexander McKee**/25-adoptedIrish & **Yellow Britches-Edna Rising Sun**/55-Kishpoko, raiding Ohio River valley/88-92, Blue Jacket War/88-94, Council Detroit Aug. 1796, Superintendent of Indian Affairs-CAN 1796, Capt.-**with British Army**-War of 1812, killed in battle, husband about 1790 of **Therese Askin**/75, father of Catherine McKee/91 & Alexander McKee/92-3/8th Kishpoko-Chippewa-Metis

  985. McKee, Thomas - 3/8th Kishpoko-Metis born about 1800-died 1844 KS - son of **Alexander McKee**/75& **Charlotte Brown**/82, moved to KS about 1843, husband before 1838 of **Catherine Quoqua**/1805-Wyandot, father of Mary

McKee/1838-3/16th Kishpoko-Wyandot-Metis

986.	McLemore, Charles (1) aka Headman-Chief Charles Macklemore – 1/4th Chalakatha-Metis born 1709 Bertie Co NC-died 1785 Bertie Co NC – son of **James McLemore**/1667 & **Fortune Gilliam**/1675, a trader on the frontier, very influential with the Cherokee & Shawnee, husband by 1729 Bertie Co NC of **Quatsis Atawaya Greenwood**/12, father of John McLemore (2)/30, Robert-Thigh McLemore/32 & others-all 19/32nd Chalakatha-Kishpoko-Black-Metis

987.	McLemore, Ganelugi Run-after aka Carnalougeache – 19/64th Chalakatha-Kishpoko-Black-**Cherokee**-Metis born 1775 Running Water TN-died after 1817 - daughter of **Robert-Thigh McLemore**/31 & **Betsy Aniwadi**/41-Cherokee, Wolf Clan Cherokee through mother, aunt of Elizabeth McLemore/1804 (wife of James Lowery/90), wife 1st 1790 TN of **Major John Lowery**/68-11/32nd Chalakatha-Pekowi-Metis, 2nd 1817 TN of **John Wagonmaster Benge**/87-9/32nd Chalakatha-Pekowi-Thawikila-Creek-Cherokee Metis, mother **with Lowery** of John Lowery Jr/90, Jenny Lowery/95 & Elizabeth Lowery/96-all 3/8th Chalakatha-Pekowi-Kishpoko-Black-Cherokee-Metis, **with Benge** of William Benge/1818, Pickens Benge/1820, James Benge/1823, John Benge/1825, Thomas Benge/1826, Robert Benge/1827, Ellis Benge/1828, Mary Polly Benge/1829, Martin Benge/1830 & Catherine Benge/1831-all 13/32nd Chalakatha-Pekowi-Kishpoko-Thawikila-Black-Creek-Cherokee-Metis

988. McLemore, Happy – 19/64th Chalakatha-Kishpoko-Black-**Cherokee**Metis born 1755 Running Water TN-died 1837 Madison Co KY – daughter of
Robert-Thigh McLemore/32 & **Betsy Aniwadi**/41-Cherokee, Wolf Clan Cherokee through mother, wife 1769 Bertie Co NC of **Ned Welch**/49white(Metis?), mother of David Welch/70-9/32nd Chalakatha-Kishpoko-Black-Cherokee-Metis

989. McNair, David aka Peaghtucha-Thakoska – Chalakatha born about 1780 OH-died after 1831 - Capt.-with U.S. Army-War 1812 & Creek War/1813, a warrior at Wapaghonettat 1817, Treaty 1817, 1831, husband 1801 of **Delilah Emelia Vann**/87, father of Elizabeth McNair/1805, Mary Ann McNair/1806, Nicholas Byer McNair/1810, Martha P. McNair/1812, Clement Vann McNair/1814-all 19/32nd Chalakatha-Pekowi-Thawikila-Creek-Cherokee-Metis

990. McPherson, James aka **Squalakalee**-Skwalakalee-Red-faced Man[78] - adopted-white-(later adopted-**Ottawa**) born about 1770-died after 1830 -

captured 1781 KY by **Joseph Brant & George Girty**, Fallen Timber/94, returned to whites 1795 after Treaty Greenville, **with U.S. Army**-Prophet's Town/1811-War 1812-Thames/1813, a warrior at Lewistown 1817, Treaty 1817, husband 1st 1788 OH **Mekoche Woman**/72, 2nd 1809 of **White Woman**(adopted-Ottawa), father **with Mekoche** of Henry McPherson/88, James McPherson Jr/90- both ½ Mekoche-Metis, children **with White-Ottawa Woman** unknown

991. McQueen, Elder Daughter of Daniel aka **Mother of Seekaboo**- Niece of Metheotashe - 1/2 Pekowi-**Creek**-Metis born about 1755 AL-died after 1770 - daughter of **Middle Sister of Metheotashe Opessa**/35 aka Middle Daughter of Loyparkaweh Opessa & **Daniel McQueen**/36-1/2 Creek-Metis, granddaughter (mother's side) of **Loyparkoweh Opessa**/1700, granddaughter (father's side) of **James McQueen**/1700-white & **Katherine Fraser**/05-Creek, sister of **Joseph McQueen**/60, 1st cousin of **Tecumseh,** wife about 1769 AL of **Father of Seekaboo**/50-Kishpoko, mother of Seekaboo/70-3/4th Kishpoko-Pekowi-CreekMetis

992. McSwain, Elizabeth - 1/4th Kishpoko-Metis born about 1782 TN-died after 1814 - daughter of **Nancy Fawling Downing** (Pettit Critterden)/46-1/2 Kishpoko-Metis & **Alexander McSwain**/40-white, Wolf Clan Cherokee, wife by 1800 of **David Welch**/70-7/64th Chalakatha-Kishpoko-Black-Metis, mother of George W. Welch/1802, Sidney Welch/1804, Mary Polly Welch/1812 & Elizabeth Jane Welch/14-all 11/64th Chalakatha-Kishpoko-Black-Metis

993. McSwain, Margaret Peggy - 1/4th Kishpoko-Metis born about 1778-died after 1822 - daughter of **Nancy Fawling Downing**/46-1/2 Kishpoko-Metis & **Alexander McSwain**/40-white, Wolf Clan Cherokee, 2nd wife 1792 of **Avery Vann Jr**/68-1/8th Chalakatha-Cherokee Metis, mother of Joseph Teaulte Vann/92, David Vann/94, Charles Vann/96, Margaret Vann/98, Sarah Vann/1800, Elizabeth Vann/1802, Avery Vann (3)/1804, Mary Vann/1806, Nancy Vann/1808, Clement Vann/1810, Claire Vann/1812, Jennie Vann/1814, Sarah Vann (2)/1816, Keziah Vann/1818, Elizabeth Vann (2)/1820, Eliza Vann/1822-all 3/16th Chalakatha-Kishpoko-**Cherokee**-Metis

994. Meamepetoo – Thawikila born about 1770 OH-died after 1817 - raiding Ohio River valley/88-92, Blue Jacket War/88/94, a warrior from Hog Creek 1817, Treaty 1817

995. Meanymsekah – Mekoche born about 1750 OH-died after 1786 – Cornstalk War/68-77, raiding Ohio-Big Sandy-New River valleys/72, Point Pleasant/74-78, Blue Jacket War/77-82, raiding KY-VA-OH/77-81, Boonesboro/78, Blue Licks/82, Crawford/82, Treaty 1786

996. Meensheka – Mekoche born about 1780 OH-died after 1817 – no part in

War 1812, a warrior at Wapaghonettat 1817, Treaty 1817

997. Meewensheka – Mekoche born about 1785-died after 1817 – no part in War 1812, a warrior at Wapaghonettat 1817, Treaty 1817

998. Megish aka Megeesh – Kishpoko born about 1770 OH-**killed** 1814 - raiding Ohio River valley/88-92, Blue Jacket War/87-94, raiding OH-KYVA/95-1810, Prophet's Town/1811, Brownstown/1812-Monguagon/1812-1st Amherstburg/1812-Frenchtown/1813-Ft. Meigs/1813-2nd Amherstburg/1813 & Thames/1813 **with Tecumseh**, killed 1814 in battle by U.S. troops

999. Mekallona – Pekowi born about 1660 OH-died after 1700 - living in PA by 1700

1000. Mekataillikoe – Chalakatha born about 1710 PA-died after 1751 - raiding PA/40, living with Creeks in AL 1751

1001. Menal – Mekoche born about 1770 OH-died after 1815 – scout-**with U.S. Army**-War 1812, living in Apple Creek MO 1815, a **minor Chief in MO**, wife & children unknown

1002. Menechootusa aka Menechootoosa – Chalakatha born about 1710 PA-died after 1751 - raiding PA/40, living with Creeks in AL 1751

1003. Menewaulakoosee aka Menewaulakoose Puckenshinwa-Menewaulakoose-**Menewalakosi-Lying Piled in a Hollow**[79] - 3/4th KishpokoPekowi-Creek-Metis born 1766 OH-died after 1819 MO - 2nd daughter of **Puckenshinwa**/35 & **Metheotashe Opessa**/40, moved to Apple Creek village MO **with Metheotashe** 1779, wife 1782 MO of **Antoine Francois Maisonville**/60-adopted-French/Canadian, mother of Francois Maisonville/913/8th Kishpoko-Pekowi-Creek-Metis (confused with her sisters by some white histories)

1004. Meouseka aka Meooseka – Pekowi born about 1740 MD-died after 1787 – Cornstalk War/58-77, raiding Ohio-New River valleys/58, Pontiac War/62-66, Bushy Run/63, raiding New-Greenbrier-Jackson River valleys/63, raiding Little Kanawha-Big Sandy-Ohio-New River valleys/72, Point Pleasant/74-75-78, Blue Jacket War/77-82, raiding KY-VA-OH/77-81, Boonesboro/78, Blue Licks/82, Crawford/82, living in OH 1787

1005. Meshenewa – Chalakatha born about 1770 OH-died after 1817 - raiding Ohio River valley/88-92, Blue Jacket War/87-94, Prophet's Town/1811, Brownstown/1812-Monguagon/1812-1st Amherstburg/1812-Frenchtown/1813-Ft. Meigs/1813-2nd Amherstburg/1813 & Thames/1813 **with Tecumseh**, Treaty

1817

1006. Mesheway – adopted-Illinois born about 1750 IL-died after 1820 – Cornstalk War/70-77, raiding Ohio-Little Kanawha-Big Sandy-New River valleys/72, Point Pleasant/74-78, Blue Jacket War/77-94, raiding KY-VAOH/77-81, Crawford/82, raiding Ohio River valley/88-92, Prophet's Town/1811, Brownstown/1812-Monguagon/1812-1st Amherstburg/1812-Frenchtown/1813-Ft. Meigs/1813-2nd Amherstburg/1813 & Thames/1813 **with Tecumseh**, moved to CAN 1815, husband about 1770 (OH-IN?) of **Kishpoko Woman**/55-same clan as Tecumseh

1007. Messaliketa aka Messaleeketa – Chalakatha born about 1720 PA-died after 1751AL - raiding PA/40, living with Creeks in AL 1751

1008. Messhawa – Mekoche born about 1740 OH-died after 1794 – from the Sandusky OH area, adopted mother 1790 of **Charles Johnston**-white, from the **Lewis Band**, wife about 1755 OH of **Mekoche Man**/35, widowed before 1790

1009. Messhawano – Kishpoko born about 1755 OH-died 1813 – Blue Jacket War/77-94, Point Pleasant/78, raiding Ohio River valley/81-92, Prophet's Town/1811, Brownstown/1812-Monguagon/1812-1st Amherstburg/1812Frenchtown/1813-Ft. Meigs/1813-2nd Amherstburg/1813, **killed at Thames/1813 with Tecumseh**

1010. Metchepelah – Mekoche born about 1775 OH-died after 1817 - Fallen Timber/94, no part in War 1812, a warrior from Wapaghonettat 1817, Treaty 1817

1011. Methawnasicee aka Methawnaseekee – Chalakatha born about 1760 OHdied after 1803 - raiding KY-VA-OH/77-81, Point Pleasant/78, Boonesboro/78, Crawford/82, raiding Ohio River valley/88-92, Blue Jacket War/77-94, Treaty 1803

1012. **Metheotashe aka Metheotashe Opessa-Meetheeotashe-MethotasaTurtle Laying Eggs**[80]-**Mother of Tecumseh** – Pekowi born 1740 AL-died 1789 MO - daughter of **Loyparcoweh Opessa**/05 & **Pekowi Woman**/10, a Pekowi from Souvanogee (Shawnee) village AL, 1st cousin of **Blue Jacket**/35 & siblings-(fathers were brothers), wife 1st 1755 AL of **Puckenshinwa**/35-1/2 Kishpoko-Creek-Metis, 2nd 1775 OH of **Hard Striker**/40-Pekowi-(widowed the same year), mother **with Puckenshinwa** of sons Cheeseekau/56 AL, Sauwaseekou/59 KY, Nahaaseema/65 OH, **Tecumseh**/68 OH, Kumshaka/70 OH & **Lalawethika-Tenskawatawa**/74 OH, & of daughters **Tecumapease**/58 AL, Menewaulakoose/64 OH & Vocemassussia/71 OH-all 3/4th Kishpoko-

PekowiCreek-Metis, aunt of **Tecumoplas-Margaret Collins**/42 & great-aunt of **Jane Collins**/68, moved 1759 from AL to KY, moved 1760 from KY to OH, widowed 1774-lived with relatives in the **Black Fish** family/74-79, moved 1779 to Apple Creek village MO **with Menewaulakoose**/64 & **Vocemassussia**/71, adopted mother 1760 of **Joshua Renicks**/46, 1768 of **John Sparks**/60 & **Richard Sparks-Shawtunte**/65, 1772 of **Stephen Ruddell-Big Fish**/67 & **Abraham Ruddell-Black Hawk**/64, all adopted children went to other families in extended family upon death/74 of Puckenshinwa/35, no known child **with Hard Striker**/40

1013.Miller, Christopher (1) - adopted-white born about 1760-died after 1795 OH - adopted before 1770-returned 1794 (on eve of Fallen Timber), brother of **Henry Miller**/62, translator Treaty Greenville 1795, may have brought his Shawnee family with him to whites, husband about 1780 OH of **Chalakatha Woman**/65, father of six or seven 1/2 Chalakatha-Metis children/80-95 names unknown but assumed to have surname Miller

1014.Miller, Christopher (2) - adopted-white born before 1767-died 1828 KY - captured 1782 KY-returned to whites 1793, brother of **Adam Miller**/70-adopted Delaware, scout-William Wells Co-**with U.S. Army**-Fallen Timbers/94-War of 1812, KY Representative 1818-19, KY Senate 1822-23, not known to have married while among the Shawnee

1015.Miller, Henry - adopted-white born about 1762-died after 1795 OH - adopted before 1770-returned to whites about 1793, brother of **Christopher Miller**/60, scout-William Wells Co-U.S. Army Fallen Timbers/94, translator, may have brought Shawnee family with him to whites, husband about 1782 OH of **Chalakatha Woman**/65, father of five or six 1/2 Chalakatha-Metis children/82-95 names unknown but assumed to have surname Miller

1016.Mingo Carpenter - Mekoche-(adopted-**Seneca**) born about 1770 OH-died after 1832 – Blue Jacket War/87-94, scout-**with U.S. Army**-War 1812-Thames/1813, Treaty 1831, 1832, a **Chief of Shawnee among the Seneca** 1832, moved to KS 1832, husband about 1790 OH of **Seneca Woman**/75, children unknown

1017.Mink aka **Chaquiweshe**[81]-Chakweeweshe – Mekoche born 1740 OH**killed** 1774 Point Pleasant WV – parents unknown, brother of **Otter-Kwitateh**/45 & **Brother of Mink**/50, Cornstalk War/58-74, raiding Ohio-New River valleys/58, Pontiac War/62-66, Bushy Run/63, raiding New-GreenbrierJackson River valleys/63, raiding Ohio-Little Kanawha-Big Sandy-New River valleys/72, killed with brother in Point Pleasant 1774, husband 1st

1760 of **Mekoche Woman**/45, 2nd 1774 (her 1st) of **Tecumapease**/58-3/4th Kishpoko-Pekowi-Creek-Metis, brother in law of **Tecumseh**/68, children/60-73 **with Mekoche**/45 unknown, father **with Tecumapease** of Big Horns- Capt. Logan/74-7/8th Mekoche-Kishpoko-Pekowi-Creek-Metis

1018. Mink, Brother of aka Brother of Otter-Kwitateh – Mekoche born 1750 OH-**killed** 1774 Point Pleasant WV - brother of **Mink**/40 & **OtterKwitateh**/45, Cornstalk War/68-74, raiding Ohio-Little Kanawha-Big SandyNew River valleys/72, killed with brother Mink in Point Pleasant 1774, husband 1st 1769 OH of **Daughter of Moluntha**/54-Mekoche, 2nd 1771 OH of **Sarah Rising Sun**/59-1/2 Kishpoko-Mohawk, father **with Daughter of Moluntha** of Otter (2)/70-Mekoche, **with Sarah** of Bright Horns/72-3/4th Mekoche-Kishpoko-Mohawk

1019. Miranda, George (1) - adopted white born 1700 PA-died 1792 PA - son of **Mary**/1666 & **Isaac Miranda**/1662, brother of **Samuel Miranda (1)**/1705, both married Pekowi Women, trader in PA & OH by 1736, signed 1748 Petition to stop sale of liquor to the Natives **with Peter Chartier**/1690, **Tecoomteh Opessa**/1700, **Pride Opessa**/10 & 94 Natives, Commandant of Fort on Wabash during French-Indian War/54-63, husband 1st about 1725 of **Pekowi Woman**/10, 2nd 1737 of **Ann Magdelene Many**/20-white, father **with Pekowi** of Samuel Miranda (2)/26, John Miranda/28, James Miranda (1)/30 & Abraham Miranda/32-all 1/2 Pekowi-Metis, father **with Ann** of 2 children that died by 1742

1020. Miranda, James (3) - 1/2 Pekowi-Metis born about 1745 PA-died 1816 KY - son of **Samuel Miranda**/05-white & **Pekowi Woman**/14, husband 1767 of **Susannah Owens**/50, father of Samuel Miranda (5)/68, James Miranda (4)/70, Isaac Miranda/72, Thomas Miranda/81, John Owens Miranda/82, Jonathan Miranda/84 & Elizabeth Miranda/87-all 3/8th Pekowi-Seneca-Metis

1021. Miranda, Samuel (1) - adopted white born 1705 PA-died after 1763 PA - son of **Mary**/1666 & **Isaac Miranda**/1662-white, brother of **George Miranda (1)**/1700, husband by 1729 PA of **Pekowi Woman**/14, father of George Miranda (2)/30, James Miranda (3)/45, Nancy Miranda/47, Samuel Miranda (4)/51 & other children/30-50-all 1/2 Pekowi-Metis

1022. Misemeathaquatha aka Meesemeethakwatha – Pekowi born about 1710 PA-died about 1758 OH in epidemic - raiding PA-VA/40, Council Philadelphia 1753, Braddock/55, raiding New-Shenandoah River valleys/55, raiding PA/55-56, raiding Ohio-New River valleys/58

1023. Mishaquathee aka Meeshakwathee – Chalakatha born about 1765 OH died after 1815 – Blue Jacket War/82-94, Crawford/82, raiding Ohio River valley/88-92, Fallen Timber/94, Prophet's Town/1811, Brownstown/1812 Monguagon/1812-1st Amherstburg/1812-Frenchtown/1813-Frenchtown/1813-Ft. Meigs/1813-2nd Amherstburg/1813 & Thames/1813 **with Tecumseh**, Treaty 1815

1024. Misquibelahihe aka Meeskweebelheehee – Mekoche born about 1730 OH-died after 1774 – Cornstalk War/55-74, French-Indian War/54-63, Braddock/55, raiding New-Shenandoah River valleys/55, raiding PA/55-56, raiding Ohio-New River valleys/58, Pontiac War/62-66, Bushy Run/63, raiding New-Greenbrier-Jackson River valleys/63, Council Stanwix Oct. 1768, raiding Ohio-Big Sandy-Little Kanawha-New River valleys/72, Point Pleasant/74

1025. Missilimeto aka Meeseeleemeto – Pekowi born about 1770 OH-died after 1813 - raiding Ohio River valley/88-92, Blue Jacket War/88-94, OH-KYVA/95-1810, Prophet's Town/1811, Brownstown/1812-Monguagon/1812-1st Amherstburg/1812-Frenchtown/1813-Ft. Meigs/1813-2nd Amherstburg/1813 & Thames/1813 **with Tecumseh**, wife & children unknown

1026. Missouri Mauler - 1/2 Thawikila-**Missouri**-Metis born about 1740 (IL?) died after 1779 - son of **Missouri-Metis Woman** & **Thawikila Man**, Cornstalk War/58-77, raiding Ohio-New River valleys/58, Pontiac War/62-66, Bushy Run/63 raiding New-Greenbrier-Jackson River valleys/63, raiding Ohio-Big Sandy-Little Kanawha-New River valleys/72, Point Pleasant/74, raiding KY-VA-OH/77, Boonesboro/78, moved to MO 1779, husband about 1760 (IN?) of **Thawikila Woman**/45, father of several 3/4th Thawikila-Missouri-Metis children/60-79

1027. Moffett, George aka **Kiteihoo**-Kitahoe - adopted white born about 1770 died about 1831 - captured 1779 with brother **John Moffett**/68, returned to whites 1782, translator-**with U.S. Army**-War of 1812, a warrior at Wapaghonettat 1817, Treaty 1817, husband about 1790 of **Mary Mekoche**/75, father of John Moffett/92, Margaret Moffett/94, Elizabeth Moffett/96, Louisa Moffett/98, Catherine Moffett/1800 & Jane Moffett/1802-all 1/2 Mekoche-Metis

1028. Moffett, John (1) - adopted white born about 1768-died after 1826 KS - captured 1779 with brother **George Moffett**/70-returned to whites 1785-lived mostly among tribes/85-1826, Prophet's Town/1811, Brownstown/1812 Monguagon/1812-1st Amherstburg/1812-Frenchtown/1813-Ft. Meigs/1813-2nd

Amherstburg/1813-Thames/1813 **with Tecumseh**, moved to KS 1826 with **Prophet** & **Paukeesaa**, husband about 1788 OH of **Kishpoko Woman**/73, children unknown

1029. Molder aka **LeMoule** - 1/2 Mekoche-Metis born about 1710 OH-died after 1755 - son of **Mekoche Woman** & **Coureur deBois**, raiding PA-VA/40, French-Indian War/54-63, Braddock/55, raiding New-Shenandoah River valleys/55, crippled by wound, bullet-maker in later years, husband by 1730 of **Mekoche Woman**/15

1030. Moluntha aka Mequachake-Malunthy-Molunthy – Mekoche born about 1710 OH-**murdered** 1786 OH – nephew of **Katee Mekoche**/1680-sister of his father, a **Mekoche Chief** in OH before 1749, **Head Chief of Mekoche** by 1778, **split leadership of All Shawnee** with **Black Hoof**-Thawikila in 1779 after death of **Black Fish**, raiding PA-VA/40, Cornstalk War /55-77, French-Indian War/5463, Braddock/55, raiding New-Shenandoah River valleys/55, raiding PA/55-56, raiding Ohio-New River valleys/58, Pontiac War/62-66, Bushy Run/63, sent warriors to Point Pleasant/74, Grand Council June 1762, 1763, 1782, Council Logstown 1765, Council Miami Jan. 1786, Treaty 1786, brother of ElkWabete/15, 1st cousin (his father & Cornstalk's mother were siblings) & brother in law (husband of Cornstalk's sister Nonhelema) of **Cornstalk**/10, **murdered** by Hugh McGeary while holding Treaty of 1786, under U.S. flag, **succeeded as Head Chief of his faction by Blue Jacket**/35-Kishpoko, husband 1st 1730 (AL?) of **Sister of Black Hoof**/15-Thawikila, 2nd 1754 OH of 1st cousin **Nonhelema Hokolesqua**/18-7/8th Chalakatha-Mekoche-Metis, 3rd 1760 OH of **Lacumtequa**
Cold Water/44-15/16th Chalakatha-Mekoche-Metis, 4th before 1786 of another **Younger Woman** (maybe named **Lanatumque**), father **with First Wife** of Daughter/54-1/2 Mekoche-Thawikila & likely many younger children, with **Nonhelema** of Chieska/55, Younger Daughter of Nonhelema-Younger Daughter of Moluntha/57 & Capt. Johnny/59-all 15/16th Mekoche-Chalakatha-Metis, **with Lacumtequa** of a child, children with **Younger Woman** unknown

1031. Monday, John (1) aka Jean Monde-George Monday-John Martin - adopted-French-Canadian born about 1725-died about 1790 - captured by Cherokee 1738-adopted by Shawnee 1741, Cornstalk War/55-77, French-Indian War/54-63, Braddock/55, raiding New-Shenandoah River valleys/55, raiding Ohio-New River valleys/58, **worked 1761-69 with John Swift**/12-white in his silver-mines furnishing silver to **Cornstalk,** raiding Ohio-New River valleys/72, Point Pleasant/74-75-78, raiding KY-OH-VA/77-81, husband 1745 OH of **Chalakatha Woman**/30, father of John Monday (2)/50-1/2 Chalakatha-Metis

1032. Monetoshe aka **Maneteshe-Resting Snake**[82]-Four Doves – Pekowi born about 1770 OH-died after 1815 - 1st wife 1788 OH of **Tecumseh**/68, divorced after one year, from Opessa Band Pekowi, relative/same clan as **Watmeme Opessa**/30, **Metheotashe Opessa**/40, **Resting Fish-Masemo**/60, mother of Young Tecumseh-Mahyawekawpawe aka Young Tecumseh/88-7/8th Kishpoko-Mekoche-Pekowi-Creek-Metis

1033. Montcalm - 1/4th Kishpoko-Metis born about 1740 IN-died after 1782 - son of **1/2 Kishpoko-Metis Woman** & **French/Canadian Man**, raiding OhioNew River valleys/58, Pontiac War/62-66, Bushy Run/63, raiding NewGreenbrier-Jackson River valleys/63, raiding Ohio-Little Kanawha-Big Sandy-
Kanawha River valleys/72, raiding Ohio River valley/74 **with Chief Logan**, Point Pleasant/74, raiding KY-VA-OH/75-81, Boonesboro/78, raiding Ohio River valley/81 **with Joseph Brant** & **George Girty**, Crawford/82, husband 1760 OH of **Kishpoko Woman**/44, children unknown

1034. Montreuil - 1/2 Pekowi-Metis born about 1730-died after 1806 - son of **Adopted French/Canadian Woman** & **Pekowi Man**, Cornstalk War /55-77, French-Indian War/54-63, Braddock/55, raiding New-Shenandoah River valleys/55, raiding PA/55-56, raiding Ohio-New River valleys/58, Pontiac War/62-66, Bushy Run/63, raiding New-Greenbrier River valleys/63, raiding Ohio-Kanawha-New River valleys/72, Point Pleasant/74, Blue Jacket War /7794, Boonesboro/78, raiding KY-OH-VA/77-81, Crawford/82, raiding Ohio River valley/88-92, husband 1750 OH of **Pekowi Woman**/35, children unknown

1035. Moose aka Big Deer-Big Elk-Great Elk – Chalakatha (or ChalakathaMekoche?) born 1730 PA-died about 1795 OH - half-brother of Tall Oak/20 &
Black Oak/25, uncle of Little Oak/40 & Leaning Oak/45, relative/same clan as **Cornstalk**, over 6'6" tall & big, a Chalakatha warrior, Cornstalk War /55-77, French-Indian War/54-63, Braddock/55, raiding Shenandoah-New River valleys/55, among the Cherokee/56-57 in support of the French, raiding OhioNew River valleys/58, Pontiac War/62-66, Bushy Run/63, raiding NewGreenbrier Rivers/63, raiding Ohio-New River valleys/72, Point Pleasant/74-78,
Blue Jacket War /77-94, raiding KY-OH-VA/75-81, Crawford/82, raiding Ohio River valley/88-92, husband 1750 (VA?) of **Nottoway Woman**/35, children unknown

1036. Morgan aka **Maquepranum** - 1/2 Chalakatha-Metis born about 1740 OH-died after 1816 – possible son of **George Morgan** & **Chalakatha Woman**/20, Cornstalk War /55-77, raiding Ohio-New River valleys/58, Pontiac

War/62-66, Bushy Run/63, raiding New-Greenbrier River valleys/63, raiding Ohio-Little Kanawha-Big Sandy-Kanawha River valleys/72, Point Pleasant/74-78, Boonesboro/78, Blue Jacket War /77-94, raiding KY-VA-OH/75-81, Crawford/82, raiding Ohio River valley/88-92, husband 1760 OH of **Chalakatha Woman**/45, children unknown

1037. Morning Dew – adopted-Cayuga born about 1740 OH-died after 1775 - wife about 1755 OH of **Mekoche Man**/34, widow in 1775

1038. Moss aka **LeMousse** - 1/4th Mekoche-**Delaware**-Metis born about 1740 OH-died after 1777 - son of **1/2 Mekoche-French/Canadian-Metis Woman & 1/2 Delaware-French/Canadian-Metis Man**, Cornstalk War /58-77, raiding Ohio-New River valleys/58, Pontiac War/62-66, Bushy Run/63, raiding NewGreenbrier-Jackson River valleys/63, raiding Ohio-Big Sandy-Little KanawhaNew River valleys/72, Point Pleasant/74, raiding KY-OH-VA/75-77, husband
1760 OH of **Chalakatha Woman**/45, children unknown

1039. Mound aka **LeMotte** - 1/2 Chalakatha-Metis born about 1730 IN-died after 1774 - son of **Chalakatha Woman & French/Canadian Man**, Cornstalk War /55-74, French-Indian War/54-63, Braddock/55, raiding New-Shenandoah River valleys/55, raiding PA/55-56, raiding Ohio-New River valleys/58, Pontiac War/62-66, Bushy Run/63, raiding Greenbrier-Jackson River valleys/63, stirring trouble in Ohio River valley 1767, raiding Ohio-Big Sandy-Little Kanawha-New River valleys/72, Point Pleasant/74, husband 1750 OH of **Chalakatha Woman**/34, children unknown

1040. Mountain aka **LeMontagne** - 3/4th Chalakatha-Metis born about 1740 OH-died after 1774 - son of **Chalakatha Woman & 1/2 ChalakathaFrench/Canadian Metis**, Cornstalk War /58-74, raiding Ohio-New River valleys/58, Pontiac War/62-66, Bushy Run/63, raiding New-Greenbrier River valleys/63, raiding Ohio-Little Kanawha-Big Sandy-New River valleys/72, Point Pleasant/74, over 6'6" tall & big, husband 1760 OH of **Chalakatha Woman**/45, children unknown

1041. Mouse Hunter – Kishpoko born about 1750 OH-died after 1774 – Cornstalk War /68-74, raiding Little Kanawha-Big Sandy-Kanawha River valleys/72, Point Pleasant/74, a Kishpoko warrior, relative/same clan as **Tecumseh**, wife & children unknown

1042. Moytoy, Ahneewakee aka **Ahneewakee Muskrat**-Anuwagi – Chalakatha-Pekowi born 1704 Chota TN-died 1744 Chota TN - daughter of **Oshasqua (1)-Muskrat (1)-Moytoy (5)**-Pekowi & **Swan-Wapehti Hop**/1686Chalakatha, Blind Savannah Clan Cherokee, read, spoke & ciphered in

English, wife 1st 1718 Chota TN of her uncle **Raven Hop**-Raven of Hiwassee-**Raven Moytoy**/1680-Chalakatha, 2nd 1727 Chota TN of **John Cheesquatalone Greenwood**/1700-15/16th Chalakatha-Kishpoko-Black-Metis, 3rd 1739 Chota TN of **Cornelius Dougherty**/1700-1/2 Cherokee-Metis, mother **with Raven Hop** of Bushy Head-Chiesatebe Hop/18, Savenooka Hop/20, Goohsohly-Go SlowlyGolalu Hop/22, Nancy Augustus Hop/24 & Elizabeth Raven's Sister Hop/26-all
Chalakatha-Pekowi, **with Greenwood** of John Sour Mush Greenwood/30, Skienah-Hawk (Greenwood-Moytoy)/32, Preachy (Greenwood-Moytoy/34, Skiarow (Greenwood-Moytoy)/36 Cheekee (2)/37 & Ground Squirrel-Skiuka (Greenwood-Moytoy)/38-all 31/32nd Chalakatha-Pekowi-Kishpoko-Black-Metis, adopted mother 1736 of **Amoyah Pigeon Hop**/36, mother **with Dougherty** of Jennie Dougherty/40, James Dougherty/42 & John Dougherty/44-all ½ Chalakatha-Pekowi-Cherokee-Metis

1043. Moytoy, Bad Water – **Moytoy (6)-Bad Water Muskrat (1)-Amoscossite**-Dreadful Water-Young Emperor-Tacite of Euphasse-Emperor of Tellico-Mankiller of Hiwassee – Chalakatha-Pekowi born 1722 Chota TN-died 1758 WV while raiding New River valley - son of **Swan-Wapehti Hop**/1686Chalakatha & **Muskrat (1)-Moytoy (5)**/1686-Pekowi, could cipher, read & write English, Blind Savannah Clan Cherokee, appointed Emperor 1741 but depended on the Council of his brothers, uncles & great-uncles, pro-French faction in French-Indian War/54-58, raiding New-Shenandoah River valleys/55, raiding
Ohio-New River valleys/58, husband 1742 Chota TN of **Long Hair Cherokee Woman**/26, father of Bad Water Moytoy (2) -Amoscossite (2)/48-1/2 Chalakatha-Pekowi-Cherokee

1044. Moytoy, Ounaconoa aka **Ounaconoa Muskrat** – Chalakatha-Pekowi born 1716 Chota TN-died after 1757 OH - daughter of **Swan-Wapehti Hop**/1686-Chalakatha & **Oshasqua (1)-Muskrat (1)-Moytoy (5)**/1686-Pekowi, could cipher, read & write English, Blind Savannah Clan Cherokee, wife 1734 Chota TN of **Cornstalk Hokolesqua**/10, mother of Black Beard Cornstalk/35, Black Wolf Cornstalk/40, John Wolf Cornstalk/50, Peter Cornstalk/55, Susan Cornstalk/57 & other children/34-57-all 15/16th Chalakatha-Mekoche-PekowiMetis

1045. Moytoy, Preachy aka **Preachy Greenwood**-Prachey – 31/32nd Chalakatha-Pekowi-Kishpoko-Black-Metis born 1734 Chota TN-died after 1760 TN - daughter of **Ahneewakee Muskrat**/04 & **John Cheesquatalone Greenwood**/1700, Blind Savannah Clan Cherokee, wife 1754 Chota TN of **Richard Parris**/25-white, mother of Kate Parris/56, George Parris/58 & Nellie

Parris/60-all 31/64th Chalakatha-Pekowi-Kishpoko-Black-Metis

1046. Moytoy, Elizabeth aka **Raven's Sister-Elizabeth Hop**-Elizabeth RavenElizabeth Moytoy-Elizabeth Greenwood – Chalakatha-Pekowi born 1724 Nickajack TN-died 1819 Nickajack TN - daughter of **Ahneewakee Muskrat**/04Chalakatha-Pekowi & **Raven Hop**/1680-Chalakatha, adopted daughter of **John Cheesquatalone Greenwood**/03, Blind Savannah Clan Cherokee, wife 1st 1739 Nickajack TN of **Bernard Hughes**/1719-white, 2nd 1744 Running Water TN of **John Trader Vann (2)**/15-1/2 Cherokee-Metis, 3rd 1749 Nickajack TN of **David Rowe Sr**/1720-1/8th Thawikila-Creek-Metis, mother **with Hughes** of James/39, Charles/41 & Sarah Hughes/43-all ½ Chalakatha-Pekowi-Metis, **with Vann** of John Cherokee/44, Polly -Wawli/46 & Elizabeth -Quedi Vann/48-all ½ Chalakatha-Pekowi-Cherokee-Metis, **with Rowe** of Richard Rowe (1)/50, David Rowe (2)/52 & Archibald Rowe (1)/54-all 9/16th Chalakatha-Pekowi-Thawikila-Creek-Metis

1047. Moytoy, Savanooka aka **Savanooka Hop** (1)-Raven-Savanooka RavenShawnee-Raven of Chota-Little Raven-Young Raven-Colinna-SawanookeeRaven Colonah-Savanuka – Chalakatha-Pekowi born 1720 Chota TN-died after 1792 Great Tellico TN - son of **Ahneewakee Muskrat**/04-Chalakatha-Pekowi & **Raven Hop**/1680-Chalakatha, adopted son of **John Cheesquatalone Greenwood**/03, Blind Savannah Clan Cherokee, reputed to have been the strongest man in the Cherokee Nation & unbeaten in wrestling, from the Overhills, Settico & Chota, pro-French faction in French-Indian War/54-63, Braddock/55, Cornstalk War/55-74, raiding Shenandoah-New River valleys/55, raiding Ohio-New River valleys/58, Pontiac War/62-66, Bushy Run/63, raiding New-Greenbrier-Jackson River valleys/63, Point Pleasant/74, Cherokee War/75, Treaty Sycamore Shoals 1775, Treaty Long Island 1777, Council with British 1779 **with Col. Alexander McKee**/25, **William Caldwell**/50, **Matthew Elliott**/30, **Simon Surphet, Simon**/41, **George**/46 & **James Girty**/43, **Wryneck**/25-Pekowi, **Weed**/50-Iroquois & **River Bottom**/50-Seneca, raiding KY-VA-OH/77-81, on the council of his cousin **Johnny Kitegista**/35 of Tenase, a leader of the Great Tellico faction, nephew & advisor to **Oconastota Rainmaker**/1702, husband 1748 Chota TN of **Cheekee Greenwood**/28, father **with Cheekee** of Savenooka Hop-Moytoy (2)/50 & Skootekitehi-Fire Heart Hop/52-both 61/64th Chalakatha-Kishpoko-Mekoche-Black-Metis

1048. Moytoy, Sour Mush aka **John Sour Mush Greenwood**-OokosetaOgosata – 31/32nd Chalakatha-Pekowi-Kishpoko-Black-Metis born 1730 Chota

TN-died 1820 OK – son of **John Cheesquatalone Greenwood**/03 & **Ahneewakee Muskrat-Moytoy**/04, **pro-French** faction in French-Indian War/54-63, Pontiac War/62-66, Point Pleasant/74, raiding KY-VA-OH/77-81, Treaty 1785, 1804, 1805, 1806, 1816, 1817, Blind Savannah Clan Cherokee, husband 1748 Chota TN of **Long Hair Woman**/32-Cherokee, father of Bear Meat- Yonaheheweeah Greenwood/56, Tree Greenwood/58, Charley-Tsali Greenwood/60 & Zachariah Fish Greenwood/64-all 15/64th Chalakatha-Pekowi-Kishpoko-Black-Cherokee-Metis

1049. Much Trouble – adopted-Cayuga born about 1740 OH-died after 1775 - wife about 1755 OH of **Chalakatha Man**/33, widow 1775, children unknown

1050. Muddy Man aka **LaBourbonaise** - 1/2 Kishpoko-Black-Metis born about 1750 (IL?)-died after 1800 - son of **Kishpoko Woman** & **FrenchCanadian Mulatto**, Cornstalk War/68-74, raiding Ohio-Little Kanawha-Big Sandy-New River valleys/72, Point Pleasant/74, Blue Jacket War/77-94, raiding KY-VA-OH/77-81, Boonesboro/78, Crawford/82, raiding Ohio River valley/88-92, husband 1st 1770 OH of **Kishpoko Woman**/54, 2nd 1795 (IN?) of **Miami Woman**/78, children unknown

1051. Mulatto, Blackberry - 1/2 Chalakatha-Black-Metis born 1755 OH-died after 1778 - son of **Chalakatha Man**/35 & **Peggy Mulatto**/35, Point Pleasant/74-75-78, raiding Ohio-New River valleys/75, raiding KY-VA-OH/77, Boonesboro/78, husband 1775 OH of **Chalakatha Woman**/60, any children unknown

1052. Mulatto, Cinnamon - 1/2 Chalakatha-Black-Metis born about 1762 OHdied after 1810 (MO?) - daughter of **Chalakatha Man**/35 & **Peggy Mulatto**/35, living in Apple Creek village before 1810, wife 1775 OH of **Chalakatha Man**/55, widow by 1795, mother of several children/75-95-all 3/4th Chalakatha-Black-Metis

1053. Mulatto, Julia - adopted-Mulatto born about 1720-died after 1775 OH – daughter of **Scot Pioneer** & **Black Slave Woman**, about 6' tall & light complexioned, captured & adopted 1740 PA by **Chief Hintoo-Intu** (some connection to Cornstalk family?), wife 1741 PA of **Cornstalk**/10, stayed with tribe 1775 when 3 younger sons returned to whites, mother of Sun Fish Cornstalk/42, Elijah Cornstalk/44, Absalom "Ailstock"/48, Abraham "Ailstock"/50, Michael "Ailstock"/52-all 7/16th Chalakatha-Mekoche-Black-Metis, other unknown children/41-65 likely daughters

1054. Mulatto, Mulberry - 1/2 Chalakatha-Black-Metis born about 1760 OHdied after 1790 - daughter of **Chalakatha Man**/35 & **Peggy Mulatto**/35, wife about 1775 OH of **Chalakatha Man**/55, widow in 1790, children/75-90 unknown-all 3/4th Chalakatha-Black-Metis

1055.Mulatto, Peggy - adopted-Mulatto born about 1735-died after 1765 - daughter of **Black Slave Woman** & **White Owner**, former slave, capturedadopted 1755 VA/WV, returned to whites-escaped & returned to tribe 1765, wife
1755 OH of **Chalakatha Man**-born about 1735 PA-died 1774 WV, mother of Blackberry/55, Mulberry/60, Cinnamon/62 & other children/56-74-all ½ Chalakatha-Black-Metis

1056.**Muskrat (1) aka Oshasqua**[83] (1)-**Moytoy (5)**-Ossaghqua-OshkesquaHotthashkwa[84] - Pekowi born 1686 Hiwassee TN-died 1754 Hiwassee TN – parents unknown but killed 1698 by Creeks, from the Meaurroway-Straight Tail band, adopted son 1698 of **Trader Tom Carpenter (2)-Moytoy (2)**/1660-3/4th Chalakatha-Metis & **Nancy Chalakatha**/1664, taught to read, speak & cipher in English by stepfather, some connection to either Nancy/1664 & the Hop family, husband 1703 of adopted sister (possible relative) **Swan-Wapehti Hop**/1686Chalakatha, father of daughters Ahneewakee/04, Ounacona/16, Tame Deer/20, sons Oshasqua (2-Muskrat (2)/18 & Bad Water-Moytoy (6)/22 & other unknown children/05-31-all ½ Chalakatha-Pekowi, adopted father 1708 of nephew **John
Watts Sr**/04-7/8th Chalakatha-Pekowi-Metis

1057.Muskrat (2) aka Oshasqua (2) -Ossaghqua-Oshkeshqua-Hothashkwa – Chalakatha-Pekowi born 1718 Chota TN-died after 1774 OH – son of **Oshasqua-Muskrat-Moytoy (5)**/1686-Pekowi & **Swan-Wapehti Hop**/1686Chalakatha, read, spoke & ciphered in English, allied with **Savannah Tom Carpenter (2)**/1698, **Robert-Thigh-Cauquillehaneh McLemore**/31, **John French**/10, **Capt. French**/12, **Rainmaker (3)**/06 & **John Lantaniak**/20adopted-French/Canadian in pro-French faction French-Indian War/54-63, Braddock/55, raiding New-Shenandoah River valleys/55, raiding Ohio-New
River valleys/58, Pontiac War/62-66, moved to the Ohio valley between 1766-74, Bushy Run/63, raiding New-Greenbrier-Jackson River valleys/63, raiding Ohio-Big Sandy-Little Kanawha-New River valleys/72, Point Pleasant/74, a **Pekowi Chief** in OH before 1774, relative/same clan as Metheotashe Opessa, **called an uncle of Tecumseh**, wife & children unknown

1058.Muskrat Man – Mekoche-(adopted-**Seneca**) born about 1780 OH-died after 1832 KS – **with U.S. Army-**War 1812-Thames/1813, Treaty 1832, move to KS 1832, husband about 1800 OH of **Seneca Woman**/85, children unknown

1059.**Muskrat Tail**[85] – Kishpoko born about 1790 OH-**killed** 1813 Thames - Prophet's Town/1811, Brownstown/1812-Monguagon/1812-1st Amhersburg/1812-Frenchtown/1813-Ft. Meigs/1813-2nd Amherstburg/1813 & **killed at Thames**/1813 **with Tecumseh**, wife & child unknown

1060.Musquakonokah aka **Muskwakonokah**[86]-**Red Pole** – Mekoche born about 1750 OH-died after 1786 - raiding Ohio-Little Kanawha-Big SandyKanawha-New River valleys/72, Point Pleasant/74-78, raiding KY-VA-OH/7781, Blue Licks/82, Crawford/82, Treaty 1786

1061.Musquanako aka Muskwanako – Chalakatha born about 1715 PA-died about 1758 OH in epidemic - raiding PA/40, Council Ft. Pitt Nov. 1753, raiding New-Shenandoah River valleys/55, raiding PA/55-56, raiding Ohio-New River valleys/58

Section XII
Nahaasema to Oxonoxy (N-O)

N

1062. Nahaasema aka Nahaaseema, Nahasimo[87] Puckenshinwa - 3/4th Kishpoko-Pekowi-Creek Metis born 1764 OH-**killed** 1788 KY - 3rd son of **Puckenshinwa**/35 & **Metheotashe Opessa**/40, Blue Jacket War/82-88, raiding KY-OH-VA/82, raiding Ohio River valley/88, **killed 1788 in KY raid**, husband aout 1785 OH of **Kishpoko Woman**/69, possible children unknown

1063. Nakacheka aka Nakacheeka-Nakachika – Mekoche born about 1780 OHdied after 1817 - no part in War 1812, a warrior at Wapaghonettat 1817, Treaty 1817

1064. Nakanapasepa – Chalakatha-Mekoche born about 1729 PA-died about 1758 OH in epidemic – son of **Father of Black Fish**/05 & **Mother of Black Fish**/10, brother of **Black Fish**/25, Kwatooka/27, French-Indian War/54-58, raiding New-Shenandoah valleys/55, raiding PA/55, Braddock/55, raiding PA/55-56, raiding Ohio-New River valleys/58, wife & children unknown

1065. Nameawah – Chalakatha born about 1785 OH-died after 1817 – no part in War 1812, a warrior at Lewistown 1817, Treaty 1817

1066.	Naneskaka – Mekoche born about 1770 OH-died after 1817 - raiding Ohio River valley/88-92, Blue Jacket War/87-94, no part in War 1812, a warrior at Wapaghonettat 1817, Treaty 1817

1067.	Napawita aka **Napaweeta** – Kishpoko born about 1780 OH-died after
1825 – brother of **Napawitha**/82 & **Sister**/84, raiding OH-KY-VA/99-1810, Prophet's Town/1811, Brownstown/1812-Monguagon/1812-1st Amherstburg/1812-Frenchtown/1813-Ft. Meigs/1813-2nd Amherstburg/1813 & Thames/1813 **with Tecumseh**, move to CAN 1815, move back to OH 1825, Treaty 1825, husband about 1800 OH of **Chalakatha Woman**/84

1068. Nawalippa aka **Nawaleepa** – Chalakatha born about 1775 OH-died after 1817 - Fallen Timber/94, no part in War 1812, a warrior at Lewistown 1817, Treaty 1817

1069. Nayabeepee – Chalakatha born about 1770 OH-died after 1817 - raiding Ohio River valley/88-92, Blue Jacket War/87-94, part in War 1812, a warrior at Lewistown 1817, Treaty 1817

1070. Naywalee – Chalakatha born about 1770 OH-died after 1817 - raiding Ohio River valley/88-92, Blue Jacket War/88-94, no part in War 1812, a warrior at Lewistown 1817, Treaty 1817

1071. Neahmensieeh aka Neeahmensee – Mekoche born about 1760 OH-died after 1803 - raiding KY-OH-VA/77-81, Crawford/82, raiding Ohio River valley/88-92, Blue Jacket War/77-94, Treaty 1803

1072. Neecheumata aka Neecheoomata– Chalakatha born about 1750 (OHAL?)-died after 1774 – Cornstalk War/68-74, raiding Ohio-Little Kanawha-Big
Sandy-New River valleys/72, Point Pleasant/74

1073. Needle in Hand – Pekowi born about 1750 OH-died after 1782 - wife about 1765 OH of **Pekowi Man**/45, widow in 1782

1074. Neenatakoshee aka Ninatakoshe – Mekoche born about 1780 OH-died after 1817 - scout-**with U.S. Army**-War 1812-Thames/1813, Treaty 1817

1075. Negro Wife aka Black Wife-Black Woman - adopted-Mulatto born about 1725-died after 1774 - daughter of **Scot Pioneer** & **Black Slave Woman**, former slave, taken in PA raids of 1740, adopted 1740-never returned to whites, sister of **Julia**/20-wife of **Cornstalk**/10 & **Black Horse**/30 both mulattoes taken in PA 1740, wife 1740 PA of **Chalakatha Man**/20-(from Okowellos band?), widow 1774, mother of several 1/2 Chalakatha-Black children/40-65-names unknown

1076. Nehquakahuka aka Nekwakahooka – Chalakatha born about 1770 OH died after 1817 - raiding Ohio River valley/88-92, Blue Jacket War/87-94, no part in War 1812, a warrior from Hog Creek 1817, Treaty 1817

1077. Neihebuketha aka Neehebookshe-Nayhebookseh - Chalakatha born about 1730 PA-died after 1765 – Cornstalk War/55-65, French-Indian War/5463, Braddock/55, raiding New-Shenandoah River valleys/55, raiding PA/55-56, raiding Ohio-New River valleys/58, Pontiac War/62-65, Bushy Run/63, raiding New-Greenbrier-Jackson River valleys/63, Council Logstown 1765

1078. Nekulisika aka Neculissika-Nekooleeseeka - adopted-white born about 1740-died after 1774 - adopted before 1750-forced to return to whites-returned to tribe 1765, Cornstalk War/58-74, raiding Ohio-New River valleys/58, Pontiac War/62-66, Bushy Run/63, raiding New-Greenbrier River valleys/63, raiding Ohio-Big Sandy-Little Kanawha-New River valleys/72, Point Pleasant/74, husband about 1760 OH of **Chalakatha Woman**/45, children unknown

1079. Nelawachika aka Nelawacheeka – Kishpoko born about 1780-died after 1825 - raiding OH-KY-VA/99-1810, Prophet's Town/1811, Brownstown/1812-Monguagon/1812-1st Amherstburg/1812-Frenchtown/1813-Ft. Meigs/1813-2nd Amherstburg/1813 & Thames/1813 **with Tecumseh**, moved to CAN 1815, returned to OH about 1825, Treaty 1825

1080. Neltawaptha aka Neltawapseh – Chalakatha born about 1710 PA-died after 1756 OH - raiding PA/40, Council Ft. Pitt Nov. 1753, Braddock/55, raiding New-Shenandoah River valleys/55, raiding PA/55-56

1081. Nemakoshe – Mekoche born about 1770 OH-died after 1817 - raiding Ohio River valley/88-92, Blue Jacket War/87-94, no part in War 1812, a warrior at Wapaghonettat 1817, Treaty 1817

1082. Nenessica aka Nenesseeka - Mekoche born about 1750 OH-died after 1788 – Cornstalk War/68-77, raiding Ohio-Little Kanawha-Big Sandy-New River valleys/72, Point Pleasant/74-75-78, Blue Jacket War/77-88, raiding KY-VA-OH/77-81, Crawford/82, raiding Ohio River valley/88, captured **Thomas Ridout**/70-white 1788

1083. Nepaho – Mekoche born about 1770 OH-died after 1817 – Blue Jacket War/87-94, no part in War 1812, a warrior at Wapaghonettat 1817, Treaty 1817

1084. Nequakabuchka aka Nekwakabooshka – Thawikila born about 1750-died after 1817 – from **Black Hoof** band, Cornstalk War/68-77, raiding Ohio-Little Kanawha-Big Sandy-New River valleys/72, Point Pleasant/74-78, Blue Jacket

War/77-94, raiding KY-OH-VA/77-81, Crawford/82, raiding Ohio River valley/88-92, Blue Jacket War/77-94, no part in War 1812, an elder at Hog Creek 1817

1085. Nequetaghaw aka Nekwataghaw - Mekoche born about 1750 OH-died after 1795 – Cornstalk War/68-77, raiding Ohio-New River valleys/72, Point Pleasant/74-78, Blue Jacket War/77-94, raiding KY-OH-VA/77-81, Crawford/82, raiding Ohio River valley/88-92, Treaty Greenville 1795

1086. Nereraha (1) aka Nerrar-Nehher – Chalakatha born about 1740 (OHPA?)-died after 1784 – Cornstalk War/58-77, raiding Ohio-New River valleys/58, Pontiac War/62-66, Bushy Run/63, raiding New-Greenbrier-Jackson River valleys/63, raiding Ohio-Big Sandy-Little Kanawha-New River valleys/72, Point Pleasant/74-75-78, Blue Jacket War/77-84, raiding KY-VA-OH/77-81, Crawford/82, husband 1760 OH of **Chalakatha Woman**/45, father of Young Nereraha/80

1087. Nereraha, Young aka Nerrer-Nehher - Chalakatha born about 1780-died after 1817 – son of **Nereraha (1)** /40 & Chalakatha Woman/45, no part in War 1812, a warrior at Lewistown 1817, Treaty 1817

1088. Nesopekwa – adopted-Cayuga born about 1740 OH-died after 1775 – Cornstalk War/58-75, raiding Ohio-New River valleys/58, Pontiac War/62-66 Bushy Run/63, raiding New-Greenbrier-Jackson River valleys/63, raiding OhioBig Sandy-Little Kanawha-New River valleys/72, raiding Ohio River valley/74 **with Chief Logan**, Point Pleasant/74-75, husband 1760 OH of **Chalakatha Woman**/44, children unknown

1089. Nesselogonee - adopted-Chippewa born about 1745 (MI?)-died after 1788 – Cornstalk War/63-77, Pontiac War/63-66, Bushy Run/63, raiding NewGreenbrier-Jackson River valleys/63, raiding Ohio-Little Kanawha-Big Sandy-
New River valleys/72, raiding Ohio River valley/74 **with Chief Logan**, Point Pleasant/74, Blue Jacket War/77-88, Boonesboro/78, raiding KY-VA-OH/77-81, Crawford/82, raiding Ohio River valley/88, husband 1765 OH of **Kishpoko Woman**/50, children unknown

1090. Nettle Carrier aka Nettle Carrier Tahchee (1)-**Talotiskee (1)**-Nettle Carrier Attakullakulla-Nettle Carrier Carpenter-Utaledangisi-TaledanigiskiTaledanigisgi-Hemp Carrier-Old Hemp - 3/16th Chalakatha-Thawikila-Creek**Cherokee**-Metis born 1756 Toqua TN-died after 1819 Cherokee Nation (TN?) - son of **Tahchee Carpenter**/36 & **Place Priber**/38, grandson of

Attakullakulla Carpenter, 1st cousin of **Dragging Canoe**, 2nd cousin of **Double Head**, Red Paint Clan Cherokee, Treaty Sycamore Shoals 1775, Council Coyatee 1792, Ish Station 1793, Council Hanging Maw Town-survived attack by John Beard's renegade militia 1793, Capt. John MacIntosh Co-**with U.S. Army**-Creek War/1813, Treaty 1805, 1819, husband 1775 (TN?) of **Susannah Catherine Cherokee**/60, father of Talotiskee (2)-Nettle Carrier (2) Tahchee/76-3/32nd Chalakatha-Thawikila-Creek-Cherokee-Metis

1091.Nettle Flower – Kishpoko born about 1750 OH-died after 1782 - wife about 1765 OH of **Kishpoko Man**/45, widow in 1782

1092.Netumpsika aka Netaumpsiko-Netaumpsico-Netaumpsiko-Netoompseeka-Nethawamsika - 1/2 Mekoche-Metis born about 1750 OH-died after 1810 - son of **Mekoche Man** & **Adopted-White Woman**, brother of **Nosewetamah**/40, returned to whites-returned to tribe 1765, Cornstalk War/68-77, raiding Ohio-Little Kanawha-Big Sandy-New River valleys/72, Point Pleasant/74-75-78, Blue Jacket War/77-94, raiding KY-VA-OH-PA/77-81, Crawford/82, raiding Ohio River valley/83-89, moved to MO about 1795, listed as a leader in 1799, husband about 1770 OH of **Mekoche Woman**/55, children unknown

1093.Neverville - 1/2 Pekowi-Metis born about 1710 (IN?)-died 1759 - son of **Pekowi Woman** & **Mr. Nieverville**-French/Canadian, French-Indian War/54-63, Braddock/55, raiding New-Shenandoah River valleys/55, raiding Ohio-New River valleys/58, living **with Shawnee** in OH 1759, husband about 1730 (IN?) of **Mekoche Woman**/15, children unknown

1094.Newabetuka aka Newabetooka - Mekoche born about 1770 OH-died after 1817 - raiding Ohio River valley/88-92, Blue Jacket War/88-94, no part in War 1812, a warrior at Wapaghonettat 1817, Treaty 1817

1095.Newalocheye aka Newalochee – Chalakatha born about 1710 PA-died after 1756 - raiding PA/40, Council Ft. Pitt Nov. 1753, Braddock/55, raiding New-Shenandoah River valleys/55, raiding PA/55-56

1096.Newasa – Chalakatha born about 1780-died after 1817 – no part in War 1812, a warrior at Lewistown 1817, Treaty 1817

1097.Newchekonno aka Neucheconner-Neuconneh-Nuchekonner-Neucheconno–Nechikonner. Pekowi born about 1690 PA-died after 1748 - living on Allegheny River 1737, raiding PA/40, fled with Peter Chartier as chief of his band from Chartier's Old Town to mouth of the Scioto at Lower Shawnee Town in 1745, living in Ohio by 1747.

1098. Newland, Benjamin - adopted-white born about 1750-died after 1800 - adopted about 1755-returned to whites 1795, Cornstalk War/68-77, raiding OhioLittle Kanawha-Big Sandy-New River valleys/72, Point Pleasant/74-75-78, Blue Jacket War/77-94, raiding KY-VA-OH/77-81, Crawford/82, raiding Ohio River valley/88-92, husband 1769 OH of **Chalakatha Woman**/54, father of Sarah Newland/70, Richard Newland/80 & other children/70-80-all 1/2 ChalakathaMetis

1099. Nianymseka aka Neeaneemseka-Nianimisico-Neinimsico - Mekoche born about 1750-died after 1799 – Cornstalk War/68-77, raiding Ohio-Little Kanawha-Big Sandy-New River valleys/72, Point Pleasant/74-78, Blue Jacket War/77-94, raiding KY-VA-OH/77-81, raiding Ohio-New River valleys/75-81, Crawford/82, raiding Ohio River valley/88-92, Council Ft. Finney 1786 **with Moluntha, Capt. Johnny, Aweeconee, Nianimissico, Wapachcawela, Red Pole, Nihipeewa**, female-**Cawechile** & **Black Snake**, Treaty Greenville 1795, listed as a leader in 1799

1100. Nichapressika aka Neechapresseeka – Chalakatha born about 1730 PAdied after 1765 – Cornstalk War/55-65, French-Indian War/54-63, Braddock/55, raiding New-Shenandoah River valleys/55, raiding PA/55-56, raiding Ohio-New
River valleys/58, Pontiac War/62-65, Bushy Run/63, raiding New-Greenbrier-Jackson River valleys/63, Council Logstown 1765

1101. Nichinissieve aka Neecheeneeseewa – Mekoche born about 1755 OHdied after 1786 - Point Pleasant/74-78, Blue Jacket War/77-82, raiding KY-VA-OH/75-81, Crawford/82, Treaty 1786

1102. Nihinessiko aka Nehinissico-Neeheeneseeko - Mekoche born about 1750 OH-died after 1786 – Cornstalk War/68-77, raiding Ohio-Little KanawhaBig Sandy-New River valleys/72, Pleasant/74-75-78, Blue Jacket War/77-86, raiding KY-VA-OH/75-81, Crawford/82, Council Ft. Finney 1786 **with Moluntha, Capt. Johnny, Aweeconee, Nianimissico, Wapachcawela, Red
Pole, Nihipeewa**, female-**Cawechile** & **Black Snake**, Treaty Ft. Finney 1786

1103. Nihipeewa[88] aka Neeheepeewa – Mekoche born about 1745 OH-died after 1786 – Cornstalk War/63-77, raiding Ohio-Little Kanawha-Big Sandy-New River valleys/72, Point Pleasant/74-78, Blue Jacket War/77-86, raiding KY-OHVA/75-81, Crawford/82, Council Ft. Finney 1786 **with Moluntha, Capt. Johnny, Aweeconee, Nianimissico, Wapachcawela, Red Pole, Nihipeewa**, female-**Cawechile** & **Black Snake**, Treaty Ft. Finney 1786

1104.**Nika aka Wild Goose**[89]-Nitka-Ni'ka-Neeka – Pekowi born about 1650 (IL-OH?)-assassinated in 1687 with LaSalle - guide with LaSalle on expeditions up to their deaths, traveled to Europe with him more than once, associated **with Martin Chartier** and **the Wolf.**

1105.Nikipohok aka Neekeepohok – Chalakatha born about 1710 PA-died about 1758 OH in epidemic - raiding PA/40, Council Ft. Pitt 1753, Braddock/55, raiding New-Shenandoah River valleys/55, raiding PA/55-56, raiding Ohio-New River valleys/58

1106.**Nimwha** aka Nimwha Hokolesqau-Nimwha Okowellos-**Nihipuwa**[90] – 7/8th Chalakatha-Mekoche-Metis born 1720 PA-died after 1786 likely OH - son of **Okowellos**/1674 & **Katee Mekoche**/1680, to AL with father 1725-returned to PA by 1730, a **Chief of the Shawnee among the Delaware** 1750, **Cornstalk War** /55-77, French-Indian War/54-63, Braddock/55, raiding New-Shenandoah River valleys/55, raiding PA/55-56, raiding Ohio-New River valleys/58, Pontiac War/62-66, Bushy Run/63, raiding New-Greenbrier-Jackson River valleys/63, Council Muskingum Nov. 1764, Council Logstown 1765, Council Ft. Pitt 1765, raiding Ohio-Little Kanawha-Big Sandy-New River valleys/72, **an emissary to the Delaware for Cornstalk** 1774, Point Pleasant/74-78, Treaty Camp Charlotte 1774, hostage of whites winter 1774-75, Council Ft. Pitt 1775 with **Corn Stalk**, **Silver Heels**, **Wryneck** & **Blue Jacket**, Council Ft. Pitt 1776, **succeeded Red Hawk as Chief of Shawnee among the Delaware 1777**, **Blue Jacket War** /77-86, Blue Licks/82, Crawford/82, Council Ft. Pitt 1785, Council Ft. Pitt 1786, Treat 1786, husband 1739 OH of **Delaware Woman**/23, children unknown

1107. Ninihica aka **Ninihica Mayapple**-Ninihica Hop-Nephew (3) of Standing Turkey-Old Hop – Chalakatha-Kishpoko born 1721 Settico TN-**killed 1776 PA** - son of **May Apple**/1690-Kishpoko & **Ghigoneli Hop**/1694-Chalakatha, halfbrother of **John French**/10 & **Capt. French**/12, from Settico, raiding Ohio-New River valleys/58, Pontiac War/62-66, Bushy Run/63, raiding New-JacksonGreenbrier River valleys/63, raiding Ohio-Little Kanawha-Big Sandy-New River valleys/72, Point Pleasant/74, Cherokee War/75, **killed by Americans** while held prisoner, husband 1741 Running Water TN of **Blind Savannah Woman**/28, children/42-76 unknown

1108. Nitaskeka aka Neetaskeka - Mekoche born about 1770 OH-died after 1817 – Blue Jacket War/87-94, raiding Ohio River valley/88-92, no part in War 1812, a warrior at Wapaghonettat 1817, Treaty 1817

1109.No Tail aka **Potchetee**-Man Without a Tail – Mekoche born about 1790 OH-died after 1817 – no part in War 1812, a warrior at Wapaghonettat 1817,

Treaty 1817

1110. Nokskahway – Kishpoko born about 1795 (OH-IN?)-died after 1850 - Prophet's Town/1811, Brownstown/1812-Monguagon/1812-1st Amherstburg/1812-Frenchtown/1813-Ft. Meigs/1813-2nd Amherstburg/1813 & Thames/1813 **with Tecumseh**, moved to CAN 1815, returned to OH-moved to KS 1826 **with Prophet & Paukeesaa**, grandson-in-law of **Tecumseh**, husband 1836 KS of **Nahswahpama**[91] **Tecumseh**/1820, children unknown

1111. Nolawat – Chalakatha born about 1780 OH-died after 1817 – no part in War 1812, a warrior from Lewistown 1817, Treaty 1817

1112. Nonhelema aka **Nonhelema**[92] **Hokolesqua**-Grenadier Squaw-Warrior Woman of the Shawnee- Nonhelema Okowellos – 7/8th Chalakatha-MekocheMetis born 1718 PA-died after 1786 OH - daughter of **Okowellos Hokolesqua**/1674 & **Katee Mekoche**/1680, about 6'6" tall-well built & attractive, moved to AL by 1725 with Okowellos' band-returned to PA by 1730, a **Chalakatha village Chief** by 1750, **Cornstalk War** /55-74, French-Indian War/54-63, Pontiac War/62-66, established Nonhelema's village on Sippio Creek of Sciota River OH before 1773, **an emissary to the Shawnee for Cornstalk** 1774, **only woman warrior** Point Pleasant/74, Grand Council 1782, Council Miami 1-1786, fingers cut off of her right hand to the 1st knuckle by whites following murder of Moluntha during Benjamin Logan's attack on Moluntha's village 1786, moved to Apple Creek MO area following death of Molunthareturned to OH home to die, wife 1st 1734 PA of **Chalakatha Chief**/14-widowed 1754, 2nd 1754 OH of 1st cousin **Moluntha**/10-Mekoche, 3rd (liaison) 1762 OH of **Richard Butler**/42-white-(adopted-Seneca), mother **with Chalakatha Chief** of Elder Daughter/45 & Middle Daughter/50-both 15/16th Chalakatha-MekocheMetis, **with Moluntha** of Chieska/55, Younger Daughter/57 & Capt. Johnny/59all 15/16th Chalakatha-Mekoche-Metis, **with Richard Butler** of Capt. Butler/63-7/16th Chalakatha-Mekoche-Metis, adopted mother of **niece Fanny Butler**/553/16th Chalakatha-Creek-Metis (daughter of her half-sister **Elizabeth**/26 & **John Butler** (1)-Sugantah-Lodging Pole/30-white-adopted Seneca), often confused in white histories with her sisters & nieces

1113. Nopamago – Chalakatha born about 1770 OH-died after 1817 - raiding Ohio River valley/88-92, Blue Jacket War/88-94, a warrior from Lewistown 1817, Treaty 1817

1114. Nosewetamah aka Nosewelamah - 1/2 Mekoche-Metis born about 1740 PA-died after 1774 - son of **Mekoche Man** & **Adopted-White Woman**, brother of **Netumpsika**/50, Cornstalk War/58-74, raiding Ohio-New River valleys/58,

Pontiac War/62-66, Bushy Run/63, raiding New-Greenbrier-Jackson River valleys/63, returned to whites-returned to tribe 1765, raiding Ohio-KanawhaNew River valleys/72, Point Pleasant/74, husband about 1760 OH of **Mekoche Woman**/45, father of several 3/4th Mekoche-Metis children/60-74

1115. Nowpour – Chalakatha born about 1780 OH-died after 1817 – no part in War 1812, a warrior from Lewistown 1817, Treaty 1817

1116. Nuadee, John aka Shawanaw-**Oshawahnoo**-John Nahdee-**John Naudee** – 1/2 Kishpoko-**Ottawa** born about 1770-died 1870 – son of **Kishpoko Woman & Ottawa Man**, raiding Ohio River valley/88-92, Blue Jacket War/88-94, **traveled with Tecumseh**/95-1811, Brownstown/1812-Monguagon/1812-1st Amherstburg/1812-Frenchtown/1813-Ft. Meigs/1813-2nd Amherstbueg/1813 & Thames/1813 **with Tecumseh**, said to have buried Tecumseh, moved to CAN 1815, remained with the Chippewa when band returned to U.S. 1825, husband of **Chippewa Woman**, children unknown

1117. Nutimaes, Ben - 1/2 Pekowi-**Delaware** born about 1705 PA-died after 1760 - son of **Pekowi Woman**/1680 & **Nutimaes**/1670-Delaware, half-brother of **Elizabeth Nutimaes**/1700, associated with brother-in-law **Poxinosa**/1670-Pekowi, wife & children unknown

1118. Nutimaes, Elizabeth – Pekowi born about 1700 PA-died after 1754 – daughter of **Pekowi Woman**/1680 & **Pekowi Man**/1675-(of Pheasant band), adopted daughter by 1705 PA of **Nutimaes**/1670-Delaware, a Christian Pekowi, half-sister of **Ben Nutimaes**/05-(same Pekowi mother), 2nd wife about 1716 of **Poxinosa**/1670, mother of Teatapercaum/17, Elder Daughter/18, Awanoos/19, Younger Daughter/20 & Kolapeka/21 & 3 other children-all Pekowi

1119. Nuussome aka Noossomee – Chalakatha born about 1780 OH-died after 1817 – no part in War 1812, a warrior from Lewistown 1817, Treaty 1817

O

1120. Ochipway aka Ocheepway – Mekoche born about 1770 OH-died after 1817 – Blue Jacket War/88-94, no part in War 1812, a warrior at Wapaghonettat 1817, Treaty 1817

1121. Oconastota aka **Oconastota Rainmaker**-Aganstata-Groundhog SausageAganustata-Pounding Meat in a Mortar-Cunne Shoate - 1/2 Chalakatha-

Cherokee born 1702 Chota TN-died 1783 - son of **Elder Sister of Old Hop**/1685-Chalakatha & **Young Rainmaker**/1685-Cherokee, Blind Savannah Clan Cherokee, delegation to ENG 1730, pro-British faction (against French & Shawnee) in French-Indian War/55-63, **Principal Man of Chota** after death of uncle Old Hop 1761, shared power/authority with his brother Kitegista/08, Pontiac War/62-66, Cherokee War/75, Treaty Sycamore Shoals 1775, **Principle Chief** of Cherokee 1775-80, husband 1st 1718 Chota TN of **Ahneewakee (Anuwagi-Aniwadi) Red Paint**/04-1/2 Thawikila-Creek, 2nd 1735 Chota TN of 1st cousin **Quatsis Fox**/08-1/2 Chalakatha-Cherokee, 3rd 1738 Chota TN of **Lucy Ward (1)**/14-adopted-white, father **with Red Paint** of Ostenaca/18, Ollie Nionee/20, Shallelocke/22, Jennie/24 & Terrapin (1)/26-all 1/2 ChalakathaThawikila-Creek-Cherokee, **with Fox** of Quatsis Oconastota/36-1/2 ChalakathaCherokee, **adopted father** of her sons Terrapin Watts-Terrapin (2)/26 & Bark Watts/28-both 11/16th Chalakatha-Pekowi-Cherokee-Metis, **with Ward** of Lucy Ward Oconastota/42-1/4th Chalakatha-Cherokee-Metis

1122. Okowellos aka **Okowellos Hokolesqua**-Akowellos-Hokowellos-Hakowellos-Stalk of Plant -3/4th Chalakatha-Metis born 1674 PA-died 1758 in epidemic OH – son of **Hokolesqua Chalakatha**/1630 & **Pashmere Carpenter (1)**/1637-1/2 Chalakatha-Metis, in TN before 1704, a **Chalakatha Chief** in OH by 1707, **King of the Upper Shawnee** in PA 1723, **Chief of the Shawnee on the Savannah River** AL 1725, a **major Chalakatha Chief** in PA 1730, **Chief of the Shawnee in AL** 1755, **Head Chief of Chalakatha in OH** 1758, over 6' tall, associated at times with **Straight Tail**-Pekowi, **Opessa**-Pekowi, **Poxinosa**Pekowi, **Pheasant**-Pekowi & **White Fish**-Pekowi -all major Shawnee chiefs of his time, also some connection with Standing Turkey-Old Hop/1688-Chalakatha & family, husband 1st 1695 PA of **Katee Mekoche**/1680, 2nd 1713 PA of

Delaware Woman/1695, 3rd 1725 AL of **Creek Woman**/09, children/95-03 **with Katee** unknown but likely daughters, father **with Katee** of daughter Wakuta/04(wife of **Thomas Greenwood**), child/06, child/08, son **Cornstalk**/10, daughter/12-(wife of **Mr. Francis & Old Belt**), son Keeweeton/14, daughter Cawechile/16-(wife of **Cold Water**), daughter **Nonhelema**/18, son **Nimwha**/20, son **Red Hawk**/22 & son **Silverheels** Hokolesqua/24-all 7/8th ChalakathaMekoche-Metis, **with Delaware** of son Wakeeampea/14, Ewikunwee/16, Naythakiena/18 & **Bukangolas**/20-all 3/8th Chalakatha-Delaware-Metis, **with Creek Wife** of daughters Elizabeth/26 & Catherine-Kitty Hokolesqua/28-both 3/8th Chalakatha-Creek-Metis

1123. Old Belt aka **Kaighswaghtaniant** - Seneca born about 1700-died after 1762 - 3rd husband after 1745 of **Older Daughter of Okowellos**/12-7/8th Chalakatha-Mekoche-Metis (his last wife), adopted father of **Silver Heels-Aroas**/30 & **Counasona**/35

1124. Old Chelelagatehee aka Old Chalakatha – Chalakatha born about 1765 TN-died after 1814 - a Chalakatha from Running Water (Shawnee) village, Capt. John Brown Co-**with U.S. Army**-Creek War/1813, husband about 1785 TN of **Chalakatha Woman**/70, children unknown

1125. Onawaskine – Thawikila born about 1775 (AL?)-died after 1832 - Fallen Timber/94, a warrior in Hog Creek village 1817, moved to KS 1832

1126. One Eyed Charlie – Mekoche born about 1750 OH-died after 1777 - blinded in one eye in battle with whites, Cornstalk War/68-77, raiding OhioLittle Kanawha-Big Sandy-New River valleys/72, Point Pleasant/74-75, raiding KY-VA-OH/77

1127. Onowaskemo aka Ononwashim – Chalakatha born about 1770 OH-died after 1817 – Blue Jacket War/88-94, raiding Ohio River valley/88-92, raiding OH-KY-VA/95-1810, Prophet's Town/1811, Brownstown/1812-Monguagon/1812-1st Amherstburg/1812-Frenchtown/1813-Ft. Meigs/1813-2nd Amherstburg/1813 & Thames/1813 **with Tecumseh**, Treaty 1817

1128. Opakeita aka Opakeyeeta - Pekowi born about 1680 MD-died after 1732 (MD?) - **Pekowi chief** that remained in MD when most of the Pekowi-MekocheThawikila from MD-PA moved to OH.

1129. Opakethwa – Pekowi born about 1690 PA-died after 1732 (PA?) - **Pekowi chief** that remained in PA when most of the Pekowi-Mekoche-Thawikila from MD-PA moved to OH

1130. Opeatako – Chalakatha born about 1700 PA-died after 1756 OH - raiding PA/40, Council Ft. Pitt Nov. 1753,

1131. Opessa aka Opethatha-Ophesaw-Ophessaw-Wopaththa-WawpaythiWapatha-Swan[93]-Opessa Straight Tail – Pekowi born 1675-died shortly after 1760 PA - son of **Straight Tail-Meaurroway**/1630 & **Pekowi Woman**/35, succeeded father as a **Pekowi Chief** in MD/PA by 1700 (resigned 1711) & **Pekowi Chief** again in MD/PA by 1723, Treaty Wm. Penn 1701, Council 1706, gave up position as Chief in MD 1711 to join the Delaware chief Sassoonan, returned to MD 1722, was in AL 1735, returned to north MD/east PA again by 1749-Council Philadelphia Aug. 1749, moved to OH about 1750, succeeded **Pheasant-Kakawatchekee**/1680 as **Head Pekowi Chief in OH** 1752, Council

Tioga Point May 1756, Council Ft. Pitt Aug. 1760, brother in law (through Sister) of **Peter Chartier**/1690, connected with **Poxinosa**, **White Fish (1)** & **Okowellos Hokolesqua** (Head Chiefs of bands), great-grandfather of **Tecumseh**/68, husband by 1695 MD of **Pekowi Woman**/1680, father of Snow White/1695, Tecoomteh/1700, Loyparkoweh-Waywayti/05 & Lawaquaqua-Pride Opessa/10-all Pekowi

1132. Opessa, Lawagqua aka Lawoughqua-Lawagkwa-**Elder Brother of Blue Jacket** – Pekowi-Kishpoko born 1733 PA-died after 1774 – trading with Ohio Fur Co. in PA **with Blue Jacket** & **Wabete** by early 1750's, Cornstalk War/55-74, French-Indian War/54-63, Braddock/55, raiding New-Shenandoah River valleys/55, raiding PA/55-56, raiding Ohio-New River valley/58, Pontiac War/62-65, Bushy Run/63, raiding New-Greenbrier-Jackson River valleys/63, Council Logstown PA 1765, a **Pekowi Chief** in OH 1760's-70's, returned captives to Ft. Pitt 1765, raiding Ohio-Little Kanawha-Big Sandy-New River valleys/72, Point Pleasant/74, wife & children unknown

1133. Opessa, Loyparkaweh aka **Loapeckeway-Lawpakaway**[94]-**Wawwaythi**[95]-Waywayti-Waywaytee – Pekowi born about 1705 MD-died after 1760 OH - son of **Opessa**/1675 & **Pekowi Woman**/1680, grandson of **Meaurroway-Straight Tail**/1630, in north MD/east PA from birth-1711 with Opessa, in west PA 1711-23 with father **Opessa**, returned to north MD/east PA area with **Opessa** 1723, moved to AL with **Opessa** 1735-left a wife & children in AL with relatives/clan members, in north MD/east PA by 1749, a **Pekowi Chief** in north MD/east PA by 1753- Council Philadelphia 1753 after **Opessa** moved to OH, in OH by 1755, French-Indian War/54-60, Braddock/55, raiding NewShenandoah River valleys/55, raiding PA/55-56, raiding Ohio-New River valleys/58, a minor **Pekowi Chief in OH** after death of **Opessa**, husband 1725 MD of **Pekowi Woman**/10, father of Tecumsapah-Margaret/25-wife of Thomas McKee, Older Daughter/27-mother of Tecumoplas, Watmeme/30-wife of Black Fish, Middle Daughter/35-wife of Daniel McQueen, Younger Daughter/38-wife of Isadore Chesne & Metheotashe Opessa/40-wife of Puckenshinwa, grandfather of Tecumoplas/42 & **Tecumseh**/68

1134. Opessa, Pride aka **Lawaquaqua-LawachkamikeeLawakwakwa**[96] – Pekowi born about 1710 MD-died 1753 SC - son of **Opessa**/1675 & **Pekowi Woman**/1680, with **Opessa** in north MD/east PA birth-1711, in west PA with Opessa 1711-23, returned to north MD/east PA with **Opessa** 1723-35, remained in north when **Opessa** took band to AL 1735, signed Petition to PA 1738 with **Peter Chartier**/1690, **George Miranda**/1700, brother Tecoomteh/1700 & 94 Natives to stop the sell of liquor to Natives, a **Pekowi**

Chief in north MD/east PA by 1738, raiding PA/40, captured on trip to the south to locate Pekowi of the south & died in SC prison/53, husband 1st 1730 east PA of **Rising Sun**/15-Kishpoko, 2nd by 1739 east PA of a widow **Mother of Black Fish**/10-Mekoche, father **with Rising Sun** of Lawagqua-Elder Brother of Blue Jacket/33, **Blue Jacket**- Weyapiersenwha-Whirlpool /35, Wabete-Elk-Younger Brother of Blue Jacket/37 & Sally Opessa-sister of Blue Jacket/39-all KishpokoPekowi, **with Mother of Black Fish** of Red Pole/40-Mekoche-Pekowi, stepfather of **Black Fish**/25, Kwatooka/27, Nakanapaseka/29-all Chalakatha-Mekoche

1135. Opessa, Snow White aka **Blanceneige**-*Wapakonee-Daughter/Sister of Opessa-Wife of Peter Chartier – Pekowi born about 1695 TN-died after 1734 (PA?) - daughter of **Opessa**/1675 & **Pekowi Woman**/1680, a Pekowi in the north mostly, wife 1710 PA of **Peter Chartier**/1690-1/2 Pekowi-Metis, mother of Francois Chartier/12, Rene-Pale Stalker Chartier/25, Anna Chartier/30 & others-all 3/4th Pekowi-Metis

1136. Opessa, Swan aka Wapehti-Wife of Blue Pocket-Wife of Swearingen - 3/4th Pekowi-Metis born about 1767-died after 1800 - daughter of **Wabete-Elk Opessa**/37 & **Ms. Baby**/52, wife about 1783 of **Blue Pocket**-Duke Swearingen/63-adopted-white, children unknown

1137. Opessa, Tecoomteh aka **Tecomteh**[97] – Pekowi born about 1700 MD-died after 1738 (MD?) - son of **Opessa**/1675 & **Pekowi Woman**/1680, 1st warrior of band 1738, signed Petition to PA to stop the sell of liquor to Natives 1738 with brother **Pride**/10, **Peter Chartier**/1690, **George Miranda**/1700 & 94 other Natives, wife & children unknown

1138. Opessa, **Wabete aka Elk**[98]-Younger Son-**Younger Brother of Blue Jacket** – Pekowi-Kishpoko born 1737 OH-died after 1774 OH - son of **Pride Opessa**/10-Pekowi & **Rising Sun**/15-Kishpoko, a Pekowi-Kishpoko warrior, younger **brother of Blue Jacket**/35, trading with OH Fur Co. in PA in early 1750's with Lawagqua & Blue Jacket, Cornstalk War/55-74, French-Indian War/54-63, Braddock/55, raiding New-Shenandoah River valleys/55, raiding PA/55-56, raiding Ohio-New River valley/58, Pontiac War/62-65, Bushy Run/63, raiding New-Greenbrier-Jackson River valleys/63, raiding Ohio-Little KanawhaBig Sandy-New River valleys/72, Point Pleasant/74, father in law of **Blue Pocket** Swearingen/63-adopted-white, husband 1757 OH of **Shawnee Woman**/42, 2nd 1766 OH of **Ms. Baby**/52-1/2 Pekowi-Metis, children/57-66 **with Shawnee** unknown, father **with Baby** of Swan-Wapehti Opessa/68-3/4th Pekowi-Metis - (some children may have been called Blue Jacket's)

1139. **Opossum**[99] – Pekowi born about 1750 OH-died after 1794 – Cornstalk War/68-77, raiding Ohio-Big Sandy-Little Kanawha-New River valleys/72, Point Pleasant/74-78, Blue Jacket War/77-95, raiding KY-VAOH/75-81, Crawford/82, raiding Ohio River valley/88-92

1140. **Oquanoxa aka Okwanosha** – Kishpoko born about 1765 OH-died after 1820 – Blue Jacket War/88-94, raiding OH-KY-VA/95-1810, Prophet's Town/1811, Brownstown/1812-Monguagon/1812-1st Amherstburg/1812Frenchtown/1813-Ft. Meigs/1813-2nd Amherstburg/1813 & Thames/1813 **with Tecumseh**, moved to CAN 1815, a minor **Chief** in 1820

1141. **Orphan aka L'Ophelin** - 1/2 Kishpoko-Metis born about 1750 (KY-IN?)-died after 1795 - son of **Kishpoko Woman** & **French/Canadian Man**, Cornstalk War/68-77, raiding Ohio-Little Kanawha-Big Sandy-New River valleys/72, Point Pleasant/74, Blue Jacket War/77-94, raiding KY-VA-OH/7581, Crawford/82, raiding Ohio River valley/88-92, husband about 1770 OH of **Pekowi Woman**/55, father of several 3/4th Pekowi-Kishpoko-Metis children/7095

1142. **Osborne, Mary Polly Brock** - daughter of **Aaron Brock (1)-Red Bird Carpenter**/31, wife 1773 NC of **Ephriam Washington Osborne Sr**-white born 1752 NC-died 1852 KY, mother of Elizabeth Osborne/73, George Osborne/75, James Osborne/77, Jesse Osborne/79, Ephriam W. Osborne Jr/81, Rebecca Osborne/83, Rhoda Osborne/85, Mary Polly Osborne/87, Hiram Osborne/89-all 7/64th Chalakatha-**Cherokee**-Metis-all grandchildren of Red Bird/31

1143. **Oshaishe aka Oshaeeshe-Oshaithe** - Mekoche born about 1775died after 1817 - Fallen Timber/94, no part in War 1812, a warrior from Wapaghonettat 1817, Treaty 1817

1144. **Oshawahnah** - Kishpoko born about 1790 OH-died 1870 - Prophet's Town/1811, Brownstown/1812-Monguagon/1812-1st Amherstburg/1812Frenchtown/1813-Ft. Meigs/1813-2nd Amherstburg/1813 & Thames/1813 **with Tecumseh**, moved to CAN 1815, returned to OH about 1825, moved to KS 1826 **with Prophet** & **Paukeesaa Tecumseh**, wife & children unknown

1145. **Ossitahiwa aka Osseetaheewa** – Chalakatha born about 1730 PA-died after 1765 OH – Cornstalk War/55-65, French-Indian War/54-63, Braddock/55, raiding New-Shenandoah River valleys/55, raiding PA/55-56, raiding Ohio-New River valleys/58, Pontiac War/62-65, Bushy Run/63, raiding New-Greenbrier-Jackson River valleys/63, Council Logstown 1765

1146.Ossoghqua aka Ossogkwa – Chalakatha born about 1710 PAdied after 1758 OH - raiding PA/40, a **Chalakatha Chief** in OH 1748, FrenchIndian War/54-58, Braddock/55, raiding New-Shenandoah River valleys/55, raiding PA/55-56, raiding Ohio-New River valleys/58, wife & children unknown

1147.Othawee – Mekoche born about 1775 OH-died after 1817 - Fallen Timber/94, no part in War 1812, a warrior at Wapaghonettat 1817, Treaty 1817

1148.Othoaway – Pekowi born about 1720 PA-died after 1759 OH - raiding PA/40, French-Indian War/54-59, Braddock/55, raiding New-Shenandoah River valleys/55, raiding PA/55-56, raiding Ohio-New River valleys/58, Council Ft. Pitt Aug. 1759

1149.**Otter (1) aka Kwitateh**[100]-Kweetatay – Mekoche born about 1745 OH**murdered** 1781 OH – brother of **Mink**/40 & **Brother of Mink**/50, Cornstalk War/68-77, raiding Ohio-Kanawha-New River valleys/72, Point Pleasant/74-7578, raiding KY-VA-OH/75-81, murdered by **Martin Wetzel**, wife & children unknown

1150.Otter (2) – Mekoche born about 1770 OH-died after 1815 MO/KS - son of **Brother of Mink**/50 & **Daughter of Moluntha**/54, a Mekoche warrior, raiding Ohio River valley/88-92, Blue Jacket War/88-94, scout-**with U.S. Army**-War 1812-Thames/1813, half-brother through father of **Bright Horns**/70, 1st cousin through **Mink**/40 of **Big Horn-Capt. Logan**/74 & through **Tecumpease**/58 of **Tecumseh**/68 & through mother of **Capt. Johnny**/65, grandson of **Moluntha**/10-Mekoche & **Sister of Black Hoof**/15-Thawikila, great-nephew of **Black Hoof**/30, moved to MO/KS after 1815, husband 1790 OH of **Otter's Wife**/75, children unknown

1151.Otter, Wabethe aka **Sister of White Otter** – Chalakatha born about 1743 (PA?)-died after 1775 OH – daughter of **Father of White Otter**/15 & **Mother of White Otter**/20, wife about 1758 OH of **John Smith**/30-adopted Irish, mother of Ann Smith/59, John Smith Jr/65, Mary Smith/72 & other 1/2 Chalakatha-Metis children/60-75

1152.Otter Lifter, Polly Vann aka Wawli-Mary Christianna - wife 1759 Running Water TN of **Otter Lifter**-Cherokee born 1740 TN-died after 1793, mother of Levi Otterlifter/60 & Robert Otterlifter/62-both 1/4th Chalakatha-Pekowi-Cherokee-Metis

1153.Owens, Daughter of Tanacharisson - wife about 1735 (PA?) of **John Owens**-white born about 1700-died 1764, mother of David Owens/36, George Owens/38, John Owens Jr/40, Susannah Owens/50 & other children/36-64-all 1/4th Pekowi-**Seneca**-Metis

1154.Owens, David (1) - 1/4th Pekowi-Seneca-**Metis** born about 1736 PA-died before 1800 IN - son of **Daughter of Tanacharisson**/20 & **John Owens**/1700-white, trading with Ohio Fur Co. in PA in 1750s, lived & traded **among the Shawnee & Delaware**, scout-translator **for Bouquet with Colonial Army** 1764, scout-translator for Dunmore **with Colonial Army** 1774, Capt. in VA Militia **with U.S. Army**-in Revolution-but demoted, **murdered his Pekowi Wife & 3 children** 1764 for scalps, **with George Rogers Clark** at building of Ft. Jefferson, husband about 1755 PA of **Pekowi Woman**/40, later wife or wives unknown, father of three 5/8th Pekowi-Seneca children that he murdered

1155.Owens, George (1) - 1/4th Pekowi-Seneca-Metis born about 1738 PA-died 1789 IN - son of **John Owens**/1700-white & **Daughter of Tanacharisson**/20, husband about 1760 PA of a **White Woman**/40, father of George Owens Jr/61 & Thomas Owens/63-both 1/8th Pekowi-Seneca Metis

1156.Owens, John (2) aka John Owens Jr - 1/4th Pekowi-SenecaMetis born about 1740-died 1781 - son of **John Owens (1)**/1700-white & **Daughter of Tanacharisson**/20, husband about 1760 of **Susannah Pekowi**/45, father of David Owens (2)/61, John Owens (3)/63, Vincent Owens/65, George Owens (3)/67, Hannah Owens/68, Mary Owens/69, James Owens/71, Sarah Owens/73, Judith Owens/75-all 5/8th Pekowi-Seneca-Metis

1157.Owens, Susannah - 1/4th Pekowi-Seneca-Metis born about 1746 PA-died 1825 KY - daughter of **Daughter of Tanacharisson**/20 & **John Owens**-white, wife 1767 of **James Miranda (3)**/45-1/2 Pekowi-Metis, mother of Samuel Miranda (4)/68, James Miranda (4)/70, Isaac Miranda/72, Thomas Miranda/81, John Owens Miranda/82, Jonathan Miranda/84 & Elizabeth Miranda/87-all 3/8th Pekowi-Seneca Metis

1158.**Owl aka Mehathwa**[101] – Kishpoko born about 1755 OH-died after 1774 - raiding Ohio-Little Kanawha-Big Sandy-New River valleys/72, Point Pleasant/74

1159.Owl, George – adopted-Miami-Delaware born about 1775 OHdied after 1815 – son of **Miami Man** & **Delaware Woman**, brother of **John Owl**/70Fallen Timber/94, Prophet's Town/1811, Brownstown/1812-Monguagon/1812-1st Amherstburg/1812-Frenchtown/1813-Ft. Meigs/1813-2nd Amherstburg/1813-Thames/1813 **with Tecumseh**, living in Apple Creek MO 1815, husband about 1795 OH of **Kishpoko Woman**/80, father of several 1/2 Kishpoko-Delaware-Miami children/95-1815

1160.Owl, John – adopted-Miami-Delaware born about 1770 OH-died after 1815 – son of **Miami Man** & **Delaware Woman**, brother **George Owl**/75,

Blue Jacket War/87-94, Prophet's Town/1811, Brownstown/1812-Monguagon/1812-1st Amherstburg/1812-Frenchtown/1813-Ft. Meigs/1813-2nd Amherstburg/1813-Thames/1813 **with Tecumseh**, living in Apple Creek MO 1815, husband about 1790 OH of **Kishpoko Woman**/75, father of several 1/2 Kishpoko-Delaware-Miami children/90-1815

1161.Oxonoxy aka Ocksonocksee – Kishpoko born about 1790 OH-died after 1827 - Prophet's Town/1811, Brownstown/1812-Monguagon/1812-1st Amherstburg/1812-Frenchtown/1813-Ft. Meigs/1813-2nd Amherstburg/1813 & Thames/1813 **with Tecumseh**, move to CAN 1815, return to OH about 1825, move to KS 1826 **with Prophet** & **Paukeesaa**, wife & children unknown

Chapter XIII
Paciter to Pushwepako (P)

P

1162.Paciter, Wynima - adopted-white born about 1740-died after 1765 - adopted before 1750-returned to whites-returned to tribe 1765, living with tribe in OH 1765, wife about 1755 OH of **Chalakatha Man**/35, children unknown

1163.Pahaweon – Kishpoko born about 1785 OH-died after 1817 CAN - Prophet's Town/1811, Brownstown/1812-Monguagon/1812-1st Amherstburg/1812-Frenchtown/1813-Ft. Meigs/1813-2nd Amherstburg/1813 & Thames/1813 **with Tecumseh**, move to CAN 1815

1164.Paheto aka Paheetoo – Mekoche born about 1785 OH-died after 1817 – no part in War 1812, a warrior at Wapaghonettat 1817, Treaty 1817

1165.**Painted Pole aka Muskwakonah**[102] – Mekoche born about 1740 OHdied after 1805 (OH?) – Cornstalk War/58-77, raiding Ohio-New River valleys/58, Pontiac War/62-66, Bushy Run/63, raiding New-Greenbrier-Jackson River valleys/63, raiding Ohio-Little Kanawha-Big Sandy-New River valleys/72, Point Pleasant/74-78, Blue Jacket War/77-94, raiding KY-OH-VA/75-81, Crawford/82, raiding Ohio River valley/88-92, Grand Council Sept. 1792, Treaty 1786, 1805

1166.Palakishaw aka Palakeeshaw – Chalakatha born about 1710 PA-died in epidemic about 1758 OH - raiding PA/40, a **Chalakatha Chief** in OH by 1748, French-Indian War/54-58, Braddock/55, raiding New-Shenandoah River valleys/55, raiding PA/55-56, raiding Ohio-New River valleys/58, wife & children unknown

1167. Palaskee – Mekoche born about 1780 OH-died after 1817 - no part in War 1812, a warrior at Wapaghonettat 1817, Treaty 1817

1168. Pamitchepetoo aka Pameetchepetoo – Mekoche born about 1775 OH died after 1817 – Fallen Timber/94, no part in War 1812, a warrior at Wapaghonettat 1817, Treaty 1817

1169. Pankoor – Mekoche born about 1775 OH-died after 1817 - Fallen Timber/94, no part in War 1812, a warrior at Wapaghonettat 1817, Treaty 1817

1170. Panther – Kishpoko born about 1770 OH-died after 1817 - traveled 1795-1812 **with Tecumseh**, a relative/same clan **as Tecumseh**, Brownstown/1812-Monguagon/1812-1st Amherstburg/1812-Frenchtown/1813-Ft. Meigs/1813-2nd Amherstburg/1813 & Thames/1813 **with Tecumseh**, a warrior at Lewistown 1817, Treaty 1817

1171. **Panther aka Meshepeshe**[103] – Chalakatha born about 1740-**murdered 1791** - Cornstalk War/58-77, raiding Ohio-New River valleys/58, Pontiac War/62-66, Bushy Run/63, raiding New-Greenbrier-Jackson River valleys/63, raiding Ohio-Big Sandy-Little Kanawha-New River valleys/72, a **Chalakatha Chief** 1772, Point Pleasant/74-75-78, Blue Jacket War/77-91, Boonesboro, raiding KY-OH-VA/77-81, Crawford/82, raiding Ohio River valley/88, Harmar/90, **murdered 1791 by whites** with son Gray Fox, **succeeded by Chiuxca**/40, husband 1760 OH of **Chalakatha Woman**/45, father of Gray Fox/61

1172. Papamousse aka Papamoosee – Mekoche born about 1770 OH-died after 1825 – Blue Jacket War/87-94, no part in War 1812, a warrior at Wapaghonettat 1817, Treaty 1817, 1825, living in Apple Creek MO 1817

1173. Papashow – Mekoche born about 1790 OH-died after 1817 - no part in War 1812, a warrior from Wapaghonettat 1817, Treaty 1817

1174. Papaskootepa aka Papaskooteepa – Thawikila born about 1780 OH-died after 1817 - no part in War 1812, a warrior at Hog Creek 1817, Treaty 1817

1175. Paquiwesee aka Paquawesee-Pakweewesee - 1/2 Thawikila-Metis born about 1740 OH-died after 1774 (AL?) - son of **Thawikila Man** & **AdoptedWhite Woman**, a Thawikila warrior, Cornstalk War/58-74, raiding Ohio-New
River valleys/58, Pontiac War/62-66, Bushy Run/63, raiding New-GreenbrierJackson River valleys/63, returned to whites-returned to tribe 1765,

raiding OhioBig Sandy-Little Kanawha-New River valleys/72, Point Pleasant/74, moved
south with the Thawikila/74, appears to have remained in AL, husband about 1760 OH of **Thawikila Woman**/45

1176.Parks, Billy Lawnoetuchu aka Lawnoeetoochoo - 1/4th Thawikila-Metis born about 1798 OH-died after 1854 KS - son of **John Parks**-SCO & **Maria Metis**/70, **with U.S. Army**-War 1812-Thames/1813-Seminole War/1837, a warrior at Hog Creek 1817, moved to KS before 1837, Treaty 1854, husband about 1818 OH of **Thawikila Woman**/1800

1177.Parks, Joseph aka Capt. Parks-Joso-**Pasahtahkahta**-Runs Against Something - 1/4th Thawikila-Metis born about 1790 OH-died 1859 Johnson Co KS - son of **Maria Metis**/70-1/2 Thawikila-Metis & **John Parks**-white, a Thawikila warrior & headman, raised & educated by Lewis Cass, to D.C. 1802 with **Wayweleapee**/60, **John Perry**/75, **Spy Buck**/70, **Quaskee Black Hoof**/60 & **Francois Duchoquet**/66, a Thawikila at Hog Creek 1817, Treaty 1826, 1831, 1854, delegate to D.C. 1831, moved to KS 1833, Capt-**with U.S. Army**-War 1812-Seminole War/1837, husband about 1815 OH of **Catherine Racer**/1800Wyandot-Metis, father of John Parks/1816, Emily Parks/1820, Sally Parks/1822,
Margaret Parks/1824, Nancy Parks/1835-all 1/8th Thawikila-Wyandot-Metis

1178. Parks, Julia – 1/4th Thawikila-Metis born 1806 OH-died 1829 OH – daughter of **Maria Metis**/70 & **John Parks**-SCO, wife 1824 OH of **Pascal Fish**/1804, mother of Locust Paschal Fish/1825-1/4th Chalakatha-Mekoche-Pekowi-Thawikila-Metis

1179. Parks, Maria aka Maria Metis - 1/2 Thawikila-Metis born about 1770 OH-died after 1806 - daughter of **Thawikila Woman** & **French/Canadian Man**, 1st wife about 1785 OH of **John Parks-SCO**, mother of children/85-89,
Joseph Parks/90, children/91-95, Samuel Parks/96, Billy Parks/98, children/99-1805, Julia Parks/1806-all 1/4th Thawikila-Metis

1180. Parks, Samuel - 1/4th Thawikila-Metis born 1796 (TN?)-died 1841 TN - son of **Maria Metis**/70 & **John Parks**-SCO, a Thawikila warrior, Treaty 1819, **lived with Cherokee & Wyandot**, husband 1814 Bradley Co TN of **Susannah Fox-Taylor**/98, father of Ruth Parks/1816, Almira Parks/1818, Jennie
Parks/1820, George Washington Parks/1822, Thomas Jefferson Parks/1824,

Richard Parks/1826, Calvin Parks/1828, William Parks/1830, Mary Ann Parks/1832, Robert C. Parks/1834, John Ross Parks/1836, Samuel Parks Jr/1838all 9/32nd Chalakatha-Thawikila-Mekoche-Creek-Cherokee-Metis

1181. Parris, Cheekee Greenwood (2) – wife 1750 Chota TN of **George Parris**-white born 1720 IRE-died 1797 Rutherford Co NC-(son of **George Parris**/1685 & **Sarah Parris** = a brother of **Richard Parris**/25), children/50-60 (surnamed **Parris**?) unknown

1182. Parris, Preachy Greenwood aka Preachy Moytoy-Prachey - Blind Savannah Clan Cherokee, wife 1754 Chota TN of **Richard Parris**-white born 1725 likely IRE-died 1794 Bahamas-(son of **George Parris**/1685 & **Sarah Parris** = a brother of **George Parris**/20), trading partner of **Nathaniel Gist**/30 in Cherokee country following French-Indian War/54-63), mother of Kate Parris/56, George Parris/58, Nellie Parris (1)/60-all 31/64th Chalakatha-Pekowi-Kishpoko-Black-Metis

1183. Pashaway – Kishpoko born before 1790 OH-died after 1820 CAN - Prophet's Town/1811, Brownstown/1812-Monguagon/1812-1st Amherstburg/1812-Frenchtown/1813-Ft. Meigs/1813-2nd Amherstburg/1813 & Thames/1813 **with Tecumseh**, move to CAN 1815

1184. Patakoma – Mekoche born about 1790 OH-died after 1817 – no part in
War 1812, a warrior from Wapaghonettat 1817, Treaty 1817

1185. Pauley, Margaret aka Yellow Gold - adopted-white born 1752 (VA?)died 1843 - adopted daughter 1779-83 of **Wababakahto-White Bark**/32Chalakatha, returned to whites before 1789, wife 1779 OH of **Son of White
Bark**/58, children/79-83 unknown

1186. Payakootha aka Paytakootha **Flying Cloud** –Thawikila born about 1735 OH-died after 1779 MO – Cornstalk War/55-77, French-Indian War/54-63, Braddock/55, raiding New-Shenandoah River valleys/55, raiding PA/55-56, raiding Ohio-New River valleys/58, Pontiac War/62-66, Bushy Run/63, raiding New-Greenbrier-Jackson River valleys/63, raiding Ohio-Big Sandy-Little Kanawha-New River valleys/72, Point Pleasant/74-78, moved to AL 1774-back to OH 1778-to MO 1779, husband 1755 OH of **Thawikila Woman**/40, father of
Young Payakootha-Young Flying Cloud/60

1187. Payakootha, Young aka Young Flying Cloud – Thawikila born 1768

OH-died 1838 Montgomery Co IN – son of **Flying Cloud (1)-Payakootha**/35 & **Thawikila Woman**/40, living in Apple Creek MO 1810, husband 1788 OH of **Little Vine**/73-Thawikila, father of daughter Ulethi Kisathwa/1810

1188. Paytokothe aka Paytokoseh – Mekoche born about 1780 OH-died after
1817 – no part in War 1812, a warrior at Wapakonetta 1817, Treaty 1817

1189. Peapakseka aka Peeapakseeka – Mekoche born about 1770 OH-died after 1817 - raiding Ohio River valley/88-92, Blue Jacket War/88-94, no part in
War 1812, a warrior at Wapaghonettat 1817, Treaty 1817

1190. Pedanquit aka Pedankweet - Kishpoko born about 1770 OH-died after 1836 KS - Blue Jacket War/87-94, raiding OH-KY-VA/95-1810, Prophet's
Town/1811, a **Kishpoko Chief** by 1812, Brownstown/1812-Monguagon/1812-1st Amherstburg/1812-Frenchtown/1813-Ft. Meigs/1813-2nd Amherstburg/1813 & Thames/1813 **with Tecumseh**, moved to CAN 1815, returned to OH 1825, move to KS 1826 **with Prophet** & **Paukeesaa**, wife & children unknown

1191. Peehatha – Kishpoko born about 1770 OH-died after 1831 KS - raiding
Ohio River valley/88-92, Blue Jacket War/88-94, raiding OH-KY-VA/95-1810, Prophet's Town/1811, Brownstown/1812-Monguagon/1812-1st Amherstburg/1812-Frenchtown/1813-Ft. Meigs/1813-2nd Amherstburg/1813 & Thames/1813 **with Tecumseh**, moved to CAN 1815, returned to OH 1825, moved to KS 1826 **with Prophet** & **Paukeesaa**, Treaty 1831

1192. Peekishinoah aka **Young Eagle**-Peekeesheenoah – Kishpoko born about
1755 OH-died about 1792 – son of Bad Eagle-**Waughapelethee**/35 & **Kishpoko Woman**/40, Point Pleasant/74, Blue Jacket War/77-92, raiding KY-VA-OH/7581, Crawford/82, raiding Ohio River valley/88, Harmar/90, wounded at St. Clair/91, later died from wounds/92, relative/same clan (Panther) as **Tecumseh**, husband 1st about 1776 OH of **Mary Bayles**/63-adopted white, 2nd 1782 OH of **Kishpoko Woman**/65, father **with Bayles** of Teliskwatawa Bayles/77-1/2 Kishpoko-Metis, children/83-92 **with Kishpoko** unknown

1193. Peetahlahwah – Kishpoko born about 1770 OH-died after 1832 KS - raiding Ohio River valley/88-92, Blue Jacket War/88-94, raiding OH-KYVA/95-1810, Prophet's Town/1811, Brownstown/1812-Monguagon/1812-1st Amherstburg/1812-Frenchtown/1813-Ft. Meigs/1813-2nd Amherstburg/1813 &

Thames/1813 **with Tecumseh**, moved to CAN 1815, returned to OH 1825, moved to KS 1826 **with Prophet & Paukeesaa**, Treaty 1832

1194. Peewalitotha aka Peewaleetotha - 1/2 Mekoche-Metis born about 1755 OH-died after 1783 - daughter of **Mekoche Man & Adopted-white Woman**, wife 1770 OH of **Mekoche Man**/50, widow in 1783, children unknown

1195. Pekatheseka – Mekoche born about 1770 OH-died after 1817 - raiding Ohio River valley/88-92, Blue Jacket War/88-94, no part in War 1812, a warrior at Wapaghonettat 1817, Treaty 1817

1196. Peliska aka Peleeska –Thawikila born before 1790 OH-died after 1817 - a warrior at Hogs Creek village 1817, from **Black Hoof** band-maybe a relative

1197. Pelmetachemo – Kishpoko born about 1780 KY-died after 1826 KS - raiding OH-KY-VA/99-1810, Prophet's Town/1811, Brownstown/1812Monguagon/1812-1st Amherstburg/1812-Frenchtown/1813-Ft. Meigs/1813-2nd Amherstburg/1813 & Thames/1813 **with Tecumseh**, moved to CAN 1815, returned to OH 1825, moved to KS 1826 **with Prophet & Paukeesaa**

1198. Pemenpiah aka Pemenpeeah – Mekoche born about 1670 OH-died after 1745 Oh – a **Mekoche Chief** in OH 1710, father of Pemanich Pemeniah/35, grandfather of Charlotte Pemanich Bouganville/58-1/2 Mekoche-Metis

1199. Pemitacamchika aka Pemeetacamcheeka – Kishpoko born about 1780 OH-died after 1826 KS - raiding OH-KY-VA/99-1810, Prophet's Town/1811, Brownstown/1812-Monguagon/1812-1st Amherstburg/1812-Frenchtown/1813-Ft. Meigs/1813-2nd Amherstburg/1813 & Thames/1813 **with Tecumseh**, moved to CAN 1815, returned to OH 1825, Treaty 1825, moved to KS 1826 **with Prophet & Paukeesaa** 1826

1200. Pemotah – Mekoche born about 1780 OH-died after 1817 – no part in War 1812, a warrior at Wapaghonettat 1817, Treaty 1817

1201. Penascoh – Pekowi born about 1660 OH-died after 1700 PA - a **Pekowi Chief** in MD-PA **with Straight Tail** 1700

1202. Penatheywa – Thawikila born about 1770 OH-died after 1817 - raiding Ohio River valley/88-92, Blue Jacket War/88-94, no part in War 1812, a warrior at Hog Creek 1817, Treaty 1817

1203. Perrot, Nicholas - 1/2 Mekoche-Metis born about 1730-died after 1774 - son of **Mekoche Woman**/15 & **Francois Perrot**/10-adopted French/Canadian, Cornstalk War/55-74, French-Indian War/54-63, Braddock/55, raiding New-Shenandoah River valleys/55, raiding Ohio-New River valleys/58, Pontiac War/62-66, Bushy Run/63, raiding New-Greenbrier-Jackson River valleys/63, raiding Ohio-Big Sandy-Little Kanawha-New River valleys/72, Point Pleasant/74, husband about 1750 OH of **Mekoche Woman**/35, children unknown

1204.Perry, John aka **Lolliway**-Pemthala-Capt. Perry – Mekoche born about 1775 OH-died 1843 KS – parents unknown, brother of **William Perry**/70, Delegation to Congress 1802 with **Wayweleapee**/60, **Quaskee Black Hoof**/60, **Spybuck**/70, **Joseph Parks**/90 & **Francois Duchoquet**/66, John Logan's scouts**with U.S. Army**-War of 1812, captured at Ft. Meigs/1813 & released by **Tecumseh**, Treaty 1832, Joseph Parks Co-**with U.S. Army**-Seminole War/1837, Treaty 1815, 1817, 1831, 1832, became **Head Chief** at Wapaghonettat 1830 OHsucceeding **Black Hoof**/30, **Co-Chief** 1835 KS with brother **William Perry**/70, may have lived in NC with brother William 1795-1800, living in Apple Creek MO 1815, return to OH by 1830, moved to KS 1832, husband about 1795 of **Mekoche Woman**/80, father of Yakouaichika Perry/96, Yawachika Perry /98, daughter/1815, James Perry/1822, Thomas Perry/1825, son/1827

1205.Perry, William aka Kaketchheka-**Kayketchheka** – Mekoche born about 1770 OH-died before 1844 – parents unknown, brother of John Perry/75, Blue Jacket War/88-94, may have lived in N.C. with brother John 1795-1800, Capt. John Logan's scouts-**with U.S. Army**-War 1812, captured at Ft. Meigs/1813 & released by **Tecumseh**, Treaty 1832, a warrior at Wapaghonettat 1817, Treaty 1817, moved to KS 1828 with Young Cornstalk/42, **2nd chief** in KS 1833, **cochief** with brother John in KS 1835, Joseph Parks Co-**with U.S. Army**-Seminole War/1837, husband 1st about 1790 OH of **Mekoche Woman**/75, 2nd about 1826 of **Elizabeth Fleehart**/1810-white, children/90-1825 **with Mekoche** unknown, father **with Fleehart** of Phoebe Perry/1828-1/2 Mekoche-Metis

1206.Perthius aka Pertheeus - 1/2 Pekowi-Black Metis born about 1725 PAdied after 1758 - son of **Pekowi Man** & **Adopted-Mulatto Woman**/05, FrenchIndian War/54-63, Braddock/55, raiding New-Shenandoah River valleys/55, raiding Ohio-New River valleys/58, husband 1745 OH of **Chalakatha Woman**/30, children unknown

1207.Pertik aka Perteek – Pekowi born about 1710 PA-died about 1758 OH in epidemic - a **Pekowi Chief with Poxinosa** in PA, Treaty 1752, Braddock/55, raiding New-Shenandoah River valleys/55, raiding PA/55-56, raiding Ohio-New River valleys/58

1208.Peshequakame aka Pesheekwakamee – Mekoche born about 1780 OHdied after 1817 - raiding KY-OH-VA/99-1810, Prophet's Town/1811, Brownstown/1812-Monguagon/1812-1st Amherstburg/1812-Frenchtown/1813-Ft. Meigs/1813-2nd Amherstburg/1813 & Thames/1813 **with Tecumseh**, a warrior at Wapaghonettat 1817, Treaty 1817

1209. Petalla aka One Eye-Old Yie-**Petalla Cornstalk** - adopted white born about 1730 (PA?)-**murdered** 1777 WV - adopted son of **Cornstalk**/10, taken 1740 in PA-never returned to whites (same series of raids that **Julia Mulatto**/20 was taken), Cornstalk War/55-77, Braddock/55, raiding New-Shenandoah River valleys/55, raiding PA/55-56, raiding Ohio-New River valleys/58, Pontiac War/62-66, Bushy Run/63, raiding New-Greenbrier-Jackson River valleys/63, raiding Ohio-Big Sandy-Little Kanawha-New River valleys/72, Point Pleasant/74, raiding KY-OH-VA/77, blinded in one eye in battle with whites, **murdered 1777** with Cornstalk/10, Ellinipsico/45 & Red Hawk/25 at Ft. Randolph/Point Pleasant WV, **tortured & mutilated by whites** before his death, **the white son-in-law of Cornstalk mentioned in history of the murder**, husband 1st about 1750 OH of adopted sister **Catherine Cornstalk (1)**/34, 2nd about 1765 OH of adopted sister **Elizabeth Cornstalk**/45-(to raise her children by **John Swift**-white), any children of his own by either wife unknown

1210. Peters, Isaac – adopted-Delaware born about 1760 OH-died after 1805 – son of **Richard** or **John Peters**, Blue Jacket War/77-94, Boonesboro/78, Point Pleasant/78, Blue Licks/82, Crawford/82, raiding Ohio River valley/88-92, Treaty 1805, husband 1st 1780 OH of **Kishpoko Woman**/65, 2nd 1792 OH of **Sontonegoo** (Girty Ironside)/60-adopted-Mohawk, children/80-92 **with Kishpoko** unknown (likely surname Peters), step-father of **Simon Girty Jr** aka **Simon Peters**/76 & **Quasay Girty**/78-both 1/2 Mohawk-Metis, any children **with Sontonegoo** unknown

1211. Petiska aka Peteeska – Thawikila born about 1785 OH-died after 1817 - Fallen Timber/94, from the **Black Hoof** band, possibly a relative, a warrior from Hog Creek 1817, Treaty 1817

1212. Petro, Mary See aka **Mary Cornstalk** - wife 1783 of **Leonard Petro (1)**-former adopted-white born 1750 PA-died 1824 Warren Co. OH, (daughter of **Cornstalk**/10 & **Catherine Vanderpoole** (Sharp-See)/25-white), mother of Margaret Petro/88, Michael See Petro/90 & John Petro/92-all 7/32nd Chalakatha-Mekoche-Metis

1213. Pettit, Thomas - 1/4th Kishpoko-Metis born about 1765-died after 1810 - son of **Nancy Fawling Downing**/46 & **William Pettit**/40-white, Wolf Clan **Cherokee**, husband 1st about 1785 of **Cherokee Woman**/70, 2nd 1795 of **Catherine Barnes**/80-white, 3rd 1796 of **Catherine Hughes**/66-3/4th Chalakatha-Pekowi-Metis, children/85-95 **with Cherokee** unknown, father **with Barnes** of James Pettit/96-1/8th Kishpoko-Metis, **with Hughes** of Rachel Pettit/96, Thomas Pettit Jr/97, Elizabeth Pettit/98, Agnes Pettit/99, Benjamin Pettit/1800,

Washington Pettit/1801, Nancy Pettit/1802, William Pettit/1803, 1 daughter & 2 other sons/1805-10-all ½ Kishpoko-Chalakatha-Pekowi-Metis

1214.Pewaypee – Mekoche born about 1790 OH-died after 1817 – no part in War 1812, a warrior from Wapaghonettat 1817, Treaty 1817

1215.Pewiatchee aka Peweeache - adopted-Seneca born about 1780 OH-died after 1832 KS - scout-**with U.S. Army**-War 1812-Thames/1813, Treaty 1831, 1832, move to KS 1832, husband about 1800 OH of **Chalakatha Woman**/85, father of several 1/2 Chalakatha-Seneca children/1800-25

1216.Phillips, Philip – adopted-Dutch born about 1735 (HOL?)-died after 1785 - adopted 1750 PA, trading in OH by 1756, Cornstalk War/62-77, **with Shawnee** in Pontiac War/62-64-Bushy Run/63, raiding New-Greenbrier-Jackson River valleys/63, translator-Treaty Ft. Stanwix 1768, raiding Ohio-Little Kanawha-Big Sandy-New River valleys/72, Point Pleasant/74, raiding Ohio-New River valleys/75, raiding KY-VA-OH/77-81, often lived **with ShawneeMunsee-Delaware**, husband 1755 OH of **Pekowi Woman**/40, father of Jacob Phillips/56, Charles Phillips/60 & Joseph Phillips/85-all ½ Pekowi-Metis

1217. Pitesawa aka Peetesawa – Mekoche born about 1750 OH-died after 1786 – Cornstalk War/68-77, raiding Ohio-New River valleys/72, Point Pleasant/7475-78, Boonesboro/78, Blue Jacket War/77-86, raiding KY-VA-OH/77-81, Blue Licks/82, Crawford/82, Council Miami Jan. 1786

1218.Plants Corn – Chalakatha born about 1750 OH-died after 1775 - wife about 1765 OH of **Chalakatha Man**/45, widow in 1775

1219.Pluggy aka Plukkemehnote – ½ Kishpoko-**Mohawk** born about 1720 (WV?)-died 1776 (OH?) – son of **Mohawk Man** & **Kishpoko Woman**, raiding PA/40, Cornstalk War/55-76, French-Indian War/54-63, Braddock/55, raiding New-Shenandoah River valleys/55, raiding PA/55-56, raiding Ohio-New River valleys/58, Pontiac War/62-66, Bushy Run/63, raiding New-Greenbrier-Jackson River valleys/63, Grand Council 1763, raiding Ohio-Little Kanawha-Big Sandy-New River valleys/72, raiding Ohio River valley/74 **with Chief Logan**, Point Pleasant/74-75, a leader of a mixed-tribe Mingo band

1220.Pokechaw aka Pokeshaw – Chalakatha born about 1770 OH-died after 1820 – brother of **Wapacanaugh**/75, Blue Jacket War/87-94, raiding Ohio River valley/88-92, no part in War 1812, a warrior at Wapaghonettat 1817, Treaty 1817, husband 1790 OH of **Mekoche Woman**/74

1221.Pompey - adopted-Black born about 1740-died after 1778 - former slave, adopted by 1755, never returned to whites, Cornstalk War/62-77, Pontiac War/62-66, Bushy Run/63, raiding New-Jackson-Greenbrier River valleys/63, raiding Ohio-Little Kanawha-Big Sandy-New River valleys/72, Point Pleasant 1774/75/78, Boonesboro/78, moved to MO 1779, husband about 1760 OH of **Thawikila Woman**/44, father of Young Pompey/65-1/2 Thawikila-Black

1222. Poor Boy aka Thin Boy – Kishpoko born about 1750-died after 1778 – Cornstalk War/68-77, raiding Ohio-Little Kanawha-Big Sandy-Kanawha-New River valleys/72, Point Pleasant/74-75-78, raiding KY-OH-VA/77, Boonesboro/78

1223. Poor Raccoon aka **Chequisheghar**-Thin Raccoon – adopted-Miami born about 1760 OH-died after 1815 – Blue Jacket War/77-94, Crawford/82, raiding Ohio River valley/83-89, raiding OH-VA-KY/95-1810, Prophet's Town/1811, **left Prophet & Tecumseh** after Prophet's Town, Treaty 1814, 1815, living in Apple Creek MO 1815, husband about 1780 OH of **Kishpoko Woman**/65, father of several 1/2 Kishpoko-Miami children/80-1810

1224. Poor Wolf aka Thin Wolf – Chalakatha born about 1735 (AL?)-died after 1775 - Cornstalk War/55-77, French-Indian War/54-63, Braddock/55, raiding New-Shenandoah River valleys/55, raiding Ohio-New River valleys/58, Pontiac War/62-66, Bushy Run/63, raiding New-Greenbrier-Jackson River valleys/63, raiding Ohio-Big Sandy-Little Kanawha-New River valleys/72, Point Pleasant/74-75, husband about 1755 AL of ½ **Chalakatha-Creek Woman**/38

1225. Pope, Abraham - adopted-white born about 1775-died after 1813 - son of **William Pope**-white, adopted about 1780 OH, never fully returned, raiding OH-KY-VA/95-1810, Prophet's Town/1811, Brownstown/1812, Monguagon/1812, 1st Amherstbug/1812, Frenchtown/1813, Ft. Meigs/1813, 2nd Amherstbug/1813 & Thames/1813 **with Tecumseh**, husband about 1795 of **Mekoche Woman**/80(**daughter of a Chief?**), father of several 1/2 Mekoche-Metis children/94-1813 with surname Pope

1226. Popsikona aka Popseekona – ½ Chalakatha-Cherokee born about 1760 (VA?)-died about 1810 Monroe Co WV - daughter of **Chalakatha Man** & **Cherokee Woman**, sister of **Elvira**, wife about 1775 VA/WV of **Chalakatha Man**, widow before 1790, children unknown

1227. Popsonawamuh – Pekowi born about 1760 OH-died after 1790 - wife about 1775 OH of **Pekowi Man**/54, widow in 1790

1228. Porcupine – Chalakatha born about 1770 OH-died after 1817 - Blue Jacket War/88-94, raiding Ohio River valley/88-92, raiding OH-KY-VA/95-1810, Prophet's Town/1811, Brownstown/1812-Monguagon/1812-1st Amherstburg/1812-Frenchtown/1813-Ft. Meigs/1813-2nd Amherstburg/1813 & Thames/1813 **with Tecumseh**, a warrior at Lewistown 1817, Treaty 1817

1229. Porcupine Woman – Kishpoko born about 1740 OH-died after 1770 - wife about 1755 OH of **Kishpoko Man**/34, widow in 1770

1230. Powder Horn (1) - 1/2 Thawikila-Metis born about 1740-died after 1800 MO - son of **Thawikila Man** & **Adopted White Woman**, Cornstalk War/58-77, raiding Ohio-New River valleys/58, Pontiac War/62-66, Bushy Run/63, raiding New-Greenbrier-Jackson River valleys/63, raiding Ohio-Little Kanawha-Big Sandy-Kanawha River valleys/72, Point Pleasant/74-78, raiding KY-OH-VA/7781, Crawford, raiding Ohio River valley/88-92, Blue Jacket War/77-94, moved to
MO before 1800 with family-band, husband about 1760 OH of **Thawikila Woman**/45, father of Little Captain/70, Little Powder Horn/75 & Shot Pouch/80all 3/4th Thawikila-Metis

1231. Powder Horn, Little aka Young Powder Horn-Powder Horn (2) - 3/4th Thawikila-Metis born about 1775 OH-died after 1832 MO - son of **Powder Horn (1)**/40 & **Thawikila Woman**/45, moved to MO before 1800 with familyband, associated **with James Onothe Rogers**/78-1/2 Chalakatha-MekochePekowi-Metis & **Jimmy Rogers**/70-adopted white, scout-**with U.S. Army**-War
1812, wife & children unknown

1232. Powless, Margaret Brant - wife of **Powless Powless**-Mohawk born about 1785 OH-died 1851, mother of Catherine Powless/1804, Joseph Brant Powless/1806, Susannah Powless/1808, Margaret Powless/1810, George Powless/1812, Rachel Powless/1814, Abraham Powless/1816, Ellen Powless/1821 & Jacob Powless/1825-all 1/8th Chalakatha-Mohawk-Metis

1233. **Poxinosa aka Paxinosa-Pakshinotha**[104]-Pakshinosha-**Hard Striker**From another Place-Bukshenoatha-Bukshinosa - Bachsinosa - Pekowi born about 1670 OH-died late 1760 OH - Council with N.Y. Gov. Donegon 1690, Treaty with William Penn 1701, a **Pekowi Chief** by 1701, succeeded relative **Pheasant**/1680 as **Head Chief of Pekowi in PA** 1744, Treaty 1752, Grand Council Philadelphia 1755, Council Tioga Point 1756, Easton 1757, Ft. Pitt Aug. 1760, associated **with Shikellimus**-Seneca & **Teedyuskung**-Delaware, **Opessa, Okowellos** & **White Fish**-all Shawnee, moved from PA to OH about 1758, husband 1st about 1690 PA of **Pekowi Woman**/1675, 2nd about 1716 PA of **Elizabeth Nutimaes**/1700-Pekowi, children/1690-1715 **with Pekowi** unknown, father **with Elizabeth** of Teatapercaum/17, Elder Daughter/18, Awanoos/19, Younger Daughter/20 & Kolapeka/21 & 3 other children-all Pekowi.

1234. Poxinosa, Awanoos – Pekowi born about 1719 PA-died about 1758 OH in epidemic - son of **Poxinosa**/1670 & **Elizabeth Nutimaes**/1700-Pekowi, a

Pekowi warrior, raiding PA/40, French-Indian War/54-58, Braddock/55, raiding New-Shenandoah River valleys/55, raiding PA/55-56, raiding Ohio-New River valleys/58, wife & children unknown.

1235. Poxinosa, Elder Daughter of aka Wife of Peter Spelman – Pekowi born about 1718 PA-died after 1757 - daughter of **Poxinosa**/1670 & **Elizabeth Nutimaes**/1700-Pekowi, moved to OH before 1750, wife about 1733 of **Peter Spelman**/1705 aka **Ooligsaha**-Owiligasho-adopted German, mother of Sabra Spelman/35-1/2 Pekowi-Metis

1236. Poxinosa, Elizabeth Nutimaes - a Christian Pekowi, half-sister of **Ben Nutimaes**/05, 2nd wife about 1716 PA of **Poxinosa**/1670, mother of Teatapercaum/17, Elder Daughter/18, Awanoos/19, Younger Daughter/20 & Kolapeka/21 & 3 other children-

1237. Poxinosa, Kolapeka aka Kolapechka-Kolapecha-Copelin – Pekowi born about 1721 PA-died after 1758 (OH?) - youngest son of **Poxinosa**/1670 & **Elizabeth Nutimaes**/1700, a Pekowi warrior, raiding PA/40, French-Indian War/54-58, Braddock/55, raiding New-Shenandoah River valleys/55, raiding Ohio-New River valleys/58, wife & children unknown

1238. Poxinosa, Teatapercaum – Pekowi born about 1717 PA-died after 1766 - son of **Poxinosa**/1670 & **Elizabeth Nutimaes**/1700, raiding PA-VA/40, Cornstalk War/55-66, French-Indian War/54-63, Braddock/55, raiding NewShenandoah River valleys/55, raiding PA/55-56, Pontiac War/62-66, wife & children unknown

1239. Poxinosa, Younger Daughter of aka Wife of Francois Chartier – Pekowi born about 1720 PA-died after 1740 - daughter of **Elizabeth Nutimaes**/1700 & **Poxinosa**/1670, a Pekowi, associated with the Delaware & may have lived among them, wife 1734 PA of **Francois Chartier**-15/16th Pekowi-Metis, mother of Nancy Nadachine/34-31/32nd Pekowi-Metis

1240. Pretty Bird – Chalakatha born about 1745 OH-died after 1775 - wife about 1760 OH of **Chalakatha Man**/39, widow in 1775

1241. Priber, Ooloosta Rainmaker aka Oolootah – 2nd wife 1738 TN of **Christian Priber**-white born 1697 GER-died 1753 Frederica GA, mother of Great Priber-Drags Blanket/39-1/4th Chalakatha-**Cherokee**-Metis

1242. Priber, Susan Moytoy Carpenter – 1st wife 1730 Tellico Plains TN of **Christian Gottleib Priber**-white born 1697 GER-died 1753 Frederica GA, mother of Susanna Caroline/Catherine Priber/30, Grand Priber/32 & Place Priber/34-all 7/32nd Chalakatha-**Cherokee**-Metis

1243. Price, Nancy Rogers - wife of 1799 **Looney Price Sr**-white born about 1780-died after 1808, mother of Looney Price Jr/99, Moses Price/1804 & Alzira Price/1808-all 1/64th Chalakatha-Cherokee-Metis

1244. Pride aka Pride Opessa-**Lawaquaqua**-Lawachkamikee- Lawakwakwa – Pekowi born about 1710 MD-died 1753 SC - son of **Opessa**/1675 & **Pekowi Woman**/1680, with **Opessa** in north MD/east PA birth-1711, in west PA with Opessa 1711-23, returned to north MD/east PA with **Opessa** 1723-35, remained in north when **Opessa** took band to AL 1735, signed Petition to PA 1738 with **Peter Chartier**/1690, **George Miranda**/1700, brother **Tecoomteh**/1700 & 94 Natives to stop the sell of liquor to Natives, a **Pekowi Chief** in north MD/east PA by 1738, raiding PA/40, captured on trip to the Pekowi in the south & died in SC prison/53, husband 1st 1730 east PA of **Rising Sun**/15-Kishpoko, 2nd by 1739 east PA of a widow **Mother of Black Fish**/10Mekoche, father **with Rising Sun** of Lawagqua-elder Brother of Blue Jacket/33,
Blue Jacket- Weyapiersenwha-Whirlpool /35, Wabete-Elk-younger Brother of Blue Jacket/37 & Sally Opessa-sister of Blue Jacket/39-all Kishpoko-Pekowi, **with Mother of Black Fish** of Red Pole/40-Mekoche-Pekowi, step-father of **Black Fish**/25-Chalakatha-Mekoche.

1245. Proctor, Celia Downing - wife about 1835 of **William Proctor**-whiteborn 1806-died 1858-(nephew of **William Davis**/92-great-nephew of **Jeremiah Davis**/77), sister of 1st wife **Dicey Downing**/1808, granddaughter of **Tecumseh** & **Tahneh-Dark Star-Naomi**-Chickamauga, mother of Adam Proctor/1836, Archibald Proctor/1839, Rachel Proctor/1842 & Nancy Proctor/1844-all 5/32nd Kishpoko-Pekowi-Creek-Cherokee-Metis

1246. Proctor, Dicey Downing - wife about 1823 of **William Proctor**-white born about 1806-died 1858-(nephew of **William Davis**/92-great-nephew of **Jeremiah Davis**/77), sister of 2nd wife **Celia Downing**/1814, granddaughter of **Tecumseh** & **Tahneh-Dark Star-Naomi**-Chickamauga, mother of Sarah Proctor/1824, Johnson Proctor/1828, Ezekial Proctor/1831, Elizabeth Proctor/1834-all 5/32nd Kishpoko-Pekowi-Creek-Cherokee-Metis

1247. Proctor, Nancy Davis - sister of **Virginia Jane Davis**/86, wife 1814 of **William Proctor**-white born 1792-died 1837-(nephew of Jeremiah Proctor/77), mother of Cynthia M. Proctor/1816, William Alexander Davis Proctor/1819, Mary Ann G. Proctor/1821, Elizabeth I. Proctor/1823, Eliza Ann Proctor/1825, Susan Caroline Proctor/1830 & Francis Marion Proctor/34-all 1/16th Chalakatha-Thawikila-Creek-Cherokee-Metis

1248. Proctor, Virginia Jane Davis - sister of Nancy Davis/96, wife 1805 of **Jeremiah Proctor**-white born 1777 VA-died 1839 AL-(uncle of William Proctor/92), mother of Eliza Proctor/1805, William Davis Proctor/1806, Mary B. Proctor/1807, Micajah Alexander Proctor/1808, children/1809-13, Robert Tinker Proctor/1814, Clarissa Proctor/1819 & Elizabeth Ann Proctor/1824-all 1/16th Chalakatha-Thawikila-Creek-Cherokee-Metis

1249. Promise Maker – adopted-Delaware born about 1730 PA-died after 1774 – Cornstalk War/55-74, French-Indian War/54-63, Braddock/55, raiding NewShenandoah River valleys/55, raiding PA/55-56, raiding Ohio-New River valleys/58, Pontiac War/62-66, Bushy Run/63, raiding New-Greenbrier-Jackson River valleys/63, raiding Ohio-Big Sandy-Little Kanawha-New River valleys/72, Point Pleasant/74, husband about 1750 OH of **Pekowi Woman**/34, children unknown

1250. Proud Boy – Chalakatha born 1740 Running Water TN-died after 1764 – Blind Savannah Clan Cherokee, Cornstalk War/58-63, raiding Ohio-New River valleys/58, Pontiac War/62-64, Bushy Run/63, raiding New-Greenbrier-Jackson River Valleys/63, 2nd husband 1759 Running Water TN of **Place Priber**/38-7/32nd Chalakatha-Cherokee-Metis, children unknown

1251. Pryor, John – white born about 1750-**killed** 1794 KY – husband 1775 OH of **Chalakatha Woman**/60, father of Nancy Pryor/76-(wife of **Robert MClelland**/71-adopted white), Robert L. Pryor/77, Eliza Pryor/78, Jane Pryor/79, James Pryor/80-all 1/2 Chalakatha-Metis

1252. **Puckenshinwa aka Pukenshinwa-Puckinshinoawa-Alights from Flying**[105]-Alight From Flying-Something That Drops - 1/2 Kishpoko-CreekMetis born 1735 AL-**killed** 1774 Point Pleasant WV - son of **Kishpoko Man** & **Older Daughter of James McQueen**/20-1/2 Creek-Metis, a Kishpoko from AL, moved to KY 1759-to OH 1760, French-Indian War/54-63-(54-58 in south-59-63 in KY-OH), Cornstalk War/55-74, Pontiac War/63-66, Bushy Run/63, raiding New-Greenbrier-Jackson River valleys/63, raiding Ohio-Little Kanawha-Big Sandy-New River valleys/72, **Head Chief of Kishpoko in OH** by 1770, **killed** in battle at Point Pleasant/74, Grand Council June 1762, Sept. 1762, 1763, Council Bouquet Oct. 1764, brother of **Older Sister**=1st Wife of **Blue Jacket**/39 & **Younger Sister**=Wife of **David Francis**/45, husband 1755 AL of **Metheotashe Opessa**/40-Pekowi, father of son **Cheeseekau**/56 AL, daughter **Tecumapease**/58 AL, sons Sauwaseekou/60 KY, Nahaaseema/64 OH, daughter Menewaulakoose/66 OH, sons **Tecumseh**/68 OH, Kumshaka/70 OH, daughter Vocemassussia/72 OH & son Lalawethika-Tenskawatawa-**Shawnee Prophet**/74 OH -all 3/4th Kishpoko-Pekowi-Creek-Metis, adopted father 1760 of **Joshua**

Renicks/46, 1768 of **John Sparks**/60 & **Richard Sparks**/57, 1772 of **Stephen Ruddell**/67, uncle of (by Sister/45) John Francis/60, **Josiah Francis**/65 & Joseph Francis/70

1253. Puckenshinwa, Metheotashe Opessa - wife 1755 AL of **Puckenshinwa**/35-1/2 Kishpoko-Creek-Metis, moved to KY 1759 with Cheeseekau & Tecumapease, moved to OH 1760 after birth of Sauwaseekou, remaining children all born in OH, mother of sons **Cheeseekau**/56, Sauwaseekou/60, Nahaaseema/64, **Tecumseh**/68, Kumshaka/70 & Lalawethika-**Tenskawatawa**/74 & daughters **Tecumapease**/58, Menewaulakoose/66 & Vocemassussia/72-all 3/4th Kishpoko-Pekowi-Creek-Metis

1254. Puckenshinwa, Older Sister of - 1/2 Kishpoko-Creek-Metis born 1739 AL-died about 1774 OH - daughter of **Kishpoko Man** & **Daughter of James McQueen**/20-1/2 Creek-Metis, appears to have returned north with father, 1st wife 1st 1755 OH of **Blue Jacket**/35-Kishpoko-Pekowi, remarried when Blue Jacket married Margaret Moore-white, 2nd 1762 OH of **Isadore Chesne**/35-Wyandot-Metis, mother **with Blue Jacket** of Young Blue Jacket-Young Whirlpool/56, Spybeech/58, Wayweleapee/60 & George Blue Jacket (1)/62-all 3/4th Kishpoko-Pekowi-Creek-Metis, **with Chesne** of Anthony Shane-Chesne/63 & Joseph Shane-Chesne/65-both 1/4th Kishpoko-Creek-Wyandot-Metis

1255. Puckenshinwa, Younger Sister of - 1/2 Kishpoko-Creek-Metis born 1745 AL-died after 1805 - daughter of **Kishpoko Man** & **Daughter of James McQueen**/20-1/2 Creek-Metis, aunt of **Tecumseh**, wife 1759 of **David Mumagechee Francis**/40-7/16th Chalakatha-Mekoche-Metis-(adopted Creek), mother of John Francis/60, Josiah Francis/65, Joseph Francis/70 & Susan Francis/75-all 15/32nd Chalakatha-Kishpoko-Mekoche-Creek-Metis

1256. Pucksinekau – Kishpoko-Pekowi born about 1735-died about 1823 - son of **Sister of Pheasant (1)** aka **Sister of Kakawatchekee (1)**/1695 & **Kishpoko Man,** brother of **Hard Striker**/30 & **Catherine**/38, Cornstalk War/55-77, French-Indian War/54-63, Braddock/55, raiding New-Shenandoah River valleys/55, raiding PA/55-56, raiding Ohio-New River valleys/58, Pontiac War/62-66, Bushy Run/63, raiding New-Greenbrier-Jackson River valleys/63, raiding Little Kanawha-Big Sandy-Ohio-New River valleys/72, Point Pleasant/74-75-78, Blue Jacket War/77-94, raiding KY-VA-OH/75-81, Blue Licks/82, Crawford/82, raiding Ohio River valley/88-92, husband about 1752 (OH?) of **Mary Ice**/37-adopted white, father of Young Pucksinekau/53, Red Hair/55 & other 1/2 Kishpoko-Pekowi-Metis children

1257. Pumpkin Boy aka **Pumpkin Boy Carpenter** aka Pumpkin Boy Great Eagle-Eyahchutlee-Iyahuwagiatsutsa-No Pumpkins – 7/32nd

ChalakathaCherokee-Metis born 1741 Great Tellico TN-killed 1792 Ish Station TN in battle - son of **Great Eagle Carpenter**/02 & **Wurteh Tawsee Fox**/05, from the Overhills, Red Paint Clan Cherokee, Pontiac War/62-66, Point Pleasant/74, Cherokee War/75, Treaty Sycamore Shoals 1775, raiding KY-OH-VA/77-80, husband 1761 Great Tellico TN of **Chaueka Cherokee**/45, father of Young
Pumpkin Boy/68 & Catherine Pumpkin/82-both 7/64th Chalakatha-Cherokee-Metis, other unknown children/65-90 likely

1258. Pushwepako – Pekowi born about 1720 PA-died after 1774 - wife about 1735 PA of **Pekowi Man**/14, widow in 1774

1259. Pyatt, Elizabeth – Pekowi born about 1735 PA-died after 1784 - wife 1750 of **Jacob Pyatt**/25-adopted white, mother of Jacob Pyatt Jr/51, Benjamin Pyatt/53, James Pyatt/55, Thomas Pyatt/57, Robert Pyatt/59, Rebecca Pyatt/61, Rachel Pyatt/63, Mary Pyatt/65, Diana Pyatt/67, Susanna Pyatt/69, Elizabeth Pyatt/71-all 1/2 Pekowi-Metis

Chapter XIV
Quaghoquona to Runs With Ax (Q – R)

Q

1260. Quaghoquona aka Kwagahkwona – Mekoche born about 1770 OH-died after 1817 - raiding Ohio River valley/88-92, Blue Jacket War/87-94, no part in War 1812, a warrior at Wapaghonettat 1817, Treaty 1817

1261. Quaho aka Kwaho – Mekoche born about 1770 OH-died after 1817 - raiding Ohio River valley/88-92, Blue Jacket War/87-94, no part in War 1812, a warrior at Wapaghonettat 1817, Treaty 1817

1262. Quailaisha aka Kwaeelaeesha – Mekoche born about 1775 OH-died after 1817 – Fallen Timber/94, no part in War 1812, a warrior at Wapaghonettat 1817, Treaty 1817

1263. Quamapea aka Kwamapee – Kishpoko born about 1780 OH-died after 1826 KS - raiding KY-OH-VA/99-1810, Prophet's Town/1811, Brownstown/1812-Monguagon/1812-1st Amherstburg/1812-Frenchtown/1813-Ft. Meigs/1813-2nd Amherstburg/1813 & Thames/1813 **with Tecumseh**, moved to

CAN 1815, returned to OH 1825, Treaty 1825, moved to KS 1826 **with Prophet & Paukeesaa**

1264. Quanaqua aka Kwanakwa – Mekoche born about 1770 OH-died after 1817 – Blue Jacket War/87-94, no part in War 1812, a warrior at Wapaghonettat 1817, Treaty 1817

1265. Quaquesha aka Kwakwesha – Mekoche born about 1775 OH-died after 1817 - Fallen Timber/94, no part in War 1812, a warrior at Wapaghonettat 1817, Treaty 1817

1266. Quarkee aka Kwarkee – Kishpoko born about 1770 OH-died after 1831 KS - raiding Ohio River valley/87-92, Blue Jacket War/87-94, raiding OH-KY-VA/95-1810, Prophet's Town/1811, Brownstown/1812-Monguagon/1812-1st Amherstburg/1812-Frenchtown/1813-Ft. Meigs/1813-2nd Amherstburg/1813 & Thames/1813 **with Tecumseh**, moved to CAN 1815, returned to OH about 1825, moved to KS 1826 **with Prophet & Paukeesaa**, Treaty 1831

1267. Quedaska aka Kweedaska – Thawikila born about 1770 OH-died after 1817 – Blue Jacket War/87-94, no part in War 1812, a warrior at Hog Creek 1817

1268. Quelenee aka Kweelenee-Quelana-Qwelana-Quilna-Quilina - Thawikila born about 1785 OH-died 1878 KS/OK – no part in War 1812, a warrior at Hog Creek & Wapaghonettat 1817, Treaty 1817, 1831, 1854, moved to KS about 1832, husband 1805 OH of **Thawikila Woman**/89

1269. Quelou aka Kweeloo - 1/2 Pekowi-Metis born about 1730 PA-died after 1755 OH - son of **Pekowi Woman** & **White Man**, French-Indian War/54-55, Braddock/55, raiding New-Shenandoah River valleys/55, husband about 1750 OH of **Pekowi Woman**/35, father of 1 son & 1 daughter/50-55

1270. Quemauto aka Kweemawto – Chalakatha born about 1770 OH-died after 1817 - raiding Ohio River valley/88-92, Blue Jacket War/87-94, raiding OH-KY-VA/95-1810, Prophet's Town/1811, Brownstown/1812-Monguagon/1812-1st Amherstburg/1812-Frenchtown/1813-Ft. Meigs/1813-2nd Amherstburg/1813 & Thames/1813 **with Tecumseh**, a warrior at Lewistown 1817, Treaty 1817

1271. Quinaska aka Kweenaska - Thawikila born about 1770 OH-died after 1817 - raiding Ohio River valley/88-92, Blue Jacket War/87-94, no part in War 1812, a warrior at Hog Creek 1817, Treaty 1817

1272. Quinton, Lydia Critterden - wife 1815 of **Samuel Quinton**-white born about 1790-died 1870, mother of William Quinton/1816, Jennie Quinton/1818, Nelly Quinton/1819, Edith Elizabeth Quinton/1820-all 1/4th Chalakatha-

Kishpoko-Pekowi-**Cherokee**-Metis

1273. Quitewee aka Quitawek-Quitawec-Kweetawek – Mekoche born about 1770 OH-died after 1817 - raiding Ohio River valley/87-92, Blue Jacket War/8794, scout-**with U.S. Army**-War 1812, a **War Chief** at Wapaghonettat 1817,
Treaty 1817

1274. Quotowamee aka Kwotowamee – Mekoche born about 1770 OH-died after 1817 - raiding Ohio River valley/87-92, Blue Jacket War/87-94, no part in War 1812, a warrior at Wapaghonettat 1817, Treaty 1817

R

1275. Rabbit (1) aka **Patakeenotha**[106] – Pekowi born about 1745 PA-died after 1774 – Cornstalk War/62-74, Pontiac War/62-66, Bushy Run/63, raiding NewGreenbrier-Jackson River valleys/63, raiding Ohio-Kanawha-Big Sandy-Little
Kanawha River valleys/72, Point Pleasant/74

1276. Raccoon aka **Shapatha**[107] – Kishpoko born about 1740-died after 1780 – Cornstalk War/58-77, raiding Ohio-New River valleys/58, Pontiac War/62-66, Bushy Run/63, raiding New-Greenbrier-Jackson River valleys/63, raiding Ohio-Big Sandy-Little Kanawha-New River valleys/72, Point Pleasant/74, raiding KY-OH-VA/77-80, husband 1760 OH of **Kishpoko Woman**/45, father of Young Raccoon/80

1277. Raccoon, Young aka Young Shapatha - Kishpoko born about 1780 OH**killed** Thames 1813 - son of **Raccoon-Shapatha**/40 & **Kishpoko Woman**/45, raiding OH-KY-VA/99-1810, Prophet's Town/1811, Brownstown/1812Monguagon/1812-1st Amherstburg/1812-Frenchtown/1813-Ft. Meigs/1813-2nd Amherstburg/1813, **killed at Thames/13 with Tecumseh**, wife & children unknown

1278. Ragsdale, Eleanor Harnage - wife before 1810 of **John Ragsdale**-white born about 1790-died after 1824 (brother of Isaac Ragsdale/95), mother of Benjamin Ragsdale/1810, Elizabeth Ragsdale/1812, Isaac Ragsdale/1814, Thomas Ragsdale/1816, John Ragsdale Jr/1818, William Ragsdale/1820, Ezekial Ragsdale/1822, Susan Ragsdale/1824-all 1/16th Chalakatha-**Cherokee**-Metis

1279. Ragsdale, Elizabeth Jane Welch - wife 1830 of **Isaac Ragsdale**/1814, mother of David Welch Ragsdale/1831 & Winnie Jane Ragsdale/1832-both 7/64th Chalakatha-Kishpoko-Black-**Cherokee**-Metis

1280.Rainbow, Elizabeth – Pekowi born about 1760 VA-died after 1785 - sister of **James Rainbow**/65, wife of **William Rogers**-white born about 1750died after 1785, mother of John Nolichucky Rogers/79 & Robert Rogers/85-both 1/2 Pekowi-Metis, other children likely

1281.Rainey, Matthew - 5/16th Chalakatha-Kishpoko-Pekowi-Creek-Metis born about 1815 IN-died 1881 IN - son of **Serena Skwato Tecumseh**/99 & **William Rainey**/75-white, grandson of **Tecumseh**/68 & **White Wing Cornstalk**/70, husband 1836 of **Mary Polly Johnson**/1818-white, father of Nancy Rainey/1838, Eliza Jane Rainey/1840, Andrew Jackson Rainey/1841, Caroline Rainey/1842, Sarah Elizabeth Rainey/1843, Mary Elizabeth Rainey/1845, William H. Rainey/1848, Enoch Rainey/1849, Sylvester Rainey/1854, Martha Marie Rainey/1856, Florence Rainey/1859 & Mahala Rainey/1861-all 5/32nd Chalakatha-Kishpoko-Pekowi-Creek-Metis

1282.Rainmaker (1) aka Amadohityi-**Water Beaver** – Cherokee born 1640 TN-died 1710 TN – could recall when the "white Indians aka Welsh" left TNNC-KY for MO before 1670, husband 1665 of **Quatsey (1)**/1650-Wolf Clan Cherokee, from the Valley Towns-Little Hiwassee-Taseetchee, father of Elder Daughter/1672, Younger Daughter/1674, sons Tistoe/1676, Oukahula/1678, **Rainmaker (2)-Young Rainmaker** /1680-(husband of **Elder Sister of Old Hop**/1680), daughters **Quatsey (2)-Susan**/1682-(1st wife 1697 of **Savannah Tom Carpenter (1)**/1680 & 1700 of **Tsula Fox-Smallpox Conjurer**/1670), Nancy/1684-(2nd wife 1700 of **Savannah Tom Carpenter (1)**/1680 & 2nd wife 1710 of his brother **White Owl Carpenter**/1678) & **Sugi**/1690-(wife of **Old Hop**)-all Wolf Clan Cherokee, & adopted father 1694 of daughters **Elder Sister of Old Hop**/1684, **Oolootah Hop**/1692 & **Ghigoneli Hop**/1694-Chalakatha (sisters of **Old Hop**-Standing Turkey/1688)

1283.Rainmaker (2) aka **Young Rainmaker-Pigeon of Tellico** - Cherokee born about 1680 Great Tellico TN-**killed** 1741 TN in battle - son of **Rainmaker (1)**/1640 & **Quatsey (1)**/1650-both Cherokee, Wolf Clan Cherokee, delegation to ENG 1730, shared leadership **with Tsula Fox-Smallpox Conjurer -Jacob the Conjurer**/1670-Cherokee from 1710 until 1730 when the Cherokee Chiefs & **Alexander Cummings** for the British selected him Emperor of the Cherokee, 1st British appointed Cherokee Emperor 1730, a **Principal Chief** of Cherokee 1730-41, **killed 1741 in same battle as White Owl Carpenter**, husband about 1700 of **Elder Sister of Old Hop**/1684, father of son Oconastota Rainmaker/02, child/04, son Cloggoittah Rainmaker/06, daughter Ooloosta Rainmaker/08, sons Kitegista-Skalilosken Rainmaker/10, Tathtowe Rainmaker /12, Gray Eagle Rainmaker/14, Oukahoukah Rainmaker/16 & Kallannah Rainmaker/18-all 1/2 Chalakatha-Cherokee

1284. Rainmaker (3) aka **Rain Conjurer**-Rainmaker Fox-Amadahiyi**Ootossetih**-Mankiller - Cherokee born 1702 Settico TN-died after 1763
Overhills TN - son of **Quatsey Rainmaker (2)**/1682-Cherokee & **Tsula Fox-Smallpox Conjurer-Jacob the Conjurer**/1670-Cherokee, great-grandson of Rainmaker (1)/1640, half-brother (through father) of Rising Fawn (1)/06 & Quatsis Fox/08-both 1/2 Chalakatha-Cherokee, Wolf Clan Cherokee, associated with **Savannah Tom Carpenter (2)** /1698, **Robert-Thigh-Cauquillehaneh McLemore**/31, **John French**/10, **Capt. French**/12, **Muskrat (2)**/18 & **John Lantaniak**/20-adopted-French/Canadian in pro-French faction French-Indian War/54-63 with , raiding New-Shenandoah River valleys/55, raiding NewJackson-Greenbrier River valleys/63, from the Overhills & Settico, a **Principal Chief of Cherokee** 1741-63, husband about 1722 TN of **Cherokee Woman**/07, children unknown

1285. Rainmaker, Ooloosta aka Oolootah - 1/2 Chalakatha-**Cherokee** born 1708-died after 1739 - daughter of **Young Rainmaker**/1680-Cherokee & **Elder Sister of Old Hop**/1684-Chalakatha, namesake of aunt **Oolootah Hop**/1692, granddaughter of Rainmaker (1)/1640, Blind Savannah Clan Cherokee, wife 1st 1726 of **Rising Fawn Fox (1)**/06-1/2 Chalakatha-Cherokee, 2nd by 1738 of **Christian Priber**/1697-white, mother with **Rising Fawn (1)** of Rising Fawn Fox (2)/26 & others/28-38-all 1/2 Chalakatha-Cherokee, mother **with Priber** of Great Priber-Drags Blanket/39-1/4th Chalakatha-Cherokee-Metis

1286. Ran in Thorns – Kishpoko born about 1750 OH-died after 1785 - raiding Ohio-Little Kanawha-Big Sandy-New River valleys/72, Point Pleasant/74-78, raiding KY-VA-OH/75-81, Crawford/82

1287. Rattlesnake aka **Miseethawee**[108]-Meeseethawee – Mekoche born about 1745 OH-died after 1780 – Cornstalk War/62-74, Pontiac War/62-66, Bushy
Run/63, raiding New-Greenbrier-Jackson River valleys/63, raiding Ohio-Little Kanawha-Big Sandy-New River valleys/72, Point Pleasant/74, Blue Jacket War/77-80, Boonesboro/78, raiding KY-VA-OH/75-80

1288. Rattlesnake – adopted-Cherokee born about 1750 TN-died after 1782 – Cornstalk War/70-77, raiding New-Kanawha-Ohio-Big Sandy-Little Kanawha
River valleys/72, Point Pleasant/74, raiding KY-VA-OH/75-81, Blue Jacket War/77-82, Boonesboro/78, Crawford/82, lived in KY-OH **with Shawnee**, husband about 1770 KY of **Kishpoko Woman**/55, father of several 1/2

Kishpoko-Cherokee children/70-82

1289.　　　Raven (3) - Chalakatha born about 1740 OH-died after 1780 – Cornstalk War/58-77, raiding Ohio-New River valleys/58, Pontiac War/62-66, Bushy Run/63, raiding New-Greenbrier-Jackson River valleys/63, raiding Ohio-Big Sandy-Little Kanawha-New River valleys/72, Point Pleasant/74-75-78, Blue Jacket War/77-80, Boonesboro/78, raiding KY-VA-OH/77-80

1290.　　　Raven Calls – adopted-Kickapoo born about 1730 (IL?)-died after 1778 – Cornstalk War/55-77, French-Indian War/54-63, Braddock/55, raiding New-Shenandoah River valleys/55, raiding Ohio-New River valleys/58, Pontiac War/62-66, Bushy Run/63, raiding New-Greenbrier-Jackson River valleys/63, raiding Ohio-Big Sandy-Little Kanawha-New River valleys/72, Point Pleasant/74-78, raiding KY-VA-OH/75-77, Boonesboro/78, husband 1750 (IN?) of **Mekoche Woman**/35, children unknown

1291.　　　Razor – Chalakatha born about 1780 OH-died after 1817 - raiding OHKY-VA/99-1810, Prophet's Town/1811, Brownstown/1812-Monguagon/1812-1st Amherstburg/1812-Frenchtown/1813-Ft. Meigs/1813-2nd Amherstburg/1813 & Thames/1813 **with Tecumseh**, a warrior at Lewistown 1817, Treaty 1817

1292.　　　Reaume, Agathe LaSalle - 1/2 Pekowi-Metis born about 1710-died 1778 - 2nd wife 1733 of **Hyacinth Reaume**/04-white, mother of Jacques Reaume/36, Joseph Reaume/38, Jean Baptiste Reaume/40, Agathe Reaume/42, Claude Reaume/44, Catherine Reaume/46, Julia Reaume/48, Mary Ann Reaume/50-all 1/4th Pekowi-Metis

1293. Reaume, Charles (1) aka **Old Reaume** - 1/2 Pekowi-Metis born about 1710-died after 1779 - son of **Pekowi Woman** & **Coureur-debois Reaume**white-(a brother of **Robert Reaume**/1688? – Charles/10 = a cousin of Hyacinth Reaume/04 & Pierre Reaume/09?)), raiding PA/40, French-Indian War/54-63, Braddock/55, Cornstalk War/55-66, raiding New-Shenandoah River valleys/55, raiding PA/55-56, raiding Ohio-New River valleys/58, Pontiac War/62-66, Bushy Run/63, living **with Peter Chartier** band 1747, Council Miami 1779, husband by 1730 of **Pekowi Woman**/15, father of Charles Reaume Jr/33, Piero Reaume/40, Margaret Reaume/45-all 3/4th Pekowi-Metis, many other children likely

1294. Reaume, Charles (2) aka Charles Jr - 3/4th Pekowi-Metis born 1733-died 1813 - son of **Old Charles Reaume (1)**/10 & **Pekowi Woman**/15, Cornstalk

War/55-77, raiding New-Shenandoah River valleys/55, raiding Ohio-New River valleys/58, Pontiac War/62-66, Bushy Run/63, raiding New-Jackson-Greenbrier River valleys/63, raiding Ohio-Little Kanawha-Big Sandy-New River valleys/72, Point Pleasant/74, raiding KY-VA-OH/75-81, Boonesboro/78, Crawford/82, raiding Ohio River valley/88-92, Blue Jacket War/77-94, husband by 1752 of **Pekowi Woman**/36, father of Charles Reaume (3)/52-7/8th Pekowi-Metis

1295. Reaume, Charles (3) - 7/8th Pekowi-Metis-(adopted-Chippewa) born about 1752-died 1823 - son of **Charles Reaume Jr**/33 & **Pekowi Woman**/36, Cornstalk War/72-77, raiding Ohio-Little Kanawha-Big Sandy-New River valleys/72, Point Pleasant/75-78, raiding KY-OH-VA/77-81, Crawford/82, raiding Ohio River valley/88-92, Blue Jacket War/77-94, **with British Army-War of 1812**, husband about 1772 of **Sanguenette Chippewa**/55, father of Margaret Reaume/1800-7/16th Pekowi-Chippewa-Metis

1296. Reaume, Jean Baptiste (1) - 1/4th Pekowi-Metis-(Chippewa) born about 1740-died 1807 - son of **Hyacinth Reaume**/04-white & **Agathe LaSalle**/10, Cornstalk War/62-77, Pontiac War/62-66, Bushy Run/63, raiding NewGreenbrier-Jackson River valleys/63, raiding Ohio-Little Kanawha-Big SandyNew River valleys/72, Point Pleasant/74-78, raiding KY-VA-OH/75-81, Crawford/82, raiding Ohio River valley/88-92, Blue Jacket War/77-94, husband 1st 1763 of **Agathe Lootman Barrios**/45-1/2 Chippewa Metis, 2nd 1787 of **Mary Louisa Robert**/70-1/2 Chippewa-Metis, father **with Barrios** of Agathe Louise Reaume/70-1/8th Pekowi-Chippewa-Metis

1297. Reaume, Joseph - 1/4th Pekowi-Metis born 1739-died 1796 - son of **Hyacinth Reaume**/04-white & **Agathe LaSalle**/10, Cornstalk War/58-77, raiding Ohio-New River valleys/58, Pontiac War/62-66, Bushy Run/63, raiding New-Greenbrier-Jackson River valleys/63, raiding New-Ohio-Big Sandy-Little Kanawha River valleys/72, Point Pleasant/74, raiding KY-VA-OH/75-81, Boonesboro/78, Crawford/82, raiding Ohio River valley/88-92, Blue Jacket War/77-94, husband 1st 1758 of **Pekowi Woman**/40, 2nd 1787 of **Mary Ann Robert**/68-1/2 Chippewa-Metis, children unknown

1298. Reaume, Margaret (1) - 3/4th Pekowi-Metis born about 1745-died after 1767 - daughter of **Old Charles Reaume** (1)/10 & **Pekowi Woman**/15, wife about 1765 of **Joseph Howard**/40-white, children unknown

1299. Reaume, Margaret (2) - 7/16th Pekowi-Chippewa-Metis born about 1800died after 1817 - daughter of **Charles Reaume (3)**/52 & **Sanguenette**/55-Chippewa, wife 1817 of **Jean Baptiste Rousson**/95, children unknown

1300. Reaume, Marguerite - 1/2 Pekowi-Metis born about 1732-died after 1756

- daughter of **Marie Therese**/1714 & **Pierre Reaume (1)**/1709-white, wife about 1756 of **Charles Bouron**/20-Huron-Metis, children unknown

1301.Reaume, Marie Therese – Pekowi born about 1714-died after 1750 - wife about 1729 of **Pierre Reaume**/1709-white, mother of Pierre Reaume (2)/30, Marguerite Reaume/32, Pierre Reaume (3)/34, child/36, child/38, Suzanne Reaume/40 & maybe other children/41-50-all 1/2 Pekowi-Metis

1302.Reaume, Mary Ann - 1/4th Pekowi-Metis born 1750-died after 1765 - daughter of **Agathe LaSalle**/10 & **Hyacinth Reaume**/04-white, wife 1765 of **Pierre Barron**/45-white, children unknown

1303.Reaume, Piero (1) aka Pierre Reaume (4) - 3/4th Pekowi-Metis born about 1740-died after 1763 - son of **Charles Reaume (1)**/10 & **Pekowi Woman**, raiding Ohio-New River valleys/58, Pontiac War/62-63, Bushy Run/63, raiding New-Jackson-Greenbrier River valleys/63, husband 1760 of **Maria Josette Metis**/45-Ottawa-Metis, father of Piero Reaume (2)/60-3/8th Pekowi-OttawaMetis

1304.Reaume, Piero (2) aka Pierre Reaume Jr-Pierre (5) - 3/8th PekowiOttawa-Metis born about 1760-died after 1780 - son of **Piero Reaume (1)**/40 & **Maria Josette Metis**/45-Ottawa-Metis, husband about 1780 of **Maria Jeanne Campeau**/64-Ottawa-Metis, children unknown

1305.Reaume, Pierre (1) – adopted-French-Canadian born about 1709-died 1789 - son of **Robert Reaume**/1668-white & **Elizabeth Brunet**, brother of **Hyacinth Reaume**/04, raiding PA/40, Cornstalk War/55-72, French-Indian War/54-63, Braddock/55, raiding New-Shenandoah River valleys/55, raiding PA/55-56, raiding Ohio-New River valleys/58, Pontiac War/62-66, Bushy Run/63, raiding New-Jackson-Greenbrier River valleys/63, raiding Ohio-Little Kanawha-Big Sandy-New River valleys/72, husband 1st about 1729 of **Marie Therese**/14-Pekowi, 2nd 1738 **Suzanne Hubert LaCroix**/20-white, father **with Marie Therese** of Pierre Reaume (2)/30, Marguerite Reaume/32, Pierre Reaume (3)/34, child/36, child/38, Suzanne Reaume/40 & maybe other children/41-50-all 1/2 Pekowi-Metis, **with LaCroix** of Charlotte Susanne Reaume/38, child/40, Bonaventure Reaume/42 & Veronique Reaume/44-all white

1306.Reaume, Pierre (2) - 1/2 Pekowi-Metis born about 1730-died after 1763 - son of **Pierre Reaume (1)**/09-white & **Marie Therese**/14-Pekowi, French/Indian War/54-63, Cornstalk War/55-63, Braddock/55, raiding New-Shenandoah River valleys/55, raiding Ohio-New River valleys/58, Pontiac War/62-63, Bushy Run/63, raiding New-Jackson-Greenbrier River valleys/63, husband about 1754 of **Marie Josette Pilot**/39-Huron-Metis, father of Stephen Louis/60-1/4th Pekowi-Huron-Metis

1307. Reaume, Pierre (3) - 1/2 Pekowi-Metis born 1734-died after 1764 - son of **Pierre Reaume (1)**/09 & **Marie Therese**/14-Pekowi, 2nd son called Pierre, Pontiac War/62-63, husband 2nd 1763 of **Marie Catherine Dubois**/48-Ottawa Metis, father of Mary Reaume/64-1/4th Pekowi-Ottawa-Metis

1308. Reaume, Suzanne - ½ Pekowi-Metis born about 1740-died after 1782 - daughter of **Marie Therese**/14-Pekowi & **Pierre Reaume (1)**/09-white, 3rd wife about 1760 of **Jacques Duperon Baby**/33-white, mother of James Baby/62, Suzanne Baby/66, Therese Baby/67, Francois Baby/68, Jean Baptiste Baby/70, Archangel Baby/74, Anthony Baby/75, Pierre Baby/76, Monica Baby/77, Daniel Baby/78 & Louis Baby/82-all 1/4th Pekowi-Metis (all of Baby's legitimate children?)

1309. Red Bear – Chalakatha born about 1755 AL-died after 1794 (AL?) - from Souvanogee (Shawnee) village AL, a Chalakatha in the **Okowellos** band, raiding TN-KY-VA/75-92 **with Shawnee & Chickamaugua**, Blue Jacket War/77-94, husband about 1775 AL of **Creek Woman**/60, father of several 1/2 Chalakatha-Creek children/75-94

1310. Red Beast aka LeBete Rouge - 1/2 Kishpoko-Black (**Ottawa** by marriage) born 1735 (PA?)-died after 1772 - son of **Kishpoko Woman**/10 & **African**/1700-adopted-Black, known for red hair, reddish skin, tattoos & scarring, a large violent warrior, Cornstalk War/55-72, raiding New-Shenandoah River valleys/55, raiding PA/55-56, raiding Ohio-New River valleys/58, Pontiac War/60-66, Bushy Run/63, raiding New-Jackson-Greenbrier River valleys/63, raiding Ohio-New-Big Sandy-Little Kanawha River valleys/72, associated with the Canadian Metis, husband 1755 OH of **Ottawa Woman**/40, father of several 1/4th Kishpoko-Black-Ottawa children/55-72

1311. Red Bird aka Red Bird Carpenter (1) -**Aaron Brock (1)**-Red Bird Great Eagle-Taleonteeskee-Cusawah-Tuchuwor-Tsisquaya-Totsuwha-DotsuwaTochuwar-Quagi – 7/32nd Chalakatha-**Cherokee**-Metis born 1727 Great Tellico TN-**murdered** 1796 Clay Co. KY - son of **Great Eagle Carpenter**/02 & **Wurteh Tawsee Fox**/05, Red Paint Clan Cherokee, **Chief of Taluegue**-Red Bird village, could speak, read & write English & cipher white style, Pontiac War/6266, allied **with Cornstalk**/62-77, Point Pleasant/74, Cherokee War/75, Blue Licks/78, a Chickamauga, Pigeon Co-Cherokee scouts-**with U.S. Army**Revolution after 1778, took white-Christian name for marriage from about 1749after 1764, returned to Native name after death 1764 of Susanna Caroline Priber, moved to Barrens TN 1778, moved back to KY 1789, **murdered by whites** with friend **Crippled Will**-Cherokee, husband 1748 Great Tellico TN of

his half-niece **Susanna Caroline Priber**/30-7/32nd Chalakatha-Cherokee-Metis, father of Red Bird Carpenter (2)-Aaron Brock Jr- **Tsisquaya**-Little Red Bird/48, Mahala
Susannah White Deer-Unegahiwiya Brock/50, Jesse Hungry Fox-Gayasihatsula Brock/52, George Brock/54, Reuben Brock/56, John Fire Raven-Atsilagolanu Brock/58, Mary Polly Tame Dove-Ulunitagni Brock/60, James ThunderstormUnalasgiunula Brock/62 & Amon Brock/64-all 7/32nd Chalakatha-CherokeeMetis

1312. Red Cat of Cliff – Chalakatha born about 1765 OH-died after 1790 – Blue Jacket War/82-94, Crawford/82, raiding Ohio River valley/88-89, Harmar/90, Fallen Timber/94

1313. Red Crow – Kishpoko born about 1745 KY-died after 1795 – Cornstalk War/62-77, Pontiac War/62-66, raiding Ohio-Little Kanawha-Big Sandy-New River valleys/72, Point Pleasant/74-78, Blue Jacket War /77-94, raiding KY-OH-VA/75-81, Crawford/82, raiding Ohio River valley/88-92

1314. Red Eagle – Thawikila born about 1740 AL-died after 1779 MO – moved from AL to OH 1755, Cornstalk War/58-77, raiding Ohio-New River valleys/58, a **Thawikila Chief** 1760, Pontiac War/62-66, Bushy Run/63, raiding New-Jackson-Greenbrier River valleys/63, raiding Ohio-Big Sandy-Little Kanawha-New River valleys/72, Point Pleasant/74-78, raiding KY-OH-VA/75-77, Boonesboro/78, from **Black Hoof**'s faction, move to MO 1779 with **Black Stump, Kikusgowlawa, Yellow Hawk, Red Snake** & 400 families

1315. Red Eye aka Hutqueote-Hootkweeote-Arrow - adopted-Seneca born about 1750 (PA?)-died 1830 OH - Cornstalk War/68-77, raiding Ohio-Little Kanawha-Big Sandy-New River valleys/72, Point Pleasant/74-78, Blue Jacket War /77-94, raiding KY-VA-OH/75-81, Boonesboro/78, Crawford/82, raiding Ohio River valley/88-92, husband 1770 OH of **Chalakatha Woman**/55, children unknown

1316. Red Fish – Pekowi born about 1730 (PA?)-died after 1782 OH – Cornstalk War/55-77, French-Indian War/54-63, Braddock/55, Pontiac War/6266, Point Pleasant/74-78, Blue Jacket War/77-82, raiding Ohio-New River valleys/75-81, Crawford/82

1317. **Red Fox**[109] – Chalakatha born about 1750 OH-died after 1790 – Cornstalk War/68-77, raiding Big Sandy-Little Kanawha-Ohio-New River valleys/72, Point Pleasant/74-78, Blue Jacket War/77-90, raiding KY-VA-OH/75-81, Boonesboro/78, Crawford/82, raiding Ohio River valley/88-90

1318. Red Giant aka LeGeant Rouge-Big Indian-Big Injun – Chalakatha born about 1750 along the Great Lakes (IN-IL?)-**killed** 1788 Marietta OH – Chalakatha warrior, moved to OH valley about 1770, Cornstalk War/70-77, raiding Ohio-Little Kanawha-Big Sandy-New River valleys/72, Point Pleasant/74, Blue Jacket War/77-88, raiding KY-VA-OH/75-81, Boonesboro/78, Crawford/82, raiding Ohio River valley/88, shot in forehead on west bank of Ohio River from flatboat, **body exhumed by whites shortly after 1800**, about 8' tall, born in the north-west, husband 1766 (IN-IL?) of **Buffalo's Daughter**/50Chalakatha, father of Long Stepper/67, Big Corn/69, River Willow/71 & Little Giant/73-(all children over 6'6" tall)

1319. Red Giant, **Big Corn** aka Elder Daughter of – Chalakatha born about 1769 (IN-IL?)-died after 1788 - daughter of **Red Giant**/50 & **Buffalo's Daughter**/50, about 6'6" tall, wife 1783 OH of **Chalakatha Man**/62, children unknown

1320. Red Giant, **Buffalo's Daughter** aka Wife of Red Giant – Chalakatha, wife 1766 Great Lakes area (IN-IL?) of **Red Giant**/50, over 6' tall & heavy, mother of Long Stepper/67, Big Corn/69, River Willow/71 & Little Giant/73-all Chalakatha

1321. Red Giant, **Long Stepper** aka Elder Son of – Chalakatha born about 1767 (IN-IL?)-died after 1795 - son of **Red Giant**/50 & **Buffalo's Daughter**/50, about 7' tall & big, a Chalakatha warrior, Blue Jacket War/82-94, raiding Ohio River valley/82-92, Fallen Timber/94, wife & children unknown

1322. Red Giant, **River Willow** aka Younger Daughter of – Chalakatha born about 1771 OH-died after 1788 - daughter of **Red Giant**/50 & Buffalo's Daughter/50, about 6'6" tall & slender, wife about 1785 OH of **Chalakatha Man**/65, children unknown

1323. Red Giant, **Young** aka Little Giant-Younger Son of – Chalakatha born about 1773-died after 1788 - son of **Red Giant**/50 & **Buffalo's Daughter**/50, about 7' tall, a Chalakatha warrior, raiding Ohio River valley/88, wife & children unknown

1324. Red Hair aka Red Hair Pucksinekau- Red Hair-Red Hair Ice-Red Haired Man - 1/2 Kishpoko-Pekowi-Metis born about 1755 OH-died after 1775 - son of **Pucksinekau**/35 & **Mary Ice**/37-adopted-white, raiding Ohio-Big Sandy-Little Kanawha-New River valleys/72, Point Pleasant/74-75, husband about 1775 KY of **Kishpoko-Cherokee Woman**/60, children unknown

1325. Red Hatchet – Kishpoko born about 1745 OH-died after 1780 – Cornstalk War /72-77, raiding Ohio-Little Kanawha-New-Big Sandy River valleys/72, Point Pleasant/74, Blue Jacket War /77-80, Boonesboro/78, raiding KY-OH-VA/75-80

1326. **Red Hawk** aka Red Hawk Hokolesqua-**Miskapelathee**[110]-Misquapolathe-Red Hawk Okowellos – 7/8th Chalakatha-Mekoche-Metis born 1722 PA-died 1777 Point Pleasant WV - son of **Okowellos**/1674 & **Katee Mekoche**/1680, a **Mekoche Chief** by 1759, **Cornstalk War** /55-77, FrenchIndian War/54-63, Braddock/55, raiding New-Shenandoah River valleys/55, raiding PA/55-56, raiding Ohio-New River valleys/58, Pontiac War/62-66, Bushy Run/63, raiding New-Greenbrier-Jackson River valleys/63, raiding Ohio-Little Kanawha-New-Big Sandy River valleys/72, Point Pleasant/74, **Chief of Shawnee among the Delaware** about 1764, Council Ft. Pitt Aug. 1759, Council Ft. Pitt Aug.-Sept. 1762, Council Lancaster Aug. 1762, hostage of **Bouquet** winter of 1764-65 with **Cornstalk, Wakeeampea, Ewikunwee** & **Naythakeina**, often represented Cornstalk at Councils/60-74, Treaty 1765, **an emissary/carried wampum to Dragging Canoe for Cornstalk** before Point Pleasant 1774, Camp Charlotte 1774, **murdered at Ft. Randolph**/Point Pleasant WV 1777 with **Cornstalk**, nephew **Ellinipsico** & adopted nephew **Petella**, husband 1st 1742 PA/OH of a **Mekoche Woman** & 2nd about 1754 OH of a **Delaware Woman**, children unknown

1327. Red Horse (1) – Mekoche born about 1730 OH-died after 1786 – Cornstalk War /55-77, raiding Ohio-New River valleys/58, Pontiac War/62-66, Bushy Run/63, raiding New-Jackson-Greenbrier River valleys/63, raiding OhioLittle Kanawha-Big Sandy-New River valleys/72, Point Pleasant/74, Blue Jacket War /77-86, Boonesboro/78, raiding KY-VA-OH/75-81, Crawford/82, a **Mekoche Chief** in Moluntha's village 1786, survived Col. Benjamin Logan's raid 1786, adopted father of **Priscilla Estes**-adopted white, husband 1750 OH of **Karalo**/35-Mekoche

1328. Red Iron aka Hot Iron - 1/2 Mekoche-Delaware-Black-Metis born about 1750 (OH-PA?)-died after 1795 - son of **Mekoche Man** & **Delaware-BlackMetis Woman**, known for his reddish skin & hair, Cornstalk War/68-77, raiding Ohio-Big Sandy-Little Kanawha-New River valleys/72, Point Pleasant/74-75,

Blue Jacket War/77-94, raiding KY-OH-VA/75-81, Crawford/82, raiding Ohio River valley/88-92, husband 1770 OH of **Mekoche Woman**/54, children unknown

1329. Red Pigeon – Pekowi born about 1770 OH-died after 1790 – Blue Jacket War/87-90, raiding Ohio River valley/88-89, Harmar/90

1330. Red Pole aka **Mesquakinoe**-Mesquakunigou-Meskwakeeno – PekowiMekoche (Thawikila by marriage) born about 1740 (PA?)-died 1797 PA - son of **Pride Opessa**/10-Pekowi & **Mother of Black Fish**/10-Mekoche, reverted to mother's division-Mekoche with death of Pride 1753, then raised by mother's 3rd husband **Mekoche Man**/10, grandson of **Opessa**/1680, half-brother of **Blue Jacket**/35 (through Pride/10) & of **Black Fish**/25 (through Mother/10), a **Mekoche Chief** 1778, Cornstalk War/58-77, raiding Ohio-New River valleys/58, Pontiac War/62-66, Bushy Run/63, raiding New-Greenbrier-Jackson River valleys/63, raiding Ohio-Little Kanawha-New-Big Sandy River valleys/72, Point Pleasant/74-78, raiding KY-OH-VA/75-81, Blue Jacket War/77-82, Boonesboro/78, Crawford/82, Council Detroit May 1783, attended Treaty Ft. Finney 1786, Council Sept. 1792, Council Dec. 1792, delegation to **Thomas McKee** 1792, Treaty Greenville 1795, a **Thawikila Chief** (by marriage?) before 1797, cousin of **Metheotashe**/40 (through his uncle Loyparkoweh) & uncle of **Tecumseh**/68, died returning from Council with whites in Philadelphia, husband about 1760 OH of **Thawikila Woman**/45, children unknown

1331. Red Satan – adopted-Cherokee born about 1750 TN-died after 1792 OH – Cornstalk War/68-77, raiding Ohio-Little Kanawha-Big Sandy-New River valleys/72, Point Pleasant/74, Blue Jacket War/77-94, raiding KY-OH-VA/7581, Crawford/82, raiding Ohio River valley/88-92, lived in KY-OH **with Shawnee**, an especially vicious warrior, husband 1770 KY of **Chalakatha Woman**/54, children unknown

1332. Red Snake – Thawikila born about 1740 AL-died after 1779 – Cornstalk War/58-74, raiding Ohio-New River valleys/58, Pontiac War/62-66, Bushy Run/63, raiding New-Greenbrier-Jackson River valleys/63, raiding Ohio-Little Kanawha-New-Big Sandy River valleys/72, Point Pleasant/74, moved to AL 1774, returned to OH 1779, moved to MO 1779 with **Black Stump, Kikusgowlawa, Yellow Hawk, Red Eagle** & 400 families, wife & children unknown

1333. Red Star – Pekowi born about 1740 AL-died after 1780 - wife about 1755 AL of **Kishpoko Man**/35, widow in 1780

1334. Red Wasp – Kishpoko born about 1760 OH-died after 1782 – Blue Jacket War/77-82, raiding KY-VA-OH/77-81, Point Pleasant/78, Blue Licks/82,

Crawford/82

1335. **Red Woodpecker aka Miskwakawithe-Meeskwakaweethee**[111] - Kishpoko born about 1765 OH-died after 1794 - Blue Jacket War/82-94, Crawford/82, raiding Ohio River valley/88-92, Fallen Timber/94

1336. Reed, Susannah Melinda - 3/4th Chalakatha-Mekoche-Black-Metis born about 1798 CAN-died 1861 OH - daughter of **Capt. Reed**/50 & **Rachel McKee**/82, granddaughter of **Col. Alexander McKee**/25-adopted Irish & **Candis LaForce**/60, wife 1816 of **Lewis Adams**/85-free Mulatto, mother of William Francis Adams/1818, Melinda Adams/1820, Mary Ann Adams/1824, Isaac Adams/1825, David Adams/1826, Lewis Adams Jr/1829, Francis Reno Adams/1832, Margaret Ann Adams/1835, Sarah Leah Adams/1836 & Hulda Susan Adams/1839-all 3/8th Chalakatha-Mekoche-Black-Metis

1337. Renicks, James Logan aka **James Logan-Walk by the Water**[112] - ½ Pekowi-Metis born about 1774 OH-died after 1843 (KS?) - son of **Joshua Renicks**/46-adopted white & **Pekowi Woman**/50, husband 1st about 1794 of **Pekowi Woman**/80, 2nd 1843 KS of **Cowapease**/1825-Mekoche, father **with Pekowi** of Nancy Logan/1825 & other children/94-1825 all named Logan-all 3/4th Pekowi-Metis, children **with Cowapease** unknown

1338. Renicks, John Logan aka **John Logan-Capt. Logan** - ½ Pekowi-Metis born about 1772 OH-died about 1813 (apparently killed in war) - son of **Joshua Renicks**/46-white & **Pekowi Woman**/50, scout-translator-**with U.S. Army**-War of 1812, husband about 1799 OH of **Elizabeth**/83-Mekoche, father of twins Jain & John Logan (Renicks) Jr/99-both 3/4th Pekowi-Mekoche-Metis

1339. Renicks, Joshua - adopted-white born about 1746-died 1784 MI - son of **Peggy** & **Robert Renicks,** adopted 1st 1757 by **Unknown Shawnee**-then 1760 adopted by **Puckenshinwa**/35 (maybe original adopted parents died or killed?), didn't return with his mother Peggy & 6 siblings 1765, raiding Ohio-Little Kanawha-Big Sandy-New River valleys/72, raiding Ohio River valley/74 **with Chief Logan**, Point Pleasant/74-75-78, raiding KY-VA-OH/75-81, Boonesboro/78, a **minor Mingo Chief** (of Shawnee among the Mingo?) before 1782, Crawford/82, a **Wea-Miami Chief** 1783 IN, moved to MI with band before his death, husband 1st about 1766 OH of **Pekowi Woman**/50, 2nd 1780 OH of **Polly Butler**/65-3/16th Chalakatha-Creek-Metis, 3rd 1783 IN of **WeaMiami Woman**, father **with Pekowi** of John Logan Renicks/72 & James Logan Renicks/74-both 1/2 Pekowi-Metis, **with Polly** of Daughter/83-3/32nd Chalakatha-Creek-Metis, **with Wea-Miami** of Robert Renicks/85-1/2 Wea-Miami-Metis

1340. Resolute Man aka **Ononaskemo-Ononwahim** – Thawikila born about 1770 OH-died after 1817 – a relative of the **Black Hoof** family, raiding Ohio River valley/88-92, Blue Jacket War/87-94, a **Thawikila Chief** from Hog Creek 1817, Treaty 1817

1341. Resting Fish aka **Masemo** – Pekowi born about 1760-died after 1792 - raiding KY-VA-OH/77-81, Point Pleasant/78, Boonesboro/78, Crawford/82, raiding Ohio River valley/88-90, Harmar/90, St. Clair/91, from Opessa Band, a relative/same clan as **Watmeme Opessa** (Black Fish)/30, **Metheotashe Opessa** (Puckenshinwa)/40 & **Monetoshe-Resting Snake** (Tecumseh)/70

1342. Rice - adopted-white born about 1760-died after 1794 - adopted about 1766-never returned, Blue Jacket War/77-94, Point Pleasant/78, Boonesboro/78, raiding KY-OH-VA/77-81, Crawford/82, raiding Ohio River valley/88-92, husband about 1780 OH of **Mekoche Woman**/65, father of several 1/2 Mekoche-Metis children/80-94

1343. Ridahak aka Reedahak – Mekoche born about 1740 OH-died after 1780 – Cornstalk war/58-74, raiding Ohio-New River valleys/58, Pontiac War/62-66, Bushy Run/63, raiding New-Greenbrier-Jackson River valleys/63, raiding Ohio-Little Kanawha-Big Sandy-New River valleys/72, Point Pleasant/74-78, raiding KY-OH-VA/75-80

1344. Rides Log – adopted-Cayuga born about 1750 OH-died after 1788 (OH?) – Cornstalk War/68-77, raiding Ohio-Little Kanawha-New-Big Sandy River valleys/72, raiding Ohio River valley/74 **with Chief Logan**, Point Pleasant/7478, raiding KY-OH-VA/75-81, Blue Jacket War/77-88, raiding Ohio River valley/81 **with Joseph Brant & George Girty**, Crawford/82, raiding Ohio River valley/88, husband about 1770 OH of **Chalakatha Woman**/55, father of several 1/2 Chalakatha-Cayuga children/70-88

1345. Ridge, John – 15/64th Chalakatha-Thawikila-Kishpoko-Pekowi-BlackCreek-**Cherokee**-Metis born 1800 GA-died 1839 - son of **Major Ridge**/71 & **Susannah Wickett**/74, **murdered Doublehead**/35 1807 **with James Sanders**/76, Major Ridge Co-**with U.S. Army**-Creek War/1813, Treaty 1826, 1832, 1835-leading to Trail of Tears, **murdered 1839** with father Major Ridge, cousins Elias Boudinot, John Walker Jr & nephew John Jack Walker, husband 1824 (GA?) of **Sarah Northup**/1805-white, father of Andrew Jackson Ridge/1825, John Rollin Ridge/1827, Clarinda Ridge/1828, Herman D. Ridge/1830, Susan Catherine Ridge/1832, Aeneas Ridge/1834 & Flora Chamberlin Ridge/1838-all 7/64th Chalakatha-Thawikila-Kishpoko-Pekowi-Black-Creek-Cherokee-Metis

1346.Ridge, Sarah – 15/64th Chalakatha-Thawikila-Kishpoko-Pekowi-BlackCreek-**Cherokee**-Metis born 1813 GA-died after 1851 OK - daughter of **Major Ridge**/71 & **Susannah Wickett**/74, operated a tavern, wife 1st about 1830 of **Charles Pix**/1810-white, 2nd 1836 of **George W. Paschal**/1810-Cherokee-Metis, children/1830-35 **with Pix** unknown, mother **with Paschal** of George W. Paschal Jr/1841, Ridge Paschal/1845 & Emily Agnes Paschal/1847-all 7/64th Chalakatha-Thawikila-Kishpoko-Pekowi-Black-Creek-Cherokee-Metis

1347.Riley, Gulustiyu Doublehead - sister of 2nd wife **Nigodigeyu**/64, 2nd known wife 1785 TN of **Samuel Riley**-white born 1747 MD-died 1819 Blue Springs TN (British Loyalist?-had a brother **James Riley** among the Chickasaw), mother of Richard Riley (1)/88, Nancy Riley/90, Mary Polly Riley/91, Elizabeth Riley/92, John Riley/93, Lucy Riley/94, Eleanor Riley/95, Sarah Riley/96, Louisa Riley/97, Judge Looney Riley/98, Lewis Riley/99, Rachel Riley/1800-all 7/64th Chalakatha-**Cherokee**-Metis

1348.Riley, Nigodigeyu Doublehead - **sister of Gulustiyu**/64, 1st known wife 1780 TN of **Samuel Riley**-white born 1747 MD-died 1819 Blue Springs TN (former British Loyalist?-Samuel had a brother **James Riley** said to be among the Chickasaw), mother of Samuel Riley (2)/80, William Riley/82, Edward Riley/84, George Riley/86, Susan Riley/88, James Riley/90, Richard Riley (2)/92, Catherine Riley/94, Nelson Riley/96, Martha Riley/98, Madison Riley/1800-all 7/64th Chalakatha-**Cherokee**-Metis

1349.Rising Fawn (1) aka **Rising Fawn Fox** (1)-Rising Fawn Conjurer (1) – ½ Chalakatha-**Cherokee** born 1706 Settico TN-died 1751 Settico TN – son of **Tsula Fox-Smallpox Conjurer**/1670-Cherokee & **Quatsis Hop**/1682-Chalakatha, a **Headman from Settico**, husband 1st 1726 of **Ooloosta Rainmaker**/10-1/2 Chalakatha-Cherokee, 2nd 1738 of **Ghigoneli Bowles**/23-1/2 Chalakatha-Metis, father **with Rainmaker** of Rising Fawn Fox (2)/26 & others/28-38-all 1/2 Chalakatha-Cherokee, father **with Bowles** of Rising Fawn (3)/40-1/2 Chalakatha-Cherokee-Metis

1350.Rising Fawn (2) aka Rising Fawn Fox (2)-Rising Fawn Conjurer (2) – ½ Chalakatha-**Cherokee** born 1726 Chota TN-died after 1756 – son of **Rising Fawn (1)** /06 & **Ooloosta Rainmaker**/10, wife (likely Cherokee) & children unknown

1351.Rising Fawn (3) aka **Kenoteta**-Kenotahaka-Rising Fawn Fox(3)-Rising Fawn Conjurer (3) - 1/2 Chalakatha-**Cherokee** born 1740 Settico TN-died shortly after 1776 - son of **Rising Fawn (1)**/06 & **Ghigoneli Bowles**/23, a **Headman from Settico**, served on council of **Bad Water Moytoy**, pro-British faction in French-Indian War/54-63, Red Paint Clan Cherokee, husband 1st 1760 Settico TN of **Unknown Woman**/45, 2nd 1772 Settico TN of his half-sister **Ghigoneli Watts**/52, children/60-72 **with Unknown** Woman not known, father **with Watts** of Rising Fawn (4)/72, Catherine Rising Fawn/74 & Polly Rising Fawn/76-all 21/32nd Chalakatha-Pekowi-Cherokee-Metis

1352.Rising Fawn, Catherine aka Catherine Fox – 21/32nd Chalakatha-Pekowi-Cherokee-Metis born 1774 Settico TN-died 1835 AL - daughter of **Ghigoneli Watts**/52 & **Rising Fawn Fox (3)**/40, Red Paint Clan Cherokee, wife 1790 Settico TN-but moved quickly to AL of **John Gunter (2)**/60-white, mother of Samuel Gunter/96, Aky Gunter/98, Martha Jane Gunter/1800, Edward Gunter/1803, Elizabeth Hunt Gunter/1804, John Gunter (3)/1806 & Catherine Gunter/1810-all 21/64th Chalakatha-Pekowi-Cherokee-Metis

1353.Rising Fawn, Polly aka Polly Fox – 19/32nd Chalakatha-Pekowi-Cherokee-Metis born 1776 Settico TN-died after 1817 (TN?) - daughter of **Ghigoneli Watts**/52 & **Rising Fawn Fox (3)**/40, Red Paint Clan Cherokee, wife 1st 1790 of **John Smith**/70-Cherokee, 2nd 1810 of **Young Bald Ridge**/70Cherokee, mother **with Smith** of Jackson Smith/91, Dorcas Smith/93, Thomas
Pig Smith/95 & Walter Smith/1800 & **with Bald Ridge** of Elizabeth Baldridge/1810 & Delia Baldridge/1815-all 21/64th Chalakatha-Pekowi-Cherokee-Metis

1354.Rising Sun – Kishpoko born 1715 PA-died after 1765 OH - daughter of **Unknown Kishpoko parents**, lived in a mixed Kishpoko-Mohawk community in PA, wife 1st 1730 PA of **Pride Opessa**/10-Pekowi, widowed 1753, wife 2nd 1753 OH of **Kishpoko Man**/10-from the same mixed Kishpoko-Mohawk community that had moved to OH, widowed 1758, wife 3rd 1758 PA of **Mohawk Man**/10-from the same mixed Kishpoko-Mohawk community that had moved to OH, widowed by 1765, mother **with Pride** of Lawagqua-Elder Son/33, Blue Jacket/35, Wabete-Elk-Younger Son/37 & Sally Opessa/39-all PekowiKishpoko, **with Kishpoko** of No Worries-Mary Louise Sanschagrin/54) & Yellow Britches-Edna Rising Sun/56-Kishpoko, mother **with Mohawk** of Sarah Rising Sun/59-1/2 Kishpoko-Mohawk**,** relative (by marriage to her uncle) of **Metheotashe Opessa/40,** grandmother of **Bright Horn**/72-3/4th Kishpoko-Mohawk & of **Billy Caldwell**/76-1/4th Kishpoko-Mohawk-(adopted Chippewa)

1355.Rising Sun, No Worries aka **Marie Louise Sanschagrin**-1st Half-sister of Blue Jacket-2nd wife of **Col. Matthew Elliott**-adopted white – Kishpoko born 1754 OH-died 1826 - daughter of **Rising Sun**/15 & **Kishpoko Man**/10, sister of **Yellow Britches-Edna**/56, half-sister of **Blue Jacket**/35 & siblings, half-sister of

Sarah Rising Sun/59, 2nd wife 1769 PA of **Col. Matthew Elliott**/30-adopted Irish, mother of Isabella Elliott/70, Matthew Elliott Jr/72, William Elliott/75, Alexander Elliott/80-all 1/2 Kishpoko-Metis, likely other unknown children

1356. Rising Sun, Sarah aka 3rd Half-sister of Blue Jacket-wife of Brother of Mink-wife of William Caldwell-Sarah Caldwell-wife of James Colwell-wife of William Vance - 1/2 Kishpoko-Mohawk born 1759 OH-died after 1796 Gallia Co. OH - daughter of **Rising Sun**/15-Kishpoko & **Mohawk Man**/10, half-sister of **No Worries-Marie Louise Sanschagrin**/54 & **Yellow Britches-Edna**/56, half-sister of **Blue Jacket**/35, wife 1st 1772 OH of **Brother of Mink**/50Mekoche,widowed 1774, 2nd 1776 OH of **William Caldwell Sr**/50white,seperated 1778, 3rd 1779 WV of **James Colwell**/57-white, 4th 1789 WV of **William Vance**/55-1/4th Pekowi-Metis, abandoned **Bright Horn**/72 1776 when she married **William Caldwell**/55, abandoned **Billy Caldwell**/77 1779 & moved to WV, went by name of Sarah Caldwell in marriages to **Colwell & Vance**, mother **with Brother of Mink** of Bright Horn/72-3/4th Mekoche-KishpokoMohawk, **with Caldwell** of Billy Caldwell/77-1/4th Kishpoko-Mohawk-Metis, **with Colwell** of James Colwell/80, Jacob Colwell/82, Sarah Colwell/84 & Martha Patsy Colwell/86 & **with Vance** of Thomas Vance/90 & Christina Vance/96-all 3/8th Kishpoko-Pekowi-Mohawk-Metis

1357. Rising Sun, Yellow Britches aka Edna-Daughter of Rising Sun-2nd Halfsister of Blue Jacket- 2nd wife of **Col. Alexander McKee**-adopted white – Kishpoko born 1756 OH-died after 1793 OH – daughter of **Rising Sun**/15 & **Kishpoko Man**/10, sister of **No Worries-Marie Louis Sanschagrin**/54, halfsister of **Blue Jacket**/35 & siblings, half-sister of **Sarah Rising Sun**/59, 2nd wife 1769 PA of **Col. Alexander McKee**/25-adopted-Irish, mother of Thomas McKee/70, Elizabeth McKee/72, Alexander McKee/75, Catherine McKee/80 & at least 2 other children by 1780-all 1/2 Kishpoko-Metis

1358. River Bottom – adopted-Seneca born about 1750 OH-died after 1781 – Cornstalk War/68-77, raiding Ohio-Little Kanawha-Big Sandy-New River valleys/72, raiding Ohio River valley/74 **with Chief Logan**, Point Pleasant/74, raiding OH-KY-VA/75-81, raiding Ohio River valley/81 **with Joseph Brant**, Council with British 1779 **with Alexander McKee**/25, **Wryneck** Shawnee/30, **William Caldwell**/50, **Simon**/41-**James**/43-**George Girty**/46, **Savenooka Raven**/20-Chalakatha-Pekowi, **Simon Surphet**-cousin of McKee & **Weed**/50-Iroquois, husband about 1770 of **Kishpoko Woman**/55, father of several ½ Kishpoko-Seneca children/70-81

1359. River Man aka **LeRiviere** – adopted-Chippewa-Metis born about 1730died after 1778 - son of **Chippewa Woman** & **Coureur-debois**, French-Indian War/54-63, Braddock/55, Cornstalk War/55-77, raiding New-Shenandoah River valleys/55, raiding PA/55-56, raiding Ohio-New River valleys/58, Pontiac War/62-66, Bushy Run/63, raiding New-Greenbrier-Jackson River valleys/63, raiding Ohio-Big Sandy-New River valleys/72, Point Pleasant/74, raiding KYVA-OH/77, Boonesboro/78, husband 1750 OH of **Chalakatha Woman**/35, children unknown

1360. Robin aka Blue Tail-Skitlewa-**Skilloway**[113] - Mekoche-(adopted-**Seneca**) born about 1770 OH-died after 1832 KS – Blue Jacket War/87-94, scout-**with U.S. Army**-War of 1812, a **Chief at Lewistown** 1817, Treaty 1817, 1831, 1832, moved to KS 1832, husband about 1788 of **Adopted White Woman**/73, father of Joseph White aka Red-headed Skilloway/90-1/2 Mekoche-Metis

1361. Rogers, Elizabeth aka Betsy - 1/2 Chalakatha-Mekoche-Metis born about 1784 OH-died 1814 MO - daughter of **Parlie Blackfish**/50 & **Lewis Rogers**/50adopted white, granddaughter of **Black Fish**/25, wife by 1800 OH of **Mackinaw Beauchemie**/70-adopted-Chippewa Metis, children unknown

1362. Rogers, Elizabeth Emory (Tahlonteeskee-Due) - Long Hair Clan **Cherokee**, 1st known wife 1773 Great Tellico TN of **John Headman Rogers**/40white born 1740 (NC?), mother of Charles Rogers/74, Aky Ulusquatogu Rogers/76, John Hellfire Rogers/78, Nancy Rogers/80, James Rogers/82-all 3/64th Chalakatha-Cherokee-Metis

1363. Rogers, Henry (1) aka **Chinwa Rogers** - adopted-white born about 1755 VA-died about 1803 MO - adopted about 1760 with brother **Lewis Rogers**/50, adopted son & son-in-law of **Black Fish**/25, raiding Ohio-Little Kanawha-Big Sandy-New River valleys/72, Point Pleasant/74-75-78, raiding KY-OH-VA/7581, Crawford/82, Blue Jacket War/77-94, moved to MO about 1795, a **village Chief in MO** until his death, husband about 1775 OH of **Cheletha Black Fish**/60, father of Polly Rogers/80 & William Rogers/85-both 1/2 Chalakatha-Mekoche-Pekowi-Metis

1364. Rogers, Henry (2) – 3/4th Thawikila-Chalakatha-Mekoche-Pekowi-Metis born 1794 MO-died before 1857 KS – son of **Lewis Indian Rogers**/76 & **Thawikila Woman**/82, husband 1814 MO of **Betsy Jane Fish**/98-1/2 Chalakatha-Metis, father of Miss Rogers/1815, Graham Rogers/1818, Samuel Rogers/1820, James Rogers/1822, William Wilson Rogers/1824, Henry Foxall Rogers/1832, Lewis Rogers/1834, Thomas Johnson Rogers/1836 & Jane Celequa

Rogers/1838-all 5/8th Chalakatha-Thawikila-Mekoche-Pekowi-Metis

1365. Rogers, James (1) aka **Onothe** - 1/2 Chalakatha-Mekoche-Pekowi-Metis born about 1778 OH-died after 1846 KS - son of **Parlie Blackfish**/50 & **Lewis Rogers**/50-adopted white, **with U.S. Army**-War 1812, moved to MO 1795 **with Black Bobb band**, associated **with Shot Pouch**/80, **Powder Horn**/75 & **Little Captain**/70-all 3/4th Thawikila-Metis (brothers), a **village Chief** on the Marmec River MO after 1800, established Rogers' village-Rogerstown MO, scout **with Fremont** 1841, scout **with Wharton** 1846, husband 1797 MO of **Thawikila Woman**/80, father of Lewis Rogers/98, George Washington Rogers/1800, Thomas Jefferson Rogers/1802, James Rogers/1804, Elder Daughter/1806, Middle Daughter/1808, Younger Daughter/1810, Andrew Jackson Rogers/1812all 3/4th Chalakatha-Thawikila-Mekoche-Metis

1366. Rogers, James (2) – 3/64th Chalakatha-**Cherokee**-Metis born 1782 Great Tellico TN-died after 1824 - son of **Elizabeth Emory**/48 & **John Headman Rogers**/40-white, Long Hair Clan Cherokee, husband 1st 1800 of **Charity Coody**/80-1/8th Chalakatha-Cherokee-Metis, 2nd 1811 of her niece **Nancy Coody**/90-7/64th Chalakatha-Cherokee-Metis, father **with Charity** of Little John Rogers/1800-5/64th Chalakatha-Cherokee-Metis, **with Nancy** of Delilah Rogers/1812, Martha Rogers/1814, Jefferson Rogers/1816, Ruth Rogers/1818, William Rogers/1820, Julia Rogers/1822 & Elizabeth Rogers/1824-all 5/64th Chalakatha-Cherokee-Metis

1367. Rogers, James (3) - 3/4th Chalakatha-Thawikila-Mekoche-Metis born about 1806 MO-died after 1842 OH - son of **James Onothe Rogers**/78 & **Thawikila Woman**/80, lived at Rogers' village-Rogerstown MO, escaped removal by returning to OH & passing as white, husband about 1834 OH of **Matilda Coffman**/1819-white (possible Metis), father **with Coffman** of Hiram Rogers/1834, Julia Rogers/1836, Eliza Rogers/1838, Sarah (Elizabeth) Rogers/1840, Elizabeth Rogers/1842, Margaret Rogers/1844 & Ann Rogers/1846-all 3/8th Chalakatha-Thawikila-Mekoche-Metis

1368. Rogers, James (4) – 5/8th Chalakatha-Thawikila-Mekoche-Pekowi-Metis born 1822 MO-died after 1847 KS – son of **Henry Rogers**/94 & **Betsy Jane Fish**/98, husband about 1842 KS of **Sally Parks**/1822, father of John H. Rogers/1847-3/8th Chalakatha-Thawikila-Mekoche-Pekowi-Metis

1369. Rogers, Jimmy (1) - adopted-white born about 1770-died about 1819 MO - adopted about 1776, taken in PA in group of 7 children with **Mrs. Rachel Kennedy**, translator-**with U.S. Army**-War of 1812, a **village Chief in MO** before death, moved to MO about 1800 **with Charles Phillips**/60 & **Joseph**

Jackson/83, husband 1st 1790 OH of **Thawikila Woman**/75, 2nd about 1805 MO of **Abigail Unknown**/87-adopted white, father **with Thawikila** of Jimmy Rogers (2)/91 & Lewis Rogers (4)/93-both 1/2 Thawikila-Metis, **with Abigail** of Abram Rogers/1806-white Shawnee (**Jimmy/70 is not related to Lewis Rogers/50, Henry Chinwa Rogers/55, Joseph Rogers/55 or James Onothe Rogers/78**)

1370. Rogers, John Headman - white born about 1740 (NC?)-died after 1795 (TN?) - son of **Trader Rogers**-white & **Unknown Wife**, husband 1st 1773 Great Tellico TN of **Elizabeth Emory**/48-7/64th Chalakatha-Cherokee-Metis, 2nd 1787 TN of **Aisley Vann**/72-3/8th Chalakatha-Pekowi-Cherokee-Metis, 3rd 1788 TN of Emory's daughter **Jennie Due**/64-19/64th Chalakatha-Cherokee-Metis, father **with Emory** of Charles Rogers/74, Aky Ulusquatogu Rogers/76, John Hellfire Rogers/78, Nancy Rogers/80 & James Rogers/82-all 3/64th ChalakathaCherokee-Metis, **with Vann** of Polly Ann Rogers/94-3/16th Chalkatha-Pekowi-Cherokee-Metis, **with Due** of Martha Rogers/88, Annie Rogers/90, Joseph Rogers/92, William Charles Rogers/93, Susanna Rogers/94 & Tiana Rogers/95 all 9/64th Chalakatha-**Cherokee**-Metis

1371. Rogers, John Hellfire aka Chief John-Capt. John-Hellfire Jack – 3/64th Chalakatha-**Cherokee**-Metis born about 1778-died 1846 D.C. - son of **Elizabeth Emory**/48 & **John Headman Rogers**/40-white, Long Hair Clan Cherokee, Capt**with U.S. Army**-Creek War/1813, **Head Chief AR Cherokee** 1839-46, husband
1st 1798 of 1st cousin **Ailsey Fawling**/68-3/64th Chalakatha-Cherokee-Metis, 2nd 1804 Great Tellico TN of **Elizabeth Coody**/86-7/64th Chalakatha-CherokeeMetis, father **with Fawling** of Polly Ann Rogers/99 & Isaac Rogers/1800-both 3/64th Chalakatha-Cherokee-Metis, **with Coody** of Cynthia Rogers/1808,
Thomas Lewis Rogers/1816, Charles Coody Rogers/1818, George Washington Rogers/1820, W. D. Nelson Rogers/1824, Granville Rogers/1826 & Randolph Rogers/1828-all 5/64th Chalakatha-Cherokee-Metis

1372. Rogers, John Nollichucky aka Nollichucky Jack-Nolitsugi - 1/2 PekowiMetis born about 1779 GA-died 1851 - son of **Elizabeth Rainbow**/60-Pekowi &
William Rogers/50-white, husband 1804 of **Sarah Sonicooie**/82, father of Robert Rogers/1804, William Rogers/1805, Joseph Rogers/1806, Johnson Rogers/1808, Lovely Rogers/1810, Mary Cordery Rogers/1812, George Waters Rogers/1816, Cynthia Rogers/1820, Annie Chapel Rogers/1822, Henry Curtis Rogers/1824, Jackson Rogers/1826 & John Pendergrass Rogers/1830-all 5/16th Chalakatha-Pekowi-Thawikila-Creek-**Cherokee**-Metis

1373. Rogers, Joseph (1) – adopted-white born about 1755-**killed** 1780 OH - adopted about 1765-never returned, killed during his **uncle George Rogers Clark's attack 1780 on Pickaway village**, husband 1775 OH of **Chalakatha Woman**/60, father of some 1/2 Chalakatha-Metis children/75-80 that may have used surname Rogers

1374. Rogers, Lewis (1) aka **Capt. Rogers** - adopted-white born about 1750 VA-died after 1819 MO - adopted about 1760 with brother **Henry Rogers**/55, adopted son 1760 OH & son in law 1771 OH of **Black Fish**/25, **village Chief in OH & MO**, Cornstalk War/68-77, raiding Ohio-Little Kanawha-Big Sandy-New River valleys/72, Point Pleasant/74-75-78, took little part in Blue Jacket War/7794, moved to MO about 1779 with Thawikila, **Chief of Black Fish-Rogers band in MO**, succeeded as **Chief by William Jackson-Fish**-adopted white, husband by 1771 OH of **Parlie Blackfish**/56, father of Nancy Rogers/72, Mary Rogers/74, Lewis Rogers/76, James Rogers/78, William Rogers/80, Martha Rogers/82, Elizabeth Rogers/84, Parlie Rogers/86-all 1/2 Chalakatha-Mekoche-Pekowi-Metis

1375. Rogers, Lewis (2) aka **Indian Rogers**-Lewis Jr - 1/2 Chalakatha-Mekoche-Pekowi-Metis born about 1776 OH-died 1838 Howard Co MO - son of **Parlie Blackfish**/50 & **Lewis Rogers**/50-adopted white, **with U.S. Army**-War 1812, husband about 1793 MO of **Thawikila Woman**/78, father of Henry Rogers/94 & Lewis Rogers/96-both 3/4th Thawikila-Chalakatha-Mekoche-Pekowi-Metis

1376. Rogers, Lewis (3) - 1/2 Thawikila-Metis born about 1793 OH-died after 1829 - son of **Jimmy Rogers (1)**/70-adopted white & **Thawikila Woman**/75, namesake of **Chief Lewis Rogers** (1)/50-no relation, wife & children unknown

1377. Rogers, Lewis (4) - 3/4th Thawikila-Chalakatha-Mekoche-Pekowi-Metis born about 1796 MO-died before 1857 KS - son of **Lewis Indian Rogers**/76 & **Thawikila Woman**/78, associated in MO **with Black Bob** band, lived in Rogers' village-Rogerstown MO, husband about 1815 MO of **Maria**/99-Thawikila, children unknown

1378. Rogers, Martha Rogers aka **Polly** - 1/2 Chalakatha-Mekoche-PekowiMetis born about 1782 MO-died after 1800 - daughter of **Parlie Blackfish**/50 &
Lewis Rogers (1)/50-adopted white, 3rd wife about 1797 MO of **William Jackson Fish**/60-adopted white, mother of Elizabeth Nakease Fish/98, William Jackson Jr/1800, Miss Fish/1802, Pascal Fish/1804, John Ficklin Fish/1806, Charles Salahnewe Fish/1808 -all 1/4th Chalakatha-Mekoche-Pekowi-Metis

1379. Rogers, Mary (1) – ½ Chalakatha-Mekoche-Pekowi-Metis born 1774

OH-died about 1795 MO – daughter of **Lewis Rogers**/50 & **Parlie Black Fish**/60, wife 1790 MO of **Mackinaw Beauchemie**/70, children/90-95 unknown

1380. Rogers, Nancy – ½ Chalakatha-Mekoche-Pekowi-Metis born about 1772 OH-died after 1832 KS – daughter of **Lewis Rogers**/50 & **Parlie Black Fish**/50, wife 1787 MO of "**Won't Work**" **White Man**, 2nd by 1795 MO of "**Won't Hunt**" **White Man**, 3rd by 1810 of **John Cohun**/70-Delaware, children/87-1809 **with White Men** unknown, mother **with Cohun** of George Cohun/1825-1/4th Chalakatha-Mekoche-Pekowi-Delaware-Metis

1381. Rogers, Parlie aka Polly (2)-Mary Elizabeth-Betsy - 1/2 ChalakathaMekoche-Metis born about 1786 MO-died 1847 - daughter of **Lewis Rogers (1)**/50-adopted white & **Parlie Blackfish**/50, wife 1st about 1802 OH of **Chalakatha Man**, 2nd 1814 OH of **Mackinaw Beauchemie**/70-adoptedChippewa-Metis, children/1802-13 **with Chalakatha** unknown, mother **with Beauchemie** of Annie Beauchemie/1815, Alexander Beauchemie/1816, William Beauchemie/1817, Martha Beauchemie/1818, Louisa Beauchemie/1819, Julia Ann Beauchemie/1820 & John Beauchemie/1822-all 1/4th Chalakatha-Mekoche-Pekowi-Chippewa-Metis

1382. Rogers, Polly - 1/2 Chalakatha-Mekoche-Pekowi-Metis born about 1780 OH-died about 1803 MO - daughter of **Henry Rogers**/55-adopted white & **Cheletha Black Fish**/60, wife about 1795 MO of **Mackinaw Beauchemie**/70adopted-Chippewa-Metis, children/95-1800 unknown

1383. Rogers, Robert Choastoee - 1/2 Pekowi-Metis born about 1785-died after 1820 - son of **Elizabeth Rainbow**/60-Pekowi & **William Rogers**/50-white, husband 1st 1803 of **Nancy Cordery**/88, 2nd 1807 of **Lucy Sonicooie**/84 (halfsister of Nancy Cordery-sister of Elizabeth Sonicooie), 3rd 1810 of **Elizabeth Sonicooie**/86 (half-sister of Nancy Cordery & sister of Lucy Sonicooie), 4th about 1816 of **Elizabeth Harnage**/98-1/8th Chalakatha-Cherokee-Metis, father **with Cordery** of Ira Rogers/1803, John Roger/1804 & William Rogers/1805, **with Lucy Sonicooie** of Nancy Rogers/1813, Catherine Rogers/1814, Robert Rogers Jr./1815, John Rogers II/1818 & James Rogers/1820-all 5/16th Chalakatha-Pekowi-Thawikila-Creek-**Cherokee**-Metis, any children **with Elizabeth Sonicooie**/85 unknown, **with Harnage** of Jennie Rogers-/1816-5/16th Chalakatha-Pekowi-**Cherokee**-Metis

1384. Rogers, Talhina aka Tiana-Titania-Tenia-Hiana - 9/64th Chalakatha**Cherokee**-Metis born about 1790 TN-died 1838 - daughter of **Jennie Due**/66 &

John Headman Rogers/40-white, Long Hair Clan Cherokee, niece of **Chief John Jolly** & **Tahlonteeskee**, wife 1st 1817 of **David Gentry**/80-white, 2nd 1832 of **Sam Houston**/93-adopted-white, children unknown

1385. Rogers, William (1) - 1/2 Chalakatha-Mekoche-Pekowi-Metis born about 1780 MO -died 1829 KS - son of **Parlie Blackfish**/56 & **Lewis Rogers (1)**/50adopted white, husband 1st 1797 of **Kansa Woman**/82, 2nd 1799 of 1825 KS of **Otoe Woman**/84, 3rd 1806 of **Pawnee Woman**/91, 4th 1808 KS of **Omaha Woman**/95, father **with Kansa** of William David Rogers/97 & Lewis Rogers/99both 1/4th Chalakatha-Mekoche-Pekowi-Kansa-Metis, **with Otoe** of Felicita Rogers/1800 & Elizabeth Rogers/1806-both 1/4th Chalakatha-Mekoche-Pekowi-Otoe-Metis, **with Pawnee** of William Rogers/1807- 1/4th Chalakatha-MekochePekowi-Pawnee-Metis, **with Omaha** of Mary Rogers/1808 & Margaret Rogers/1810-both 1/4th Chalakatha-Mekoche-Pekowi-Omaha-Metis

1386. Rogers, William (2) - 1/2 Chalakatha-Mekoche-Pekowi-Metis born about 1785 OH-died after 1860 KS - son of **Cheletha Black Fish**/60 & **Henry Rogers**/55-adopted-white, **Principal Chief 1860** of Fish-Jackson band **with Pascal Fish**/92, husband 1st about 1805 MO of **Shawnee Woman**/90, children unknown

1387. Rose, Edward aka Cut Nose-Five Scalps-Nez Coupe – 1/4th ChalakathaBlack-Metis born 1780 (KY-OH)-**killed** 1833 Yellowstone – son of **Little Black Cat**/50-1/2 Chalakatha-Black-Metis& **Mr. Rose**-likely a Jewish trader, born around Falls of the Ohio, grew up in the Louisville KY area, tip of his nose bit off in a brawl with a "big Chillicothean i.e. Chalakatha", in New Orleans in 1798, in St. Louis 1807, joined the Crows 1808, with **Jedediah Smith** 1823, a well known scout, trader & frontiersman in the west, any wives & children unknown

1388. Roseberry, Wife of William - Chalakatha born about 1775-died after 1793 - wife about 1790 TN of **William Roseberry**-white born about 1770-killed 1793 Hanging Maw's Town N.C. in attack by John Beard's renegade militia, mother of a couple of 1/2 Chalakatha-Metis children/90-93 possibly named Roseberry

1389. Ross, Daniel – white born 1760 SCO-died after 1800 - husband 1st 1785 of **Mary McDonald**/70, 2nd 1788 of (sister of Mary) **Mollie McDonald**/72-both 1/4th Chalakatha-Cherokee-Metis, father **with Mary**/70 of Elizabeth Ross/86, Jennie Ross/87, Lewis Ross/88, Susanna Ross/90, Annie Ross/92, Maria Ross/94 & Margaret Ross/03, **with Mollie**/72 of David Ross/88, John Ross/90, Andrew

Tlostama Ross/95-all 1/8th Chalakatha-**Cherokee**-Metis

1390. Ross, John Golden – white born 1787 SCO-died 1858 - orphaned at sea in transit, nephew of **Daniel Ross**/60-white, husband 1819 of 1st cousin **Elizabeth Ross**/86, **with U.S. Army-**Creek War/1813-Battle of New Orleans/1815, father of William Potter Ross/1820-1/16th Chalakatha-**Cherokee**Metis

1391. Ross, Tavener - adopted-white born about 1740-died after 1780 Butler Co PA - adopted about 1755, Cornstalk War/58-74, Pontiac War/62-66, Bushy Run/63, raiding New-Greenbrier-Jackson River valleys/63, returned to whitesreturned to tribe 1765, raiding Ohio-Little Kanawha-New-Big Sandy River valleys/72, Point Pleasant/74, returned to whites after Point Pleasant/74, spy-**with John Gibson Co**/78, settled in Butler Co PA, husband about 1760 OH of **Chalakatha Woman**/45, father of several 1/2 Chalakatha-Metis children/60-74 possibly named Ross

1392. Rough Woman – adopted-Seneca born about 1750 OH-died after 1789 – a large, strong-featured woman, wife about 1765 OH of **Mekoche Man**/44, widow in 1789

1393. Round Man – Kishpoko born about 1715 PA-died after 1772 – a short, heavy-set warrior, raiding PA/40, French-Indian War/54-63, Braddock/55, Cornstalk War/55-72, raiding New-Shenandoah River valleys/55, raiding PA/5556, raiding Ohio-New River valleys/58, Pontiac War/62-66, Bushy Run/63, raiding New-Jackson-Greenbrier River valleys/63, raiding Ohio-Little Kanawha-
Big Sandy-New River valleys/72

1394. Round Thing aka Something Round – Pekowi born about 1740 PA-died after 1778 - wife 1765 OH of **Pekowi Man**/45, widow in 1778

1395. Rowe, Archibald (1) – 9/16th Chalakatha-Pekowi-Thawikila-**Creek**Metis born 1754 Nickajack TN-died after 1820 Audrain Co. MO - son of **Elizabeth Raven's Sister Hop**/24 & **David Rowe (1)**/20, Blind Savannah Clan Cherokee, husband 1774 Nickajack TN of **Chalakatha Woman**/59-Blind Savannah, father of Richard Rowe (2)/78, David Rowe (3)/82 & Archibald Rowe (2)/93-all 25/32nd Chalakatha-Pekowi-Thawikila-Creek-Metis

1396. Rowe, David (2) aka **David Rowe Jr** – 3/16th Chalakatha-PekowiThawikila-**Creek**-Metis born 1752 Nickajack TN-**killed** 1777 Point Pleasant WV
- son of **Elizabeth-Raven's Sister Hop**/24 & **David Rowe (1)**/20, Blind Savannah Clan Cherokee, killed while on trip north to speak to **Cornstalk**,

husband 1772 of **Chalakatha Woman**/55-Blind Savannah, any children/72-77 unknown

1397. Rowe, Richard (1) – 9/16th Chalakatha-Pekowi-**Creek**-Metis born 1750 Nickajack TN-**killed** 1777 Point Pleasant WV - son of **Elizabeth-Raven's Sister Hop**/24 & **David Rowe (1)**/1720, Blind Savannah Clan Cherokee, killed while on trip to north to speak to **Cornstalk**, husband 1769 Nickajack TN of **Blind Savannah Woman**/54-Chalakatha, father of Susannah Rowe/70 & Samuel Rowe/75-both 25/64th Chalakatha-Pekowi-Creek-Cherokee-Metis, a couple of other children likely

1398. Rowe, Richard (2) – 25/32nd Chalakatha-Pekowi-**Creek**-Metis born 1778 GA-died 1842 - son of **Archibald Rowe (1)**/54 & **Chalakatha Woman**/60, Cherokee-Creek interpreter, Blind Savannah Clan Cherokee, husband 1798 of **Wolf Clan Woman**/80-Cherokee, father of Sugi Rowe/98, Ollie Rowe/1804, Mary Rowe/1808, Catherine Rowe/1810, Elizabeth Rowe/1815, Judge David Ustusutli Rowe/1820, Polly Rowe/1821 & Arch Rowe/1826-all 25/64th Chalakatha-Pekowi-Thawikila-Creek-Cherokee-Metis

1399. Ruddehega – Pekowi born about 1700 PA-died about 1758 (epidemic?) – a **Pekowi Chief**, King of the **West Susquehanna Shawnee** 1757, raiding PA/40, French-Indian War/54-57, Braddock/55, raiding New-Shenandoah River valleys/55, raiding PA/55-56, raiding Ohio-New River valleys/58

1400. Ruddle, Abraham aka **Black Hawk** - adopted-white born about 1764 VA-died 1857 AR - adopted about 1772-returned to whites 1795, son of **Isaac Ruddle**, adopted by different family/same clan as brother Stephen Ruddle, raiding Ohio River valley/81 **with Joseph Brant & George Girty**, Blue Licks/82, Crawford/82, raiding Ohio River valley/88-92, Blue Jacket War/81-94, abandoned Shawnee Wife & family when he returned to whites 1795, had outer rims of ears trimmed off, wore earrings & ear-bobs, translator-spy-scout-**with U.S. Army**-War 1812, moved to AR about 1820, husband 1st 1782 of **Kishpoko Woman**/68, 2nd 1797 of **Mary Culp**/80-white, father **with Kishpoko** of several 1/2 Kishpoko-Metis children/82-95 names unknown, **with Culp** of Abraham Ruddle Jr/98, Daniel Ruddle/1800, America Ann Ruddle/1802, Sally Ruddle/1804, Elizabeth Ruddle/1806 & Esther Ruddle/1808-all white

1401.Ruddle, George - adopted white born 1757 VA-died 1846 AR - adopted 1772-returned to whites 1795, brother of **Isaac Ruddle**-uncle of Abraham,

Stephen & Sarah, Blue Jacket War/77-94, husband 1st about 1777 OH of **Kishpoko Woman**/62, 2nd 1797 of **Theodosia Linn**/60-adopted white, children unknown

1402. Ruddle, Sarah - adopted white born about 1770-died after 1832 - adopted 1780-returned to whites 1795, daughter of **Isaac Ruddle**, sister of Abraham & Stephen, left Shawnee family when she returned to whites, wife 1st 1785 of **Kishpoko Man**, 2nd 1796 of **Thomas Davis**/68-1/2 Kishpoko-Cherokee-(brother of **Susanna Davis**/82), mother **with Kishpoko** of several 1/2 Kishpoko-Metis children/85-95, **with Davis** of Sarah Ruddle Davis/98-1/4th Kishpoko-CherokeeMetis

1403. Ruddle, Stephen aka **Big Fish-Sinnanatha**[114] - adopted-white born 1768 VA-died 1845 IL - adopted about 1772-returned to whites 1795, son of **Isaac Ruddle**, translator, adopted son 1772 OH of **Puckenshimwa**/35-adopted brother of **Tecumseh**/68, then 1774 OH of **Black Fish**/25, moved to MO 1779 with Shawnee mother **Watmeme Blackfish**/30 after death 1778 of Black Fish, raiding Ohio River valley/88-92, Blue Jacket War/88-94, abandoned Shawnee Wife & family when he returned to whites after death of Watmeme about 1795, husband 1st about 1788 OH of **Kishpoko Woman**/73, 2nd 1797 of **Catherine Kingery**/80white, 3rd 1809 of **Susanna Davis**/82-1/2 Kishpoko-Cherokee-(sister of **Thomas Davis**/78), 4th 1834 of **Rachel Wood**/15-white, father **with Kishpoko** of several 1/2 Kishpoko-Metis children/88-95, children with **Kingery, Davis & Wood** unknown

1404. Rum Cup – adopted-Seneca born about 1745 PA-died after 1785 OH – a fort Indian in PA-associated closely with white men at forts, living in Mingo village in OH by 1770, wife 1st about 1760 PA of **White Man**, 2nd by 1770 OH of **Mekoche Man**, mother **with White Man** of Little Rum Cup/60-Seneca-Metis, children **with Mekoche** unknown

1405. Runs Fast – ½ Mekoche-Seneca born about 1780-died after 1831 – son of **Mekoche Woman & Seneca Man**, scout-**with U.S. Army**-War 1812-Thames/1813, Treaty 1831

1406. Running Bird – Thawikila born about 1740 (OH?)-died after 1777 - wife about 1755 OH of **Thawikila Man**/34, widow in 1777

1407. Running Otter – Kishpoko-(adopted **Cayuga**) born about 1760 OH-died after 1816 – Blue Jacket War/77-94, raiding KY-VA-OH/77-81, Point Pleasant/78, raiding Ohio River valley/81 **with Joseph Brant & George Girty**, Blue Licks/82, Crawford/82, raiding Ohio River valley/88-92, Prophet's

Town/1811, Brownstown/1812-Monguagon/1812-1st Amherstburg/1812Frenchtown/1813-Ft. Meigs/1813-2nd Amherstburg/1813 & Thames/1813 **with**
Tecumseh, moved to CAN 1815, husband 1st 1780 OH of **Kishpoko Woman**/65, 2nd 1810 (IN?) of **Cayuga Woman**/95, children unknown

1408.Runs on Ridge – Chalakatha born about 1770 OH-died after 1794 - raiding Ohio River valley/88-92, Blue Jacket War/87-94

1409.Runs with Ax – Mekoche born about 1750 OH-died after 1785 - wife about 1765 OH of **Mekoche Man**/44, widow in 1785

Section XV
Sachachewa to Silversmith (S)

S

1410. Sachachewa aka Sachachooa – Mekoche born about 1770 OH-died after 1817 - raiding Ohio River valley/88-92, Blue Jacket War/88-94, a warrior at Wapaghonettat 1817, Treaty 1817

1411.Sak – ½ Chalakatha-Cherokee born about 1744 TN-died after 1774 – son of **Marhalonak**/10 & **Chalakatha Woman**/15, scout **with father Marhalonak**/10 & brothers Tok/42, Sark/46 & Loho/48-Pontiac War/62-66, Bushy Run/63 **with Colonial Army** & Point Pleasant/74 **with Andrew Lewis**, husband 1764 TN of **Cherokee Woman**/50, children unknown

1412.Sally aka Sally Kishpoko-Sally Kishpoko-Metis – ½ Kishpoko-Metis born 1760 OH-died after 1815 – daughter of **Kishpoko Man** (maybe a Kishpoko Chief?) & **Adopted White Woman**, wife 1775 OH of **Caesar (3)**/40-adopted-Black, mother with **Caesar** of Caesar (6)/75, Sally's White Son/80 & Sally's Black Son/85 & others/76-1805-all 1/4th Kishpoko-Black-Metis, living in Apple Creek MO 1815

1413.Sally's Black Son aka Black Son of Caesar (3) - 1/4th Kishpoko-BlackMetis born 1785 OH-died after 1832 KS - son of **Sally Kishpoko**/60 & **Caesar (3)**/40, called "black son" because of darker skin, raiding OH-KY-VA/18021810, Prophet's Town/1811, Brownstown/1812-Monguagon/1812-1st Amherstburg/1812-Frenchtown/1813-Ft. Meigs/1813-2nd Amherstburg/1813 &

Thames/1813 **with Tecumseh**, moved to CAN 1815, returned to OH 1825, Treaty 1832, move to KS 1832, husband 1805 OH of **Kishpoko Woman**/90, father of several 5/8th Kishpoko-Black-Metis children/1805-15

1414. Sally's White Son aka White Son of Caesar (3) - 1/4th Kishpoko-Black-Metis born 1780 OH-died after 1815 - son of **Sally Kishpoko**/60 & **Caesar (3)**/40, called "white son" because of lighter skin, raiding KY-OH-VA/99-1810, Prophet's Town/1811, Brownstown/1812-Monguagon/1812-1st Amherstburg/1812-Frenchtown/1813-Ft. Meigs/1813-2nd Amherstburg/1813 & Thames/1813 **with Tecumseh**, moved to CAN 1815, either died in CAN or didn't return to the U.S., husband about 1800 (IN?) of **Kishpoko Woman**/85, father of several 5/8th Kishpoko-Black-Metis children/1800-15

1415. Sanataiowanah aka Sanataeeowana– Pekowi born about 1700 PA-died about 1758 (epidemic?) – from **Straight Tail** band, living in PA by 1725, raiding PA/40, living in OH by 1748, Braddock/55, raiding New-Shenandoah River valleys/55, raiding PA/55-56, raiding Ohio-New River valleys/58

1416. Sanders, Agnes (1) – 23/64th Chalakatha-Mekoche-**Cherokee**-Metis born 1790 GA-died after 1851 - daughter of **Susannah (Corn Tassel) Carpenter**/49 & **Mitchell Sanders (1)**/50, twin of David Sanders, Bird Clan Cherokee, wife before 1803 of **Jacob Alberty**/86-white, mother of Delilah Alberty/1803, Johnson Alberty/1804, Lydia Alberty/1805, Moses Alberty/1808, Sarah Alberty/1810, Nancy Alberty/1811-all 11/64th Chalakatha-Mekoche-CherokeeMetis

1417. Sanders, Alexander (1) - 1/2 **Wyandot**-Metis born about 1772 OH-died after 1815 - son of **Samuel Sanders (1)**/45-adopted-white-(adopted Shawnee & Wyandot) & **Wyandot Woman**/55, Blue Jacket War/90-94, raiding Ohio River valley/95-1810, Prophet's Town/1811, Brownstown/1812-Monguagon/1812-1st Amherstburg/1812-Frenchtown/1813-Ft. Meigs/1813-2nd Amherstburg/1813 &
Thames/1813 **with Tecumseh**, husband about 1792 (OH?) of **Wyandot Woman**/75, children unknown

1418. Sanders, Alexander Jeremiah – 23/64th Chalakatha-Mekoche-**Cherokee**-Metis born 1772 TN-died after 1821 – oldest son of **Susannah Corn Tassel Carpenter**/49 & **Mitchell Sanders (1)**/50, Capt.-**with U.S. Army**-Creek War/1813-under Col. Gideon Morgan, Bird Clan Cherokee, **murdered** (his uncle/2nd cousin) Chief **Double Head** 1807 **with his brother James Sanders**/76 & **John Ridge** & also **murdered Chief James Vann** 1809 **with Edmund &**

William Fawling, husband 1st 1793 of **Margaret Watts**/78-21/64th Chalakatha-Pekowi-Cherokee-Metis, 2nd 1794 of **Peggy Sonicooie**/80-1/8th ChalakathaThawikila-Creek-Cherokee-Metis, children **with Watts** unknown, father **with**
Sonicooie of George Sanders/94, Mitchell Sanders (2)/95, John Sanders/96, Thomas Jefferson Sanders/97, Jennie Sanders/98, Richard Daniel Sanders/99, Andrew Jeremiah Sanders/1800, Mary Polly Sanders/1801 & Ellis Sanders (2)/1802-all 13/64th Chalakatha-Thawikila-Mekoche-Creek-Cherokee-Metis

1419. Sanders, Elder Daughter of Samuel - 1/2 Pekowi-Metis born about 1762 KY-died after 1815 - daughter of **Samuel Sanders (1)**/45-adopted white & **Pashika Pekowi**/50, wife 1775 (OH?) of **Adam Brown**/47-adopted white(Wyandot), mother of Mary Brown/75, Joseph Brown/78, Theresa Brown/79, Samuel Brown/80, Charlotte Brown/81, John D. Brown/83, James Brown/84,
Daughter/85, Adam Brown Jr/86, Matthew Brown/87, Daughter/88 & Julia Ann Brown/90-all 1/4th Pekowi-Metis-(Wyandot)

1420. Sanders, James Topee aka James Saunders - 1/2 Pekowi-Metis born about 1768 KY-died after 1817 - son of **Samuel Sanders (1)** /45-adopted-white & **Pashika Pekowi**/50, raiding Ohio River valley/88-92, Blue Jacket War/86-94, a warrior at Wapaghonettat 1817, Treaty 1817, husband about 1788 OH of **Mekoche Woman**/53, children unknown

1421. Sanders, Miss aka Daughter of Ellis Sanders - 1/2 Mekoche-Metis born about 1748 VA-died after 1778 - daughter of **Ellis Sanders**/20-white & **Mekoche Woman**/30, sister of **Mitchell Sanders** (1)/50, wife by 1778 of **Arthur Starr**/44-Irish, mother of Moses Starr/78-1/4th Mekoche-Metis

1422. Sanders, Mitchell (1) - 1/2 Mekoche-Metis born 1750 VA-died after 1791 NC - son of **Ellis Sanders**/20-white & **Mekoche Woman**/30, brother of **Miss Sanders**/48-wife of **Arthur Starr**/44-Irish, husband 1769 Running Water TN of **Susannah (Corn Tassel) Carpenter**/49, father of Alexander Jeremiah Sanders/72, George Goguyelesgi Sanders/74, James Sanders/76, John Sanders/78, twins-Jennie & Nancy Sanders/82, Andrew Snake Sanders/88, twinsAgnes & David Sanders/90-all 23/64th Chalakatha-Mekoche-Cherokee-Metis

1423. Sanders, Samuel (1) aka Samuel Saunders - adopted-white-(later adopted-**Wyandot & Cherokee**) born about 1745 ENG-died 1815 CAN - came from ENG to VA as indentured labor, then escaped to KY 1760, adopted by Shawnee 1760, never completely returned to whites, Cornstalk War/63-77, raiding Ohio-Little Kanawha-Big Sandy-New River valleys/72, Point

Pleasant/74-75-78, Blue Jacket War/77-94, raiding KY-OH-VA/77-80, Crawford/82, raiding Ohio River valley/88-92, translator Treaty 1808, father in law of **Adam Brown**-adopted white Wyandot, moved to CAN 1815 **with son Samuel Sanders Jr, Prophet** & **Paukeesa**, husband 1st 1764 KY of **Pashika Pekowi**/50, 2nd about 1771 OH of **Wyandot Woman**/55, 3rd after 1772 (TN-OH?) of **Cherokee Woman**/55, father **with Pashika** of Elder Daughter/62, Younger Daughter/64, James Sanders/68, Samuel Sanders(2) -Samuel Sanders Jr-Young Sanders/70-all 1/2 Pekowi-Metis, **with Wyandot** of Alexander Sanders/72-1/2 Wyandot-Metis & **with Cherokee** of unrecorded 1/2 Cherokee-Metis children likely named Sanders or Saunders

1424. Sanders, Samuel (2) aka Samuel Sanders Jr-Young Sanders-Young Saunders-Samuel Saunders Jr - 1/2 Pekowi-Metis born about 1770 KY-died after 1826 - son of **Samuel Sanders (1)**/45-adopted-white & **Pashika Pekowi**/50, raiding Ohio River valley/88-92, Blue Jacket War/88-94, **with British Army** War of 1812-Thames/13 **with Tecumseh**, moved to CAN 1815 **with father Samuel, Prophet** & **Paukeesa**, moved back to OH then to KS 1826 **with Prophet** & **Paukeesaa**, husband 1795 OH of **Wyandot Woman**/75, father of Theresa Sanders/98-1/4th Pekowi-Wyandot-Metis

1425. Sanscriante, Jean Baptiste – adopted-**Ottawa**-Metis born about 1730died 1812 – Cornstalk War/55-77, French-Indian War/54-63, Braddock/55, Pontiac War/62-66, Point Pleasant/74, Boonesboro/78, raiding OH-KY-VA/7781, raiding Ohio River valley/81 **with Joseph Brant**, Crawford/82, captured by George Rogers Clark 1779 with **Antoine Francois Maisonville**/50, husband about 1754 OH of **Kishpoko Woman**, children unknown

1426. Sansregret, Jean Louis – adopted-Cree-Metis born about 1725-died after 1755 - son of **Cree Woman** & **Coureur deBois**, French-Indian War/54, Braddock/55, raiding New-Shenandoah River valleys/55, husband about 1750 (OH?) of **Chalakatha Woman**/35, father of three known children/50-55-all 1/2 Chalakatha-Cree-Metis

1427. Sarcoxie, George aka George Blue Jacket – 1/2 Pekowi-Metis born 1836 (KS?)-died after 1856 – son of **Mr. Sarcoxie**-white & **Eliza Chowapea**/1818 Pekowi, adopted son of **Henry Blue Jacket**/99, wife & children unknown

1428. Sark – 1/2 Chalakatha-Cherokee born about 1746-died after 1774 – son of **Marhalonak**/10 & **Chalakatha Woman**/15, scout **with Andrew**

Lewis & whites-Pontiac War/62-66-Bushy Run/63-Point Pleasant/74, with father **Marhalonak**/10 & brothers **Tok**/40, **Sak**/44 & **Loho**/48, husband 1766 TN of **Cherokee Woman**/52, children unknown

1429.   Sasesequa aka Sasasekwa – Chalakatha born about 1750 OH-died after
1775 – Cornstalk War/68-75, raiding Ohio-Little Kanawha-New-Big Sandy River valleys/72, Point Pleasant/74-75

1430. Saucy Jack – Mekoche born about 1780 OH-died after 1820 - scout-**with U.S. Army**-War 1812-Thames/1813

1431. Saunahoe – Chalakatha born about 1770 OH-died after 1817 - raiding Ohio River valley/88-92, Blue Jacket War/88-94, raiding OH-KY-VA/95-1810, Prophet's Town/1811, Brownstown/1812-Monguagon/1812-1st Amherstburg/12Frenchtown/1813-Ft. Meigs/1813-2nd Amherstburg/1813 & Thames/1813 **with**
Tecumseh, a warrior at Lewistown 1817, Treaty 1817

1432. Sauwaseekou aka Sauwaseekou aka Sauwaseekou Puckenshinwa**Panther Crouching for Prey**[115] - 3/4th Kishpoko-Pekowi-Creek-Metis born 1760 KY-**killed** 1791 OH - 4th son of **Puckenshinwa**/35 & **Metheotashe Opessa**/40, a Kishpoko warrior, born in KY during move from AL to OH, Blue Jacket War/7791, raiding KY-OH-VA/77-80, Crawford/82, raiding Ohio River valley/88, killed 1791 at St. Clair, husband by 1780 OH of **Kishpoko Woman**/65, children unknown

1433. Savage Hawk – Kishpoko born about 1750 OH-died after 1794 – Cornstalk War/68-77, raiding New-Ohio-Little Kanawha-Big Sandy River valleys/72, Point Pleasant/74-75-78, Blue Jacket War/77-94, raiding KY-VAOH/77-81, Boonesboro/78, Crawford/82, raiding Ohio River valley/88-92, Fallen
Timber/94

1434. Savage Heart – adopted-Delaware born about 1730-died after 1770 - French-Indian War/54-63, Braddock/55, raiding New-Shenandoah River valleys/55, raiding PA/55-56, raiding Ohio-New River valleys/58, Pontiac War/62-66, Bushy Run/63, raiding New-Greenbrier-Jackson River valleys/63, husband about 1750 OH of **Chalakatha Woman**/34, children unknown

1435. Savannah Jack aka John Hague Jr - 1/2 Thawikila-Metis born about 1775-died after 1840 - son of **John Hague**/30-adopted-white-(later adopted-Creek) & **Thawikila Woman**/54, moved south after Fallen Timber/94, a Chickamauga in TN, trader from Tallapoosa after 1795, a Red Stick Creek associated **with Charles & William Weatherford, with Natives**-Creek War/1813, living with Spanish in FL after Creek War/1813, "a blood-thirsty, fiendish, cruel man", said to be husband of **Shawnee, Creek, Black & White Women**, father of many children by all, names unknown

1436. Savannah King – Chalakatha born before 1710 VA-died after 1746 TN - **Principal Chief 1746** of the Shawnee-among-the-Cherokee, diplomat between Shawnee & Overhill Cherokee, some relation to the **Hokolesqua-Okowellos-Cornstalk** family

1437. Savannah Tom (1) aka **Savannah Tom Carpenter (1)**-Thomas Carpenter (4)-Corn Planter (4)-**Moytoy (3)** – 7/8th Chalakatha-Metis born 1680 Chota TN-died 1710 Oconee SC - son of **Nancy Chalakatha**/1664 & **Trader Tom Carpenter (2)-Moytoy (2)**/1660, from Chota & Running Water TN, associated with Old Hop-Chalakatha & Rainmaker (2)-Cherokee, could cipher, read & write English, husband 1st 1697 Upper Hiwassee VA of **Susan-Quatsey (2) Rainmaker**/1682, separated 1700, 2nd 1700 of her sister **Nancy Rainmaker**/1683-Cherokee, father **with Susan-Quatsey** of Savannah Tom Carpenter (2)-Corn Planter (5)/1698-7/16th Chalakatha-Cherokee-Metis, **with Nancy** of Great Eagle Carpenter/02, Elizabeth Tassel Carpenter/04, Attakullakulla Carpenter/06, Corn Tassel Carpenter/08 & Susan Moytoy Carpenter/10-all 7/16th Chalakatha-Cherokee-Metis

1438. Savannah Tom (2) aka **Savannah Tom Carpenter (2)**-Thomas Carpenter (5)-Corn Planter (5) – 7/16th Chalakatha-**Cherokee**-Metis born 1698 Running Water TN-died after 1763 – son of **Savannah Tom Carpenter (1)Corn Planter (4)-Moytoy (2)**/1680 & **Susan-Quatsey (2) Rainmaker**/1682, could cipher, read & write English, associated **with Robert-Thigh-Cauquillehaneh Mclemore/31, French John French/10, Capt. French/12 & John Lantaniak/20-**adopted French-Canadian in pro-French faction during the French-Indian War, said to have had Shawnee, Cherokee, Creek, black & white wives, children unknown

1439. Sawauwone – Kishpoko born about 1750 OH-died after 1784 - raiding Ohio-Little Kanawha-New-Big Sandy River valleys/72, Point Pleasant/74-78, raiding KY-OH-VA/77-81, Blue Licks/82

1440. Saweeto – Pekowi born about 1740 PA-died after 1784 - raiding OhioNew River valleys/58, Pontiac War/62-66, Bushy Run/63, raiding NewGreenbrier-Jackson River valleys/63, raiding Ohio-New-Little Kanawha-Big
Sandy River valleys/72, Point Pleasant/74, Boonesboro/78, raiding KY-VA-OH/77-81, Crawford/82

1441.　　　Sawquaha aka Sawkwaha – Chalakatha born about 1780 OH-died after 1817 - raiding OH-KY-VA/99-1810, Prophet's Town/1811, Brownstown/1812-Monguagon/1812-1st Amherstburg/1812-Frenchtown/1813-Ft. Meigs/1813-2nd Amherstburg/1813 & Thames/1813 **with Tecumseh**, a warrior at Lewistown 1817, Treaty 1817

1442.　　　Saylok – Chalakatha born about 1750 OH-died after 1817 – Cornstalk War/68-77, Point Pleasnt/74, Blue Jacket War/77-94, raiding KY-VA-OH/77-81, Crawford/82, raiding Ohio River valley/88-92, scout-**with U.S. Army**-War 1812-Thames/1813, a warrior at Lewistown 1817, Treaty 1817

1443.　　　Scotowe aka Skotowe – Chalakatha born about 1780 OH-died after 1817
- raiding OH-VA-KY/99-1810, Prophet's Town/1811, Brownstown/1812Monguagon/1812-1st Amherstburg/1812-Frenchtown/1813-Ft. Meigs/1813-2nd Amherstburg/1813 & Thames/1813 **with Tecumseh**, a warrior at Lewistown 1817, Treaty 1817

1444. Scott, Elizabeth - 1/16th Chalakatha-Thawikila-Creek-**Cherokee**-Metis born 1774-died 1825 - daughter of **Sarah Gosaduisga Hicks**/58 & **Walter Scott**/50-white, Wolf Clan Cherokee, wife 1st 1788 of **Chief James Vann**/663/8th Chalakatha-Pekowi-Cherokee-Metis, 2nd 1790 of **Edward Adair**/55Cherokee-Metis, 3rd 1793 of **William Burgess**/60-white, 4th 1794 of **John Shepherd**/60-1/2 Thawikila-Creek-Cherokee-Metis, 5th 1802 of **Edward Springston**/60-Cherokee-Metis, 6th 1803 of **Mr. Vaught**/60-white, 7th 1807 of **Pleasant Rose**/60-white, mother **with Chief James** of James Vann (4)/88-7/32nd Chalakatha-Pekowi-Thawikila-Creek-Cherokee-Metis, **with Adair** of Walter Scott Red Wat Adair/90, James Adair/91, Edward Adair Jr/92-all 1/32nd Chalakatha-Thawikila-Creek-Cherokee-Metis, **with Burgess** of William Burgess II/93-1/32nd Chalakatha-Thawikila-Creek-Cherokee-Metis, **with Shepherd** of John Shepherd Jr/95, Mary Shepherd/97, Mahala Shepherd/99 & Sally Shepherd/1801-all 9/32nd Thawikila-Chalakatha-Creek-Cherokee-Metis, **with Springston** of Edley Springston/1802 & Jennie Springston/1803-both 1/32nd Chalakatha-Thawikila-Creek-Cherokee-Metis, **with Vaught** of Charles Vaught/1804 & James B. Vaught/1806-both 1/32nd Chalakatha-Thawikila-Creek-Cherokee-Metis, **with Rose** of Tilghman Rose/1807-1/32nd Chalakatha-Thawikila-Creek-Cherokee-Metis

1445.Scott, Margaret Peggy - 1/16th Chalakatha-Thawikila-Creek-**Cherokee**Metis born about 1780-died 1820 - daughter of **Sarah Gosaduisga Hicks**/58 & **Walter Scott**/50-white, Wolf Clan Cherokee, wife 1st 1795 of 5th cousin/uncle

Doublehead/40, 2nd 1797 of **John Clement Vann (1)**/68, 3rd 1798 of **Chief James Vann**/66, 4th 1809 GA of **Joseph Crutchfield Jr**/88-1/8th Chalakatha-Cherokee-Metis, mother **with Doublehead** of Two Heads Doublehead/94 & Double Head (2)/96-both 9/64th Chalakatha-Thawikila-Pekowi-Creek-Cherokee-Metis, **with John Clement** of Delilah Vann/98-7/32nd Chalakatha-Thawikila-Pekowi-Creek-Cherokee-Metis, **with Chief James** of David Vann (3)/99 & Judge John Vann/1801, Lucy Ayouku Vann/1803, Little John Vann /1805, Elizabeth Vann/1807 & James Vann (6)/1809 -all 7/32nd Chalakatha-ThawikilaPekowi-Creek-Cherokee Metis, any children **with Crutchfield** unknown

1446.Scott, Mary Polly - 1/16th Chalakatha-Thawikila-Creek-**Cherokee**-Metis born about 1782-died after 1842 - daughter of **Sarah Gosaduisga Hicks**/58 & **Walter Scott**/50-white, Wolf Clan Cherokee, wife 1st 1798 of **Chief James Vann**/66-3/8th Chalakatha-Pekowi-Cherokee-Metis, 2nd 1800 of **Eliphus Holt**/80-1/4th Thawikila-Metis, 3rd 1824 of **William R. Campbell Jr**/80-7/64th Chalakatha-Pekowi-Cherokee-Metis, mother **with Chief James** of Robert Robin Vann/98-7/32nd Chalakatha-Thawikila-Pekowi-Creek-Cherokee-Metis, **with Holt** of William Holt/1801-5/32nd Chalakatha-Thawikila-Creek-Cherokee-Metis, any children **with Campbell** unknown

1447.Scott, Nancy - 1/16th Chalakatha-Thawikila-Creek-**Cherokee**-Metis born about 1776 TN-died 1855 - daughter of **Sarah Gosaduisga Hicks**/58 & **Walter Scott**/50-white, Wolf Clan Cherokee, wife 1792 of **John Thornton**/70-white, mother of William Thornton/93, James Thornton/94, Charles Thornton/95, twins John Thornton Jr & Amos Thornton/96, Riley Thornton/97, twins Delilah Thornton & Wiley Glover Thornton /98, twins Elizabeth Thornton & Smith Taladu Thornton/99-all 1/32nd Chalakatha-Thawikila-Creek-Cherokee-Metis

1448.Scott, Richard - 1/16th Chalakatha-Thawikila-Creek-**Cherokee**-Metis born about 1778-died after 1835 - son of **Sarah Gosaduisga Hicks**/58 & **Walter Scott**/50-white, Wolf Clan Cherokee, husband about 1800 of **Polly Wadeyohe**/86-Cherokee, father Alexander Scott/1801, Richard Scott Jr/1808, George Scott/1810, Harry Scott/1812, Betsy Scott/1814, Nancy Scott/1816, Darkey Scott/1818, Elsie Scott/1822, John Scott/1824 & Lizzie Scott/1826-all 1/32nd Chalakatha-Thawikila-Creek-Cherokee-Metis

1449. Scott, Sarah - 1/8th Chalakatha-Thawikila-Creek-**Cherokee**-Metis born 1784-died 1830 - daughter of **Sarah Gosaduisga Hicks**/58 & **Walter Scott**/50white, Wolf Clan Cherokee, wife 1st 1801 of 5th cousin/uncle **Doublehead**/407/32nd Chalakatha-Cherokee-Metis, 2nd before 1807 of **George McDonald**/751/4th Chalakatha-Cherokee-Metis, 3rd 1824 of **Alexander Copeland**/85-white, mother **with Doublehead** of William Doublehead/1801 & Double Head (3)/1802-both 5/32nd Chalakatha-Thawikila-Creek-Cherokee-Metis, **with**
McDonald of Collin McDonald/1808-3/16th Chalakatha-Thawikila-Creek-Cherokee-Metis, any children **with Copeland** unknown

1450. See, Catherine Vanderpool Sharpe - adopted-white born 1720 NY-died 1806 IN - daughter of Adam Vanderpoole, adopted 1763 **with all 7 of her children**-returned to whites 1765 **with 6 children** (leaving **Elizabeth**/54) **plus daughter Mary Cornstalk See**/64-7/16th Chalakatha-Mekoche-Metis & **granddaughter Margaret Peggy (2) Cornstalk See**/64-15/32nd ChalakathaMekoche-Metis, wife 1st 1740 of **John Sharpe**/10-white, 2nd 1744 of **Fredrick
See**/10-white, 3rd 1763 of **Cornstalk**/10-7/8th Chalakatha-Metis, 4th after 1765 of **John Hardy**-white, mother **with Sharpe** of John Sharpe Jr/41 & William Sharpe/43, **with See** of Margaret Peggy See (1)/44, Lois Sarah See/46, Mary Catherine See/48, Michael See/50, Elizabeth See/54, George See/56 & John See/58-all white, **with Cornstalk** of **Mary (Cornstalk) See**/64-7/16th Chalakatha-Mekoche-Metis

1451. See, Elizabeth - adopted-white born 1754 Hampshire Co. WV-died 1807 Adams Co. OH - daughter of **Catherine Vanderpoole Sharpe**/20 & **Fredrick See**/10, adopted 1763-returned to whites about 1775, wife 1st 1769 of **Young Cornstalk**/44-15/16th Chalakatha-Mekoche-Metis, 2nd 1776 of **John Peter Shoemaker**/50-white, mother **with Young Cornstalk** of White Wing/70 & Cornstalk (3)/72-both 15/32nd Chalakatha-Mekoche-Metis, **with Shoemaker** of several children/76-91

1452. See, John - adopted-white born 1758 VA-died 1837 IN - son of **Catherine Vanderpoole Sharpe**/20 & **Fredrick See**/10, adopted 1763-returned to whites 1765-returned to tribe 1765-returned to whites after 1769, adopted into Cornstalk family with mother Catherine & sisters Margaret Peggy (1)/44, Lois Sarah/46, Mary Catherine/48 & Elizabeth/54, ransomed 1765 for $100 by his uncle Michael See, stationed at Ft. Randolph WV/1776-77-**witnessed murder of former adopted father Cornstalk**, scout-**with U.S. Army**-Revolution, lived on frontier, husband 1780 of **Margaret Elizabeth Jarrett** aka **Garrett**/56-former adopted white, father of John See Jr/1800 & 12 more children/81-1802

1453.See, Lois Sarah – adopted-white born 1746-died after 1786 – daughter of **Catherine Vanderpoole Sharp**/20 & **Fredrick See**/10, captured 1763-returned to whites 1765, wife 1763 OH of **Newa Cornstalk**/38-15/16th ChalakathaMekoche-Metis, mother **with Newa** of Son of Newa/64-15/32nd ChalakathaMekoche-Metis (son stayed with Newa when she returned to whites 1765)

1454.See, Margaret Peggy (1) – adopted-white born 1744-died after 1784 – daughter of **Catherine Vanderpoole Sharp**/20 & **Fredrick See**/10, captured 1763-returned to whites 1765, wife 1763 OH of **Walker Cornstalk**/36, mother **with Walker** of a Son of Walker Cornstalk/64-15/32nd Chalakatha-Mekoche-Metis,(left Son with Walker when she returned to whites)

1455.See, Margaret Peggy (2) aka **Margaret Peggy Cornstalk**-Margaret Peggy Ellinipsico – 15/32nd Chalakatha-Mekoche-Metis born 1764 OH-died after 1800 - only child of **Ellinipsico Cornstalk**/46 & **Mary Catherine See**/48adopted white, returned to whites 1765 with mother, grandmother & family, husband & children unknown

1456.See, Mary aka **Mary Cornstalk** – 7/16th Chalakatha-Mekoche-Metis born 1764 OH-died 1824 Warren Co. OH - only child of **Cornstalk**/10 & **Catherine Vanderpoole See**/25-adopted white, returned to whites with mother1765, wife about 1780 of former adopted Shawnee **Leonard Petro**/50-white, mother of Margaret Petro/88, Michael See Petro/90 & John Petro/92-all 7/32nd Chalakatha-Mekoche-Metis

1457.See, Mary Catherine - adopted white born 1748-died after 1800 - daughter of **Catherine Vanderpoole** Sharp/25-white & **Fredrick See**/10-white, adopted 1763-returned to whites 1765, lived after 1780 at Chillicothe OH with Mr. Johnson likely a former adopted white, wife 1st 1763 OH of **Ellinipsico Cornstalk**/46, 2nd by 1780 of **James Johnson**/45-white, mother **with Ellinipsico** of Margaret Peggy (Cornstalk) See (2)/64-15/32nd Chalakatha-Mekoche-Metis, **with Johnson** of John Apatathe Johnson /80-white-Shawnee

1458.Seekaboo - 3/4th Kishpoko-Pekowi-**Creek**-Metis born about 1770 ALdied after 1815 (FL?) - son of **Daughter of Daniel McQueen**/55 & **Kishpoko Man**/50, Blue Jacket War/87-94, multi-lingual prophet, traveled with & interpreted for his 2nd cousin Tecumseh/68 1795-1812, Ft. Mims/1813 with uncle **Peter McQueen**/80-1/2 Creek-Black Metis, a **Warpicanata Chief** 1812, a Red Stick, fled to Seminoles in FL 1815, grandson of **Middle Sister of Metheotashe**/35 & **Daniel McQueen**/36-1/2 Creek-Metis (mother's side), greatgrandson of **James McQueen**/1700-white & **Katherine Fraser**/05-Creek (father's side), great-grandson of **Loyparkoweh Opessa**/1700-Pekowi (mother's

side), 2nd cousin of John Francis/60, **Josiah Francis**/65, **Joseph Francis**/70 & Susannah
Francis/75 & of **Tecumseh**/68 & of **Osceola**/1802

1459. Seekeboo – Kishpoko born about 1760 OH-died after 1783 - wife about 1775 OH of **Kishpoko Man**/55, widowed at Crawford/82

1460. Sekochquana aka Sekochkwana – Chalakatha born about 1710 PA-died about 1758 OH in epidemic - raiding PA/40, Council Ft. Pitt Nov. 1753, Braddock/55, raiding New-Shenandoah River valleys/55, raiding PA/55-56, raiding Ohio-New River valleys/58

1461. Seney, David - 1/2 Chalakatha-Metis born 1760-died 1817 - son of **Solomon Seney**-white & **Christian Chalakatha Woman**, lived as white, husband of **Averilla Snow**/74-1/2 Chalakatha-Metis, father of Elizabeth Seney/95, Mary Seney/97, Joshua Seney/99, Fanny Seney/1801, Jane Seney/1803, Hemsley Seney/1805, Ira Seney/1807, Martha Seney/1808, Katherine Seney/1810, David Seney Jr/1817-all 1/2 Chalakatha-Metis

1462. Sequeheton aka Sekweeheton – Mekoche born about 1700 PA-died about 1758 OH in epidemic – living in PA 1725, raiding PA/40, a **Mekoche Chief** in OH by 1748, Cornstalk War/55-58, French-Indian War/54-58, Braddock/55, raiding New-Shenandoah River valleys/55, raiding PA/55-56, raiding Ohio-New River valleys/58

1463. **Sequoyah** aka George Gist-George Guess-Sowgli-Sikwayi-Pig's FootHorse – 37/64th Chalakatha-Pekowi-**Cherokee**-Metis born 1758 Great Tellico
TN-died 1843 MX - son of **Wurteh Watts**/44 & **Nathaniel Gist**/30, Red Paint Clan Cherokee, raised by step-grandfather **Red Horse-Sagwiligigagei**/20Cherokee, grandson of **Christopher Gist**/05-white & (by Wurteh) of **Oousta White Owl Carpenter**/25 & **John Watts Sr**/04, **created Cherokee alphabet & syllabary**, from Will's Town AL, delegate to D.C. 1828, Treaty 1828, John McLemore Co-**with U.S. Army**-Creek War/1813-Horseshoe Bend/1814, fingers cut off to 1st knuckle by Cherokee-American conspiracy to stop his writing, a blacksmith & silversmith by trade, moved to AR 1815, moved to OK 1829, died on trip to MX with son **Teesey Gist (1)**/89, **Standing Bowles**/99, **Standing Man Bowles**/88 & **Worm, John Elijah, Oowositi, Cahtata, Tallatoo & Coteska**-all (allegedly) Cherokee looking for the Shawnee-Cherokee in MX, half-brother (through Wurteh) of Chief **John Jolly**/57, **Tahlonteeskee**/60,
Martin-Utana-Tail Benge/81, **Robert-Chief Bench Benge**/62, **Richard Benge**/63, **Catherine Benge**/64, **Tashliske-White Path Benge**/65 & **Lucy**

Benge/66, step-brother of **Tobacco Will** (Red Horse)/61, husband 1st 1779 of **Utiyu Ughui**/65-Cherokee-(divorced 1787), 2nd 1787 of **Sally Waters**/70-1/4th Chalakatha-Pekowi-Metis, 3rd about 1798 of **Wokteeyah Langley**/85-CreekMetis, 4th 1802 **Lucy Campbell**/82-21/64th Chalakatha-Pekowi-Cherokee-Metis, 5th 1806 **Tsiyosa Cherokee**, 6th 1815 of his half-niece **Sally Benge**/97-21/64th Chalakatha-Pekowi-Cherokee-Metis, 7th 1817 AR **Ukatiya Tsoiyuka**/96Cherokee, 8th 1826 AR of **Sally Agadiya Waters**/90-1/4th Chalakatha-PekowiCherokee-Metis, father **with Utiyu** of daughters Eyagu Sequoyah/80, Ooloosta
Sequoyah (1)/82, Gooneki Sequoyah (1)/84 & Atoyah Sequoyah (1)/86-all 9/32nd Chalakatha-Pekowi-Cherokee-Metis, father **with Sally Waters** of Teeseey Gist (1)/89, George Gist Jr (1)/90, Polly Gist (1)/92, Lightning Bug Gist-Richard Gist (1)/94 & Tishali Gist (1)/95-all 13/32nd Chalakatha-Pekowi-Cherokee-Metis, father **with Langley** of Oolootsa Gist (2)/99 & Gooneki Gist (2)/1800-both 9/32nd Chalakatha-Pekowi-Creek-Cherokee-Metis, father **with Campbell** of Richard Gist (2)/1802-29/64th Chalakatha-Pekowi-Cherokee-Metis, father **with Tsiyosa** of George Wagon-wheel/1806, Polly Gist (2)/08 & Teesey Gist (2) Gist/12-all 9/32nd Chalakatha-Pekowi-Cherokee-Metis, father **with Benge** of Robert Gist.1816-29/64th Chalakatha-Pekowi-Cherokee-Metis, father **with Tsoiyuka** of Rachel Ayuqui Gist/1818, Andrew Gist/20, Oolootsa Gist (3)/22 & Patsy Gist/24-all 9/32nd Chalakatha-Pekowi-Cherokee-Metis, father **with Sally Agadiya Waters** of Joseph Gist/1827, Lucinda Gist/29, Susan Gist/31, Elizabeth Gist/33 & Mary Gist/35-all 13/32nd Chalakatha-Pekowi-Cherokee-Metis

1464. Setakosheka - Mekoche born about 1770 OH-died after 1817 - raiding Ohio River valley/88-92, Blue Jacket War/88-94, no part in War 1812, a warrior at Wapaghonettat 1817, Treaty 1817

1465. Setepakothe – Mekoche born about 1780 OH-died after 1817 – no part in War 1812, a warrior at Wapaghonettat 1817, Treaty 1817

1466. Shade - Mekoche born about 1720 OH-**murdered** 1786 OH - raiding PA/40, French/Indian War/54-63, Braddock/55, raiding New-Shenandoah River valleys/55, raiding PA/55-56, raiding Ohio-New River valleys/58, Pontiac War/62-66, Bushy Run/63, raiding New-Greenbrier-Jackson River valleys/63, raiding Ohio-Little Kanawha-New-Big Sandy River valleys/72, Point Pleasant/74-78, Boonesboro/78, Council Aug. 1776, **murdered**/86 in Col. Benjamin Logan's attack on Moluntha's village

1467. Shakes Earth – adopted-Cherokee born about 1745 TN-died after 1778 - Pontiac War/62-66, Bushy Run/63, raiding New-Jackson-Greenbrier River valleys/63, raiding Ohio-Little Kanawha-Big Sandy-New River valleys/72, Point

Pleasant/74-78, raiding KY-VA-OH/77, Boonesboro/78, over 6'6" tall & heavy, husband about 1765 KY of **Chalakatha Woman**/50

1468. Shammakabe – Pekowi born about 1768 OH-died after 1790 - raiding Ohio River valley/88-90, Harmar/90

1469. Shane, Anthony aka Antoine Chesne - 1/4th Kishpoko-Creek-WyandotMetis born about 1763 OH-died 1834 - son of **Isadore Chesne**/35-1/2 WyandotMetis & **Older Sister of Puckenshinwa**/39, same clan (Panther) as **Tecumseh**, scout-**with U.S. Army**-Revolution-Blue Jacket War-War of 1812, translator, Treaty 1817, 1818, 1829, 1832, son in law of **Black Fish**/25, husband before 1785 OH of **Lemateshe Blackfish**/58, father of David Dushane/85, Elder Daughter/87, John Shane/90, Younger Daughter/92 & Charles Chesne/95-all 5/8th Kishpoko-Chalakatha-Mekoche-Pekowi-Creek-Wyandot-Metis, step-father of **David Deshane**/80-1/2 Chalakatha-Mekoche-Pekowi-Wyandot-Metis-(son of **Lamateshe Blackfish & Capt. Joseph Dusquene**)

1470. Shane, Joseph aka Joseph Chesne - 1/4th Kishpoko-Creek-WyandotMetis-(adopted **Seneca**) born about 1765 OH-died after 1832 - son of **Isadore Chesne**/35 & **Older Sister of Puckenshinwa**/39, same clan (Panther) as Tecumseh, lived with Lewistown Chalakatha band, moved to KS 1832, husband about 1785 OH of **Seneca Woman**/70, father of Joseph Shane (2)/92-1/8th Kishpoko-Creek-Seneca-Wyandot-Metis

1471. Shapoquata aka Shapokwata – Mekoche born about 1760 OH-died after 1817 – Blue Jacket War/77-94, raiding KY-VA-OH/77-81, Boonesboro/78, Crawford/82, raiding Ohio River valley/88-92, a warrior at Wapaghonettat 1817, Treaty 1817

1472. Sharp Stick – Kishpoko born about 1760 OH-died after 1782 – Blue Jacket War/77-82, Point Pleasant/78, Boonesboro/78, raiding KY-OH-VA/77-81, Blue Licks/82

1473. Shashekopeah – Thawikila born about 1770-died after 1817 - raiding Ohio River valley/88-92, Blue Jacket War/88-94, a warrior from Hog Creek 1817, Treaty 1817

1474. Shaukawkee – Chalakatha born about 1750 OH-died after 1778 – Cornstalk War/68-77, raiding New-Ohio-Big Sandy-Little Kanawha River valleys/72, Point Pleasant/74-78, raiding KY-OH-VA/77-78

1475. Shawabaghke – Mekoche born about 1770 OH-died after 1817 - raiding Ohio River valley/88-92, Blue Jacket War/88-94, a warrior at Wapaghonettat 1817, Treaty 1817

1476. Shawala - Mekoche-(adopted-**Sioux**) born about 1710 (IN?)-died after 1763 - Cornstalk War/55-63, French-Indian War/54-63, Braddock/55, raiding New-Shenandoah River valleys/55, raiding PA/55-56, raiding Ohio-New River valleys/58,Bushy Run/63, apparently moved north-west with wife's band, husband about 1730 (IN-IL?) of **Sioux Woman**/14, children unknown

1477. Shawanoe aka Shawnee - ½ Kishpoko-Chippewa born about 1760 (OHMI?)-died after 1813 – son of **Chippewa Man** & **Kishpoko Woman**, Blue Jacket War/77-94, raiding KY-VA-OH/77-81, Crawford/82, raiding Ohio River valley/88-92, raiding OH-KY-VA/95-1810, Prophet's Town/1811, Brownstwon/1812-Monguagon/1812-1st Amherstburg/1812-Frenchtown/1813-Ft. Meigs/1813-2nd Amherstburg/1813 & Thames/1813 **with Tecumseh**, husband about 1780 OH of **Kishpoko Woman**/65, father of several 3/4th Kishpoko-Chippewa children/80-1810

1478. Shawnaha – Thawikila born about 1760-died after 1817 – Blue Jacket War/79-94, raiding KY-OH-VA/79-81, Blue Licks/82, Crawford/82, raiding Ohio River valley/88-92, no part in War 1812, an elder at Hog Creek 1817, some connection with **Black Hoof** family

1479. Shawnee Billy (1) - 1/2 Chalakatha-**Chickasaw** born about 1780 (TNAL?)-died after 1818 - son of **Chalakatha Man** & **Chickasaw Woman**, lived with Chickasaw, husband about 1800 TN of **Chickasaw Woman**/85, father of several 1/4th Chalakatha-Chickasaw children/1800-1818

1480. Shawnee Billy (2) aka **Billy Fisher** - ½ Chalakatha-Metis born 1786died after 1817 – son of **Fredrick Fisher**/40-adopted-white & **Chalakatha Woman**/65, scout-**with U.S. Army-**War of 1812, a warrior from Lewistown 1817, Treaty 1817

1481. Shawnee Prophet aka **Lalawethika**[116] Puckenshinwa-TenskawatawaOpen Door[117]-Laulewashika-Lalawetheeka-Rattling Sound in Brush - 3/4th Kishpoko-Pekowi-Creek-Metis born 1774 OH-died 1837 KS - youngest son of **Puckenshinwa**/35 & **Metheotashe Opessa**/40, a Kishpoko, only one of triplet sons to survive infancy, youngest brother of **Tecumseh**, Fallen Timbers/94, Council Greenville 1795, move to IN 1798, defeated by **William Henry Harrison** at Prophet's Town aka Tippicanoe/1811, took little active (warrior) part in Tecumseh's campaign of 1795-1810 or War of 1812, moved to CAN with band of followers & family of Tecumseh 1815, returned to OH 1825, moved to KS 1826 with nephew **Paukeesaa Tecumseh**, married 5 times, husband 1st about 1788 OH of **Kishpoko Woman**/62, again by 1814 (IN-OH?) of **Pricilla Perkins**/95-adopted white, other 3 wives unknown for now, father **with**

Kishpoko of John Prophet/90, 1 other son & 3 daughters-all 7/8th KishpokoPekowi-Creek-Metis, **with Perkins** of Marcia Bates/1814-3/8th Kishpoko-Pekowi-Creek-Metis, children **with other wives** unknown

1482. Shawnoe – adopted-Cayuga born about 1750 OH-died after 1774 – Cornstalk War/68-74, raiding Ohio-Little Kanawha-Big Sandy-New River valleys/72, raiding Ohio valley/74 **with Chief Logan**, Point Pleasant/74, husband about 1770 OH of **Kishpoko Woman**/55, children unknown

1483. Shawyanaka aka Shaweeanaka – Thawikila born about 1780 OH-died after 1817 – no part in War 1812, a warrior at Hog Creek 1817, Treaty 1817, some connection with **Black Hoof** family

1484. Shemagauashik aka Shemagaushe – Chalakatha born about 1770 OHdied after 1817 - raiding Ohio River valley/88-92, Blue Jacket War/88-94, no part in War 1812, a warrior at Hog Creek 1817, Treaty 1817, husband 1790 OH of **Black Hoof** family **Thawikila Woman**/74

1485. Shemakee aka Shemaka – Mekoche born about 1790 OH-died after 1817 – no part in War 1812, a warrior at Wapaghonettat 1817, Treaty 1817

1486. Shemay aka Sam – Mekoche born about 1780 OH-died after 1817 - scout-**with U.S. Army**-War 1812-Thames/1813, a warrior at Wapaghonettat 1817, Treaty 1817

1487. Shepherd, Agnes aka Aggy - 1/2 Thawikila-Creek-**Cherokee**-Metis born about 1754-died 1833 KY - daughter of **Thawikila Woman** & **Mr. Shepherd**Creek-Cherokee-Metis, sister of **John Shepherd Sr**/60, wife 1771 of **George All Chief Sizemore**/45-1/2 Shawano-Metis, mother of Minerva Winifred Sizemore/72, John Rockhouse Sizemore/76, Edward Ned Sizemore/78, George Golden Hawk Sizemore/83, Susan Sizemore/84, Ruth Sizemore/87, Rhoda Sizemore/88, Henry Hunting Shirt Sizemore/90-all 1/4th Shawano-Thawikila-Creek-Cherokee-Metis

1488. Shepherd, John - 1/2 Thawikila-Creek-**Cherokee**-Metis born about 1760-died after 1800 - son of **Thawikila Woman** & **Mr. Shepherd**-CreekCherokee-Metis, brother of Agnes-Aggy Shepherd/54, husband 1st about 1780 of

Unknown Woman (White, Creek, Shawnee or Cherokee?) 2nd 1796 of **Elizabeth Scott**/74-1/16th Chalakatha-Thawikila-Creek-Cherokee-Metis, children/80-96 **with 1st Wife** unknown, father **with Scott** of John Shepherd Jr/95, Mary Shepherd/97, Mahala Shepherd/99 & Sarah Shepherd/1801-all 9/32nd

Thawikila-Chalakatha-Creek-Cherokee-Metis

1489. Sheshe – Mekoche born about 1770 OH-died after 1817 - raiding Ohio River valley/88-92, Blue Jacket War/88-94, no part in War 1812, a warrior at Wapaghonettat 1817, Treaty 1817

1490. Sheshecapea aka Sheshekapea – Thawikila born about 1780 OH-died after 1817 – no part in War 1812, a warrior from Hog Creek 1817, some connection with **Black Hoof** family

1491. Shesheloo – Mekoche born about 1780 OH-died after 1817 – no part in War 1812, a warrior at Wapaghonettat 1817, Treaty 1817

1492. Shiabwasson aka Sheeabwasson – Mekoche born about 1780 OH-died after 1817 – no part in War 1812, a warrior at Wapaghonettat 1817, Treaty 1817

1493. Shiatwa aka Sheeatewa – Chalakatha born about 1785 OH-died after 1817 – no part in War 1812, a warrior at Wapaghonettat 1817, Treaty 1817

1494. Shields, Nancy White – Pekowi born about 1770 (PA?)-died after 1800, wife by 1790 of **John Shields**-white born 1769 Augusta Co VA-died 1809 IN(son of **Robert Shields** & **Nancy Stockton**), mother of Jennie Shields/90, Nancy Shields/92, Janette Martha Shields/95-all ½ Pekowi-Metis

1495. Shilling – Chalakatha born before 1780 OH-died after 1817 - scout-**with U.S. Army**-War 1812-Thames/1813, Treaty 1817, a warrior at Lewistown 1817

1496. Shinagawmaashe – Thawikila born about 1760 OH-died after 1817 – Blue Jacket War/77-94, raiding KY-OH-VA/77-81, Point Pleasant/78, Crawford/82, raiding Ohio River valley/88-92, a warrior at Hog Creek 1817

1497. Shoe Boots aka Shoe Boots Carpenter-**Shoe Boots Attakullakulla**-Shoe Boots (1)-Dasigiyang-**Tuskorigo** – 15/32nd Chalakatha-Thawikila-Creek**Cherokee**-Metis born 1746 Great Tellico TN-died 1829 Thompson Ferry GA - son of **Attakullakulla Carpenter**/08 & **Ollie Nionee Oconastota**/20, raiding KY-OH-VA/77-81, Boonesboro/78, Blue Licks/82, Crawford/82, raiding Ohio River valley/88-92, Blue Jacket War/77-94, wounded at St. Clair/91, Fallen Timber/94, lived **with Shawnee in OH** 1790-1803, Capt.-**with U.S. Army**-Creek War/1813, Horseshoe Bend/1814, husband 1st 1770 Running Water TN of **Bird Clan Cherokee Woman**/50, 2nd 1775 Shawnee Village OH of **Lecha**/60Chalakatha, 3rd 1794 Shawnee Village OH of **Clarinda Allington** (Arrington)/80-adopted white, 4th 1805 Shawnee Village OH of **Dolly Black**/90former slave, children/70-75 **with Bird Clan** unknown, father **with**

Lecha of Shoe Boots (2)-Young Shoe Boots-Dasigiyagi/75-47/64th Chalakatha-ThawikilaCreek-Cherokee-Metis, **with Clarinda** of John Allington (Shoe Boots)/94, Sally
Allington (Shoe Boots)/96, William Allington (Shoe Boots)/98-all 15/64th Chalakatha-Thawikila-Creek-Cherokee-Metis, **with Dolly** of Thomas Shoe Boots/1806, Ollie Shoe Boots/1810 & Napoleon Bonaparte (Shoe Boots)/1820 & other children- all 15/64th Chalakatha-Thawikila-Creek-Cherokee-Black-Metis

1498. Shoe Boots, Young aka Shoe Boots (2)-Shoe Boots Carpenter (2)-Shoe Boots Attakullakulla (2)-Dasigiyagi-Boots-**Chulio**-Tsuliowa-Chuleah-Chulcoah-Chilioah-**Gentleman Tom**-Thomas Carpenter (7) – 47/64th ChalakathaThawikila-Creek-**Cherokee**-Metis born 1775 Shawnee Village OH-died after
1851 Cherokee Nation (OK?) - son of **Shoe Boots Carpenter (1)**/50 & **Lecha**/60-Chalakatha, grandson of **Attakullakulla**, delegate to D.C. 1791, Fallen Timber/94 with father, **lived in OH with Shawnee** with father's band in OH 1794-1803, **with U.S. Army**-Creek War/1813-Horseshoe Bend/14, Treaty 1791, 1792, 1794, 1805, 1806, 1816, 1819, husband 1st 1794 Shawnee Village OH of **Chalakatha Woman**/78, 2nd 1804 Running Water TN of **Nancy Hughes**/74-47/64th Chalakatha-Cherokee-Metis, children unknown

1499. Shorey, Annie - Cherokee-Metis born about 1745 TN-died 1815 TN - daughter of **William Shorey**/20-white & **Ghigooie Cherokee**/30, Bird Clan Cherokee, from the Overhills-then Lookout Mountain TN, 2nd wife 1769 of **John Titasgisgi McDonald**/35-1/2 Chalakatha-Metis, mother of Mary McDonald/70, Mollie McDonald/72, Charles McDonald/74 & George McDonald/76-all 1/4th Chalakatha-**Cherokee**-Metis

1500. Shorey, Elizabeth - Cherokee-Metis born about 1762 TN-died after 1800 - daughter of **William Shorey**/20-white & **Ghigooie Cherokee**/30, Bird Clan Cherokee, wife 1st (known) about 1794 of **Major John Lowery**/68, 2nd 1796 TN of his brother **Major George Lowery**/70-both 11/32nd Chalakatha-Pekowi-Metis, mother **with Major John** of Elizabeth Lowery/95, **with Major George** of Peggy Lowery/96, Archibald Lowery (1)/97, Washington Lowery (1)/98, Charles Lowery (2)/1801-11/64th Chalakatha-Pekowi-**Cherokee**-Metis

1501. Short Wolf – Thawikila born about 1730 PA-died after 1774 – Cornstalk War/55-72, French-Indian War/54-63, Braddock/55, raiding New-Shenandoah River valleys/55, raiding PA/55-56, raiding Ohio-New River valleys/58, Pontiac War/62-66, Bushy Run/63, raiding New-Greenbrier-Jackson River valleys/63, raiding Ohio-Little Kanawha-Big Sandy-New River valleys/72, Point Pleasant/74, moved to AL 1774

1502. Short, Thomas - 3/8th Pekowi-Kishpoko-Metis born about 1795 Maumee River OH-died after 1833 (MI?) - son of **Sally Blue Jacket**/76 & **William Short**/74-white, grandson of Blue Jacket/35, husband after 1815 OH of **Wyandot Woman**, father of Joseph Short/1833-3/16th Pekowi-Kishpoko-Wyandot-Metis

1503. Shot Pouch aka **Shot Pouch** Powderhorn-**Petatwa**[118] - 3/4th ThawikilaMetis born about 1780 OH-died after 1826 MO/KS - son of **Powder Horn (1)**/40 & **Thawikila Woman**/45, scout-**with U.S. Army**-War 1812-Thames/13, Treaty 1832, wife & children unknown

1504. Showngame – Mekoche born about 1780 OH-died after 1817 – no part in War 1812, a warrior at Wapaghonettat 1817, Treaty 1817

1505. Shucking Corn – Pekowi born about 1720 PA-died after 1774 - wife about 1735 PA of **Pekowi Man**/15, widow in 1774

1506. Silver Fish – Chalakatha born about 1740 PA-died after 1785 - Cornstalk War/58-77, raiding Ohio-New River valleys/58, Pontiac War/62-66, Bushy Run/63, raiding New-Greenbrier-Jackson River valleys/63, raiding Ohio-New-Big Sandy-Little Kanawha valleys/72, Blue Jacket War/77-85, Point Pleasant/74-75-78, raiding KY-VA-OH/77-81, Boonesboro/78, Crawford/82

1507. Silver Heels (1) aka **Silver Heels Hokolesqua (1)-Halowas**[119]-Silverheels Okowellos (1) – 7/8th Chalakatha-Mekoche-Metis born 1724 PA-died 1804 OH - son of **Okowellos**/1674 & **Katee Mekoche**-1680, **Cornstalk War**/55-77, French-Indian War/54-63, Braddock/55, raiding New-Shenandoah River valleys/55, raiding PA/55-56, raiding Ohio-New River valleys/58, Pontiac War/62-66, Bushy Run/63, raiding New-Greenbrier-Jackson River valleys/63, a **Chalakatha Chief, an emissary to the Shawnee for Cornstalk** 1774, Point Pleasant/74-78, **Blue Jacket War** /77-94, Boonesboro/78, Crawford/82, raiding Ohio River valley/88-92, Council Camp Charlotte 1774, Council Ft. Woods 1775, Council Ft. Pitt 1775 with Cornstalk, Nimwha, Wryneck & Blue Jacket, over 6' tall, husband about 1744 of **Shawnee Woman**/30, father of Silverheels (4)-Halowas (2)-**Young Halowas**/60, Daughter/70, Sarah Silverheels/75 & other unknown children/44-74-all 15/16th Chalakatha-Mekoche-Metis

1508. Silver Heels (2) aka Silverheels Hokolesqua (2) -**Aroas (1)**-HaroasSilverheels Okowellos (2) – 15/16th Chalakatha-Mekoche-Metis-adopted **Seneca** born 1732 OH/PA-**killed** 1770 IN/IL - son of **Daughter of Okowellos**/12 & **Chalakatha Man**/10, adopted son after 1745 of **Old Belt**/1700-Seneca, brother of Counasona/35, grandson of **Okowellos**/1674, scout-spy **for whites-**

Shawnee Heritage

FrenchIndian War/54-63-Ft. Necessity/54-Braddock/55--Pontiac War/62-66, translatorguide for **George Morgan**-white after Pontiac War, **killed about 1770 below Louisville KY**, husband 1752 OH of **Mekoche Woman**/35, father of Daughter/52, Aroas (2)-**Young Aroas**-Silverheels Hokolesqua(3)/60-both 31/32nd Chalakatha-Mekoche-Metis-adopted Seneca

1509.Silver Heels (3) aka Hokolesqua, Silverheels Hokolesqua (3) -Aroas (2)**Young Aroas** - 31/32nd Chalakatha-Mekoche-Metis-(adopted **Miami**) born 1760 OH-died after 1825 - son of **Aroas-Silverheels (2)**/32 & **Mekoche Woman**/35, adopted Seneca, great-grandson of **Okowellos**/1674, translator-guide for **George Morgan**-white after death of his father, scout-spy **with whites**-Blue Jacket War/80-94-Crawford/82, Treaty 1809, husband 1780 IN of **Miami Woman**/65, children unknown

1510.Silver Heels (4) aka Silverheels Hokolesqua (4)-**Young Halowas** – 15/16th Chalakatha-Mekoche-Metis born 1760 OH-died after 1832 KS - son of **Halowas-Silver Heels (1)**/24 & **Chalakatha Woman**/30, grandson of **Okowellos**/1674, a Chalakatha, **Blue Jacket War** /77-94, raiding Ohio River valley/88-92, scout-**with U.S. Army-**War 1812-Thames/1813, an Elder at Lewistown OH 1817, Treaty 1817, moved to KS by 1832, nephew of **Cornstalk**/10, husband 1780 OH of **Shawnee Woman**/65, father of Moses Silverheels/82, Silverheels (5)-Halowas (3)/82

1511.Silver Heels (5) aka Silverheels Hokolesqua (5) -**Halowas (3)** – 31/32nd Chalakatha-Mekoche-Metis born 1782 OH-died after 1854 KS – son of **Silverheels (4)-Halowas (2)**/60 & **Chalakatha Woman**/65, great-grandson of **Okowellos**/1674, scout-**with U.S. Army-**War of 1812-Thames/1813, a warrior at Lewistown OH 1817, moved to KS by 1832, Treaty 1854, wife & children unknown

1512.Silversmith – Chalakatha born about 1780 OH-died after 1832 KS - scout-**with U.S. Army-**War 1812-Thames/1813, a warrior at Lewistown 1817, Treaty 1817, 1832, move to KS 1832

Section XVI
Singing Crow to Sycks (S continued)

S (continued)

1513. Singing Crow - adopted-Cherokee born about 1740 TN-died after 1775 - wife about 1755 TN of **Kishpoko Man**/35, widow 1775, mother of several 1/2 Kishpoko-Cherokee children/55-75

1514. Sister of Cornstalk – see **Wakuta** Hokolesqua/04, **Wife of Mr. Francis & Old Belt**/12, **Cawechile Hokolesqua**-Wife of Cold Water/17, **Nonhelema** Hokolesqua/18, **Elizabeth Hokolesqua**/26 & **Catherine-Kitty Hokolesqua**/28

1515. Sits Down aka **Willaquashena**-Weelakwashena – Mekoche born before 1780 OH-died after 1817 - scout-**with U.S. Army**-War 1812-Thames/1813, Treaty 1815, 1817

1516.   Sits in Shadow – Kishpoko born about 1760 OH-died after 1790 – Blue Jacket War/77-90, raiding KY-VA-OH/77-81, Crawford/82, raiding Ohio River valley/88-90, Harmar/90

1517.   Sitting Bear - Mekoche-(adopted-**Seneca**) born about 1770 OH-died after 1832 KS - raiding Ohio River valley/88-92, Blue Jacket War/88-94, scout-**with U.S. Army-**War 1812-Thames/1813, Treaty 1832, move to KS 1832, husband 1790 OH of **Seneca Woman**/75, children unknown

1518. Sitting Bird – Pekowi born about 1760 OH-died after 1790 - wife about 1775 of **Pekowi Man**/55, widowed at Harmar/90, mother of several children/7590

1519. Six Fingers – Chalakatha born about 1730 PA-died after 1770 - wife about 1745 OH of **Chalakatha Man**/25, widow in 1770, mother of several children/45-70

1520. Sizemore, Edward Ned – ½ Shawano-Metis born about 1721 VA-died **(likely hung as a Tory)** 1780 Ashe Co NC – (oldest?) son of **Edward Sizemore**white & **Shawano Woman**, husband about 1741 VA of **Mary Spears**/26-(likely ½ Shawano-Metis-daughter of **John Spears**-white & **Shawano Woman**), father of Edward Ned Sizemore/42, John Sizemore/44, Lydia Sizemore/46, Owen Sizemore/47, Sally Sizemore/48, George Sizemore/49, Hiram Sizemore/51, Ephriam Sizemore/53, Rebecca Sizem,ore/55, Henry Sizemore/56 & Phillip Sizemore/58-all ½ Shawano-Metis

1521. Sizemore, George All Chief – ½ Shawano-Metis born about 1745 VA-

Shawnee Heritage

died 1822 KY – youngest son of **Edward Sizemore**-white & **Shawano Woman**, husband (2nd?) 1771 of **Agnes Shepherd**/54, father of Minerva Winifred Sizemore/72, John Rockhouse Sizemore/74, Edward Ned Sizemore/76, George Golden Hawk Sizemore/78, Susan Sizemore/80, Sarah Ann Sizemore/82, Ruth Sizemore/84, Rhoda Sizemore/86 & Henry Hunting Shirt Sizemore/88-all 1/4th Shawano-Thawikila-Creek-**Cherokee**-Metis

1522.Skapakake – Mekoche born about 1770 OH-died after 1817 - raiding Ohio River valley/88-92, Blue Jacket War/87-94, a warrior at Wapaghonettat 1817, Treaty 1817

1523.Skekakumsheka aka Skekakoomsheka – Kishpoko born about 1780 OHdied after 1817 - a warrior at Wapaghonettat 1817, Treaty 1817, husband about 1800 OH of **Mekoche Woman**/85

1524.Skepakeskeshe – Mekoche born about 1785 OH-died after 1817 - a warrior at Wapaghonettat 1817, Treaty 1817

1525.Skepakutchika aka Skeakootcheeka – Chalakatha born about 1790 OHdied after 1817 - a warrior from Wapaghonettat 1817, Treaty 1817, husband about 1810 OH of **Mekoche Woman**/94

1526.Skinny Man - adopted-Cherokee born 1740 TN-died after 1778 OH - raiding Ohio-New River valleys/58, Pontiac War/62-66, Bushy Run/63, raiding New-Greenbrier-Jackson River valleys/63, Point Pleasant/74, raiding KY-VAOH/77, Boonesboro/78, **living with Shawnee-Cherokee in KY** 1774, husband 1760 TN of **Chalakatha Woman**/45, father of several 1/2 Chalakatha-Cherokee children/60-78

1527.Skotta – Chalakatha born about 1780 OH-died after 1817 - raiding OHKY-VA/99-1810, Prophet's Town/1811, Brownstown/1812-Monguagon/1812-1st Amherstburg/1812-Frenchtown/1813-Ft. Meigs/1813-2nd Amherstburg/1813 & Thames/1813 **with Tecumseh**, Treaty 1817

1528.**Skunk aka Sekakwa**[120] – Kishpoko born about 1755 OH-died after 1791 - Point Pleasant/74-75-78, raiding KY-VA-OH/77-81, Crawford/82, raiding Ohio River valley/88-89, Harmar/90 & St. Clair/91

1529.Sleeping Wolf – Kishpoko born about 1760 KY-died after 1794 - raiding KY-VA-OH/77-81, Point Pleasant/78, Boonesboro/78, Blue Licks/82, Crawford/82, raiding Ohio River valley/88-92, Blue Jacket War/77-94

1530. Sloan, Margaret Rogers – wife 2nd 1835 St. Lois MO of **Thomas Sloan** white born 1809 NJ-died after 1870 NE, mother of William Edward Slaon/1847,
Arteminia Sloan/1848, John Sloan/1849, Elizabeth Sloan/1851-all 1/8th Chalakatha-Mekoche-Pekowi-Omaha-Metis

1531. Slone, Barthena Brock - wife 1790 of **Thomas Slone** white born about 1770-died 1855 KY, mother of William Henry Slone/91, Thomas Slone Jr/93, Rebecca Slone/95, Nancy Slone/97, child/99, child/1801, Elizabeth Slone/1803, children/04-09, Mary Polly Slone/1810, Lavina Slone/1814, Jane Slone/1820, Barthena Slone/1822, Arra Slone/1824 & Samuel Slone/1828-all 3/64th Chalakatha-**Cherokee**-Metis

1532. Small Loud Voice – Pekowi born about 1730 AL-died after 1772 - wife about 1745 PA of **Pekowi Man**/24, widow in 1772

1533. Small Wolf – adopted-Delaware born about 1735 PA-died after 1770 - Cornstalk War/55-70, French-Indian War/55-63, Braddock/55, raiding NewShenandoah River valleys/55, raiding PA/55-56, raiding Ohio-New River valleys/58, Pontiac War/62-66, Bushy Run/63, raiding New-Greenbrier-Jackson River valleys/63, husband 1755 OH of **Pekowi Woman**/39, children unknown

1534. Smiling Face – Chalakatha born about 1760 OH-died after 1785 - wife about 1775 OH of **Chalakatha Man**/55, widowed at Crawford/82

1535. Smith, Ann - 1/2 Chalakatha-Metis born about 1759 OH-died after 1804 Gallia Co OH - daughter of **John Smith**/30-adopted-Irish & **Wabethe Otter**/43, living on Sciota River OH before 1774, wife 1774 OH of **John Ewing**/47adopted white, mother of William Ewing/75, Susanna Ewing/76, Andrew Ewing/77, John Smith Ewing/78, Elizabeth Ewing/79, Nancy Ann Ewing/80, Jeanette Ewing/81, Sarah Ewing/82, Lydia Ewing/83 & Samuel Ewing/84-all 1/4th Chalakatha-Metis

1536. Smith, Archilla – 7/64th Chalakatha-**Cherokee**-Metis born 1784-died by hanging 1841 – son of **Cabin Smith**-Cherokee & **Older Daughter of Great Eagle Carpenter**/49, husband by 1816 of **Agnes Fields**/94-9/64th Chalakatha-Kishpoko-Black-Cherokee-Metis, father of Rachel Smith/1820, Arthur Smith/1826, Elizabeth Smith/1830, John Smith/1832, Charles Smith/1834, Samuel Houston Smith/1836 & Eliza Smith/1838-all 1/8th Chalakatha-Kishpoko-Black-Cherokee-Metis

1537. Smith, Dorcas – 19/64th Chalakatha-Pekowi-**Cherokee**-Metis born about 1793-died after 1819 - daughter of **Polly Rising Fawn**/75 & **John Smith**/70-Cherokee, Red Paint Clan Cherokee, wife 1810 of **John Sanders**/78-23/64th

Chalakatha-Mekoche-Cherokee-Metis, mother **with Sanders** of Agnes Sanders/1810, Edward Sanders/1811, David Sanders/1812, twins Isaac & Benjamin Sanders/1813, Robert Sanders/1814, Elizabeth Sanders (2)/1815, Alexander Sanders/1817, twins Moses & Charles Sanders/1818 & Margaret Sanders/1819-all 21/64th Chalakatha-Mekoche-Pekowi-Cherokee-Metis

1538. Smith, Hannah – Chalakatha born about 1755-died about 1824 VA/WV - wife about 1770 of **Benjamin Smith**-white born about 1750-died before 1824 VA, may have come to WV-Kanawha valley with children, mother of David Smith/70, Aaron Smith/72, Jemima Smith/75 & Benjamin Smith Jr/80-all 1/2 Chalakatha-Metis

1539. Smith, Jemima - 1/2 Chalakatha-Metis born about 1775 VA-died after 1825-likely WV - daughter of **Hannah Chalakatha**/55 & **Benjamin Smith**/50white, wife 1st 1795 Botetourt Co VA of **John Green**/75, 2nd 1820 WV of **Mr. Dawson**/75-Shawnee-Metis, mother **with John** of Catherine Green/96, Sarah Green/97, Hannah Green/99, Margaret Green/1800, Elizabeth Green/1805, Edward Green/1808 & Miranda Green/1818-all ½ Chalakatha-Pekowi-**Cherokee**-Metis

1540. Smith, Mary - 1/2 Chalakatha-Metis born about 1772 OH-died after 1815 - daughter of **John Smith (1)**/30-adopted Irish & **Wabethe Otter**/43, living on Sciota River OH before 1774, wife about 1790 OH of **William Barbee**-white born about 1770-died before 1815, mother of William BarbeeJr/91, Sarah Barbee/93, Nancy Barbee/94, Susanna Barbee/95, Mary Barbee/99, Lucy Barbee/1800 & Melinda Barbee/1803-all 1/4th Chalakatha-Metis

1541. Smoking Fire – adopted-Cayuga-Metis born about 1720-died after 1760 - daughter of **Cayuga Woman** & **White Man**, wife about 1735 of **Mekoche Man**/15, widow 1760, mother of several 1/2 Mekoche-Cayuga-Metis children/35-60

1542. Snake aka **Peteasuva**-Petasue-Petayo-Petaza - adopted-Wyandot born about 1740-died after 1794 - Cornstalk War/58-77, raiding Ohio-New River valleys/58, Pontiac War/62-66, Bushy Run/63, raiding New-Greenbrier-Jackson River valleys/63, Point Pleasant/74-78, raiding KY-VA-OH/77-81, Crawford/82, raiding Ohio River valley/88-92, Blue Jacket War/77-94, Council Detroit Apr. 1781, Jan. 1783, July 1783, Council Miami Oct. 1792, Grand Council Sept. 1792, husband by 1770 of **Mekoche Woman**/50, father of Timothy Snake/70 & James Snake/75-both 1/2 Mekoche-Wyandot

1543. Snake, James - 1/2 Mekoche-Wyandot born about 1775 OH-died after 1832 - son of **Snake-Peteasuva**/40-Wyandot & **Mekoche Woman**/50, Fallen

Timber/94, raiding OH-KY-VA/95-1810, Prophet's Town/1811, Brownstown/1812-Monguagon/1812-1st Amherstburg/1812-Frenchtown/1813-Ft. Meigs/1813-2nd Amherstburg/1813 & Thames/1813 **with Tecumseh**, wife & children unknown

1544. Snake, John – Mekoche born about 1750 OH-died after 1781 - son of **Big Snake**/20 & **Mekoche Woman**/25, a Mekoche warrior, Cornstalk War/6877, raiding Ohio-Little Kanawha-Big Sandy-New River valleys/72, Point Pleasant/74-78, Blue Jacket War/77-81, raiding KY-VA-OH/77-81, Boonesboro/78, nephew of **Helizikinopo Cornstalk**/15, wife & children unknown

1545. Snake, Thomas – Mekoche born about 1755 OH-died after 1781 - son of **Big Snake**/20 & **Mekoche Woman**/25, a Mekoche warrior, Cornstalk War/7277, raiding Ohio-New-Little Kanawha-Big Sandy River valleys/72, Point Pleasant/74-78, Blue Jacket War/77-81, raiding KY-VA-OH/77-81, Boonesboro/78, nephew of **Helizikinopo Cornstalk**/15, wife & children unknown

1546. Snake, Timothy aka **Timootha** - 1/2 Mekoche-Wyandot born about 1770 OH-died after 1857 - son of **Snake-Peteasuva**/40-Wyandot & **Mekoche Woman**/50, raiding Ohio River valley/88-92, Blue Jacket War/88-94, raiding OH-KY-VA/95-1810, Prophet's Town/1811, Brownstown/1812-Monguagon/1812-1st Amherstburg/1812-Frenchtown/1813-Ft. Meigs/1813-2nd Amherstburg/1813 & Thames/1813 **with Tecumseh**, wife & children unknown

1547. Snapping Turtle – Chalakatha born about 1740 PA-died after 1774 – Cornstalk War/58-74, raiding Ohio-New River valleys/58, Pontiac War/62-66, Bushy Run/63, raiding New-Greenbrier-Jackson River valleys/63, raiding OhioNew-Big Sandy-Little Kanawha River valleys/72, Point Pleasant/74

1548. Snidow, Joshua - adopted-white born about 1764-died after 1812 - captured 1774 WV with brother **Theopilus Snidow**/63-returned to whites 1795, Blue Jacket War/82-94, Crawford/82, raiding Ohio River valley/88-92, husband about 1784 OH of **Chalakatha Woman**/68, father of several 1/2 Chalakatha-Metis children/85-95

1549. Snidow, Theopilus - adopted-white born about 1763-died after 1812 - captured 1774 WV with brother **Joshua Snidow**/64-returned to whites 1795, Blue Jacket War/79-94, Crawford/82, raiding Ohio River valley/88-92, husband about 1783 OH of **Chalakatha Woman**/68, father of several 1/2 Chalakatha-Metis children/84-95

1550. **Snow Falling aka Saisaigonokwe**[121]-Josephete Morandiere - 1/2

Kishpoko-**Ottawa** born about 1780 MI-died after 1820 - daughter of **Brother of Kitchibashigigan**-Ottawa & **Kishpoko Woman**, niece & adopted daughter of **Kitchibashigigan**/40-Ottawa Chief, close relative/same clan (Panther) as **Tecumseh**, wife before 1800 of **Etienne Augustin Robert de la Morandiere**/80-Chippewa-Metis, children unknown

1551. Snow on Flowers – Chalakatha born before 1730 PA-died after 1774 - wife about 1745 PA of **Chalakatha Man**/25, widow in 1774

1552. **Something Round aka Wawilaway**[122] -**Waweelaway** – Chalakatha born about 1750 OH-**murdered** 1804 OH – Cornstalk War/68-77, raiding OhioNew-Little Kanawha-Big Sandy River valleys/72, Point Pleasant/74-75-78, Blue Jacket War/77-94, raiding KY-VA-OH/77-81, Crawford/82, raiding Ohio River valley/88-92, **murdered** by whites

1553. Sonataiowaneh aka Sonataeeowaneh – Chalakatha born about 1710 PAdied about 1758 (epidemic?) - raiding PA/40, a **Chalakatha Chief** in OH by 1748, French-Indian War/54-57, Braddock/55, raiding New-Shenandoah River valleys/55, raiding PA/55-56, raiding Ohio-New River valleys/58

1554. Songo – Kishpoko born about 1775 OH-died after 1820 - wife about 1790 OH of **Kishpoko Man**/70, widow in 1820

1555. Sonicooie, Sugi Hop aka Daughter of Attakullakulla - wife 1763 TN of **Sonicooie (1)**-Cherokee born 1743 (TN-AL?)-died after 1770 (TN-AL?), mother of Susannah Sonicooie/63, Young Sonicooie/65, Nancy Sonicooie/68-all 1/4th Chalakatha-Thawikila-Creek-Cherokee

1556. Sontonegoo - adopted-Mohawk born about 1760 (OH?)-died after 1792 - daughter of **Cookoocheee**/45 & **Cokundiawthah**/40, sister of **Black Loon**/62, **White Loon**/64 & **Wapunno**/66-all adopted Mohawk, adopted sister 1792-93 (6 months) of **Oliver Spencer**-white, wife 1st about 1776 of **Simon Girty**/41-white(adopted Seneca), 2nd before 1785 of **George Ironside**/60-adopted white, 3rd 1792 of **Isaac Peters**/60-adopted-Delaware, mother **with Girty** of Simon Girty Jr aka Simon Peters/76 & Quasay Girty/78-both 1/2 Mohawk-Metis, children/85-91 **with Ironside** unknown, any children **with Peters** unknown

1557. Sore Knee – Kishpoko born about 1740 OH-died after 1774 - crippled in one leg by wound, Cornstalk War/58-74, raiding Ohio-New River valleys/58, Pontiac War/62-66, Bushy Run/63, raiding New-Greenbrier-Jackson River valleys/63, raiding Ohio-New-Little Kanawha-Big Sandy River valleys/72, Point Pleasant/74

1558. Sour Mouth - 1/2 Mekoche-Metis born about 1745 OH-died after 1774 - son of **Mekoche Man** & **Adopted White Woman**/(25?), returned to whitesreturned to tribe 1765, Cornstalk War/68-74, raiding Ohio-Little Kanawha-Big Sandy-New River valleys/72, Point Pleasant/74, husband 1765 OH of **Mekoche Woman**/50, father of some 3/4th Mekoche-Metis children/65-74

1559. Sour Mush, Charley aka **Tsali**-Charley-Tsali Greenwood – 15/64th Chalakatha-Pekowi-Kishpoko-Black-**Cherokee**-Metis born 1760 Chota TN**executed by whites** 1839 - son of **John Sour Mush Greenwood**/28 & **Long Hair Woman**/32, **Chief of Running Water** (Shawnee) village 1792, Council Coyatee 1792, a Chickamaugua, leader of a band of the "wild Indians" (Shawnee & cherokee mix?) that refused to be forced to OK, **executed by U.S. troops** 1839 with 4 sons for refusal to move west, husband about 1st 1780 Running Water TN of **Kishpoko Woman**/65, 2nd 1800 Running Water TN of **White Woman**/80, father **with Kishpoko** of nine 39/64th Kishpoko-Chalakatha-Pekowi-BlackCherokee-Metis children/80-1800, **with White Woman** of eight 7/64th Chalakatha-Pekowi-Kishpoko-Black-Cherokee-Metis children/1800-20

1560. Sour Plum - 1/2 Chalakatha-Metis born about 1740 PA-died after 1774 - son of **Chalakatha Man** & **Adopted White Woman**, Cornstalk War/58-74, raiding Ohio-New River valleys/58, Pontiac War/62-66, Bushy Run/62, raiding New-Jackson-Greenbrier River valleys/63, raiding Ohio-Little Kanawha-Big Sandy-New River valleys/72, raiding Ohio River valley/74 **with Chief Logan**, Point Pleasant/74, fled with family to western OH/eastern IN village to avoid returning to whites 1765, husband 1760 OH of **Chalakatha Woman**/45, father of several 3/4th Chalakatha-Metis children/61-74

1561. Sour Plums - 1/2 Mekoche-Metis born about 1750 OH-died after 1765 - daughter of **Adopted White Woman**/ (25?) & **Mekoche Man**, returned to whites-returned to tribe 1765, wife 1765 OH of **Mekoche Man**/44, children unknown

1562. Southern Man – adopted-Creek born about 1740 AL-died after 1777 - raiding Ohio-New River valleys/58, Pontiac War/62-66, Bushy Run/63, raiding New-Jackson-Greenbrier River valleys/63, raiding Ohio-Big Sandy-Little Kanawha-New River valleys/72, Point Pleasant/74, raiding KY-OH-VA/77, lived **with OH-KY Shawnee**, husband about 1760 KY of **Chalakatha Woman**/45, children unknown

1563. Sowanowane – Chalakatha born about 1740 PA-died after 1774 – Cornstalk War/58-74, raiding Ohio-New River valleys/58, Pontiac War/62-66, Bushy Run/63, raiding New-Greenbrier-Jackson River valleys/63, raiding Ohio-

New-Big Sandy-Little Kanawha River valleys/72, Point Pleasant/74

1564. Sowards, Esther – 15/32nd Chalakatha-Mekoche-Metis born 1781-died 1847 - daughter of **Esther Cornstalk**/51 & **Thomas Sowards**/46-white, granddaughter of **Cornstalk**/10, wife 1st 1801 of **Robert Carlisle**/76-white, 2nd 1830 of **Herman Hatfield**/90-white, mother **with Carlisle** of Frances Carlisle/1805-15/64th Chalakatha-Mekoche-Metis

1565. Sowards, Griffin aka Griffin Tipsword- Griffin Sword- Griffin Tipscord – 15/32nd Chalakatha-Mekoche-Metis born 1773-died 1845 IL - son of **Esther Cornstalk**/51 & **Thomas Sowards**/46-white, grandson of **Cornstalk**/10, husband 1790 of **Ruth Abbott**/74-1/2 Chalakatha-Metis, father of Andrew Jackson Sowards-Tipsword/99, Douglas Sowards-Tipsword/1800, Miliston Sowards-Tipsword/1801, John Adams Sowards-Tipsword/1803, Isaac Sowards-Tipsword/1805, Desha Sowards-Tipsword/1807, Rebecca Sowards-Tipsword/1809, Thomas Sowards-Tipsword/1814, Carlin Sowards-Tipsword/1815-all 31/64th Chalakatha-Mekoche-Metis

1566. Spamaghelbee – Mekoche born about 1785 OH-died after 1817 - 2nd wife before 1805 of **Capt. John Logan** aka **Big Horn**/74, a widow at Wapaghonettat 1817, Treaty 1817, mother of James Logan/1805-15/16th Mekoche-Kishpoko-Pekowi-Creek-Metis, step-mother of Red Leaf/90, Aqueshka/95 & Cagashee/96

1567. Sparks, Frances Nash – (former adopted white) 1st wife about 1782 of **Richard Sparks Shawunte Sparks**/57-adopted white, mother of Mary Polly Sparks/83 (married a Wall), Jesse Sparks/85, Catherine Sparks/88 (married a McClure), Charity Sparks/90 (married a Budd & a Cooper & a Printy), Elizabeth Sparks/92 (married a Breazeale) & Eleanor Sparks/94 (married a Printy)-all white (but with Shawnee connections through adoption at least)

1568. Sparks, John - adopted-white born about 1760-**killed** 1782 KY - brother of **Richard Shawtunte Sparks**/57, captured about 1770-never returned, adopted son 1768 of **Puckenshinwa**/35, adopted brother of **Tecumseh**/68, then 1774 of **Black Fish**/25, raiding OH-KY-VA/77-81, Boonesboro/78, Blue Licks/82, Crawford/82, killed in KY raid, husband about 1780 OH of **Chalakatha Woman**/65, father of a couple of 1/2 Chalakatha-Metis children/81-82, including Richard Sparks (2)/81-1/2 Chalakatha-Metis

1569. Sparks, Richard (1) aka **Shawtunte** - adopted-white born about 1757 N.J.-died 1813 MS - brother of **John Sparks**/60, captured about 1762-returned to whites by Treaty of Camp Charlotte 1775, **with U.S. Army-**Revolution-scout**with Crawford**-St. Clair, **with Piomingo's Chickasaw scouts**-St. Clair/91-with U.S. Army-Fallen Timber/94, Capt.-**in U.S. Army-**War 1812-Creek

War/1813, later Colonel, 1st U.S. "official" to enter OK territory, adopted son 1768 of **Puckenshinwa**/35, adopted brother of **Tecumseh**/68, then 1774 of **Black Fish**/25, husband 1st before 1783 of **Francis Nash**/60-adopted white, 2nd 1797 of
Ruth Sevier/83-white (daughter of Governor John Sevier), father **with Nash** of Mary Polly Sparks/83-(Wall), Jesse Sparks/85, Catherine Sparks/88-(McClure), Charity Saprks/90-Budd-Cooper-Printy, Elizabeth Sparks/92-(Breazeale), Eleanor Sparks/94-(Printy)-white, many of these names have Native connections & will be researched as much as possible

1570. Sparks, Richard (2) - 1/2 Chalakatha-Metis born about 1781 OH-died after 1830 - son of **John Sparks**/60-adopted white & **Chalakatha Woman**/70 associated **with the Shawnee** for most of his life, husband about 1802 (OH?) of
Chalakatha Woman/87, children unknown but named Sparks

1571. Sparks, Ruth Sevier - white born about 1780 TN-died 1824 KY - daughter of **Catherine Sherrill**/45 & **Governor John Sevier**/45-white, 2nd wife 1797 of **Richard Shawtunte Sparks**/57-white-adopted Shawnee, (wife 2nd 1816 of **Daniel Vertner**-white born 1785-died after 1824), mother **with Sparks** of Catherine/98, Polly/1800, Elizabeth/1802, Eleanor/1804, Charity Sparks/1806 white (note-all these names shared with Richard's children by Frances Nash)

1572. Spear Warrior aka **Cithiskananothe**[123] – Chalakatha born about 1750 OH-died after 1781 - Cornstalk War/68-77, raiding Ohio-New-Little Kanawha-Big Sandy River valleys/72, Point Pleasant/74-78, raiding KY-VA-OH/77-81, Blue Jacket War/77-81

1573. Spelman, Sabra - 1/2 Pekowi-Metis born about 1735 PA-died after 1757 - daughter of **Elder Daughter of Poxinosa**/18-Pekowi & **Peter Spelman** aka Ooligasha-Owligascho/05-adopted German, a Pekowi woman, husband & children unknown

1574. Spicer, Susan Francis - 1st cousin of **Tecumseh**/68, great-niece of **Cornstalk**/10, wife 1800 of **Thomas Spicer**/83-1/2 Seneca-Metis, mother of Mary Ann Francis aka Mary Ann Spicer/1801 & Elizabeth Walah Spicer/1805 both 15/64th Chalakatha-Mekoche-Kishpoko-Creek-**Seneca**-Metis

1575. Split Log aka Sounehooway-Toontroontora-Thomas Splitlog - Wyandot born about 1755 OH-died 1838 - Point Pleasant/74, Crawford/82, raiding Ohio River valley/88-92, Blue Jacket War/77-94, raiding OH-KY-VA/95-10, Prophet's

Town/1811, Brownstown/1812-Monguagon/1812-1st Amherstburg/1812Frenchtown/1813-Ft. Meigs/1813-2nd Amherstburg/1813 & Thames/1813 **with**

Tecumseh, succeeded **Roundhead** as **Head Chief** of Wyandots 1816, Treaty 1817, brother in law of **Tecumseh**, son in law of **Metheotashe**, husband about 1785 OH of **Vocemassussia Puckenshinwa**/70, divorced before 1792, father with **Vocemassussia** of some unknown 3/8th Kishpoko-Pekowi-Creek-Wyandot-Metis children/85-90 names unknown

1576. Spotted Man – adopted-1/2 Mohawk-Black born about 1750 OH-died after 1810 - son of **Mohawk Man** & adopted **Black Woman**, lived with the Mingo in OH, Cornstalk War/68-77, raiding Ohio River valley **with Chief Logan**/74, raiding PA-OH-KY-VA/75-81, Crawford/82, Blue Jacket War/77-94, moved to MO 1795, living in Apple Creek MO 1810, husband about 1770 OH of **Thawikila Woman**/55, father of several 1/2 Thawikila-Mohawk-Black children/70-1800

1577. Spring Grass – Thawikila born about 1735 (AL?)-died after 1764 - wife about 1750 OH of **Thawikila Man**/30, widow in 1764, mother of several children/50-64

1578. Springston, Elizabeth Scott (Vann-Adair-Burgess-Shepherd) - wife 5th 1802 of **Edward Springston**-Cherokee-Metis born about 1760-died after 1803 (brother of John Springston/62), mother of Edley Springston/1802 & Jennie Springston/1803- both 1/32nd Chalakatha-Thawikila-Creek-**Cherokee**-Metis

1579. Springston, Nancy Drumgoole (Doublehead) aka Nannie the Pain - wife 2nd 1810 TN of **John Springston**-Cherokee-Metis born about 1762-died after 1814 (brother of **Edward Springston**/60), mother of Isaac Springston/1811 & Anderson Springston/1814-both 3/64th Chalakatha-Pekowi-**Cherokee**-Metis

1580. Spybuck aka Saukothkaw-Tahkaska-Spybuck Chieska-Spybuck Moluntha – 9/16th Mekoche-Chalakatha-Creek-Metis born about 1780 OH-died after 1831 - son of **Polly Butler**/65 & **Chieska Moluntha**/55, a Chalakatha warrior, grandson of **Moluntha**/10, great-nephew of **Cornstalk**/10, delegate to D.C. 1802 with **Wayweleapee**/60, **John Perry**/75, **Quaskee Black Hoof**/60, **Joseph Parks**/90 & **Francois Duchoquet**/66, scout-**with U.S. Army**-War 1812-Thames/1813, Treaty 1817, 1831, a warrior at Hog Creek & Wapaghonettat 1832, husband 1795 OH of **Daughter of Col. Barbee**/80-white, father of George Spy Buck/96, Daughter of Spy Buck/98, John Spy Buck/1802 & Young Spy Buck/1806-all 9/32nd Mekoche-Chalakatha-Creek-Metis

1581.Spy Buck, Young – 9/32nd Mekoche-Chalakatha-Creek-Metis born about 1806 OH-died after 1840 - son of **Spy Buck Moluntha**/80 & **Daughter of Col. Barbee**/80-white, Joseph Parks Co-**with U.S. Army**-Seminole War/1837 with brother John Spybuck/1802, raiding Apaches 1840 with **James Kirker, Francois Duchouquet (2) & Pegleg Smith**, wife & children unknown

1582.Squesenau aka Skwesenaw – Chalakatha born about 1770 OH-died after 1817 - raiding Ohio River valley/88-92, Blue Jacket War/88-94, no part in War 1812, a warrior at Lewistown 1817, Treaty 1817

1583.**Squirrel aka Anequepi**[124] – Thawikila born about 1750 OH-died after 1832 – Cornstalk War/68-77, raiding New-Little Kanawha-Big Sandy-Ohio River valleys/72, Point Pleasant/74-78, Blue Jacket War/77-94, raiding KY-VAOH/77-81, Crawford/82, wounded at Benjamin Logan's raid/86, raiding Ohio River valley/88-92, scout-**with U.S. Army**-War 1812, captured by British at Ft. Meigs/1813, **released by Tecumseh**, husband 1775 of **Daughter of Black Hoof**/61, father of James Squirrel/1800

1584.St. Jean, Jean - 1/2 Pekowi-Metis born about 1720 IL-died after 1757 - son of **Pekowi Woman** & **Mr. St. John**-Coureur deBois, raiding PA/40, FrenchIndian War/54-57, Braddock/55, raiding New-Shenandoah River valleys/55, husband about 1740 of **Pekowi Woman**/25, children unknown

1585.Standing Bird – Kishpoko born about 1765 OH-died after 1795 - wife about 1780 OH of **Kishpoko Man**/59, widowed at Fallen Timber/94

1586.Standing Corn – Chalakatha born before 1700 OH-died after 1740 - living in PA by 1730, raiding PA/40

1587.Standing Crane – Thawikila born about 1770 OH-died after 1792 - raiding Ohio River valley/88-92, Blue Jacket War/87-92

1588.Standing Stone – adopted-Wyandot born about 1770 OH-died 1850 - raiding Ohio River valley/88-92, Blue Jacket War/87-94, scout-**with U.S. Army**War 1812-Thames/1813, husband about 1790 OH of **Mekoche Woman**/84

1589.Stands and Shoots aka **LeTendrendresse** - 1/2 Pekowi-Metis born about 1715 (IL?)-died after 1755 - son of **Pekowi Woman** & **Coureur deBois**, raiding PA/40, French-Indian War/54, Braddock/55, raiding New-Shenandoah River valleys/55, husband about 1735 (IN?) of **Mekoche Woman**/20

1590.**Stands Firm aka Wasegoboah**[125] - adopted-Chippewa-Metis born about 1755 (MI?)-**killed** Thames 1813 - son of **White Sturgeon-Namegousse**/30Chippewa, brother of **Yellow Cloud-Sawacota**/60 & **Mad**

Sturgeon/65Chippewa, adopted Chalakatha, Cornstalk War/72-77, raiding Ohio-Little Kanawha-Big Sandy-New River valleys/72, Point Pleasant/74-75-78, Blue Jacket War/77-94, Boonesboro/78, raiding KY-VA-OH/77-81, Crawford/82, Council Miami Jan. 1786, raiding Ohio River valley/88-92, Prophet's Town/1811, Brownstown/1812-Monguagon/1812-1st Amherstburg/1812-Frenchtown/1813-Ft. Meigs/1813-2nd Amherstburg/1813 & **killed at Thames/13 at the side of brother in law Tecumseh**, 2nd husband 1775 OH of **Tecumapease**/58, father of LaNannette/80-3/8th Kishpoko-Pekowi-Chippewa-Creek-Metis

1591. Stands in the Water – Chalakatha born about 1755 OH-died about 1843 KS - a Chalakatha warrior, raiding Ohio-Little Kanawha-Big Sandy-New River valleys/72, Point Pleasant/74-78, raiding KY-VA-OH/77-81, Crawford/82, raiding Ohio River valley/88-92, Blue Jacket War/77-94, moved to KS about 1826, son in law of **White Wolf-John Ward**/30-adopted white, husband about 1775 OH of **Sutawanee Ward**/60-1/2 Chalakatha-Metis, children unknown

1592. Stands Under Tree – Mekoche born about 1762 OH-died after 1782 - raiding Ohio-New River valleys/80-81, Crawford/82

1593. Starniker – Shawano born about 1710 VA-died after 1756 – **with Colonial Army**-French-Indian War/54-56, scout **for Andrew Lewis** 1756

1594. Starr, Moses - 1/4th Mekoche-Metis born 1778-died after 1798 - son of **Miss Sanders**/49 & **Arthur Starr**/44-Irish, husband 1798 of **Mary Dean**/83white, father of Alexander Starr/1801, Ellis Sanders Starr/1802 & John Starr/1803-all 1/8th Mekoche-Metis

1595. Starr, Nancy Harlan – Wolf Clan **Cherokee**, wife 1794 of **Caleb Starr**white born about 1764 PA-died 1848 OK-(nephew of **Arthur Starr**/44), mother of Ezekial Starr/1794, Mary Pauline Starr/95, James Nagisi Starr/96, Ruth Starr/99, Sarah Starr/1804, Thomas Starr/1805, George Harlan/1806, Joseph McMinn Starr/1808, Rachel Starr/1810, Nancy Starr/1811, Deborah Starr/1817 & Ellis Starr/1820-all 1/64th Chalakatha-Cherokee-Metis

1596. Stevens, Frank aka Francis Stevens - adopted-white born about 1700died after 1734 - trading on Allegheny River by 1734, husband about 1729 (PAMD-WV?) of **Pekowi Woman**/14, father of Frank Stevens Jr/30 & John Stevens/32-both 1/2 Pekowi-Metis

1597. Stewert, Anna – 1/8th Pekowi-Kishpoko-Metis born 1802 WV-died 1872 IN – daughter of **Elizabeth Stewert**/86 & **Unknown Man**, came to OH 1804 **with Stewert family**, great-granddaughter of **Blue Jacket**, wife 1818 OH of **Samuel Miranda**/1800-11/16th Pekowi-Seneca-Metis

1598. Stewert, Elizabeth - 1/4th Pekowi-Kishpoko-Metis born about 1786 WV died after 1820 - daughter of **Nancy Blue Jacket Moore**/65 & **James Stewert**/65-white, granddaughter of **Blue Jacket**/35, unmarried 1801 WV of **Unknown Man**, wife 1809 OH of **Thomas Miranda**/81-3/8th Pekowi-SenecaMetis, mother **with Unknown** of Anna Stewert/1802-1/8th Pekowi-Kishpoko-Metis, children **with Miranda** unknown

1599. Stewert, Nancy Moore aka Nancy Blue Jacket - wife about 1785 WV of **James Stewert**-white born 1765-died 1830 Logan Co OH, moved to OH 1804, living at Lewistown 1817, mother of Elizabeth Stewert/86, Henry Stewert/88, Margaret Stewert/90, John Stewert/92 & Sarah Ann Stewert/94-all 1/4th Pekowi-Kishpoko-Metis

1600. Stewert, Sarah Ann - 1/4th Pekowi-Kishpoko-Metis born about 1794 WV-died after 1812 - daughter of **Nancy Moore Blue Jacket Moore**/65 & **James Stewert**/65-white, granddaughter of **Blue Jacket**/35, wife 1812 OH of **Jonathan Miranda**/84-3/8th Pekowi-Seneca-Metis, children unknown

1601. Stone Fish – Pekowi born about 1740 (OH?)-died after 1785 – Cornstalk War/58-77, raiding Ohio-New River valleys/58, Pontiac War/62-66, Bushy Run/63, raiding New-Greenbrier-Jackson River valleys/63, raiding Ohio-NewLittle Kanawha-Big Sandy River valleys/72, Point Pleasant/74-75, Blue Jacket War/77-82, husband 1st 1760 of **Pekowi Woman**/45, 2nd 1779 OH of **Delaware Woman**/62, children/60-78 **with Pekowi** unknown, father **with Delaware** of Young Stone Fish/80-1/2 Pekowi-Delaware

1602. Stone Fish, Young – ½ Pekowi-Delaware born about 1780 OH-died 1875 KS – son of **Stone Fish**/40 & **Delaware Woman**, Prophet's Town/1811, Brownstown/1812-Monguagon/1812-1st Amherstburg/1812-Frenchtown/1813-Ft. Meigs/1813-2nd Amherstburg/1813 & Thames/1813 **with Tecumseh**, moved to CAN 1815, returned to OH 1825, moved to KS with **Prophet** & **Paukeesaa** 1826, when he died he was the last surviving supporter of **Tecumseh**, husband 1800 OH of **Kishpoko Woman**/84, children unknown

1603. Stoneking, Judith – Pekowi-Chalakatha born 1725 PA-died after 1755 - daughter of **Stone King**/1700 & **Pekowi Woman**/05, wife 1740 PA of **Thomas Coyle**/20-adopted white, mother of Margaret Coyle/40, George Coyle/45 & Thomas Coyle Jr/50-all 1/2 Pekowi-Chalakatha-Metis

1604. Stood in Front – adopted-Delaware born about 1750 (OH?)-died after 1794 – Cornstalk War/72-77, raiding Ohio-Little Kanawha-Big Sandy-New River valleys/72, Point Pleasant/74-75-78, Blue Jacket War/77-94, raiding KY-

VA-OH/77-81, Crawford/82, raiding Ohio River valley/88-92, husband about 1770 OH of **Chalakatha Woman**/55, father of several 1/2 Chalakatha-Delaware children/70-94

1605. Stookey, Jacob – adopted-white-(**Wyandot**) born about 1740-died after 1814 - adopted before 1755-avoided returns/65-75-95, returned to whites 1802, Cornstalk War/58-77, raiding Ohio-New River valleys/58, Pontiac War/62-66, Bushy Run/63, raiding New-Greenbrier-Jackson River valleys/63, raiding Ohio-Little Kanawha-Big Sandy-New River valleys/72, Point Pleasant/74-75, blue Jacket War/77-94, raiding KY-OH-VA/77-81, Point Pleasant/78, Boonesboro/78, Crawford/82, raiding Ohio River valley/88-92, Fallen Timber/94, Treaty 1814, husband 1st about 1760 OH of **Chalakatha Woman**/45, 2nd about 1790 OH of **Wyandot Woman**/75, father of numerous 1/2 Chalakatha-Metis children/60-90, father of some 1/2 Wyandot-Metis children/90-1814

1606. Straight Man aka **Pahtecoosawa** – Chalakatha born about 1780 OH-died after 1832 - raiding OH-VA-KY/99-1810, Prophet's Town/1811, **left Tecumseh** after Prophet's Town, moved to KS 1832

1607. **Straight Tail aka Meaurroway**[126] - Pekowi born about 1630 OH-died about 1710 PA - a **Pekowi Chief** before 1670, succeeded as **Head Pekowi Chief** 1700 by Pheasant-Kakawatchekee/1680, husband 1650 of **Pekowi Woman**/35, grandfather (through Opessa) of **Snow White Opessa**/1695, **Tecoomteh Opessa**/1700, **Loyparcoweh Opessa**/05 & **Pride Opessa**/10, grandfather (through Sewatha) of **Peter Chartier**/1690, great-grandfather (through Loyparkoweh) of **Metheotashe**/40 & great-grandfather (through Pride) of **Blue Jacket**/35 & **Red Pole**/40, great-great-grandfather of **Tecumseh**/68, father of Sewatha/1660, Snow White (1)/1665, John White/1670, **Opessa**/1675

1608. Strikes Twice – adopted-Cayuga born about 1750 OH-died after 1791 – Cornstalk War/72-77, raiding Ohio-New-Little Kanawha-Big Sandy River valleys/72, raiding Ohio River valley/74 **with Chief Logan**, Point Pleasant/7475-78, Blue Jacket War/77-91, raiding KY-OH-VA/77-81, Crawford/82, raiding Ohio River valley/88-90, Harmar/90, St. Clair/91, husband about 1770 OH of **Kishpoko Woman**/55, father of several 1/2 Kishpoko-Cayuga children/70-91

1609. Strikes With Stick – Chalakatha born about 1720 PA-died after 1763 - wife about 1735 PA of **Chalakatha Man**/15, widow in 1763

1610. Striking Snake – Chalakatha born about 1720 PA-died after 1768 – Cornstalk War/55-68, French-Indian War/54-63, Braddock/55, raiding NewShenandoah River valleys/55, Pontiac War/62-66, Bushy Run/63, raiding New-Greenbrier-Jackson River valleys/63

1611. Striped Cat - Mekoche-(adopted-**Delaware**) born about 1750 OH-died after 1796 - wife about 1765 OH of **Delaware Man**/45, widow in 1796, children unknown

1612. Striped Snake - adopted-Delaware born about 1745 OH-died after 1796 - wife about 1760 OH of **Pekowi Man**/40, widow in 1796

1613. Strong Buffalo – adopted-Seneca born about 1740 OH-died after 1775 – Cornstalk War/55-74, Ohio-New River valleys/58, Pontiac War/62-66, Bushy Run/63, raiding New-Greenbrier-Jackson River valleys/63, raiding New-OhioLittle Kanawha-Big Sandy River valleys/72, raiding Ohio River valley/74 **with Chief Logan**, Point Pleasant/74-75, husband about 1760 OH of **Chalakatha Woman**/45

1614. Strong Neck – Kishpoko born about 1750 OH-**killed** 1790 OH – Cornstalk War/68-77, raiding Ohio-New-Little Kanawha-Big Sandy River valleys/72, Point Pleasant/74, Blue Jacket War/77-90, raiding KY-VA-OH/7781, Crawford/82, raiding Ohio River valley/88-90, **killed at Harmar**/90

1615. Strong, Jenny Jane Callahan - wife 1790 of **William S. Strong** white born about 1768 VA-died 1848 KY-(son of **Daniel Strong**-IRE), mother of Edward Strong/91, John Strong/93, Moses Strong/95, Thomas Strong/97, William Strong Jr/99, Mary Polly Strong/1803, Alexander Strong/1808, Isaac Strong/1810, Isabella Strong/1812 & Henry Harrison Strong/1814-all 3/64th Chalakatha-**Cherokee**-Metis

1616. Stuart, Bushyhead Oonodutu aka Donodutu-Bushyhead (3) - 3/64th Chalakatha-**Cherokee**-Metis born 1760 Great Tellico TN-died after 1835 OK - son of **Susannah Emory (1)**/44 & **Col. John Stuart**/30-white, Long Hair Clan Cherokee, **with U.S. Army-**Creek War/1813, husband 1st 1780 TN of **Cherokee Woman**/65, 2nd 1803 of **Nancy Gourd Foreman**/86-19/64th Chalakatha-Pekowi-Cherokee-Metis, children/80-1802 **with Cherokee** unknown, father **with Foreman** of Jesse Bushyhead/1804, Isaac Bushyhead/1808, George Bushyhead/1810, Nancy Otahki Bushyhead/1811, Charles Bird Bushyead/1814, Jacob Bushyhead/1816, Susan C. Bushyhead/1818-all 11/64th Chalakatha-Pekowi-Cherokee-Metis

1617. Succopanus – adopted-Seneca born before 1740 (OH?)-died about 1798 – Cornstalk War/58-77, raiding Ohio-New River valleys/58, Pontiac War/62-66, Bushy Run/63, raiding New-Greenbrier-Jackson River valleys/63, raiding OhioNew-Little Kanawha-Big Sandy River valleys/72, raiding Ohio River valley/74 **with Chief Logan**, Point Pleasant/74, raiding OH-KY-VA/75-81, Crawford/82, raiding Ohio River valley/88-92, Blue Jacket War/77-94, adopted father 1781 of **Jonathan Alder**/73-white, husband of **Winecheoh**/40-Kishpoko, father of Sally Succopanus/65, Mary Succopanus/67 & Hannah Succopanus/69-all 1/2 Kishpoko-Seneca

1618. Succopanus, Hannah (1) – ½ Kishpoko-**Seneca** born about 1769 OH died after 1855 KS - daughter of **Succopanus**/40-Seneca & **Winecheoh**/40 Kishpoko, sister of Sally/65 & Mary/67, adopted sister of **Jonathan Alder**/73 white, wife 1883 OH of **Ben Dickerson**/30-adopted white, mother of Hannah Succopanus (2)-Hannah Dickerson/84-1/4th Kishpoko-Seneca-Metis

1619. Succopanus, Hannah (2) aka Hannah Dickerson – 1/4th Kishpoko**Seneca**-Metis born 1784 OH-died after 1820 – daughter of **Hannah Succopanus**/70 & **Ben Dickerson**/30, wife 1812 OH of **Isaac Zane Jr**/80-Wyandot-Metis, mother of John Zane/1812, Isaac W. Zane/1815, Noah Zane/1818, Sarah Zane/1820-all 1/4th Kishpoko-Seneca-**Wyandot**-Metis

1620. Succopanus, Mary - 1/2 Kishpoko-Seneca born about 1767 OH-died after 1815 - daughter of **Succopanus**/40-Mingo & **Winecheoh**/40-Kishpoko, sister of **Sally**/65 & **Hannah**/69, adopted sister of **Jonathan Alder**/73-white, wife about 1785 OH of **John Lewis**/65-Chalakatha, no children

1621. Succopanus, Sally - 1/2 Kishpoko-Seneca born about 1765 OH-died after 1800 - daughter of **Succopanas**/40-Seneca & **Winecheoh**/40-Kishpoko, sister of **Mary**/67 & **Hannah**/69, adopted sister of **Jonathan Alder**/73-white, wife 1780 OH of **Chalakatha Man**/60-(a cousin of **John, George & Tom Lewis**-maybe a son of **Polly Kizer & Lewis' Uncle**), children unknown

1622. Succopanus, Winecheoh aka Winecho – Kishpoko born about 1740-died about 1792 - wife of **Succopanus**/40-Seneca, mother of Sally/65, Mary/67 & Hannah/69-all 1/2 Kishpoko-**Seneca**, adopted mother 1781 of Jonathan Alder/73 white

1623. Sugar – Thawikila born before 1750 OH-died after 1775 - wife about 1765 OH of **Thawikila Man**/44, widow in 1775

1624. Sugar Cone - 1/2 Kishpoko-Metis born about 1725 (IL?)-died after 1775 - daughter of **Kishpoko Woman & Coureur deBois**-white, wife about 1740 (IN?) of **Kishpoko Man**/21, widow in 1775

1625. **Sugar Tree aka Melassatequi-Melassatekwee**[127] – Mekoche born about 1730 OH-died after 1778 - wife about 1745 OH of **Mekoche Man**/25, widow in 1778, adopted mother of **Simon Kenton**-white

1626. Sumanavitch, Lucky aka Lucky Somenuvich[128]-Sonnovitch - 1/2

Chalakatha-Metis born about 1730 (PA?)-died after 1772 - son of **Chalakatha Woman** & **Slavic White Man**, Cornstalk War/55-72, French-Indian/54-63, Braddock/55, raiding New-Shenandoah River valleys/55, raiding Ohio-New River valleys/58, Pontiac War/62-66, Bushy Run/63, raiding New-JacksonGreenbrier River valleys/63, raiding Ohio-New-Little Kanawha-Big Sandy River valleys/72, husband about 1750 OH of **Chalakatha Woman**/35, children unknown

1627.   Sun King aka **Quetawah**-Kweetawah – Chalakatha born before 1770 OH-died after 1814 - raiding Ohio River valley/88-92, Little Turtle War/90-94, raiding KY-OH-VA/95-1810, Prophet's Town/1811, Brownstown/1812Monguagon/1812-1st Amherstburg/1812-Frenchtown/1813-Ft. Meigs/1813-2nd Amherstburg/1813 & Thames/1813 **with Tecumseh**, Treaty 1814

1628.   Sundial – ½ Thawikila-Creek born about 1750 AL-died after 1785 – daughter of **Thawikila Man** & **Creek Woman**, wife about 1765 OH of **Thawikila Man**/45, widow in 1785

1629.   Sunrise aka **Sowaget** – Chalakatha born about 1780 OH-died after 1817 – no part in War 1812, from Lewistown 1817, Treaty 1817

1630. Sutton, Benjamin - adopted-white born about 1735-died after 1780 - adopted 1740 (PA?), **traveled 1763 with White Eyes**-Delaware, journeyed down & up the Ohio-Missouri-Mississippi & other rivers, traveled west to the Rocky Mountains, traveled south to St. Augustine, visited among Shawnee, Delaware, Miami, Illinois, Chickasaw, Mandan & other tribes, husband about 1765 (OH/KY?) of **Pekowi Woman**/50, father of David Sutton/66, children/67-79, Elijah Sutton/80, Sarah Sutton/82-all 1/2 Pekowi-Metis

1631. Swamp Water aka Through the Swamp-Thick Swamp Water-Stands in the Swamp-Paughpi-Popee[129] – Kishpoko born about 1770 OH-died after 1826 (IN?) - raiding Ohio River valley/88-92, Fallen Timber/94, traveled/95-98 **with Tecumseh** (same clan-Panther), raiding OH-KY-VA/99-1810, Prophet's Town/1811, Brownstown/1812-Monguagon/1812-1st Amherstburg/1812Frenchtown/1813-Ft. Meigs/1813-2nd Amherstburg/1813 & Thames/1813 **with Tecumseh**, moved to CAN 1815, returned to OH 1826, moved to IN 1826 & lived among Miami, husband 1st 1790 OH of **Kishpoko Woman**/75, 2nd 1827 IN of **Miami Woman**/1810, children unknown (some connection with **Abraham Pope**/75-adopted white-maybe lived in same Miami village ?)

1632. Swapee aka Swappee – Mekoche born about 1770-died after 1817 - raiding Ohio River valley/88-92, Blue Jacket War/87-94, a warrior at Wapaghonettat 1817, Treaty 1817

1633. Swaunakou – Chalakatha born about 1780 OH-died after 1817 - raiding OH-KY-VA/99-1810, Prophet's Town/1811, Brownstown/1812-Monguagon/1812-1st Amherstburg/1812-Frenchtown/1813-Ft. Meigs/1813-2nd Amherstburg/1813 & Thames/1813 **with Tecumseh**, a warrior at Lewistown 1817, Treaty 1817

1634. Swift, John aka Jonathan Swift-George Swift - adopted-white born 1712 PA-died 1800 VA - trading in Ohio River valley before 1750, lived most of 1750-69 **with Ohio Shawnee**, except **with Colonial Army**- Braddock/55, mined silver & counterfeited English, French & Spanish coins 1761-69 in WV-KY-VA furnishing silver & coins for **Cornstalk**/10, himself & associates, assisted mainly by **John Monday**/25, **Joshua McClintock**/30 & **James Ireland**/40-all adopted whites (with Shawnee wives & Metis children), left for east coast 1769, imprisoned in ENG during Revolution, returned in 1790 but was unable to locate 16+ mines in drainages of the Kentucky-Big Sandy-Tug-Great Kanawha River valleys due to blindness, associated with **Dragging Canoe**, **John Watts Sr**, **Christopher Gist**, **Doublehead**, **Nathaniel Gist**, **Sam Blackburn**, Abram Flint, Herman Staley, Isaac Campbell, Shadrack Jefferson, Pierre St. Martin, Andrew Renound, Jeremiah Bates, Alexander Bartel, Henry Hazlitt, Moses Fletcher & Seth Montgomery-engraver, husband 1760 OH of **Elizabeth Cornstalk**/4415/16th Chalakatha-Mekoche-Metis, father of four 15/32nd Chalakatha-MekocheMetis children/60-66 names unknown, abandoned wife & children 1769

1635. Swift Water – adopted-Cayuga born about 1740 PA-died after 1778 OH – Cornstalk War/58-77, raiding Ohio-New River valleys/58, Pontiac War/62-66, Bushy Run/63, raiding New-Jackson-Greenbrier River valleys/63, raiding NewOhio-Big Sandy-Little Kanawha River valleys/72, raiding Ohio River valley/74 **with Chief Logan**, Point Pleasant/74-75-78, husband about 1760 OH of **Pekowi Woman**/45

1636. Swift Wolf – Kishpoko born about 1735 (AL?)-died after 1772 – Cornstalk War/58-72, raiding Ohio-New River valleys/58, Pontiac War/62-66, Bushy Run/63, raiding New-Jackson-Greenbrier River valleys/63, raiding Ohio-New-Little Kanawha-Big Sandy River valleys/72

1637. Sycks, Christina - adopted-white born about 1762-died after 1797 - adopted about 1772-returned to whites about 1795, wife 1st about 1777 OH of

Chalakatha Man, 2nd 1790 of **Joseph Munger**/64-adopted white, mother **with Chalakatha** of at least five 1/2 Chalakatha-Metis children/77-89, **with Munger** of two daughters/90-94, left **Chalakatha & Munger** families 1795 when she returned to whites

1638.Sykes, Little Man - 1/4th Pekowi-Metis born about 1765-died before 1826 - son of **1/2 Pekowi-Metis Woman**/40 & **Trader Sykes**-white, white first name unknown, Blue Jacket War/83-94, raiding OH-KY-VA/95-1810, Prophet's Town/1811, Brownstown/1812-Monguagon/1812-1st Amherstburg/1812Frenchtown/1813-Ft. Meigs/1813-2nd Amherstburg/1813 & Thames/1813 **with**
Tecumseh, about 5' tall, moved to CAN about 1815-may not have returned in 1825, husband 1785 & 1793 of **two 1/2 Kishpoko-Metis Sisters**, father of 16 children/85-1815-(11 daughters & 5 sons) -all 3/8th Kishpoko-Pekowi-Metis with surname Sykes

Section XVII
Tahchee to Two Clouds (T)

T

1639. Tahchee aka Tahchee Carpenter (1) -Datsi-Tatsi-Tahchee Attakullakulla – 15/32nd Chalakatha-Thawikila-Creek-**Cherokee**-Metis born 1736 Great Tellico TN-died before 1830 Audrain Co MO – son of **Attakullakulla Carpenter**/08 & **Ollie Nionee Oconastota**/20, Cornstalk War/58-74, raiding Ohio-New River valleys/58, Pontiac War/62-66, Bushy Run/63, raiding New-Jackson-Greenbrier River valleys/63, Point Pleasant/74, Cherokee War/75, Pigeon Co-Cherokee scouts-**with U.S. Army**-Revolution, moved to MO about 1810, Wolf Clan Cherokee, husband 1st 1755 Great Tellico TN of **Place Priber**/38-7/32nd Chalakatha-Cherokee-Metis, 2nd 1756 Great Tellico TN of **Ailsey Red Paint**/40-Cherokee, 2nd 1770 of **Susannah Catherine Red Horse**/42-Cherokee, father **with Priber** of Nettle Carrier-Talotiskee/56-3/16th Chalakatha-ThawikilaCherokee-Metis, **with Ailsey** of Giyosta Tahchee/56, Ooloosta Tahchee/60 &
Major Ridge/71-all 15/64th Chalakatha-Thawikila-Creek-Cherokee-Metis, **with Susannah** of Young Tachchee/85-15/64th Chalakatha-Thawikila-Creek-Cherokee-Metis

1640. Tahlonteeskee (1) aka Talonutisgi – 7/32nd Chalakatha-**Cherokee**-Metis born about 1743 Great Tellico TN-**killed** 1792 in battle Buchanan Station TN - son of **Oousta Carpenter**/23 & **Cherokee Man**/19, brother of **Tahnoyanteehee**/41, Council Coyatee 1792, a Chickamauga, husband 1762 Tomatly TN of **Elizabeth Emory**/48-7/64th Chalakatha-Cherokee-Metis, father of Tahlonteeskee (3) -Aaron Price/63-5/32nd Chalakatha-Cherokee-Metis

1641. Tahlonteeskee (2) aka Tahlonteeskee Bloody Fellow-Tahlonteeskee Benge-Tallotuskee-Tallunteeskee-Talluntusky-Tallotiskee-Talohuskee-Tashiskee – 53/64th Kishpoko-Chalakatha-Pekowi-**Cherokee**-Metis born 1760 Great Tellico TN-died 1819 AR - son of **Wurteh Watts**/44 & **Bloody Fellow**/40Kishpoko, adopted son of **John Trader Benge**/35, Red Paint Clan Cherokee, a Chickamauga, led raids on whites 1792, Blue Jacket War/82-94, operated House of Entertainment 1801-1810, move to AR **with Chief Bowl** 1810, Treaty 1806, **Principal Chief of AR Cherokee** 1810-19, succeeded by half-brother Chief **John Jolly**/57, Red Paint Clan Cherokee, husband 1st 1780 of **Elizabeth Tassel**/60-7/64th Chalakatha-Cherokee-Metis, 2nd 1795 of **Jennie Jane Lowery**/80-11/32nd Chalakatha-Pekowi-Cherokee-Metis, children/80-95 **with Tassel** unknown, father **with Lowery** of Tahlonteeskee (4)/95-37/64th Kishpoko-Chalakatha-Pekowi-Cherokee-Metis

1642. Tahlonteeskee (3) aka **Aaron Price**-Talonutisgi-Talotiskee - 5/32nd Chalakatha-**Cherokee**-Metis born 1763 Great Tellico TN-died 1844 AR - son of **Elizabeth Emory**/48 & **Tahlonteeskee (1)**/42, Long Hair Clan Cherokee, a Chickamauga, Buchanan Station 1792, Treaty 1805 **with Double Head**, Capt. John Brown Co–**with U.S. Army**-Creek War/1813, wounded at Horseshoe Bend/1814, husband 1784 TN of **Cherokee Woman**/69, father of Tahlonteeskee (5)-Aaron Price Jr/95-5/64th Chalakatha-Cherokee-Metis

1643. Tahlonteeskee (4) – 37/64th Kishpoko-Chalakatha-Pekowi-**Cherokee**Metis born about 1795-died after 1814 - son of **Tahlonteeskee (2)** /60 & **Jennie Jane Lowery**/80, Capt. John Brown Co-**with U.S. Army**-Creek War/1813, wounded at Horseshoe Bend/1814, wife & children unknown

1644. Tahlonteeskee (5) aka **Aaron Price Jr**- 5/64th Chalakatha-**Cherokee**Metis born 1795 TN-died after 1830 - son of **Tahlonteeskee (3)**-**Aaron Price**/63 & **Cherokee Woman**/69, Capt. John Brown Co-**with U.S. Army**-Creek War/1813, wounded at Horseshoe Bend/14, husband before 1820 of **Neli**

Cherokee/1800, father of Lydia Price/1830-1/32nd Chalakatha-Cherokee-Metis 1645. Taiapee aka Taeeapee – Mekoche born about 1770 OH-died after 1817 - raiding Ohio River valley/88-92, Blue Jacket War/87-94, a warrior at Wapaghonettat 1817, Treaty 1817

1646. Taideteso aka Taeedeteso – Chalakatha born about 1790 OH-died after 1817 - Prophet's Town/1811, Brownstown/1812-Monguagon/1812-1st Amherstburg/1812-Frenchtown/1813-Ft. Meigs/1813-2nd Amherstburg/1813 & Thames/1813 **with Tecumseh**, Treaty 1817

1647. Takepee – Chalakatha born about 1765 OH-died after 1817 – Blue Jacket War/83-94, a warrior at Wapaghonettat 1817, Treaty 1817

1648. Talking Rabbit – Pekowi born about 1720 PA-died aboput 1758 OH in epidemic - raiding PA/40, French-Indian War/54, Braddock/55, raiding NewShenandoah River valleys 1755, raiding PA/55-56, raiding Ohio-New River valleys/58

1649. Tall Doe – Chalakatha born about 1740 PA-died after 1774 - wife about 1755 OH of **Chalakatha Man**/35, about 6' tall, widow 1774, mother of several children/55-73

1650. Tall Oak – Chalakatha born about 1720 PA-died after 1778 OH - raiding PA/40, Cornstalk War/55-77, French-Indian War/54-63, Braddock/55, raiding New-Shenandoah River valleys/55, raiding PA/55-56, raiding Ohio-New River valleys/58, a **Chalakatha Chief** by 1763, Pontiac War/62-66, Bushy Run/63, raiding New-Jackson-Greenbrier River valleys/63, raiding Ohio-New-Little Kanawha-Big Sandy River valleys/72, Point Pleasant/74-78, brother of **Black Oak**/25, half-brother of **Moose-Big Deer-Big Elk**/30, about 6'6" tall, relative & same clan as **Cornstalk**, husband 1740 PA of **Chalakatha Woman**/25, father of Little Oak/40 & Leaning Oak/45

1651. Tame Cat – adopted-Cherokee born about 1750 TN-died after 1778 (OH?) - wife about 1765 TN of **Kishpoko Man**/45, widow in 1778, mother of several 1/2 Kishpoko-Cherokee children/65-74

1652. Tame Deer aka Tame Deer Muskrat-Nanih-**Tame Deer Moytoy** - Chalakatha-Pekowi born 1720 Chota TN-died after 1760 Cheowee NC - daughter of **Wapehti-Swan Hop**/1686-Chalakatha & **Oshasqua-Muskrat-Moytoy (5)**/1686-Pekowi, Blind Savannah Clan Cherokee, could cipher, read & write English, Treaty Sycamore Shoals 1775, wife 1735 of (possible relative) **All Bones White Owl Carpenter**/20-7/16th Chalakatha-Cherokee-Metis, mother of All Bones Carpenter (2)/50-23/32nd Chalakatha-Pekowi-**Cherokee**-Metis

1653. Tame Doe aka Tame Doe Carpenter-**Tame Doe White Owl**-Nanih-Tame Deer-Nancy – 7/16th Chalakatha-**Cherokee**-Metis born 1718 Great Tellico TN died after 1775 Chota TN - daughter of **Nancy Rainmaker**/1683 & **White Owl Carpenter**/1678, could cipher, read & write English, Wolf Clan Cherokee, Treaty Sycamore Shoals 1775, wife 1735 Chota TN of **Francis WardShayaqustuego-Five Killer**/12-adopted-white, mother of Long Fellow (Ward) Fivekiller/36, Nancy Wild Rose (Ward) Fivekiller/38 & Little Fellow (Ward) Fivekiller/40-all 7/32nd Chalakatha-Cherokee-Metis

1654. Tame Wolf – Kishpoko born about 1775 OH-died after 1815 - Fallen Timber/94, raiding OH-KY-VA/95-1810, Prophet's Town/1811, **left Tecumseh** after Prophet's Town, living in OH 1815

1655. **Taming Buck aka Tamininipakwa-Tamininipaquah-Tammony Buck-Domini Buck-Corn Blade**[130] Chief - Pekowi born about 1710 PA-died about 1758 OH (epidemic?) - raiding PA/40, a major **Pekowi Chief** by 1748, Council Logstown 1752, Ft. Pitt Nov. 1753, Cornstalk War/55-58, French-Indian War/54-58, Braddock/55, raiding New-Shenandoah River valleys/55, raiding PA/55-56, raiding Ohio-New River valleys/58

1656. Tanacharisson, Daughter of - 1/2 Pekowi-**Seneca** born about 1720-died after 1756 - daughter of **Tanacharrison**/1700-Seneca & **Pekowi Woman**/05, wife about 1735 of **John Owens**/1700-white, mother of David Owens/36, GeorgeOwens/38, John Owens Jr/40, Susannah Owens/50 & others 1/4th Pekowi-Seneca children/35-64

1657. Tanacharisson, Johnny aka **Capt. Johnny**-Straight Arm-WelepachonHeylepacheion-Assilcius-Isreal- 1/2 Pekowi-**Seneca** born about 1722 PA-died after 1766 (OH?) - son of **Tanacharisson**/1700-Seneca & **Pekowi Woman**/05, scout-**with Colonial Army**-French-Indian War/54-63-Braddock/55-Pontiac War/63-66-Bushy Run/63, Treaty 1764, husband of **Seneca Woman**/30, children unknown

1658. Tanner, John aka **Shashawwabenee**-White Indian - adopted-white(later-**Ottawa**) born about 1780-died 1847 - adopted 1789 **by Shawnee**-then adopted by **Gishkawgi**/50-Ottawa, trader, translator, returned to whites 1817 KY, husband about 1800 of **Older Daughter of Gishkawgi**/85-Ottawa, about 1805 of **Younger Daughter of Gishkawgi**/90-Ottawa, about 1810 OH of **Shawnee Woman**/95, 1818 KY of **White Woman**/1800, children unknown (but likely surname Tanner)

1659. Tassel, Elizabeth Euguioote aka **Elizabeth Tassell (1)**-Elizabeth

Euguioote Carpenter – 7/16th Chalakatha-**Cherokee**-Metis born 1704 Great Tellico TN-died 1755 Tellico Plains TN - daughter of **Nancy Rainmaker**/1683 & **Savannah Tom Carpenter (1)-Moytoy (3)**/1680, step-daughter of her uncle **White Owl Carpenter**/1678, from the Overhills, Long Hair Clan Cherokee (?), could cipher, read & write English, wife 1726 Great Tellico TN of **Ludovic Grant**/1698-white, mother of Mary Grant/27 & Susannah Catherine Grant/28both 7/32nd Chalakatha-Cherokee-Metis

1660. Tassel, Elizabeth (2) aka Elizabeth Great Eagle Tassel-Elizabeth Tassel Carpenter (2) – 7/64th Chalakatha-**Cherokee**-Metis born 1760 Great Tellico TNdied after 1830 TN - daughter of **Corn Tassel Great Eagle Carpenter**/30 & **Cherokee Woman**/40, namesake of aunt **Elizabeth Euguioote Tassel Carpenter**/06, wife 1st 1780 of **Tahlonteeskee (2)**/60-53/64th KishpokoChalakatha-Pekowi-Cherokee-Metis, 2nd 1782 of **Joseph Coody**/66-1/8th Chalakatha-Cherokee-Metis, children/80-82 **with Tahlonteeskee** unknown, mother **with Coody** of Sarah Coody/83, Elizabeth Coody/86 & Nancy Coody/90all 7/64th Chalakatha-Cherokee-Metis

1661. Teachenosen – Thawikila born about 1730 PA-died after 1774 - FrenchIndian War/54-63, Braddock/55, Cornstalk War/55-74, raiding New-Shenandoah River valleys/55, raiding PA/55-56, raiding Ohio-New River valleys/58, Pontiac War/62-66, Bushy Run/63, raiding New-Jackson-Greenbrier River valleys/63, raiding Ohio-Big Sandy-Little Kanawha-New River valleys/72, Point Pleasant/74, moved to AL 1774

1662. Tecumapease aka Crossing The Water[131]-Tecumesa-Tecumapease Puckenshinwa - 3/4th Kishpoko-Pekowi-Creek-Metis born 1758 AL-died before 1825 CAN - oldest daughter of **Metheotashe Opessa**/40-Pekowi & **Puckenshinwa**/35-1/2 Kishpoko-Creek-Metis, oldest sister of **Tecumseh**/68 & **Lalawethika-Prophet**/74, a Kishpoko, moved to CAN 1815 with family, died while in CAN, wife 1st by 1773 OH of **Mink -Chaquiweshe**/40-Mekoche, widowed 1774, 2nd 1775 OH of **Stands Firm -Wasegobah**/60-adoptedChippewa, widowed 2nd time 1813, mother **with Mink** of Big Horns-Capt. Logan-John Logan/74-7/8th Mekoche-Kishpoko-Pekowi-Creek-Metis, **with Stands Firm** of LaNanette Tecumapease-Nanette-Maryanne/80-3/8th KishpokoPekowi-Creek-Chippewa-Metis, other children/75-1805 **with Stands Firm** likely, (confused with her younger sisters by some white histories)

1663.**Tecumqualuska aka Graybeard**[132]- Tecumqualuska Cheeseekau - 7/8th Kishpoko-Pekowi-Creek-Metis born 1777 OH-died after 1848 OK - son of **Cheeseekau** (Puckenshinwa)/56 & **Kishpoko Woman**/60, came south 1789 with father & uncle Tecumseh, remained with step-mother **Daughter of Dragging Canoe**/56 & Chickamauga after death of **Cheeseekau** 1792, from Running Water (Shawnee) village, moved west on Trail of Tears, husband about 1795 of **Chickamaugua Woman**/80, father of Johnson Graybeard/1821-7/16th Kishpoko-Pekowi-Creek-Cherokee-Metis

1664.**Tecumoplas Margaret**[133] aka Tecumoplas Margaret Opessa (for lack of a better surname) – Pekowi born 1742 MD-died after 1791 (WV?) - daughter of **Older Sister of Metheotashe** aka **Older Daughter of Loyparkaweh Opessa**/27 & **Pekowi Man**/22, a Pekowi in the North, 1st cousin of **Tecumseh**, wife 1767 (or maybe by 1757?) WV of **Rupert Collins**-white born about 1740-died after 1791, mother of Jane Collins/68, Parker Collins/80 & at least 6 other children/69-82 (or 11 children/59-82?) -all 1/2 Pekowi-Metis 1665.

Tecumsapah Margaret[134] aka Tecumsapah Margaret Opessa – Pekowi born about 1725-died after 1769 - daughter of **Loyparkoweh Opessa**/05 & **Pekowi Woman**/10, aunt of **Tecumseh**, wife about 1737 PA of **Thomas McKee (1)**/1695-adopted-Irish, step-mother of **Thomas McKee**/20-adoptedDelaware & **Col. Alexander McKee**/25-adopted-Shawnee, mother of Alexander McKee/38, Nancy McKee/40, Hugh McKee/42, Catherine McKee/44, Thomas McKee/50, John McKee/54, James McKee/55-all 1/2 Pekowi-Metis

1666. **Tecumseh aka Panther in the Sky**[135]-Panther Leaping at PreyTecumseh Puckenshinwa-Tecumshe-Tecumthe-Tecoomteh-Tecoomti - Tecomteh- 3/4th Kishpoko-Pekowi-Creek-Metis born 1768 Chillicothe OH-**killed 1813 Thames River CAN** - 4th son of **Puckenshimwa**/35 & **Metheotashe Opessa**/40, a Kishpoko war chief, raiding Ohio River valley/88-90, Blue Jacket War/86-94, lived-raided 1790-92 **with Chickamaugua** & brother **Cheeseekua**/56 in TN-KY-VA-NC-GA-AL, raiding OH-WV-VA-KY/93-99, titled as a British Colonel-War 1812, Brownstown/1812- Monguagon/1812-1st Amherstburg/1812-Frenchtown/1813-Ft. Meigs/1813-2nd Amherstburg/1813, **killed at Thames**/1813, Council Miami 1786, Grand Council 1791, traveled much of 1795-1811 soliciting support for united Native force, Council Vincennes July & Aug. 1810, Council Amherstburg Mar. 1812, Council Massinawa May 1812, met with **Isadore Chesne** near Ft. Wayne June 1812, met with **Col. Brock** at Amherstburg July 1812, reportedly a member of the Masons in CAN, last great leader of Eastern Natives though never more than a War Chief if that, **brothers =** Cheeseekau/56, Sauwaseekou/60, Nahaaseema/66, Kumshaka/70, Lalawethika

/74, **sisters** = Tecumapease/58, Menewaulakoose/64, Vocemassussia/71, brother in laws = by **Tecumapease** = **Mink**/50 & **Stands Firm**/55, by **Vocemassussia** = **Split Log**/50 & **George Ironside**/60, by **Menewaulakoosee** = **Antoine Francois Maisonville**/60, nephew of **Black Fish**/25, double-nephew of **Blue Jacket**/35(by mother's uncle & father's sister), brother in law of **Clear Water Baby** (Blue Jacket), **Ms. Baby** (Opessa), **Suzanne Baby** (Caldwell) & **James Baby**, 1st cousin of **Tecumoplas Collins**/42-(by mother's sister), nephew of **Red Pole**/40(mother's 1st cousin), 2nd cousin/uncle of **Seekaboo**/70-(by mother's niece), cousin by marriage of **Anthony Shane**/60-(husband of 2nd cousin **Lemateshe Blackfish**), step-2nd cousin of **Bright Horns**/80-(son of step-1st cousin **Sarah**

Rising Sun/59), 1st cousin of **Big Horns-Capt./John Logan**/74-(son of sister **Tecumapease & Mink**), 1st cousin of **Otter**/70-(nephew of uncle **Minkhusband of Tecumapease**), uncle/3rd cousin of **David Deshane**/80-(son of 2nd cousin **Lematashe Blackfish**), 1st cousin of **John Francis**/60, **Josiah Francis**/65, **Joseph Francis**/70 & **Susan Francis**/75-(by father's sister), step-son 1775 OH of **Hard Striker**/40-(killed the same year), relative/same clan as **Swamp Water**/70, **Elk in Water-Tekuntequa**/70, **Turkey Foot (2)**/70, **Turkey Foot (3)**/90 & **Turtle**/70, husband 1st 1788 OH of **Monetoshe**/70-Pekowi, 2nd 1789 OH of **Mamate Baby**/74-1/2 Kishpoko-Metis, 3rd 1790 OH of **Adopted White Girl**/77, 4th 1790 Running Water TN **Dark Star-Tahneh-**

Shawnee Heritage

Naomi/75Chickamauga, 5th 1793 OH of **White Wing-Big Nancy Cornstalk**/70-15/32nd Chalakatha-Mekoche-Metis, 6th 1800 IN of **Wasigezeegoqua**/85-Pottawamee, 7th by 1805 IN **Winnipegoosqua**/90-Chippewa, father **with Monetoshe** of Mahyawekawpawe/88-7/8th Kishpoko-Pekowi-Creek-Metis, **with Mamate** of Naythahwaynah/90-5/8th Kishpoko-Pekowi-Creek-Metis, **with White Girl**/77 of Michelana/90-3/8th Kishpoko-Pekowi-Creek-Metis, **with Dark Star** of Lydia Tecumseh/90, Tecumtequah/92 & Cherokee Daughter/94-all 3/8th KishpokoPekowi-Creek-Cherokee-Metis, **with White Wing** of Paukeesaa/94, Adjala/96 & Serena/98-all 39/64th Kishpoko-Chalakatha-Mekoche-Pekowi-Creek-Metis, with **Wasigezeegoqua** of Pottawamee Son/1801, Elder Pottawamee Child/1803 & Younger Pottawamee Child/1805-all 3/8th Kishpoko-Pekowi-Creek-Pottawamee-Metis, with **Winnipegoosqua** of four 3/8th Kishpoko-Pekowi-Creek-Chippewa Metis children/1806-08-10-12, other unknown children with unknown women possible

1667. Tecumseh, Adjala – 39/64th Kishpoko-Chalakatha-Pekowi-MekocheCreek-Metis born 1796 OH-died after 1826 (OH-KS?) - son of **Tecumseh**/68 & **White Wing Cornstalk**/70, a Kishpoko warrior, Prophetstown/1811, Brownstown/1812-Monguagon/1812-1st Amherstburg/1812-Frenchtown/1813-Ft. Meigs/1813-2nd Amherstburg/1813 & Thames/1813 **with Tecumseh**, moved to CAN 1815 with band, returned to OH 1826, husband 1816 CAN of **Kishpoko Woman**/1800, children unknown

1668. Tecumseh, Dark Star aka Tahneh-Naomi – Chickamauga (Shawnee or Cherokee or Shawnee-Cherokee) born about 1775 TN-died after 1813 (MO-TN?) - 4th wife 1790 Running Water TN of **Tecumseh**/68, remained in TN with children when Tecumseh returned to OH, moved to MO before 1812 with Daughter/94, may have returned to TN after 1813, mother of Lydia Tecumseh/90, Tecumtequah/92 & Daughter of Tecumseh/94-all 3/8th Kishpoko-Pekowi-Creek-Cherokee-Metis

1669. Tecumseh, Lydia - 3/8th Kishpoko-Pekowi-Creek-Cherokee-Metis born about 1790 TN-died after 1824 AR - daughter of **Tecumseh**/68 & **Dark StarTahneh-Naomi**/75-Cherokee, sister of Tecumtequah/92 & Daughter/94, moved to AR after 1814, wife 1808 of **Moses Downing**/88-1/4th Kishpoko-Cherokee-Metis, mother of Dicey Downing/1808, Cash Downing/1812, Celia Downing/1814-all 5/16th Kishpoko-Pekowi-Creek-Cherokee-Metis

1670.Tecumseh, Mahyawekawpawe aka Young Tecumseh[136]-True Stepper-**McLaughlin** - 7/8th Kishpoko-Pekowi-Creek-Metis born about 1788 OH-died 1868 KS - son of **Tecumseh**/68 & **Monetoshe**/70-Pekowi, a Kishpoko warrior, Prophetstown/1811, Brownstown/1812-Monguagon/1812-1st Amherstburg/1812-Frenchtown/1813-Ft. Meigs/1813-2nd Amherstburg/1813 & Thames/1813 **with Tecumseh**, Treaty 1817, moved to KS **with Prophet** & **Paukeesaa** 1826, took white name of McLaughlin, husband before 1826 of **Tawpama Shawnee**/1800, father of 4 or 5 children-at least one a daughter

1671.Tecumseh, Mamate Baby - 2nd wife 1789 of **Tecumseh**/68, mother of Naythahwaynah/90-5/8th Kishpoko-Pekowi-Creek-Metis, died shortly after birth of son

1672.Tecumseh, Michelana aka Machielaini[137]-**Tecumseh's Son** - 3/8th Kishpoko-Pekowi-Creek-Metis born 1790 OH-died after 1839 (AR-OK?) - son of **Tecumseh**/68 & **Adopted White Woman**/77, a Kishpoko warrior/leader, Prophetstown/1811, Brownstown/1812-Monguagon/1812-1st Amherstburg/1812Frenchtown/1813-Ft. Meigs/1813-2nd Amherstburg/1813 & Thames/1813 **with Tecumseh**, living in Apple Creek MO 1815, moved to KS 1826, led group of mixed Natives from KS to AR 1839, wife & children unknown

1673.Tecumseh, Monetoshe[138] aka Four Doves-Manetohse-**Resting Snake** - Opessa Band Pekowi, relative/same clan as **Watmeme Opessa**/30, **Metheotashe Opessa**/40, **Resting Fish-Masemo**/60,, 1st wife 1787 OH of **Tecumseh**/68, mother of Mahyawekawpawe-Young Tecumseh/88-7/8th Kishpoko-PekowiCreek-Metis, divorced when son was one year old

1674.Tecumseh, Naythahwaynah aka Panther Seizing Prey[139]-**Young Tecumseh** - 5/8th Kishpoko-Pekowi-Creek-Metis born about 1790 OH-died about 1826 KS - son of **Tecumseh**/68 & **Mamate Baby**/74, a Kishpoko warrior, Prophetstown/1811, Brownstown/1812-Monguagon/1812-1st Amherstburg/1812Frenchtown/1813-Ft. Meigs/1813-2nd Amherstburg/1813 & Thames/1813 **with Tecumseh**, moved to CAN 1815, returned to OH about 1825, moved to KS with **Prophet** & half-brother **Paukeesaa** 1826, died shortly after arriving in KS, husband 1810 OH of **Sokomsee Kishpoko**/95, father of twins Maythahskse &
Waylahse/1816, Jim Fry/1818, Nahswahpama/1820, Pahsequahmease/1822 & Big Jim Tecumseh/1824-all 13/16th Kishpoko-Pekowi-Creek-Metis

1675.Tecumseh, Paukeesaa aka Tecumseh Jr-Pugeshashenwa-PahkeesaPahguesahah-Puchetha-Puggeesha-Panther Watching Prey[140] –

39/64th Kishpoko-Chalakatha-Pekowi-Mekoche-Creek-Metis born 1794 OH-died 1843 KS - son of **Tecumseh**/68 & **White Wing Cornstalk**/70, Prophetstown/1811, Brownstown/1812-Monguagon/1812-1st Amherstburg/1812-Frenchtown/1813-Ft. Meigs/1813-2nd Amherstburg/1813 & Thames/1813 **with Tecumseh, Head Chief of Shawnee in CAN** 1815 at 21 years old, succeeded by **Yealabaheah** as Head Chief in CAN before 1825, moved back to OH, moved KS 1826 with his uncle **the Prophet**/74, a **Kishpoko Chief** in KS after 1826, husband 1815 CAN of **Kishpoko Woman**/1800, father of John Tecumseh/1820-51/64th Kishpoko-Chalakatha-Pekowi-Mekoche-Creek Metis

1676.Tecumseh, Serena aka Skwato – 39/64th Kishpoko-Chalakatha-PekowiMekoche-Creek-Metis born 1798 IN-died 1833 IN - daughter of **Tecumseh**/68 &
White Wing Cornstalk/70, a Kishpoko, granddaughter-(by White Wing) of **Young Cornstalk**/42 & **Elizabeth See**/54-adopted white & (by Tecumseh) of **Metheotashe Opessa**/40 & **Puckenshinwa**/35, 3rd wife 1808 (OH-IN?) of **William Rainey**/76-Irish, mother of Matthew Rainey/15-19/64th Kishpoko-Chalakatha-Pekowi-Mekoche-Creek-Metis

1677.Tecumseh, Sokomse – Kishpoko born about 1795 OH-died 1867 OK - daughter in law of **Tecumseh**, wife 1st 1815 (OH-CAN?) of **Naythahwaynah Tecumseh**/90, 2nd 1826 of **Wapakwaha**/95-Kishpoko, mother **with Naythahwaynah** of Waylahskse & Maythahskse/1816, Jim Fry/1818, Nahwahpama/1820, Pahsaquawmease/1822 & Big Jim Tecumseh/1824-all 13/16th Kishpoko-Pekowi-Creek Metis (married 2nd to **Wapakwaha**/95 after death 1826 of Naythahwaynah)

1678.Tecumseh, Tecumtequah aka Cross the Water[141]- TakomtequaTaykoomteeqwa - 3/8th Kishpoko-Pekowi-Creek-Cherokee-Metis born 1792 NCdied after 1826 MN?) - son of **Tecumseh**/68 & **Dark Star-Tahneh-Naomi**/75Cherokee, moved to OH about 1810, Prophetstown/1811, Brownstown/1812Monguagon/1812-1st Amherstburg/1812-Frenchtown/1813-Ft. Meigs/1813-2nd
Amherstburg/1813 & Thames/1813 **with Tecumseh**, a **Kishpoko Chief** at Wapaghonettat 1817, Treaty 1814, 1817, moved to KS 1826 with uncle **Prophet** & half-brother **Paukeesaa**, moved north by 1820 to Dakotas or Montana, husband 1st about 1810 OH of **Kishpoko Woman**/85, 2nd about 1820 of **Seeshemeteh Flathead**/1805, children/1810-20 **with Kishpoko** unknown, father **with Seeshemeteh** of Angelica Josephete Cahkatshee Tecumtequah/1821-3/16th Kishpoko-Pekowi-Creek-Cherokee-Flathead-Metis, father in law of **Louis**

Tellier-Metis

1679. Tecumseh, Wasigezeegoqua aka Pottawamee Wife of - Pottawamee born about 1785-died after 1813 - 6th wife about 1800 of **Tecumseh**/68, mother of Pottawamee Son/1801, Elder Pottawamee Child/03 & Younger Pottawamee Child/05-all 3/8th Shawnee-Creek-Pottawamee-Metis, moved with children to WI after death of Tecumseh at Thames/13 (descendants in Prairie Band Pottawatomie today)

1680. Tecumseh, Waylahkse aka One Of Grace - 13/16th Kishpoko-PekowiCreek-Metis born about 1816 CAN-died 1869 KS - daughter of **Naythahwaynah Tecumseh**/90 & **Sokomsee**/95-Kishpoko, granddaughter of **Mamate Baby**/74 & **Tecumseh**/68, twin to **Maythahskse**, wife about 1834 of **George Wildcat Alford**/10-Shawnee-Metis, mother of Nancy Hood-Ahlamawpama/35, David Alford-Paymetahpeasekah/40 & Nellie Hood-Nahwahtawpease/45, Thomas Wildcat Alford-Ganwahpeasaka/50-all 13/16th Kishpoko-Pekowi-Creek-Metis

1681. Tecumseh, White Wing Cornstalk aka Big Nancy-Nancy Adkins - 3rd wife 1793 OH of **Tecumseh**, about 6' tall, an occasional translator for Tecumseh, granddaughter of **Cornstalk**/10, mother of Paukeesaa/94, Adjala/96 & SerenaSkwato/98-all 39/64th Kishpoko-Chalakatha-Pekowi-Mekoche-Creek-Metis

1682. Tecumseh, White Wife - adopted-white born about 1777-died after 1795 - 3rd wife by 1790 OH of **Tecumseh**/68, captured/adopted 1788 KY, returned to whites in KY 1795, mother of Michelana Tecumseh/90-3/8th Kishpoko-Pekowi-Creek-Metis

1683. Tecumseh, Winnipegoosqua aka Chippewa Wife of - born about 1790died after 1813 - 7th wife about 1805 of **Tecumseh**/68, mother of three or four 3/8th Kishpoko-Pekowi-Creek-Chippewa-Metis children/1806-13

1684. Tellier, Angelique Josephete Tecumseh aka Cahkatstshee-Green Blanket-Kahnhopsita - 3/16th Kishpoko-Pekowi-Creek-Cherokee-**Flathead**-Metis born 1823 ID-died 1913 MN - daughter of **Seeshemteh Flathead**/05 & **Tecoomteh-Tecumtequah Tecumseh**/92, granddaughter of **Tecumseh**, wife 1841 ID of **Louis Tellier**-Metis born 1809 CAN-died after 1880 MN, mother of Nelson Tecumseh Tellier/1841, Mary Blue Eyes Tellier/1845, Cleofus-Clopis Tellier/1847, Narcissa Tellier/1849, Theodore Tellier/1851, Samuel Tellier/1853, Moses Tellier/1859, Isaac Tellier/1862 & Adeline Tellier/1864-3/32nd Kishpoko-Pekowi-Creek-Cherokee-Flathead-Metis

1685. Tenakee – Mekoche born about 1770 OH-died after 1817 – Blue Jacket

War/88-94, a warrior at Wapaghonettat 1817, Treaty 1817

1686. Tepetoseka – Mekoche born about 1770 OH-died after 1817 - raiding Ohio River valley/88-92, Blue Jacket War/88-94, a warrior at Wapaghonettat 1817, Treaty 1817

1687. Terrapin (1) aka Terrapin Oconastota (1) aka Terrapin (1) – Terrapin of Chota-Tuskasah of Chiles Tooch - 1/2 Chalakatha-Thawikila-Creek-**Cherokee** born 1726 Chota TN-died after 1794 - son of **Oconastota Rainmaker**/02 & **Ahneewakee Red Paint**/04, Red Paint Clan Cherokee, from the Overhills & Chota, Treaty Sycamore Shoals 1775, Pigeon Co-Cherokee scouts-**with U.S. Army**-Revolution, husband 1746 Chota TN of **Wolf Clan Cherokee**/30, father of Young Terrapin/50 & Terrapin Warrior/60-both 1/4th Chalakatha-Thawikila-Creek-Cherokee

1688. Terrapin (2) aka Terrapin Watts-Terrapin Oconastota (2)-Terrapin (2)Tuckasee of Etowah-Tukasi – 11/16th Chalakatha-Pekowi-**Cherokee**-Metis born 1726 Chota TN-died after 1796 GA – son of **John Watts (Sr)**/04 & **Quatsis Fox**/08, adopted son 1735 of **Oconastota**/02, Red Paint Clan Cherokee, Pigeon Co-Cherokee scouts-**with U.S. Army**-Revolution, Treaty Sycamore Shoals 1775, Tellico 1794, husband 1757 Etowah TN of **Old Jennie**/44-Cherokee, father of Polly (Watts) Terrapin/68 & Little Terrapin (Watts)-Brother Terrapin/70-both 11/32nd Chalakatha-Pekowi-Cherokee-Metis

1689. Terrapin Warrior aka Terrapin Warrior Oconastota-**Skotelawenethe** – 1/4th Chalakatha-Thawikila-Creek-**Cherokee** born 1760 Chota TN-died after 1794 (OH?) – son of **Terrapin Oconastota (1)**/26 & **Wolf Clan Woman**/30, Wolf Clan Cherokee, brother of Young Terrapin/50, raiding KYVA-OH/77-81, Crawford/82, raiding Ohio River valley/88, Blue Jacket War/7794, husband 1780 (KY-OH?) of **Kishpoko Woman**/65, children unknown but likely surname Terrapin

1690. Terror To All – Kishpoko born about 1740 KY-died after 1790 – Cornstalk War/58-77, raiding Ohio-New River valleys/58, Pontiac War/62-66, Bushy Run/63, raiding New-Jackson-Greenbrier River valleys/63, raiding Ohio-New-Big Sandy-Little Kanawha River valleys/72, Point Pleasant/74-75-78, Blue Jacket War/77-90, raiding KY-VA-OH/77-81, Crawford/82, raiding Ohio River valley/88-90, Harmar/90, an especially vicious warrior

1691. Tetetee – Mekoche born about 1770 OH-died after 1817 – Blue Jacket War/88-94, a warrior at Wapaghonettat 1817, Treaty 1817

1692. Tetewekee – Chalakatha born about 1700 PA-died after 1751 - raiding

PA/40, living with Creeks in AL 1751

1693.	Tewanima aka Tewaneema - 1/2 Thawikila-Metis born about 1750 OHdied after 1775 - daughter of **Thawikila Man** & **Adopted White Woman**, returned to whites-returned to tribe 1765, wife about 1765 OH of **Thawikila Man**/45, children unknown

1694.	Thaitcheto aka Thaeetcheto – Mekoche born about 1775 OH-died after 1817 - Fallen Timber/94, a warrior at Wapaghonettat 1817, Treaty 1817

1695.	Thaminusque aka Thameenooskwee – Chalakatha born about 1730 PA- died after 1765 - French-Indian War/54-63, Cornstalk War/55-65, Braddock/55, raiding New-Shenandoah River valleys/55, raiding PA/55-56, raiding Ohio-New River valleys/58, Pontiac War/62-65, Bushy Run/63, raiding New-Greenbrier-Jackson River valleys/63, Council Logstown 1765

1696.	Thapaeka – Chalakatha born about 1775 OH-died after 1817 - Fallen Timber/94, a warrior at Wapaghonettat 1817, Treaty 1817

1697.	Thapeshe aka Tahpeshe-Thapethee – Kishpoko born about 1790 OHdied after 1830 KS - Prophet's Town/1811, Brownstown/1812-Monguagon/1812-1st Amherstburg/1812-Frenchtown/1813-Ft. Meigs/1813-2nd Amherstburg/1813 & Thames/1813 **with Tecumseh**, moved to CAN 1815, returned to OH 1825, moved to KS 1826 **with Prophet** & **Paukeesaa**, wife & children unknown

1698.	Thaswa – Mekoche born about 1775 OH-died after 1817 – Fallen Timber/94, a warrior at Wapaghonettat 1817, Treaty 1817

1699.	Thathouakata aka Thathouskata – Mekoche born about 1770 OH-died after 1817 - raiding Ohio River valley/88-92, Blue Jacket War/88-94, a warrior at Wapaghonettat 1817, Treaty 1817

1700.	Thaway – Chalakatha born about 1775 OH-died after 1817 – Fallen Timber/94, a warrior at Wapaghonettat 1817, Treaty 1817

1701.	Thawwamcee aka Thawwamsee – Chalakatha born about 1770 OH-died after 1817 - raiding Ohio River valley/88-92, Blue Jacket War/88-94, raiding

OH-KY-VA/95-1810, Prophet's Town/1811, Brownstown/1812-Monguagon/1812-1st Amherstburg/1812-Frenchtown/1813-Ft. Meigs/1813-2nd Amherstburg/1813 & Thames/1813 **with Tecumseh**, a warrior at Lewistown 1817, Treaty 1817

1702. Thekomma aka Thecomma – Mekoche born about 1720 PA-died after 1765 OH - raiding PA/40, French-Indian War/54-63, Cornstalk War/55-65, Braddock/55, raiding New-Shenandoah River valleys/55, raiding PA/55-56, raiding Ohio-New River valleys/58, Pontiac War/62-65, Bushy Run/63, raiding New-Jackson-Greenbrier River valleys/63, Council Logstown 1765

1703. Thekosema – Chalakatha born about 1710 PA-died 1758 OH in epidemic
- raiding PA/40, Council Ft. Pitt Nov. 1753, French-Indian War/54-58, Braddock/55, raiding New-Shenandoah River valleys/55, raiding PA/55-56, raiding Ohio-New River valleys/58

1704. Theocheepa aka Theecheapei-Theacheepa - adopted-white born about 1740-died after 1774 - adopted before 1750 PA, returned to whites-returned to tribe 1765, Cornstalk War/58-74, raiding Ohio-New River valleys/58, Pontiac War/62-66, Bushy Run/63, raiding New-Jackson-Greenbrier River valleys/63, raiding Ohio-New-Little Kanawha-Big Sandy River valleys/72, Point Pleasant/74, husband about 1760 OH of **Kishpoko Woman**/45, children unknown

1705. Thick Neck aka **Nawillingong** – adopted-Miami born about 1780 INdied after 1815 - Prophet's Town/1811, Brownstown/1812-Monguagon/1812-1st Amherstburg/1812-Frenchtown/1813-Ft. Meigs/1813-2nd Amherstburg/1813Thames/1813 **with Tecumseh**, living in Apple Creek MO 1815, husband about 1800 of **Kishpoko Woman**/85-(same clan/Panther as **Tecumseh**), father of several 1/2 Kishpoko-Miami children/1800-15

1706. Thin Warrior – Kishpoko born about 1750 OH-died after 1783 – Cornstalk War/68-77, raiding Ohio-New-Big Sandy-Little Kanawha River valleys/72, Point Pleasant/74-78, Blue Jacket War/77-82, raiding KY-VA-OH/75-81, Blue Licks/82

1707. Thistle – adopted-Cayuga born about 1730 (OH?)-died after 1782 – Cornstalk War/55-77, French-Indian War/54-63, Braddock/55, raiding Shenandoah-New River valleys/55, raiding PA/55-56, raiding Ohio-New River valleys/58, Pontiac War/62-66, Bushy Run/63, raiding New-Jackson-Greenbrier River valleys/63, raiding Ohio-New-Little Kanawha-Big Sandy River valleys/72, raiding Ohio River valley/74 **with Chief Logan**, Point Pleasant/74-78, raiding KY-VA-OH/75-81, Blue Jacket War/77-82, Crawford/82, husband about 1750

OH of **Kishpoko Woman**/35, children unknown

1708. Thokutchema aka Thokootcheema – Mekoche born about 1770 OH-died after 1817 - raiding Ohio River valley/88-92, Blue Jacket War/88-94, a warrior at Wapaghonettat 1817, Treaty 1817

1709. Thompson, Jack – ½ Chalakatha-Metis born 1766-died after 1819 – son of **John Thompson**-white & **Chalakatha Woman**, brother of William Thompson/68, husband 1786 of **Jennie Vann (1)**/70, father of Laugh at Mush Thompson/86, Necooie Thompson/88 & William Thompson (2)/90-all 7/16th Chalakatha-Pekowi-Cherokee-Metis

1710. Thompson, John (2) – ½ Chalakatha-Metis born 1775-**killed** 1815 ILMO – son of **John Thompson**-white & **Chalakatha Woman**, enlisted in **Lewis & Clark** expedition 1799, husband 1795 of **Peggy Unknown**/80, children/95-1815 unknown

1711. Thompson, William (1) - 1/2 Chalakatha-Metis born 1768-died after 1800 - son of **John Thompson**-white & **Chalakatha Woman**, brother of **Jack Thompson**/66 & **John Thompson**/75, husband 1786 of **Mary Johnston**/70white, father of Rachel Thompson/86-1/4th Chalakatha-Metis

1712. Thompson, William (2) – 11/16th Chalakatha-Pekowi-**Cherokee**-Metis born 1790-died after 1832 - son of **Jennie Vann**/70 & **Jack Thompson**/66, husband 1st about 1808 of **Nancy Merrell**/96-Cherokee-Metis, 2nd about 1818 of **Elizabeth Fields**/91-5/64th Chalakatha-Thawikila-Creek-Cherokee-Metis, 3rd about 1832 of **Louisa Jane Blackburn**/1817-7/16th Chalakatha-PekowiCherokee-Metis, children **with Fields & Blackburn** unknown, father **with Merrell** of Elizabeth Thompson/1808, Alexander Thompson/1810, Sally Thompson/1812, Charles Thompson/1814 & Nancy Thompson/1816-all 11/32nd Chalakatha-Pekowi-Cherokee-Metis

1713. Thornton, Riley - 1/32nd Chalakatha-Thawikila-Creek-**Cherokee**-Metis born about 1797-died after 1846 - son of **Nancy Scott**/76 & **John Thornton**/70white, husband 1st about 1817 of **Eliza Quatie**/1800-Cherokee, 2nd before 1840 of **Rebecca Mitchell**/1820-3/32nd Chalakatha-Pekowi-Thawikila-CherokeeCreek-Chickasaw-Metis, father **with Quatie** of Thomas Thornton/1828, George Thornton/1829 & Osceola Thornton/1830-all 1/64th Chalakatha-ThawikilaCreek-Cherokee-Metis, **with Mitchell** of Mary Ann Thornton/1844 & Ailsey Thornton/1846-both1/16th Chalakatha-Thawikila-Pekowi-Creek-Cherokee-Chickasaw-Metis

1714. Thornton, Smith Taladu aka **Tullahtoo-Cricket** - 1/32nd ChalakathaThawikila-Creek-**Cherokee**-Metis born about 1799-died 1865 - son of **Nancy
Scott**/76 & **John Thornton**/70-white, twin of Elizabeth Thornton, husband 1st 1820 of **Cherokee Woman**/1805, 2nd 1840 of **Caroline Daniel**/1824-1/16th Kishpoko-Cherokee-Metis, 3rd 1850 of **Lucy Critterden**/1828-21/64th Chalakatha-Mekoche-Kishpoko-Pekowi-Cherokee-Metis, children/1820-39 **with Cherokee** unknown, father **with Daniel** of William H. Thornton/1842, Nancy Jane/1844 & Fannie Delilah Thornton/1848-all 3/64th Kishpoko-ChalakathaThawikila-Creek-Cherokee-Metis, **with Critterden** of Elizabeth Thornton/1851,
Jacob Thornton/1854 & Francis Marion Thornton/1856- all 11/64th Chalakatha-Mekoche-Kishpoko-Pekowi-Thawikila-Creek-Cherokee-Metis

1715. Three Springs – adopted-Seneca born about 1730 PA-died after 1765 OH - wife about 1745 OH of **Chalakatha Man**/24, widow in 1765

1716. **Tiger Face aka Mashepesheewinqua**[142] - adopted-Miami born about 1760 OH-died after 1815 - Blue Jacket War/77-94, Crawford/82, raiding OHKY-VA/95-1810, Prophet's Town/1811, Brownstown/1812-Monguagon/1812-1st Amherstburg/1812-Frencthown/1813-Ft. Meigs/1813-2nd Amherstburg/1813Thames/1813 **with Tecumseh**, living in Apple Creek MO 1815, husband about 1780 OH of **Kishpoko Woman**/65, father of several 1/2 Kishpoko-Miami children/80-1810

1717. Timberlake, Henry – white born about 1730 VA-died 1769 ENG – brother of **Richard Timberlake**/25, 2nd husband 1761 Running Water TN of **Sokinney Oconastota**/39, father of Elizabeth Timberlake/62-3/8th Kishpoko-Chalakatha-Thawikila-Creek-**Cherokee**-Metis

1718. Timberlake, Richard – white born about 1725 VA-died after 1769 (TN?) – brother of **Henry Timberlake**/30, husband 1759 Running Water TN of **Sokinney Oconastota**/39, father of Richard Timberlake Jr/60-3/8th Kishpoko-Chalakatha-Thawikila-Creek-**Cherokee**-Metis

1719. Timberlake, Richard Jr – 3/8th Kishpoko-Chalakatha-Thawikila-Creek**Cherokee**-Metis born 1760 Running Water TN-died after 1835 - son of **Sokinney Oconastota**/39 & **Richard Timberlake**/30-white, husband 1st 1775 Running Water TN of **Ollie Critterden**/58-1/4th Chalakatha-Pekowi-Cherokee-Metis, 2nd 1782 of her sister **Aisley Critterden**/60-1/4th Chalakatha-PekowiCherokee-Metis, 3rd 1787 of **Patsy Brown**/60-3/8th Chalakatha-Cherokee-Metis,
4th 1797 of (half-1st cousin of Patsy) **Nancy Ann Brown**/78-1/8th Chalakatha-

Cherokee-Metis, also husband 5th of **Unknown Woman**, father **with Ollie** of Richard Timberlake (3)/75, Benjamin Timberlake/77, Peggy Timberlake/78, Charles-Red Timberlake/79, Lizzie Timberlake/80 & Levi Timberlake/84, **with Aisley** of Celia Timberlake/94 & Black Fox Timberlake/96-all 5/16th ChalakathaKishpoko-Thawikila-Pekowi-Creek-Cherokee-Metis, children **with Patsy** unknown, **with Nancy** of Charles Timberlake/98-1/4th Kishpoko-Chalakatha-Thawikila-Creek-Cherokee-Metis, children with **Unknown Woman** unknown

1720. Tok – ½ Chalakatha-Cherokee born about 1742-died after 1774 – son of **Marhalonak**/10 & **Chalakatha Woman**/15, scout **with Andrew Lewis & whites**-Pontiac War/62-66 & Point Pleasant/74 with father Marhalonak/10 & brothers Sak/44, Sark/46 & Loho/48, husband 1762 of **Cherokee Woman**/48, children unknown

1721. Tomahawk, Joe – Pekowi born about 1779 OH-died after 1818 - brother of **John Tomahawk**/81,scout-**with U.S. Army**-War of 1812-Thames/1813, Treaty 1817, living with whites 1818, wife & children unknown

1722. Tomahawk, John – Pekowi born about 1781 OH-died after 1818 - brother of **Joe Tomahawk**/79, scout-**with U.S. Army**-War of 1812-Thames/1813, Treaty 1817, living with whites 1818, wife & children unknown

1723. Tonaout – Chalakatha born about 1780 OH-died after 1817 - Treaty 1817, a warrior from Lewistown 1817

1724. Tooley, Charles Jr - 1/2 Chalakatha-Metis born about 1780-died after 1840 - son of **Chalakatha Woman**/60 & **Charles Tooley**/50-white, husband about 1800 of **Chalakatha Woman**/85, about 1830 of **Mekoche Woman**/1815, father with **Chalakatha** of Elizabeth Tooley/1810-3/4th Chalakatha-Metis, with **Mekoche** of Sarah Tooley/1839-3/4th Chalakatha-Mekoche-Metis

1725. Toothed Fish – adopted-Seneca born about 1745 (OH?)-died after 1782 – Cornstalk War/62-77, Pontiac War/62-66, raiding Ohio-New-Little Kanawha-Big Sandy River valleys/72, raiding Ohio River valley/74 **with Chief Logan**, Point Pleasant/74, Blue Jacket War/77-82, raiding OH-KY-VA/75-81, Crawford/82, husband about 1765 OH of **Chalakatha Woman**/50, children unknown

1726. Toposheka – Mekoche born about 1780 OH-died after 1817 - a warrior at Wapaghonetta 1817, Treaty 1817

1727. Toshena aka Tosheshena – Chalakatha born about 1785 OH-died after 1817 - a warrior at Wapaghonetta 1817, Treaty 1817

1728. Totah – Mekoche born about 1790 OH-died after 1817 - a warrior from

Wapaghonettat 1817, Treaty 1817

1729. Totigose aka Toteegosee – Kishpoko born about 1780 OH-died after 1826 KS - raiding OH-KY-VA/99-1810, Prophet's Town/1811, Brownstown/1812-Monguagon/1812-1st Amherstburg/1812-Frenchtown/1813-Ft. Meigs/1813-2nd Amherstburg/1813 & Thames/1813 **with Tecumseh**, moved to CAN 1815, returned to OH about 1826, moved to KS **with Prophet & Paukeesaa**, husband 1800 OH of Chalakatha Woman/84, children unknown

1730. Totintiontonna aka Toteenteeontonna – Chalakatha born about 1710 PAdied 1758 OH in epidemic - French-Indian War/54-58, Braddock/55, raiding Shenandoah-New River valleys/55, raiding PA/55-56, raiding Ohio-New River valleys/58

1731. **Trotter aka Manemepahtoo**[143] – Mekoche born about 1790 OH-died after 1817 - scout-**with U.S. Army**-War 1812-Thames/1813, a warrior at Wapaghonettat 1817, Treaty 1817

1732. Troxell, Catherine (1) - 3/8th Pekowi-Metis born 1772 VA/PA-died after 1791 (VA?) - daughter of **Anna Chartier**/30 & **David Troxell**/30-white, wife 1791 Augusta Co VA (WV?) of **Michael Rodgers**/70-white, children unknown

1733. Troxell, Catherine (2) aka Katy – 19/64th Chalakatha-Pekowi-CherokeeMetis born 1782 Wayne Co KY-died 1844 Scott Co TN - daughter of **Big Jake Troxell**/58 & **Corn Blossom Doublehead**/58, wife 1798 Wayne Co KY (church 1803) of **Jonathan Blevins**/79-Cherokee-Metis, mother of child/99, child/1801, child/03, Timothy Blevins/1805, Pleasant Blevins/1806, Jonathan Blevins (2)/1808, Mary Polly Blevins/1809, Tarlton Blevins (2)/1810, Jacob Blevins/1811 & Ada Blevins/1812-all 9/64th Chalakatha-Pekowi-Cherokee-Metis

1734. Troxell, Catherine (3) – 5/8th Pekowi-Metis born 1784 Pulaski Co VAdied after 1850 IN – daughter of **George Troxell**/56 & **Elizabeth Chartier**/60, wife by 1804 KY of **James Burton**-white, children unknown

1735. Troxell, Elizabeth (1) – 3/8th Pekowi-Metis born 1764 MD/PA-died 1851 McCreary Co KY – daughter of **Anna Chartier**/30 & **David Troxell**/30, twin of Mary, sent south 1779 with **Big Jake** for raising, wife (1780?) KY of **Benjamin Burke**-white (or Metis son of **Mary Burke**-former captive?) born 1755-died 1828, children unknown

1736. Troxell, Elizabeth (2) aka Betty – 19/64th Chalakatha-Pekowi-CherokeeMetis born 1796 Wayne Co KY-died 1850 KY - daughter of **Big Jake**

Troxell/58 & **Corn Blossom Doublehead**/58, wife 1812 KY of **James Vaughn**/90-white (or a Vann Metis?), mother of Nancy Vaughn/1813, Elizabeth Vaughn/1816, Matilda Margaret Vaughn/1824, John Vaughn/1827, James Vaughn/1829, Hiram Vaughn/1835, Malinda Vaughn/1837 & Rebecca Jane Vaughn/1839-all 9/64th Chalakatha-Pekowi-Cherokee-Metis

1737. Troxell, Fredrick - 3/8th Pekowi-Metis born 1762 MD/PA-died 1824 Sullivan Co TN - son of **Anna Chartier**/30 & **David Troxell**/30-white, came south 1779 with **Big Jake**, husband by 1785 (KY-OH?) of **Anna Hess**/65, children unknown

1738. Troxell, George aka George Jacob – 3/8th Pekowi-Metis born 1756 PAdied 1843 Dekalb Co AL – son of **Anna Chartier**/30 & **David Troxell**/30, PA Militia-**with U.S. Army**-Revolution, came south 1779 with **Big Jake**, apparently was wounded & fled Yahoo Falls 1810 & died after arriving in AL, husband 1st about 1776 (PA?) of **Elizabeth Chartier**/60-7/8th Pekowi-Metis, 2nd 1806 Washington Co MD of **Elizabeth Brewer**/83-white (?), 3rd 1823 Wayne Co KY of **Elizabeth Blevins**/96-(white or Metis?), father **with Chartier** of Peter Troxell/81, Catherine Troxell/84, Jane Marie Troxell/1800, Jacob William Troxell/1803 & others-all 5/8th Pekowi-Metis, children **with Brewer** unknown, **with Blevins** of Elizabeth Troxell/1824-3/16th Pekowi-Metis (or something elsedepending on mother's line)

1739. Troxell, Jacob (1) aka Big Jake - 3/8th Pekowi-Metis born 1758 MD/PA**killed** 1810 Yahoo Falls KY - son of **Anna Chartier**/35 & **David Troxell**/30white, PA Militia-**with U.S. Army**-Revolution 1776-79, came to KY 1779 with older brother **George Troxell**/56, younger brothers **John Troxell**/60, **Fredrick Troxell**/62, **Peter-Little Jake (1) Troxell**/66 & sister **Elizabeth Troxell**/64-twin of Mary, Blue Jacket War/80-94, (the **Jacob George Troxell** that died after 1810 was likely Jake's brother **George Troxell**/56 who came south with Jake in 1779), husband 1779 KY of **Corn Blossom Doublehead**/58, father of Jacob-Little Jake (2) Troxell Jr/80, Catherine Troxell/82, Peter Troxell/84, Mary Polly Troxell/86, Margaret Peggy Troxell/88, child/90, child/92, child/94, Elizabeth Troxell/96,
Sarah Troxell/98, William Troxell/1800-all 19/64th Chalakatha-Pekowi-Cherokee-Metis

1740. Troxell, Jacob (2) aka Jacob Jr-Little Jake (2) – 19/64th Chalakatha-Pekowi-**Cherokee**-Metis born 1780 Loudon Co VA-**killed** 1810 Yahoo Falls KY - son of **Big Jake Troxell**/58 & **Corn Blossom Doublehead**/58, husband 1803 Wayne Co KY of **Jane Stephenson**/85-white, father of Jacob-Little Jake Troxell (3)/1804, Mary Polly Troxell/1806, William S. Troxell/1808 & George

Washington Troxell/1810-all 9/64th Chalakatha-Pekowi-Cherokee-Metis

1741. Troxell, Jacob (3) aka Little Jake (3) – 9/64th Chalakatha-Pekowi-**Cherokee**-Metis born 1804 Wayne Co KY-died 1880 Parmleysville KY – son of **Jacob-Little Jake (2) Troxell**/80 & **Jane Stephenson**/85, alleged to have killed & scalped 9 men, wife & children unknown

1742. Troxell, Jacob William – 5/8th Pekowi-Metis born 1803 KY-died after 1850 – son of **George Troxell**/56 & **Elizabeth Chartier**/60, husband 1821 Wayne Co KY of **Sally Abbott**/1806-white (?), children unknown

1743. Troxell, Margaret Peggy – 19/64th Chalakatha-Pekowi-**Cherokee**-Metis born 1788 Wayne Co KY-died after 1850 Wayne Co KY - daughter of **Big Jake Troxell**/58 & **Corn Blossom Doublehead**/58, wife 1805 Wayne Co KY of **James Bell**/78-5/8th Chalakatha-Pekowi-Metis, mother of David Bell/1807, Mary Polly Bell/1810, Tarlton Bell/1812, Jacob Bell/1816, William Bell/1818, Elizabeth Bell/1820, Malinda Bell/1822, Anna Bell/1828, twins Telitha & Eliza Bell/1830, Martha Bell/1832 & Permilia Bell/1834-all 29/64th Chalakatha-Pekowi-Cherokee-Metis

1744. Troxell, Peter (1) aka Little Jake (1)-Chief Peter (1) - 3/8th Pekowi-Metis born 1766 Fredrick Co MD-**killed** 1810 Yahoo Falls KY - son of **Anna Chartier**/30 & **David Troxell**/30-white, moved to KY 1779 with **Big Jake**, Blue Jacket War/80-94, husband 1st 1784 KY of **Rachel Chambers**/68-white, 2nd 1786 KY of **Standing Fern Cherokee**/70, no known children **with Chambers**, children/86-1810 **with Fern** unknown but may have included a son Peter Troxell -Chief Peter Troxell

1745. Troxell, Peter (2) aka Little Jake (3)-Chief Peter (2) – 19/64th Chalakatha-Pekowi-**Cherokee**-Metis born 1784 Wayne Co KY-died after 1820 KY – son of **Corn Blossom Doublehead**/58 & **Big Jake Troxell**/58, survived Yahoo Falls, known later as **Chief Little Jake & Chief Peter**, husband 1805 KY of **Elizabeth Metis**/93-1/2 Pekowi-Metis, children/1805-20 unknown but may have included a son Peter Troxell-Chief Peter

1746. Troxell, Peter (3) – 5/8th Pekowi-Metis born 1781 KY (or VA?)-died after 1824 KY – son of **George Troxell**/56 & **Elizabeth Chartier**/60, husband 1802 Wayne Co KY of **Sally Saratte**/86, children unknown

1747. Troxell, Sarah – 19/64th Chalakatha-Pekowi-**Cherokee**-Metis born 1798 Wayne Co KY-died 1885 (KY-TN?) - daughter of **Big Jake Troxell**/58 & **Corn Blossom Doublehead**/58, wife 1818 Wayne Co KY of **Thomas Bell**/87-5/8th Chalakatha-Pekowi-Metis, mother of Mary Bell/1820, James Bell/1822, Malinda Bell/1830, Nancy Bell/1834, Relitha Bell/1837, Martha Bell/39 & Matilda

Bell/1843-all 29/64th Chalakatha-Pekowi-Cherokee-Metis

1748. Troxell, William aka Little Loud Wolf – 19/64th Chalakatha-Pekowi**Cherokee**-Metis born 1800 Wayne Co KY-died 1882 Jackson Co AL - son of **Big Jake Troxell**/58 & **Corn Blossom**/58, **wounded at Yahoo Falls**/10, husband 1820 Wayne Co KY of **Catherine Farris**/1802-white, father of Elizabeth Troxell/1822, Thomas Elias Troxell/1824, James Troxell/1826, Jacob Troxell/1828, Lucinda Troxell/1830, Canzida Troxell/1834, John Troxell/1836, William H. Troxell/1840, Susan Troxell/1842, Nancy Troxell/1844 & Emanuel Taylor Troxell/1846-all 9/64th Chalakatha-Pekowi-Cherokee-Metis

1749. Tucker, Charles (1) - 1/2 Mekoche-Metis born about 1780-died after 1860 - son of **William Tucker**/40-adopted white & **Mekoche Woman**/60, moved to KS 1832, Treaty 1854, brother of William (2)/85 & Thomas M/90, Joseph Parks Co-**with U.S. Army**-Seminole War/1837, **sub-Chief of FishJackson band** 1860, husband 1800 (OH?) of **Mekoche Woman**/85, father of Charles Tucker (2)/1805-3/4th Mekoche-Metis

1750. Tucker, Charles (2) – 3/4th Mekoche-Metis born 1805-died after 1871 OK – son of **Charles Tucker**/80 & **Mekoche Woman**/85, husband about 1825 of **Mary White Woman**/1810-white, father of Charles Tucker (3)/1826-3/8th Mekoche-Metis

1751. Tucker, Charles (3) – 3/8th Mekoche-Metis born 1826-died after 1871 – son of **Charles Tucker**/1805 & **Mary White Woman**/1810, husband of **Unknown Woman**, father of Maria Tucker/1855, John M. Tucker/1857, Joshua Tucker/1860 & other children/1827-1854-all 3/16th Mekoche-Metis

1752. Tucker, Thomas M - 1/2 Mekoche-Metis born 1790-died after 1850 - son of **Mekoche Woman**/60 & **William Tucker (1)**/40-adopted white, in **Mason Co. WV** about 1815, husband by 1831 of **Sarah Peck (Vanmetre)**/95-1/4th Chalakatha-Metis, father of William Tucker (3)/1832 & Mary Tucker/1835-both 3/8th Chalakatha-Mekoche-Metis

1753. Tucker, William (1) - adopted-white born about 1740 NJ-died after 1815 - adopted about 1755-returned to whites about 1776-continued association with Tribe, Pontiac War/62-66, Bushy Run/63, raiding New-Greenbrier-Jackson River valleys/63, raiding Ohio-Little Kanawha-Big Sandy-New River valleys/72, Point Pleasant/74, translator-**with** - Revolution & War of 1812, sons William Tucker Jr/85 & Thomas Tucker/90 joined him in moving to **Mason Co WV** about 1815, husband about 1779 OH of **Mekoche Woman**/60, father of Charles Tucker/80, William Tucker Jr/85, Thomas Tucker/90 & several earlier children-all 1/2 Mekoche-Metis

1754. Tucker, William (2) aka William Jr - 1/2 Mekoche-Metis born about 1785-died after 1826 - son of **Mekoche Woman**/60 & **William Tucker (1)**/40adopted-white, in **Mason Co. WV** about 1815, husband 1814 of **Emily Mekoche**/1800, father of John W. Tucker/1814, James Tucker/1820, Jacob Tucker/1826, Emily Tucker/1827-all 3/4th Mekoche-Metis

1755. Tudors, Stephen – adopted-white born 1770 VA-died 1843 KY – adopted 1772 VA, husband 1793 (NC?) of **Morning Dawn**/78-Pekowi, father of Elizabeth Tudors/95, Leatha Tudors/97, Mary Polly Tudors/1800 & Winnie Tudors/1806-all ½ Pekowi-Metis

1756. Turkey (1) aka **Pelewais**-Peleways[144] – Chalakatha born about 1730 PA**killed** 1780 OH - French-Indian War/54-63, Braddock/55, Cornstalk War/55-77, raiding Shenandoah-New River valleys/55, raiding PA/55-56, raiding Ohio-New River valleys/58, Pontiac War, Bushy Run/63, raiding New-Jackson-Greenbrier
River valleys/63, raiding Ohio-Little Kanawha-Big Sandy-New River valleys/72, Point Pleasant/74 & 78, Blue Jacket War/77-80, raiding KY-OH-VA/77-80, killed in raid 1780

1757. Turkey (2) aka **Plawough** – Chalakatha-Pekowi born about 1745 OHdied after 1817 – son of **Pekowi Man** & **Chalakatha Woman**, Cornstalk War/62-77, Pontiac War/62-66, Bushy Run/63, raiding New-Jackson-Greenbrier
River valleys/63, raiding Ohio-Little Kanawha-Big Sandy-New River valleys/72, Point Pleasant/74-78, raiding OH-KY-VA/75-81, Crawford/82, raiding Ohio River valley/88-92, Blue Jacket War/77-94, relative of **Metheotashe** (through father) & of **Black Fish** (through mother), husband 1765 OH of **Pekowi Woman**/50, father of Young Turkey/69

1758. Turkey (3) aka **Young Turkey**-Plawough (2) – Pekowi-Chalakatha born about 1769 OH-died after 1813 - son of **Turkey (2)-Plawough**/45 & **Pekowi Woman**/50, raiding Ohio River valley/88-92, Blue Jacket War/86-94, traveled 1795-1811 **with relative Tecumseh**, Brownstown/1812-Monguagon/1812-1st Amherstburg/1812-Frenchtown/1813-Ft. Meigs/1813-2nd Amherstburg/1813 & Thames/1813 **with Tecumseh**, wife & children unknown

1759. Turkey Foot (1) - adopted-Ottawa born about 1750 (IN?)-**killed** 1794 OH – Cornstalk War/68-77, raiding Ohio River valley/74 **with Chief Logan**, raiding Ohio-Little Kanawha-Big Sandy-New River valleys/77-81, Point Pleasant/74-78, Blue Jacket War/77-94, Boonesboro/78, raiding Ohio River valley/81 **with Joseph Brant** & **George Girty**, Crawford/82, raiding Ohio River valley/88-93, **succeeded Little Turtle** as leader of the united bands 1794 **with Blue Jacket**/35, **killed at Fallen Timber**/94, husband 1769 OH of **Kishpoko**

Woman/55-(Panther clan), father of Turkey Foot (2)/70-1/2 Kishpoko-Ottawa

1760. Turkey Foot (2) - 1/2 Kishpoko-**Ottawa** born about 1770 OH-**killed** 1813 Thames - son of **Kishpoko Woman**/55 & **Turkey Foot (1)**/50-adopted Ottawa, over 6'6" & heavy, relative-same clan (Panther) as **Tecumseh**, lived **with Shawnee, then with Pottawamee** at Prophet's Town, raiding Ohio River valley/88-92, Blue Jacket War/87-94, raiding OH-VA-KY/95-99, **traveled with Tecumseh**/99-1810, Prophet's Town/1811, Brownstown/1812-Monguagon/1812-1st Amherstburg/1812-Frenchtown/1813-Ft. Meigs/1813-2nd Amherstburg/1813 & Thames/1813 **with Tecumseh**/13, **killed at Thames**/1813, husband 1789 OH of **Kishpoko Woman**/74-(Panther clan?), father of Turkey Foot (3)/90-3/4th Kishpoko-Ottawa

1761. Turkey Foot (3) - 3/4th Kishpoko-**Ottawa** born 1790 OH-died after 1832 KS - son of **Kishpoko Woman**/74 & **Turkey Foot (2)**/70, Prophet's Town/1811, Brownstown/1812-Monguagon/1812-1st Amherstburg/1812-Frenchtown/1813-Ft. Meigs/1813-2nd Amherstburg/1813 & Thames/1813 **with Tecumseh**, moved to KS 1832, husband about 1815 OH of **Kishpoko Woman**/99, father of Jacob Turkey Foot/1816-7/8th Kishpoko-Ottawa

1762. Turned Up Nose – Pekowi born about 1740 (PA?)-died after 1771 - wife about 1755 OH of **Pekowi Man**/24, widow in 1771

1763. Turnip Seed – Chalakatha born about 1770 OH-died after 1810 - wife about 1785 OH of **Chalakatha Man**/65, widowed at Fallen Timber/94

1764. **Turtle (1) aka Namatha**[145] – Chalakatha born about 1740 PA-died after 1774 - raiding Ohio-New River valleys/58, Pontiac War/62-66, Bushy Run/63, raiding New-Jackson-Greenbrier River valleys/63, raiding Ohio-New-Little Kanawha-Big Sandy River valleys/72, Point Pleasant/74, father of Young Turtle-Young Namatha/60

1765. **Turtle (2) aka Big Turtle-Shenkagkela**[146] (1) – Chalakatha born about 1750 OH-died after 1817 - from the **Black Fish** band, brother of **Barshaw Turtle**/65, Cornstalk War/68-77, raiding Little Kanawha-Big Sandy-Kanawha River valleys/72, Point Pleasant/74-75-78, raiding KY-OH-VA/75-81, Blue Jacket War/77-94, Boonesboro/78, Blue Licks/82, Crawford/82, raiding Ohio River valley/88-92, a **Chalakatha Chief** in OH by 1787, wounded at Ft. Recovery/94, Treaty 1817, husband 1770 OH of **Kishpoko Woman**/55-(Panther clan), father of Young Turtle-Shekaghkela/70-Chalakatha-Kishpoko (**not Daniel Boone**)

1766. Turtle (3) aka Young Turtle-**Young Shenkagkela** – ChalakathaKishpoko born about 1770 OH-died after 1817 – son of Big Turtle-

Shenkagkela/50 & Kishpoko Woman/55, raiding Ohio River valley/88-92, Blue Jacket War/87-94, **traveled with Tecumseh** 1795-1812, Brownstown/1812Monguagon/1812-1st Amherstburg/1812-Frenchtown/1813-Ft. Meigs/1813-2nd Amherstburg/1813 & Thames1813 **with Tecumseh**, Treaty 1817, relative/same clan (Panther) as **Tecumseh**, wife & children unknown

1767. Turtle (4) aka Young Turtle-**Young Namatha** – Chalakatha born about
1760 OH-died after 1778 - son of **Turtle (1)-Namatha**/40, Point Pleasant/78, Boonesboro/78, wife & children unknown

1768.Turtle At Home aka Turtle At Home Carpenter-**Turtle At Home Attakullakulla**-Sullicooahwolu-Fulaquokoko-Snapping Turtle - 15/32nd Chalakatha-Thawikila-Creek-**Cherokee**-Metis born 1750 Great Tellico TN-died after 1813 Running Water TN – son of **Attakullakulla Carpenter**/08 & **Ollie Nionee Oconastota**/20, Wolf Clan Cherokee, Cherokee War/75, Pigeon CoCherokee scouts-**with U.S. Army**-Revolution, **Headman at Running Water** (Shawnee) village 1792, operated ferry at Nickajack TN, Capt. in John Speers Co-**with U.S. Army**-Creek War/1813, Treaty 1805, 1806, husband 1770 Nickajack TN of **Ahyague Cherokee**/55, father of Tsinyahnehnaw (Turtle at Home) Carpenter/77 & others-all 15/64th Chalakatha-Thawikila-CreekCherokee-Metis

1769.**Turtle's Heart aka Kitehi-Keetehee**[147] – adopted-Delaware born about 1730 PA-died after 1783 OH – Cornstalk War/55-77, French-Indian War/54-63, Braddock/55, raiding Shenandoah-New River valleys/55, raiding PA/55-56, raiding Ohio-New River valleys/58, Pontiac War/62-66, Bushy Run/63, Grand Council 1763, Council Bouquet Oct. 1764, Council Ft. Pitt 1764 with **Capt. Johnny**-Delaware, **Beaver**-Delaware, **Capt. Pipe**-Delaware, **Simon Girty**white-adopted Seneca, **White Wolf-John Ward**-white-adopted-Shawnee & **Thomas Hickman**-white-(adopted Delaware), Logstown 1765, Stanwix Oct. 1768, raiding Ohio-New-Big Sandy-Little Kanawha River valleys/72, Point Pleasant/74-78, Blue Jacket War/77-82, raiding KY-OH-VA/77-81, Crawford/82, husband about 1750 OH of **Pekowi Woman**/35, children unknown

1770.Tutawtut aka Tutaw-Tutal-Totall-Tutal-Tootaw-Tootal - 1/2 PekowiMetis - born about 1760 (IL?)-died after 1817 - son of **Pekowi Woman** & **French-Canadian Man**, raiding KY-OH-VA/77-81, Point Pleasant/78, Crawford/82, raiding Ohio River valley/88-92, Blue Jacket War/77-93, scout**with U.S. Army**-Fallen Timber-War 1812, husband about 1779 OH of **Pekowi Woman**/64, father of Mary Tutal/80-3/4th Pekowi-Metis

1771.Twisted Man aka **LeTortu** – adopted-**Ottawa**-Metis born about 1730died after 1780 - son of **Ottawa Woman** & **French/Canadian Man**, may have gotten name from some sort of physical deformity, French-Indian War/54-63, Braddock/55, Cornstalk War/55-77, raiding Shenandoah-New River valleys/55, raiding PA/55-56, raiding Ohio-New River valleys/58, Pontiac War/62-66, Bushy Run/63, Point Pleasant/74, Boonesboro/78, raiding KY-OH-VA/77-80, husband about 1750 OH of **Chalakatha Woman**/35, children unknown

1772.Two Clouds – adopted-Miami born about 1760 OH-died after 1791 - wife about 1775 OH **Mekoche Man**/55, widowed at St. Clair/91

Chapter XVIII
Ugly Man to White Bark (U-W)

U

1773. Ugly Man – adopted-Cherokee born about 1740 TN-died after 1775 OH – Cornstalk War/58-75, raiding Ohio-New River valleys/58, Pontiac War/62-66, Bushy Run/63, raiding New-Jackson-Greenbrier River valleys/63, Point Pleasant/74-75, husband about 1760 KY of **Kishpoko Woman**/45, children unknown

1774.Uhseshemaki – adopted-Delaware born about 1735 PA-died after 1765 – Cornstalk War/55-65, French-Indian War/54-63, Braddock/55, raiding NewShenandoah River valleys/55, raiding PA/55-56, raiding Ohio-New River valleys/58, Pontiac War/62-65, Bushy Run/63, raiding New-Jackson-Greenbrier River valleys/63, husband about 1755 OH of **Mekoche Woman**/40, children unknown

1775.Under Elms – adopted-Cayuga born about 1760 OH-died after 1805 - wife about 1775 OH of **Kishpoko Man**/55, widow in 1778

1776.Uphill Man aka **Thakatcheway**-Goes Up The Hill – Mekoche born about 1785 OH-died after 1817 - a warrior at Wapaghonettat 1817, Treaty 1817

1777.Used Her Ax – Chalakatha born about 1740 PA-died after 1776 - wife about 1755 OH of **Chalakatha Man**/35, widow in 1776

V

1778. Vamauweke - Chalakatha born about 1770 OH-died after 1817 - raiding Ohio River valley/88-92, Blue Jacket War/88-94, a warrior at Lewistown 1817, Treaty 1817

1779. Vance, William – 1/4th Pekowi-Metis born 1755 VA-died after 1796 WV-OH – son of **Rachel Castle (1)**/40 & **John Vance (1)**-white, 4th husband 1st 1775 VA of **Unknown Woman**/60, 2nd 1790 WV of **Sarah Rising Sun**/59-1/2 Kishpoko-Mohawk, children/75-90 **with Unknown Woman** unknown, father **with Sarah** of Thomas Vance/91 & Christina Vance/96-both 3/8th Kishpoko-Pekowi-Mohawk-Metis

1780. Vann, Avery (1) - 1/4th Chalakatha-**Cherokee**-Metis born 1748 Davidson Co NC (TN)-died after 1795 Davidson Co NC (TN) - son of **Edward Ned Vann**/20 & **Charity Barnes**/25, great-nephew of **Old Hop**, husband 1767 Davidson Co NC (TN) of **Bird Clan Woman**/50-Cherokee, father of Avery Vann (2)/68-1/8th Chalakatha-Cherokee-Metis

1781. Vann, Chief James aka Tikalohi-Crazy James – 3/8th Chalakatha-Pekowi-**Cherokee**-Metis born 1766 GA-**murdered** 1809 GA - son of **Joseph Vann (1)**/38 & **Polly Wawli Vann**/46, raiding with the Chickamauga/85-92, Cavett's Station 1793, Blind Savannah Clan Cherokee, associated with the New Order Cherokee, Treaty 1804, 1806, **murdered** by **Alexander Jeremiah Sanders, Edmund & William Fawling**-the latter were brothers of his brother-in-law **John Fawling** that Chief James had killed in a duel, husband 1st 1784 GA of **Dawnee**/70-Kishpoko, 2nd 1786 GA of **Elizabeth Hicks (2)**/66-1/8th Chalakatha-Thawikila-Creek-Cherokee-Metis, 3rd 1788 GA of **Elizabeth Scott**/74-1/16th Chalakatha-Thawikila-Creek-Cherokee-Metis-(sister of Margaret Peggy Scott/80 & Mary Polly Scott/82), 4th 1792 GA of **Nancy Ann Brown**/781/8th Chalakatha-Cherokee-Metis, 5th 1796 of **Jennie Foster**/79-1/8th Thawikila-Cherokee-Metis, 6th 1798 GA of **Margaret Peggy Scott** aka **Peggy CherokeeCherokee Peggy**/80-1/16th Chalakatha-Thawikila-Creek-Cherokee-Metis-(sister of Elizabeth Scott/74 & Mary Polly Scott/82), 7th 1799 GA of **Mary Polly Scott**/82-1/16th Chalakatha-Thawikila-Creek-Cherokee-Metis-(sister of Elizabeth Scott/74 & Margaret Peggy Scott/80), **father with Dawnee** of Jesse Vann/84 & Edward Vann/86-both 11/16th Chalakatha-Kishpoko-Pekowi-Cherokee-Metis, **with Hicks** of Delilah Emelia Vann/87-1/4th Chalakatha-Pekowi-ThawikilaCreek-Cherokee-Metis, **with Elizabeth Scott** of James Vann/88-7/32nd Chalakatha-Pekowi-Thawikila-Creek-Cherokee-Metis, **with Brown** of Mary Gahoga Vann/93, John James Vann/94 & Joseph-Rich Joe Vann/95-all 1/4th

Chalakatha-Pekowi-Cherokee-Metis, with **Foster** of Sarah Vann/97-1/4th Chalakatha-Thawikila-Pekowi-Cherokee-Metis, **with Margaret Peggy Scott** of David Vann/99, Judge John Vann/1801, Lucy Ayouku Vann/1803, Little John Vann/1805, Elizabeth Vann/1807 & James Vann/1809-all 7/32nd ChalakathaThawikila-Pekowi-Creek-Cherokee-Metis, **with Mary Polly Scott** of RobertRobin Vann/99-7/32nd Chalakatha-Thawikila-Pekowi-Creek-Cherokee-Metis

1782. Vann, Clement (1) - 1/4th Chalakatha-**Cherokee**-Metis born 1744 GAdied 1832 GA - son of **Edward Vann**/20 & **Charity Barnes**/25, great-nephew of **Old Hop**, husband 1st 1766 Davidson Co NC (TN) of 1st cousin **Elizabeth Quedi Vann**/44, 2nd 1775 Davidson Co NC (TN) of her sister/his 1st cousin **Polly Wawli Vann**/46, father **with Elizabeth** of Mary Vann/67, Alice Vann/69, John Clement Vann/71 & Mary Vann/78-3/8th Chalakatha-Pekowi-Cherokee-Metis, children/75-86 **with Polly** unknown

1783. Vann, Edith (1) - 1/4th Chalakatha-**Cherokee**-Metis born 1750 Davidson Co NC (TN)-died after 1804 - daughter of **Edward Ned Vann**/20 & **Charity Barnes**/25, great-niece of Old Hop, wife 1765 Davidson Co NC (TN) of **Arthur Archibald Coody**/40-white, mother of Joseph Coody (1)/66, Arthur Archer Coody/68, Lewis Coody/70, James Coody/72, Edward Ned Coody/74, Zephaniah Coody/76, Elizabeth Coody/78, Rachel Coody/79, Charity Coody/80 & Joseph Coody (2)/82-all 1/8th Chalakatha-Cherokee-Metis

1784. Vann, Edward (1) - 1/2 **Cherokee**-Metis born about 1720-died 1773 - son of **John Trader Vann (1)**/1690-white & **Cherokee Woman**/1695, brother of **John Trader Vann (2)**/15, husband 1st about 1737 of **Mary Barnes**/20-1/2 Chalakatha-Metis, 2nd about 1744 of Mary's sister **Charity Barnes**/26-1/2 Chalakatha-Metis, father **with Mary** of Joseph Vann/38, Jennie Vann/40, James Vann/42 & Edward Ned Vann (1)/44, **with Charity** of Clement Vann/44, Thomas Vann/46, Avery Vann (1)/48, Edith Vann/50 & Susanna Vann/52-all 1/4th Chalakatha-Cherokee-Metis

1785. Vann, Edward Ned (1) aka Edward (2) - 1/4th Chalakatha-**Cherokee**Metis born 1744 Davidson Co NC (TN)-died 1833 SC - son of **Edward Vann**/20 & **Mary Barnes**/20, great-nephew of **Old Hop**/1690, husband 1762 SC of **Mary King**/46-1/2 Thawikila-Chickasaw, father of Edward Ned Vann (2)/63, Margaret Vann/66, William Vann/70, Edith Vann/74, Vashti Vann/76 & Mason Vann/77all 3/8th Chalakatha-Thawikila-Chickasaw-Cherokee-Metis

1786. Vann, Elizabeth Quedi aka Elizabeth (1) – ½ Chalakatha-Pekowi**Cherokee**-Metis born 1748 Running Water TN-died 1784 Davidson Co.

NC - daughter of **Raven's Sister-Elizabeth Hop-Moytoy**/24 & **John Trader Vann (2)**/15, wife 1st 1762 Running Water TN of her 1st cousin **Joseph Vann (1)** aka John Joseph Vann/38-1/4th Chalakatha-Cherokee-Metis, 2nd 1766 Davidson Co. NC (TN) of his half-brother/her 1st cousin **Clement Vann (1)**/44-1/4th Chalakatha-Cherokee-Metis, mother **with Joseph** of Joseph David Vann/63 & Mary Vann/65, **with Clement** of Mary Vann/67, Alice Vann/69, John Clement Vann/71 & Mary Vann/74-all 3/8th Chalakatha-Pekowi-Cherokee-Metis

1787. Vann, James (1) - 1/4th Chalakatha-**Cherokee**-Metis born 1742 Davidson Co NC (TN)-died 1800 GA - son of **Edward Vann**/20 & **Mary Barnes**/20, great-nephew of **Old Hop**, husband 1762 Davidson Co NC (TN) of **Bird Clan Woman**/45-Cherokee, father of Josiah Vann/70, Isaac Vann/75 & James Vann/80-all 1/8th Chalakatha-Cherokee-Metis, guardian of nephews **Edmund Rock Crutchfield**/86 & **Joseph Crutchfield**/88-(sons of his sister **Susanna Vann**/52) upon the death of their father **John Crutchfield**/50-white (**Not Chief James Vann**)

1788. Vann, Jennie (2) – 3/8th Chalakatha-Pekowi-**Cherokee**-Metis born 1770 GA-died after 1818 - daughter of **Joseph Vann (1)**/38 & **Polly Wawli Vann**/46, wife 1st about 1786 of **Jack Thompson**/70-1/2 Chalakatha-Metis, 2nd before 1813 of **Judge James Brown**/80-1/8th Chalakatha-Cherokee-Metis, mother **with Thompson** of Laugh At Mush Thompson/86, Necooie Thompson/88 & William Thompson/90-7/16th Chalakatha-Pekowi-Cherokee-Metis, children **with Brown** unknown

1789. Vann, John Cherokee aka John (3) – ½ Chalakatha-Pekowi-**Cherokee**Metis born 1744 Running Water TN-died of smallpox 1805 Running Water TN - son of **Elizabeth Hop-Raven's Sister**/24 & **John Trader Vann (2)**/15, Blind Savannah Clan Cherokee, appointed as official translator 1770 by Alexander
Cameron, husband 1st 1762 Running Water TN of **Agnes Weatherford**/47-3/8th Shawano-Metis, 2nd 1766 Running Water TN of **Catherine French**/48-3/4th Chalakatha-Black-Metis, 3rd 1788 (GA?) of **Polly Terrapin-Watts**/68-11/32nd Chalakatha-Pekowi-Cherokee-Metis, father **with Weatherford** of Keziah Vann/63-7/16th Chalakatha-Pekowi-Shawano-Cherokee-Metis, **with French** of John Oowayne-John (4)-Uwani Vann/66, Rebecca Vann/74, Otiyu Vann/76, Lucinda Vann/80 & others/67-84-all 5/8th Chalakatha-Pekowi-Black-Cherokee-Metis, **with Terrapin-Watts** of George Vann/90, John Boy Vann/92-both 27/64th Chalakatha-Pekowi-Cherokee-Metis

1790. Vann, John Oowayne aka John (4)-Uwani-John Wayne – 5/8th Chalakatha-Pekowi-Black-**Cherokee**-Metis born 1766 Running Water TN-died after 1814 - son of **John Cherokee Vann**/44 & **Catherine French**/48, Capt. James Foster Co-**with U.S. Army**-Creek War/1813, husband 1787 TN of **Mary Cherokee**/70, father of Edith Vann/88, Nancy Vann/90, Isaac Vann/92, Mary Vann/94, Rebecca Vann/96, Edward Vann/98 & Nellie Vann/1800-all 5/16th Chalakatha-Pekowi-Black-Cherokee-Metis

1791. Vann, John Trader (2) - 1/2 **Cherokee**-Metis born 1715 Cheowee TNdied 1770 Great Tellico TN - son of **John Trader Vann (1)**/1690-white & **Cherokee Woman**/1695, brother of **Edward Vann (1)**/20, husband 1st about 1735 of **Unknown Woman**/20, 2nd husband 1744 of **Elizabeth Hop-Raven's Sister**/24, children/35-44 **with Unknown Woman** unknown, father **with Elizabeth-Raven's Sister** of John Cherokee Vann/44, Polly Wawli Vann/46, Elizabeth Quedi Vann/48-all ½ Chalakatha-Pekowi-Cherokee-Metis

1792. Vann, Joseph (1) aka John Joseph - 1/4th Chalakatha-**Cherokee**-Metis born 1738 Davidson Co. NC (TN)-died 1800 (GA?) - son of **Mary Barnes**/20 & **Edward Ned Vann**/20, great-nephew of **Old Hop**, translator 1775, Treaty Sycamore Shoals 1775, husband 1st 1762 Running Water TN of his 1st cousin **Elizabeth Quedi Vann**/46-1/2 Chalakatha-Pekowi-Cherokee-Metis, 2nd 1765 of her sister/his 1st cousin **Polly Wawli Vann**/47-1/2 Chalakatha-Pekowi-CherokeeMetis, father **with Elizabeth Quedi** of Joseph David Vann/63 & Mary Vann/65, **with Polly Wawli** of Chief James-Tikalohi Vann/66, Jennie Vann/70, Aisley Vann/72 & Nancy Vann/74-all 3/8th Chalakatha-Pekowi-Cherokee-Metis

1793. Vann, Joseph (4) aka **Rich Joe** – 1/4th Chalakatha-Pekowi-CherokeeMetis born 1795 GA-died 1844 IN - son of **Chief James Vann**/66 & **Nancy Ann Brown**/78, Capt. John Brown Co-**with U.S. Army**-Creek War/13, moved west 1836, killed on the Ohio River when boiler of his steamship "Lucy Walker" exploded, husband 1st 1820 of **Polly Blackwood**/1805-Cherokee-Metis, 2nd 1822 of his step-sister (through his father's 1st wife Elizabeth Scott) **Jennie Springston**/1804-1/32nd Chalakatha-Thawikila-Creek-Cherokee-Metis, no known children/1820-22 **with Blackwood**, father **with Springston** of James Springston Vann/1822, Mary Frances Vann/1824, John Shepherd Vann/1826, Joseph W. Vann/1828, Minerva Vann/1830, Delilah Amelia Vann/1834, Henry Clay Vann/1838-all 5/64th Chalakatha-Thawikila-Pekowi-Creek-Cherokee-Metis

1794. Vann, Joseph Teaulte aka Joseph (5)-**Poor Joe-Tequelto**-Big Joe - 3/16th Chalakatha-Kishpoko-**Cherokee**-Metis born about 1792-died 1877 - son of **Avery Vann (2)**/68 & **Margaret Peggy McSwain**/78, Wolf Clan Cherokee, husband 1st 1812 of **Unknown Woman**, 2nd 1825 of **Catherine Rowe**/1810, 3rd 1830 her sister **Elizabeth Rowe**/1815-both 25/64th Chalakatha-Pekowi-CreekCherokee-Metis, children/1812-25 with **Unknown Woman** unknown, father **with Catherine** of Mary Frances Vann/1825 & Clarinda Rebecca Vann/1828, **with Elizabeth** of David Rowe Vann/1831, Louisa Jane Vann/1833, Jennie Tsinosa Vann/1838 & Kiamitia Elizabeth Vann/1840-all 9/32nd Chalakatha-Pekowi-Creek-Cherokee-Metis

1795. Vann, Keziah (1) – 7/16th Chalakatha-Pekowi-Shawano-**Cherokee**-Metis born 1763 Running Water TN-died 1849 N C - daughter of **John Cherokee Vann**/44 & **Agnes Weatherford**/46, wife 1781 of **Martin Maney**/48-white, mother of Nancy Maney/83, John J. Maney/85, William Maney/87, James Maney/90-all 7/32nd Chalakatha-Pekowi-Shawano-Cherokee-Metis

1796. Vann, Keziah (2) - 3/16th Chalakatha-Kishpoko-**Cherokee**-Metis born about 1818-died after 1832 - daughter of **Avery Vann (2)**/68 & **Margaret McSwain**/78, Wolf Clan Cherokee, wife 1832 of **Robert Webber (2)**/1812-5/8th Chalakatha-Kishpoko-Cherokee-Metis, children unknown

1797. Vann, Polly aka **Wawli**-Polly Otterlifter-Mary Christianna – ½ Chalakatha-Pekowi-**Cherokee**-Metis born 1746 Running Water TN-died 1835 GA - daughter of **Raven's Sister-Elizabeth Hop-Moytoy** (Hughes)/24 & **John Trader Vann (2)**/15, Blind Savannah Clan Cherokee, sister of **John Cherokee Vann**/44 & **Elizabeth Quedi Vann**/48, wife 1st 1759 Running Water TN of **Otter Lifter**/40-Cherokee, 2nd 1765 Running Water TN of 1st cousin **Joseph Vann (1)**/38-1/4th Chalakatha-Pekowi-Cherokee-Metis, 3rd 1775 Davidson Co. NC of his half-brother/her 1st cousin **Clement Vann (1)**/44-1/4th Chalakatha-Pekowi-Cherokee-Metis, mother **with Otter Lifter** of Levi Otterlifter/60 & Robert Otterlifter/62-both 1/4th Chalakatha-Pekowi-Cherokee-Metis, **with Joseph** of Chief James Tikalohi Vann/66, Jennie Vann/70, Aisley Vann/72 & Nancy Vann/74-all 3/8th Chalakatha-Pekowi-Cherokee-Metis, any children **with Clement Vann** unknown

1798. Vann, Susanna - 1/4th Chalakatha-**Cherokee**-Metis born 1752 Davidson Co NC (TN)-died 1800 GA - daughter of **Edward Ned Vann (1)**/20 & **Charity Barnes**/25, great-niece of Old Hop, wife 1st 1767 of **Unknown Man**, 2nd 1783 Running Water TN of **John Crutchfield**/50-white, children/67-82 **with Unknown** not known, mother **with Crutchfield** of Rachel Crutchfield/84, Edmund Rock Crutchfield/86 & Joseph Crutchfield/88-all 1/8th ChalakathaCherokee-Metis, both sons taken in by their uncle James Vann (1)/42 upon death of their father John in 1810

1799. Vann, Thomas (1) - 1/4th Chalakatha-**Cherokee**-Metis born 1746 GAdied 1839 AL - son of **Edward Ned Vann (1)**/20 & **Charity Barnes**/25, greatnephew of Old Hop, husband 1st 1766 Running Water TN of **Blind Savannah Woman**/50, 2nd by 1779 of **Anna Cherokee**/60, children/66-78 **with Blind Savannah** unknown, father **with Anna** of Bryan Vann/80, Sarah Vann/81, Thomas Vann Jr/82, Dempsey Vann/83, Lazarus Vann/84, Edward Hare Vann/93 & Mary Vann (3)/94-all 1/8th Chalakatha-Cherokee-Metis

1800. Vaudon - 1/2 Mekoche-Metis born about 1715 OH-died after 1755 - son of **Mekoche Woman** & **Coureur deBois**-Canadian, French-Indian War/54, Braddock/55, raiding New-Shenandoah River valleys/55, husband about 1735 OH of **Mekoche Woman**/20

1801. Vaught, Elizabeth Scott (Vann-Adair-Burgess-Shepherd-Springston) - wife 1803 of **Mr. Vaught** (aka Vogt)-white born about 1760-died after 1804, mother of Charles Vaught/1804 & James Vaught/1806-both 1/32nd ChalakathaThawikila-Creek-**Cherokee**-Metis

W

1802. Wabapusito aka Wabapooseeto – Chalakatha born about 1760 OH-**killed** 1782 KY - son of **Wababakahto-White Bark**[148], Blue Jacket War/78-82, raiding KY-VA-OH/77-82, Point Pleasant/78, Blue Licks/82, killed with brother 1782 in KY raid

1803. Wabekesheke – Thawikila born about 1770-died after 1817 - raiding Ohio River valley/88-92, Blue Jacket War/88-94, a warrior at Hog Creek 1817, Treaty 1817

1804. Wabemek aka Wabemec – Mekoche born about 1770-died after 1817 - raiding Ohio River valley/88-92, Blue Jacket War/88-94, a warrior at Wapakoneta 1817, Treaty 1817

1805. Wabepee aka White Color-White Man (3) - white-Shawnee born about 1770 OH-died after 1817 - son of **White Man's Wife (1)**/50 & **White Man (2)**/50-both adopted white, raiding Ohio River valley/88-92, Blue Jacket War/8894, raiding Ohio River valley/95-1810, Prophet's Town/1811, Brownstown/1812Monguagon/1812-1st Amherstburg/1812-Frenchtown/1813-Ft. Meigs/1813-2nd Amherstburg/1813 & Thames/1813 **with Tecumseh**, a **Mekoche Chief** at Wapaghonettat before 1817, Treaty 1817, husband about 1790 OH of **White**

Man's Wife (2)-Wife of Wabepee/70-Mekoche, father of several 1/2 Mekoche-Metis children/90-1817

1806. Waggoner, Barbara - 3/4th Chalakatha-Metis born 1805-died after 1844 - daughter of **Peter Waggoner (2)**/84 & **Chalakatha Woman**/88, wife 1824 of **George P. Clark**/1800-1/8th Pekowi-Metis-(Wyandot), mother of Sarah Clark/1825, Mary Clark/1828, Archibald Clark/1830, Samuel Clark/1832, Peter Clark/1834, Eliza Jane Clark/1836, Elizabeth Clark/1838, Catherine Clark/1841 & George Henry Clark/1844-all 7/16th Chalakatha-Pekowi-Metis-(Wyandot)

1807. Waggoner, John Peter - adopted-white born about 1745-died after 1812 - son of **John Waggoner**-white, adopted about 1755, returned to whites 1812, Cornstalk War/63-77, Point Pleasant/74-75-78, Blue Jacket War/77-94, raiding KY-OH-VA/77-81, Crawford/82, raiding Ohio River valley/88-92, husband about 1765 OH of **Chalakatha Woman**/50, father of Peter Waggoner (2)/84 & several other 1/2 Chalakatha-Metis children/65-95, only Peter (2)/84 returned to whites with him 1812

1808. Waggoner, Peter (1) - adopted-white born about 1775-died after 1803 - son of **Brother of John Peter Waggoner**-Son of John Waggoner, grandson of **John Waggoner**-white, captured **with 2 sisters** 1792 by **Tecumseh**, adopted 1792-returned to whites 1803, nephew of **John Peter Waggoner**/45, cousin of **Peter Waggoner**/84-1/2 Shawnee-Metis, husband about 1795 OH of **Kishpoko Woman**/80, father of John Waggoner/96 & several other children/95-1803-all 1/2 Kishpoko-Metis, only John Waggoner/96 returned to whites with him 1803, likely abandoned Shawnee family 1803

1809. Waggoner, Peter (2) - 1/2 Chalakatha-Metis born 1784-died 1885 - son of **John Peter Waggoner**/45-adopted-white & **Chalakatha Woman**/50, returned to whites about 1812 with father, husband about 1803 OH of **Chalakatha Woman**/88, father of Barbara Waggoner/1805 & about four more 3/4th Chalakatha-Metis children/1803-1812, likely abandoned Shawnee family 1812

1810. Wagunetee – Chalakatha born about 1745 OH-died after 1774 – Cornstalk War/63-74, raiding Ohio-New-Little Kanawha-Big Sandy River valleys/72, Point Pleasant/74

1811. Wahepelathee aka **White Hawk**[149] – Kishpoko born about 1770 OH-died after 1823 - raiding Ohio River valley/88-92, Blue Jacket War/88-94, raiding OH-KY-VA/95-1810, Prophet's Town/1811, Brownstown/1812-Monguagon/1812-1st Amherstburg/1812-Frenchtown/1813-Ft. Meigs/1813-2nd Amherstburg/1813 & Thames/1813 **with Tecumseh**, moved to CAN 1815, returned to OH & moved to MO about 1825

1812. Wahwailainne aka Wawelainni-Wahwawwlaeennee– Kishpoko born about 1770 OH-died after 1832 KS - raiding Ohio River valley/88-92, Blue Jacket War/77-94, Prophet's Town/1811, Brownstown/1812-Monguagon/1812-1st Amherstburg/1812-Frenchtown/1813-Ft. Meigs/1813-2nd Amherstburg/1813 & Thames/1813 **with Tecumseh**, moved to CAN 1815, returned to OH about 1817, Treaty 1817, 1825, 1832, move to KS 1832, husband 1790 OH of **Chalakatha Woman**/74

1813. Waits By Water – adopted-Cayuga born about 1740 PA-died after 1764 OH - wife about 1755 OH of **Chalakatha Man**/35, widow in 1764, mother of several 1/2 Chalakatha-Cayuga children/55-64

1814. Wakonathecha – Mekoche born about 1720 PA-died after 1759 - raiding PA/40, French-Indian War/54-59, Braddock/55, raiding New-Shenandoah River valleys/55, raiding PA/55-56, raiding Ohio-New River valleys/58, Council Ft. Pitt Aug. 1759

1815. Wakpelleawee – Chalakatha born about 1710 PA-died after 1751 AL - raiding PA/40, living with Creeks in AL 1751

1816. Wakumsee aka Wacumsee-Wakumthe - Chalakatha born about 1770 OH-died after 1817 - raiding Ohio River valley/88-92, Blue Jacket War/88-94, a warrior at Lewistown 1817, Treaty 1817

1817. Walathe aka Walaseh – Chalakatha born about 1770 OH-died after 1817 – Blue Jacket War/88-94, a warrior from Lewistown 1817, Treaty 1817

1818. Walker, Jennie – 25/64th Chalakatha-Mekoche-**Cherokee**-Metis born 1772 Chota TN-died after 1836 OK - daughter of **John Walker (1)**/52 & **Catherine Kingfisher**/52, Wolf Clan Cherokee, wife 1st 1785 **Thomas FoxTaylor**/60-1/4th Chalakatha-Thawikila-Creek-Cherokee-Metis, 2nd 1789 **John Gotaquasgi MacIntosh**/70-Chickasaw-Metis, mother **with Fox-Taylor** of Charles Fox-Taylor III/86, Richard Fox-Taylor/87, Thomas Fox-Taylor Jr/88 & Susannah Fox-Taylor/89-all 5/16th Chalakatha-Mekoche-Thawikila-Creek-Cherokee-Metis & **with MacIntosh** of John MacIntosh Jr/90, Nellie MacIntosh/92 & Maria MacIntosh/95-all 3/16th Chalakatha-Mekoche-Cherokee-Chickasaw-Metis

1819. Walker, John (2) aka **John Walker Jr** – 25/64th Chalakatha-Mekoche**Cherokee**-Metis born 1770 Chota TN-**murdered** 1839 TN - son of **John Walker (1)**/52 & **Catherine Kingfisher**/52, Wolf Clan Cherokee, Treaty 1806, 1816, 1817, 1819, General Staff-**with U.S. Army**-Creek War/1813, murdered 1839 with his son **John Jack Walker**/1800, uncle **Major Ridge**/55, & cousins

Elias Boudinot/72 & **John Ridge**/75, husband 1st 1795 of **Susannah Fields (1)**/66-1/2 Chalakatha-Pekowi-Metis, 2nd 1800 of **Elizabeth Lowery (Sevier)**/7711/32nd Chalakatha-Pekowi-Metis, father **with Fields** of Susan Walker/95 & Carter Thigh Walker/95-both 7/16th Chalakatha-Mekoche-Pekowi-CherokeeMetis, **with Lowery** of John Jack-John (3) Walker/1800-23/64th Chalakatha-
Mekoche-Pekowi-Cherokee-Metis

    1820.   Walking Bear - Kishpoko-(adopted-**Cherokee-Chickamauga**) born about 1760-**killed** 1810 KY - raiding KY-VA-OH/77-81, Point Pleasant/78, Blue Licks/82, Crawford/82, raiding Ohio River valley/88-92, Blue Jacket War/77-94, raiding TN-KY-VA-OH/95-10, living **with Cherokee** in east KY 1792-1810, **killed at Yahoo Falls**/10, husband about 1780 KY of **Cherokee-Chickamauga Woman**/65, children unknown

    1821.   Walking Stick aka Capt. John-**Willopothee** – Chalakatha born about
1770 OH-died 1843 KS - raiding Ohio River valley/88-92, Blue Jacket War/88-94, Delegation to Congress 1802, Capt-Shoe Boots Co-**with U.S. Army**-Creek War/1813, moved to KS 1832, husband about 1789 KY of **Cherokee Woman**/75, father of John Walkingstick/90, Tetolenust Walkingstick/91, Elsie Walkingstick/92-all 1/2 Chalakatha-Cherokee

    1822. Walks Bent – adopted-Delaware born about 1750 OH-died after 1778 OH - wife about 1765 OH of **Mekoche Man**, widow 1778, children unknown

    1823. Walks Far – Chalakatha born about 1730 PA-died after 1775 - wife about 1745 OH of **Chalakatha Man**/25, widow 1775, children unknown

    1824. Wallasee – Chalakatha born about 1770 OH-died after 1817 - raiding Ohio River valley/88-92, Blue Jacket War/88-94, raiding Oh-KY-VA/95-1810, Prophet's Town/1811, Brownstown/1812-Monguagon/1812-1st Amherstburg/1812-Frenchtown/1813-Ft. Meigs/1813-2nd Amherstburg/1813 & Thames/1813 **with Tecumseh**, a warrior at Lewistown 1817, Treaty 1817

    1825. Walters, Ephriam - adopted-white born 1744-died after 1794 - adopted 1756-returned to whites 1764, brother of **John Walters**/43, husband 1766 of **Mary Debolt**/50-5/8th Pekowi-Metis, father of several children/66-94-all 5/16th Pekowi-Metis

    1826. Walters, John - adopted-white born 1743-died after 1783 - adopted 1756returned to whites 1765-returned to tribe 1783, brother of **Ephriam Walters**/44, adopted son of **Yougashaw**/10, scout-**with U.S. Army**-

Crawford/82, husband 1763 of **Daughter of Yougashaw**/48-Pekowi, children unknown

1827. Wanechataka – Mekoche born about 1710 PA-died about 1758 OH in epidemic- raiding PA/40, Council Ft. Pitt Nov. 1753, Braddock/55, raiding NewShenandoah River valleys/55, raiding PA/55-56, raiding Ohio-New River valleys/58

1828. Wapacanaugh – Mekoche born before 1790 OH-died after 1825 - brother of **Pokechaw**, Prophet's Town/1811, Brownstown/1812-Monguagon/1812-1st Amherstburg/1812-Frenchtown/1813-Ft. Meigs/1813-2nd Amherstburg/1813 & Thames/1813 **with Tecumseh**, moved to CAN 1815, returned to OH about 1825

1829. Wapakwaha – Kishpoko born about 1795 OH-died 1840 KS - Prophet's Town/1811, Brownstown/1812-Monguagon/1812-1st Amherstburg/1812Frenchtown/1813-Ft. Meigs/1813-2nd Amherstburg/1813 & Thames/1813 **with Tecumseh**, moved to CAN 1815, returned to OH 1825, moved to KS 1826 **with Prophet & Paukeesaa**, 2nd husband 1826 of **Sokomse Tecumseh**-(widow 1826 of **Naythahwaynah Tecumseh**), **step-father of** Waylahskse/1810, Jim Fry/1812, Nahswahpama/1814, Pahsequawmease/1816, Big Jim Tecumseh/1824.

1830. Wapatanequa - 1/2 Thawikila-Metis born 1755 OH-died after 1779 - son of **Thawikila Man**/35 & **Wapatonequa**/40-adopted white, returned to whites with mother-returned to tribe 1765, raiding Ohio-Little Kanawha-Big SandyNew River valleys/72, raiding VA-KY-OH/75-77, Point Pleasant/74-75-78, not part of group that went to AL/74, moved to MO 1779, husband about 1775 OH of **Thawikila Woman**/60, father of two known 3/4th Thawikila-Metis children/75-79

1831. Wapatonequa - adopted-white born 1740-died after 1779 (MO?) - adopted 1750, returned to whites-returned to tribe 1765, wife about 1755 OH of **Thawikila Man**/35, widow in 1775, not part of group that went to AL/74, moved to MO 1779, mother of Wapatanequa/55 & several other children/55-74-all ½ Thawikila-Metis

1832. Wapekawpa – Chalakatha born about 1730 PA-**killed** 1765 - FrenchIndian War/54-63, Braddock/55, raiding New-Shenandoah River valleys/55, raiding Pa/55-56, raiding Ohio-New River valleys/58, Pontiac War/62-65, Bushy
Run/63, raiding New-Jackson-Greenbrier River valleys/63, Council Logstown 1765, killed by a Kickapoo

1833. Wapemeskuletisesa aka Wapemeskooleteesesa – Chalakatha born about 1710 PA-died after 1751 AL - raiding PA/40, living with AL Creeks 1751

1834. Wapeskeahathew – Mekoche born about 1760 OH-died after 1817 – Blue Jacket War/78-94, Point Pleasant/78, raiding KY-VA-OH/77-81, Crawford/82, raiding Ohio River valley/88-92, Prophet's Town/1811, **left Tecumseh** after Prophet's Town/1811

1835. Wapeskeka – Thawikila born before 1790 OH-died after 1817 – no part in War 1812, from **Black Hoof** band-family, a warrior from Hogs Creek village 1817

1836. Wapeskekahathew – Chalakatha born about 1760 OH-died after 1786 – Blue Jacket War/78-94, raiding OH-KY-VA/77-81, Point Pleasant/78, Crawford/82, living in Moluntha's village 1786

1837. Wapunnoo - adopted-Mohawk born about 1766-died after 1792 - son of **Coohcoochee**/45 & **Cokundiawthah**/40, brother of **Sotonegoo** (Girty Ironside)/60, **Black Loon**/62, **White Loon**/64-all adopted-Mohawk-Shawnee, adopted brother 1792-93 (6 months) of **Oliver Spencer**-white, Blue Jacket War/86-92, Crawford/82, Harmar/90, St. Clair/91, husband about 1786 OH of **Kishpoko Woman**/70, father of four 1/2 Kishpoko-Mohawk children/86-92

1838. Waquiwas aka Wahkweewas – Kishpoko born about 1780 OH-died after 1826 KS - raiding OH-KY-VA/99-1810, Prophet's Town/1811, Brownstown/1812-Monguagon/1812-1st Amherstburg/1812-Frenchtown/1813-Ft. Meigs/1813-2nd Amherstburg/1813 & Thames/1813 **with Tecumseh**, Treaty 1817, 1825, living in Apple Creek MO 1815, moved to KS 1826 with **Prophet** & **Paukeesa**, wife & children unknown

1839.   Ward, Bryant (1) – adopted-white born 1710 ENG-died after 1760 SC – son of **Edmund Ward**/1680-white & **Mrs. Ward**/1685-white, brother of **James Ward**/1700, **Francis Ward-Five Killer**/12 & **Lucy Ward**/14, immigrated 1732 with father & Francis, in SC by 1735, a fur-trader, husband 1st 1735 SC of **Anna Pekowi**/20, 2nd 1756 Chota TN of his niece (daughter of his brother Francis/Five Killer) **Nancy Fivekiller-Ward**/38-7/32nd Chalakatha-Cherokee-Metis, father **with Anna** of Lucy Ward/36, Bryant Ward (2)/38, 4 other children/39-49 & John Jack Ward/50-1/2 Pekowi-Metis, **with Nancy** of Elizabeth Ward (1)/57-7/64th Chalakatha-Cherokee-Metis

1840.   Ward, Elizabeth (1) – 7/64th Chalakatha-**Cherokee**-Metis born about 1757 Chota TN-**killed** 1794 Chota TN - daughter of **Nancy Five Killer** (Kingfisher) **Ward**/38 & **Bryant Ward (1)**/10-adopted-white, Wolf Clan Cherokee, half-sister (through Bryant) of **John Jack Ward**/50-1/2 Pekowi-Metis, & half-sister (through Nancy) of

Catherine Kingfisher/52 & **Five Killer-Little Fellow Kingfisher**/55-both 7/64th Chalakatha-Cherokee-Metis, wounded 1793 in attack by **John Beard**'s renegade militia, killed in battle, wife 1st 1776 of **Joseph Martin Jr**/40-1/2 Pekowi-Metis, 2nd 1788 of **Daniel Hughes**/60-3/4th Chalakatha-Kishpoko-Pekowi-Metis, mother **with Martin** of John Martin/76, Nancy Martin/78, James Martin/80-all 19/64th Chalakatha-Pekowi-Cherokee-Metis & **with Hughes** of Rachel Hughes/90-27/64th Chalakatha-Kishpoko-Pekowi-Cherokee-Metis

1841. Ward, Elizabeth (2) - 3/8th Chalakatha-Pekowi-**Cherokee**-Metis born 1778 Chota TN-died after 1822 - daughter of **Catherine McDaniel**/53 & **John Jack Ward**/50, Wolf Clan Cherokee, half-sister of **James Bryant Ward**/92-1/4th Pekowi-Cherokee-Metis, wife 1st 1798 of **Bernard Hughes Tsuyogonisgi Hughes**/77-3/4th Chalakatha-Kishpoko-Pekowi-Metis, 2nd about 1808 of **John Cox**/88-white, 3rd 1812 of **Gideon Franklin Morris** aka Walosi-Frog/92-white, 4th 1813 of **Elijah Sutton**/82-1/2 Pekowi-Metis, children/98-1818 with **Hughes** and children/1808-11 **with Cox** unknown, mother **with Morris** of George Morris/1812-3/16th Chalakatha-Pekowi-Cherokee-Metis, mother **with Sutton** of Henrietta Sutton/1814, Loretta Sutton/1816, Catherine Sutton/1818, Harriett Sutton/1820 & John Ward Sutton/1822-all 7/16th Chalakatha-Pekowi-CherokeeMetis

1842. Ward, Francis aka **Five Killer**-Shayaqustuego-Raven of Chota-Kollanah – adopted-white born 1712 ENG-died 1755 Nachestown TN in battle – son of
Edmund Ward/1680-white & **Mrs. Ward**/1685-white, brother of **James Ward (1)**/1700, **Lucy Ward (1)**/14 & **Bryant Ward**/10, emigrated 1732 to VA with father James & brother Bryant, delegation to ENG later, killed in same battle as his son in law **Kingfisher**, husband 1735 Chota TN of **Tame Doe Carpenter**/167/16th Chalakatha-Cherokee-Metis, father of Long Fellow Ward-Fivekiller/36, Nancy Wild Rose Ward-Fivekiller/38 & Little Fellow Ward-Fivekiller/40-all
7/32nd Chalakatha-Cherokee-Metis

1843. Ward, James (1) – adopted white born 1700 ENG-died after 1725 (VA?)
– son of **Edmond Ward**/1680 & **Mrs. Ward**, brother of **Francis-Five Killer Ward**/12, **Lucy Ward (1)**/14 & **Bryant Ward**/10, immigrated before 1725, husband by 1725 VA of **Kishpoko Woman**/10, father of Lucy Ward (3)/25-1/2 Kishpoko-Metis

1844. Ward, John aka **White Wolf**-Wapamowawa[150] - adopted-white born about 1741-**killed** 1793 OH - adopted about 1745-never returned, adopted Chalakatha, raiding Ohio-New River valleys/58, Pontiac War/62-66, Bushy

Run/63, raiding New-Jackson-Greenbrier River valleys/63, Point Pleasant/74-78, Boonesboro/78, Crawford/82, raiding Ohio River valley/88-92, Blue Jacket War/77-93, Council Ft. Pitt 1764 with **Capt. Johnny**-Delaware, **Capt. Pipe**Delaware, **Beaver**-Delaware, **Turtle's Heart**-adopted-Delaware, **Simon Girty**adopted Seneca & **Thomas Hickman**-adopted Delaware, Council Logstown 1765, killed in raid with **Tecumseh**, husband about 1758 OH of **Chalakatha Woman**/44, father of John Jr-Young White Wolf/58, Sutawanee/60 & Joseph Ward/62-all 1/2 Chalakatha-Metis

1845. Ward, John Jack – ½ Pekowi-Metis born 1750 SC-died 1815 SC - son of **Bryant Ward**/10-adopted-white & **Anna Pekowi**/20, husband 1st 1771 Chota TN of **Catherine McDaniel**/53-1/4th Chalakatha-Cherokee-Metis, 2nd 1791 Chota TN of **Cherokee Woman**/76, father **with McDaniel** of James Ward/72, George Ward/74, Samuel Ward/76, Elizabeth Ward/78, Susan Ward/80, Bryan Ward/82, Nancy Ward/84, Charles Jackson Ward/86, Lucy Ward/88 & John S. Ward/90-all 3/8th Chalakatha-Pekowi-Cherokee-Metis, **with Cherokee** of James Bryant Ward/92-1/4th Pekowi-Cherokee-Metis

1846. Ward, John Jr aka **Young White Wolf** - 1/2 Chalakatha-Metis born about 1758-died after 1794 - son of **White Wolf** aka **John Ward**/41-adoptedwhite & **Chalakatha Woman**/44, a Chalakatha, raiding KY-OH-VA/77, Point Pleasant/74-78, Boonesboro/78, Crawford/82, raiding Ohio River valley/88-92, Blue Jacket War/77-94, brother of **Sutawanee Ward**/60 & **Joseph Ward**/62, husband 1777 OH of **Chalakatha Woman**/60, children unknown

1847. Ward, Joseph - 1/2 Chalakatha-Metis born about 1762-**killed** 1793 KY - son of **White Wolf-John Ward**/41-adopted white & **Chalakatha Woman**/44, a Chalakatha warrior, brother of **John Ward Jr-Young White Wolf**/58 & **Sutawanee Ward**/60, Blue Jacket War/80-93, raiding Ohio River valley/81 **with Joseph Brant & George Girty**, Crawford/82, raiding Ohio River valley/88-92, Harmar/90, St. Clair/91, **killed in KY raid** with Tecumseh, husband 1783 OH of **Kishpoko Woman**/65, children unknown

1848. Ward, Lucy (1) - white born 1714 ENG-died after 1780 Chota TN – daughter of **Edmund Ward**/1680 & **Mrs. Ward**, sister of James Ward/1700, Bryant Ward/10 & Francis Ward/12-all adopted-whites, Treaty Sycamore Shoals 1775, wife 1738 Chota TN (his 3rd) of **Oconastota Rainmaker**/02, mother **with Oconastota** of Lucy Ward Oconastota/42-1/4th Chalakatha-Cherokee-Metis

1849. Lucy (3) – ½ Pekowi-Metis born 1735 SC-died after 1758 – daughter of **Bryant Ward**/10-adopted-white & **Anna Pekowi**/20, husband & children unknown

1850. Ward, Lucy (4) aka Lucy Ward Oconastota - 1/4th Chalakatha-**Cherokee**-Metis born 1742 Chota TN-died after 1758 - daughter of **Oconastota Rainmaker**/02 & **Lucy Ward (1)**/14-adopted white, husband & children unknown

1851. Ward, Lucy (5) - 3/8th Chalakatha-Pekowi-**Cherokee**-Metis born 1788 Chota TN-died after 1822 - daughter of **Catherine McDaniel**/53 & **John Jack Ward**/50, Wolf Clan Cherokee, half-sister of James Bryant Ward/92-1/4th Pekowi-Cherokee-Metis, wife about 1803 of **Unknown Man**, children unknown

1852. Ward, Susan - 3/8th Chalakatha-Pekowi-**Cherokee**-Metis born 1780 Chota TN-died after 1828 - daughter of **Catherine McDaniel**/53 & **John Jack Ward**/50, Wolf Clan Cherokee, half-sister of James Bryant Ward/92, wife by 1802 of **William England**/80-Creek or Creek-Metis-(brother of **Elizabeth England**/88-wife of **James Bryant Ward**/92), mother of Matilda England/1812, Joseph England/1814, Hepsie England/1816, Sabra England/1817, Tillman England/1818, William England Jr/1820, Chapman England/1822 & Emily England/1824-all 3/16th Chalakatha-Pekowi-Creek-Cherokee-Metis

1853. Ward, Sutawanee - 1/2 Chalakatha-Metis born about 1760-died after 1778 - daughter of **John White Wolf Ward**/41-adopted-white & **Chalakatha Woman**/44, a Chalakatha, sister of **John Ward Jr-Young White Wolf**/58 & **Joseph Ward**/62, wife about 1775 OH of **Stand in the Water**/55-Chalakatha, children unknown

1854. Warm Skirt – Pekowi born about 1750 OH-died after 1780 - wife about 1765 OH of **Pekowi Man**/44, widow in 1780

1855. Wasewwela aka Wasoowela – Mekoche born about 1770 OH-died after 1817 - raiding Ohio River valley/88-92, Blue Jacket War/88-94, no part in War 1812, a warrior at Wapaghonettat 1817, Treaty 1817

1856. Washington, George aka Queshawksey-**Keeshawksee** - Mekoche(adopted-**Seneca**) born about 1764 OH-died about 1843 KS - scout-translator **with U.S. Army**-Revolution, Treaty Greenville 1795, Treaty 1817, husband about 1784 of **Martha Washington**/70-Seneca, father of George Washington Jr/85, James Washington/87, John Washington/95-all 1/2 Mekoche-Seneca

1857. Wasina aka **Waseena**-Wasinwa – Kishpoko born about 1770 OH-**killed** 1813 Thames - raiding Ohio River valley/88-92, Blue Jacket War/88-94, raiding OH-KY-VA/95-1810, Prophet's Town/1811, Brownstown/1812-

Shawnee Heritage

Monguagon/1812-1st Amherstburg/1812-Frenchtown/1813-Ft. Meigs/1813-2nd Amherstburg/1813, **killed at Thames**/13 **with Tecumseh**, wife & children unknown

1858.Watchdog aka **LeMolosse**-Molossee - 1/2 Pekowi-Metis born about 1750 OH-died after 1821 - son of **Pekowi Woman** & **French/Canadian Man**, Cornstalk War/68-77, Point Pleasant/74, Blue Jacket War/77-94, raiding KYOH-VA/77-81, Boonesboro/78, raiding Ohio River valley **with Joseph Brant & George Girty**/81, Crawford/82, raiding Ohio River valley/88-92, husband about 1770 OH of **Pekowi Woman**/55

1859.Waters, Catherine McKee - wife 1818 of **Thomas George Waters (2)**white born 1798-died after 1826, mother of Alexander Joseph/1820, twins John & James Waters/1822 & Thomas George Waters (3)/1825-all 1/4th KishpokoMetis

1860.Waters, George Morgan aka George Morgan Watters - 1/4th ChalakathaPekowi-Metis born about 1772-died 1855 - son of **Sarah Hughes**/43 & **Col. Thomas Waters**/45-white, brother of **Sally Wild Rose Waters**/75, Blind Savannah Clan Cherokee, educated in ENG by his father, husband 1st about 1789 of **Lydia Wolf**/70-1/4th Chalakatha-Pekowi-Cherokee-Metis, 2nd 1797 of **Susan Bigby**/77-1/16th Chalakatha-Thawikila-Creek-Cherokee-Metis, 3rd 1803 **Catherine Fife**/85-white, father **with Wolf** of Sally Agadiya Waters/90-1/4th Chalakatha-Pekowi-Cherokee-Metis, children/97-03 **with Bigby** unknown, father **with Fife** of Wilhelmina Clarke Waters/1805, Thomas Jefferson Waters/1809 & Sarah Margaret Waters/1810, Catherine Waters/1814-all 1/8th Chalakatha-Pekowi-Metis

1861.Waters, Sally aka Wild Rose-Tsidunigisdi-Sally Watters – 1/4th Chalakatha-Pekowi-Metis born about 1770-died after 1828 - daughter of **Sarah Hughes**/43 & **Col. Thomas Waters**/45-white, Blind Savannah Clan Cherokee, wife 1st 1788 (TN?) of **Sequoyah-George Gist**/58-37/64th Chalakatha-PekowiCherokee-Metis, 2nd 1798 of **Young Puppy**/70-Cherokee, mother **with Sequoyah** of Teeseey Gist/88, George Gist Jr-Sequoyah Jr/90, Polly Gist/92, Richard-Lightning Bug Gist/94 & Tisahli Fox Gist/96-all 13/32nd Chalakatha-Pekowi-**Cherokee**-Metis, children **with Young Puppy** unknown

1862.Waters, Sally Agadiya – 1/4th Chalakatha-Pekowi-**Cherokee**-Metis born 1790-died after 1851 - daughter of **George Morgan Waters**/72 & **Lydia Wolf**/70, Bird Clan Cherokee (but should be Blind Savannah if following mother's Clan), 8th wife 1826 AR of **Sequoyah-George Gist**/59, mother of Joseph Gist/1827, Lucinda Gist/1829, Susan Gist/1831, Elizabeth Gist/1833 & Mary Gist/1835-all 13/32nd Chalakatha-Pekowi-Cherokee-Metis

1863. Wathakapee – Mekoche born about 1790 OH-died after 1835 KS - wife about 1815 OH of **Mekoche Man**/85, moved to KS about 1832, widow in 1835

1864. Watie, David aka **Oowatie** - 7/32nd Chalakatha-Thawikila-Creek**Cherokee**-Metis born 1770 GA-died 1842 OK - son of **Killancea Carpenter (2)**/40 & **Giyosti Tahchee**/57, husband 1st 1790 GA of **Unknown Woman**/74, 2nd 1805 GA of **Susanna Charity Reese**/85-Cherokee-Metis, children/90-1805 **with Unknown** not known, father **with Reese** of Isaac-Stand Watie/1806, Galagina-Buck-Elias Boudinot/1808, Nancy Watie/1809, Mary Ann Watie/1810, Thomas Black Watie/1812, Elizabeth Watie/1814, John Alexander Watie/1815, Charles Edwin Watie/1816 & Susan Watie/1818-all 7/64th Chalakatha-Thawikila-Creek-Cherokee-Metis

1865. Watts, Bark aka **Bark Oconastota** – 11/16th Chalakatha-Pekowi**Cherokee**-Metis born 1728 Chota TN-died 1754 TN of smallpox – son of **John Watts (Sr)**/04 & **Quatsis Fox**/08, adopted son 1735 of **Oconastota**/02, Red Paint Cherokee, a medicine man, died of smallpox caught while doctoring the ill, husband 1748 Chota TN of his adopted sister **Jennie Oconastota**/24-1/2 Chalakatha-Thawikila-Creek-Cherokee, father **with Jennie** of Bark Watts (2)Bark Oconastota (2)/50-21/32nd Chalakatha-Pekowi-Thawikila-Creek-CherokeeMetis

1866. Watts, Betty Tuni aka **Betty Toney** – 19/64th Chalakatha-Pekowi Thawikila-Creek-**Cherokee**-Metis born 1838-died after 1851 – daughter of **Peach Eater Watts**/84 & **Jennie Catateehee**/1820, husband & children unknown

1867. Watts, Capt. John aka John (5) – 9/16th Chalakatha-Pekowi-ThawikilaCreek-**Cherokee**-Metis born 1782 NC-died after 1850 Greene Co MO - son of **Wurtegua Attakullakulla Carpenter**/60 & **John-Young Tassel-Watts Jr**/48, husband 1800 Willstown AL of **Mary Polly (1)-Ooloosta Benge**/85-21/64th Chalakatha-Pekowi-Cherokee-Metis, father of Mary Chiouke/1810, John Watts (7)/1815, Martha Watts/1818 & Cecilia Watts/1820-all 7/16th Chalakatha-Thawikila-Pekowi-Creek-Cherokee-Metis

1868. Watts, Elizabeth (1) – 21/32nd Chalakatha-Pekowi-**Cherokee**-Metis born 1750 Willstown AL-died after 1790 - daughter of **Oousta (White Owl-Great Eagle) Carpenter**/23 & **John Watts Sr**/04, Red Paint Clan Cherokee, wife 1st 1765 (AL?) of **Unknown Man**, 2nd 1779 (AL?) of **William R. Campbell**/60white, 3rd 1789 AL of **Leckickee Natchez**/50-Creek, children/65-79

with **Unknown Man** not known, mother **with Campbell** of William R. Campbell Jr/80, Lucy Campbell/82, Elizabeth Campbell/86, Diana Campbell/88- all 21/64th
Chalakatha-Pekowi-Cherokee-Metis, **with Natchez** of Nancy Natchez/90-21/64th Chalakatha-Pekowi-Creek-Cherokee-Metis

1869. Watts, Elizabeth (2) – 7/16th Chalakatha-Pekowi-**Cherokee**-Metis born 1786 AL-died 1852 - daughter of **Nancy Oousta Hanging Maw**/60 & **JohnYoung Tassel-Watts Jr**/48, wife by 1810 of **Mr. Couch**/86-white, mother of Isaac Couch/1820-7/32nd Chalakatha-Pekowi-Cherokee-Metis

1870. Watts, Ghigoneli aka Forget Me Not-Chekawnahler – 11/16th Chalakatha-Pekowi-Metis born 1752 Running Water TN-died about 1804 TN - daughter of **Ghigoneli Bowles**/23 & **John Watts Sr**/04, Red Paint Clan
Cherokee (?), namesake of mother & great-aunt, wife 1st (his 2nd) 1769 Nickajack TN of **George Lowery (1)**/40-white, 2nd 1772 Settico TN of her half-brother **Rising Fawn Fox (2)**/30-1/2 Chalakatha-Cherokee, no children of record **with Lowery**, mother of **with Rising Fawn** of Rising Fawn (3)/72, Catherine/74 & Polly Rising Fawn/76-all 21/32nd Chalakatha-Pekowi-Cherokee-Metis

1871. Watts, John (1) – ½ Chalakatha-Metis born 1662 VA-**killed** 1708VA by Catawba – son of **Thomas Watts (1)**/1642-white & **Elizabeth Chalakatha**/1645, could cipher, read & write English, husband 1682 of **Chalakatha Woman (2)**/1665, father of Thomas Watts (2)/1682-3/4th Chalakatha-Metis

1872. Watts, John (2)–**John Watts Sr**-Little Tassel-Old **Forked Tongue** – 7/8th Chalakatha-Pekowi-Metis born 1704 VA-died 1779 Great Tellico TN – son of **Thomas Watts (2)**/1682 & **Sister of Oshasqua-Muskrat**/1684-Pekowi, adopted son 1708 of **Swan-Wapehti Hop**/1688 & his uncle **Oshasqua (1)Muskrat (1)-Moytoy (5)**/1686 when his family was killed by Catawba, could cipher, read & write English, French-Indian War/54-63, raiding NewShenandoah River valleys/55, raiding Ohio-New River valleys/58, Pontiac
War/62-66, raiding New-Jackson-Greenbrier River valleys/63, **associated with John Swift** silver-mining & counterfeiting/61-69, associated with **Cornstalk, Dragging Canoe, Doublehead, Nathaniel Gist, Sam Blackburn**, Abram Flint, Herman Staley, Isaac Campbell, Shadrack Jefferson, Pierre St. Martin, Andrew Renound, Jeremiah Bates, Alexander Bartel, Henry Hazlitt & Moses Fletcher on the frontier, husband 1st 1724 Settico TN of **Quatsis Fox**/08-1/2 ChalakathaCherokee, 2nd 1735 of **Unknown White Woman**/20, 3rd 1743 Great Tellico TN of **Oousta Carpenter**/22-7/16th Chalakatha-Cherokee-Metis, 4th 1747

Running Water TN of **Ghigoneli Bowles**/23-1/2 Chalakatha-Metis, father **with Fox** of
Terrapin/26, Bark/28 & other children/24-35-all 11/16th Chalakatha-PekowiCherokee-Metis, children/35-43 with **Unknown White Woman**/20 unknown, father **with Oousta** of Wurteh Watts/44, John Watts Jr-John (3)/48, Elizabeth Watts/52 & Unacata-White Mankiller Watts/54-all 21/32nd Chalakatha-Pekowi-Cherokee-Metis, **with Ghigoneli** of Nancy Watts/48, Ghigoneli Watts-Ghigoneli Bowles (2)/50 & John Watts (4)-John Bowles-Chief Bowl/56-all 11/16th Chalakatha-Pekowi-Metis

1873. Watts, John (3) - **John Watts Jr**-Kunoskeskie-**Young Tassel**-CoatoheeCorn Tassel of Toquo – 21/32nd Chalakatha-Pekowi-**Cherokee**-Metis born 1746 Wills Town AL-died 1808 Dekalb Co. AL - son of **Oousta (White Owl-Great Eagle) Carpenter**/23 & **John Watts (1)**/04, could cipher, read & write English, Red Paint Clan Cherokee, Treaty Sycamore Shoals 1775, Council Coyatee 1792, **succeeded Dragging Canoe as Chickamauga Chief** 1792 **with** Standing Turkey (2)-**Little Turkey**/15-(son of Old Hop-Standing Turkey), raiding TN 1788 with Major Ridge, wounded 1792 while leading attack on Buchanan Station-with 200 Cherokee, 80 Creek & 30 Shawnee, Council Hanging Maw Town 1793-survived attack by **John Beard**'s renegade militia, husband 1st 1768 Great Tellico TN of **Deer Clan Woman**/53, 2nd 1778 Great Tellico TN of **Wurtegua (Attakullakulla) Carpenter**/60-15/32nd Chalakatha-ThawikilaCreek-Cherokee-Metis, 3rd 1780 Great Tellico TN of **Nancy Oousta Hanging Maw**/50-7/32nd Chalakatha-Cherokee-Metis, father **with Deer Clan Woman** of Margaret Watts/78-21/64th Chalakatha-Pekowi-Cherokee-Metis, **with Wurtegua** of Mink Watts/80, Capt. John Watts/82, Soup-Chulusatah Watts/84 & Fish Tail-Fork-tail Watts/86-all 9/16th Chalakatha-Pekowi-Thawikila-Creek-CherokeeMetis, **with Nancy** of Thomas Watts/82, Two Wood/84, Peach Eater/86, Elizabeth Watts (2)/88 & Councilor John Watts-John (5)/92-all 7/16th Chalakatha-Pekowi-Cherokee-Metis

1874. Watts, Nancy aka Nannie-Nannte-Nionee-Ooloosta – 11/16th Chalakatha-Pekowi-Metis born 1748 Great Tellico TN-died after 1786 - daughter of **Ghigoneli Bowles**/23 & **John Watts Sr**/04, Blue Holly Clan Cherokee, wife 1767 Nickajack TN of **George Lowery (1)**/40-white, mother of Major John Lowery/68, Major George Lowery/70, Elizabeth Lowery/76, Sarah Lowery/78, Jennie Lowery/80, Aky Lowery/82 & Nellie Lowery/86-all 11/32nd Chalakatha-

Pekowi-Metis

1875. Watts, Terrapin aka **Terrapin Oconastota (2)**-Terrapin (2)-Tuckasee of Etowah-Tukasi – 11/16th Chalakatha-Pekowi-**Cherokee**-Metis born 1726 Chota TN-died after 1796 GA – son of **John Watts (Sr)**/04 & **Quatsis Fox**/08, adopted son 1735 of **Oconastota**/02, Red Paint Clan Cherokee, Pigeon Co-Cherokee scouts-**with U.S. Army**-Revolution, Treaty Sycamore Shoals 1775, Tellico 1794, husband 1757 Etowah TN of **Old Jennie**/44-Cherokee, father of Polly (Watts) Terrapin/68 & Little Terrapin (Watts)-Brother Terrapin/70-both 11/32nd Chalakatha-Pekowi-Cherokee-Metis

1876. Watts, Thomas (1) – white born 1642 ENG-**killed** 1708 VA by Catawba – associated with Carpenter, Greenwood, Ward families (all English that married into the Shawnee in the 1600's), husband 1660 of **Elizabeth Chalakatha**/1645, father of John Watts (1)/1662-1/2 Chalakatha-Metis

1877. Watts, Thomas (2) – 3/4th Chalakatha-Metis born 1682-**killed** 1708 VA by Catawba – son of **John Watts (1)**/1662-1/2 Chalakatha-Metis & **Chalakatha Woman (2)**/1665, husband 1700 VA of **Sister of Oshasqua-Muskrat**/1684Pekowi, father of John Watts (2)-John Watts Sr/1704-7/8th Chalakatha-PekowiMetis

1878. Watts, Wurteh aka Betsy-Molly Running Wolf – 21/32nd ChalakathaPekowi-**Cherokee**-Metis born 1744 Great Tellico TN-died 1779 NC - daughter of **John Watts Sr**/04 & **Oousta (White Owl-Great Eagle) Carpenter**/23, Red Paint Clan Cherokee (through mother)-later Bird Clan (by marriage?), wife 1st
1757 Great Tellico TN of **Robert Due-Chief Jolly-Jaulee**/40-1/2 ShawneeMetis, 2nd 1758 of **Nathaniel Gist**/30-1/2 Pekowi-Metis, 3rd 1759 Great Tellico TN of **Bloody Fellow**/40-Kishpoko, 4th 1760 of **John Trader Benge**/30-white, possibly 5th of **Nathaniel Lawson**-white, mother **with Due** of Chief John Jolly/58-37/64th Chalakatha-Pekowi-Cherokee-Metis, **with Gist** of Sequoyah-George Gist/59-37/64th Chalakatha-Pekowi-Cherokee-Metis, **with Bloody Fellow** of Tahlonteeskee (2)-Tahlonteeskee Bloody Fellow-Tahlonteeskee (Benge)-53/64th Kishpoko-Chalakatha-Pekowi-Cherokee-Metis, **with Benge** of Martin-Utana-Tail Benge/61, Robert-Chief Bench Benge/62, Richard Benge/63, Catherine Benge/64, Tashliske-White Path Benge/65 & Lucy Benge/66-all 21/64th Chalakatha-Pekowi-Cherokee-Metis, children **with Lawson** unknown

1879. Waupaukawda – Chalakatha born about 1750 OH-died after 1786 – Cornstalk War/68-77, raiding Ohio-Little Kanawha-Big Sandy-New River valleys/72, Point Pleasant/74-75-78, Blue Jacket War/77-82, raiding KY-OH-VA/77-81, Crawford/82, Treaty 1786

1880. **Waupaukowelo, Waupaucowela**[151] – Mekoche born about 1740 OH died after 1786 – Cornstalk War/58-77, raiding Ohio-New River valleys/58, Pontiac War/62-66, Bushy Run/63, raiding New-Jackson-Greenbrier River valleys/63, raiding Ohio-Little Kanawha-Big Sandy-New River valleys/72, Point Pleasant/74-75-78, Blue Jacket War/77-82, Boonesboro/78, raiding OH-KY-VA/77-81, Crawford/82, Treaty 1786

1881. **Wawaleepesheeka** – Mekoche born about 1790 OH-died after 1817 - a warrior at Wapaghonettat 1817, Treaty 1817

1882. **Wawatashewa aka Wawatashoowa** – Thawikila born about 1775 AL died after 1817 - Fallen Timber/94, a warrior from Hog Creek 1817, Treaty 1817

1883. **Wayashikee aka Wayasheekee** – Pekowi born about 1750 OH-died after 1790 - wife about 1765 OH of **Pekowi Man**/45, widowed at Harmar/90, mother of several children/65-90

1884. **Waymataiba aka Waymataeeba** – Kishpoko born about 1750 OH-died after 1817 – Cornstalk War/68-77, raiding Ohio-New-Little Kanawha-Big Sandy River valleys/72, Point Pleasant/74-75-78, raiding KY-VA-OH/77-81, Crawford/82, raiding Ohio River valley/88-92, Blue Jacket War/77-94

1885. **Waythapamatha** – Chalakatha born about 1750 OH-died after 1795 – Cornstalk War/68-77, raiding Ohio-New-Little Kanawha-Big Sandy River valleys/72, Point Pleasant/74-78, raiding KY-OH-VA/75-81, Blue Jacket War/77-94, Crawford/82, raiding Ohio River valley/88-92, Treaty Greenville 1795

1886. **Wayweejaytin aka Wayweejayteen** – Kishpoko born about 1760 OH**killed** 1794 OH - raiding KY-OH-VA/77-81, Crawford/82, raiding Ohio River valley/88-92, Blue Jacket War/87-94, killed 1794 at Fallen Timber

1887. **Weasau aka Wausawsa** – Thawikila born about 1724 AL-died after 1798 (AL?) - in OH by 1754, Cornstalk War/55-74, French-Indian War/54-63, Braddock/55, raiding New-Shenandoah River valleys/55, raiding PA/55-56, raiding Ohio-New River valleys/58, Pontiac War/62-64, Bushy Run/63, raiding New-Jackson-Greenbrier River valleys/63, a **Thawikila Chief** in OH before 1763, raiding Ohio-New-Big Sandy-Little Kanawha River valleys/72, Point Pleasant/74, moved to AL 1774-after Point Pleasant/74, **King of the Sawanogi (Shawnee among the Creek)** 1798, brother of **Wife of Moluntha**/15, **Black Stump**/20, **Kikusglowlawa**/22, **Capt. Johnny**/26, **Yellow Hawk**/28, **Black Hoof**/30 & **Kishkalwa-Tiger Tail**/35, husband about 1754 OH of **Thawikila Woman**/40, father of Young Weasau/60

1888. Weasau, Young aka Weasau (2) -Wausawsa (2) – Thawikila born about 1760 OH-**killed** 1814 AL - son of **Waesau**/24 & **Thawikila Woman**/40, a Thawikila warrior among the Sawanogi (Shawnee among the Creeks) 1798, Capt. Frogg Co-**with U.S. Army**-Creek War/1813-**killed in battle** 1814 at Horseshoe Bend, husband about 1780 AL of **Thawikila-Creek Woman**/64, children unknown

1889. Weasel in House – Kishpoko born about 1750 OH-died after 1780 - Point Pleasant/74-78, Boonesboro/78, raiding KY-OH-VA/75-80

1890. Weathaksheka – Mekoche born about 1780 OH-died after 1817 - a warrior at Wapaghonettat 1817, Treaty 1817

1891. Weatherford, Agnes – 3/8th Shawano-Metis born 1747 VA-died after 1765 – daughter of **Martin Weatherford**/26 & **Mary Jane**/31-½ ShawanoMetis, 1st wife about 1765 of **John Cherokee Vann**/46-3/8th Chalakatha-Pekowi-Cherokee-Metis, mother of Keziah Vann/63-7/16th Chalakatha-Pekowi-Shawano-Cherokee-Metis

1892. Weatherford, Charles (5) – 3/8th Shawano-Metis born 1752 Lunenburg Co VA-died after 1800 GA – son of **Martin Weatherford**/26 & **Mary Jane**/31½ Shawano-Metis, moved to AL before 1778 with **Samuel Sims**, associated with **Lachlan McGillivray**, husband 1780 AL of **Sehoy (III) Tuckabatchee**/59-3/4th Creek-Metis, father of Chief **William Red Eagle** Weatherford/81, John David Weatherford/83, Elizabeth Weatherford/85, Washington Weatherford/87, Major Weatherford/88, Rosanna Weatherford/89 & Polly Weatherford/90-all 3/16th Shawano-Creek-Metis

1893. Weatherford, Martin – 1/4th Shawano-Metis born 1726 James City VAdied 1805 Harbor Island Bahamas – son of **Charles Weatherford**/05 & **Mary Cornet-Cupboard**/08, husband 1st 1747 VA of **Mary Jane**/31-½ ShawanoMetis, 2nd 1775 Augusta GA **Isabella Archer**/60-white, father **with Mary Jane** of Agnes Weatherford/47, William Weatherford/48, James Weatherford/50, Charles Weatherford/52, Elenor Weatherford/53, John Weatherford/54,
Catherine Weatherford/56-all 3/8th Shawano-Metis, **with Archer** of Henrietta Weatherford/76, John William Weatherford/77, William Henry Weatherford/78, Catherine Weatherford/79, Charles Cameron Weatherford/80, Richard Weatherford/81, Charlotte Weatherford/83, Sarah Weatherford /84 & Isabella Weatherford/85-all 1/8th Shawano-Metis

1894. Weatherford, Susannah Shawano – Shawano born about 1659 VA-died after 1690 – wife about 1673 VA of **William Weatherford-Whitheford**-white born 1645 York Co VA-died 1732 (VA?), mother of Richard Weatherford/1674, Thomas Weatherford/1676, William Weatherford/1678, John Weatherford/1682, James Weatherford/1684, Charles Weatherford/1686 & Ann Weatherford/1690all ½ Shawano-Metis

1895. Weatherford, Wilkerson – 1/8th Shawano-Metis born 1726 New Kent Co VA-died 1790 Mecklenburg Co NC – son of **William Weatherford**/02 & **Susanna Wilkerson**/10, husband 1753 NC of **Susanna**/36-1/8th Shawano-Metis, father of Hilkiah Weatherford/54, Agnes Weatherford/56, Ursula Weatherford/58, William Weatherford/60 & John Weatherford/62-all 1/8th Shawano-Metis

1896. Weatherford, William (2) – ½ Shawano-Metis born 1678 James City Co VA-died 1756 Lunenburg Co VA – son of **Susannah Shawano**/1659 & **William Weatherford(1)-William Whitheford**/1645, husband 1699 VA of **Susanna Waller**/1685-white, father of John Weatherford/1700, William Weatherford/02, Lucy Weatherford/05 & Major Weatherford/15-all 1/4th Shawano-Metis

1897. Weatherford, William (3) – 1/4th Shawano-Metis born 1702 New Kent Co VA-died after 1730 – son of **William Weatherford**/1678 & **Susanna Waller**/1685-white, husband about 1728 VA of **Susannah Wilkerson**/10, father of Wilkerson Weatherford/26, John Weatherford/28, Major Weatherford/30, Richard Weatherford/32 & Elizabeth Maria Weatherford/34-all 1/8th ShawanoMetis

1898. Weatherford, William Red Eagle aka Lamochattee-HopnicafutsahiaStraight Talker-Truth Teller – 3/16th Shawano-**Creek**-Metis born 1781 AL-died
1824 Baldwin Co AL – son of **Charles Weatherford**/52 & **Sehoy Tuckabatchee**/59, husband 1st about 1794 AL of **Mary Polly Moniac**/83-CreekMetis, 2nd 1812 AL of **Sopoth Thlanie**/85-Creek, 3rd 1817 (under white law) of
Mary Stiggens/97-Natchez-Metis, , father **with Moniac** of Charles Weatherford/95 & Mary Polly Weatherford/97, **with Thlanie** of William Weatherford Jr/1813, **with Stiggens** of Alexander McGillivray Weatherford/1818, Mary Levitia Weatherford/1820-all 3/32nd Shawano-CreekMetis

1899. Weaver, Mary McDaniel – wife 1770 NC of **William Weaver**-white born 1750-died 1836 Ashe Co. NC, mother of Joshua Weaver/85-1/8th Chalakatha-**Cherokee**-Metis

1900.	Webber, William (2) – ½ Chalakatha-Metis born 1712 Chota TN- died 1751 Chota TN – son of **Quatsis Hop**/1684-Chalakatha & **William Webber (1)**/1680-ENG, husband 1st 1726 of **Unknown Woman**, 2nd 1738 of **Lucy Ward (3)**/25-1/2 Kishpoko-Metis, children/26-38 **with Unknown Woman** unknown, father **with Ward** of William Webber (3)-Capt. Will/40-1/2 Chalakatha-Kishpoko-Metis

1901.	Webber, William (3) aka **Capt. Will**-Red-haired Will - ½ ChalakathaKishpoko-Metis born 1740 Chota TN-died after 1796 TN - son of **Lucy Ward (2)**/25 & **William Webber (2)**/12, adopted son 1751 of his aunt **Catherine Webber**/10 & **May Apple**/1690-Kishpoko upon death of his parents, called a half-brother of **Ostenaco Oconastota**/19, from Nequassee & Running Water TN, raiding New-Ohio-Little Kanawha-Big Sandy River valleys/72, Point Pleasant/74, raiding KY-OH-VA/77, Treaty 1785, Council with Blount 1792, moved west 1796, husband about 1760 (TN?) of **Sarah Bird Clan**/45-Cherokee, father of William Webber (4)/62, other children/63-71, Susan Webber/72, Robert Webber/74, Archibald Webber/76, David Webber/78, Elizabeth-Betsy Webber/80-all 1/4th Chalakatha-Kishpoko-Cherokee-Metis

1902.	Wechquessinah aka Wechkweesseena - 1/2 Mekoche-Metis born about 1750 OH-died after 1765 - daughter of **Adopted White Woman** & **Mekoche Man**, returned to whites-returned to tribe 1765, wife about 1765 OH of **Mekoche Man**/44, children unknown

1903.	Wechequewissainah aka Wechekweeweesaneah – adopted-Delaware born about 1740 PA-died after 1764 - raiding New-Ohio River valleys/58, Pontiac War/62-64, Bushy Run/63, raiding New-Jackson-Greenbrier River valleys/63, husband about 1760 OH of **Chalakatha Woman**/45

1904.	Weed aka **Theueteseepuah**-Theeooeeteseepaw – adopted-Iroquois born about 1750 (PA?)-died after 1817 – Cornstalk War/72-77, raiding Ohio-Little Kanawha-Big Sandy-New River valleys/72, raiding Ohio River valley/74 **with Chief Logan**, Point Pleasant/74, raiding OH-KY-VA/75-81, Crawford/82, raiding Ohio River valley/88-92, Blue Jacket War/77-94, raiding OH-KYVA/95-1810, Prophet's Town/1811, Council with British 1779 with **Alexander McKee**/25, **Wryneck**/25-Pekowi, **William Caldwell**/50, **Matthew Elliott**/30,

Simon Girty/41, **James Girty**/43 & **George Girty**/46, **Simon Surphet**McKee's cousin, Savenooka Raven Hop/20 & **River Bottom**/45-Seneca, a elder warrior at Lewistown 1817, Treaty 1817, husband about 1770 OH of **Chalakatha Woman**/55

1905. Wekonnathaka – Chalakatha born about 1730 PA-**killed** 1774 Point Pleasant WV - French-Indian War/54-63, Braddock/55, raiding New-Shenandoah River valleys/55, raiding PA/55-56, raiding Ohio-New River valleys/58, Pontiac War/62-65, Bushy Run/63, raiding New-Jackson-Greenbrier River valleys/63, Council Logstown 1765, raiding Little Kanawha-Big Sandy-Ohio-New River valleys/72, **killed** Point Pleasant/74

1906. Welch, David - 9/32nd Chalakatha-Kishpoko-Black-Metis born 1770 Madison Co KY-died 1814 (War of 1812?) – son of **Happy McLemore**/55 & **Ned Welch**/49-white, husband 1st 1791 Madison Co KY of his 1st cousin **Catherine Little Cat Brock**/73-19/32nd Chalakatha-Kishpoko-Black-CherokeeMetis, 2nd 1800 KY of **Elizabeth McSwain**/82-1/4th Kishpoko-Metis, father **with Brock** of Nicholas Welch/93, John Welch/95 & Thomas Welch/99-all 7/16th Chalakatha-Kishpoko-Black-Cherokee-Metis, **with McSwain** of George W. Welch/1802, Sidney Welch/1804, Mary Polly Welch/1812 & Elizabeth Jane Welch/1814-all 17/64th Chalakatha-Kishpoko-Black-Metis

1907. Welch, Happy McLemore – wife 1769 NC of **Ned Welch**-white born 1749 Bertie Co NC-died after 1770 (KY?), mother of David Welch/70-9/32nd Chalakatha-Kishpoko-Black-Metis

1908. Welewenaka – Thawikila born about 1780 OH-died after 1817 - a warrior from Hog Creek 1817, from **Black Hoof** band-family, Treaty 1817

1909. Wells, William aka Apekonit-Wild Carrot-Black Snake - white(adopted-**Miami**) born 1770 PA-**killed** 1812 - adopted about 1775 KY-returned to whites 1794-after Fallen Timbers, **adopted son of Porcupine**-Gaviahatte-Eel Miami, known for his red hair, raiding Ohio River valley/88-92, Blue Jacket War/87-94, Treaty Greenville/95, 1805, 1809, Indian Agent-trader-translator, Capt. of scouts-**with U.S. Army**-War 1812-killed in War, son in law of **Nonhelema** Hokolesqua/20 & of **Little Turtle**-Miami, husband 1st 1785 OH of **Youngest Daughter of Nonhelema**/57, 2nd about 1790 (OH-IN) of **Tukemung Little Turtle**/75-Miami, father **with Youngest Daughter of Nonhelema** of William Wayne Wells/86 & Mary Wells/88-both 15/32nd Chalakatha-Mekoche-

Metis-(Miami)

1910. Welviesa aka Welveesa – Mekoche born about 1775 OH-died after 1817 - Fallen Timber/94, a warrior from Wapaghonettat 1817, Treaty 1817

1911. Weseloutha aka Weselootha – Chalakatha born about 1720 PA-died after 1759 OH - French-Indian War/54-59, Braddock/55, raiding New-Shenandoah River valleys/55, raiding PA/55-56, raiding Ohio-New River valleys/58, Council Ft. Pitt Aug. 1759

1912. **Wesheshemo**[152] – Mekoche born about 1780 OH-died after 1817 - a warrior at Wapaghonettat 1817, Treaty 1817

1913. Wespata – Chalakatha born about 1785 OH-died after 1817 - a warrior from Lewistown 1817, Treaty 1817

1914. West, Elizabeth - 1/2 Chalakatha-Metis born about 1774-died after 1812 - daughter of **Chalakatha Woman** & **Trader West**-white (or Metis blood going back to Jamestown?), wife 1794 of **Samuel Candy Jr**/69-3/64th ChalakathaCherokee-Metis, mother of Thomas Tsatagadihi Candy/92, Ollie Candy/93,
Nancy Candy/96, George Washington Candy/99, Sam Candy III/1800, John Walker Candy/1803 & Peggy Candy/1808-all 17/64th Chalakatha-CherokeeMetis

1915. West, George - 1/2 Chalakatha-Metis born about 1790-died after 1843 - son of **Chalakatha Woman** & **Trader West**-white(or Metis blood going back to Jamestown?), husband 1st 1815 of **Elizabeth Vann**/1800-7/16th ChalakathaKishpoko-Pekowi-Cherokee-Metis, 2nd 1825 of **Unknown Woman**, children unknown

1916. West, Jacob - 1/2 Chalakatha-Metis born about 1785-died 1843 AR - son of **Chalakatha Woman** & **Trader West**-white(or Metis blood going back to Jamestown?), husband 1808 of **Sarah Harlan**/88, father of Bluford West/1808, Eliza West/1809, John Walker West/1811, Rosa West/1815, Ellis West/1817, George Harlan West/1818, Ezekial West/1820-all 17/64th Chalakatha-CherokeeMetis

1917. Wewachee – Chalakatha born about 1770 OH-died after 1817 - raiding Ohio River valley/88-92, Blue Jacket War/88-94, a warrior at Lewistown 1817, Treaty 1817

1918. Weythapamatha – Mekoche born 1760 OH-died after 1795 OH – Blue Jacket War/77-94, raiding KY-OH-VA/77-81, Blue Licks/82, raiding Ohio River valley/88-92, Treaty Greenville 1795

1919. Whirlwind aka **Wishekuane**-Weeshekooanee – Chalakatha born 1750 OH-died after 1792 OH – Cornstalk War/68-77, raiding Ohio-New-Big SandyLittle Kanawha River valleys/72, Point Pleasant/74-78, Blue Jacket War/77-92, raiding KY-VA-OH/77-81, Crawford/82, raiding Ohio River valley/88-92,
Harmar/90 & St. Clair/92

1920. Whistler – Chalakatha born 1730 PA-died 1758 OH in epidemic - French-Indian War/54-58, Braddock/55, raiding New-Shenandoah River valleys/55, raiding PA/55-56, raiding Ohio-New River valleys/58

1921. White Alligator - 1/2 Thawikila-**Creek**-Metis born 1740 AL-died after 1779 - son of **Thawikila Woman** & **1/2 Creek-Metis Man**, moved north about 1755, Cornstalk War/55-77, French-Indian War/57-63, raiding Ohio-New River valleys/58, Pontiac War/62-66, Bushy Run/63, raiding New-Jackson-Greenbrier River valleys/63, raiding Ohio-Little Kanawha-Big Sandy-New River valleys/72, raiding Ohio River valley **with Logan**/74, Point Pleasant/74, moved to AL 1774, returned to OH 1778, moved to MO 1779, husband about 1760 OH of **Thawikila Woman**/45, children unknown

1922. White Arms – adopted-1/2 Delaware-Metis born about 1750-died after 1785 - daughter of **Delaware Woman** & **White Man**, didn't return to whites 1765, wife about 1765 OH of **Mekoche Man**/45, widow 1785, children unknown

1923. White Bark aka **Wababakahkahto** – Chalakatha born about 1732 PA-died of illness 1783 OH - French-Indian War/54-63, Braddock/55, Cornstalk War/55-77, raiding New-Shenandoah River valleys/55, raiding PA/55-56, raiding Ohio-New River valleys/58, Pontiac War/62-66, Bushy Run/63, raiding NewJackson-Greenbrier River valleys/63, raiding Ohio-Big Sandy-Little KanawhaNew River valleys/72, Point Pleasant/74-78, Boonesboro, father of Son/58husband of **Margaret Pauley**, Wabapusito/60, adopted father 1779 of **Margaret Pauley**/52-white

Section XIX
White Beaver to Young (W - Z)

W (*continued*)

1924. White Beaver – adopted-Kickapoo born about 1730 (IN-IL?)-died after 1770 - wife about 1745 (IN?) of **Kishpoko Man**/24, widow in 1770

1925. White Bird (1) aka **Wapepillose**-Ouapipelene-Wapepeelosee – Thawikila born about 1760 OH-died 1835 – moved to AL with family/74, returned to OH/78, raiding OH-KY-VA/78-79, Point Pleasant/78, Boonesboro/78, moved to MO 1779, living in Apple Creek MO 1794, a **minor Thawikila Chief** in MO

1926. White Bird (2) -1/2 Pekowi-Metis born about 1760 OH-died after 1795 – daughter of **Pekowi Man** & **Adopted White Woman**, wife about 1775 OH of **Pekowi Man**/54, widow in 1795

1927. White Cap aka White Caps in the Water – Chalakatha born about 1740 PA-died after 1799 – Cornstalk War/58-77, raiding Ohio-New River valleys/58, Pontiac War/62-66, Bushy Run/63, raiding New-Jackson-Greenbrier River valleys/63, raiding Ohio-New-Little Kanawha-Big Sandy River valleys/72, Point Pleasant/74-78, Blue Jacket War/77-94, raiding KY-VA-OH/77-81, Crawford/82, raiding Ohio River valley/88-92, listed as a leader in 1799, wife & children unknown

1928. White Carp – Pekowi born about 1740 (PA?)-died after 1785 - raiding Ohio-New River valleys/58, Pontiac War/62-66, Bushy Run/63, raiding NewJackson-Greenbrier River valleys/63, raiding Ohio-Little Kanawha-Big Sandy-
New River valleys/72, Point Pleasant/74, raiding KY-VA-OH/77-81, Crawford/82

1929. White Corn – Chalakatha born about 1745 PA-died after 1778 OH - wife about 1760 OH of **Chalakatha Man**/40, widow 1778

1930. White Deer – Kishpoko born about 1780-died after 1854 KS - raiding OH-KY-VA/99-1810, Prophet's Town/1811, Brownstown/1812-Monguagon/1812-1st Amherstburg/1812-Frenchtown/1813-Ft. Meigs/1813-2nd Amherstburg/1813 & Thames/1813 **with Tecumseh**, Treaty 1817, 1854, moved to KS before 1832, husband 1800 OH of **Chalakatha Woman**/84

1931. White Elk aka **Wapemashehawey** – Chalakatha born about 1720 PAdied after 1762 - French-Indian War/54-62, Braddock/55, raiding NewShenandoah River valleys/55, raiding PA/55-56, raiding Ohio-New River valleys/58, Council Ft. Pitt Aug. 1762 (**not Col. Alexander McKee**)

1932. White Face - 1/2 Pekowi-Metis born about 1730 OH-died after 1765 - daughter of **Pekowi Woman** & **Coureur deBois**, wife about 1745 OH of **Pekowi Man**, widow 1765, didn't return to whites 1765, husband & children unknown

1933. White Feather aka Nawabasheka-**Wapawasheka** – Chalakatha born about 1750 OH-died after 1819 – Cornstalk War/68-77, raiding Ohio-New-Little Kanawha-Big Sandy River valleys/72, Point Pleasant/74-75-78, Blue Jacket War/77-94, raiding KY-VA-OH/77-81, Crawford/82, raiding Ohio River valley/88-92, a minor **village Chief** in OH before 1800, a warrior at Wapaghonettat 1817, Treaty 1817, moved west after 1817, father of John White Feather/95

1934. White Fish – Pekowi born about 1705 PA-died after 1778 OH – a **Chief in PA** by 1740, raiding PA/40, French-Indian War/54-63, Braddock/55, very old at Treaty Ft. Pitt 1776, possibly relative of **Poxinosa & Opessa**, accidentally blinded in one eye while bird-hunting 1778

1935. **White Hawk aka Wapepelethee**[153] – Kishpoko born about 1745 OHdied after 1778 – Cornstalk War/62-76, Pontiac War/62-66, raiding NewJackson-Greenbrier River valleys/63, raiding Ohio-Little Kanawha-Big Sandy-New River valleys/72, Point Pleasant/74-75-78, Boonesboro/78

1936. White Head - adopted-white born about 1750-died after 1777 - adopted about 1755-returned to whites-returned to tribe 1765, known for her whiteblonde hair, 2nd wife about 1765 OH of **Chalakatha Man**/30

1937. White Heart – adopted-Ottawa born about 1760 (MI?)-died after 1795 - wife about 1775 (OH-IN?) of **Kishpoko Man**/54, widow in 1795

1938. White Horse – Pekowi born about 1730 PA-died before 1815 (MO?) – Cornstalk War/55-77, French-Indian War/54-63, Braddock/55, raiding NewShenandoah River valleys/55, raiding PA/55-56, raiding Ohio-New River valleys/58, Pontiac War/62-66, Bushy Run/63, raiding New-Jackson-Greenbrier River valleys/63, raiding Ohio-New-Little Kanawha-Big Sandy River valleys/72, Point Pleasant/74-78, Blue Jacket War/77-82, raiding KY-OH-VA/77-81, Crawford/82, moved west before 1794, husband about 1755 OH of **White Horse Woman**/40

1939. White Legs - adopted-white born about 1740-died after 1765 - adopted about 1753, living in OH before 1765-didn't return to whites 1765, wife about 1755 OH of **Kishpoko Man**/35, children unknown

1940. White Light aka **Wapameeto** – Kishpoko born about 1760 OH-died after 1795 - Blue Jacket War/77-94, Point Pleasant/78, raiding KY-OH-VA/77-81, Crawford/82, raiding Ohio River valley/88-92, Fallen Timber/94

1941. **White Loon aka Wawpawwawqua-Wapawaqua**[154] - adopted-Mohawk born about 1764 OH-died after 1832 KS - son of **Coocoochee**/45 &

Cokundiawthah/40-both adopted-Mohawk, joined Ohio Shawnee with family 1769, brother of **Sotonegoo** (Girty Ironside)/60, **Black Loon**/62, **Wapunnoo**/66, adopted brother 1792-93 (6 months) of **Oliver Spencer**-white, raiding Ohio River valley/88-92, Blue Jacket War/82-94, husband about 1784 OH of **Kishpoko Woman**/67, children unknown

1942. White Man (1) aka **LeBlancquerre** - 1/2 Kishpoko-Chippewa-Metis born about 1710 IN-died after 1755 - son of **Kishpoko Woman** & **ChippewaFrench/Canadian Metis**, raiding PA/40, French-Indian War/54, Braddock/55, raiding New-Shenandoah River valleys/55, husband about 1730 OH of **Kishpoko Woman**/15, children unknown

1943. White Man (2) - adopted white born about 1745-died after 1805 OH - adopted about 1755-never returned to whites, raiding Ohio-Little Kanawha-Big Sandy-New River valleys/72, raiding Ohio River valley/74 **with Chief Logan**, Point Pleasant/74-75-78, Blue Jacket War/77-94, raiding Ohio-New River valleys/77-81, Crawford/82, raiding Ohio River valley/88-92, husband about 1770 OH of **White Man's Wife**/50-adopted white, father of Wabapee-White Man (3)/70 & several more children/70-95-all white-Shawnee

1944. White Man (4) aka Wakawuxsheno-**Wakawooksheno** – adopted-1/2 **Seneca**-Metis born about 1770-died after 1817 - son of **Seneca Woman** & **White Man**, raiding Ohio River valley/88-92, Blue Jacket War/87-94, scout**with U.S. Army**-Prophet's Town/1811-War 1812-Thames/1813, Treaty 1817, husband 1st about 1790 OH of **Mekoche Woman**/75, 2nd about 1810 OH of **Seneca Woman**/95, several children by each wife/91-1817

1945. White Otter aka Wabawasena-**Wapawasena** – Chalakatha born about 1740 PA-died after 1774 – Cornstalk War/58-74, raiding Ohio-New River valleys/58, Pontiac War/62-66, Bushy Run/63, raiding New-Jackson-Greenbrier River valleys/63, raiding Ohio-New-Big Sandy-Little Kanawha River valleys/72, Point Pleasant/74, adopted brother of **John Ewing**/47-adopted white, wife & children unknown

1946. White Otter, Mother of – Chalakatha born about 1720 PA-died of smallpox 1766 OH – wife by 1739 of **Father of White Otter**/15, widowed 1763, mother of **White Otter**/40, **Wabethe Otter**/43 & others/42-62, adopted mother 1763 OH of **John Ewing**/47, mother in law about 1759 of **John Smith**/30-adopted-Irish

1947. White Otter, Sister of aka **Wabethe** – Chalakatha born about 1743 (PA?)-died after 1775 OH – daughter of **Father of White Otter**/15 & **Mother of**

White Otter/20, wife about 1758 OH of **John Smith**/30-adopted Irish, mother of Ann Smith/59, John Smith Jr/65, Mary Smith/72 & other 1/2 Chalakatha-Metis children/60-75

1948. White Owl (1) aka **White Owl Carpenter**-White Owl Raven-**Moytoy (4)**-**Caulanna**-Collanah-**Moytoy (4)** – 7/8th Chalakatha-Metis born 1678 Running Water TN-**killed** 1741 in battle – son of **Trader Tom Carpenter (2)Moytoy (2)**/1660 & **Nancy Chalakatha**/1664, Long Hair Clan Cherokee, could cipher, read & write English, delegation to ENG 1730, leader of the 7 Cherokee Clans, killed in same battle as **Young Rainmaker**, husband 1st about 1698 of **Unknown Woman**, 2nd 1711 of **Nancy Rainmaker**/1683-Cherokee, children/1698-1711 **with Unknown Woman** not known, father **with Nancy** of Killaneca-Buck Carpenter/12, Killaqua Carpenter/14, Betsy Carpenter/16, Tame Doe Carpenter/18, All Bones-Flying Squirrel Carpenter/20, Oousta Carpenter/22 & Bushy Head Carpenter/24-all 7/16th Chalakatha-Cherokee-Metis, **adopted father of** Great Eagle Carpenter/02, Elizabeth Tassel Carpenter/04, Attakullakulla Carpenter/06, (Old) Corn Tassel Carpenter/08 & Susan Moytoy Carpenter/10-(all children of his brother **Savannah Tom Carpenter (1)-Moytoy (3)** & **Nancy Rainmaker**), adopted father of **Amoyah Pigeon Moytoy**/15-15/16th Chalakatha-Metis (son of his sister **Pashmere Carpenter (2)**/1681)

1949. White Owl, Betsy aka **Betsy Carpenter** – 7/16th Chalakatha-CherokeeMetis born 1716 Great Tellico TN-**killed by hanging** 1803 GA - daughter of
Nancy Rainmaker/1683 & **White Owl Carpenter (1)**/1678, could cipher, read & write English, Wolf Clan Cherokee, wounded 1793 by **John Beard**'s renegade militia, hung by whites 1803 GA, wife 1st 1732 Great Tellico of **Unknown Man**, 2nd 1749 Running Water TN of **Hanging Maw**/10-Cherokee, children/32-48 **with Unknown** not known, mother **with Maw** of Willico Maw/50, Thomas Jacob Maw/55 & Nancy Maw/60-all 7/32nd Chalakatha-Cherokee-Metis

1950. White Owl, Tame Doe aka **Tame Doe Carpenter**-Nanih-Tame DeerNancy – 7/16th Chalakatha-**Cherokee**-Metis born 1718 Great Tellico TN-died after 1775 Chota TN - daughter of **Nancy Rainmaker**/1683 & **White Owl Carpenter**/1678, could cipher, read & write English, Wolf Clan Cherokee, Treaty Sycamore Shoals 1775, wife 1735 Chota TN of **Francis WardShayaqustuego-Five Killer**/12-adopted-white, mother of Long Fellow (Ward) Fivekiller/36, Nancy Wild Rose (Ward) Fivekiller/38 & Little Fellow (Ward) Fivekiller/40-all 7/32nd Chalakatha-Cherokee-Metis

1951. White Thunder – Pekowi born about 1730 PA-**killed** 1774 WV – scout**with Colonial Army-**French-Indian War/54-63-Braddock/55-Pontiac War/6266-Bushy Run/63, **returned allegiance to Tribe** 1766, Cornstalk War/66-74, raiding Ohio-Little Kanawha-Big Sandy-New River valleys/72, killed Point Pleasant/74, wife & children unknown

1952. White Tree - Chalakatha-(adopted-**Seneca**) born about 1780 OH-died after 1832 KS - scout-**with U.S. Army-**Prophet's Town/1811-War 1812-Thames/1813, Treaty 1832, moved to KS 1832, husband about 1800 OH of **Seneca Woman**/85, children unknown

1953. White Turkey – Kishpoko born about 1790 OH-died about 1845 - Prophet's Town/1811, Brownstown/1812-Monguagon/1812-1st Amherstburg/1812-Frenchtown/1813-Ft. Meigs/1813-2nd Amherstburg/1813 & Thames/1813 **with Tecumseh,** moved to CAN 1815, returned to OH about 1825, moved to KS 1826 **with Prophet** & **Paukeesaa**, wife & children unknown

1954. White, John aka John White Straight Tail - Pekowi born about 1670-died after 1751 – son of **Straight Tail** aka **Meaurroway**/1630 & **Pekowi Woman**/1635, brother of Sewatha, uncle of Peter Chartier, a **Pekowi Chief** in PA and AL/1751, wife & children unknown (surnames likely White).

1955. White, Joseph aka Red-headed Skilliway-Skilloway-Chilloway-Gillaway-Skulloway-Wappa-Wampa-Wappan-Wabba-Galloway - 1/2 Mekoche-Metis born about 1790 OH-died after 1854 KS - son of **Adopted White Woman**/73 & **Robin-Blue Tail-Skilloway**/70, scout-**with U.S. Army-**Prophet's Town/1811-War 1812-Thames/1813, Treaty 1832, 1854, move to KS 1832, husband about 1810 OH of **Seneca Woman**/95, father of Matilda White/1828-1/4th Mekoche-Seneca-Metis

1956. White, Matilda - 1/4th Mekoche-Seneca-Metis born 1828 OH-died 1852 - daughter of **Joseph White**/90 & **Seneca Woman**/95, wife 1845 of **Fredrick Chouteau**/1809-white, mother of Fredrick Chouteau/1845, Peter Chouteau/1846, Loho Chouteau/1847, Charles Pierre Chouteau/1849, Emily Chouteau/1850 & Julia Chouteau/1851-all 1/8th Mekoche-Seneca-Metis

1957. White, Peter aka White Madoc – Pekowi born about 1778-died after 1813 – descendant of **John White Straight Tail**/1670, was the last **Chief of White Plains PA** village, sold land to whites & moved to N.Y. with Christian Natives, wife & children unknown

1958. Wickett, Kate Parris aka Kate Parris Wicked - Blind Savannah Clan Cherokee, wife 1769 Chota TN of **Wicked**-Cherokee born 1749 TN-died after 1780, mother of Elizabeth Ann Wickett/72, Susannah Wickett/74, Young

Wicked/76 & Charlotte Wickett/80-all 15/64th Chalakatha-Kishpoko-Pekowi-Black-**Cherokee**-Metis

1959. Wide Bones – adopted-Cherokee born about 1740 TN-died after 1774 (OH?) – Cornstalk War/58-74, raiding New-Ohio River valleys/58, Pontiac War/62-66, Bushy Run/63, raiding New-Jackson-Greenbrier River valleys/63, raiding Ohio-Little Kanawha-Big Sandy-New River valleys/72, Point Pleasant/74, husband about 1760 KY of **Chalakatha Woman**/45, children unknown

1960. Wide Mouth – Chalakatha born about 1740 PA-died after 1775 OH – Cornstalk War/58-75, raiding Ohio-New River valleys/58, Pontiac War/62-66, Bushy Run/63, raiding New-Jackson-Greenbrier River valleys/63, raiding New-Ohio-Little Kanawha-Big Sandy River valleys/72, Point Pleasant/74-75

1961. **Wild Cat aka Peshewa**[155] - Chalakatha born about 1740 PA-**killed** 1773 - a Chalakatha warrior, Cornstalk War/58-73, raiding Ohio-New River valleys/58, Pontiac War/62-66, Bushy Run/63, raiding New-Jackson-Greenbrier River valleys/63, raiding Ohio-New-Big Sandy-Little Kanawha River valleys/72, killed 1773, husband 1760 OH of **Chalakatha Woman**/45, father of Young Wild Cat/61

1962. Wild Cat, Young aka Young Peshewa – Chalakatha born 1761 OH-died 1795 - son of **Wild Cat-Peshewa**/40 & **Chalakatha Woman**/45, a Chalakatha warrior, Blue Jacket War/78-94, Point Pleasant/78, raiding KY-OH-VA/77-81, Crawford/82, raiding Ohio River valley/88-92, killed in raid after Fallen Timber/94, wife & children unknown

1963. **Wild Goose (2) aka Neeakee-Neeakethoh-Nika**[156] – Pekowi born about 1740 PA-**killed** 1774 WV – Cornstalk War/58-74, raiding Ohio-New River valleys/58, Pontiac War/62-66, Bushy Run/63, raiding New-Jackson-Greenbrier River valleys/63, raiding Ohio-New-Little Kanawha-Big Sandy River valleys/72, killed at Point Pleasant/74

1964. Wild Night aka Wild at Night – Kishpoko born about 1765 OH-died after 1783 – Blue Jacket War/77-82, Point Pleasant/75-78, raiding Ohio River valley/77-81, Crawford/82

1965. Wild Wing – Kishpoko born about 1775 OH-died after 1794 - raiding OH-VA-KY-TN/93, Fallen Timber/94

1966. Willesque aka Willeskay – Chalakatha born about 1770 OH-died after 1817 – Blue Jacket War/88-94, raiding Ohio River valley/88-92, Fallen Timber/94, no part in War 1812, a Chalakatha warrior at Lewistown 1817, Treaty 1817

1967. Williams, Abraham - 1/2 Thawikila-Metis-(adopted **WyandotDelaware**) born about 1750 Newcomer's Town -died 1812 OH - son of **Elizabeth Thawikila**/37 & **Isaac Williams**/17-white, translator, trader, Treaty Greenville 1795, 1817, husband 1st about 1769 OH of **Thawikila Woman**/55, 2nd 1790 OH of **Mary Castleman**/77-adopted-white-Delaware, father **with Thawikila** of William Williams (1)/70, Thomas Williams/72, George Pamothoway Williams/75 & Archibald Williams/85-all 3/4th Thawikila-Metis-(adopted Wyandot-Delaware), **with Mary** of William Williams (2)/91, Sally Williams/95 & George Isaac Williams/97-all 1/4th Thawikila-Metis-(adopted Delaware-Wyandot)

1968. Williams, Archibald - 3/4th Thawikila-Metis-(adopted-**DelawareWyandot**) - born about 1780 OH-died after 1820 - son of **Abraham Williams**/50 & **Thawikila Woman**/55, husband about 1806 of **Sarah Delaware**/91, living in **Mason Co. WV** by 1820

1969. Williams, George **Pamothoway** - 3/4th Thawikila-Metis-(adopted**Wyandot**) born about 1775-died after 1831 - son of **Abraham Williams**/50 & **Thawikila Woman**/55, scout-**with 1st U.S. Army Reg.**-1791, from Hog Creek 1817, Treaty 1817, 1829, 1831, living in **Mason Co. WV** by 1820, husband of **Mary Wyandot**/80

1970. Williams, George Isaac - 1/4th Thawikila-Metis born about 1797 Erie Co OH-died after 1820 - son of **Abraham Williams**/50 & **Mary Castleman**/72white-(adopted-Delaware), Prophet's Town/1811, Brownstown/1812Monguagon/1812-1st Amherstburg/1812-Frenchtown/1813-Ft. Meigs/13-2nd Amherstburg/1813 & Thames/1813 **with Tecumseh** & **Roundhead**, husband about 1820 of **Wyandot Woman**/1805, children unknown

1971. Williams, Sally – 1/4th Thawikila-Metis-(**Delaware**) – born 1795 Erie Co OH-died after 1830 KS - daughter of **Mary Castleman**/77 & **Abraham Williams**/50, 2nd wife 1810 OH of **Solomon Journeycake**/70-Delaware, mother of Charles Journeycake/1811-1/8th Thawikila-Delaware-Metis

1972. Williams, Thomas - 3/4th Thawikila-Metis-(adopted **DelawareWyandot**) born about 1772-died after 1820 - son of **Abraham Williams**/50 & **Thawikila Woman** /55, with **1st U.S. Army Reg.** 1791, lived with DelawareWyandot before moving to **Mason Co. WV** before 1820

1973. Williams, William (1) - 3/4th Thawikila-Metis-(adopted-**Wyandot & Chippewa**) born about 1770 OH-died after 1825 WV - son of **Abraham Williams**/50 & **Thawikila Woman**/55, scout-**Sam Brady's Rangers-1st U.S.**

Army Reg. 1791, scout-**with U.S. Army**-Fallen Timbers 1794, husband 1795 of **Mary Fox**/80-Chippewa, lived with Wyandot & Chippewa before moving to **Mason Co. WV** before 1820, father of Abraham Williams/1808-3/8th ThawikilaChippewa-Metis

1974. Williams, William (2) - 1/4th Thawikila-Metis-(adopted-**Wyandot**) born about 1791 OH-died after 1844 - son of **Mary Castleman**/77-white & **Abraham Williams**/50, moved to **Mason Co. WV** before 1820, husband about 1810 of **Sarah Wyandot**/91, father of William Henry Williams/1819, John Williams/1823, Sarah H. Williams/1832, Tabitha A. Williams/1835, Esom H. Williams/1844, 1 son & 2 daughters/1810-1835-all 1/8th Thawikila-WyandotMetis

1975. Wilson, Ankee Greenwood – 2nd wife 1749 Nickajack TN of **James Wilson**-white born 1712 ENG-died by drowning 1766 GA, mother of Thomas Wilson (1)/50, Kateeyah Wilson (1)/62 & others/51-66-all 15/32nd Chalakatha-Kishpoko-Black-Metis

1976. Wilson, Catherine – 31/64th Chalakatha-Kishpoko-Black-Metis - born 1770-died after 1800 - daughter of **Mary McCreary**/55 & **Thomas Wilson (1)**/50, 1st wife about 1786 of **Alexander McDaniel**/58-1/4th ChalakathaCherokee-Metis, sister of 2nd wife **Mary Wilson**/72, mother of James McDaniel/90, Catherine McDaniel/96, Mary McDanile/98 & John B. McDaniel/1800-all 23/64th Chalakatha-Kishpoko-Black-Cherokee-Metis

1977. Wilson, Charles – 5/32nd Chalakatha-Kishpoko-Thawikila-Black-Creek**Cherokee**-Metis born 1782-died after 1815 - son of **Mary Hicks**/62 & **Thomas Wilson (1)**/50, 2nd husband about 1799 (OH?) of **Sally Blue Jacket**/76-3/4th Kishpoko-Pekowi-Metis, left Sally when she joined followers of Tecumseh to go to CAN, father of Thomas Wilson (3)/1800-29/64th Chalakatha-Kishpoko-Thawikila-Black-Creek-Cherokee-Metis

1978. Wilson, Elizabeth – 5/32nd Chalakatha-Kishpoko-Thawikila-BlackCreek-**Cherokee**-Metis born 1784-died after 1805 – daughter of **Mary Hicks**/62 & **Thomas Wilson (1)** /50, wife by 1805 of **James Edwards**-white, mother of Eliza Edwards/1805-5/64th Chalakatha-Kishpoko-Thawikila-Black-Creek-Cherokee-Metis

1979. Wilson, George (1) – 11/32nd Chalakatha-Kishpoko-Thawikila-BlackCreek-**Cherokee**-Metis - born 1782 Nickajack TN-died 1850 (OK?) - son of **Ooloosta Tahchee**/60 & **Thomas Wilson (1)**/50, apparently went with his father, John Speers Co-**with U.S. Army**--Creek War/1813-Horseshoe Bend/1814, 2nd husband 1810 of **Nanquese-Ruth (2) Drumgoole**/90, father of William Wilson/1811, Elizabeth Wilson/1814, Archibald M. Wilson/1815, Alexander Drumgoole Wilson/1817, Mary Jane Wilson/1821, Rebecca Wilson/1823, George W. Wilson/1825, Ruth Wilson/1827, John Wilson/1828, Anderson Springston Wilson/1830 & Malinda Wilson/1834-all 11/64th Chalakatha-Kishpoko-Thawikila-Pekowi-Black-Creek-Cherokee-Metis

1980. Wilson, James - adopted-white born 1715 ENG-died by drowning 1766 GA - trader, soldier, husband 1st 1734 Nickajack TN of **Nancy Greenwood**/20, 2nd 1749 Nickajack TN of her sister **Ankee Greenwood**/29-both 15/16th Chalakatha-Kishpoko-Black-Metis, father **with Nancy** of William Wilson (1)/35, **with Ankee** of Thomas Wilson (1)/50 & Kateeyah Wilson (1)/62-all 15/32nd Chalakatha-Kishpoko-Black-Metis

1981. Wilson, Kateeyah (1) – 15/32nd Chalakatha-Kishpoko-Black-Metis born 1762 Nickajack TN-died 1794 Nickajack TN in Major Orr raids – daughter of **Ankee Greenwood**/29 & **James Wilson**/12-white, husband & children unclear

1982. Wilson, Kateeyah (2) – 5/32nd Chalakatha-Thawikila-Kishpoko-BlackCreek-**Cherokee**-Metis born 1780 Nickajack TN-**murdered** 1801 GA by Doublehead - daughter of **Thomas Wilson (1)**/50 & **Mary Hicks**/62, 5th wife 1796 TN of 4th cousin **Doublehead**/40, mother of Tassel Doublehead/97, Alcy Doublehead/98, Susannah Doublehead/99, Peggy Doublehead/1800-all 3/16th Chalakatha-Thawikila-Kishpoko-Black-Creek-Cherokee-Metis

1983. Wilson, Mahala – 5/32nd Chalakatha-Kishpoko-Thawikila-Black-Creek**Cherokee**-Metis born about 1786 NC-died after 1817 - daughter of **Thomas Wilson (1)**/50 & **Mary Hicks**/62, wife 1st 1804 of **Isaac Fiddler Callahan**/84-7/64th Chalakatha-Cherokee-Metis, mother of Mahala Callahan/1805 & Juba Callahan/15 – both 1/8th Chalakatha-Kishpoko-Thawikila-Black-Creek-Cherokee-Metis

1984. Wilson, Mary – 31/64th Chalakatha-Kishpoko-Black-Metis born 1772died after 1813 - daughter of **Thomas Wilson (1)**/50 & **Mary McCreary**/55, 2nd wife 1788 of **Alexander McDaniel**/58-1/4th Chalakatha-Cherokee-Metis, sister of 1st wife **Catherine Wilson**/70, mother of Lucy McDaniel/88, Eleanor McDaniel/90 & Sukey McDaniel/1813-all 23/64th Chalakatha-Kishpoko-Black-Cherokee-Metis

1985. Wilson, Thomas (1) – 15/32nd Chalakatha-Kishpoko-Black-Metis born 1750 Nickajack TN-died after 1818 MO – son of **James Wilson**/15-white &

Ankee Greenwood/29, with **John Gibson Botetourt Volunteer Co**-Point Pleasant/74, husband 1st about 1769 of **Mary McCreary**/55-1/2 ChalakathaMetis, 2nd 1779 of **Mary Hicks**/62-1/8th Chalakatha-Thawikila-Creek-CherokeeMetis, 3rd (simultaneously?) 1780 Nickajack TN of **Ooloosta Tahchee**/58-15/64th Chalakatha-Thawikila-Creek-Cherokee-Metis, father **with McCreary** of Catherine Wilson/70, Mary Wilson/72 & William Wilson (2)/90 & other children/74-88-all 31/64th Chalakatha-Kishpoko-Black-Metis, **with Hicks** of Kateeyah Wilson (2)/80, Charles Wilson/82, Elizabeth Wilson/84 & Mahala Wilson/86-all 5/32nd Chalakatha-Kishpoko-Thawikila-Black-Creek-CherokeeMetis, **with Tahchee** of Thomas Wilson (2)/80 & George Wilson/82-both
11/32nd Chalakatha-Thawikila-Kishpoko-Black-Creek-Cherokee-Metis

1986. Wilson, Thomas (2) aka Thomas Wilson Jr – 11/32nd ChalakathaKishpoko-Thawikila-Black-Creek-**Cherokee**-Metis born 1780 Nickajack TNdied after 1830 - son of **Ooloosta Tahchee**/60 & **Thomas Wilson (1)**/50, apparently went with his father, husband 1st 1808 of **Katie Killachulla**/86Cherokee, 2nd 1815 of **Jane S. Lloyd**/90-white, father **with Killachulla** of Mary
Polly Wilson/1806-5/32nd Chalakatha-Kishpoko-Thawikila-Black-Creek-Cherokee-Metis, children **with Lloyd** unknown

1987. Wilson, Thomas (3) – 29/64th Chalakatha-Kishpoko-Pekowi-ThawikilaBlack-Creek-**Cherokee**-Metis born about 1800-died after 1815 - son of **Sally Blue Jacket** (Short)/76 & **Charles Wilson**/82, grandson of **Blue Jacket**/35, taken by father when Sally left with followers of Tecumseh for CAN, wife & children unknown

1988. Wilson, William (1) – 15/32nd Chalakatha-Kishpoko-Black-Metis born 1735 Nickajack TN-died 1796 IN - son of **James Wilson**/15-white & **Nancy Greenwood**/20, with **John Gibson-Botetourt Volunteer Co**-Point Pleasant/74, represented **George Morgan**-white at Council 1776 with **Cornstalk**/10, **White Eyes**-Delaware, **John Montour**-Seneca Metis & Wyandot **Half-King**, husband about 1755 TN of **Chalakatha Woman**/40, father of John Wilson/70-47/64th Chalakatha-Kishpoko-Black-Metis

1989. Wilson, William (2) – 31/64th Chalakatha-Kishpoko-Black-Metis born 1790 (TN?)-died 1834 Trail - son of **Thomas Wilson (1)**/50 & **Mary McCreary**/55, husband 1st 1810 of Unknown Woman, 2nd 1824 of half-niece (daughter of his half-sister Kateeyah) **Peggy Doublehead**/1800-3/16th Chalakatha-Thawikila-Kishpoko-Creek-Cherokee-Metis, father **with**

Doublehead of Elzrah Wilson/1825, George Wilson/26, Bird Wilson/27, Jane Wilson/28, Gilbert Bird Wilson/29-all 21/64th Chalakatha-Kishpoko-Thawikila-Black-Creek-Cherokee-Metis

1990. Wind from Water – Chalakatha born about 1740 PA-died after 1795 - wife about 1755 OH of **Hog Head**/30, widow in 1795, children unknown

1991. Winney, Cornelius - adopted-Seneca born about 1770 OH-died after 1832 KS - scout-**with U.S. Army**-War 1812-Thames/1813, Treaty 1832, move to KS 1832, husband 1790 OH of **Mekoche Woman**/75, children unknown

1992. Winter Wind – Thawikila born about 1730 AL-died after 1760 - wife about 1745 OH of **Thawikila Man**/20, widow in 1760

1993. Wishenaska aka Weeshenaska – Chalakatha born about 1750 OH-died after 1800 – Cornstalk War/68-77, raiding Ohio-New-Big Sandy-Little Kanawha River valleys/72, Point Pleasant/74, Blue Jacket War/77-94, raiding KY-OHVA/77-81, Crawford/82, raiding Ohio River valley/88-92, Fallen Timber/94

1994. Wiwelipa aka Wiweliipea-Weewelleepah – Kishpoko born about 1760 OH-died after 1838 KS - raiding KY-OH-VA/77-81, Crawford/82, raiding Ohio River valley/88-92, Blue Jacket War/77-94, raiding OH-KY-VA/95-10, a **Kishpoko Chief** in OH 1790, Prophet's Town/1811, Brownstown/1812Monguagon/1812-1st Amherstburg/1812-Frenchtown/1813-Ft. Meigs/1813-2nd Amherstburg/1813-Thames/1813 **with Tecumseh**, Treaty 1817, 1831, moved to KS before 1832, husband about 1780 OH of **Chalakatha Woman**/66

1995. Wochequeaka aka Wohcheekweeaka-Wocheque-Wocheekwa – Chalakatha born about 1785 OH-died after 1817 – no part in War 1812, a warrior from Lewistown 1817, Treaty 1817

1996. **Wolf aka Muweesha-Meshewawa**[157] – Mekoche born about 1750 OHdied 1817 - brother of **Nutsheway**-Wolf's Brother/60, Cornstalk War/68-77, raiding Ohio-Little Kanwha-Big Sandy-New River valleys/72, Point Pleasant/74, Blue Jacket War/77-94, Boonesboro/78, raiding KY-OH-VA/77-81, Crawford/82, raiding Ohio River valley/88-92, raiding OH-KY-VA/95-1810, Brownstown/1812-Monguagon/1812-1st Amherstburg/1812-Frenchtown/1813-Ft. Meigs/1813-2nd Amherstburg/1813-Thames/1813 **with Tecumseh**, Treaty 1817, a warrior at Wapaghonettat 1817

1997. Wolf, Black Poddee aka Black Poddee Cornstalk – 31/32nd ChalakathaMekoche-Pekowi-Metis born 1785 OH-died before 1846 KS - daughter of **John Wolf Cornstalk (1)**/50 & **Chalakatha Woman**/60, moved to KS by 1832, husband & children unknown

1998. Wolf, Peter Temestetee – 31/32nd Chalakatha-Mekoche-Pekowi-Metis born 1770 OH-died after 1815 - son of **John Wolf Cornstalk (1)**/50 & **Chalakatha Woman**/55, Blue Jacket War/87-94, living in Apple Creek MO 1815, wife & children unknown

1999. Wolf's Brother aka Nutsheway-**Nootsheway** – Mekoche born about 1760 OH-died after 1815 - brother of **Meshewawa-Wolf**/50, Blue Jacket War/77-94, raiding KY-VA-OH/77-81, Crawford/82, raiding Ohio River valley/88-92, raiding OH-KY-VA/95-1810, Prophet's Town/1811, Brownstown/1812Monguagon/1812-1st Amherstburg/1812-Frenchtown/1813-Ft. Meigs/1813-2nd Amherstburg/1813-Thames/1813 **with Tecumseh**, Treaty 1815, a warrior at Wapaghonettat 1817

2000. Woodruff, Margaret Petro - wife 1826 of **Moses Woodruff**-white born 1787 NJ-died 1838 IN - granddaughter of **Cornstalk**/10, mother of Esquire Woodruff/1827 & Martin Woodruff/1828-both 7/64th Chalakatha-MekocheMetis

2001. Wopekenee – Pekowi born about 1720 PA-died about 1758 OH in epidemic - raiding PA/40, Council Ft. Pitt Nov. 1753, Braddock/55, raiding New-Shenandoah River valleys/55, raiding Ohio-New River valleys/58,

2002. Wopemonga – Chalakatha born about 1730 PA-died after 1765 - FrenchIndian War/54-63, Braddock/55, raiding New-Shenandoah River valleys/55, raiding Ohio-New River valleys/58, Pontiac War/62-65, Bushy Run/63, raiding New-Greenbrier-Jackson River valleys/63

2003. Wopeypelethay – adopted-Miami born about 1710 OH-died after 1759 - raiding PA/40, French-Indian War/54-59, Braddock/55, raiding NewShenandoah River valleys/55, raiding PA/55-56, raiding Ohio-New River valleys/58, Council Ft. Pitt Nov. 1753, Aug. 1759, husband about 1730 OH of **Mekoche Woman**/15, father of several 1/2 Mekoche-Miami children/30-59

2004. Wopesquittee aka Wohpeeskweettee – Chalakatha born about 1780 OHdied after 1817 - a warrior at Lewistown 1817, Treaty 1817

2005. Wopthema – Mekoche born about 1710 PA-died about 1755 - raiding PA/40, Council Ft. Pitt Nov. 1753, Braddock/55, raiding New-Shenandoah River valleys/55

2006. Wosheta – Chalakatha born about 1770 OH-died after 1817 - raiding Ohio River valley/88-92, Blue Jacket War/87-94, a warrior at Lewistown 1817, Treaty 1817

2007. Wrynek aka Aquilsa-Aquilisa-Akweeleesa-Hakweelsa-Crooked Neck-Aquilsika-Akweelseeka-Hakwilsikia[158] - Pekowi born about 1725 PA died 1784 OH - called "**Wrynek = "Irish term for wounded or scarred**" by the Irish pioneers (**McKee, Elliott** etc.) because of a large scar on his neck & head received in battle that left his head angled, Cornstalk War/55-77, French-Indian War/54-63, Braddock/55, raiding New-Shenandoah River valleys/55, raiding PA/55-56, raiding Ohio-New River valleys/58, Pontiac War/62-66, Bushy Run/63, raiding New-Greenbrier-Jackson River valleys/63, raiding Ohio-Little Kanawha-New-Big Sandy River valleys/72, Point Pleasant/74-78, Blue Jacket War/77-82, raiding KY-OH-VA/75-81, Boonesboro/78, Crawford/82, Council Ft. Pitt 1775 **with Corn Stalk, Silver Heels, Nimwha & Blue Jacket**, Council **with George Rogers Clark** 1778, Council with British 1779 with **Alexander McKee**/25, **William Caldwell**/50, **Matthew Elliott**/30, **Simon Girty**/41, **George Girty**/46, **James Girty**/30, McKee's cousin **Simon Surphet**, **Savenooka Raven**/20, **Weed**/50-Iroquois & **River Bottom**/50-Seneca, **Principal Chief of Pekowi** in OH 1779-84, husband about 1745 OH of **Catherine Hokolesqua**/28-3/8th Chalakatha-Creek-Metis, children unknown

2008. Wyckoff, Charity Gertrude – Pekowi born about 1726 MD-died after 1746 - a Pekowi, wife 1745 of **Samuel Wyckoff** (1)-white born about 1725-died after 1746, mother of Elizabeth Wyckoff/46, Geertje Wyckoff/52, John Wyckoff/54, Samuel Wyckoff Jr/60, Jacob Wyckoff/64, Peter Wyckoff/66-all 1/2 Pekowi-Metis

2009. Wylahlahpiah – Chalakatha born about 1770 OH-died 1843 KS - raiding Ohio River valley/88-92, Blue Jacket War/88-94, raiding OH-KY-VA/95-1810, Prophet's Town/1811, Brownstown/1812-Monguagon/1812-1st Amherstburg/1812-Frenchtown/1813-Ft. Meigs/1813-2nd Amherstburg/1813 & Thames/1813 **with Tecumseh**, moved to CAN 1815, returned to OH about 1825, moved to KS **with Prophet & Paukeesaa** 1826, husband 1790 OH of **Kishpoko Woman**/75

2010. Wynimwa aka Wyneemwa – Mekoche born about 1750 OH-died after 1774 - raiding Ohio-Little Kanawha-New-Big Sandy River valleys/72, Point Pleasant/74

2011. Wysaoskeka aka Wysayoskeeka – Chalakatha born about 1780 OH-died after 1825 - raiding OH-KY-VA/99-1810, Prophet's Town/1811, Brownstown/1812-Monguagon/1812-1st Amherstburg/1812-Frenchtown/1813-Ft. Meigs/1813-2nd Amherstburg/1813 & Thames/1813 **with Tecumseh**, moved to

CAN 1815, returned to OH about 1825, Treaty 1825, moved to KS **with Prophet & Paukeesaa** 1826, husband 1800 OH of **Kishpoko Woman**/85

X – No entries.

Y

2012. Yankee Bill – adopted-Seneca born about 1780 OH-died after 1832 - scout-**with U.S. Army-**War 1812-Thames/1813, Treaty 1831, 1832, move to KS 1832, husband about 1800 OH of **Mekoche Woman**/85, father of several 1/2 Mekoche-Seneca children/1800-30

2013. Yarontee – Thawikila born about 1760 OH-died after 1778 - raiding KYVA-OH/77, Boonesboro/78

2014. Yaunts, John aka John Three Rivers-Yauntkaha - 1/4th PekowiDelaware-**Metis** born about 1718 NJ-died after 1790 PA - son of **1/2 PekowiDelaware Woman** & **John Francaneur**-French, husband by 1750 PA of **Nancy Nadachine Chartier**/34-7/8th Pekowi-Metis, father of John Yaunts Jr/55-9/16th Pekowi-Delaware-Metis

2015. Yaunts, John Jr - 9/16th Pekowi-Delaware-**Metis** born about 1755 PAdied after 1801 - son of **John Yaunts**/17 & **Nancy Nadachine Chartier**/34, great-grandson of **Peter Chartier**/1690, husband about 1780 PA of **Mary Mast**/60-Delaware-Metis, father of Fredrick Yaunts/80, Rebecca Yaunts/1801 & other children-all 9/32nd Pekowi-Delaware-Metis

2016. Yaunts, Rebecca - 9/32nd Pekowi-Delaware-**Metis** born about 1801 PAdied 1895 - daughter of **John Yaunts Jr**/55 & **Mary Mast**/60, wife 1819 of **Jesse Hoover**/99-white, mother of Eli Hoover/1820, Delilah Hoover/1822, Elizabeth Hoover/1824, Solomon Hoover/1826, Mary Hoover/1828, Benjamin Hoover/1830, Sarah Hoover/1832 & Fredrick Hoover/1834-all 9/64th Pekowi-Delaware-Metis

2017. Yeager, Christina - 3/4th Delaware-**Metis** born 1785 PA-died 1877 WV - daughter of **John George Yeager**/61-1/2 Delaware-Metis & **Delaware Woman**, sister of George John Yeager/86 & Maria Yeager/87, wife about 1804 PA of **John King (2)** aka **King John (2)**/84, moved to **Mason Co. WV** about 1824, mother of William Richard KIng/1805, Peter King/1807, John King Jr/1809, George King/1811, James King/1812, Elizabeth King/1813, Hugh King/1816,

Levi King/1817, Jacob King/1818, Alexander King/1820, Mary King/1822, Francis King/1823, Delila King/1824, Christina King/1826, Sarah Martha King/1828, Catherine King/1831-all 1/2 Mekoche-Delaware-Metis

2018. Yealabaheah – Kishpoko born about 1770 OH-died after 1826 KS – Blue Jacket War/87-94, raiding OH-KY-VA/95-1810, Prophet's Town/1811, Brownstown/1812-Monguagon/1812-1st Amherstburg/1812-Frenchtown/1813-Ft. Meigs/1813-2nd Amherstburg/1813 & Thames/1813 **with Tecumseh**, a **Kishpoko Chief** while Shawnee were in CAN 1816-25, succeeded Paukeesaa Tecumseh as **Head Chief** in Canada 1816, returned to OH 1825, moved to KS 1826 with Prophet & Paukeesaa, wife & children unknown

2019. **Yellow aka Othawsa**[159] – Mekoche born about 1770 OH-died after 1817 - raiding Ohio River valley/88-92, Blue Jacket War/87-94, no part in War 1812, a warrior at Wapaghonettat 1817, Treaty 1817

2020. Yellow Buzzard – Chalakatha born about 1755 AL-died after 1800 - a Chickamauga, raiding AL-TN-VA-KY-OH **with Shawnee & Cherokee**/75-92, Blue Jacket War/77-94, husband about 1775 AL of **Creek Woman**/60, father of several 1/2 Chalakatha-Creek children/75-1800

2021. Yellow Cat - adopted-Creek born about 1730 AL-died after 1770 – Cornstalk War/55-70, French-Indian War/54-63, Braddock/55, raiding NewShenandoah River valleys/55, raiding PA/55-56, raiding Ohio-New River valleys/58, Pontiac War/62-66, Bushy Run/63, raiding New-Jackson-Greenbrier River valleys/63, lived **with Shawnee in OH**, husband about 1750 (OH?) of **Chalakatha Woman**/35, children unknown

2022. Yellow Cloud (1) aka Sowaghkota-**Sawacota** – adopted-Chippewa born about 1760 (MI?)-**killed** 1813 Frenchtown - son of **White Sturgeon**/30Chippewa, brother of **Stands Firm**-Wasegoboah/55-adopted Chippewa & **Mad Sturgeon**/65-Chippewa, brother in law of Tecumapease Puckenshinwa, Blue Jacket War/77-94, raiding KY-OH-VA/77-81, Point Pleasant/78, Crawford/82, raiding Ohio River valley/88-92, raiding OH-KY-VA/95-1810, Prophet's Town/1811, Brownstown/1812-Monguagon/1812-1st Amherstburg/1812 **with Tecumseh, killed** at Frenchtown/1813, husband about 1780 OH of **Mekoche Woman**/65, father of Yellow Cloud (2)-Sowaghkota/80-1/2 Mekoche-Chippewa

2023. Yellow Cloud (2) aka **Sowaghkota** - 1/2 Mekoche-Chippewa born about 1780 OH-died after 1817 - son of **Yellow Cloud (1)-Sawacota**/60-adopted Chippewa & **Mekoche Woman**/65, raiding OH-KY-VA/99-1810, Prophet's

Town/1811, Brownstown/1812-Monguagon/1812-1ˢᵗ Amherstburg/1812Frenchtown/1813-Ft. Meigs/1813-2ⁿᵈ Amherstburg/1813 & Thames/1813 **with**

Tecumseh, a warrior at Wapaghonettat 1817, Treaty 1817, husband about 1800 (OH-IN?) of **Mekoche Woman**/85, children unknown

   2024. Yellow Corn – Chalakatha born about 1700 PA-died after 1755 - wife about 1715 PA of **Chalakatha Man**/1695, widow 1755

   2025. **Yellow Feather aka Othawakeska-Yellow PlumeOuthowwaheshegath**[160] - Mekoche born about 1770 OH-died after 1817 - raiding Ohio River valley/88-92, Blue Jacket War/88-94,no part in War 1812, a

Mekoche Chief at Wapaghonettat before 1817, Treaty 1815, 1817

   2026. **Yellow Hawk aka Othawapeelethee**[161] – Thawikila born about 1728 AL-died after 1817 MO – moved from AL to OH/55, Cornstalk War/55-77, French-Indian War/55-63, Braddock/55, raiding New-Shenandoah River valleys/55, raiding Ohio-New River valleys/58, Pontiac War/62-66, Bushy Run/63, raiding New-Jackson-Greenbrier River valleys/63, raiding Ohio-Little Kanawha-New-Big Sandy River valleys/72, Point Pleasant/74-78, a **Thawikila Chief** by 1768, moved to Creeks in AL 1774 after Point Pleasant/74, returned to OH 1778, moved to MO 1779 with **Black Stump, Kikusgowlawa, Red Eagle, Red Snake** & 400 families, **succeeded Black Snake as Civil Chief** of Black Hoof's faction 1785, Treaty 1817, brother of **Wife of Moluntha**/15, **Black Stump**/20, **Kikusglowlawa**/22, **Weasau**/24, **Capt. Johnny**/26, **Black Hoof**/30 & **Kishkalwa-Tiger Tail**/35, husband by 1750 AL of **Duck Laying Eggs**/30-Thawikila, children unknown

   2027.Yellow Hawk, **Duck Laying Eggs aka Sheshepukwawalo**[162] – Thawikila born about 1730 AL-died after 1779 MO – moved to OH 1755, moved to AL 1774 with band, returned to OH 1778, moved to MO about 1779, wife by 1750 AL of **Yellow Hawk**/28-Thawikila, children unknown

   2028.Yellow Legs aka **Yellow Legs Caesar** - 1/2 Thawikila-Black born 1745 OH-died after 1790 (MO?) - daughter of **Caesar (2)-Black Ceasar**/10 & **Thawikila Woman**/25, sister of **Black Face**/40 & **Young Caesar**/50, may have moved to AL 1774, then returned to OH 1778, then moved to MO with the Thawikila 1778, wife 1760 OH of **Thawikila Man**, widow 1774 (he was killed at Point Pleasant/74), likely wife 2ⁿᵈ 1775 AL of **2ⁿᵈ Thawikila Man**, mother of several 3/4ᵗʰ Thawikila-Black children/61-90

   2029.Yellow Water aka Wethawakaskia-**Othawethawakaskia-**

Oweethawakaskeea – Mekoche born about 1770 OH-died after 1814 - raiding Ohio River valley/88-92, Blue Jacket War/88-94, raiding OH-KY-VA/95-1810, Prophet's Town/1811, Brownstown/1812-Monguagon/1812-1st Amherstburg/1812-Frenchtown/1813-Ft. Meigs/1813-2nd Amherstburg/1813 & Thames/1813 **with Tecumseh**, Treaty 1814

2030. Yougashaw – Pekowi born about 1710 PA-died after 1764 – Cornstalk War/55-63, French-Indian War/54-63, Braddock/55, raiding New-Shenandoah River valleys/55, raiding PA/55-56, raiding Ohio-New River valleys/58, Pontiac War/62-64, Bushy Run/63, raiding New-Jackson-Greenbrier River valleys/63, adopted father 1756 of **John Walters**/43-white, father of Daughter/48-(wife 1763 of **John Walters**-adopted white)

2031. Young Elk - Mekoche born about 1770 OH-died after 1795 – son of **Little Elk**/40 & **Mekoche Woman**/45, a Mekoche warrior, raiding Ohio River valley/88-92, Blue Jacket War/88-94, grandson of **Elk-Wabete**/15, great-nephew of **Moluntha**, wife & children unknown

2032. Young Fox aka Young **Wahkoceethee** – Mekoche born about 1760 OHdied after 1778 - son of **Fox-Wahkoceethee**/40 & **Mekoche Woman**/45, raiding
KY-VA-OH/77, Point Pleasant/78, Booneboro/78

2033. Young Hawk aka Young Hawkawepilathy-Young Hokawepeelathee - Thawikila born about 1752 OH-died after 1779 – son of **Hawk**/30 & **Thawikila Woman**/35, Cornstalk War/70-77, raiding Ohio-Little Kanawha-Big Sandy-New River valleys/72, Point Pleasant/74-75-78, raiding KY-OH-VA/75-78, left father's family & moved to MO 1779, wife & children unknown

2034. Young Raccoon aka **Young Shapatha** - Kishpoko born about 1780 OH**killed** Thames 1813 - son of **Raccoon-Shapatha**/40 & **Kishpoko Woman**/45, raiding OH-KY-VA/99-1810, Prophet's Town/1811, Brownstown/1812Monguagon/1812-1st Amherstburg/1812-Frenchtown/1813-Ft. Meigs/1813-2nd Amherstburg/1813, **killed at Thames/1813 with Tecumseh**, wife & children unknown

2035. Young Stranger – Chalakatha (or Chalakatha-mix blood) born about 1740 (MI?)-died after 1776 - from the Great Lakes, Cornstalk War/60-75, raiding Ohio-New River valleys/58, Pontiac War/62-66, Bushy Run/63, raiding New-Jackson-Greenbrier River valleys/63, raiding Ohio-Little Kanawha-NewBig Sandy River valleys/72, Point Pleasant/74-75, husband 1760 OH of **Chalakatha Woman**/45, children unknown

2036. Young Turtle aka Young Namatha – Chalakatha born about 1760 OHdied after 1778 - son of **Turtle (1)-Namatha**[163]/40 & **Chalakatha Woman**/45, Point Pleasant/78, Boonesboro/78, wife & children unknown

2037. Young, Betty aka Sore Knees - adopted-white born about 1740-died after 1775 - captured before 1755-returned to whites-rejoined tribe 1765, wife 1755 OH of **Mekoche Man**, mother of John Totala Young/70 & several other 1/2 Mekoche-Metis children/55-75

2038. Young, John **Totala** - 1/2 Mekoche-Metis born about 1770 OH-died after 1832 KS - son of **Betty Sore Knees Young**/40-adopted white & **Mekoche Man**, raiding Ohio River valley/88-92, Blue Jacket War/88-94, scout-**with U.S. Army**-Prophet's Town/1811-War 1812-Thames/1813, Treaty 1831, 1832, 2nd **Mekoche Chief** in OH 1832, moved to KS 1832, husband about 1790 OH of **Mekoche Woman**/75, father of William Young/90-3/4th Mekoche-Metis

Greenville Treaty 1765

About The Author

Don Greene is proudly in his second half-century of life. Tested as a genius as a child, Don had read the Bible, World Book Encyclopedia, Encyclopedia Britannica and Webster Dictionary from cover to cover before he was twelve years old. Don attended two State Colleges and two Universities, over a period of nearly twenty years, all the while working six days a week and becoming a labor, social and political activist. While majoring and humbly excelling in American Literature Don still found time to pick up courses in everything from labor law to anthropology and philosophy.

Don has had a few poems, stories and articles published in various publications, from labor papers to poetry and ancient history magazines and a long series of letters to the editors of several West Virginia papers. Don has written over five hundred columns for the "Communicator" from Clay County West Virginia and continues the bi-weekly column, addressing everything from national politics to Shawnee history. Please visit his column under "Don Greene-the WV Radical" at www.claywestvirgina.com to see some of his rambling thoughts. A sometimes painter, Don enjoys doing landscapes in his self-taught style and has works in several homes in West Virginia and is trying to find the time to do some of the rugged Appalachian horizons around his home.

A long first marriage gave Don three wonderful children, one son, Cody, lost in a tragic car accident in 1978. From his daughter Kelly and son Keegan, Don is now the grandfather of three beautiful girls, Kady, Kennedy and Kelsie and a grandson Keegan Jr. Through his second marriage Don has inherited two beautiful step-daughters, Annie Green and Sarah Huskins. Annie lives a few miles away, while Sarah makes her home with Don and Patty. They have given Don seven marvelous grandchildren. Annie's are Taylor, Isabella, James and Jacob, all as cute and ornery little rascals as you've ever seen. Sarah has given Don two great joys that live with him and his wife Patty, Emily Huskins and Gabriella Clark and another grandson Elijah Clark who lives with his father, all eleven cute as buttons and nearly as precocious as Don was as a Korean War era babe.

After a long career in highway construction and excavation work that led Don all over West Virginia, Virginia and North Carolina, Don decided to change trades and became a millwright, ending up working in the nuclear industry for General Electric and Westinghouse from Maryland to Iowa.

Feeling a passion for fair pay and treatment for good work Don entered into a long record of labor activity in the early 70's, serving for years as a union steward, officer and organizer. Don's labor activity led him into local politics and Don was elected four times to public office in his home county and hometown and failed in three other bids for office in the same. For the last thirty years Don has known every Governor of West Virginia by his first name, visited the U.S. Senator in his home, and had Congressmen and State officers visit him in his own home.

Seldom satisfied with merely passing gently through life, Don has been an activist in the most sincere way in politics, social issues, environmental causes, labor, matters concerning senior citizens and the impoverished, served on many boards and committees on various and sundry matters as well as on several societies and committees concerning things of historical interest. As a public advocate he strongly represented many citizens in actions against public boards and commissions, often with great success. Don located and registered with the State of West Virginia three small, badly ravaged Adena mounds in Mason County West Virginia, now humbly named the Greene Mounds 1, 2 and 3. Don has tried for nearly a decade to get some officials interested in investigating what appears to be a major mound along the Kanawha River in Mason County and the last remnant of a complex of mounds, petroglyphs and burials there.

After five heart attacks in two years ended his career in public work, Don recovered to begin his research into the Shawnee in earnest, originally intending to put forth an encyclopedia of Native Americans from the 1700's Don soon realized that his true passion was for the Shawnee and their erroneously recorded history. Beginning with ascertaining what Natives that participated in the Battle of Point Pleasant in 1774, Don expanded his research to include anyone and everyone that had any Shawnee blood in the 1700's. Merging his research with that of Noel Schutz, a noted scholar of the Shawnee, Don has maintained a website containing some of his work for nearly a decade at www.shawneetraditions.com/Names and encourages anyone that has Shawnee ancestry to visit there. Using his prodigious memory, years of research, much intuitive thought and maybe a little psychic ability Don has pieced together the trails of many families among the Shawnee and the part-white Shawnee Metis, and gained a new understanding of the role the Shawnee played in the true history of the United States from the earliest arrival of the Europeans until the sad times of the removal of the Native Americans to the west and beyond that into current times. Don maintains contacts with most of the Shawnee Bands in several States and has conversed with the Tribes in Oklahoma as well. His work is being used by many groups and families.

Don can now be found high in the mountains of Ashe County North Carolina, between Pond and White Top Mountains, enjoying the tranquility of the highlands with his love Patty, continuing his Great Work daily, playing with his granddaughters, puttering around the gardens and arbors on his hillside home, conversing and exchanging information on the Shawnee with friends far and wide via the Internet, phone and mail, volunteering a little of his time, especially to the Ola Belle Reed Mountain Music Festival. Please visit us at www.olabellefest.com to find out about this wonderful lady and our well received and rapidly growing festival in her honor in Lansing, North Carolina.

Don and little Emily attend church at Pleasant Chapel Baptist church next door to them where Don is known to sing an occasional solo when the Spirit moves him. While he is pretty sure that his battered vocals aren't the easiest thing to listen to, they assuredly come from the heart and have been likened by some to the black spirituals sung by the slaves, with all of Don's hand-clapping and swaying.

Enjoy the work of this modern day Mike Fink and be sure to call on him if you ever need a friend.

The photo accompanying this book was taken by Don's sweetheart Emily Lynn Huskins age three and a half and he feels it may be the best one taken of him in many years. Old Don gives kudos to his Golden Sun Child, Emily's Shawnee name.

APENDIX I

Introduction to Shawnee Names by

Noel Schutz

My contributions are relatively straight forward and have to do with the linguistic aspects of Shawnee names. Don has invested the thousands of hours necessary to compile the information in this foundational work and I have only added the translation and/or interpretation of Shawnee names. I commend Don Greene on this monumental task that he has undertaken.

I began work on sorting out the linguistic aspects of Shawnee names for my dissertation (published 1975) and wanted to put up some of this information, both that which appeared in the dissertation and from my own notes, on the webstite, Shawnee Traditions.com. Then by fortuitous circumstance Don and I came into contact and I discovered his treasure chest of Shawnee personages. Since my work had been the analyzing of names to determine clan and division affiliations, this was indeed a welcomed happenstance and Don agreed to take over the Shawnee Names portion of the website – the portion that has received the most attention over the years and been the cornerstone of the site..

In this Introduction I will discuss the social milieu in which the Shawnee lived and how their names reflected their place in the network of relations in their

nation.

SHAWNEE SOCIAL ORGANIZATION

One cannot understand Shawnee names without understanding how they functions as part of Shawnee Social Organization when the Shawnee were an autonomous nation. We are fortunate to have comparative data from the Kispokoo tribe that is very helpful. They appear to have separated from the Shawnee at no great distance before the historic period and their language and culture show great similarities to the Shawnee and, most importantly, their naming and clan system is virtually identical to that of the Shawnee, with many of the names close cognates with known clan affiliations.. And the social organization of the Kickapoo probably reflects the earlier organization of the disparate pre-contact bands that separated to roam the eastern half of the continent and then in early historical times a number of tribes leagued into a single confederacy. This confederation had social implications that put the Shawnee culture in a state of flux over past three centuries, the final resolution of which had not been completed when they lost political automony after the first quarter of the 1800s. We have ethnohistorical material from the Shawnee Prophet, Blackhoof, and the Blue Jacket family on this consolidation or leaguing of the groups (*nekutithipe*).

As best as can be reconstructed, each Shawnee from the early 1700s until modern times belonged to four social groups. The first are the several divisions of the tribe that were probably in the mid-1600s and earlier separate tribes with mutually intelligible dialects. The second group is the organization of clans into "phratries" (a larger social grouping within the tribe with each consisting of a number of clans). And the third is the clan affiliation withing a phratry and, finally, the individual lineages (families) that involve the marriage of individuals among clans and phratries.

In the late period of Shawnee automomy and the early period of their removal to the west, the phratry system was being developed. The development was necessitated by the fact that each of the tribes that leagued together had overlapping groups of clans. This caused social imbalance with the resulting large number of clans. For example, one clan might have a Thunder Clan and another not, one might have a Buffalo Clan and another did not, etc. Since intermarriage between the confederated tribes was unhindered, the clans became a jumble and the Shawnee began sorting them out by putting similar clans within larger phratries that were in common for all the divisions. See charts I and II for the reconstruction and process of accommodation and change I am proposing.

A single tribe would have had a number of clans; the ideal of twelve was seldom obtained, but about that more or less. NOTE: I am here using "clan" as an informal term for that called a "patri-sib" or gens in anthropological usage (patrilineal descent - in the father's clan -with marriage to someone outside the clan).

Chart I – the pre-Shawnee Nation tribal organization for each tribe.

Example: Kickapoo These Clans: Eagle, Turkey, Bear, Fox, Racoon, Elk, Buffalo, Water, Thunder, Man, Stone. Water an inceptive phratry Turtle, Fish and swimming birds. It is closely associated with Thunder Clan. paired in

TRIBE	
CLAN 1	CLAN 7
CLAN 2	CLAN 8
CLAN 3	CLAN 9
CLAN 4	CLAN 10
CLAN 5	CLAN 11
CLAN 6	CLAN 12

clans are exogamous (they must marry someone from another clan) and Berry, patrilineal (succession of is property, clan and with chieftonnship, etc., are though the male line). Sometimes clans are social functions.

We can get a view of what the social organization was by looking a Mexican Kickapoo for which we have data from the early 1940s when a Mrs. Lewis A. Harmon collected Kickapoo names from the tribal role and elicited means and the clan affiliation shown by the names. Kickapoo is very close linguistically to Shawnee and its social structure probably reflects the type of social organization of the Shawnee Nation before it was formed by the leaguing of a number of preShawnee groups with little dialectal and cultural variation. The tribe was divided roughly into a dozen or so exogamous clans. A child was named into a clan at a meeting of the clan which the child was an infant (about four months old). Each clan ideally had its own totemic creature (Eagle clan, Bear clan, Elk clan, Fox clan, Racoon clan, Man or Chief clan) or things pertaining to nature (Berry clan, Tree clan, Stone clan, Water clan, Thunder clan [weather, thunder, rain, sky, clouds]). So the emblem of the Eagle Clan was the eagle, the emblem of the Turkey clan was a turkey, the emblem of the Tree clan was the tree, etc. The name given a child revealed the clan affiliation of the name-bearer. In one case, however, the clan had several totemic creatures that approach the phratry system, perhaps showing where this system in Shawnee had its roots. Thus things pertaining to the Water clan included reference to water *per se* (water flowing downstream) or to fish, water birds such as the duck, swan, sea gull, and Turtle. Likewise, Thunder clan had several items of reference (and may have been included in or closely associated with the Water clan).

A point of interest comes from the interrogation in the Carolinas of Itawachcomequa who was arrested as he strayed while looking for Peter Chartier in the south. He told the authorities that "I am a Shavanah [the southern term for Shawnee], and Head of a Town. We are distributed by different names, the Cow, the Bear, the Buffalo. There are also the Wolf Shavanahs and other names given us." Note the reference to "names given us" in reference to the totems. This interview/interrogation occurred in 1753.

Comparing Chart I above with Chart II below of the social organization of the Shawnee Nation (as reconstructed) shows a vast difference in complexity. And this chart does not show the whole of it. Within the subtribes were subdivisions as well. In the late 1600s and early 1700s the Pekowi were divided into two bands: the Potomac Pekowi of Maryland who went from Fort St. Louis in he Illinois country through a detour to the the Cumberland, Carolina, and then northward, while another group of Pekowi came to western Pennsylvania directly from Ohio. They both had separate chiefs of and councils during this period. Another example is the Thawikila subtribe who resided mostly in the south with only brief intrusions into Pennsylvania and then later a short stay in Ohio before returning each time to the south. Among the Potomac, or Lower Susquehannah, Shawnee, in fact, were another group of Thawiikilas who seemed to have remained with the Potomac Shawnee a bit more contantly than other bands of this tribe. referred to as "Shawkerawque" (Shaw-ke-raw-que for Thawii-ki-la-ki) in 1698.

Further, the Thawiikila as not a single entity, but three bands each with its own council: the Thawikila proper, the Spitothaki, and the Tahogaleki (who belonged to the Tawikila according to Gatchet with the Spitothaki a third band).

The identity of the "Spitotha" has been in doubt. Some have thought the Mekoche and some the Kispoko, but Gatschet had this information long ago. It was from the south and said to be of the Thawikila, but with a separate council.

The "Tahogalewi" (Tahogale, Tahogaria, Taogria,Tongaaria, Tohogaleagas, etc.) were placed by cartographers on the Tennessee and Savannah Rivers and said to be a band of Yuchi (see Jeffery's Atlas where at a point on Savannah River above Augusta it reads "Hughchees or Hogoleges Old Town deserted in 1715 and an island "Huhgchee" also called "Uchee Island").

These two groups were also on the Chattahoochee River among the Lower Creeks, which seems to have been there home ground. Hodge, however, has "Taogarias, Taogria" as Shawnee despite Swanton who labels them as Yuchi. Given Gatchet's data from the field, it would seem certain that Tahogalewi and Taogaria are alternate names for these Shawnee Tahogaleki. It is noteworthy that in all but one instance, these groups are at or near the location of groups identified Shawnee (Chaoenons, Savanas, etc.). There identification as Yuchi is therefore suspect.

Chart II – The Emergence of a Phratry System showing the five best known subtribes and the five phratries.

CHALAKA	THAWIKILA	MEKOCHE	KISHPOKO	PEKOWI	
↑	↑	↑	↑	↑ d	
All phratries are in all subtribes whether or not all clans are in all subtribes		The development simplifie he system to avoid prolems in ineraction between clans.			
↑	↑	↑	↑		↑
Bird (fowl) Phratry "Turkey Phratry"†	Round-footed Phratry "Wolf Phratry"	Hoofed Phratry "Horse Phratry"	Water Phratry "Turtle Phratry"	Rabbit stands alone "Rabbit"	
Turkey	Owl	Wolf	Racoon	Horse	Deer	Turtle	Duck (Swan?)	
Turkey is the totemic emblem and Turkey and Owl are the associate leaders (grandfathers).	Wolf is the totemic emblem and Wolf and Racoon the associate leaders (grandfathers)	Horse (formerly Deer?) is the totemic emblem and Horse and Deer the associate leaders (grandfathers)	Turtle is the totemic emblem and Turtle and Duck (earlier Swan?) the asssociate leader (grandfathers)	Rabbit has no partner and is the only member of s the group.	

Shawnee Heeritage

Totemic clans: Turkey, Owl, Eagle, Hawk, Buzzard, including 'wading birds' like Loon and Crane.but not 'swimming birds' like duck and swan.	Totemic clans - Wolf, Racoon, panther, bear, beaver, etc. Voegelin had a Racoon group as a separate non- carnevorous group along with Bear.	Totemic clans - Horse, Deer, Elk, Buffalo, etc. Includes both single and split hooved cratures. It is said that anciently Deer was the principle totem.	Totemic clans - Turtle, Fish, Snake, and 'swimming birds' including Duck, Swan, Goose, Pelican, etc. Swan had prominence among the Pekowi.	(Perhaps in former times other gentle animals like the squirrel were included in this group.)
The Shawnee used the emblemic totem as the name of the phratry (2nd line of heading). I will use the terms on the first line of the headings to keep from confusing them; for example, the Turtle Phratry with Turtle Clan. That is, a name that indicates Snake Clan will be a member of the Water (Turtle) Phratry, and the like. The Kickapoo tribe used Water Clan for the one that included turtle. This was the only group among the Kickapoo that had multiple totems; all others were separate clans – for example, Turkey and Eagle were separate clans. This indicated an emerging Phratry among the Kickapoo while among the Shawnee it was a development nearing its completion when the tribe ceased to have an autonomous existence.				

This system provides a picture a bit different from the simpler one of the Kickapoo where there are a group of exogamous clans with no intermediate social groups between then and the tribe as a whole. And in the more rudimentary tribal organization there would be both clan councils as well as an overall tribal council. It would seem that for the Shawnee until the loss of tribal autonomy that clans functioned and were exogamous; that is, for example, a member of the Turtle tribe could not marry someone of the turtle tribe, but one could marry anyone else of a different clan within or without the Water Phratry, with the result that that a man and wife are of necessity of different clans. Totemic emblems of clans, such as an image of a turtle, may have been placed here and there, and we do have a report they were put on graves. For the Shawnee and Kickapoo the descent (and thus the name) was in the father's line (patri-lineal sibs or gens – the technical names of this sort of clan). These ideal situations, however, did not always seem to have held even in the late 1700s. Sometimes female children seemed to have bee named into their mother's clan and sometimes even a male child might be named into an illustrious clan on the mother's side.

By the late 19th century and onward, the numerous totemic clans were grouped into the above indicated phratries with information from Voegelin, Gatschet and Lewis Henry Morgon. Gatschet called them phratries and Vogelin "Name Groups" (since the social functions of the clans had largely been lost and remaining functions were largely liturgical and in joking relationships in the second quarter of the 1900s).

Even as late as the early 1900s, however, there were pairings between clans which would seem to indicate marriage preferences at an earlier period, or the like. Voegelin reported such pairings and Truman Michelson (unpublished manuscript in the Bureau of American Ethnology) did likewise. Voegelin reported that Turtle and Turkey and Horse and Round-footed men (paired with different phratries) were "friends" that can team up joking with other clans, but Racoon (Coon) and Rabbit were on their own. Coon and Turtle had an adversary joking relationship because it is said Coon running along the river bank ate turtle eggs and this is the reason they taunt each other so much in joking. In ritual activities, clans take different tasks and there are taboos about which clans can do what depending on the clan of the deceased. The Shawnee Prophet reported that a member of the Panther Clan led a war party to war and a member of the Wolf Clan let the party back to the village on their return. Michelson reported that Bear and Elk, Wolf and Fox, Panther and Wildcat, Eagle and Turkey and Turtle and Turkey formed pairs but that Coon and Rabbit stood alone as in Voegelin's material.

I will use one name for the phraties and the totem name for the clans. For example, *peleewom'shomi* refers specifically to the turkey clan itself while *peleewileni* "Turtle People" can refer to the phratry of which turkey is the emblem after Gatschet's usage. The clan designation, *ho'somi* 'totem', has the same stem as the kinship term grandfather since this term covers a large group of more distant relatives of which the father's or mother's father is the closet relative of this group. See the forthcoming book Don and I are preparing that will include details on the kinship system. The book is tentatively entitled: *Shawnee Heritage II: Famous Shawnee Chiefs and Warriors and their Families*.

THE STRUCTURE AND MEANING OF SHAWNEE NAMES

The meaning and linguistic structure of Shawnee names is not a simple matter. First of all, there are several types of names which, when possible, need to be distinguished. The most important are the names given a child shortly after his birth and which I will refer to as the "totemic name" or sometimes "clan name". These names will form the bulk of this discussion. However, there are two other types of names that occur in the historical records that must be mentioned since we know many historic individuals only thorugh these other kinds of names. First of all, as in many societies, an individual is often given a nickname by his friends and family as he grows up in his community. These may be shortened forms of his clan name, a pet name given by parents or others, or a word or phrase that captures some aspect of the individual's physical appearance or character. A further note should be made that colonists and pioneers often took the nickname of a Shawnee and made their own modifications of the name either in abbreviating it, associating it with some common English name or circumstances, or simplyi by recording it in a somewhat distorted fashion. Further, settlers and chroniclers often gave their own names to personages, as the brother of Tecumseh widely referred to as the "Shawnee Prophet" and to another great Shawnee as "Blue Jacket". There is even another type and that is a nickname which consists of a shortened form of the totemic name. In many cases, this looks like a non-totemic nickname and thus the clan affiliation remains in doubt.

A second type of name is one in which an individual takes up to mark some significant event or turning point in his or her life. This name was not necessarily meant to supercede the clan name – thought it might in fact eclipse it – but was the one with which the person preferred to be addressed or referenced in a titular manner. A notable example of this involves Tecumseh's brother, the Shawnee Prophet. The Shawnee Prophet's name can also be used to show how distortions creep in. Taking his totemic name as somehow descriptive of the Shawnee Prophet's character at birth or in his latter life, many have recorded their idea about the meaning of his totemic name in a dismissive manner. Thus, it is translated as "Loud Mouth" and such, whereas in fact the name actually indicates the rattling sound made by a rattlesnake, and thus assigns him to this totemic clan. These intercultural distortions represent not the original meaning of the name but rather the attitudes and negative discrimination of whites. This treatment of Shawnee names at all costs must be dispensed with in this work to clear the record once and for all.

This brings us to the Shawnee clan, or totemic, name – which is the most important name a Shawnee can bear. In a very natural sense it is the individual's *real* name. In essence, names bear the same significance in the closely related Kickapoo, Fox and Sauk. Priscilla Wanatee of the Fox tribe (http://www.pbs.org/riverofsong/music/e1-meskwaki.html) has noted that similar to the practices of the Shawnee, "…we still carry on the practice of a naming ceremony for a newborn child; the baby's name is determined by the father's clan affiliation or in the case of a member of another tribe, the mother's clan names can be used. The child's name is picked and used so that the Creator will know and identify the "new human being" as part of the earth, and the name is intended to protect the baby's spirit while very young and living on this earth."

It is worth noting that the names collected in the early forties from among the conservative Mexican Kickapoo have cognate words and very similar clan indentifications. Among all these groups – Kickapoo, Sauk, Fox and Shawnee – the name belongs to the clan and identifies the infant as a member of that clan.

Below we will discuss this under two headings in which first the ritual conferring of the name is described and secondly the linguistic structure and interpretation of Shawnee names is discussed.

1. The Ritual Conferring of Shawnee Names.

The Shawnee naming ceremony, like other cultural aspects of this noble tribe, differs a it from subtribe to subtribe, but not in its essential characteristics. For example, we have recorded the practice of one group naming the child 4 to 6 months after birth and another practice of naming them annually, usually at the Spring or Fall Bread dance. The following detailed presentation from Voegelin's discussion of Shawnee names was applicable at least to the Kispoko in the 1930s.

During the period of seclusion of the mother and child after birth (from 1 to 9 days), the father asks to old men or women to come to his home on the evening of the ninth day after the birth of the baby. These name-givers are preferably advanced in years who have some gift for bestowing names. Voegelin collected the following text of instructions to the candidates for the name-giver:

> We called you here this evening be cause I want you to name my childe in the morning; tomorrow tht child will have been born ten days. You folks study about this matter over and over; think about the animals [connected with the name groups]—how they act, how they move, everything like that. Tonight think about the turtles, chickens, the wolf, deer, coon, rabbit; study about them. When you go to sleep, keep this thought with you; maybe you will dream about tht name, some way. If you don't dream about it, maybe you'll just think about it, and so find a good name. And you must not be angry when we take only one of the names you offer; we will be glad to hear both names, when you have found them iin the morning.

It must be noted that by the 1930s when this text was collected, the Shawnee had lost the original patrilinial sib organization in which the child took the totem ("name group" in Voegelin's terminology) of the father's clan. Nevertheless, the clans retained ritual functions in worship, funerals, dances, and the like. and the task of choosing the name was a solumn event. If a name-giver has a dream or contemplates feathers *(-piiwe)* the name will be associated with the Turkey [feathered creatures] clan or if he dreams of water (-*kami*) it will be the Turtle [water creatures] Clan. Ideally, the name found should not be a duplicate of any name used before by a living or deceased person insofar as this can be determined. Duplications do occasionally occur and because of the limited number of stems involved for different clans, the same names can be found generations apart.

On the morning of the tenth day, the women relatives of the infant rise well before daylight to prepare the naming breakfast. The mother cleans herself in her hut of seclusion where the child was born, but then brings the child with her to the family dwelling where the kinfolks, paternal and material, are assembled. If the name givers are women, they sponge bathe the child; if men, the mother performs this task.

The mother then sits with the child as the name-givers stand to offer their selections and the parents choose one. If the parents do not agree on a choice, the mother's decision is the deciding factor as the the one who gave birth to the child. The father then announces which name has been chosen. The name-giver is presented with a short string of white, finely cut beads to use in conferring the name on the child. The selected name-giver then holds the child and addresses the Creator at length discussing the naming tradition and the animal names involved and just why this name was chosen.

Returning the child to the mother, the name-giver finishes his speech, then he holds the string of beads in his extended hands and bestows the name: "That is why everyone will call him — (mentions the name again); from this morning on they will call him —; everybody all the time will call him ——."

Having pronounced the name four times, the name-giver ties the string of beads around the child's neck. They are worn by the child until the string breaks after which the mother will save them for the child (though they are in many cases lost). Then the relatives gather around and generally use the name in their remarks and they all have breakfast. The mother will use her fingertip to dip into each dish and let the child lick it off. After breakfast the relatives give the child small gifts. A few days later, the mother may present the name-giver with a gift (a shirt or length of cloth or even a horse). The Cherokee Shawnee and the Eastern Shawnee (Mekoche and Chalaka), but not the Absentee Shawnee (Thawikila, Pekowi or Kishpoko), sometimes confer a name on a child after the spring or fall Bread Dance. Gatschet has references to the naming occurring after about four months after birth as well as to an annual naming time for different groups. It is obvious that earlier there were varying practices among the subtribes, and, in fact, naming was probably done by clan conclaves in the earlier historical period as was the case among the Kickapoo.

In the case of illegitimate children the child is named in the same manner but, of course, the father is not present. Presumably, the child would take the clan name of the mother in such a case. It is not certain what would happen in the case of a deceased husband. In such a case, the wife has the option of selecting a brother of her husband (the levirate, but with the category "brother" including certain male relatives other than siblings of the same parent(s)). But if the mother does choose a male member of her deceased husband's clan, she returns to her own family and clan. Does the child then take the name of the mother's clan? This issue cannot be resolved from the historical record as we now have it, but the ideal of naming in the father's clan was clearly not always the case. Tecumseh's family may be a case in point. Tecumseh's mother was of the distinguished Turtle Clan in the Pekowi subtribe while the father, though a noted Kispoko warrior, was Shawnee by virtue of his mother's side since his father is believed to have been Creek. Since he did not receive his name from a patri-sib but from his mother's side, perhaps the prominence of Tecumseh's mother's family led to the children being named into her phratry (with Turtle and Snake names).

We have the following information from Gatschet: "When father & mother were of the same clan, the child was called from that clan, but the ancients had to be there by all means, who had to invent the name. All the turtles, for instance, were kámi; (kámsi in women) kamisika or kamthénui. Tekumthi was (turtle) 'walking across'... But when "...father and mother were of different clans, the girls were generally, but not always placed into the mother's clan & named after it; the boys not always placed in the father's clan. For instance, when they had lost children; changes of names & hence of clan...". At an earlier period the name indicated the father's clan, but at some point, even as early as the late 1700s, the practice begain to shift as clan membership had fewer and fewer political implications and began to be reserved primarily for ritual purposes.

This situation points to a further problem. How to tell what phratry (group of clans) from the meaning of a name. In fact, it is the interpretation of the name giver that provides the information and friends and family know this from the name givers speech during the naming ceremony. Over time, however, the allusions can be lost and not even native speakers of Shawnee always knew what the clan assignment is for some names. This situation results at times in some false interpretations – we might even say folk etymologies or educated guesses by native Shawnee speakers. Thus we have more than one interpretation for Tecumseh's name based on an alternative stem that sounds like the one in his name. Other instances of the loss of knowledge of the original interpretation by the name giver are also found.

Name changing follows the same procedure but in a much abbreviated form, but it adds the discarding of the original, unsuccessful, name to the ritual. Names may be unsuccessful for several reasons. First, the name bearer may be sickly.

The parents or a shaman decide if the name is at fault. Secondly, the name may be unsuccessful if the name did not agree with the individual bearing it. Duplication is another factor. If someone living or dead is found to bear the same name, it might be changed. In the case of a living person who is the namesake, if he or she were to die, there is a danger the name bearer will die as well. Morgan in the late 19th century in Kansas reported another reason for a name change that accords with the ancient patrilineal tradition. The successor of a chief, in the old days, was often the oldest son (or another son if the oldest was not suitable to the task). However, in the absence of a son or suitable male child, the chief's sister's son might be chosen. However, the sister's son would bear the name of his mother's clan which would of necessity (ideally) differ from that of the uncle (since one could not marry one of his or her own patri-sib). In one case Morgan cited, the nephew's name was changed to the totem of his uncle so that he could succeed him as chief. I suspect this might have also happened in the case of a son-in-law succeeding as chief since he would also of necessity have been of a different clan than his wife (the chief's daughter). Of course, if a brother of the chief succeeded him, which was frequently the case and even perhaps the first option, there was no necessity of name change since brothers (in an extended since) were of the same clan.

2. The Linguistic Structure and Interpretation of Shawnee Names.

WORD FORMATION		
Initial Stem (This stem normally provides the primary meaning of the name)	**Prefinal stem(s)** (indicates actions, characteristics or physical features of the totem)	**Final Element** (designates the sex of the name bearer with common actions or features)

meth-	'whole, all, uninterrupted' 'good, well'	-miyee - piiwe -kam(i) - 'kawe/kawi -piye(e)	'paths' 'feathers' 'water' 'tracks'	-'shi	'to recline or be in a situation or position' (f.)
weshi/ wele- mayaaw	'straight, right, correct' 'yellow' 'firm'		'extending in a line, across an expanse of water, extending hither'	-'shika	'something that reclines or drops down by action of legs or feet' (m.)
hathawaahaayiita -pem-	'along, over, around, by			-skaka	'action or situation by means of feet' (m.)
	'fowl' 'crossing, flat, at right angles', 'going along, along there'	-aalow-, -alw- -pto	'tail' 'to run'	-shimo -'the/ -'tha -pama -'kwe	'to voice, having voice, noise' (m.) 'to move by legs or wings' (m) 'looking at someone' (f.) 'woman, female'
pelee- haashit-					
halem-					

> *Metha-miyee-'shi* 'Travels All Over (along all the paths)' – Horse Phratry (f.)
> *Metha-skaka* 'Steps on All of It (of hoof}' – Horse Phratry (m.)
> *Metha-kam-shika* 'Whole Body in the Water' – Turtle Phratry (m.)
> *Wele-piwe-'shi* 'Fine Feathers' – Turkey Phratry (f.)
> *Mayaawi-'shimo* 'Right Sounding Voice' –Turkey Phratry (m.)
> *Hothawaa-kam-'shi* 'Reclines in Yellow Water' – Turtle Phratry (f.)
> *Hothaawa-thakaka* 'Puts Foot in Something Yellow' – Round-footed Phratry (m.)
> *Pem-kawi-'-shi* 'Tracks Go By' – Round-footed (Wolf) Phratry (f.)
> *Halem'kawi'shi* 'Tracks Go Back' (Go along so tracks go back behind). Roundfooted, Wolf (f.)
> *Haayiitaapama* 'Looks at Someone Firmly' – Bird Phratry (f.)
> *Hayiitaa-thakaka* 'Stamps Firmly' – Rabbit (m.)
> *Pem-'the* 'Passes By' – Round-footed (m.)
> *Mayaaw-'tha* 'Flying Straight' (m.) – Bird Phratry, Eagle Clan.
> *Pele-'kwa* 'Eagle Woman' From *pelee-* 'fowl' Eagle is *pelee'thi*. Eagle Clan (f.)
> *Haashite-kam-'tha* 'Crossing the Water'[1]. Water Phratry, Turtle Clan. *Wanak-aalwi* "Raises Tail"[2]. Rabbit (m.).
>
> f. = female name, m. = male name.
>
> [1] *Haashit-* (+ *-ee-, -ashk-*) 'position of one thing relative to another (crossing, flat, at right angles)' [SS:434]. Gatschet noted with this name that ofTecumseh: "Tekumthi was turtle 'walking across'; "All the turtles, for instance, were *kámi* (*kámsi* in woman) *kamisika* or *kamthénuī*". He assigned this to Duck or Turtle Clan).
>
> [2] With respect to names ending in *–aalow-/-alw-* 'tail' (non-initial doublet), Gatschet has the note from a Shawnee "…to hold up the tail, therefore rabbit or skunk clan."

Initial stems. *Initial or primary stems generally define the meaning of the name.* They are the most open class that could be virtually any stem. However, in practice, stems having to do with the behavior, character or looks of totems are of course favored. For example, colors, particularly white, black and yellow, occur frequently. Sometimes the primary stem has a vague demonstrative (*tee'-* 'at that place') or locative meaning (*pem'* 'along, over, by, around'), but generally they derive from full nominal and verbal words.

Prefinal stems. *Prefinal or secondary stems provide the meaning which points to the clan of the name bearer.* It does this by allusion to actions or situations characteristic of the totem of the clan to which the name bearer belongs. This is a small class of stems and some of them are used exclusively or most often to indicate specific clans. For example, *-kam(i),* concerning an expanse of water, always refers to the Turtle Clan, and *-shimo*, voice, almost always refers to Turkey Phratry (Turkey and Owl Clans usually), but I sometimes for Wolf Clan since the noises made by both are unusual (gobbling, hooting, howling). References to feathers (*piiwe*), flying or wings indicate the Fowl Phratry. Some stems, however, can be suitable for more than one clan. The stem *piye(e)-* has a meaning that can point to a line of horses, ducks flying or swimming in a line, or of a turtle in a pool. In many cases, the combination of all the stems is involved in interpreting the meaning of a name. Sometimes the final stem is not translated at all since the primry stem holds the essential meaning.

Final elements. These most always determine the sex of the named person. There is a smaller set for women. The meaning of these stems is not always translated.

- Female: -*'shi* 'to recline or to be in a situation', -*pama* 'to look at someone', -*'kwe* 'woman'.

- Male: -*'shika* 'something that reclines or drops down by action of legs or feet', -*skaka* (alternate -*thaka*) 'in an action or situation through feet', -*'shinwa* 'alight, crop down', -*pawi* 'to stand', -*'the/'tha* 'to move by action of feet or wings', -*'shimo* 'to voice, having a voice', -*pto* 'to run', -*'the/-'tha* 'to move by means of legs or wings; go, walk, fly'.

NOTE: There are two final elements which sound like –*tha/'the*. These can cause confusion.

- The ending –*tha* 'person' and its inanimate equivalent, *thi/'thi* 'creature' (or inanimate object). The former may occur with legitimate clan names, names of membership in a group, or as names of totemic guardian spirits. And the latter occurs as part of the names of a number of animals, but may occur as part of a name with the proper prefinal stems. Examples: *Chalakatha* 'person, member of this subtribe'), *skoteetha* 'fire person' (guardian spirit of fire), *waapethi* 'swan', *pelee'thi* 'eagle'.

- The diminutive endings –*tha* 'little' (animate) and –*thi* 'little' (inanimate). Either of these may occur on legitimate clan names with the proper accompanying prefinal stem(s), but more often occur with nicknames. Examples: *Chakakamtha* 'Little Water' (Turtle Clan; real clan name from *Chak-* + *-'a/-i* 'small' + *kam(i)* "water" + *-thi* 'inanimate diminutive' and with animate ending: *Tootiitha* 'Little Frog (Frenchman)' (nickname), *piilitha* 'Little Billy' (nickname; English loanword).

A final word on names has to do with shortened forms. Sometimes longer clan names were abbreviated and the longer form never appeared in the historical record. This means that we do not always know whether it is a clan name or a nickname. Words like *Miina* 'Blackberry' are almost always nicknames since they indicate the name of the object only. Sometimes these nicknames, acquired later in life, are preserved and used in the community to the exclusion of the original clan name. Blue Jacket would be another such instance since the word for jacket is an English loanword, indicating the origin of the name was from whites and it was translated into Shawnee.

This brings us to a final point on interpretation. Lacking one or more translations by Shawnee of the meaning of a name it is sometimes still possible to determine the meaning from the stems involved, but it is always conjectural as the names often have allusions with which native speakers might be familiar, but of which we are clueless. Such translation conjectures will have a question mark or comment. In the instance of an English translation without a Shawnee word we are on very thin ice indeed. If it is a common name or one in which the stems seem obvious I have made the leap, but put an asterisk before the conjectural Shawnee word. When there is only an English name there are two possibilities: 1) if it is something simple like "Berry" or "Owl" it is reasonable to just give those in Shawnee without comment; however, 2) if the name seems more complicated but has some possibility of being reconstructed, it will be put with an asterisk to indicate that it has not been verified by native speakers.

In the entries, those names analyzed are indicated in bold red and put as Endnotes (sowing up in gray in the black and white print edition).

I hope all will enjoy Don's monumental effort and I am pleased to make my modest contribution.

Noel Schutz
August 8, 2007

Guide to Pronouncing Shawnee Names

The phonetic alphabet used in the analysis of Shawnee names follows general American linguistic usage except for two sounds: 1) what is usually written "s" by some researchers and "š" by others is her written with the usual English pronunciation as "sh" (as in "*sh*ip"), and 2) what is technically written as "θ" is here written as "th" (as in the word "*th*ing"). Otherwise, it will be familiar to linguists.

1. Consonants

The sounds [**p, t, ch** and **k**] sounds, though similar to English have some differences. Between vowels they may sometimes sound like b, d, dzh (as the "j" in **j**udge) in the speech of men. This is just a phonetic variation and not significant in Shawnee, though folks who wrote down names wrote sometimes one or the other ("b" for "p", for example). For non-native speakers it is best to ignore the slight differences and pronounce them like English is the best course:

"**p**" as in **p**ad, "**t**" as in **t**ad, ch as in **ch**urch and "**k**" as in **c**ool

Also regarding people who wrote down Shawnee names it may be noted that sometimes the sounds "t" and "k" were spoken so weakly they were missed.

The sounds [**th, sh**] dound pretty much like the English sounds in *th*ing and *sh*ip (though "sh" sometimes sounds a bit like "s" to English ears, especial before consonants (like"sk" and "sp" which I still write as shk and shp as they are not quite like the English "s").

"**th**" as in **th**ing, "**sh**" as in **sh**ip

The sound [**h**] occurs at the beginning of words and is comparable to the sound in the English word *help*. Initial "h" is lightly pronounced and often missed by those writing down Shawnee names, so that it appeared they begin with a vowel.

The sound written with a raised comma, [**'**], does not occur in English as a regular sound, but can be heard in exclamations like "uh-oh" where it is written with a dash. It is a catch in the throat called a glottal stop and occurs in many languages. It occurs between vowels and before consonants. When it occurs before consonants, it has a rasping (frication) quality such that Gatschet wrote it as a combination of [**'**] and [h] = 'h or χ (sometimes sounds a bit like "sh"), but a quick catch is sufficient.

"**h**" as in **h**elp, "**'**" as in **uh-oh**

The sounds [m, n, l] are much like English, except m and l are pronounced more lightly. In addition, "m" at the beginning of words is often voiceless and those who wrote down names often missed it.

The semi-vowels [w, y] are pronounced much as in English with "y" as in *yes* and "w" as in *west*. Recorders of Shawnee names often missed the "y" and wrote a sequence of vowels instead.

2. Vowels

There are only four vowels, both short and long: [i, e, o, a]. Long vowels are written as double vowels [ii, ee, oo, aa].

The pronunciation of each vowel can vary a great deal.

"**i**" as in b**ee**t, **ea**t or *it* or *bet*. A large phonetic range. Probably "i" as in *it* is best most of the time. Many write "i" only for these but write "e" as a separate vowel in a five vowel broad phonetic *notation*. This e is more like e than the one following. Examples: *Thawiikila* (Thah-wee-kee-lah) 'Shawnee divison'; *Mekoch**e*** (Maykoh-chay) 'Shawnee division'; also heard as *Mekoch**i*** or *Mekuch**i*** (or even *Mekuch**e***).

"**e**" as in *mad or sometimes almost like h**a**y.* though it is also pronounced in many words with the sound as in "**ea**t" in many words. Example: *P**e**kowi* (Pay-koh-wee) 'Shawnee division'; also sometimes heard as *P**i**kowi*, etc.

"**o**" as in *s**o**up* or *s**o**ap*. Sometimes like "o" and sometimes like "u". Example: *Kishpoko* (keesh-poh-koh) 'Shawnee dividion'; also heard as *Kishpukoo* or *Kishpuku*. Note the consonants do not distinguish k and g and one or the other might be heard so that sometimes you get *kishpugo*, etc.

"**a**" as in **Oh!**, *h**o**t* or *f**a**ther or c**a**r*. Example: Chalak**a**atha (member of a Shawnee division).

ENDNOTES

Analysis of Selected Shawnee Names

1

Attakullakulla Carpenter-Leaning Wood. *Hote'koo-* from *hote'kwi* 'wood, log'. See *hote'ko* 'logs'.

2

Autumn Leaf aka Pahkotasisqui. Perhaps Pakwatashishiki 'dry leaf' from pakw/peekw//piikw 'dry, dryness' and a non-initial doublet for *m'shishki* 'leaf'. See *hashishki* 'earth'. Another possibility is *pakw-* 'plant, plant-like, leaf-shaped' + *shishki* 'dirt, ground' in the since of leaves falling to the ground in autumn.

3

Aweecony. From *hawikanwi* 'shade, shadow'.

4 Waughapelethee. 'Bald Eagle'. *Waapeele'thi* 'bald eagle' (literally 'white eagle'from *waap-* 'white' + *pele'thi* 'eagle' [*pelee-* 'fowl' + *-thi*

'creature' (analogous to -*tha* 'person'). Eagle Clan, Bird (Turkey/Eagle) Phratry.

5
Matchemento 'Bad Snake'. *Machimaneto* 'bad snake' or 'devil' (*mat-/mach-* 'bad, ugly' + *maneto* 'snake; supernatural power'). Snake Clan in the Water (Turtle/Duck) Phratry.

6
Baker, Boling aka *Kikpelethee*. Perhaps from *Kekewapelethee* 'Hawk' as in 'Tame Hawk' below. from *kekewa* 'hawk' + *pelee'thi* 'eagle'. Fowl (Turkey) Phratry.

7
Amaghqua 'Beaver'. *Hame'kwa* 'Beaver'. Beaver Clan, Round-footed Phratry (Wolf/Beaver Phratry).

8
Big Hominy aka Missemediqueety. **M'shimethekwiti* 'Big Hominy' from *mshi-* 'big' + "methekwite" 'hominy, pounded and boiled' (from Denny and Butler). See Miami *mitokatwi* 'cooked hominy'). The alternate name "Misemeathaquatha" might be thename form or just a variant way of writing it.

9
Spemica Lawba 'High Horn'. A particle, *spemeki* (*sp-* 'up, raised, high' + *-emeki*) 'high, raised up'+ a non-initial stem for horn; perhaps –*laaka* as in *pshekthiwilaaka* 'deer horn' (*holaaka* 'dish'). Deer Clan, Hoofed (Horse/Deer) Phratry.

10
Sepettekenathe 'Big Rabbit'. *Mshipetakine* 'Big Rabbit' from *mshi-* 'big' + *petakine"thi* 'rabbit'.The initial "m" in *mshi-* is often voiceless and thus not heard by non-native speakers. This happens in many names, as in Big Snake below.
Rabbit Clan (no Phratry for rabbits. Rabbits stand alone).

11   Shemenetoo 'Big Snake'. *Mshimaneto* from *mshi-* 'big' + *maneto* 'snake; supernatural power'. Snake Clan, Water (Turtle/Duck) Phratry.

12 Shekaghkela 'Big Turtle'. *Mshikakila* 'Big Turtle' from *mshi-* 'big' + *ka'kila* 'water turtle' (derived from *kasky-* 'rough surface'). Turtle Clan, Water (Turtle/Duck) Phratry.

13   Mugwa 'Black Bear'. *M'kwa* 'Bear'. Bear Clan, Round-footed (Wolf/Beaver) Phratry.

14   Cottawahcothi 'Black Body'. *M'kateewethi* 'One who is black' from m'kateewethi 'he is black'. See also *waapakoche* 'he has a white body'. Here 'body' is not expressed.

15   Black Cat (1) aka Piktwaposetha-Pekatwaposetha. Possibly *Pekichatwapooshitha* 'Black Cat' from *pooshiitha* 'house cat' (literally, 'Little pussycat' from *pooshi-* from pussycat Engish loanword, with the diminutive –*tha*). Perhaps (pe)*pekich-* 'dark' is used rather than the word for black? The exact form cannot be recovered from the information at hand. The Shawnee word for cat is *peshi*; however in this name an English loan word is used. Probably a knickname.

16   Mkahdaywahmayquah 'Black Fish'. *Mkateewaameekwa* from *mkateewa* 'it is black' + *-ameekwa* 'fish' (non-initial stem). Fish clan, Water (Turtle/Duck) Phratry.

17 Lematashe. *Lemata'shi* 'Lies sloping downward (?)' (allusion to position in the water?) from *lemat-* 'down' + *'shi* 'reclines, lies' (feminine name ending) See the masculine equivalent *lemachshinwa* 'he lies on an incline sloping downward'.
Note also the name for a species of fish, *lemachtheewameekwa* 'leper sturgeon'. Turtle/Duck Phratry, Fish Clan.

18   Catahekassa – Black Hoof. M'kateekashe 'black hoof' From *m'katee-* 'black' + *-kashe* 'hoof (sometimes 'fingernail, toenail'). Horse or Deer Clan, Hoofed Phratry.

19   Falling Tree aka Pht-Peethatha. From *pth-/path-* 'detached portion' + *-tha* 'moving'? (but this usually implies action of feet or wings). Analysis uncertain.

20 Rabbit (1) aka Nenookse. Possibly *Naanook'shi* 'Lying in the mud (?)' from *naanooka(w)-* 'muddy, boggy' + 'shi 'reclining, lying, resting' (feminine name ending).

21 Rabbit (2) aka Neneksa. Possibly *Nenek'shi* 'trembling nervously?'. See *Nenekakam'shi* (Gatschet, "refers to water", *ninekipiyeshka* 'he ripples it (refers to water)' (turtle). But also Voegelin has a description of neneki 'shaking nervously, nervously perceptive' as "he is nervously looking for a place to alight (as a bird flying or a man in an airplane)".

22 Black Loon aka Cawtawawwawqua-Kahtahwawwahkwah. *M'kateewamakwa* 'Black Loon' from *M'katee(w)-* + *makwa* 'loon'. Bird Phratry, Turkey or Eagle Clan. Also Waapimakwa 'White Loon'.

23 Shemeneto 'Black Snake'. *Mshimaneto* 'big snake' from *mshi-* 'big' + *maneto* 'snake'; black is *mkatee-* and Gatschet gives his name properly as "*Mkatewimanito*". Snake Clan, Water Phratry.

24 Aquewelene 'Blanket Man'. *hakwa-* 'up on top, covering' + *-leni* 'man' (noninitial doublet of hileni). See *nitakhwa* 'I put a blanket on top of him'. Clan?

25 Bloody Fellow aka Ninatoogah. Probably *Neenaw'tooka* 'Warrior' from *neenaw'to* 'warrior'.

26 Ouiskelotha – Blue Bird. *Wiskilo'tha* 'bird' (with non-initial doublet for bird – *skilo'tha,* with *-'tha* 'to fly'. The stem for blue does not occur though such words are found (see *wiipekwiskilo'tha* 'Thrush' (= 'grayish bird'). This is would seem to be a nickname or pet name.

27 Blue Jacket. Rendered in Shawnee as *Skipaki Chekiti* 'Blue Jacket' from *skipaki* 'blue' + *chekiti* 'jacket' (English loan word. Gatshet transcribed "Skípagi tchékiti"). It would seem to be a nickname seeing that it involves an English loan word. Possibly given by whites and translated back into Shawnee. This name was also given others, but we do not know the circumstances which broutht it about.

28 Blue Jacket aka Weyapiersenwha 'Whirlpool'. *Weyapiyeshinwa* 'whirlpool'. From Waa*wiyaa-* 'round, around, circular' + *piye(e)* 'to come, extend hither' + *shinwa* 'reclines, lies, comes to rest'. The notion of a 'pool' is sometimes supplied by the stem *piye,* as in the name *Welepiye'shi* 'One who is in a fine pool' (with *wele-* from *howesi/howele-* 'good, well'}. The same name with the

ending *–piye'shi* would be the feminine name equivalent (*'shi* 'coming to rest') of the masculine *–piye'shinwa* with *shinwa* (coming to rest, reclining, lying). A more common masculine name would end in *-skwaka*. The allusion would be to the circular movement of water as in a whirlpool (note Miami *waia*sitwa 'whirlwind'). This has the form of a birthname, but his alternate name Big Rabbit does as well. Perhaps he officially changed his clan name rather than simply taking on a nickname. The name of a man might be changed to accomodate his becoming a member of a different clan for purposes such as being eligible to be a chief. Water Clan? and Phratry (there was no Water Clan as such in our records for Shawnee, but the closely rrelated Kickapoo tribe had names with water references which did not seem to be connected with an animal totem.

29 Blue Jacket aka Sepettekenathe 'Big Rabbit-in youth' *Mshipetekenathe* 'big rabbit' from *mshi-* 'big' + *petakine-* 'rabbit' + '*the*. Rabbit Clan. The translation may indicate that his name was changed later in life since he was born a Pekowi. This clan was popular among the Pekowi and while it existed into the 20th century, it was already rare by the time Gatschet did his field work.

30 Blue Jacket, George Jr aka Nawahtahtha. Perhaps *Nawata'tha* 'Pass By Without Stopping, Pass By At Random (?)'. From *naawat-* 'unintentional, uncertain, uninterrupted'. See *ninaawachipem'the* 'I went by there without stopping', *nawachipto* 'he ran by at random', *ninaawataapama* 'I chanced to look at him'.

31 Blue Jacket aka Mathahpease. Probably Methapiye'shi 'Lying stretched out' (?) (in the water?)' Turtle clan? (f.). See the male name *methakamshika* 'Whole body in the water'. Turtle Clan (m.)

32 Hokantitakarchi 'Bony Legs'. From *ho'kani* 'bone' + (perhaps, *tiltii-* 'smallish' or some combination with *–tee-*; 'body, person, individual') + '*kaachi* 'legs'. Appears to be a nickname.

33 Bowman, Billy aka Two Goose-Neshwaueshwa. *niishwi* 'two, pair, double, paired together'. The ending is not the usually words for goose.

34 Bright Horn aka Wathethewela. *Wa'theethewile* 'bright horn' from *wa'thete* 'it shines' (*wa'thee-* 'illumination') + *-wile* 'horn' (*pe'shiwile* 'deer horn'). Deer Clan, Hoofed Phratry.

35

Buffalo aka Moothooshwah. *M'thoothwa, me'thoothwa* 'buffalo, cow' (see *msime'thoothwa* 'big buffalo'; *manetoowim'thoothwa* 'sacred buffalo'). Buffalo Clan?, Hoofed Phratry.

36
   Bukangolas 'Breaks to Pieces'. Perhaps **Pokenkola* 'One who breaks something by hand' (* marks conjectural) from *pok-* (< *po'k* 'mashing, breaking') + *-en-* 'by hand' + *ko* < 'ko' 'cutting'? + *-l-* 'direct toward' + *-a* 'inanimate goal'. See *nipokkola* 'I gutted him, cut out his guts'; *nipo'kin*a 'I cracked it open, broke it by hand').

37 Chiesatebe 'Bushy Head'. Unidentified intial stem 'bushy' + *-tepee* 'brain, head'.

38
   Tamenatha. Perhaps **Taaminatha* 'Corn Person' or "Little Corn' from *taami(n)a-* 'corn' + *-tha* 'person' or 'diminutive' (see taaminaapo 'corn whisky' with –aapo 'liquid'. The expression *taamina'kiithi* 'corn person' does occur (perhaps derived from the verb *taamine'ki* 'it is productive of corn')

39
   Kekewepelethee 'Tame Hawk'. *Kekewapelethee* 'hawk' from *kekewa* 'hawk' + *pelee'thi* 'eagle' (< *pelee-* 'fowl' + -*'thi* 'creature' [the counterpart of –'tha 'person']).

40   Taumee Elene 'Corn Man'.
taami- 'corn' + *hileni* 'man'.

41   Nepikeweewa. Initial step: *nepi* 'water'.

42
   Penegashegan 'Change of feathers'. *pen-* '(movement) downward' (see *penawe* 'he is shedding' = pen + *-awa* 'downy feathers') + *-ka* 'splits off' + *sheka* 'hangs down'. The allusion seems to be the shedding of feathers.

43
   Wacanackshina-Wokonuckshenoah 'White one alights'?? (or reclines) from *Wa'kanaky-* 'White' + *-shinwa* 'lies, reclines, alights' (perhaps referring to a swan or goose alighting on the water???). See also *wa'kanakya* 'it is white', *weewa'kanakithita* 'white horse' (also *waapim'sheewe* 'white horse'). m. Possibly Water Phratry (swimming birds such as duck, goose, swan along with turtle, fish, snake).

44 Cheeseekau "Sting'. *Chi'shika* from *chi'sh-* 'pierce, break, sting' + *-shika* masculine name ending parallel to female *-shi* (-shi 'coming to rest' + -ka 'action of feet' (used for snake clan in names like *Washikapiyeshika* 'strung out in a line' [Gatschet]). See also *nichi'tha* (with alaternate form *thi'sh-*) 'I (*ni*)

stung him (as an insect might)'. If this alludes to the sting of a snake bite, this wouild be Snake Clan, Water (Turtle/Duck) Phratry.

45   Passquankake 'Gun Shot'. Perhaps *Paahkwaanikaka*. Cp. *Pepkwaanani* 'it shoots' (Miami language: *papikwani* 'gun') and *Pepkwanwi* 'report of a gun (the noise of a gunshot). Probably *paash*(y)- 'emergence from and opening" + *kwaani* 'gun' + *-kaka* (masculine name ending).

46   Child in Blanket aka Aquewa Apetotha. From *hakwa-* 'on top of' (used for blanket in the sense of a covering) + *hapelo'the* 'baby, child'.

47   Wepenipe 'Cold Water'. *Weepi* 'cold, chilly' + *nepi* 'water'.

48   Hokoleskwa 'Corn Stalk'. *Hokoweshkwa* 'Corn Stalk' from *hokoleshkwa* 'cornstalk without the ears of corn' (also *holeshkwa* 'cornstalk'). The non-initial stem *-ashkwa* concerns plants as in also *taamin-ashkwa* 'cornstalk' and *kawashkwi* 'wheat'.

49   Waynaypooechseekwa 'Stout Man' < ??? + a*po-che* 'belly' [see –eche 'rounded thing'] + *-shika* (var. Wneypuechsika, Waynaypooechseeka).

50   Keightughqua aka Corn Stalk. perhaps *ke'ta-* 'worn out, old; reborn'.

51   Heleeneepseeko 'Native Warrior'. *Hilenawee* 'person, Indian' (as opposed to white man) + *-shika* 'masculine name ending'.

52   Pomeatha 'Passes By'. *Pem'the* 'he goes/passes by' [SS:93] from *pem-* 'along, by, over, around, movement around' + -'*the* 'going, passing, walking, flying'. Wolf clan, Round-footed (Wolf/Beaver) Phratry.

53   Pisakethe 'Deer". *Pshekthi* 'deer'.

54   Wabete 'Elk'. From *msiwaapiti* 'elk'.

55   Skootekitehi 'Fire Heart'. From *shkote* 'fire' + -*tehi* 'heart. Probably a nickname.

56   Pepikwa 'Flea'. From *papikwa* 'flea'. A nickname.

57   Flying Cloud aka Paytakootha. Perhaps *Paathkootha (< *poothkwa* 'cloud' [where kwa > koo + '*tha* 'flying']) derived from *poothkwatwi* 'it is cloudy' and *piipoothkwatwi* 'it is alternately cloudy and clear' (from *pooth-* 'foamy, cloudy' + '*kwa-twi* 'concerning the sky'?). Gatschet reported "Puthkwa" 'clouds'. See

paathkwa'ki 'rain cloud' Notably, a Thunderbird is *wapoothi* (See also *waputhi*, Gatschet).

58   Pemethata 'Turkey Flying By'. *Pemthaata* 'flying by' from *pem-* 'along, by over, around' + *'tha* 'going, walking, flying' + *-ta* 'in reference to inanimate goal (see *nipem'thaata* 'I pass by, over it' {SS:93]). Turkey Clan, Bird (Turkey/Eagle) Phratry.

59   Niewekilechi 'Four Fingers'. From *niyeewi* 'four' + *-lechi* 'finger, hand, toe'. Nickname.

60   Fox aka Wahkoceethee. *Waakoche'thi* 'Fox' from *waakoche'thi* 'fox'.

61   Spemcia Elene 'Big Man'. From *shpemiki* 'up, up high' (can be seen as 'tall') + *hileni* 'man'.

62   Kishanositee 'Hard Man'. *Kiishinachi* (leni) 'Difficult (man)' from *kiishinaachi* 'difficult, hard to get along with' [SS:300]. Nickname because, as the Moravians said, he was difficult to deal with..

63   Hard Striker aka Pucksinekau. **Pakshinka* 'Hard Striker' from *pak-* 'strike, pound' + *shi(n)-* 'come to rest' + *-ka* 'action by legs'. The ending probably is not reflected in the translation being a common masculine name ending. See also Pakshinosa (also called Hard Striker?).

64   Hawk aka Hawkawepilathy-Hokawepeelathee. A species of hawk (?) from – *pelee'thi* 'eagle'. See also *Kekewapelethee* 'hawk' from *kekewa* 'hawk' + *pelee'thi* 'eagle'.

65   Heap aka Akopee. Probably from haakw- 'piled up' (as in haakwate 'it is piled up').

66   Cawechile. See *kawi* 'briar, thorn' and *kawishi* 'briary plant, stalk of bush'.

67   Counasona. From *koona* 'snow'.

68   Hop, Wapethi 'Swan'. *Waapethi* 'Swan'.

69   Kemepemo 'Lies in Wait'. **Kimipimo* 'lies stealthily' from *kim(i)-* 'unobserved, secretly, sneakily' + *piim-* 'on one side, sideways, crooked, harm, evil'. Gatschet has "pimo lie there, refers to quadrupeds, 'roundfooted' clan." Wolf Clan, Round-footed Phratry.

70   Kishkalawa (1) aka Keeshkalawa. *Kishkaalowa* 'Cut Tail' from *kiisk-* 'cut, cut off, break' +

-*aalowa* 'tail'. See *kishkaalowe'shinwa* 'he has a tail completely cut off'.

71 Weepaykweleekwa 'Grey Eyes'. From *wiipekiwa* 'gray' + -l- + -y'kwe 'woman'.

72 Kumskaka 'Cat Flying in Air'. *Kamshkaka* 'moving across or stepping in the water (through action of feet)' from *kami-* 'water' + *-shka-* 'to move, general bodily movement + -ka 'located at legs'. Voegelin gives the gloss for *-shkaka* as "one who is an actor, or a situation, through use of feet." This form –*shkaka* /*thkaka* occurs frequently as a male name ending. See discussion under Tecumseh below and elsewhere. The translation given, Cat Flying in the Air, was probably a confusion by Drake of Tecumseh's name with the allusion ot the sacred water panther.

73 Kwatooka 'He Who Is Afraid'. *Kwteka 'One who is afraid' from *kwta-* 'fear' + *-ka* 'one who' (participle).

74 LaForce, Cottawahcothi 'Black Body'. See *m'kateewethi* 'he is black'.

75 Little Moon aka Tebethtakishthok. See *tepe'kishthwa* 'night luminary, moon' from *tep'ki-* 'night' + *kishthwa* 'luminary, month'.

76 Little Sun aka Kisathoitakishok. From *kiishathwa* (> *kiishatho-*) from *kiisha'thwa* beside *Kiishthwa* 'luminary, month' (sun is *kiishekikiishthwa* 'day luminary, sun').

77 Long Tail aka Chakalawa. See –*aalowe* 'tail'. However, *chak-* 'small' not long. Rabbit Clan.

78 McPherson, James aka Skwalakalee-Red-faced Man. See *m'shkw-* 'red'.

79 Menewalakosi-Lying Piled in a Hollow. From *menw-* 'bunched, piled'. + *waal'kwa* 'scooped out' + *-shi* 'lying' (woman's name ending).

80 Metheotashe -Turtle laying her eggs in the sand'. From *meth-* 'whole, entire, all' + *-oote-* 'directed motion' + *-shi* 'coming to rest, lying, reclining' (feminine name ending). The allusion would be the motion of a turtle in the sand when laying eggs. See names like *Methakamsika* 'Whole body lying in the water, lying entirely in the water'. If the ending is –*shki*, as Drake has it in his *Life of Tecumseh*, , this might refer to non-initial doublet of *hashishi* 'earth, land, clay, sand' which would fit the translation.. Turtle Clan, Water Phratry.

81 Mink aka Chaquiweshe. *Saakweewe'thi* 'mink'.

82

Monetoshe 'Resting Snake'. *Maneto* 'snake" plus the feminine name ending – *shi* 'reclining, resting'.

83 Muskrat (1) aka Oshasqua. Hothaskwa 'muskrat'.

84 Muskrat (1) aka Oshasqua-Hotthashkwa. *Hothashkwa* 'muskrat'.

85 Muskrat Tail. *Hothashkwaalowe* 'Muskrat Tail'. Note that Oppossum is *hothashkwaalowe'thi* 'Muskrat-tail creature'.

86 Muskwakonokah. *M'skwa'kuna* 'red (tree, made so by climbing)' from m'skw- 'red, blood' + probably *kwa'kuna* 'holding'. Gatschet has for this person's name "*mskwa'hkuna* 'red (tree)' with the explanation by a Shawnee that the tree was made red by taking the bark off, by bears, etc., climbing up (holding) the tree. *kwa'hkuna.* Bear clan." Bear Clan, Round-footed Phratry.

87 Nahaseemo. *Naha'shimo* 'One who speaks properly/correctly' or perhaps "One who speaks well" (as opposed to good which would be *weshi-'shimo*); from *n'h- (+ -a, -i)* 'expertly, correctly, properly, virtuously, curiously, suspiciously' + *shimo* 'voice, sound' (a masculine name ending). See a cognate in Miami: *nahachimwa* 'one who reports correctly'. The ending -*'shimo* 'voice in all of Voegelin's material it Turkey Clan and in Gatschet Turkey Phratry (Owl clan once) as well except for one example of the howl of a wolf (Wolf Clan). Always a male name in all data. Gatschet as *Na'swi'shimo* 'Pretty Good Sounding Voice' from *na'swi* 'pretty' + -*'shimo* and puts it in the Owl Clan for the Shawnee involved. Turkey Clan, Bird Phratry.

88 Nihipeewa. Perhaps *N'hipeewa 'One who has correct feathers (?)' from *n'h- (+ -a, -i)* 'expertly, correctly, properly, virtuously, curiously, suspiciously' + – *piiwe* 'feathers, hair'. Gatschet has "fine feather, down (eagle clan)". Eagle Clan, Bird (Turkey/Eagle) Phratry.

89 Nika aka Wild Goose. *Nika* 'Wild Goose'. Water (Turkey/Duck) Phratry.

90 Nimwha aka Nihipuwa-Niemwha. Conjectural. Perhaps Niim'ha 'Carry a Flag (on him, as a horse)' from *niim-* 'carrying aloft (as a flag)'. See *niniim'ha* 'I am carrying a flag on him (a horse).' Or maybe *Niipaw'ha* 'One who makes someone Stand (?)' from *niipawi* 'standing' + transitivizing –'h- (+ -w-, -a). or *Niimpawa (?) with the ending *–pawa* 'standing'. See *niniipaw'ha* 'I made him stand up', *niteleiw'ha* 'I made him manly (tough)'. Need more data.

91

Nahswahpama. *Naashwepama* 'One who looks at someone nicely'. For the initial stem, Gatschet has the name "Nahswesimo" [*Naasweshimo*] 'Pretty Good Sounding Voice' (Owl Clan, m.), with the note "na'swi pretty"; but the stem is *naashwi* 'it is fancy, decorous' (as in *ninaashwaapama* 'I looked at him nicely, decorously' [SS:380]. Voegelin has the ending in the name *Mayataapama* 'One who looks at queer things' (doubtful clan affiliation, f.). From Mayataa- 'it is nice, pretty, decorous' + -*pama* 'looking at someone'. –*pama* is a female name ending that occurs with Turkey, Turtle and undetermined clan affiliation.

92
Nonhelema 'Grenadier Squaw' aka 'Warrior Woman'. Perhaps *naan*- 'near, not quite' + *hileni* 'man' + -*ma*. This is similar to the translation given as "Not a man" except that would imply an English or French negative (not, non). The stem *naan*- is native Shawnee. A more chancy interpretation is noon- 'suckle' (*noonwa* 'he is suckling (at breast or bottle)'. A man with breasts? Probably not the latter. Nickname.

93
Opessa 'Swan'. *Waapetha* 'Swan'.

94
Loapeckeway aka "Opessah's son". Perhaps *Laapalkawa* 'Restepping Somebodies Tracks' from *Laap*- 'the same repeated + -*l*- 'transitivizer, action directed toword someone or something' + -*kawe* 'tracks' _ + -a '3rd person'. Or *Lapakawe* 'Restepping Tracks' with *Laap*- 'the same repeated' + -*kawe* 'tracks'. See *ni lapalkawa* 'I am restepping somebodies tracks'. Round-footed Phratry, Wolf Clan.

95
Wawwaythi. Perhaps *Wawiyeethi* 'One who is Round' from *wawiy*- 'round, around, circular'. See *wa(a)wiyeethi* 'he is round'. Probably nickname.

96
Opessa, Pride aka Lawaquaqua-Lawachkamikee-Lawakwakwa. Possibly *Laawaakami'ki* 'Water is Insufficient' from *Laaw*- 'insufficient, diminishing' + *kami* 'concerning water' + -'*ki* 'watery'. See *laawaakami* 'insufficient water' and ending –'*ki* in *ta'nepiw'kiki* 'place where water is abumdant' (with stem for water *nepi*-). Also Miami *sipiwi* [river, Shawnee *thipi*-] *nätawikamki* 'the river is sandy'.

97 Tekomteh. *Tekamthe* 'Crossing the water'. Uncertain about final –teh. If –the then it is virtually the same as his nephews name (Tecumseh)

which is unlikely. Otherwise it is from *te'-* 'there' + *-kam* 'concerning water'. Turtle Clan, Water Phratry.

98   Wabete aka Elk. *Waapiti* 'Elk".

99

Opossom. *Hothashkwalowe'thi* 'Opossum' (muskrat-tail creature) from *hothaskwa* 'Muskrat" + *-aalowe* 'tail' + '*thi* "creature'.

100 Otter (1) aka Kwitateh. *Kitate* 'Otter'.

101

Owl aka Mehathwa. *Miyaathwe* 'Common Gray Owl' from *miyaa-* 'owl'; see also *miyaalwe* 'hoot owl' and *mshimiyaalwe* 'horned oot owl' (literally big hoot owl with *mshi-* 'big').

102

Painted Pole aka Muskwakonah. *M'skwa'kuna* 'red (tree, made so by climbing)' from m'skw- 'red, blood' + probably *kwa'kuna* 'holding'. Gatschet has for this person's name "*mskwa'hkuna* 'red (tree)' with the explanation by a Shawnee that the tree was made red by taking the bark off, by bears, etc., climbing up (holding) the tree. *kwa'hkuna.* Bear clan." Bear Clan, Round-footed Phratry. Same name as Red Pole.

103   Panther aka Meshepeshe. *M'shipeshi* 'Panther' from *mshi* (< m'shi;) 'big' + *peshi* 'cat'. See also *peshwa* 'wildcat'.

104   Poxinosa aka Pakshinotha. *Paakshinotha* 'Hard Striker'. There are two stems, one is *paak-/pak-* 'hard, strong, firm, taut, staccato movement' and the other is pak- 'strike, pound'. For the former see *paakiikwe'shinwa* 'he hit his face (*iikwe*) against something', *nipaakhwa* 'I beat him (as on a drum, with repeated movements). For the later see *pake* 'strike, poiund' and *pakamaaka* 'war club'. See Miami *päkamaka* 'I strike/buffet him with something'. The non-initial stem + *shino-* (< *-shi(n)* 'coming to rest' + -*wa* 'he' or 'one who') + -'*tha* 'movement by legs or wings; going, walking, flying' or *–tha* 'person' do not seem to come into the translation. The sequencing of two non-final stems often occurs, but this one (*shinwa* + -*tha*) is not found elsewhere and seems odd. However, the entire meaning transmitted in the translation is resident in the primary stem.

105

Puckensinwah 'Alights from flying'. *Pakenshinwa* 'Comes to rest from another place' from *pak-* 'away from another place' (perhaps + *-en-* 'by movement of hand') + *shi-n-* 'coming to rest' + *-wa* 'he' (see *pakshinwa* 'he alighted from flying' [SS:76] – the best translation). Eagle Clan, Turkey/Eagle Phratry. Cognate stems for the same clans are used in names in Kickapoo: "Puckke-shin-no" 'Going to light on a tree' (Eagle Clan) and "Pah-ke-che-moke" 'Turkey lighting on a tree' (Turkey Clan).

106 Patakeenotha 'Rabbit'. *Petakine'thi* 'rabbit' (but with the human person *-'tha* rather than the creature ending *-'thi*). Rabbit Clan.

107 Shapaatha 'Racoon'. *Thepa'tha* 'Racoon' from *(ha')thepati* 'racoon' with the stem *(ha')thepa-* + *-'tha* 'person' (as for Rabbit above, and elsewhere). Racoon Clan, Round-footed Phratry.

108 Rattlesnake aka Miseethawee. *M'shiithwe* 'rattlesnake'. Water Phratry, Snake Clan (m.)

109 Red Fox. *M'skwa"kiitha* 'Red fox' with *m'skwa-* 'red'.

110 Red Hawk aka Miskapelathee. *M'skwapiilethi* 'Red Hawk' from *m'skwa-* 'red' + *pelee-* 'bird' + *-thi* 'creature' (parallel in some ways to *–tha* 'person'). Bird Phratry, Eagle Clan.

111 Red Woodpecker aka Meeskwakaweethee. Perhaps *M'skwakaawi'thi* "Red Briar/Thorn Bird (?)' from *m'skw-* 'red, blood' + perhaps *–kaawi* 'briar, thorn' + *-'thi* 'creature'. Non-final stem uncertain.

112 James Logan-Walk by the Water. Perhaps *Pemkam'the* 'Walking By the Water' from *pem-* + *kam-* + *'the*. See *Pam'the* 'Go/Walk By'. This is not attested.

113 Robin aka Blue Tail aka Skitlewa-Skilloway.*Skipakaalowa* 'Blue Tail' from *Skipaki* 'blue' + *-aalowa* 'tail'. Robin is *pepche*.

114 Ruddle, Stephen aka Sinnanatha 'Big Fish'. *M'shiname'tha* 'Big Fish' from *m'shi-* 'big" + *name'tha* 'fish'.

115 Sauwaseekou 'Panther Crouching for Prey". Primary stem uncertain. Could be *Saawe'shika* 'lying on the pathway' from *saawe-* 'open pathway' or *Thaawa'shika* 'One who reclines in yellow (in water?) from *(ho)thawa-* 'yellow' + *'shika* mascline name ending from *-'shi* 'reclining, lying, coming to rest" + *-ka* 'located at legs'). If the first stem, then the translation of "Panther Crouching"

would seem to allude to be crouching along a path to leap on prey. If this is so, it would refer to the Round-footed Phratry that would include wolf and panther. However, if the primary stem is *thaawa-* 'yellow' then we have other possibilities. In Voegelin's material, yellow was always *hothaaka-* in names; however, Gatschet has the shorted form (*Thaawawa'shi* 'yellow-furred', female name with –*'shi*). See then *(ho)thaawakam'shi* 'One who reclines in yellow water' (Turtle Clan), *(ho)thaawipiiwe'shi* 'One who has yellow feathers' (Turkey Clan) and *(ho)thaawathkaka* 'One who puts his foot in something yellow' (Roung-footed Phratry, could be wolf or panther totem). Without a second noninitial stem, it is difficult to know the correct interpretation.

116 Shawnee Prophet aka **Lalawethika** 'Rattling Sound in the bush'. *Lalawe'thika* 'Rattling Noise' from *lalawee-/lalalawe-* 'rattling' + *'thika/'shika* masculine name ending (-'thi is an alternate of –'shi 'lying, resting, reclining' + -ka 'located at feet').. See *lalalweewa* 'it makes a rattling noise going through the brush' and *nilalalawe'ke* 'I make a rattling noise going through the brush' and *lalaweenika* 'rattle from rattlesnake'. Snake Clan, Water (Turtle/Duck) Phratry. The ascription of translations such as "Loud Mouth" and such, implying that his name was bestowed up the Prophet because of character flaws, flies in the face of both the naming system which designates a person's clan and the correct analysis of the name itself.

117 Shawnee Prophet aka Tenskawatawa 'Open Door'. **Thenwi-* 'to be open' + *shkwaate* 'door(way)' + *-wa*. Not a totemic name but a nickname taken on as a result of a profound spiritual experience and the inauguration of his career as a prophet.

118 Shot Pouch 'Petatwa'. *Piitalwa* 'Shot Pouch' from *piit-* 'hole' + -*alwa* 'bullets' = bullet bag. See also *piitaaka* 'sack, bag'.

119 Unidentified. Halowas, Horoas and Aroas could be something like **halowas*, but I have not identified the meaning of this name yet. Possibilities: **halowa* 'it is fading, disappearing', **halawa* "it is rejected, refused, worthless' (?).

120 Skunk aka Sekakwa. *Shekaakwa* 'skunk, skunk odor'. Round-footed Phratry.

121 Snow Falling aka Saisaigonokwe. Unidentified initial stem + *koona* 'snow' + *'kwe* 'woman'.

122 Something Round aka Wawilaway. *wawiy-* 'round, around, circular' + (?) – *aalowe* 'tail' or *-lawi* 'concerning a bear'. Analysis of non-final stem uncertain.

123 Spear Warrior aka Cithiskananothe. See *chi'th-* 'pierce, break' (should be chi'sh- before -i-).

124 Squirrel aka Anequepi. *Hanikwapi* 'Squirrel' from *hanikwa* 'squirrel' + *-api* 'sittting' (typical name ending) not reflected in translation.

125 Stands Firm aka Wasegoboah. *Wiishikaapawi* "One who stands firm' from *wiishi-* 'firm' + *-ka-* (reference to legs) + *-pawi* 'standing'. Horse Clan, Hoofed Phratry.

126 Straight Tail aka Meaurroway. *Mayaawaalowe* "Straight Tail' from *mayaaw-* 'straight, correct, right, central' + -aalw-/aalow- 'tail'. See also the verb *mayaawilawi* 'he does right' and a term applied to a war leader, meemayaaw'theeta 'one who goes correctly'.

127 Sugar Tree aka Melassatequi. *Melaashite'kwi* "Sugar Tree' from *melaashi-* 'sugar, sweetening' (from *mel-/meleny-* 'milk' (of breask, corn, sap) + *-aashi + *-te'kwi* 'tree' (see *hote'kwi* 'wood, log'). Nickname?

128 Lucky son of a bitch???

129 Thick Swamp Water aka Paughpi-Popee. See Miami *nipopi* 'soup'.

130 Taming Buck aka Tamininipaquah 'Corn Blade'. *Taaminipakwa* 'Corn Blade' from *taami(n)-* 'corn' + *pakwa-* 'plant, plant-like, leaf-shaped').

131 Tecumapease 'Crossing The Water'. *Te'kampiyeshi* 'Crossing the water' from *te'-* 'vague location' + *-kam(i)* 'water' + *piye(e)* 'coming, extending hither; long extension or expanse of something' + *-shi* 'reclining, lying, resting'. Perhaps referring to reclining in the water or in a line in the water. See Gatchet "*methakamsika*" - 'whole body in the water'. Turtle Clan, Water (Turtle/Duck) Phratry.

132 Tecumqualuska 'Graybeard'. *Te'kamkwaalushka '' from *te'-* 'vague location' + *-kam(i)* 'water' + unanalyzed "kwalushka. Has nothing to do with a graybeard – this must be a nickname. Turtle Clan, Water Phratry.

133 **Tecumoplas aka Margaret.** *Tekamoplashi* (?) from *te'-* 'vague location' + *kam(i)* 'water' + unanalyzed *-op-la* + *--sh(i)* 'reclining, lying'. Turtle Clan, Water Phratry.

134

Tecumsapah aka Margaret. *Te'kamshapa* from *te'*- 'vague location' + *-kam(i)* 'water' + *-shapa* (unanalyzed –sha + *-pa*, feminine name ending?).

135 Tecumseh 'Panther in the Sky'. This name is a bit of a puzzle. The Shawnee Prophet and others plance him in the "Panther Clan" based on the allusion to the sacred water panther who leaps from the sea at night and flies across the sky, his tail making sparks that are falling stars, and then plunging back into the sea before day. Yet the analysis of the name yields a straight forward one: *Te'kamtha/Te'kamthe* from *te'*- 'vague location' + *-kam(i)* 'water' + *-'tha/'the* 'going, walking, flying'. Normally this would be translated as "crossing the water" and automatically name him into the Turtle Clan. The initial stem *te'*- is roughly "located there (at the indicated place)" with reference to the action in or implied by the non-initial stem and ending. Usually does not figure in translations of names since the location is stated or imlied in the rest of the word.

There are no instances of all the names in Shawnee or Kikapoo of the non-initial stem *–kami* referred to any clan other than the Turtle Clan and Gatschet, specifically dealing with Tecumseh's name, makes this point. Since his father, *Pakenshinwa*, was of the Bird Phratry this would mean he was named into his mother's clan and that of his adopted father (presumably) Black Fish (Water Phratry). If my analyses of the names are correct, his older brother and the Shawnee Prophet were named into the Snake Clan, also Water Phratry. Even the ascription of the name as an allusion to the sacred water panther would involve a water creature, or perhaps a Thunder Clan as such would be in Kickapoo and not necessarily land based quadrapeds (Round-footed Phratry). In addition, his close relatives all have similar names in which the Turtle Clan is clearly indicated with no possibility of a Panther Clan affiliation: his older sister (*Tecumapease* 'Crossing The Water'), named before him, his aunt (*Tecumsapah*, his mother's older sister, who, like his mother, was of the Turtle Clan), his aunt's daughter and his first cousin (*Tecumoplas*), his nephew (*Tecumqualuska*), and his son, *Kam'shaka* 'One who moves across or steps in the water' (not "Cat Flying in the Air" for which there is not a shred of support), and his son Tecumtequah 'Cross the Water'. The evidence is therefore overwhelming that he was named into the Turtle Clan. Yet as far back as the early 1820's, the Shawnee Prophet, Tecumseh's younger brother, allotted them to the Panther Clan, the claim cannot be ignored. Given that the Shawnee Prophet's birth name could hardly be considered as a Panther Clan name, I can see only one solution. Given that the Panther Clan leads a war party out and the wolf clan back from an expedition, and given Tecumseh's preeminent leadership in war, the name was reinterpreted and the clan changed. I would suppose this a legitimate possibility for a famous warrior and his son then could be named into the same clan. This and any other interpretation must await further research for confirmation. Only one family name is ambiguous and that is Tecumseh's brother, Sauwaseekou (*Saawe'shika*) translated as 'Panther Crouching for Prey'. If *Saawe-* 'path' is he primary stem, then with the ending –'*shika* (reclining) the translation could be 'reclining, lying or resting on the pathway' but perhaps the meaning 'coming to rest by action of the legs or feet' could include the notion of crouching if the clan was known, since the interpretation of what the action of the feet is depends on the animal totem.. .I am not sure of the clan affiliation here (nor whether this is in fact the correct primary stem), but it is true that reference to pathways or tracks usually involved Round-footed creatures but also sometimes Turkey clan (Tecumshe's father's phratry). One final bit of contributing evidence is the report that "cabalistic" symbl0s, in which one of a turtle was specifically pointed out as obvious, were carved on a tree near the ground where he was buried.

I think that the reinterpretation of his name was befitting the great warrior and all agreed to this view. If the statement is true that a meteor flew overhead after Tecumseh was born, and it has passed down to us from a man who as a child lived in the same village as Tecumseh when they were young, the family tradition may have aided in the re-interpretation and it may have followed some time honored tradition among the Shawnee. But great men forge their own traditions. It may be that when the father died the mother, not taking a clan brother of her husband, returned, as was the tradition, to her own clan. It may have been at this point that they were renamed into the clan of the mother and her relative, Chief Blackfish. If so, it may not have been amiss for Tecumseh himself to receive honorary membership in the Panther Clan on the basis of his leadership and supported by a childhood portent.

136

Tecumseh, Young aka Mahyawekawpawe 'True Stepper'. *Mayaawi-* 'straight, correct, right, true' + *-ka-pawi* 'standing' (*-pawi* occurs only after one of two preposed elements, -nii (vague demonstrative) or -ka- (reference to legs). The use of
"stepper" is consistent with this, though such action of the feet often indicates Horse or Deer Clan (unlikely for Tecumshe's family) or Turkey Clan (Tecumseh's father's clan)..

137

Tecumseh, Young aka Michelana or Machielaini. *M'shileni* or *Makileni* 'Big Man' from *m'shi-* and *mak-* 'big' plus the non-initial form of *hileni* 'man'. Nickname.
138
Tecumseh, Monetoshe 'Resting Snake'. *Moneto'shi* 'Resting Snake' from *moneto* 'snake' + -*'shi* 'reclining, resting, lying.
139
Tecumseh, Young aka Naythahwaynah 'Panther Seizing Prey'. No analysis at present.
140
Tecumseh Jr. aka Paukeesaa, Pahkeesa, Puchetha, Puggeesha, Pugeshashenwa 'Panther Watching Prey'. *Pakishashinwa* '*Alight from flying*'. It is hard to get the meaning of the translation of "Panther Watching Prey' from the stems involved. It appears to be a variation of Pak(en)shinwa (Techumseh's father's name). **Pakithashinwa* 'Alighting (*shinwa*) from flying (-*tha*) away from another place (*pak-i*). Turkey/Eagle Phratry.
141
Tecumtequah 'Cross the Water'. *Te'kam'thekwe* 'Cross the water' from *te'* 'vague demonstrative' + -*kam* 'water' + -*the* 'movement by feet or wings'+ -*kwa*. Turtle Clan, Water Phratry.
142
Tiger Face aka Mashepesheewinqua. *M'shipeshiwiikwe* 'Tiger/Panther/Lion Face' from *m'si-* 'big' + -*iikwe* 'face'. Presumably Panther Clan, Round-footed Phratry.
143 Trotter aka Manemepahtoo. *Menimepto* 'running lively' (= trotter') from *men(ime)-* 'lively, having fun' + *pto* 'running'. Hoofed Phratry (horse, deer, elk, etc.).
144 Turkey (1) aka Pelewais, Peleways. *Peleewa* 'turkey, fowl, chicken'. Turkey/Eagle Phratry.
145 Turtle (1) aka Namatha. *Namatha* 'Fish'. Turtle/Duck Phratry.
146 Turtle (2) aka Big Turtle-Shenkagkela. *M'shi'ka'kile* 'Big Turtle' from *m'shi-* 'big' + *'ka'kile* 'water turtle'.
147 Turtle's Heart aka Kitehi-Keetehee. *Kitehi* 'his heart' with *ki-* + –*tehi* 'heart'
148
Wababakahto 'White Bark'. Perhaps *Waapakwatwi* 'White Bark' from waapa- 'white' + -'kwatwi
149 Go to
Wapepelethee.
150

Ward, John aka Wapamowawa 'White Wolf'. *Wapamweewa* 'White Wolf' from *waap-* 'white' + *mweewa* 'wolf'.
151

Waupaukowela 'White Horn'. *Waapawela* 'White Horn' from *waapa-* 'white' + *-wile* 'horn'; Gatschet has "wápa'hkwi wíli 'white horn' ". Deer Clan, Hoofed Phratry.
152

Wesheshemo. *Weshi'shimo* 'One who has a good voice' from *weshi-* 'good' + *-shimo* 'voice, sound'. Turkey Clan, Bird Phratry.
153

White Hawk aka Wapepelethee. *Waapapelee'thi* 'White Hawk' from *waapa-* 'white" + *pelee* 'fowl' + '*thi* 'creature'. Note *Waapalanye'thi* 'bald eagle'. Hawk totem, Bird (Turkey/Eagle) Phratry.
154

White Loon aka Wawpawwawqua. *Wapimakwa* 'White Loon'. Gatschet has "Turkey or Eagle Clan." Loons and cranes, though spending time in the water, are perhaps considered wadding rather than swimming birds (who are in the Water Phratry) and thus in the Bird Phratry.

155 Wild Cat aka Peshewa. *Peshiwa* 'wild cat'. From *peshi* 'cat'. Note *mshipeshi* 'panther' (big cat) and *manetoowim'shipeshi* 'sacred water panther' (flies unseen through the night sky across the ocean, shooting stars from sparks from his tail, and he plunges back into the sea before dawn).
156

Wild Goose (2) aka Neeakee-**Neeakethoh**-Nika. From niika 'wild goose'. Goose totem, Water (Turtle/Duck) Phratry.
157

Wolf aka Muweesha-Meshewawa. Perhaps *M'shimweewa* 'Big Wolf' from *mweewa* 'wolf'..
158

Wrynek aka Crooked Neck-Aquilsika-Akweelseeka-Hakwilsikia. *Ha'kwil'shika* 'Severe Neck' from *ha'kw-* 'severe, extreme' + '*shika*, masculine name ending. See *ha'kwanwi* 'it is severe' and *ha'kwiloke* 'he is sick'.
159

Yellow aka Othawsa. *Hothaawa* 'Yellow'.
160

Yellow Feather aka Othawakeska-Yellow Plume-Outhowwaheshegath. Hothaawashika 'Yellow Feather' from *hothaawa* 'yellow' + *–shika*, male name ending. Turkey Clan, Fowl Phratry.
161

Yellow Hawk aka Othawapeelethee. *Hathaawapeleethi* 'Yellow Hawk' from *hathaawa* 'yellow" + *pilee-* 'foul' + *-thi* 'creature'.

162 Duck Laying Eggs aka Sheshepukwawalo. From *shi'shiipa* 'duck'. See *weewaawita* 'one who is laying eggs'. Not completely analyzed.

163 Namatha 'Turtle'. *Name'tha* 'fish'. Translated the phratry of Turtle/Duck rather than the Fish Clan.

SOURCES

This is a list of some of the authors, editors and sources used in this research. The various works have been read, compared and used as reference material only. Anyone reading my work will know that I reach my own conclusions. I try to take into account the jingoism, biases and prejudices of the various Nations, Tribes and writers and allow for the discrepancies and falsehoods that have echoed for decades before reaching a decision as to who was whom in this work.

1. Abenaki, Histories of the
2. Adair, Histories of John
3. Alabama, County Histories of
4. Alabama, Histories of the
5. Albright, Edward
6. Alden, John Richard
7. Alder, Histories of Jonathan

8. Alexander, Henry

9. Alford, Thomas Wildcat

10. Algonquians of North Carolina, Histories of the

11. Allen, Robert S.

12. Alvord, Clarence W.

13. American Indian Quarterly

14. American State Papers – Indian Affairs

15. Anderson, Fred

16. Andrews, Edward D.

17. Anderson, W.R.

18. Anson, Bert

19. Apalachicola, Histories of the

20. Arkansas, County Histories of

21. Arkansas, Histories of

22. Armstrong, John

23. Aron, Stephen

24. Ashe, Geoffrey

25. Askin, John

26. Atwater, Caleb

27. Bacon, Edward

28. Bailey, Francis

29. **Bamberg, Glenn Michael – special thanks**

30. Bancroft, Hubert H.

31. Barker, Felix

32. Bear River Indians, Histories of the

33. Beckwith, Hiram

34. Belue, Ted Franklin

35. Bennett, John

36. **Bishop, Debra – special thanks**

37. Black Elk

38. Black Minquas, Histories of the

39. Black, Glenn- Collections

40. Blackfoot, Histories of the

41. Blanchard, Rufus

42. Bliss, Eugene F.

43. Blue Jacket, Histories of

44. Boone, Histories of Daniel

45. Boorstien, Daniel

46. Bowe, John P.

47. Bradley, Michael

48. British Colonial Office Papers

49. British War Office Papers

50. Brown, Dee

51. Brown, John P.

52. Brunson, Alfred

53. Burks, Samuel

54. Burnet, Jacob

55. Butler, Mann

56. Butler, Papers of Richard

57. Butterfield, Consul W.

58. Caddo, Histories of the

59. Cahokia, Histories of

60. Callender, Charles

61. Calloway, Colin G.

62. Canada, Public Archives of

63. Canda, Indian Affairs Papers of

64. Canada, Military Papers of

65. Chapman, Paul H.

66. Carter, Clarence E.

67. Cass, Lewis

68. Catawba, Histories of the

69. Catlin, George

70. Cave, Alfred A.

71. Cayuga, Histories of the

72. Chalkey, Lyman

73. **Chartier, Vernon – special thanks**

74. Cheraw, Histories of the

75. Cherokee, Histories of the

76. Chestnut, Don

77. Chiaha, Histories of the

78. Chicago, Historical Society of

79. Chickahominey, Histories of the

80. Chickamauga, Histories of the

81. Chickasaw, Histories of the

82. Chippewa, Histories of the

83. Choctaw, Histories of the

84. Chowan, Histories of the

85. Chowanock, Histories of the

86. Christian, Shirley

87. Cincinnati, Historical Society of

88. Clark, Histories of George Rogers

89. Clark, Jerry E.

90. Clark, Peter Dooyentate

91. Clark, Thomas D.

92. Clark, Histories of William

93. Collins, Lewis

94. Comstock, Jim

95. Congaree, Histories of the

96. Conoy, Histories of the

97. Coosa, Histories of the

98. Coree, Histories of the

99. **Cornsilk, David – special thanks**

100. Cotterill, R.S.

101. **Crawford, Madeleine Chartier – special thanks**

102. Creek, Histories of the

103. Croatan, Histories of the

104. Croghan, Histories of George

105. Cumberland Valley, Histories of the

106. Cummings, Pamela

107. Curnoe, Greg

108. Cusabo, Histories of the

109. Cushman, H.B.

110. Dakota, Histories of the

111. **Dally, Flory – special thanks**

112. Danzinger, Edward L.

113. Darlington, W.M.

114. Davies, Kenneth G.

115. **Davis, Dean – special thanks**

116. Davis, W.B.

117. Day, Sherman

118. Delaware, County Histories of

119. Delaware, Histories of

120. Delaware Valley, Histories of the

121. DeHass, Wills

122. Delaware, Histories of the

123. DeMarce, Virginia

124. Denissen, Christian

125. Dixon, David

126. Dockstader, Frederick J.

127. **Domer, Jean Amos – special thanks**

128. **Domer, Jessica Alyss – special thanks**

129. Donehoo, George P.

130. Dowd, Gregory E.

131. Downes, Randolph C.

132. **Downing, Gregg – special thanks**

133. Drake, Benjamin

134. Drake, Richard B.

135. Drake, Samuel G.

136. Draper, Lyman C.

137. **East, Don – special thanks**

138. Eckert, Allen

139. Edmunds, R. David

140. Encyclopedia Britannica

141. Encyclopedia, Columbia

142. Encyclopedia, Funk & Wagner

143. Encyclopedia, World Book

144. Eno, Histories of the

145. Erie, Histories of the

146. Everts & Peck

147. **Ewing, Tom – special thanks**

148. Fell, Barry

149. Fester, Robert

150. Filson Club Quarterly

151. Filson, John

152. Finley, James B.

153. FL, County Histories of

154. FL, Histories of

155. Flick, Alexander

156. **Fowler, Bob – special thanks**

157. Fox, Histories of the

158. Georgia, County Histories of

159. Georgia, Historical Society of

160. Georgia, Histories of

161. Galloway, William A.

162. Ganawese, Histories of the

163. **Garen, Stephen – special thanks**

164. Gayarre, Charles

165. Gibson, Arnell M.

166. Gilbert, Bill

167. Goss, Dwight

168. Great Lakes-Ohio Valley Ethno-history Archives

169. Green, Michael D.

170. **Greene, Chief Don – files of**

171. **Greene, Keegan Von – special thanks**

172. **Greene, Patricia Riley – extra special thanks**

173. Hagen, William T.

174. Hahn, C.F.

175. Hall, James

176. Hall, Tony

177. Hancks, David

178. **Hancock, Virginia – special thanks**

179. Hardesty, H.H.

180. Harmar, Histories of Josiah

181. Harrison, Mary Roberts

182. Harrison, William Henry

183. Harvard Historical Studies

184. Harvey, Henry

185. Hatteras, Histories of the

186. Haywood, John

187. Hearn, Histories of Samuel

188. Heckwelder, Histories John

189. Heyerdahl, Thor

190. Hildreth, S.P.

191. Hinshaw, Carlyle

192. Hitchiti, Histories of the

193. Hoberg, Walter R.

194. Hodge, Fredrick W.

195. **Holland, Dave & Samantha – special thanks**

196. Holt, Reinhart

197. Honniasont, Histories of the

198. Horowitz, David

199. Horsfield, Timothy

200. Horsman, Reginald

201. Houck, Louis

202. Howard, James H.

203. Howe, Henry

204. **Hunt, Chief Gary – special thanks**

205. Hunter, William A.

206. Huron, Histories of the

207. Hurt, R. Douglas

208. Iowa, County Histories of

209. Iowa, Histories of

210. Illinois, County Histories of

211. Illinois, Historical Society of

212. Illinois, Histories of

213. Illinois, Histories of the

214. Indiana, Academy of Science of

215. Indiana, County Histories of

216. Indiana, Historical Collections of

217. Indiana, Historical Society of

218. Indiana, Magazine of History of

219. Indiana, Histories of

220. Indian Claims Commission

221. Indians of Person Co NC, History of

222. Ironside, Histories of George

223. Iroquois, Histories of the

224. Jablow, Joseph

225. Jacob, Axel

226. Jacobs, Wilbur R.

227. James, James Alton

228. **Jaynes, Reba – special thanks**

229. Johnson, Louise Franklin

230. Johnson, Histories of Sir William

231. Johnston, Charles

232. Johnston, David A.

233. Johnston, Histories of John

234. Johnston, Michael

235. Jones, Histories of Rev. David

236. Josephy, Alan M.

237. Kanawha, Histories of the

238. Kappler, Charles J.

239. Kaskinampo, Histories of the

240. Kellogg, Louise P.

241. Kelsey, Isabel

242. Kenney, James

243. Kenton, Dena

244. Kenton, Histories of Simon

245. Kercheval, Samuel

246. **Kerns, Terri – special thanks**

247. Keyauwee, Histories of the

248. Kickapoo, Histories of the

249. Kingston, John T.

250. Kinietz, Vernon

251. Kinnaird, Lawrence

252. Klinck, Carl F.

253. Klopfenstien, Carl G.

254. Knight, Kevin

255. Koasati, Histories of the

256. Kansas, County Histories of

257. Kansas, Histories of

258. Kentucky, County Histories of

259. Kentucky, Filson Club of

260. Kentucky, State Papers of

261. Kentucky, Histories of

262. Lamb, Annette

263. **Langley, Cheryl – special thanks**

264. Lassalle Papers

265. Leach, Douglas E.

266. **Lee, Carrie – special thanks**

267. **Lehmann, Barbara – special thanks**

268. Leni Lenape, Histories of the

269. Lewis, Histories of Andrew

270. **Lewis, Chief Eagle – special thanks**

271. Lewis, Histories of Meriwether

272. Lewis, Virgil

273. Logan, Histories of Chief

274. **Longtail, Chief Gray Cloud – special thanks**

275. Lossing, Benson J.

276. Louden, Archibald

277. Lucier, Armand F.

278. Lumbee, Histories of the

279. MA, County Histories of

280. MA, Historical Society

281. MA, Histories of

282. MA, Provincial Councils of

283. Machapunga, Histories of the

284. MacIntosh, Histories of Lachlan

285. Mahican, Histories of the

286. Mallery, Arlington

287. Manahoac, Histories of the

288. Marks, Paula Mitchell

289. Marshall University, Library of

290. Martin, Ken

291. Martini, Don

292. Mascouten, Histories of the

293. Massachuset, Histories of the

294. Mastin, Betty Lee

295. Matson, Nehemiah

296. McAfee, Robert B.

297. **McClure, Jerry – special thanks**

298. McConnell, Michael N.

299. McCoy, Histories of Isaac

300. McDowell, J.L.

301. McGee, Malcolm

302. McKee, Histories of Alexander

303. McKee, Histories of Thomas

304. McKenny, Thomas L.

305. **McQuinn, Starfire – special thanks**

306. Meherrin, Histories of the

307. Menominee, Histories of the

308. Metis, Histories of the

309. MD, County Histories of

310. MD, Histories of

311. MI, County Histories of

312. MI, Historical Collections of

313. MI, Pioneer & Historical Society of

314. MI, Histories of

315. Miami, Histories of the

316. Middleton, Carol

317. Middleton, Richard

318. Mingo, Histories of the

319. Mississippi Valley, Histories of the

320. Mississippi Valley Historical Review

321. Missouri Historical Review

322. Missouri, Histories of the

323. MO, County Histories of

324. MO, Histories of

325. Mobile, Histories of the

326. Mohawk, Histories of the

327. Mohegan, Histories of the

328. Mohr, Walter H.

329. Monacan, Histories of the

330. Moneton, Histories of the

331. Montagnais, Histories of the

332. Moore, John H.

333. Moore, S.M.

334. Moorehead, Warren K.

335. Moratok, Histories of the

336. Morgan, Histories of George

337. Mosopelean, Histories of the

338. Muklasa, Histories of the

339. Munsee, Histories of the

340. Muskogee, Histories of the

341. Nanticoke, Histories of the

342. Natchez, Histories of the

343. National Archives of the U. S.

344. NC, Colonial Records of

345. NC, County Histories of

346. NC, State Records of

347. NC, Histories of

348. Nelson, Larry L.

349. Neusiok, Histories of the

350. Neutrals, Histories of the

351. NJ, County Histories of

352. NJ, Histories of

353. Noe, Randolph

354. Northwest Ohio Quarterly

355. Northwest Territory Collection

356. Nottoway, Histories of the

357. NY, County Histories of

358. NY, Library of

359. NY, Histories of

360. Occaneechi, Histories of the

361. O'Callaghan, Edmund B.

362. O'Donnell, James H.

363. OH, Archeological & Historical Society of

364. OH, County Histories of

365. OH, Historical Collections of

366. OH, Historical Society of

367. OH, Historical & Philosophical Society of

368. OH, Histories of

369. Ohio Valley, Histories of the

370. Olmsted, Earl P.

371. Oneida, Histories of the

372. Onondaga, Histories of the

373. Osage, Histories of the

374. Ottawa, Histories of the

375. PA, County Histories of

376. PA, Historical Collections of

377. PA, Historical Magazine of Western

378. PA, Historical Society of

379. PA, Provincial Councils of

380. PA, State Archives

381. PA, Histories of

382. **Paine, Myron – special thanks**

383. Pamlico, Histories of the

384. Pamukey, Histories of the

385. **Pangburn, Richard – special thanks**

386. Parker, Arthur C.

387. Parkman, Francis

388. Peckham, Howard H.

389. Pedee, Histories of the

390. Pequot, Histories of the

391. Perdue, Theda

392. Perkins, Elizabeth A.

393. Perrin du Lac, F.M.

394. Pickett, Albert James

395. Piscataway, Histories of the

396. Pittsburgh, Carnegie Library of

397. **Pope, Chief Hawk – special thanks**

398. Porter, Frank W. III

399. Pottawatomie, Histories of the

400. Powhatan, Histories of the

401. Quaife, Milo M.

402. Rappahannock, Histories of the

403. Reynolds, John

404. Rice, Otis K.

405. Ridout, Histories of Thomas

406. Roanoke, Histories of the

407. **Roush, Reba Dell Justice Greene – special thanks**

408. Royce, Charles C.

409. Saluda, Histories of the

410. Sandersson, Ivor

411. Santee, Histories of the

412. Saponi, Histories of the

413. Sauk, Histories of the

414. Saunders, William L.

415. Savannah Valley, Histories of the

416. Sawakoli, Histories of the

417. Sayre, Gordon M.

418. SC, County Histories of

419. SC, Histories of

420. Schoolcraft, Henry Rowe

421. **Scoggins, Peggy – special thanks**

422. SCOT, National Archives of

423. **Schutz, Noel – files of**

424. Seaver, James C.

425. Secotin, Histories of the

426. Seelye, Elizabeth

427. Seneca, Histories of the

428. Shakori, Histories of the

429. Shawnee, Histories of the Absentee

430. Shawnee, Histories of the Eastern

431. Shawnee, Histories of the Loyal

432. Shenandoah Valley, Histories of the

433. **Sherman, Hal – special thanks**

434. Shoemaker, Nancy

435. **Shoults, Kelly – special thanks**

436. Siberell, Lloyd E.

437. Sioux, Histories of the

438. Sipe, C. Hale

439. Sissipahaw, Histories of the

440. Smith, Dwight

441. Smith, Histories of John

442. Smith, William

443. Smith, Z.F.

444. Sosin, Jack M.

445. Spencer, Joab

446. Spencer, Histories of Oliver M.

447. St. Clair, Histories of Arthur

448. Staab, Rodney

449. Starr, Emmett

450. Steele, Ian

451. Stevens, Paul L.

452. Stiggens, George

453. Stockbridge, Histories of the

454. Stone, William L.

455. Stotz, Charles M.

456. Stuart, Charles A.

457. Stuart, Histories of John

458. Sturtevant, William C.

459. Sugaree, Histories of the

460. **Sugden, John – special thanks**

461. Sultzman, Lee

462. Susquehanna, Histories of the

463. Susquehanna Valley, Histories of the

464. Swain, George T.

465. Swanton, John R.

466. Sword, Wiley

467. Tankersley, Kenneth

468. Tanner, Helen Hornbeck

469. Tecumseh, Histories of
470. Tennessee Valley, Histories of the
471. Thatcher, B.B.
472. **Thomas, Debra – special thanks**
473. Thom, James A. & Claudia
474. Thompson, Charles
475. Thompson, Gunnar
476. Thorne, V. Keith
477. Thrapp, Dan L.
478. TN, County Histories of
479. TN, Histories of
480. **Todd, Maya Sue – special thanks**
481. Trowbridge, Charles C.
482. Troxell, Dan
483. **Truman, Tim – special thanks**
484. Tuckabatchee, Histories of the
485. Turner, Fredrick J.
486. Tuscarora, Histories of the

487. Tuskegee, Histories of the

488. Tutelo, Histories of the

489. Thwaites, Reuben G.

490. U.S. History Manuscripts

491. U.S., Annals of 1st thru 15th Congresses of

492. U.S., Congressional Documents – Indian Land Cessions 1784-1894

493. U.S., Congressional Documents 1784-1873

494. U.S., National Archives of the

495. VA, County Histories of

496. VA, Historical Register of

497. VA, Journal of Executive Council 1776-78

498. VA, Library of

499. VA, Magazine of History & Biography of

500. VA, University of

501. VA, Histories of

502. **Vann, Ironhead – special thanks**

503. **Veronese, Debrah – special thanks**

504. Voeglin, Charles F.

505. Voeglin, Ermine W.

506. Waccamaw, Histories of the

507. Wainwright, Nicholas

508. Wallace, Paul A.

509. Wampanoag, Histories of the

510. War of 1812 Manuscripts

511. Ward, Matthew c.

512. Warren, Stephen

513. Wateree, Histories of the

514. **Watters, Chief Tula – special thanks**

515. Waxhaw, Histories of the

516. Wayne, Histories of Anthony

517. Weapemeoc, Histories of the

518. Weld, Isaac

519. Wells, Histories of William

520. Weslager, C.A.

521. White Minquas, Histories of the

522. White, Richard

523. WI, County Histories of

524. WI, Historical Collections of

525. WI, Magazine of History of

526. WI, Histories of

527. Wilcox, Frank N.

528. Williams, Samuel Cole

529. Winnebago, Histories of the

530. Winyaw, Histories of the

531. Withers, Alexander Scott

532. Witthoft, John

533. **Wood, Mary Jane – special thanks**

534. Wright, J. Leitch Jr

535. **Wright, Melissa – special thanks**

536. WV, County Histories of

537. WV, State Archives of

538. WV, University of

539. WV, Histories of

540. Wyandot, Histories of the

541. Xuala, Histories of the

542. Yamasee, Histories of the

543. **Yates, Jennifer – special thanks**

544. Yuchi, Histories of the

545. Zeisberger, Diaries of David

Made in the USA
Las Vegas, NV
15 October 2021